Brief Contents

P9-CQW-086

Brief Contents

Writing First

PRACTICE IN CONTEXT

WITH READINGS

Writing First

PRACTICE IN CONTEXT

WITH READINGS

FOURTH EDITION

Laurie G. Kirszner
University of the Sciences in Philadelphia

Stephen R. Mandell
Drexel University

Bedford / St. Martin's
Boston ■ New York

For Bedford/St. Martin's

Developmental Editor: Joelle Hann
Senior Production Editor: Bill Imbornoni
Production Supervisor: Jennifer Peterson
Marketing Manager: Casey Carroll
Art Director: Lucy Krikorian
Text Design: Anne Carter
Copy Editor: Alice Vigliani
Photo Research: Shaie Dively Photosearch, Inc.
Cover Design: Joyce Weston
Cover Art: Painting *Summer #23* by Susannah Bielak
Composition: TexTech International
Printing and Binding: RR Donnelley and Sons

President: Joan E. Feinberg
Editorial Director: Denise B. Wydra
Editor in Chief: Karen S. Henry
Director of Development: Erica T. Appel
Director of Marketing: Karen R. Soeltz
Director of Editing, Design, and Production: Marcia Cohen
Assistant Director of Editing, Design, and Production: Elise S. Kaiser
Managing Editor: Shuli Traub

Library of Congress Control Number: 2008937792

Manufactured in the United States of America.

3 2 1 0 9
f e d c b

For information, write: Bedford/St. Martin's, 75 Arlington Street, Boston, MA 02116   (617-399-4000)

ISBN-10: 0-312-48760-6 (Instructor's Annotated Edition)
          0-312-48758-4 (Student Edition with Readings)
          0-312-48687-1 (Student Edition)

ISBN-13: 978-0-312-48760-7 (Instructor's Annotated Edition)
          978-0-312-48758-4 (Student Edition with Readings)
          978-0-312-48687-7 (Student Edition)

Preface for Instructors

In college, writing comes first. In fact, as soon as students set foot in a classroom, they are asked to write—to take notes, to complete assignments, to write papers, to take exams. But writing is also crucial outside the classroom: in the community and in the workplace, writing empowers people, enabling them to participate more fully in every aspect of their lives. For these reasons, writing also comes first in *Writing First: Practice in Context*, where our organization and emphasis reflect our priorities as teachers as well as the importance of writing in college and in the wider world.

In *Writing First*, writing comes first chronologically: the book begins with thorough coverage of the writing process, and most chapters begin with writing prompts. Writing is also first in importance: extensive writing practice is central to the grammar chapters as well as to the writing process chapters. In addition to an abundance of practice exercises, each grammar chapter includes a unique three-step sequence of writing and editing prompts that guides students in applying the chapter's concepts to their own writing. One thing our years in the classroom have taught us is that students learn writing skills best in the context of their own written work.

Our goals in this edition of *Writing First* remain the same as they have been from the start: to motivate students to improve their writing for college and for everyday life, and to give them the tools they need to do so. It is our hope that by practicing these skills in the context of their own writing, students will come to see writing as something at which they can succeed. To achieve our goals, we have worked hard to keep the text flexible enough to support a variety of teaching styles and to meet the needs of individual students. At the same time, we wanted to support students and instructors grappling with the realities of the developmental classroom. In this edition, we made our grammar exercises more accessible, added more help to orient both native and nonnative speakers to cultural terms and ideas, and added easy-to-follow student case-study models to the paragraph chapters. Other issues that affect the writing classroom (such as academic reading skills, research skills, ESL issues, test-taking, job hunting, and study skills) are also covered thoroughly in *Writing First*.

We wrote this book for adults—our own interested, concerned, hardworking students—and we tailored the book's approach and content to them. Consequently, we avoid exercises that present writing as a dull, pointless, and artificial activity, and we do our best to offer fresh, contemporary

examples, writing assignments, and student models. In the book's style and tone, we work hard to show respect for our audience—to treat college students as adults who can take responsibility for their own learning and for their own development as writers.

Organization

Writing First: Practice in Context has a flexible organization that permits instructors to teach various topics in the order that works best for them and their students. The book is divided into three sections: "Writing Paragraphs and Essays," "Revising and Editing Your Writing," and "Becoming a Critical Reader." The first section is a comprehensive discussion of the writing process. The second section presents a thorough review of sentence skills, grammar, punctuation, mechanics, and spelling. The third section introduces students to critical reading skills and includes nineteen professional essays, each illustrating a particular pattern of development. Finally, four appendixes—Appendix A, "Strategies for College Success"; Appendix B, "Using Research in Your Writing"; Appendix C, "Taking Standardized Assessment Tests"; and Appendix D, "Job-Hunting Strategies"— provide help with skills that students will need in other courses, on placement and assessment tests, and in campus life.

Features

Central to *Writing First* is our "student writing first" philosophy, which is supported by innovative features designed to make students' writing practice meaningful, productive, and enjoyable.

***Writing First* empowers students by teaching them essential writing skills in the context of their own writing.** A three-step exercise strand (Writing First/Flashback/Revising and Editing) gets students writing immediately and shows them how to revise and edit their original writing as they work through the chapter. By moving frequently between their own writing and workbook-style mastery exercises, students get constant practice, advice, and reinforcement of the skills they are learning.

Students get the writing and grammar help they need—in an accessible format. With four chapters on the writing process, eleven chapters on paragraph development, and a full unit on essay writing, *Writing First* provides comprehensive coverage of the process of writing paragraphs and essays. Grammar in Context boxes, cross-referenced to the book's handbook sections, integrate focused grammar coverage into the writing chapters. Three full units of grammar coverage later in the book provide clear explanations and helpful examples essential for basic writing students.

Abundant opportunities for practice and review help students learn important skills and become proficient self-editors. Hundreds of practice exercises help students master the fundamentals of writing and grammar. Chapter Review activities—featuring Editing Practices, Collaborative Activities, and Self-Assessment and Review Checklists—plus Unit

Reviews help students to think critically about their writing as they work on improving it.

The text helps students make the connection between reading and writing. *Writing First* treats reading and writing as linked processes, offering numerous professional and student examples throughout the text as well as nineteen engaging professional selections and guidelines for critical reading at the end of this edition.

Unique appendixes, plus a comprehensive chapter on ESL usage, address issues important to the basic writing classroom. "Strategies for College Success," "Using Research in Your Writing," and a new "Job-Hunting Strategies" appendix offer a broad range of practical skills to help students manage their time, take notes, complete homework, find a job, and adjust to college life. "Taking Standardized Assessment Tests" orients students to high-stakes exams while the comprehensive ESL chapter addresses concerns of special interest to nonnative speakers.

New to This Edition

The fourth edition of *Writing First* offers students more help in transferring paragraph-writing skills to essay assignments. A new "Moving from Paragraph to Essay" box at the end of each paragraph chapter connects the paragraph chapters to the drafting, revising, and editing concepts covered in the essay chapter. Checklists allow students to apply these skills to their own work.

Case studies for every rhetorical mode offer students realistic writing models. New start-to-finish drafts in the paragraph chapters show a student's writing in progress, allowing other students to see how a paragraph develops from brainstorming to final draft.

***Writing First* provides even more context to help orient students to new words and ideas.** New Culture Clues help define cultural references for both native and nonnative speakers, while additional Word Power boxes define vocabulary in exercises, instructions, and readings. More ESL tips in the Instructor's Annotated Edition will be helpful to new and experienced instructors alike.

An accessible approach makes mastering technical skills less daunting. Simplified terms, definitions, and exercises make important grammatical concepts easy for students to learn and easy to practice.

***WritingClass* with *Writing First* e-Book lets students and instructors work together online.** Designed in consultation with developmental students and instructors, the *Writing First* e-book allows students to work on skills and writing directly in the online course space with *Writing First's* advice and models at their fingertips. With integrated reporting, *WritingClass* makes it easy for teachers to monitor student progress and give immediate feedback. Even better, *WritingClass* comes preloaded with our best media for you to use when building your course: *Exercise Central*, video tutorials for challenging concepts, writing guides, and much more. ISBN-10: 0-312-55839-2 / ISBN-13: 978-0-312-55839-0

Ancillaries

Writing First is accompanied by comprehensive teaching support that includes the following items. Many resources are free. Starred items are free when packaged with the book.

Print Resources

Instructor Resources

- ■ The *Instructor's Annotated Edition* contains answers to all the practice exercises, plus numerous teaching and ESL tips that offer ideas, reminders, and cross-references that are immediately helpful to teachers at any level. ISBN-10: 0-312-48760-6 / ISBN-13: 978-0-312-48760-7
- ■ *Classroom Resources and Instructor's Guide to* WRITING FIRST, Fourth Edition, offers advice for teaching developmental writing as well as chapter-by-chapter pointers for using *Writing First* in the classroom. It contains answers to all of the book's practice exercises, sample syllabi, additional teaching materials, and full chapters on collaborative learning. ISBN-10: 0-312-48761-4 / ISBN-13: 978-0-312-48761-4
- ■ *Diagnostic and Mastery Tests to Accompany* WRITING FIRST, Fourth Edition, offers tests that complement the topics covered in *Writing First*. ISBN-10: 0-312-48762-2 / ISBN-13: 978-0-312-48762-1
- ■ *Transparency Masters to Accompany* WRITING FIRST includes numerous models of student writing and is downloadable from the *Writing First* Web site at **bedfordstmartins.com/writingfirst**.
- *■ *Teaching Developmental Writing: Background Readings,* Third Edition, is a professional resource, edited by Susan Naomi Bernstein, former cochair of the Conference on Basic Writing, that offers essays on topics of interest to basic writing instructors, along with editorial apparatus pointing out practical applications for the classroom. ISBN-10: 0-312-43283-6 / ISBN-13: 978-0-312-43283-6

Student Resources

- *■ *Supplemental Exercises to Accompany* WRITING FIRST, Fourth Edition, provides students with even more practice on essential skills. Perforated pages are easy to copy and distribute. ISBN-10: 0-312-38504-8 / ISBN-13: 978-0-312-38504-0
- *■ The *Bedford/St. Martin's ESL Workbook* includes a broad range of exercises covering grammatical issues for multilingual students of varying language skills and backgrounds. Answers are at the back. ISBN-10: 0-312-44503-2 / ISBN-13: 978-0-312-44503-4
- *■ *From Practice to Mastery* is a study guide for the Florida Basic Skills Exit Tests in reading and writing that gives students all the resources they need to practice for—and pass—the test. It includes pre- and posttests, abundant practices, and clear instruction on all the skills covered on the exam. ISBN-10: 0-312-41908-2 / ISBN-13: 978-0-312-41908-0
- *■ The *Bedford/St. Martin's Planner with Grammar Girl's Quick and Dirty Tips* includes everything that students need to plan and use their time effectively, with advice on preparing schedules and to-do lists plus blank schedules and calendars (monthly and weekly). Tips from the

popular "Grammar Girl" podcast and quick advice on fixing common grammar errors, note-taking, and succeeding on tests are integrated into the planner, along with an address book, and an annotated list of useful Web sites. The planner fits easily into a backpack or purse, so students can take it anywhere. ISBN-10: 0-312-48023-7 / ISBN-13: 978-0-312-48023-3

New Media Resources

Instructor Resources

* ✳■ **The *Testing Tool Kit: Writing and Grammar Test Bank* CD-ROM** allows instructors to create secure, customized tests and quizzes from a pool of nearly 2,000 questions covering 47 topics. It also includes 10 prebuilt diagnostic tests. ISBN-10: 0-312-43032-9 / ISBN-13: 978-0-312-43032-0
* ■ *Just-in-Time Teaching* **at bedfordstmartins.com/justintime** is a collection of course materials culled from the best handouts, teaching tips, assignment ideas, and more from our print and online resources — perfect for last-minute class preparation.
* ■ *Adjunct Central* **at bedfordstmartins.com/adjunctcentral** offers a central place for adjuncts to find practical advice for the classroom, and downloadable handouts and assignments that can be adapted as needed. The site also offers access to the Adjunct Advice blog, links to additional resources, and a free adjunct resource kit.
* ■ *Writing First* **content for course management systems** is ready for use with Blackboard, WebCT, and other popular course management systems. For more information about Bedford/St. Martin's course management offerings, visit bedfordstmartins.com/cms. ISBN-10: 0-312-48764-9 / ISBN-13: 978-0-312-48764-5

Student Resources

* ■ **The *WritingClass* with *WRITING FIRST* e-Book** was designed in consultation with developmental students and instructors, and allows students to work on skills and writing directly in the online course space (see full description above in "New to This Edition"). ISBN-10: 0-312-55839-2 / ISBN-13: 978-0-312-55839-0
* ■ **The free companion Web site at bedfordstmartins.com/writingfirst** offers helpful student and instructor resources including additional Unit Reviews, downloadable forms, and annotated paragraphs and essays that offer strong writing models in an interactive format. The site also gives access to *Exercise Central* and *Re:Writing Basics* (described below), and to many helpful learning modules for students on avoiding plagiarism, doing research, and much more.
* ■ *Exercise Central* **at bedfordstmartins.com/writingfirst** is the largest collection of grammar and writing exercises available online. This comprehensive resource for skill development and assessment contains nearly 9,000 exercises with immediate feedback and reporting, helping to identify students' strengths and weaknesses, recommend personalized study plans, and provide tutorials for common problems.
* ✳■ **The *Exercise Central to Go: Writing and Grammar Practices for Basic Writers* CD-ROM** provides hundreds of practice items to help

students build their writing and editing skills. No Internet connection is necessary. ISBN-10: 0-312-44652-7 / ISBN-13: 978-0-312-44652-9

■ *Re:Writing Basics* at **bedfordstmartins.com/rewritingbasics** is an easy-to-navigate Web site that offers the most popular and widely used free resources from Bedford/St. Martin's, including writing and grammar exercises, model documents, help with the writing process, tips on college success, instructor resources, and more.

■ *Re:Writing Plus* is a premium online resource that includes the first-ever peer review game, *Peer Factor*; innovative and interactive help with writing a paragraph; tutorials and practices that show how writing works in students' real-world experience; plus hundreds of models of writing across the disciplines and hundreds of readings. ISBN-10: 0-312-47074-6 / ISBN-13: 978-0-312-47074-6

*■ The *Make-a-Paragraph Kit* is a fun, interactive CD-ROM that includes "Extreme Paragraph Makeover" animation to teach students about paragraph development. It also contains exercises to help students build their own paragraphs, audiovisual tutorials on four of the most common errors for basic writers, and the content from *Exercise Central to Go: Writing and Grammar Practices for Basic Writers*. ISBN-10: 0-312-45332-9 / ISBN-13: 978-0-312-45332-9

Ordering Information

To order any of these ancillaries for *Writing First*, contact your local Bedford/ St.Martin's sales representative: send an email to **sales_support@bfwpub .com** or visit our Web site at **bedfordstmartins.com**

Use these ISBNs when ordering the following supplements packaged with your students' copy of ***Writing First with Readings***:

WritingClass with WRITING FIRST *e-Book* Access Card:
 ISBN-10: 0-312-38503-X; ISBN-13: 978-0-312- 38503-X
Re:Writing Plus:
 ISBN-10: 0-312-56511-9; ISBN-13: 978-0-312-56511-4
Supplemental Exercises:
 ISBN-10: 0-312-57174-7; ISBN-13: 978-0-312-57174-0
The Bedford/St.Martin's ESL Workbook:
 ISBN-10: 0-312-57171-2; ISBN-13: 978-0-312-57171-9
Exercise Central to Go CD-ROM:
 ISBN-10: 0-312-57172-0; ISBN-13: 978-0-312-57172-6
Make-a-Paragraph Kit CD-ROM:
 ISBN-10: 0-312-56510-0; ISBN-13: 978-0-312-56510-7
From Practice to Mastery:
 ISBN-10: 0-312-57173-9; ISBN-13: 978-0-312-57173-3
The Bedford/St.Martin's Planner with Grammar Girl's Quick and Dirty Tips:
 ISBN-10: 0-312-57154-2; ISBN-13: 978-0-312-57154-2

Use these ISBNs when ordering the following supplements packaged with your students' copy of ***Writing First*** without readings:

WritingClass with WRITING FIRST *e-Book* Access Card:
 ISBN-10: 0-312-55839-2; ISBN-13: 978-0-312-55839-0

Re:Writing Plus:
    ISBN-10: 0-312-57147-X; ISBN-13: 978-0-312-57147-4
Supplemental Exercises:
    ISBN-10: 0-312-57151-8; ISBN-13: 978-0-312-57151-1
The Bedford/St.Martin's ESL Workbook:
    ISBN-10: 0-312-57152-6; ISBN-13: 978-0-312-57152-8
Exercise Central to Go CD-ROM:
    ISBN-10: 0-312-57153-4; ISBN-13: 978-0-312-57153-5
Make-a-Paragraph Kit CD-ROM:
    ISBN-10: 0-312-56510-0; ISBN-13: 978-0-312-56510-7
From Practice to Mastery:
    ISBN-10: 0-312-57149-6; ISBN-13: 978-0-312-57149-8
*The Bedford/St.Martin's Planner with Grammar Girl's Quick and
Dirty Tips*:
    ISBN-10: 0-312-57148-8; ISBN-13: 978-0-312-57148-1

Note on MLA Documentation   As you may know, the Modern Language
Association publishes two versions of its guidelines for documenting
sources. The *MLA Style Manual and Guide to Scholarly Publishing* is for
scholars and graduate students. The *MLA Handbook for Writers of Research
Papers* is for undergraduate and high school students.

In May 2008, the guide for scholars was updated with new guidelines
for documenting sources. The Modern Language Association strongly discouraged publishers from updating texts intended for undergraduates to
reflect the changes in the scholars' guide. Accordingly, the coverage of
MLA documentation in *Writing First: Practice in Context* reflects the guidelines for undergraduates as put forth in the current edition of the *MLA
Handbook for Writers of Research Papers*. When the Modern Language Association publishes the new edition of this guide (anticipated in the spring
of 2009), student copies of *Writing First* will be reprinted to reflect these
new guidelines.

Acknowledgments

In our work on *Writing First*, we have benefited from the help of a great
many people.

Franklin E. Horowitz of Teacher's College, Columbia University,
drafted the earliest version of Chapter 30, "Grammar and Usage Issues for
ESL Writers," and his linguist's insight continues to inform that chapter.
Linda Stine and Linda Stengle of Lincoln University devoted energy and
vision to the preparation of the *Classroom Resources and Instructor's Guide
to WRITING FIRST*. Linda Mason Crawford of McLennan Community College drew on her extensive teaching experience to contribute teaching tips
and ESL tips to the *Instructor's Annotated Edition*. Susan Bernstein's work
on the compilation and annotation of *Teaching Developmental Writing* reflects her deep commitment to scholarship and teaching.

We thank Kristen Blanco, Stephanie Hopkins, Judith Lechner, Carolyn
Lengel, Carol Sullivan, Jessica Carroll, and Charlotte Gale for their contributions to the exercises and writing activities in the text and Linda Stine

for developing the presentation slides featured on the *Writing First* Web site. Jess Carroll, Kelly Lockmer, and Jane Maher's work in updating and revising the ancillary booklets was invaluable. Kathryn Nielsen-Dube of Merrimack College reviewed the *Writing First* fourth edition manuscript for ESL-appropriate content and drafted the new Culture Clues designed to help both native and nonnative speakers.

It almost goes without saying that *Writing First* could not exist without our students, whose words appear on almost every page of the book in sample sentences, paragraphs, and essays. We thank all of them, past and present, who allowed us to use their work.

Instructors throughout the country have contributed suggestions and encouragement at various stages of the book's development. For their collegial support, we thank Alexandra Alessandri, Miami Dade College; Nancy Armstrong, California State University; Carolyn Barr, Broward Community College; Russell Bent, Middlesex Community College; Cheyenne Bonnell, Copper Mountain College; Mary Chavarria, Pierce College; Sally Cohen, North Shore Community College; Sharon Donohue, St. Petersburg College; Carol Eisenhower, Sierra College; Cynthia Halstead, Broward Community College; Linda Hulbert, Wayne State University; Lori Kupczynski, South Texas College; Enid Leonard, Lane Community College; Paulette Longmore, Essex County College; Marci MacGregor, Broward Community College; Jeff Maryanow, College of the Sequoias; Angela Medina, Rio Hondo College; Adrienne Mews, Lane Community College; Rebecca Miller, North Shore Community College; Spencer Olesen, Mountain View College; Patricia Osterman, Palm Beach Community College; Roberta Panish, Rockland Community College; Jeanette Richey, Cabrillo College; Joseph Scherer, Community College of Allegheny County; John Sullivan, Riverside Community College; Li-Lee Tunceren, St. Petersburg College; Maria Villar-Smith, Miami Dade College; Jinhao Wang, South Texas College; Florence Williams, Palm Beach Community College.

At Bedford/St. Martin's, we thank founder and former president Chuck Christensen, president Joan Feinberg, and former Editor in Chief Nancy Perry, who believed in this project and gave us support and encouragement from the outset. We thank Erica Appel, director of development, for overseeing this edition and Nina Gantcheva, editorial assistant, for helping with numerous tasks, big and small. We are also grateful to Jennifer Peterson, production supervisor, and Bernie Onken and Bill Imbornoni, senior project editors, for guiding the book ably through production and Lucy Krikorian, art director, for once again overseeing the book's design. Thanks also go to Casey Carroll, marketing manager, and his team; crack proofreaders Julie F. Nemer and Sara Warf; and our outstanding copyeditor, Alice Vigliani. And finally, we thank our editor, Joelle Hann, whose patience, hard work, and dedication kept the project moving along.

We are grateful for the continued support of our families—Mark, Adam, and Rebecca Kirszner and Demi, David, and Sarah Mandell. Finally, we are grateful for the survival and growth of the writing partnership we entered into when we were graduate students. We had no idea then of the wonderful places our collaborative efforts would take us. Now, we know.

Laurie G. Kirszner
Stephen R. Mandell

Contents

WRITING PARAGRAPHS AND ESSAYS   1

UNIT ONE   Focus on Paragraphs   1

UNIT TWO Patterns of Paragraph Development 47

REVISING AND EDITING YOUR WRITING   243

UNIT FOUR   Writing Effective Sentences   243

UNIT SEVEN Understanding Punctuation, Mechanics, and Spelling 513

BECOMING A CRITICAL READER   573

A Student's Guide to Using *Writing First*

What *Writing First* Can Do for You

It's no secret that writing will be very important in most of the courses you take in college. Whether you write lab reports or English papers, midterms or final exams, your ability to organize your thoughts and express them in writing will help to determine how well you do. In other words, succeeding at writing is the first step toward succeeding in college. Perhaps even more important, writing is a key to success outside the classroom. On the job and in everyday life, if you can express yourself clearly and effectively, you will stand a better chance of achieving your goals and making a difference in the world around you.

Whether you write as a student, as an employee, as a parent, or as a concerned citizen, your writing almost always has a specific purpose. For example, when you write an essay, a memo, a letter, or a research paper, you are writing not just to complete an exercise but to give other people information or to tell them your ideas or opinions. That is why, in this book, we do not just ask you to do grammar exercises and fill in blanks. In each chapter, we also ask you to apply the skills you are learning to a writing assignment of your own.

As teachers—and as former students—we know how demanding college can be and how hard it is to juggle assignments with work and family responsibilities. We also know that you do not want to waste your time. That is why in *Writing First* we make information easy to find and use and include many different features to help you become a better writer.

The following sections describe key features of *Writing First*. If you take the time now to familiarize yourself with these features, you will be able to use the book more effectively later on.

How to Find Information in *Writing First*

Brief table of contents. The first page of *Writing First* shows a brief table of contents that summarizes the topics covered in this book. This feature can help you find a particular chapter quickly.

Detailed table of contents.   The table of contents that starts on page xiii provides a detailed breakdown of the book's topics. Use this table of contents to find a specific part of a particular topic.

Index.   The index, which appears at the back of the book starting on page 703, enables you to locate all the information about a particular topic. The topics appear in alphabetical order; so, for example, if you wanted to find out how to use commas, you would find the *C* section of the index and look up the word *comma*. (If the page number following a word is **boldfaced**, that tells you that on that page you can find a definition of the word.)

List of Self-Assessment Checklists.   On page xxxiii is a list of checklists designed to help you write, revise, and fine-tune the paragraphs and essays you compose for particular writing assignments.

Easy-to-use navigational tools.   At the tops of most pages of *Writing First*, you will find *quick reference corner tabs* consisting of green-and-blue boxes, each containing a number and a letter (for example, "5A"). This information tells you which chapter you have turned to and which section of that chapter you are looking at. *Cross-references* (for example, "see Chapter 25") within instructional boxes such as the *Focus* and *Grammar in Context* boxes point you to other sections of the book. Together, the tabs and the cross-references help you find information quickly.

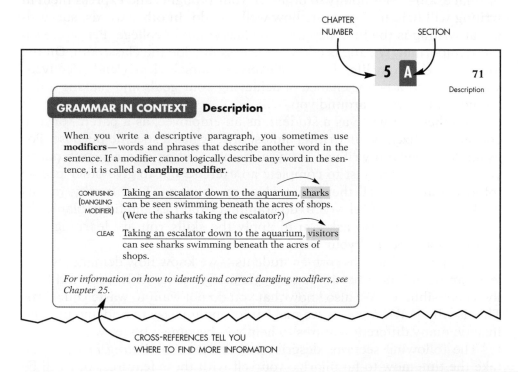

CHAPTER
NUMBER   SECTION

5 A   71
                        Description

GRAMMAR IN CONTEXT   Description

When you write a descriptive paragraph, you sometimes use **modifiers**—words and phrases that describe another word in the sentence. If a modifier cannot logically describe any word in the sentence, it is called a **dangling modifier**.

CONFUSING (DANGLING MODIFIER)   Taking an escalator down to the aquarium, sharks can be seen swimming beneath the acres of shops. (Were the sharks taking the escalator?)

CLEAR   Taking an escalator down to the aquarium, visitors can see sharks swimming beneath the acres of shops.

For information on how to identify and correct dangling modifiers, see Chapter 25.

CROSS-REFERENCES TELL YOU
WHERE TO FIND MORE INFORMATION

How *Writing First* Can Help You Become a Better Writer

Boxes.   Throughout the chapters, boxes highlight important information or ask you to complete specific tasks.

■   **Preview boxes.**   Each chapter starts with a list of key concepts that will be discussed in the chapter. Looking at these boxes before you begin the chapter will help you to get an overview.

Writing Simple Sentences

15

PREVIEW

In this chapter, you will learn

- to identify a sentence's subject (15A)
- to identify prepositions and prepositional phrases (15B)
- to distinguish a prepositional phrase from a subject (15B)
- to identify a sentence's verb (15C)

PREVIEW BOX

▸ **Word Power**

idol someone who is admired or adored

role model a person who serves as a model for other people to imitate

emulate to strive to equal or excel

■ **WRITING FIRST**

The picture above shows British soccer superstar David Beckham, who now plays for the LA Galaxy. Look at the picture, and then write about a person with whom you would like to trade places. What appeals to you about this person's life?

WRITING FIRST
ACTIVITY

245

■ *Writing First* **activity boxes.** Most chapters include a three-part writing activity that helps you apply particular skills to your own writing. Each chapter starts with a *Writing First* activity, accompanied by a visual, that asks you to write about a topic. Later in the chapter, *Flashback* and *Revising and Editing* exercises guide you to fine-tune your writing.

■ **Focus boxes.** Throughout the book, beige boxes with a maroon out-line highlight useful information, identify key points, and explain difficult concepts.

FOCUS BOX
EXPLAINING
HELPING
VERBS →

FOCUS **Helping Verbs**

Helping verbs (also called **auxiliary verbs**) include forms of *be, have,* and *do* as well as the words *must, will, can, could, may, might, should,* and *would.*

■ Some helping verbs, such as forms of *be* and *have,* combine with main verbs to give information about when the action occurs.
■ Forms of *do* combine with main verbs to form questions and negative statements.
■ Some helping verbs indicate willingness (*can*), possibility (*may*), necessity (*should*), obligation (*must*), and so on.

■ **Grammar in Context boxes.** In Chapters 3 to 11 you will find boxes that identify key grammar issues in the patterns of paragraph develop-ment. Use these boxes to increase your understanding of important issues in your writing.

GRAMMAR
IN CONTEXT
BOX FOR
ARGUMENT →

GRAMMAR IN CONTEXT **Argument**

When you write an argument paragraph, you need to show the re-lationships between your ideas. You do this by creating both com-pound sentences and complex sentences.

COMPOUND SENTENCE An emergency notification system will help
, and it
all of us communicate better. ~~It~~ will ensure
our school's safety.
Because communicating
COMPLEX SENTENCE ~~Communicating~~ with students in a crisis
, our
situation can save lives. ~~Our~~ school should
install an emergency notification system.

For more information on how to create compound sentences, see Chapter 16. For more information on how to create complex sen-tences, see Chapter 17.

■ **Moving from Paragraph to Essay boxes.** At the end of the writing chapters you will find boxes that help make connections between paragraph writing skills and essay writing skills. Checklists in the editing chapters allow you to apply these skills to your essay work.

MOVING
FROM
PARAGRAPH
TO ESSAY
BOX FOR
ARGUMENT

MOVING FROM PARAGRAPH TO ESSAY

▶ **Argument**

In addition to writing argument paragraphs, you may sometimes have to write an **argument essay**. For example, in a literature class, you may be asked to write an essay about a poem, play, or short story in which you support an argumentative thesis. In an email to a local newspaper, you might argue for a law that taxes motorists who drive into the center of the city. *For information on how to write an argument essay, see 14I.*

■ **Boxes in the margins.** In the margins of *Writing First*, you will find three kinds of notes that provide additional information. *Culture Clues* help to define concepts, customs, people, and organizations specific to the United States. These are designed to be helpful no matter where you grew up. *Word Power* boxes define words that you may find useful in working with a particular writing assignment or reading selection. Cross-references to *Exercise Central*, an online collection of over 9,000 exercises, are called *On the Web* and indicate where to find additional practice with specific skills.

■ **Culture Clue**

Take Your Daughter to Work Day was created by the Ms. Foundation for Women in 1993 in order to expose young women to career opportunities. In 2003, the program was expanded to include sons.

▶ **Word Power**

aspire to strive toward a goal

encourage to inspire with hope or confidence

nurture to nourish; to bring up

ON THE WEB
Visit *Exercise Central* at
bedfordstmartins.com/writingfirst
for more practice.

Checklists. At the end of every chapter, you will find a checklist that will help you review and apply the skills you are learning.

■ **Self-Assessment Checklists.** Chapters 1 to 14 include Self-Assessment Checklists that give you a handy way to review your understanding of basic paragraph and essay structure.

SELF-ASSESSMENT
CHECKLIST FOR →
ARGUMENT

☑ SELF-ASSESSMENT CHECKLIST:
Writing an Argument Paragraph

- Do you have a clearly worded topic sentence that states your position on this issue?

- Does your topic sentence state your position on a debatable topic?

- Does all your evidence support your paragraph's main idea?

- Have you included enough evidence to support your points, or do you need to add more?

- Do you include transitions to let readers know when you move from one point to another?

- Do you include transitions to indicate when you are addressing opposing arguments?

- Do you need to add transitions to make your argument more coherent?

- Does your paragraph end with a concluding statement that reinforces your position on the issue?

■ **Review Checklists.** All grammar chapters and some of the writing chapters end with a summary of the most important information in the chapter. Use these checklists to review material for quizzes or to remind yourself of key points.

REVIEW
CHECKLIST FOR →
WRITING SIMPLE
SENTENCES

☑ REVIEW CHECKLIST:
Writing Simple Sentences

- A sentence expresses a complete thought. The subject tells who or what is being talked about in the sentence. (See 15A.)

- A prepositional phrase consists of a preposition and its object (the noun or pronoun it introduces). (See 15B.)

- The object of a preposition cannot be the subject of a sentence. (See 15B.)

- An action verb tells what the subject does, did, or will do. (See 15C.)

- A linking verb connects the subject to a word or words that describe or rename it. (See 15C.)

- Many verbs are made up of more than one word. The complete verb in a sentence includes the main verb plus any helping verbs. (See 15C.)

Answers to Odd-Numbered Exercises.   Starting on page 691, you will find answers for some of the Practice exercises in the book. When you need to study a topic independently or when your instructor has you complete a Practice but not hand it in, you can consult these answers to see if you are on the right track.

How to Access Additional Exercises and Resources Online

Writing First's companion Web site gives you free access to *Exercise Central*, a database of over 9,000 practice exercises where you can take a diagnostic test to see the skills with which you need more help. You will also find access to *Re:Writing Basics*, a resource center with help for many issues that come up frequently in the writing classroom and in college, such as how to take good notes and how to avoid plagiarism.

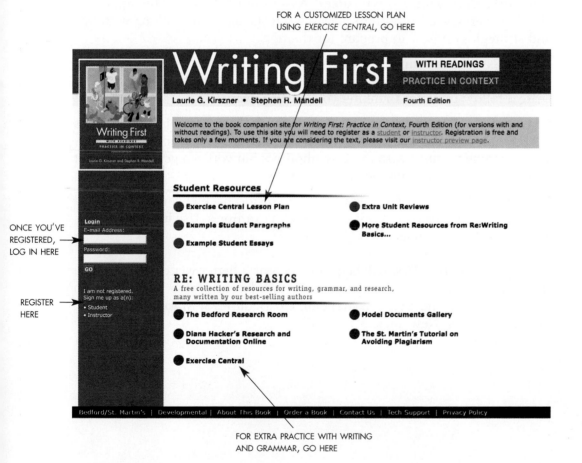

Visit **bedfordstmartins.com/writingfirst** to register. It's free and you will have to register only once. Keep a record of your username and password so that you can easily sign in on future visits.

Your Username: _____

Your Password: _____

How *Writing First* Can Help You Succeed in Other Courses

As we said earlier, writing is the key to success in college. For this reason, *Writing First* includes appendixes and other information at the end of the book that you may find especially useful in courses you take later in college. We have designed these sections so you can use them either on your own or with your instructor's help.

Appendix A: Strategies for College Success. Here you will find tips for making your semester (and your writing course) as successful as possible. Included are effective strategies for taking notes, completing homework assignments, doing well on exams, and managing your time efficiently.

Appendix B: Using Research in Your Writing. This appendix gives a short overview of the research process and shows how to document sources and create a list of works cited. A student research paper, complete with helpful marginal notes, is also included.

Appendix C: Taking Standardized Assessment Tests. This appendix gives an overview of important placement tests and exams, along with tips and strategies on how to prepare for them.

Appendix D: Job-Hunting Strategies. This appendix offers advice on how to write a résumé, draft a cover letter, prepare for a job interview, and write a follow-up letter thanking your interviewer.

List of correction symbols. The chart on the last page of the book lists marks that many instructors use when evaluating and grading student papers. Become familiar with these symbols so that you can get the most out of your instructor's comments on your work.

Review of the parts of speech. On the inside back cover you will find the eight major parts of speech defined with examples. Use it to review this essential information as often as you need.

We hope *Writing First* will help you become a better writer and student. If you have suggestions for improving this book, please send them to Laurie Kirszner and Stephen Mandell, c/o Bedford/St.Martin's, 33 Irving Place, 10th floor, New York, NY 10003.

Self-Assessment Checklists for Writing Paragraphs and Essays

Units 1–3 of *Writing First* include a number of Self-Assessment Checklists designed to help you write, revise, and fine-tune your paragraphs and essays. You can use these checklists both in your writing course and in other courses that include written assignments. The following list shows the page number for each checklist.

UNIT ONE

FOCUS ON PARAGRAPHS

Writing a Paragraph

▶ **Word Power**

primary most important

aspiration a strong desire for high achievement; an ambitious goal

■ **WRITING FIRST**

What do you think is the primary purpose of college—to give students a general education or to prepare them for specific careers? Look at the pictures above, and think about this question carefully as you read the pages that follow. This is the topic you will be writing about as you move through this chapter.

1 A

Writing is not just something you do in school; writing is a life skill. If you can write clearly, you can express your ideas convincingly to others—in school, on the job, and in your community.

Writing takes many different forms. In college, you might write a single paragraph, an essay exam, a short paper, or a long research paper. At work, you might write a memo, a proposal, or a report. In your daily life as a citizen of your community, you might write a letter or an email asking for information or explaining a problem that needs to be solved.

Writing is important. If you can write, you can communicate; if you can communicate effectively, you can succeed in school and beyond.

A Understanding Paragraph Structure

Because **paragraphs** are central to almost every kind of writing, learning how to write one is an important step in becoming a competent writer. This chapter takes you through the process of writing a paragraph. (Although a paragraph can be a complete piece of writing in itself—as it is in a short classroom exercise or an exam answer—most of the time, a paragraph is part of a longer piece of writing.)

A paragraph is a group of sentences that is unified by a single main idea. The **topic sentence** states the main idea, and the rest of the sentences in the paragraph **support** the main idea. Often, a final **concluding statement** sums up the paragraph's main idea.

Paragraph

Topic sentence   A paragraph consists of a **topic sentence** and **support**. The topic sentence states the main idea of the paragraph. This idea unifies the paragraph. The other sentences in the paragraph provide support
Supporting sentences   for the topic sentence. These sentences present details and examples to help readers understand the main idea. At the end of the paragraph is a **conclud-**
Concluding statement   **ing statement**, a final sentence that sums up the paragraph's main idea. Many paragraphs follow this general structure.

Note that the first sentence of a paragraph is **indented**, starting about one-half inch from the left-hand margin. Every sentence begins with a capital letter and, in most cases, ends with a period. (Sometimes a sentence ends with a question mark or an exclamation point.)

◆ **PRACTICE 1-1**

Bring two paragraphs to class—one from a newspaper or magazine article and one from a textbook. Compare your paragraphs with those brought in by other students. What features do all your paragraphs share? How do the paragraphs differ from one another?

B Focusing on Your Assignment, Purpose, and Audience

In college, a writing task usually begins with an assignment that gives you a topic to write about. Instead of jumping in headfirst and starting to write, take time to consider some questions about your **assignment** (*what* you are expected to write about), your **purpose** (*why* you are writing), and your **audience** (*for whom* you are writing). Answering these questions at this point will save you time in the long run.

Questions about Assignment, Purpose, and Audience

Assignment

- What is your assignment?
- Do you have a word or page limit?
- When is your assignment due?
- Will you be expected to complete your assignment at home or in class?
- Will you be expected to work on your own or with others?
- Will you be allowed to revise before you hand in your assignment?
- Will you be allowed to revise after you hand in your assignment?

Purpose

- Are you expected to express your personal reactions—for example, to tell how you feel about a piece of music or a news event?
- Are you expected to present information—for example, to answer an exam question, describe a process in a lab report, or summarize a story or essay you have read?
- Are you expected to argue for or against a position on a controversial issue?

Audience

- Who will read your paper—just your instructor or other students as well?
- How much will your readers know about your topic?
- Will your readers expect you to use formal or informal language?

■ **Culture Clue**
Writing papers on controversial issues is common in the United States. If you are uncertain whether a topic is appropriate, talk to your instructor.

◆ **PRACTICE 1-2**

Each of the following writing tasks has a different audience and purpose. Think about how you would approach each task. (Use the Questions about Assignment, Purpose, and Audience listed on page 5 to help you decide on the best strategy.) On the lines following each task, make some notes about your approach. Discuss your responses with your class or in a small group.

1. For the other students in your writing class, describe your best or worst educational experience.

   _____

   _____

   _____

   _____

2. For the instructor of an introductory psychology course, discuss how early educational experiences can affect a student's performance throughout his or her schooling.

   _____

   _____

   _____

   _____

3. Write a short letter to your community's school board in which you try to convince members to make two or three changes that you believe would improve the schools you attended or those your children might attend.

   _____

   _____

   _____

   _____

4. Write a letter to a work supervisor—either past or current—telling what you appreciate about his or her guidance and how it has helped you develop and grow as an employee.

   _____

   _____

   _____

   _____

C Finding Ideas

Once you know what, why, and for whom you are writing, you can begin the process of finding material to write about. This process is different for every writer.

Stella Drew, a student in an introductory writing course, was given the following assignment.

> Should community service—unpaid work in the community—be a required part of the college curriculum? Write a paragraph in which you answer this question.

Before she drafted her paragraph, Stella used a variety of strategies to find ideas to write about. The pages that follow illustrate the four strategies her instructor asked the class to try: *freewriting, brainstorming, clustering,* and *journal writing.*

▶ **Word Power**
curriculum all the courses required by a school

elective a course that is not required

Freewriting

When you **freewrite**, you write for a set period of time—perhaps five minutes—without stopping, and you keep going even if what you are writing doesn't seem to have a point or a direction. Your goal is to relax and let ideas flow without worrying about whether or not they are related. Sometimes, you can freewrite without a topic in mind, but at other times you will focus your attention on a particular topic. This strategy is called **focused freewriting**.

When you finish freewriting, read what you have written and underline any ideas you think you might be able to use. If you find an idea you want to explore further, freewrite again, using that idea as a starting point.

Here is Stella's focused freewriting on the topic of whether or not community service should be a required part of the college curriculum.

> Community service. Community service. Sounds like what you do instead of going to jail. Service to the community—service in the community. Community center. College community—community college. Community service—I guess it's a good idea to do it—but when? In my spare time—spare time—that's pretty funny. So after school and work and all the reading and studying I also have to do service? Right. And what could I do anyway? Work with kids. Or homeless people. Old people? Sick people? Or not people—maybe animals. Or work for a political candidate. Does that count? But when would I do it? Maybe other people have time, but I don't. OK idea, could work—but not for me.

Freewriting

◆ **PRACTICE 1-3**

Reread Stella's freewriting on the topic of community service for college students. If you were advising her, which of her ideas would you suggest she explore further? Underline these ideas in her freewriting, and then recopy them on the lines below.

_____

_____

_____

_____

_____

_____

_____

◆ **PRACTICE 1-4**

▶ **Word Power**

general education a broad range of courses from the arts and sciences

Now, it's time for you to begin the work that will result in a finished paragraph. (You already have your assignment from the Writing First box on p. 3: to write about whether the primary purpose of college is to give students a general education or to prepare them for careers.)

Your first step is to freewrite about this assignment. On a blank sheet of lined paper (or on your computer), write (or type) for at least five minutes without stopping. If you have trouble thinking of something to write, keep rewriting the last word you have written until something else comes to mind.

◆ **PRACTICE 1-5**

Reread the freewriting you did for Practice 1-4. Underline any ideas you think you might use in your paragraph. Then, choose one of these ideas, and use it as a starting point for another focused freewriting exercise.

Brainstorming

When you **brainstorm**, you record all the ideas about your topic that you can think of. Unlike freewriting, brainstorming is often scattered all over the page. You don't have to use complete sentences; single words or phrases are fine. You can underline, star, or box important points. You can also ask questions, list points, draw arrows to connect ideas, and even draw pictures or diagrams.

Stella's brainstorming on the topic of community service appears below.

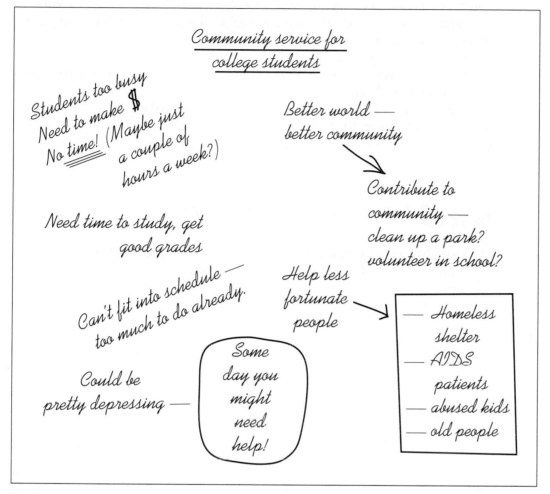

Brainstorming

◆ **PRACTICE 1-6**

Reread Stella's brainstorming notes on community service above. How is her brainstorming similar to her freewriting on the same subject (p. 7)? How is it different? If you were advising Stella, which ideas would you suggest she write more about? Which ideas should she cross out? Write your suggestions on the lines below.

Write more on these ideas: _____

_____

_____

Cross out these ideas: _____

_____

_____

◆ **PRACTICE 1-7**

On a sheet of *unlined* paper, brainstorm about your assignment: What do you think is the primary purpose of college—to give students a general education or to prepare them for careers? (Begin by writing your topic, "The purpose of college," at the top of the page.)

Write quickly, without worrying about using complete sentences. Try writing on different parts of the page, making lists, and drawing arrows to connect related ideas.

When you have finished, look over what you have written. Which ideas are the most interesting? Did you come up with any new ideas as you brainstormed that you did not discover while freewriting?

FOCUS **Collaborative Brainstorming**

Usually you brainstorm on your own, but at times you may find it helpful to do **collaborative brainstorming**, working with other students to find ideas. Sometimes your instructor may ask you and another student to brainstorm together. At other times, the class might brainstorm as a group while your instructor writes the ideas you think of on the board. However you brainstorm, your goal is the same: to come up with as much material about your topic as you can.

◆ **PRACTICE 1-8**

Working as a class or in a group of three or four students, practice collaborative brainstorming. First, decide as a group on a topic for brainstorming. (Your instructor may assign a topic.) Next, choose one person to write down ideas on a blank sheet of paper or on the board. (If your group is large enough, you might choose two people to write down ideas and have them compare notes at the end of the brainstorming session.) Then, discuss the topic informally, with each person contributing at least one idea. After fifteen minutes or so, review the ideas that have been written down. As a group, try to identify interesting connections among ideas and suggest ideas that might be explored further.

Clustering

Clustering, sometimes called *mapping*, is another strategy that can help you find ideas to write about. When you cluster, you begin by writing your topic in the center of a sheet of paper. Then, you branch out, writing related ideas on the page in groups, or clusters, around the topic. As you add new ideas, you circle them and draw lines to connect the ideas to one another and to the topic at the center. (These lines will look like spokes of a wheel or branches of a tree.) As you move from the center to the corners of the page, your ideas will get more and more specific.

Stella's clustering on the topic of community service for college students appears on page 11.

Note: Sometimes, one branch of your cluster exercise will give you all the material you need. At other times, you may decide to write about the ideas

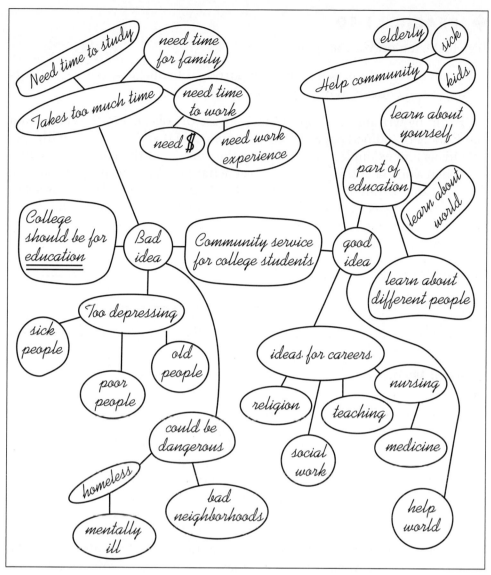

Clustering

from several branches, or to choose one or two ideas from each branch. If you find you need additional material after you finish your first cluster exercise, you can cluster again on a new sheet of paper, this time beginning with a topic from one of the branches.

◆ **PRACTICE 1-9**

Reread Stella's clustering on community service above. How is it similar to her brainstorming on the same subject (p. 9)? How is it different? If you were advising Stella, which branches of the cluster diagram would you tell her seem most promising? Why? Can you add any branches? Can you add details to extend any of her branches further? Write your suggestions on the following lines. Then, discuss them with your class or in a small group.

Most promising branches: _____

Possible new branches: _____

Additional details: _____

◆ **PRACTICE 1-10**

Try clustering on your assignment.

What do you think is the primary purpose of college—to give students a general education or to prepare them for careers?

Begin by writing your topic ("the purpose of college") in the center of a blank sheet of unlined paper. Circle the topic, and then branch out with specific ideas and examples, continuing to the corners of the page if you can.

When you have finished, look over what you have written. What are the most interesting ideas in your cluster diagram? Which branches seem most promising as the basis for further writing? What new ideas have you come up with that you did not get from your freewriting or brainstorming? Write your responses on the lines below.

Most interesting ideas: _____

Most promising branches: _____

New ideas: _____

Journal Writing

A **journal** is a notebook (or a computer file) in which you keep an informal record of your thoughts and ideas. In a journal, you can reflect, question, summarize, or even complain. When you are involved in a writing project, your journal is a place where you record ideas to write about. Here you can try to resolve a problem, restart a stalled project, argue with yourself about your topic, or comment on a draft. You can also try out different versions of sentences, list details or examples, or keep a record of interesting things you read, see, or hear.

Journal writing works best when you write regularly, preferably at the same time each day, so that it becomes a habit. Once you have started making regular entries in your journal, take the time every week or so to go back and reread what you have written. You may find material you want to explore in further journal entries—or even an idea for a paper.

FOCUS Journals

Here are some subjects you can write about in your journal.

■ *Your schoolwork* You can use your journal to explore ideas for writing assignments. Your journal can also be a place where you think about what you have learned, ask questions about concepts you are having trouble understanding, and examine new ideas and new ways of seeing the world. Writing regularly in a journal about what you are studying in school can even help you become a better student.

(continued on following page)

(continued from previous page)

■ *Your job* In your journal, you can record job-related successes and frustrations, examine conflicts with coworkers, or review how you handled problems on the job. Reading over these entries can help you understand your strengths and weaknesses and become a more effective employee. As an added bonus, you may discover work-related topics to write about in school.

■ *Your ideas about current events* Expressing your opinions in your journal can be a good way to explore your reactions to social or political issues. Your entries may encourage you to write to your local or school newspaper or to public officials—and even to become involved in community projects or political activities.

■ *Your impressions of what you see* Many writers carry their journals with them everywhere so they can record any interesting or unusual things they observe. If you get into the habit of recording what you see, you can later incorporate it into essays or other pieces of writing.

■ *Aspects of your personal life* Although you may not want to record the intimate details of your life if your instructor plans to collect your journal, such entries are the most common of all in a private journal. Writing about relationships with family and friends, personal problems, hopes and dreams—all the details of your life—can help you develop a better understanding of yourself and others.

Here is Stella's journal entry on the topic of community service for college students.

> I'm not really sure what I think about community service. I guess I think it sounds like a good idea, but I still don't see why we should have to do it. I can't fit anything else into my life. I guess it would be possible if it was just an hour or two a week. And maybe we could get credit and a grade for it, like a course. Or maybe it should just be for people who have the time and want to do it. But if it's not required, will anyone do it?

Journal Entry

◆ **PRACTICE 1-11**

Buy a notebook to use as a journal. (Your instructor may require a specific size and format, particularly if journals are going to be collected at some point, or you may be permitted to keep your journal in a computer file.)

1 **D**

Set a regular time to write for fifteen minutes or so in your journal—during your lunch break, for example, or before you go to bed. Make entries daily or several times a week, depending on your schedule and on your instructor's suggestions.

For your first journal entry, write down your thoughts about the topic you have been working on in this chapter: the primary purpose of college.

D Identifying Your Main Idea and Writing a Topic Sentence

When you think you have enough material to write about, it's time to identify your **main idea**—the idea you will develop in your paragraph.

To find a main idea for your paragraph, begin by looking over what you have already written. As you read through your freewriting, brainstorming, clustering, or journal entries, look for the main idea that your material seems to support. The sentence that states this main idea and gives your writing its focus will be your paragraph's **topic sentence**.

The topic sentence is usually the first sentence of your paragraph. The topic sentence is important because it tells both you and your readers what the focus of your paragraph will be. An effective topic sentence has three characteristics.

1. **A topic sentence is a complete sentence.** There is a difference between a *topic* and a *topic sentence*. The **topic** is what the paragraph is about. A **topic sentence**, however, is a complete sentence that includes a subject and a verb and expresses a complete thought.

TOPIC	Community service for college students
TOPIC SENTENCE	Community service should be required for all students at our school.

2. **A topic sentence is more than just an announcement of what you plan to write about.** A topic sentence makes a point about the topic the paragraph discusses.

ANNOUNCEMENT	In this paragraph, I will explain my ideas about community service.
TOPIC SENTENCE	My ideas about community service changed after I started to volunteer at a homeless shelter.

3. **A topic sentence presents an idea that can be discussed in a single paragraph.** If your topic sentence is too broad, you will not be able to discuss it in just one paragraph. If your topic sentence is too narrow, you will not be able to say much about it.

TOPIC SENTENCE TOO BROAD	Students all over the country participate in community service, making important contributions to their communities.
TOPIC SENTENCE TOO NARROW	Our school has a community service requirement for graduation.

EFFECTIVE TOPIC   Our school's community service requirement has had
SENTENCE   three positive results.

When Stella Drew reviewed her notes, she saw that they included two kinds of ideas: ideas about the value of doing community service and ideas about the problems it presents. She thought she could write about how community service requires time and commitment but is still worthwhile. She stated this idea in a topic sentence.

> Community service takes time, but it is so important that college
> students should be required to do it.

When Stella thought about how to express her topic sentence, she knew it had to be a complete sentence, not just a topic, and that it would have to make a point, not just announce what she planned to write about. When she reread the topic sentence she had written, she felt confident that it did these things. Her topic sentence was neither too broad nor too narrow, and it made a statement she could support in a paragraph.

◆ PRACTICE 1-12

Read the following items. Put a check mark next to each one that has all three characteristics of an effective topic sentence.

Examples

The common cold _____

Many people are convinced that large doses of vitamin C will prevent

the common cold.   ✔

1. Global warming, a crisis for our cities _____

2. High school science courses should teach students about the dangers of global warming. _____

3. In this paragraph, I will discuss global warming. _____

4. Buying books online _____

5. College students can sometimes save money by buying their textbooks online. _____

◆ PRACTICE 1-13

Decide whether each of the following statements could be an effective topic sentence for a paragraph. If a sentence is too broad, write *too broad* in the blank following the sentence. If the sentence is too narrow, write *too narrow* in the blank. If the sentence is an effective topic sentence, write *OK* in the blank.

1 D

Example: Thanksgiving always falls on the fourth Thursday in
November.   *too narrow*

1. Wireless computer networks are changing the world. _____

2. There are twenty computer terminals in the campus library.

   _____

3. Our school should set up a wireless network on campus. _____

4. Soccer is not as popular in the United States as it is in Europe.

   _____

5. Americans enjoy watching many types of sporting events on television.

   _____

6. There is one quality that distinguishes a good coach from a bad one.

   _____

7. Vegetarianism is a healthy way of life. _____

8. Uncooked spinach has fourteen times as much iron as steak does.

   _____

9. Fast-food restaurants are finally meeting the needs of vegetarians.

   _____

10. Medical schools in this country have high standards. _____

■ **Culture Clue**

Fast food describes
inexpensive food that
can be prepared and
served quickly, such as
hamburgers, french fries,
and milkshakes.

◆ **PRACTICE 1-14**

In Practices 1-4, 1-7, 1-10, and 1-16, you practiced freewriting, brainstorming, clustering, and journal writing. Now, you are ready to start
writing a paragraph in response to the following assignment.

> Do you think the primary purpose of college is to give students a gen-
> eral education or to prepare them for careers?

Your first step is to find a main idea for your paragraph. Look over the
work you have done so far, and try to decide what main idea your material
can best support. Then, write a topic sentence that expresses this idea on
the lines below.

Topic sentence: _____

_____

E Choosing Supporting Points

After you have stated your paragraph's main idea in a topic sentence, review your notes again. This time, look for specific examples and details to **support** your main idea. Write or type your topic sentence at the top of a blank page. As you review your notes, list all your supporting points below the topic sentence.

Stella chose several points from her notes to write about. After she read through her list of points, she crossed out three that she thought would not support her main idea.

Topic sentence: Community service takes time, but it is so important that college students should be required to do it.

- ~~Community service helps people.~~
- ~~Some community service activities could be boring.~~
- Community service can help the world.
- Community service helps the community.
- College students are busy.
- Community service takes a lot of time.
- ~~Community service might not relate to students' majors.~~
- Community service can be upsetting or depressing.
- Community service can be part of a student's education.

◆ **PRACTICE 1-15**

Now, continue your work on your paragraph about the purpose of a college education. Reread your freewriting, brainstorming, clustering, and journal writing to find the points that can best support your topic sentence. Write your topic sentence on the lines below; then, list your supporting points.

Topic sentence: _____

_____

_____

Supporting points:

- _____
- _____
- _____
- _____

Check carefully to make sure each point on your list supports your topic sentence. Cross out any that do not.

F **Arranging Supporting Points**

After you have made a list of points you think you can write about, your next step is to arrange them in the order in which you plan to discuss them in your paragraph.

When she read over her list of supporting points, Stella saw that she had two different kinds of points: some points identified the *problems* of doing community service, and other points identified the *advantages* of doing community service. When she arranged her points, she decided to group them in these two categories under the headings "Problems" and "Advantages."

Topic sentence: Community service takes time, but it is so important that college students should be required to do it.

Problems

- Community service takes a lot of time.
- College students are busy.
- Community service can be upsetting or depressing.

Advantages

- Community service helps the community.
- Community service can be part of a student's education.
- Community service can help the world.

◆ **PRACTICE 1-16**

Look over the supporting points you listed in Practice 1-15. Decide which of your points are about going to college to get an education and which are about going to college to prepare for a career. Then, arrange your points below in the order in which you plan to write about them.

Getting a general education

- _____
- _____
- _____
- _____

Preparing for a career

- _____
- _____
- _____
- _____

G Drafting Your Paragraph

Once you have written a topic sentence for your paragraph, selected the points you will discuss, and arranged them in the order in which you plan to write about them, you are ready to write a first draft.

In a **first draft**, your goal is to get your ideas down on paper. Begin your paragraph with a topic sentence that states the paragraph's main idea. Then, following the list of points you plan to discuss, write or type without worrying about correct wording, spelling, or punctuation. If a new idea—one that is not on your list—occurs to you, write it down. Don't worry about whether it fits with the other ideas. Your goal is not to produce a perfect piece of writing but simply to create a working draft. When you revise, you will have a chance to rethink ideas and rework sentences.

Because you will be making changes to this first draft later on—adding or crossing out words and phrases, reordering ideas and details, clarifying connections between ideas, and so on—leave wide margins, skip lines, and leave extra blank lines in places where you might need to add material. Feel free to be messy and to cross out; remember, the only person who will see this draft is you. (If you are typing your draft, use large type or leave extra space between lines to make the draft easier to work on.)

When you have finished your first draft, don't make any changes right away. Take a break (overnight if possible), and think about something—anything—else. Then, return to your draft, and read it with a fresh eye.

Here is the first draft of Stella's paragraph on the topic of community service for college students.

Why Community Service Should Be Required

Community service takes time, but it is so important that college students should be required to do it. When college students do community service, they volunteer their time to do good for someone or for the community. Working in a soup kitchen, raking leaves for senior citizens, and reading to children are all examples of community service. Community service can require long hours and take time away from studying and jobs. It can also force students to deal with unpleasant situations, but overall it is rewarding and helpful to others. Community service is good for the community and can be more fulfilling than playing sports or participating in clubs. Community service can also be an important part of a college education. Students can even discover what they want to do with their lives. Community service can also make the world a better place.

First Draft

◆ **PRACTICE 1-17**

Reread Stella's draft paragraph. If you were advising her, what would you suggest that she change in the draft? What should she add? What should she cross out? Write your suggestions on the following lines. Then, discuss your ideas with your class or in a small group.

Add these ideas: _____

_____

_____

Cross out these ideas: _____

_____

_____

◆ **PRACTICE 1-18**

Now, write a draft of your paragraph about the purpose of a college education, using the material you came up with for Practice 1-15. Be sure your paragraph states your main idea in a topic sentence and supports the topic sentence with specific points. If you handwrite your draft, leave wide margins and skip lines; if you type your draft, leave extra space between lines. When you are finished, give your paragraph a title.

H Revising Your Paragraph

Revision is the process of reseeing, rethinking, reevaluating, and rewriting your work. Revision usually involves much more than substituting one word for another or correcting a comma here and there. Often, it means moving sentences, adding words and phrases, and even changing the direction or emphasis of your ideas. To get the most out of the revision process, begin by carefully rereading your draft, using the checklist below to guide your revision.

☑ SELF-ASSESSMENT CHECKLIST:
Revising Your Paragraph

- ☐ Is your topic sentence clearly worded?

- ☐ Do you have enough ideas to support your topic sentence, or do you need to look back at your notes or try another strategy to find additional supporting material?

(continued on following page)

(continued from previous page)

☐ Do you need to explain anything more fully or more clearly?

☐ Do you need to add more examples or details?

☐ Should you cross out any examples or details?

☐ Does every sentence say what you mean?

☐ Can you combine any sentences to make your writing smoother?

☐ Should you move any sentences?

☐ Are all your words necessary, or can you cut some?

☐ Should you change any words to make them more specific?

☐ Does your paragraph end with a concluding statement that sums up its main idea?

Guided by the Self-Assessment Checklist on pages 20–21, Stella revised her paragraph, writing her changes in by hand on her typewritten draft.

Why Community Service Should Be Required

Community service takes time, but it is so important that college

students should be required to do it. When college students do community

service, they ~~volunteer their time to~~ do good for someone or for the

For example, they work   *rake*
community. ~~Working~~ in a soup kitchen, ~~raking~~ leaves for senior citizens,

or read   ^   ^   *These activities*
~~and reading~~ to children. ~~are all examples of community service. Community~~
^   ^   ^
important things like
~~service~~ can require long hours and take time away from studying and jobs.
However, community service is worth the time it takes.
~~It can also force students to deal with unpleasant situations, but overall it~~
^
~~is rewarding and helpful to others.~~ Community service ~~is good for the~~

for students   other college activities, such as
~~community and~~ can be more fulfilling than playing sports or participating
^   ^

in clubs. Community service can also be an important part of a college
learn about themselves, about their communities, and about their world, and
education. Students can even discover what they want to do with their   *they*
Finally,   ^   *can*
lives. ~~C~~ommunity service can ~~also~~ make the world a better place. *For all these*
^   ^
reasons, community service should be a required part of the college curriculum.

Revised Draft

When she revised, Stella did not worry about being neat. She crossed out words, added material, and changed sentences and words. When she felt her revision was complete, she was ready to move on to edit her paragraph.

Editing Your Paragraph

When you **edit**, you check for correct grammar, punctuation, mechanics, and spelling. You also proofread carefully for typographical errors that your spell checker may not identify. In addition, you check to make sure that you have indented the first sentence of your paragraph and that every sentence begins with a capital letter and ends with a period.

Remember, editing is a vital last step in the writing process. Many readers will not take your ideas seriously if your paragraph contains grammatical or mechanical errors. You can use the checklist below to guide your editing.

✔ SELF-ASSESSMENT CHECKLIST:
Editing Your Paragraph

- Are all your sentences complete and grammatically correct?
- Do all your subjects and verbs agree?
- Have you used the correct verb tenses?
- Are commas used where they are required?
- Have you used apostrophes correctly?
- Have you used other punctuation marks correctly?
- Have you used capital letters where they are required?
- Are all words spelled correctly?

For help with grammar, punctuation, mechanics, and spelling, see Units 4–7 of this text.

When Stella edited her paragraph, she began by printing out her revised draft. Then, she checked grammar, punctuation, mechanics, and spelling and looked carefully for typos. The final version of her paragraph appears next.

Why Community Service Should Be Required

Community service takes time, but it is so important that college students ——— Topic sentence
should be required to do it. When college students do community service, they
do good for someone or for the community. For example, they work in a soup
kitchen, rake leaves for senior citizens, or read to children. These activities can
require long hours and take time away from important things like studying and
jobs. However, community service is worth the time it takes. Community service ——— Supporting sentences
can be more fulfilling for students than other college activities, such as playing
sports or participating in clubs. Community service can also be an important
part of a college education. Students can learn about themselves, about their
communities, and about their world, and they can even discover what they want
to do with their lives. Finally, community service can make the world a better
place. For all these reasons, community service should be a required part of the ——— Concluding statement
college curriculum.

Final Draft

◆ PRACTICE 1-19

Reread the final draft of Stella's paragraph about community service for
college students (above) and compare it with her revised draft (page 21).
Then, answer the following questions about her revision.

1. Did Stella revise her paragraph's topic sentence? If so, why? If not, why
   not? Do you agree with her decision?

   _____

   _____

2. Did Stella add any new material to her paragraph? List any new details
   or examples on the lines below.

   _____

   _____

   Can you think of any new ideas she *should* have added? List them below.

   _____

   _____

3. What did Stella cross out? Why do you think she deleted this material?
   Do you think she should cross out any additional material?

   _____

   _____

4. Why do you think Stella added "For example" (line 4) and "However" (line 8)?

_____

_____

_____

5. Why do you think Stella added the word "Finally" in her next-to-last sentence?

_____

_____

6. In her revision, Stella added a sentence at the end of the paragraph. Do you think this sentence is necessary?

_____

◆ **PRACTICE 1-20**

Generally speaking, what kinds of changes did Stella make as she revised her paragraph? Which do you think are her most effective changes? Why? Do you think she needs to make any additional changes? Write your responses on the lines below. Then, with your class or in a small group, discuss your reactions to the final draft of Stella's paragraph.

_____

_____

_____

_____

_____

◆ **PRACTICE 1-21**

Use the Self-Assessment Checklist on pages 20–21 to evaluate the paragraph you drafted for Practice 1-18. Can you add any details or examples to support your points more fully? Should any material be crossed out because it does not support your main idea? Can anything be stated more clearly? On the following lines, list some of the changes you might make in your draft.

_____

_____

_____

_____

_____

_____

_____

_____

Now, revise your draft. Cross out unnecessary material and material you want to rewrite, and add new and rewritten material between the lines and in the margins. After you finish your revision, edit your paragraph, checking grammar, punctuation, mechanics, and spelling—and look carefully for typos. When you are satisfied with your paragraph, print out a clean copy to use in Chapter 2.

> ☑ REVIEW CHECKLIST:
> ## Writing a Paragraph
>
> - Learning to write a paragraph is an important step in becoming a competent writer. (See 1A.)
> - Before you start to write, consider your assignment, purpose, and audience. (See 1B.)
> - Use freewriting, brainstorming, clustering, and journal writing to help you find ideas. (See 1C.)
> - Identify your main idea, and write a topic sentence. (See 1D.)
> - Choose points to support your main idea. (See 1E.)
> - Arange your points in the order in which you plan to discuss them. (See 1F.)
> - Write a first draft of your paragraph. (See 1G.)
> - Revise your paragraph. (See 1H.)
> - Edit your paragraph. (See 1I.)

Fine-Tuning Your Paragraph

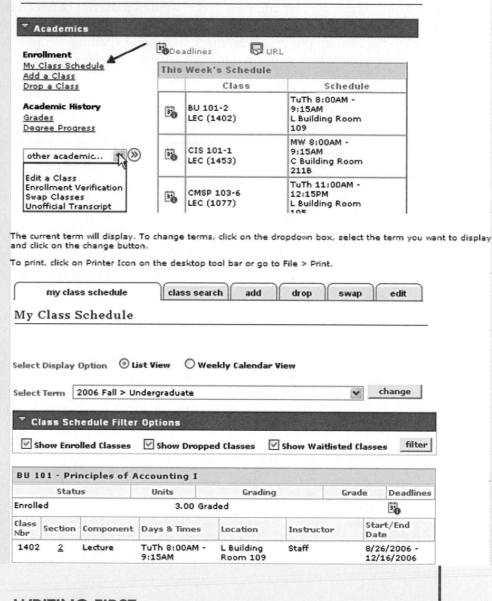

■ WRITING FIRST

The visual above shows a college student's online class schedule. In Chapter 1, you wrote and revised a paragraph about the purpose of a college education. Keep a copy of the final draft of this paragraph handy so you can continue to work on it as you go through this chapter.

As you learned in Chapter 1, a **paragraph** is a group of related sentences that develops one main idea. Every paragraph includes a **topic sentence** that states the paragraph's main idea. This topic sentence helps guide readers, and it also helps keep writers on track as they write.

A paragraph is **unified** when all of its sentences support the main idea stated in the topic sentence. A paragraph is not unified when its sentences do not support the main idea in the topic sentence. When you revise, you can make your paragraphs unified by crossing out sentences that do not support your topic sentence. The following paragraph is not unified.

Paragraph Not Unified

Although applying for a loan can be confusing, the process is not all that difficult. The first step is to determine which bank has the lowest interest rate. There are a lot of banks in my neighborhood, but they aren't very friendly. The last time I went into one, I waited for twenty minutes before anyone bothered to wait on me. Once you have chosen a bank, you have to go to the bank in person and apply, and if the bank isn't friendly, you don't want to go there. This is a real problem when you apply for a loan. If you have any questions about the application, you won't be able to get anyone to answer them. After you have submitted the application comes the hard part—waiting for approval.

After stating that applying for a loan is not difficult, the writer of the paragraph above wanders from his main idea to complain about how unfriendly the banks in his neighborhood are. For this reason, most of the sentences in the paragraph do not support the topic sentence.

The following revised paragraph is unified. When the writer reread his paragraph, he deleted the sentences that did not support his topic sentence. Then, he added sentences that did. The result is a paragraph that supports its main idea: that applying for a loan is not hard.

Paragraph Unified

Although applying for a loan can be confusing, the process is not all that difficult. The first step is to determine which bank has the lowest interest rate. ~~There are a lot of banks in my neighborhood, but they aren't very friendly.~~ ~~The last time I went into one, I waited for twenty minutes before anyone bothered to wait on me.~~ Although a half-percent difference in rates may not seem like much, over the course of a four-year loan the savings can really add up. Once you have chosen a bank, you have to go to the bank in person and apply~~., and if the bank isn't friendly, you don't want to go there. This is a real problem when you apply for a loan. If you have any questions about the application, you won't be able to get anyone to answer them.~~ Make sure you tell the loan officer exactly what rate you are applying for. Then, take the application home and fill it out, being careful not to omit any important information. If you have any problems with your credit, explain them on the application or

— *Support added*

— *Support added*

2 A

Support added—[in a separate letter. Take the application back to the bank, and ask any questions you might have. (Do not sign the application until all your questions have been answered.) After you have submitted the application comes the hard part—waiting for approval.

— Hector de la Paz (student)

◆ **PRACTICE 2-1**

Underline the topic sentence in each of the following paragraphs.

1.   Genetically modified crops can be very beneficial to a person's health. "Golden rice," for example, was created when scientists took genes from daffodils and other small plants and put them into a type of rice. These genes gave the rice a golden color. More important, the new genes enabled the rice to produce vitamin A. The Swiss scientist who created golden rice knew that about three hundred million people in China suffered from a lack of vitamin A. The lack of vitamin A can cause a person to become sick or even to go blind. In China, however, vitamins were expensive. So, if the rice the Chinese people ate contained a vitamin that they needed, eating the rice would solve a number of medical problems.

2.   Perseverance is important for a writer who wants to publish his or her first novel. J. K. Rowling, author of the Harry Potter books, first began writing the books in 1990. By 1993, she was the divorced mother of a young daughter. Rowling could not afford day care on the money she received in public assistance from the British government, and she could not get a job without paying someone to watch her child. As a result, she could write only when her daughter was asleep. When Rowling finished her first book five years later, she wanted to send a copy to publishers and keep a copy for herself, but she could not afford to make photocopies. She did not give up, though. Instead, she typed copies on her old typewriter. In 1997, *Harry Potter and the Philosopher's Stone* was bought by a publisher. Later, critics called Rowling an overnight sensation. They did not know how long that "night" had been.

3.   In the mid-nineteenth century, steamboats revolutionized transportation in America. These boats carried cargo and passengers between river towns. In some towns, passengers were met at the wharf by stage coaches that took them from place to place. In other towns, a railroad line came within walking distance of the wharf. Americans were pleased with this new type of transportation. Trips that had taken weeks by horse and carriage could now be completed in days.

4.   In 1949, the FBI asked the public for help in catching the most dangerous criminals in the United States. That year, the FBI created the "Ten Most Wanted Fugitives" list. On the list were murderers and other criminals who were considered the greatest threats to society. The FBI hoped that average Americans would help track down these fugitives, and the plan worked. With more people looking, more of the worst criminals were getting caught. Although the names on the list have changed, the program still exists today. Now, it is even easier for the public to see who is on the list

▶ **Word Power**

perseverance continued action over a long time, despite difficulties

▶ **Word Power**

revolutionize to change something radically

▪ **Culture Clue**

The *FBI* (*Federal Bureau of Investigation*) is the U.S. federal agency that runs investigations for the Attorney General. It is also responsible for safeguarding national security.

► **Word Power**
fugitive a person who is
hiding to avoid arrest

and to offer helpful information. Every week, the television show *America's Most Wanted: America Fights Back* shows pictures and videos of the most wanted fugitives and asks viewers to call with information. Since 1949, 94 percent of people whose names appeared on the list have been caught.

5. Space travelers will not be able to fly to Mars until four problems are solved. First is the problem caused by a lack of gravity, which can lead to loss of bone strength. Because we cannot create gravity on a spaceship, the astronauts who land on Mars might be unable to do their jobs once they arrive. Second, science cannot fully protect the astronauts from the cosmic rays they would be exposed to in deep space. Exposure to these rays would make the astronauts more likely to become ill or cause them to develop serious diseases, such as cancer. Third, the astronauts would have very little help if they did become ill. They would not have access to the medical help that we take for granted here on earth. Finally, astronauts might develop psychological problems because of the length of time it would take to get to Mars. Until science can solve these problems, going to Mars will be difficult, if not impossible.

◆ **PRACTICE 2-2**

The following paragraph is not unified by a topic sentence. Read it, and then choose the topic sentence below that best unifies the paragraph.

Some people save all the books they have read. They stack old paperbacks on tables, on the floor, and on their nightstands. Other people save magazines or newspapers. Still others save movie-ticket stubs or postcards. Serious collectors save all sorts of things—including old toys, guns, knives, maps, stamps, baseball cards, comic books, beer cans, movie posters, dolls, old televisions, political buttons, and even coffee mugs. Some things—such as matchbook covers or restaurant menus—may have value only to the people who collect them. Other items—such as stamps or coins—may be worth a lot of money. A few people collect items that are so large that storing them is difficult. For example, people who collect automobiles or antique furniture may have to rent a garage or even a warehouse in which to store their possessions.

Put a check mark next to the topic sentence that best expresses the main idea of the paragraph above.

1. Everyone, regardless of age or occupation, seems to have the urge to collect. _____
2. Collecting things like matchbooks and restaurant menus can be fun, but collecting jewelry or coins can be very profitable. _____
3. The things people collect are as different as the people who collect them. _____
4. In spite of the time and expense, collecting can be an interesting and fulfilling hobby. _____
5. Before you begin to collect things as a hobby, you should know what you are getting into. _____

◆ **PRACTICE 2-3**

Read the following paragraphs, and then write an appropriate topic sentence for each.

1. _____ The first—and simplest way—is to move out of the way. If a good driver does not do this, the angry driver may honk the horn, flash the lights, or tailgate the slower driver. Next, the good driver should avoid making eye contact with the angry driver. This lessens the chance that the furious driver will try to insult the good driver and make things worse. Finally, once the angry driver has passed, the good driver should consider calling the police.

2. _____ For example, Jim Morrison, lead singer of the Doors, has been the subject of a movie and several books since his death in July 1971. His grave in France is visited by fans, including many who were not even born when he was alive. Kurt Cobain, who committed suicide in 1994, is now the subject of several books, and his group, Nirvana, has an album that continues to sell well. Another example is Tupac Shakur. He was killed in 1996, but his albums still sell, and his poetry has been collected and published. Probably the biggest sign that all three singers are still remembered is the number of Web sites that claim that they are still alive.

3. _____ _____ Some people who once tried allergy shots now prefer to try vitamins and supplements. Some who suffer with back problems are giving up pain relievers and visiting acupuncturists and chiropractors instead. Still other patients try physical therapy instead of surgery to help them deal with a health problem. Some people also attend yoga classes instead of taking medication to relieve stress. Clearly, many patients are turning to nontraditional methods to help them deal with their ailments.

◆ **PRACTICE 2-4**

The following paragraphs are not unified because some sentences do not support the topic sentence. Cross out any sentences in each paragraph that do not belong.

1. The one thing I could not live without is my car. In addition to attending school full time, I hold down two part-time jobs that are many miles from each other. Even though my car is almost twelve years old and has over 120,000 miles on it, I couldn't manage without it. I'm thinking about buying a new car, and I always check the classified ads, but I haven't found anything I want that I can afford. If my old car breaks down, I guess I'll have to, though. I couldn't live without my portable tape recorder because I use it to record all the class lectures I attend. Then I can play them back while I'm driving or during my breaks at work. Three nights a week and on weekends, I work as a counselor at a home for troubled teenagers, and my other job is in the tire department at Sears. Without my car, I'd be lost.

2. The more television violence children are exposed to, the more aggressive they are as teenagers and adults. In 1960, Dr. Leonard Eron began to

study the relationship between television violence and violent behavior. He questioned parents about how they treated their children at home, including how much television their children watched. There is more violence on television today than there was then. Ten years later, he interviewed these families again and discovered that whether or not teenage sons were aggressive depended less on how they had been treated by their parents than on how much violent television programming they had watched as children. Returning in 1990, he found that these same young men, now in their thirties, were still more likely to be aggressive and to commit crimes. Thus, Eron's research suggests a link between television violence and aggression. Researchers estimate that a child today is likely to watch 100,000 violent acts on television before finishing elementary school.

3. Libraries today hold a lot more than just books. For example, many libraries now have large collections of tapes and compact discs. Many also have videotapes of both instructional programs and recent and vintage movies. Some libraries also stock DVDs. However, most people probably still get more movies from video stores than from libraries. In addition, the children's section often has games and toys young patrons can play with in the library or even check out. Most important, libraries offer computerized databases, which provide more up-to-date information than printed sources. These nonprint sources are the wave of the future for even the smallest libraries. They will allow patrons to access much more information than books or magazines ever could. People who don't know how to use a computer are going to be out of luck.

◆ PRACTICE 2-5

Read the following topic sentences. Then, on the lines that follow, write a paragraph that supports the main idea stated in the topic sentence. After you finish, make sure that the paragraphs you have written are unified.

1. Many people have too much credit-card debt. _____

_____

_____

_____

_____

_____

2. Choosing the right cell phone can be a difficult task. _____

_____

_____

_____

_____

_____

3. College involves more than just going to class. _____

_____

_____

_____

_____

_____

■ **WRITING FIRST: Flashback**

Look back at the paragraph you wrote for the Writing First activity in Chapter 1. Review your paragraph for unity. Cross out any sentences that do not support the topic sentence.

B | **Writing Well-Developed Paragraphs**

A paragraph is **well developed** when it contains enough material to support the topic sentence. A paragraph is not well developed when it does not provide the **support**—details and examples—readers need to understand or accept its main idea.

How do you determine how much support you need? The answer to this question depends on your topic sentence. If your topic sentence is relatively simple and straightforward—for example, "My school's registration process is a nightmare"—two or three well-chosen examples will probably be enough. If, however, your statement is more complicated—for example, "The plan that the mayor has presented for building a new stadium is seriously flawed"—you will have to present more support.

FOCUS | **Developing Paragraphs with Details and Examples**

Details and examples make a paragraph convincing. For example, in a paragraph on a history test, you could say that many soldiers were killed during the American Civil War. Your paragraph would be far more effective, however, if you said that over 500,000 soldiers were killed during the Civil War—more than in all the other wars in U.S. history combined.

When you check your paragraphs to make sure they are well developed, look for unsupported general statements. If you find any, add the details and examples you need to support these statements. The following paragraph is not well developed.

Paragraph Not Well Developed

> Although pit bulls were originally bred to fight, they can make good pets. Today, many people are afraid of pit bulls. These dogs are sometimes mistreated. As a result, they become more aggressive. For this reason, they are misunderstood and persecuted. In fact, some cities have taken action against them. But pit bulls do not deserve their bad reputation. In fact, they can actually make good pets.

Culture Clue
The *pit bull* is an American breed of dog with powerful jaws, a broad skull, and short hair.

The paragraph above includes a topic sentence and a series of general statements. It does not give readers specific information about how pit bulls can make good pets (which is what the topic sentence promises). In the following revised paragraph, the writer added details and examples that help readers understand the point the topic sentence makes.

Well-Developed Paragraph

> Although pit bulls were originally bred to fight, they can make good pets. It is true that their powerful jaws, short muscular legs, and large teeth are suited to fighting, and they were used for this purpose in the rural South and Southwest. It is also true that some pit bulls — especially males — can be aggressive toward other dogs. However, most pit bulls like human beings and are quite friendly. Owners report that pit bulls are affectionate, loyal, and good with children. When pit bulls behave badly, it is usually because they have been mistreated. As a recent newspaper article pointed out, the number of reported bites by pit bulls is no greater than the number of bites by other breeds. In fact, some dogs, such as cocker spaniels, bite much more frequently than pit bulls do. The problem is that whenever a pit bull attacks a person, the incident is reported. But pit bulls do not deserve their bad reputation. In fact, they can actually make good pets.
>
> —Susan Delaney (student)

Topic sentence

Details and examples

◆ **PRACTICE 2-6**

Underline the supporting details and examples in each of the following paragraphs.

1. Hearing people have some mistaken ideas about the deaf community. First, some hearing adults think that all deaf people would trade anything not to be "handicapped." Hearing people do not realize that many deaf people are proud to be part of the deaf community. They have their own language, customs, and culture. Second, many hearing people think that all deaf people read lips, so there is no need to learn sign language to communicate with them. Lip reading—or speech reading, as deaf people call the practice—is difficult. Not all hearing people say the same words

in the same way. Facial expressions can also change the meaning of the words. If hearing people make more of an attempt to understand deaf culture, communication between them will improve.

2.   Since its beginning in 1997, the Women's National Basketball Association (WNBA) has been a success in the United States. During its first season, eight teams competed in the WNBA. The WNBA has grown a lot since then in both size and popularity. Thirteen teams competed in the 2007 season, six in the Eastern Conference and seven in the Western Conference. Like the NBA, the WNBA now has a popular mid-season All-Star Game as well. In this East versus West contest every July, the best players from each conference compete against one another. Over the years, the league has grown in other ways as well. WNBA teams are involved in many community activities nationwide. Today, fans often see their favorite players off the court, working for fitness, literacy, breast cancer awareness, and other important causes.

3.   Hurricane names help weather forecasters talk about storms to the general public. Hurricanes form near the equator and move along a curved path at anywhere from five to fifty miles per hour. Often, more than one hurricane will be active at a time, so the names help people understand which storm is being discussed. Since 1979, storms in the Atlantic have been given men's and women's names beginning with all the letters of the alphabet except q, x, y, and z. In the Pacific, the practice was the same until recently, when names common to the people in that area began to be used. So, while the second storm in the Atlantic in 2002 was named Bertha, the second in the Pacific Northwest was named Boris. These names help the public keep track of hurricanes.

4.   Turtles are among the most adaptable living reptiles. They can live on land or in the water and are found everywhere in the world except Antarctica. In spring and summer, turtles search for food, including insects, fish, berries, and water plants. In winter, they hibernate in the mud of lakes or creeks or under piles of leaves and brush. Turtles range in size from several inches to as large as eight feet, which is the average length of a sea turtle called the leatherback. Unfortunately, pollution and population growth are now threatening the existence of these fascinating and harmless creatures.

> **Word Power**
> **hibernate**   to go into a sleeplike state over the winter

5.   One of the largest celebrations of the passage of young girls into womanhood occurs in Latin American and Hispanic cultures. This event is called La Quinceañera, or the fifteenth year. It acknowledges that a young woman is now of marriageable age. The day usually begins with a Mass of Thanksgiving. The young woman wears a full-length white or pastel-colored dress and is attended by fourteen friends and relatives who serve as maids of honor and male escorts. Her parents and godparents surround her at the foot of the altar. When the Mass ends, other young relatives give small gifts to those who attended, while the Quinceañera herself places a bouquet of flowers on the altar of the Virgin. Following the Mass is an elaborate party, with dancing, cake, and toasts. Finally, to end the evening, the young woman dances a waltz with her favorite escort.

◆ PRACTICE 2-7

Provide two or three supporting details for each of the following topic sentences.

1. When it comes to feeding a family on a budget, you need to shop carefully.

   _____

   _____

   _____

2. If you are dating someone at work, it is best not to let your coworkers know about it.

   _____

   _____

   _____

3. When scheduling classes, you should keep several things in mind.

   _____

   _____

   _____

4. Although many people are victims of identity theft, there are steps you can take to protect yourself.

   _____

   _____

   _____

5. Choosing the right car was harder than I thought it would be.

   _____

   _____

   _____

■ **Culture Clue**

Identity theft refers to the theft of someone's personal or financial information (credit cards, Social Security number, driver's license, and so on) with the intention of using that information illegally.

◆ PRACTICE 2-8

The following two paragraphs are not well developed. On the lines that follow each paragraph, write three questions or suggestions that might help the writer develop his or her ideas more fully.

1. Computers can be a great help for young students. Word processing can make writing assignments easier, and math drills can be fun when they are in the form of computer games. Also, when students have questions

about almost anything, they can usually find the answer on the Internet. Even very young children can do research by using computers.

_____

_____

_____

_____

_____

_____

2. It is difficult to tell much about people from the clothes they wear. For example, almost everyone today wears athletic clothes. Also, worn-out clothes do not necessarily show that people do not have enough money to buy new clothes. In fact, torn jeans are popular. In the past, wearing black was a sign of mourning. Now, wearing black has nothing to do with being sad. Many times, all clothes show is that people want to be in style.

_____

_____

_____

_____

_____

◆ **PRACTICE 2-9**

Choose one of the paragraphs from Practice 2-8. Reread it, and review your suggestions for improving it. Then, rewrite the paragraph on the lines below. Add any details and examples you think are needed to make the paragraph well developed.

_____

_____

_____

_____

_____

_____

_____

_____

_____

■ **WRITING FIRST: Flashback**

Look back at the paragraph you wrote for the Writing First
activity in Chapter 1. Is your paragraph well developed? On
the lines below, list the details and examples that you used to
support your main idea. Then, list suggestions for revision,
noting the kinds of examples and details you might add.

Details and Examples in Your Paragraph:

_____

_____

_____

_____

_____

_____

Suggestions for Revision:

_____

_____

_____

_____

_____

_____

C **Writing Coherent Paragraphs**

A paragraph is **coherent** if all its sentences are arranged in a clear, sensible
sequence and connected logically. You can make a paragraph coherent by
arranging details in a definite order and by supplying transitional words
and phrases that show the connections between sentences.

You can arrange the details and examples in a paragraph according to
time order, spatial order, or *logical order.*

Time Order

Paragraphs arranged in **time order** present events in the order in which
they occurred. News reports, historical accounts, and instructions are usually arranged in time order.

The following paragraph presents events in time order. Transitional words and phrases—for example, specific dates as well as the words *before, once, then, finally, later,* and *after*—indicate the sequence of events in the paragraph.

<u>In 1856,</u> my great-great-great-grandparents, Anne and Charles McGinley, came to the United States to start a new life. <u>Before</u> they left Ireland, their English landlords had raised the taxes on their land so high that my ancestors could not afford to pay them. It took them three years to save the money for passage. <u>Once</u> they had saved the money, they had to look for a ship that was willing to take them. <u>Then,</u> my great-great-great-grandparents were on their way. They and their ten children spent four long months on a small ship. Storms, strong tides, and damaged sails made the trip longer than it should have been. <u>Finally,</u> in <u>November 1856,</u> they saw land, and two days <u>later</u> they sailed into New York Harbor. <u>After</u> they entered the United States, they took a train to Baltimore, Maryland, where some cousins lived.

Transitional Words and Phrases

Some Words and Phrases That Signal Time Order

after	earlier	now
afterward	eventually	soon
at first	finally	then
before	later	today
during	next	dates (for example, "In June")

Spatial Order

Paragraphs that are arranged in **spatial order** present details in the order in which a viewer sees them—from top to bottom, from near to far, from right to left, and so on. Spatial order is central to paragraphs that describe what an object, place, or person looks like.

The following paragraph presents details in spatial order. Notice how the transitional words and phrases *directly in front of, next to, behind, in between, on top of, inside,* and *in the center of* establish the order in which the writer sees the details of the scene (from far to near).

▶ **Word Power**
clapboard long thin board used to cover the outer walls of some buildings and homes, especially in the northeastern United States.

The Amish school I visited was unlike any other school I had seen before. A long, tree-lined dirt road led to the small one-room wooden schoolhouse. <u>Directly in front of</u> the school was a line of bicycles and metal scooters. A small baseball diamond had been carved into the dirt in the yard <u>next to</u> the schoolhouse. <u>Behind</u> the school, two little outhouses stood next to each other with a green water pump <u>in between</u>. The schoolhouse itself was a small one-story structure. White paint curled off its clapboard siding, and a short steeple, holding a brass bell, sat firmly <u>on top of</u> the roof. <u>Inside</u> the open door, a long line of black hats hung on pegs. <u>In the center of</u> the small schoolhouse was an iron potbellied stove surrounded by the children's desks.

Transitional Words and Phrases

Some Words and Phrases That Signal Spatial Order

above	in front	on the left
behind	in the center	on the right
below	inside	on top
beside	near	over
in back	next to	under
in between	on the bottom	

Logical Order

Paragraphs that are arranged in **logical order** present ideas in a sequence that indicates why one idea logically follows another. For example, a paragraph may move from least important to most important idea, from general to specific, or from most familiar to least familiar.

The following paragraph presents ideas in logical order. Here, the transitional phrases *the first rule, the second rule,* and *the last and most ridiculous rule* establish the order in which the rules are presented—from least to most ridiculous—and thus help readers move from one point to another.

My high school had three rules that were silly at best and ridiculous at worst. The first rule was that only seniors could go outside the school building for lunch. In spite of this rule, many students went outside to eat because the cafeteria was not big enough to seat all the school's students at the same time. Understanding the problem, the teachers and the principal looked the other way as long as we returned to school before the lunch period was over. The second rule was that we had to attend 95 percent of the classes for every course. This rule meant that a person could miss only about six days of class every semester. Naturally, this rule was never enforced because if it had been, half the students would have failed. The last and most ridiculous rule, however, was that students could not throw their hats into the air during graduation. At some point in the past—no one seems to know when—a parent had complained that a falling hat could poke someone in the eye. As a result, graduating classes were told that under no circumstance could they throw their hats. Naturally, on graduation day we did what every previous graduating class had done—ignored the rule and threw our hats into the air.

Transitional Words and Phrases

Some Words and Phrases That Signal Logical Order

also	last
although	moreover
consequently	next
first…second…third	not only…but also
for example	one…another
for instance	similarly
furthermore	the least important
in addition	the most important
in fact	therefore

◆ **PRACTICE 2-10**

Read each of the following sentences carefully. If you were writing a paragraph introduced by each sentence, how would you arrange the supporting details—in time order, spatial order, or logical order? Write your answer in the blank following the topic sentence.

> **Example:** The work crews that built the Hoover Dam had to follow a definite series of steps. ___*time order*___

1. Colonial Philadelphia was laid out as a series of squares.

   _____

2. The development of modern antibiotics took some interesting and unexpected turns. _____

3. There are three reasons why the king and queen of Spain gave Columbus the money for his voyage. _____

4. The 1918 flu epidemic grew more deadly as it spread.

   _____

5. Scientists are taking steps to stop Venice from sinking into the sea.

   _____

6. The Guggenheim Museum in New York is an unusual building.

   _____

7. The life of Helen Keller is an inspiration to anyone who has a disability.

   _____

8. When he built the first Ferris wheel in 1893, George Ferris faced some big challenges. _____

9. Seeming to float above San Francisco Bay, the Golden Gate Bridge is an engineering marvel. _____

10. All young children go through the same stages as they develop.

   _____

◆ **PRACTICE 2-11**

Underline the transitional words and phrases in each of the following paragraphs. Then, decide what order—time order, spatial order, or logical order—the writer has chosen for arranging details in each paragraph. Write your answers in the blanks provided.

1. There are several reasons why today's teenage girls get only half as much exercise as boys. One reason girls get little exercise is that they watch a lot of television. However, this is not enough of an explanation because boys generally watch as much television as girls do. A more important reason is that many girls are not offered the sorts of organized athletic programs that are offered to boys. Furthermore, both parents now often work, and girls are more likely than boys to have responsibilities at home. For this reason, they have little free time to engage in physical activity. Most important, though, may be the attitude among girls that boys are not attracted to girls who are athletic. For some girls, being "feminine" means avoiding anything that might mess up their hair or make them sweat. Unless these attitudes change, the current generation of teenage girls may grow into a generation of women with serious health problems.

Order: _____

2. Although my apartment is small, it is perfect for me. As you enter my one-room apartment, the first thing you see on the left is a wooden loft. It is attached to one of the apartment's cream-colored walls. On top of the loft is my mattress. To the left of the mattress are a small bookshelf and a tiny dresser. Across from my bed are steps that lead down to the main level of the apartment. At the front of the room is my metal desk, which faces three large windows. In the middle of the room are two wooden chairs and a couch that I found in a used furniture store. At the back of the room is a small, open kitchen. A counter runs along the wall of the kitchen. Next to the counter are a refrigerator and a small closet. Above the counter are several cabinets that contain neatly stacked boxes and cans of food. Even though my apartment is small, I am very comfortable here, and I am lucky to have found it.

Order: _____

▶ **Word Power**
loft a balcony or platform, especially one for sleeping

3. The Caribbean island of Puerto Rico has a complex history. Before the 1400s, the island's inhabitants were the native Arawak Indians. In 1493, Christopher Columbus and his crew were the first Europeans to reach the island. Fifteen years later, Ponce de Leon conquered the island for Spain. The Spanish made the Arawaks slaves and forced them to work in the sugarcane fields. Eventually, these native people were completely wiped out. Soon the Arawaks were replaced by African slaves. In 1898, after the Spanish-American War, the island was given to the United States. The next year, the United States made Puerto Rico a colony under an American governor. Later, in 1917, Puerto Ricans were granted U.S. citizenship, and in 1952 the country became a U.S. commonwealth. Since then, Puerto Ricans have debated this status, with some arguing for statehood and others for independence. For now, the island remains a commonwealth, and its citizens share most of the rights and obligations of U.S. citizenship.

Order: _____

▶ **Word Power**
commonwealth a self-governing country or territory that is associated with a more powerful country

2 C

◆ **PRACTICE 2-12**

On the lines below, write a paragraph for each of the following topic sentences. After each of the paragraphs, indicate whether you arranged details in time order, spatial order, or logical order. When you have finished, reread the paragraphs, and make sure you have used transitional words and phrases to link your ideas.

■ **Culture Clue**

Elementary schools in the United States typically teach children from kindergarten through grade five or six (from the ages of five until ten or eleven).

1. There are many reasons why elementary schools should have good physical education programs. _____

_____

_____

_____

_____

_____

_____

(Details arranged in _____ order)

2. A job interview can go well if you prepare. _____

_____

_____

_____

_____

_____

_____

_____

(Details arranged in _____ order)

3. Just one look at my room tells people exactly who I am. _____

_____

_____

_____

_____

_____

_____

_____

(Details arranged in _____ order)

■ **WRITING FIRST: Flashback**

Look back at the paragraph you wrote for the Writing First activity in Chapter 1. Are all your sentences arranged in a clear, sensible order? Is this order time, spatial, or logical? List below the transitional words and phrases that signal this order to readers.

_____ _____

_____ _____

_____ _____

_____ _____

_____ _____

Now, add to your paragraph any transitions you think are needed, rearranging your sentences if necessary.

■ **WRITING FIRST: Revising and Editing**

Review the work you did for the Flashback activities on pages 32, 37, and above. Then, revise your paragraph for unity, development, and coherence, incorporating any changes or corrections you made in your Flashback activities.

CHAPTER REVIEW

◆ **EDITING PRACTICE**

Read the following paragraphs, and evaluate each one in terms of its unity, development, and coherence. First, underline each topic sentence. Then, cross out any sentences that do not support the topic sentence. Next, add transitional words and phrases where needed. Finally, be prepared to discuss in class whether additional details and examples could be added to each paragraph.

Nuclear reactor at Three Mile Island

1. In 1979, a series of errors in the nuclear generating plant at Three Mile Island, near Harrisburg, Pennsylvania, caused an accident that changed the nuclear power industry. A combination of stuck valves, human error, and poor decisions caused a partial meltdown of the reactor core. Large amounts of radioactive gases were released into the atmosphere. The governor of Pennsylvania evacuated pregnant women from the area. Other residents panicked and left their homes. The nuclear regulatory agency claimed that the situation was not really dangerous. It said that the released gases were not a health threat. Activists and local residents disagreed with this. The reactor itself remained unusable for more than ten years. Large demonstrations followed the accident, including a rally of more than 200,000 people in New York City. Some people came because the day was nice. By the mid-1980s, all new construction of nuclear power plants in the United States had stopped.

Ad featuring Joe Camel

2. Tobacco companies have consistently encouraged people to smoke. One of the earliest television ads showed two boxes of cigarettes dancing to an advertising jingle. The approach in this ad was simple: create an entertaining commercial, and people will buy the product. Many people liked these ads. Other advertisements were aimed at specific audiences. Marlboro commercials, with the rugged Marlboro man, targeted men. Virginia Slims made an obvious pitch to women by saying, "You've come a long way, baby!" Salem, a mentholated cigarette, showed rural scenes and targeted people who liked the freshness of the outdoors. Kent, with its "micronite filter," appealed to those who were health conscious by claiming that Kent contained less tar and nicotine than

any other brand. This claim was not entirely true. Other brands had less tar and nicotine. Merit and other high-tar and high-nicotine cigarettes began to target minorities. Cigarette companies responded to the national decline in smoking by directing advertising at young people. Camel introduced the cartoon character Joe Camel, which was aimed at teenagers and young adults.

3. Cities created police forces for a number of reasons. The first reason was status: after the Civil War, it became a status symbol for cities to have a uniformed police force. A police force provided a large number of political jobs. This meant that politicians were able to reward people who worked to support them. Police forces made people feel safe. Police officers helped visitors find their way. They took in lost children and sometimes fed the homeless. They directed traffic, enforced health regulations, and provided other services. Police officers kept order. Without a visible, uniformed police force, criminals would have made life in nineteenth-century cities unbearable.

Nineteenth-century police officer in uniform

◆ COLLABORATIVE ACTIVITIES

1. Working in a group, list the reasons why you think students decide to attend your school. After working together to arrange these reasons from least to most important, write a topic sentence that states the main idea suggested by your list. Finally, on your own, draft a paragraph in which you discuss the key factors that lead students to attend your school.

2. In a newspaper or magazine, find an illustration or photograph that includes a lot of details. Then, write a paragraph describing what you see in the photograph. (Include enough support—details and examples—so that readers will be able to "see" it almost as clearly as you can.) Decide on a specific spatial order—from top to bottom, from left to right, or another arrangement that makes sense to you. Use that spatial order to organize the details in your paragraph. Finally, trade paragraphs with another student, and offer suggestions that could improve his or her paragraph.

3. Bring to class a paragraph from a newspaper or a magazine. Working in a group, decide whether each of your paragraphs is unified, well developed, and coherent. If any paragraph does not conform to the guidelines outlined in this chapter, try as a group to revise it to make it more effective.

☑ REVIEW CHECKLIST:
Fine-Tuning Your Paragraph

- A topic sentence states the main idea of your paragraph. (See 2A.)

- A paragraph is unified when it focuses on a single main idea. (See 2A.)

- A paragraph is well developed when it contains enough details and examples to support the main idea. (See 2B).

- A paragraph is coherent if its sentences are arranged in a clear, sensible order and it includes all necessary transitional words and phrases. (See 2C.)

UNIT TWO

PATTERNS OF PARAGRAPH DEVELOPMENT

Exemplification

PREVIEW

In this chapter, you will learn to write an exemplification paragraph.

■ WRITING FIRST

The picture above shows the home page of Miami Dade College's Web site. Many students go to this site for information about the school and the support services offered there. Visit your school's Web site, and then write a paragraph about the programs and services your school offers to make it easier for students to adjust to college. Begin your paragraph with a topic sentence that states your main idea.

▶ **Word Power**

adapt to adjust to new surroundings

mentor an experienced and trusted advisor

facilitate to make easy

49

3 A

In Chapters 3 through 11, you will learn different ways of organizing your ideas within paragraphs: *exemplification, narration, description, process, cause and effect, comparison and contrast, classification, definition,* and *argument.* Recognizing these patterns and understanding how they help you organize your ideas will make you a more confident writer.

A   What Is Exemplification?

What do we mean when we tell a friend that a teacher is "good" or that a football team is "bad"? In class or on an exam, what do we mean when we say that a character in a play is "undeveloped" or that a particular war was "wrong"? To clarify general statements like these, we use **exemplification**—that is, we use specific examples that illustrate a general idea.

General Statement	*Specific Examples*
Today is going to be a hard day.	Today is going to be a hard day because I have a history test in the morning and a lab quiz in the afternoon. I also have to go to work an hour earlier than usual.
My car is giving me problems.	My car is burning oil and won't start on cold mornings. In addition, I need a new set of tires.

An **exemplification paragraph** explains or clarifies the idea in the **topic sentence** with specific examples. Personal experiences, class discussions, observations, conversations, and reading (for example, in newspapers and magazines or on the Internet) can all be good sources of examples.

When you write an exemplification paragraph, keep the following guidelines in mind:

- An **exemplification paragraph** should begin with a topic sentence that states the paragraph's main idea.
- The topic sentence is followed by examples that support the main idea.
- Examples should be arranged in **logical order**—for example, from least important to most important or from general to specific.
- An exemplification paragraph ends with a concluding statement that sums up its main idea.

An exemplification paragraph generally has the following structure.

```
Topic Sentence _____

Example #1 _____

_____

Example #2 _____

_____

Example #3 _____

_____

Concluding Statement _____

_____
```

The following paragraph uses several examples to make the point that some countries change their names for political reasons.

New Government, New Name

Often, when countries change their names, it is for political reasons. ——— Topic sentence
Sometimes a new government decides to change the country's name to separate
itself from an earlier government. For example, Burma became Myanmar when
a military government took over in 1989. Cambodia has had several name
changes as well. After a coup in 1970, it was called the Khmer Republic. Then,
in 1975, under communist rule, it became Kampuchea. Gaining independence
from another nation is another reason for a country to change its name. For ——— Examples presented
instance, in 1957, after gaining independence from the Great Britain, the Gold   in logical order
Coast became Ghana. Another name change occurred when the French Sudan
became Mali. After gaining independence from France in 1960, it decided to
reject its colonial past. Finally, Zimbabwe gave up its former British name,
Rhodesia, several years after winning independence. These name changes
can be confusing, but they reveal the changing political climate of the ——— Concluding statement
countries in which they occur.

—Kim Seng (student)

When you write an exemplification paragraph, be sure to include clear
transitional words and phrases. These transitions help readers follow your
discussion by indicating how each example is related to another as well as
how each example supports the topic sentence.

Transitions for Exemplification

also	for instance	specifically
besides	furthermore	the most important
finally	in addition	example
first…second…	moreover	the next example
[and so on]	one example…	
for example	another example	

GRAMMAR IN CONTEXT **Exemplification**

When you write an exemplification paragraph, always use a comma after an introductory transitional word or phrase that introduces an example.

> <u>For example</u>, Burma became Myanmar when a new military government took over in 1989.

> <u>Finally</u>, Zimbabwe gave up its former British name, Rhodesia, several years after winning independence.

For information on using commas with introductory transitional words and phrases, see 31B.

◆ **PRACTICE 3-1**

Read this exemplification paragraph; then, follow the instructions that come after it.

Jobs of the Future

Students should take courses that prepare them for the careers that will be in demand over the next ten years. For example, the health-care field will have the greatest growth. Hundreds of thousands of medical workers—such as home-care aides, physician assistants, and registered nurses—will be needed. Also, many new employees will be needed in the retail and customer-service areas. These are fields in which technology cannot completely replace human beings. In addition, certain computer fields will need many more workers. People who can work as database administrators or information systems managers will find many employment opportunities. Furthermore, education will be an attractive area for new job seekers. Many new teachers will be needed to replace the thousands who are expected to

retire during the next ten years. Students who know what jobs will be available can prepare themselves for the future.

— Liz Behr (student)

1. Underline the topic sentence of the paragraph.

2. List the specific examples the writer uses to support her topic sentence. The first example has been listed for you.

   health-care jobs
   _____

   _____

   _____

   _____

3. Circle the transitions the writer uses to connect ideas in the paragraph.

4. Underline the paragraph's concluding statement.

◆ PRACTICE 3-2

Following are four possible topic sentences for exemplification paragraphs. On the lines below, list three or four examples you could use to support each topic sentence. For example, if you were writing a paragraph about how difficult the first week of your new job was, you could mention waking up early, getting to know your coworkers, and learning new routines.

1. There is plenty to like in my neighborhood. _____

   _____

   _____

   _____

   _____

   _____

2. Part-time jobs give students opportunities to develop useful skills.

   _____

   _____

   _____

   _____

   _____

3. Good health care is sometimes difficult to find. _____

   _____

   _____

_____

_____

_____

_____

4. You can learn a lot by watching certain television shows. _____

_____

_____

_____

_____

_____

B **Writing an Exemplification Paragraph**

When Sarah Herman was asked to write a paragraph about work, she had little difficulty deciding on a topic. She had just finished a summer job waiting on tables in Sea Isle City, New Jersey. She knew, without a doubt, that this was the worst job she had ever had.

Once she had decided on her topic, Sarah brainstormed to find ideas to write about. After reviewing her brainstorming notes, she listed several examples that could support her topic sentence.

Restaurant too big

Boss disrespectful

No experience

Kitchen chaotic

Customers rude

Tips bad

> **Word Power**
> **chaotic** confused or
> disorderly

After reading her list, Sarah wrote the following topic sentence to express the main idea of her paragraph.

TOPIC SENTENCE   Being a waitress was the worst job I ever had.

After Sarah identified her main idea, she eliminated examples that she thought did not support her topic sentence. Then, she arranged the remaining examples in the order in which she thought she could discuss them most effectively: from least important to most important.

TOPIC SENTENCE: Being a waitress was the worst job I ever had.
    1. No experience
    2. Customers rude
    3. Tips bad
    4. Boss disrespectful

Using her list of points as a guide, Sarah wrote the following draft of her paragraph.

> Waiting on tables was the worst job I ever had. I had little experience as a waitress. The first day of work was so bad that I almost quit. The customers were rude. All they wanted was to get their food as fast as possible so they could get back to the beach or the boardwalk. As a result, they were often impolite and demanding. The tips were bad. It was hard to be pleasant when you knew that the table you were waiting on was probably going to leave you a bad tip. Finally, the owner of the restaurant did not show us any respect. He often yelled at us, saying that if we didn't work harder, he would fire us. He never did, but his constant threats didn't do much to help our morale.

When she finished her draft, Sarah met with her instructor. She knew she had a good topic sentence, but she also knew she needed to make some revisions. Together, she and her instructor decided on some changes that would make her paragraph better.

- She needed to make some of her examples more specific. For example, what experience did she have that made her want to quit? Exactly how were customers rude?
- She needed to add transitions to make it easier for readers to follow her discussion.
- She needed to add a concluding statement.

With her instructor's comments in mind, Sarah revised her paragraph. Here is her final draft.

▶ **Word Power**
morale a positive spirit that motivates a group to succeed

My First Job

Waiting on tables was the worst job I ever had. First, I had never worked in a restaurant before, so I had a lot to learn. Unfortunately, I forgot to bring salads to the first table I waited on. A person at the table complained so loudly that the owner had to calm him down. I was so upset that I almost quit. Second, the customers at the restaurant were often rude. All they wanted was to get their food as fast as possible so they could get back to the beach or the boardwalk. They were on vacation, and they wanted to be treated well. As a result, they were often impolite and demanding. No one ever said, "excuse me," "please," or "thank you," no matter what I did for them. Third, the tips were usually bad. It was hard to be pleasant when you knew that the table you were waiting on was probably going to leave you a bad tip, if you were lucky. Finally, the owner of the restaurant never showed his workers any respect. He would yell at us, saying that if we didn't work harder he would fire us. He never did, but his constant threats didn't do much to help our morale. Even though I got through the summer, I promised myself that I would never wait on tables again.

Examples made more specific

Transitions added

Concluding statement added

◆ **PRACTICE 3-3**

Now, you are ready to write an exemplification paragraph. Choose one of the topics below (or choose your own topic). Then, on a separate sheet of paper, use one or more of the strategies described in 1C to help you think of as many examples as you can for the topic you have chosen.

Effective (or ineffective) teachers	Things you can't do without
Qualities that make an athlete great	Terrible dates
	Extreme sports
Roommates	Role models
Challenges older students face	Rude behavior
Traditions your family follows	Politicians
Unattractive clothing styles	Acts of courage
Peer pressure	Lying
The benefits of iPods	Credit-card debt

◆ **PRACTICE 3-4**

Review your notes from Practice 3-3, and list the examples that can best help you develop a paragraph on the topic you have chosen.

_____

_____

_____

_____

◆ **PRACTICE 3-5**

Reread your list of examples from Practice 3-4. Then, draft a topic sentence that introduces your topic and communicates the main idea your paragraph will discuss.

_____

_____

_____

_____

◆ **PRACTICE 3-6**

Arrange the examples you listed in Practice 3-4 in a logical order—for example, from least important to most important.

1. _____

2. _____

3. _____

4. _____

◆ PRACTICE 3-7

Draft your exemplification paragraph.

◆ PRACTICE 3-8

Consulting the Self-Assessment Checklist below, revise your exemplification paragraph.

◆ PRACTICE 3-9

Type a final draft of your exemplification paragraph.

■ **WRITING FIRST: Revising and Editing**

Look back at your response to the Writing First activity on page 49. Consulting the Self-Assessment Checklist below, evaluate the paragraph you wrote. Then, prepare a final draft of your paragraph.

☑ SELF-ASSESSMENT CHECKLIST:
Writing an Exemplification Paragraph

■ Do you have a clearly worded topic sentence that states your paragraph's main idea?

■ Does your topic sentence state an idea that can be supported with examples?

■ Do all your examples support your topic sentence, or should some be deleted?

■ Do you have enough examples, or do you need to add more?

■ Do transitions introduce all the examples your paragraph discusses, or do you need to add transitions to make your paragraph more coherent?

■ Does your paragraph end with a concluding statement that summarizes your main idea?

MOVING FROM PARAGRAPH TO ESSAY

Exemplification

In addition to writing exemplification paragraphs, you may sometimes have to write an **exemplification essay**. For example, on a communications midterm, you might be asked to give examples of types of television news shows. In an email to a local newspaper, you might decide to give examples of quality-of-life improvements that need to be made in your neighborhood. *For information on how to write an exemplification essay, see 14A.*

Narration

PREVIEW

In this chapter, you will learn to write a narrative paragraph.

Panel 1: "DO YOU BELIEVE IN MAGIC?" IT WAS A SONG ON THE RADIO THAT PLAYED THE SUMMER I DECIDED TO MOVE MY BEDROOM INTO THE BASEMENT.

I'LL MEETCHA TOMORROW SORTA LATE AT NIGHT

Panel 2: I WAS GROWING MY HAIR OUT AND IT WAS IN AN IN-BETWEEN STAGE THAT DIDN'T MAKE SENSE TO ANYBODY. I'D WANTED LONG HAIR ALL MY LIFE. I WAS WILLING TO LOOK INSANE WHILE I WAITED FOR IT.

DO YOU BELIEVE LIKE I BELIEVE

Panel 3: THERE WERE BIG CHANGES GOING ON IN MY HOUSE. GRANDMA MOVED OUT, AND BOTH MY PARENTS WERE "SECRETLY" SEEING OTHER PEOPLE. THEY WERE NEVER AROUND.

HALT! GET OUT OF MY WAY.

NO ONE SAID YOU COULD MOVE TO THE BASEMENT.

BUG OFF.

MAKE ME.

Panel 4: I WAS LEFT TO WATCH MY TWO YOUNGER BROTHERS AND KEEP HOUSE. I WAS SUPPOSED TO STAY AT HOME ALL DAY, EVERY DAY, THE SUMMER THAT SONG PLAYED ON THE RADIO.

WE'RE HUNGRY, MAN! YOU GOTTA MAKE US FOOD, MAN!

CHICKEN POT PIES, OVEN AT 350°.

WE'RE SICK OF CHICKEN POT PIE, MAN!

I'M NOT.

■ WRITING FIRST

The four panels above are part of a graphic story from Lynda Barry's book *One! Hundred! Demons!* Look at the four panels, and then write a paragraph in which you tell the story of a difficult period in your childhood. Make sure your topic sentence states the main idea of your paragraph.

> **Word Power**
> **traumatic** emotionally damaging
>
> **dysfunctional** not functioning well

A **What Is Narration?**

Narration is writing that tells a story. For example, a narrative paragraph could tell how an experience you had as a child changed you, how the life of Martin Luther King Jr. is inspiring, or how the Battle of Gettysburg was the turning point in the Civil War.

When you write a narrative paragraph, keep the following guidelines in mind:

■ A **narrative paragraph** should begin with a topic sentence that tells readers the point of the paragraph—that is, why you are telling a particular story.

■ Events are presented in a definite **time order**, usually the order in which they occurred. Effective narrative paragraphs include only those events that tell the story and avoid irrelevant information that could distract or confuse readers.

■ A narrative paragraph ends with a concluding statement that sums up the main idea stated in the topic sentence.

A narrative paragraph generally has the following structure.

Topic Sentence _____

Event #1 _____

_____

Event #2 _____

_____

Event #3 _____

_____

Concluding Statement _____

_____

The writer of the following paragraph recounts a series of events to support the point that getting a tattoo is a lot easier than having one removed.

KBR Forever

Topic sentence ——— It only takes a few minutes to get a tattoo, but having one removed takes a

lot more time and effort. Until I met Kevin, I had never wanted a tattoo. By the

Events presented ⌐ time we had been together for three months, I was sure he was my soul mate.
in time order ⌐

Even after a year, we could not go a day without seeing or talking to each

other. When he suggested we get our initials tattooed on each other's wrists, I did not hesitate. Then, we broke up. Now, when I see that "KBR," I feel sick to my stomach. Next week, I am going to have my first laser treatment to remove the tattoo. The whole process will cost ten times what the tattoo cost, but it will be worth it. After five painful sessions, the tattoo should be gone. <u>Breaking up with Kevin was easy, but getting rid of his initials will be a lot more trouble.</u> — *Concluding statement*

—Gillian Kavsan (student)

As you arrange your ideas in a narrative paragraph, be sure to use clear transitional words and phrases, as the student writer does in the paragraph above. These signals help readers follow your narrative by indicating the order of the events you discuss.

Transitions for Narration

after	first…second…third	suddenly
as	immediately	then
as soon as	later	two hours (days, months,
before	later on	years) later
by the time	mean while	until
earlier	next	when
eventually	now	specific dates
finally	soon	(for example, "In 2006")

GRAMMAR IN CONTEXT   Narration

When you write a narrative paragraph, you tell a story. As you become involved in your story, you might forget all about sentence boundaries and begin to string events together without proper punctuation. If you do, you will create a **run-on** or a **comma splice.**

INCORRECT (RUN-ON) We had been together for three months I was sure he was my soul mate.

CORRECT We had been together for three months. I was sure he was my soul mate.

CORRECT By the time we had been together for three months, I was sure he was my soul mate.

For information on how to recognize and correct run-ons and comma splices, see Chapter 21.

◆ **PRACTICE 4-1**

Read this narrative paragraph; then, follow the instructions that come after it.

When I first came to live in a dormitory at college, I was homesick. As soon as my parents left me at school, I felt sad. My room looked cramped and empty. I couldn't see how two people could live in such a tiny space, and I missed my room at home. My roommate hadn't arrived yet, so I picked out a bed on one side of the room and started to unpack my belongings. Then, my roommate burst through the door, smiling and joking. Immediately, I felt better. We talked about our high schools and our families. Later on, we made plans to fix up the room with some posters. When it was time to eat, we went to the cafeteria for dinner. I was used to meat and potatoes; however, the cafeteria was serving salads and veggie burgers. Suddenly, I wanted to be home, eating with my family. I even missed my little sister. When I went to bed that night, I thought about the changes I would have to adapt to. Now, I realized that living away from home would be very challenging.

—John Deni (student)

1. Underline the topic sentence of the paragraph.

2. List the major events of the narrative. The first event has been listed for you.

   I felt sad.

   _____

   _____

   _____

   _____

   _____

   _____

   _____

3. Circle the transitional words and phrases the writer uses to link events in time.

4. Underline the paragraph's concluding statement.

◆ **PRACTICE 4-2**

Following are four possible topic sentences for narrative paragraphs. On the lines below, list three or four events that could support each topic sentence. For example, if you were recalling a barbecue that turned into a disaster, you could tell about burning the hamburgers, spilling the soda, and forgetting to buy paper plates.

1. One experience made me realize that I was no longer as young as I thought. _____

   _____

   _____

2. The first time I _____, I got more than I bargained for.

   _____

3. I didn't think I had the courage to _____, but when I did, I felt proud of myself. _____

   _____

   _____

4. I remember my reactions to one particular event very clearly.

   _____

   _____

   _____

B Writing a Narrative Paragraph

When Todd Kinzer's instructor asked the class to write a paragraph about an experience that had a great impact on them, Todd tried to narrow this topic by listing some experiences that he could write about.

   Accident at camp — Realized I wasn't as strong as I thought I was

   Breaking up with Lindsay — That was painful

   Shooting the winning basket in my last high school game — Sweet

   The last Thanksgiving at my grandparents' house — Happy and sad

As Todd looked over the experiences on his list, he realized that he could write about all of them. He decided, however, to focus on the last Thanksgiving he spent at his grandparents' house. This occasion was especially meaningful to him because his grandfather died right after the holiday.

Todd began his writing process by freewriting on his topic. He typed whatever came into his mind about the dinner, without worrying about spelling, punctuation, or grammar. Here is Todd's freewriting paragraph.

Thanksgiving. Who knew? I remember the smells when I woke up. I can see Granddad at the stove. We were all happy. He told us stories about when he was a kid. I'd heard some of them before, but so what? I loved to hear them. We ate so much I could hardly move. They say turkey has something in it that puts you to sleep. We watched football all afternoon and evening. I still can't believe Granddad died. I guess I have the topic for my paragraph.

When he looked over his freewriting, Todd thought he had enough ideas for a first draft of his paragraph. His draft appears below.

Last Thanksgiving, my grandparents were up early. My grandfather stuffed the turkey, and my grandmother started cooking the other dishes. When I got up, I could smell the turkey in the oven. The table was already set for dinner, so we ate breakfast in the kitchen. My grandfather told us about the Thanksgivings he remembered from when he was a boy. When we sat down for dinner, a fire was burning in the fireplace. My grandmother said grace. My grandfather carved the turkey, and we all passed around dishes of food. For dessert, we had pecan pie and ice cream. After dinner, we watched football on TV. When I went to bed, I felt happy. This was my grandfather's last Thanksgiving.

Todd knew his first draft needed a lot of work. Before he wrote the next draft, he tried to remember what other things had happened that Thanksgiving. He also tried to decide which idea was most important and what additional information could make his paragraph stronger. After he reread his paragraph, he made these changes.

- He added a topic sentence that stated his main idea.
- To unify his paragraph, he deleted sentences that did not support his main idea.
- He added transitional words and phrases to indicate the time order of events in the paragraph.
- He wrote a stronger concluding statement.

After making these changes, Todd wrote the following revised and edited version of his paragraph.

Thanksgiving Memories

Topic sentence added

This past Thanksgiving was the last one I would spend with both my grandparents. The holiday began early. At 5 o'clock in the morning, my grandfather woke up and began to stuff the turkey. About an hour later, my grandmother began cooking corn pie and pineapple casserole. At 8 o'clock, when I got up, I could smell the turkey cooking. While we ate breakfast, my grandfather told us about Thanksgivings he remembered when he was a boy. Later, my grandfather made a fire in the fireplace, and we sat down for dinner. After my grandmother

Transitions added

said grace, my grandfather carved and served the turkey. The rest of us passed around dishes of sweet potatoes, mashed potatoes, green beans, asparagus, cucumber salad, relish, cranberry sauce, apple butter, cabbage salad, stuffing, and of course, corn pie and pineapple casserole. For dessert, my grandmother served pecan pie with scoops of ice cream. After dinner, we turned on the TV and the whole family watched football all evening. Four months later, my grandfather was diagnosed with terminal cancer. For my family and me, Thanksgiving would never be the same.

■ Stronger concluding
statement added

◆ PRACTICE 4-3

Now, you are ready to write a narrative paragraph. Choose one of the topics below (or choose your own topic). Then, on a separate sheet of paper, use one or more of the strategies described in 1C to help you recall events and details to develop the topic you have chosen.

A difficult choice	An embarrassing situation
A frightening situation	A surprise
A time of self-doubt	A sudden understanding or insight
A success	Something funny a friend did
An act of violence	Unexpected good luck
A lesson you learned	A conflict with authority
A happy moment	An event that changed your life
An instance of injustice	An important decision

◆ PRACTICE 4-4

List the events you recalled in Practice 4-3 that can best help you develop a narrative paragraph on the topic you have chosen.

_____

_____

_____

_____

_____

_____

◆ PRACTICE 4-5

Reread your list of events from Practice 4-4. Then, draft a topic sentence that introduces your topic and states the main idea your paragraph will discuss.

_____

_____

_____

◆ **PRACTICE 4-6**

Write down the events you listed in Practice 4-4 in the order in which they occurred.

1. _____

2. _____

3. _____

4. _____

5. _____

◆ **PRACTICE 4-7**

Draft your narrative paragraph.

◆ **PRACTICE 4-8**

Consulting the Self-Assessment Checklist below, revise your narrative paragraph.

◆ **PRACTICE 4-9**

Type a final draft of your narrative paragraph.

■ **WRITING FIRST: Revising and Editing**

Look back at your response to the Writing First activity on page 59. Consulting the Self-Assessment Checklist below, evaluate the paragraph you wrote. Then, prepare a final draft of your paragraph.

☑ **SELF-ASSESSMENT CHECKLIST:**
Writing a Narrative Paragraph

☐ Do you have a clearly worded topic sentence that states your paragraph's main idea?

☐ Does your topic sentence give readers an idea why you are telling the story?

(continued on following page)

(continued from previous page)

- Do your details fully support your paragraph's topic sentence, or should some be added?

- Do you include enough information about the events you discuss, or do you need to add more?

- Do your transitions clearly indicate the order of events in the paragraph, or do you need to add transitions to make your paragraph more coherent?

- Does your paragraph end with a concluding statement that summarizes your main idea?

MOVING FROM PARAGRAPH TO ESSAY

Narration

In addition to writing narrative paragraphs, you may sometimes have to write a **narrative essay**. For example, in a history class, you might have to write a short essay discussing the events that led up to the American Revolution. In a letter of complaint, you might have to summarize, in time order, the problems you had with a particular product. *For information on how to write a narrative essay, see 14B.*

■ WRITING FIRST

The picture above shows a street vendor selling food. Look at the picture, and then write a paragraph in which you describe a person you encounter every day—for example, a street vendor, a bus driver, or a worker in your school cafeteria. Before you begin writing, decide what general impression you want to convey about the person you are describing.

A What Is Description?

In a personal email, you may describe a new boyfriend or girlfriend. In a biology lab manual, you may describe the structure of a cell. In report for a nursing class, you may describe a patient you treated.

When you write a **description**, you use words to paint a picture for your readers. With description, you use language that creates a vivid impression of what you have seen, heard, smelled, tasted, or touched. The more details you include, the better your description will be.

The following description is flat because it includes very few details.

FLAT   Today, I saw a beautiful sunrise.

In contrast, the description below is full of details that convey the writer's experience to readers.

RICH   Early this morning as I walked along the soft sandy
beach, I saw the sun rise slowly out of the ocean. At first,
the ocean glowed red. Then, it turned slowly to pink, to
aqua, and finally to blue. As I stood watching the sun,
I heard the waves hit the shore, and I felt the cold water
swirl around my toes. For a moment, even the small grey
and white birds that hurried along the shore seemed to
stop and watch the dazzling sight.

The revised description relies on sight (*glowed red*; *turned slowly to pink, to aqua, and finally to blue*), touch (*the soft sandy beach*; *felt the cold water*), and sound (*heard the waves hit the shore*).

When you write a descriptive paragraph, keep the following guidelines in mind:

■ A **descriptive paragraph** should begin with a topic sentence that states the main point you want to make in your paragraph (for example, "My sister's room is a pig sty" or "The wooden roller coaster in Coney Island is a work of art").

■ A descriptive paragraph should present the details that support the topic sentence in a clear **spatial order**, the order in which you observed the person, object, or scene you are describing. For example, you can move from near to far or from top to bottom.

■ A descriptive paragraph ends with a concluding statement that sums up the main idea stated in the topic sentence.

A descriptive paragraph generally has the following structure.

Topic Sentence _____

Detail #1 _____

_____

Detail #2 _____

_____

Detail #3 _____

_____

Concluding Statement _____

_____

The writer of the following paragraph uses descriptive details to support the idea that despite being an indoor mall, the Mall of America gives shoppers the sense that they are surrounded by nature.

The Mall of America

Topic sentence ——— Although Minnesota's Mall of America is all indoors, nature is everywhere. Above the polished marble interior, glass skylights let in the sun. In the center of the mall, large trees and rough timber benches surround a brightly colored amusement park. The shiny tile and glass corridors, which spread out from the center in every direction, are lined with rows of leafy plants. When watered, these plants smell damp and earthy like a park after a rainstorm. One of the corridors leads to a pale green fountain where water splashes into a shallow pool. Down another corridor, past the hissing espresso machines at one of the mall's many coffee shops, is an even wilder example of the outdoors. Taking an escalator down to the aquarium, visitors can see sharks swimming beneath the acres of shops. Even though shoppers are in an enclosed mall, they sometimes get the feeling that they are walking though a park that happens to be lined with stores.

Details arranged in spatial order

Concluding statement

— Heidi Decker (student)

As you arrange your ideas in a descriptive paragraph, be sure to use appropriate transitional words and phrases to lead readers from one detail to another.

Transitions for Description

above	in front of	outside
behind	inside	over
below	nearby	the first…the second
between	next to	the least important…
beyond	on	the most important
in	on one side…on the	the next
in back of	other side	under

GRAMMAR IN CONTEXT   **Description**

When you write a descriptive paragraph, you sometimes use **modifiers**—words and phrases that describe another word in the sentence. If a modifier cannot logically describe any word in the sentence, it is called a **dangling modifier**.

CONFUSING (DANGLING MODIFIER)   Taking an escalator down to the aquarium, sharks can be seen swimming beneath the acres of shops. (Were the sharks taking the escalator?)

CLEAR   Taking an escalator down to the aquarium, visitors can see sharks swimming beneath the acres of shops.

For information on how to identify and correct dangling modifiers, see Chapter 25.

◆ **PRACTICE 5-1**

Read this descriptive paragraph; then, follow the instructions that come after it.

The Bookmobile

In my neighborhood, the arrival of the bookmobile is something everyone looks forward to. Every other week, the bright green bookmobile parks outside my apartment building. At its door, a crowd of excited people gathers. Inside the long narrow bus, the shelves are filled with the bright, inviting spines of books. The mobile library is divided neatly into sections, just like any library. The chunky, well-worn bestsellers are on the first set of shelves. Behind them, the popular CDs and DVDs are piled in tight, organized stacks. Next to them are the many shelves of books on every topic, from cooking and home repair to politics and religion. Finally, at the back of bookmobile, four red and blue beanbag chairs sit in a cozy pile in the middle of the kids' section. Here in the bookmobile, far from the sounds of the street, readers settle in to enjoy a little quiet library time.

—Felix Jimenez (student)

1. Underline the topic sentence of the paragraph.

2. In a few words, summarize the main idea of the paragraph.

_____

_____

3. What are some of the details the writer uses to describe the book-mobile? The first detail has been listed for you.

bright green

_____

_____

_____

_____

_____

_____

4. Circle the transitional words and phrases the writer uses to lead readers from one detail to another.

5. Underline the paragraph's concluding statement.

◆ **PRACTICE 5-2**

Each of the five topic sentences below states a possible main idea for a paragraph. After each topic sentence, list three details that could help convey this main idea. For example, to support the idea that sitting in front of a fireplace is relaxing, you could describe the crackling of the fire, the pine scent of the smoke, and the changing colors of the flames.

1. One look at the stern face of the traffic-court judge told me that my appeal would be denied.

_____

_____

_____

2. The dog was at least ten years old and had been living on the streets for a long time.

_____

_____

_____

3. The woman behind the department store makeup counter was a walking advertisement for every product she sold.

_____

_____

_____

4. One of the most interesting stores I know sells vintage clothing.

_____

_____

_____

► **Word Power**
vintage old-fashioned

5. Riding the roller coaster was so exciting that I got back in line for another ride.

_____

_____

_____

B Writing a Descriptive Paragraph

When Jared Lopez was asked to write a descriptive paragraph about someone he admired, he decided to write about his uncle Manuel, who had been a father figure to him.

Because he was familiar with his topic, Jared did not have to brainstorm or freewrite to find ideas. He decided to begin his paragraph by giving a general description of his uncle and then concentrate on his uncle's most noticeable feature: his hands. Here is the first draft of Jared's paragraph.

> My uncle's name is Manuel, but his friends call him Manny. He is over six feet tall. Uncle Manny's eyes are dark brown, almost black. They make him look very serious. When he laughs, however, he looks friendly. His nose is long and straight, and it makes Uncle Manny look very distinguished. Most interesting to me are Uncle Manny's hands. Even though he hasn't worked as a stonemason since he opened his own construction company ten years ago, his hands are still rough and scarred. They are large and strong, but they can be gentle too.

After a conference with his instructor, Jared made a number of changes.

- He added a topic sentence that stated the main idea of his description.
- He added more details so that readers would have a better sense of what his uncle looked like.
- He included more transitions to move readers from one part of his description to another.
- He wrote a stronger concluding statement.

Jared made these changes as he revised and edited his draft.

5 B

- Topic sentence added

- Transitions added

- Details added

- Stronger concluding
  statement added

My Uncle Manny

My uncle Manuel is a kind and gentle person who took care of my mother and me when my father died. My uncle Manuel, or "Manny" as his friends and family call him, is over six feet tall. This is unusual for a Mexican of his generation. The first thing that most people notice about my uncle Manny is his eyes. They are large and dark brown, almost black. They make him look serious. When he laughs, however, the sides of his eyes crinkle and his face seems to light up. The next thing that stands out is his nose, which is long and straight. My mother says it makes Uncle Manny look distinguished. Below his mustache is his mouth. His dark, full lips cover bright white teeth that shine when he smiles. The most interesting thing about Uncle Manny is his hands. Even though he hasn't worked as a stonemason since he opened his own construction company ten years ago, his hands are still rough and scarred from carrying stones. No matter how much he tries, he can't get rid of the dirt under the skin of his fingers. Uncle Manny's hands are big and rough, but they can be gentle too. To me they show what he really is: a strong and gentle man.

◆ PRACTICE 5-3

Now, you are ready to write a descriptive paragraph. Choose one of the topics below (or choose your own topic). Then, on a separate sheet of paper, use one or more of the strategies described in 1C to help you come up with specific details about the topic you have chosen. If you can, observe your subject directly and write down your observations.

A favorite place	A favorite article of clothing
A place you felt trapped in	A useful object
A comfortable spot on campus	A pet
An unusual person	A building you think is ugly
Your dream house	Your car or truck
A family member or friend	The car you would like to have
A work of art	A statue or monument
A valued possession	Someone you admire
Your workplace	A cooking disaster

◆ PRACTICE 5-4

List the details you came up with in Practice 5-3 that can best help you develop a descriptive paragraph on the topic you have chosen.

_____

_____

_____

_____

_____

◆ PRACTICE 5-5

Reread your list of details from Practice 5-4. Then, draft a topic sentence that summarizes the idea you want to convey in your paragraph.

_____

_____

◆ PRACTICE 5-6

Arrange the details you listed in Practice 5-4. You might arrange them in the order in which you have observed them—for example, from left to right, near to far, or top to bottom.

1. _____

2. _____

3. _____

4. _____

5. _____

6. _____

7. _____

◆ PRACTICE 5-7

Draft your descriptive paragraph.

◆ PRACTICE 5-8

Consulting the Self-Assessment Checklist on page 76, revise your descriptive paragraph.

◆ **PRACTICE 5-9**

Type a final draft of your descriptive paragraph.

■ **WRITING FIRST: Revising and Editing**

Look back at your response to the Writing First activity on page 68. Consulting the Self-Assessment Checklist below, evaluate the paragraph you wrote. Then, prepare a final draft of your paragraph.

☑ **SELF-ASSESSMENT CHECKLIST:**
Writing a Descriptive Paragraph

☐ Do you have a clearly worded topic sentence that states your paragraph's main idea?

☐ Does your topic sentence indicate what person, place, or object you will be describing in your paragraph?

☐ Do all your examples and details help to support your paragraph's main idea, or should some be deleted?

☐ Do you have enough descriptive details, or do you need to introduce more details?

☐ Do transitions lead readers from one detail to the next, or do you need to add transitions to make your paragraph more coherent?

☐ Are your details presented in a clear spatial order?

☐ Does your paragraph end with a concluding statement that summarizes your main idea?

MOVING FROM PARAGRAPH TO ESSAY

Description

In addition to writing descriptive paragraphs, you may sometimes have to write a **descriptive essay**. For example, in a drama class, you might write an essay in which you describe a play's setting. At work, you might write a memo describing a piece of equipment you would like your department to buy. *For information on how to write a descriptive essay, see 14C.*

Process

CHAPTER 6

PREVIEW

In this chapter, you will learn how to write a process paragraph.

■ **WRITING FIRST**

The picture above shows a spinner from the game Twister. Look at the picture, and then write a paragraph in which you explain how to play your favorite board (or other indoor) game. Assume that your readers know nothing about the game.

> ▶ **Word Power**
> **compete** to work against another person in pursuit of a goal
>
> **objective** a purpose or goal
>
> **penalty** a punishment

A   What Is Process?

When you describe a **process**, you tell readers how something works or how to do something. For example, you could explain how the optical scanner at the checkout counter of a food store works, how to hem a pair of pants, or how to send a text message.

When you write a process paragraph, keep the following guidelines in mind:

■ A **process paragraph** should begin with a topic sentence that identifies both the process and the point you want to make about it (for example, "Parallel parking is easy once you know the secret" or "By following a few steps, you can design an effective résumé").

■ A process paragraph should describe the steps in the process, one at a time. These steps should be presented in strict **time order**—the order in which they occur or are to be performed.

■ A process paragraph should end with a concluding statement that sums up the point you are making about the process.

A process paragraph generally has the following structure.

Topic Sentence _____

_____

Step #1 _____

_____

Step #2 _____

_____

Step #3 _____

_____

Concluding Statement _____

_____

There are two types of process paragraphs: **process explanations** and **instructions**.

Process Explanations

In a **process explanation**, your purpose is to help readers understand how something works or how something happens—for example, how a cell phone operates or how a computer works. With a process explanation, you do not actually expect readers to perform the process.

In the following process explanation paragraph from a psychology exam, the writer explains the four stages children go through when they acquire language.

> Children go through four distinct stages when they learn language. The — Topic sentence
> first stage begins as soon as infants are born. By crying, they let people know
> when they need something or if they are in pain. The second stage begins
> when children are about a year old and are able to communicate with single
> words. For example, a child will use the word *food* to mean anything from
> "I'm hungry" to "feed the dog." The third stage begins at about twenty — Steps presented in time order
> months. During this stage, children begin to use two-word sentences, such as
> "dada car" (for "This is dada's car"). Finally, at about thirty months, children
> begin to learn the rules that govern language. They learn how to form simple
> sentences, plurals, and the past tense of verbs. No matter what language they
> speak, all children follow the same process when they learn language. — Concluding statement
>
> — Jennifer Gulla (student)

Instructions

When you write **instructions**, your purpose is to give readers the information they need to actually perform a task or activity—for example, to fill out an application, to operate a piece of machinery, or to help someone who is choking. Because you expect readers to follow your instructions, you address them directly, using **commands** to tell them what to do (*check the gauge...pull the valve*).

In the following paragraph, the writer gives instructions on how to break up with someone.

Breaking Up

> If you follow a few simple steps, breaking up with someone does not have — Topic sentence
> to be stressful. First, give the person an idea of what is coming so that it is
> not a total surprise. Make excuses for not getting together, or occasionally say
> that it might be better if the two of you spent more time apart. Second, go
> to a public place to break the news. The other person is less likely to make a
> scene if you are in a restaurant than if the two of you are alone. Next, gently
> but directly tell the other person that you want to break up. Be firm. Remember — Steps presented in time order
> that this discussion should not turn into a debate. During this process, be
> sensitive to the other person's feelings. If the person gets emotional, be
> understanding. Finally, once the break-up is complete, go out with your friends
> and have some fun. That is the best way to take your mind off the situation
> and to meet new people. By following these simple steps, you can make a
> difficult situation a little bit easier. — Concluding statement
>
> — Nicole Riddle (student)

Transitions are very important in process paragraphs like the two you have just read. They enable readers to clearly identify each step—for example, *first, second, third*, and so on. In addition, they establish a sequence that lets readers move easily though the process you are describing.

Transitions for Process

after that,	first	subsequently
after this	immediately	the first (second,
as	later	third) step
as soon as	meanwhile	the next step
at the same time	next	the last step
at this point	now	then
during	once	when
finally	soon	while

GRAMMAR IN CONTEXT **Process**

When you write a process paragraph, you may find yourself making **illogical shifts** in tense, person, and voice. If you shift from one tense, person, number, or voice to another without good reason, you may confuse your reader.

CONFUSING First, give the person an idea of what is coming so that it is not a total surprise. Excuses should be made for not getting together. (illogical shift from active to passive voice)

CLEAR First, give the person an idea of what is coming so that it is not a total surprise. Make excuses for not getting together. (consistent use of active voice)

For information on how to avoid illogical shifts in tense, person, and voice, see Chapter 24.

◆ **PRACTICE 6-1**

Read this process paragraph; then, follow the instructions that come after it.

An Order of Fries

I never realized how much work goes into making French fries until I worked at a potato processing plant in Hermiston, Oregon. The process begins with freshly dug potatoes being shoveled from trucks onto conveyor belts leading into the plant. During this stage, workers must pick out any rocks that may have been dug up with the potatoes because these could damage the automated peelers. After the potatoes have gone through the peelers, they travel on a conveyor belt through the "trim line." Here, workers cut out any bad spots, being careful not to waste

potatoes by trimming too much. Next, the potatoes are sliced in automated cutters and then fried for about a minute. After this, they continue along a conveyor belt to the "wet line." Here, workers again look for bad spots, and they throw away any rotten pieces. At this point, the potatoes go to a second set of fryers for three minutes before being moved to subzero freezers for ten minutes. Then, it's on to the "frozen line" for a final inspection. The inspected fries are weighed by machines and then sealed into five-pound plastic packages, which are weighed again by workers who also check that the packages are properly sealed. Finally, the bags are packed into boxes and made ready for shipment to various restaurants across the western United States. This complicated process goes on twenty-four hours a day to bring consumers the French fries they enjoy so much.

—Cheri Rodriguez (student)

1. Underline the topic sentence of the paragraph.

2. Is this a process explanation or instructions? _____

   How do you know? _____

3. List the steps in the process. The first step has been listed for you.

   The potatoes are unloaded, and the rocks are sorted out.

   _____

   _____

   _____

   _____

   _____

   _____

4. Circle the transitional words and phrases the writer uses to move readers from one step to the next.

5. Underline the paragraph's concluding statement.

◆ PRACTICE 6-2

Following are four possible topic sentences for process paragraphs. After each topic sentence, list three or four steps that explain the process the sentence identifies. For example, if you were explaining the process of getting a job, you could list preparing a résumé, looking at ads in newspapers or online, writing a job application letter, and going on an interview. Make sure each step follows logically from the one that precedes it.

1. Downloading music from the Internet is a simple process.

_____

_____

_____

_____

2. Getting the most out of a student-teacher conference can take some preparation.

_____

_____

_____

3. Cage-training a puppy can be a tricky process.

_____

_____

_____

_____

4. Choosing the perfect outfit for a job interview can be a time-consuming task.

_____

_____

_____

_____

B Writing a Process Paragraph

When Manasvi Bari was assigned to write a paragraph in which she explained a process she performed every day, she decided to write about how to get a seat on a crowded subway car. To make sure she had enough to write about, she made the following list of possible steps she could include.

Don't pay attention to heat

Get into the train

Get the first seat

Look as if you need help

Get to a pole

Don't travel during rush hour

Choose your time

Be alert

Squeeze in

After looking over her list, Manasvi crossed out steps that she didn't think were essential to the process she wanted to describe.

~~Don't pay attention to heat~~

Get into the train

Get the first seat

Look as if you need help

~~Get to a pole~~

~~Don't travel during rush hour~~

~~Choose your time~~

Be alert

Squeeze in

Once she had decided on her list of steps, she rearranged them in the order in which they should be performed.

Get into the train

Be alert

Get the first seat

Squeeze in

Look as if you need help

At this point, Manasvi thought that she was ready to begin writing her paragraph. Here is her first draft.

> When the train arrives, get into the car as fast as possible. Be alert. If you see an empty seat, grab it and sit down immediately. If there is no seat, ask people to move down, or squeeze into a space that seems too small. If none of this works, you'll have to use some imagination. Look helpless. Drop your books, and look as if the day can't get any worse. Sometimes a person will get up and give you a seat. If this strategy doesn't work, stand near someone who looks as if he or she is going to get up. When the person gets up, jump into the seat as fast as you can. Don't let the people who are getting on the train get the seat before you do.

When Manasvi took the draft of her paragraph to a writing center tutor, they agreed that her paragraph had enough examples and explanations. Together, they decided that she needed to make the following changes.

■ Culture Clue

Writing centers serve all students—native and non-native speakers alike—at all stages in the writing process. Most colleges have a writing center. Ask your teacher for more information.

■ She needed to add a topic sentence that identified the process and stated the point she wanted to make about it.

■ She needed to add transitions that helped readers follow the steps in the process.

■ She needed to add a concluding statement that restated the point of the process.

After she made these changes, Manasvi wrote the following revised and edited draft of her paragraph.

Surviving Rush Hour

■ Topic sentence added

Anyone who takes the subway to school in the morning knows how hard it is to find a seat, but by following a few simple steps, you should be able to get one almost every day. First, when the train arrives, get into the car as fast as possible. Be alert. As soon as you see an empty seat, grab it, and sit down

■ Transitions added

immediately. Meanwhile, if there is no seat, ask people to move down, or try to squeeze into a space that seems too small. Most of the time, people will shift to make room for you. Next, if none of this works, you'll have to use some imagination. Look helpless. Drop your books, and look as if the day can't get any worse. Sometimes a person will get up and give you a seat. Don't be shy. Take it, and remember to say thank you. Finally, if this strategy doesn't work, stand near someone who looks like he or she is about to get up. Often, people who are going to get off at the next stop begin to gather their belongings together. When the person gets up, jump into the seat as fast as

■ Concluding statement added

you can. By following these steps, you should be able to get a seat on the subway and arrive at school rested and relaxed.

◆ PRACTICE 6-3

Now, you are ready to write a process paragraph. Choose one of the topics below (or choose your own topic). Use one or more of the strategies described in 1C to help you come up with as many steps as you can for the topic you have chosen, and list these steps on a separate sheet of paper.

Making a major purchase	How to quit smoking
Strategies for winning arguments	How to save money
	How to drive in the snow

Your typical work or school day
How to be a good friend
How to discourage
   telemarketers
Your morning routine
How to use a digital camera
How to perform a particular
   household repair

How to apply for financial aid
A process involved in a hobby
   of yours
How to build something
How to make your favorite dish
How to prepare for a storm

◆ **PRACTICE 6-4**

Review your notes on the topic you chose in Practice 6-3, and decide
whether to write a process explanation or a set of instructions. Then, on
the lines below, choose the steps from the list you wrote in Practice 6-3
that can best help you develop a process paragraph on your topic.

_____

_____

_____

_____

◆ **PRACTICE 6-5**

Reread your list of steps from Practice 6-4. Then, draft a topic sentence
that identifies the process you will discuss and communicates the point
you will make about it.

_____

_____

◆ **PRACTICE 6-6**

Review the steps you listed in Practice 6-4. Then, write them down in time
order, moving from the first step to the last.

1. _____   4. _____

2. _____   5. _____

3. _____   6. _____

◆ **PRACTICE 6-7**

Draft your process paragraph.

◆ **PRACTICE 6-8**

Consulting the Self-Assessment Checklist below, revise your process paragraph.

◆ **PRACTICE 6-9**

Type a final draft of your process paragraph.

■ **WRITING FIRST: Revising and Editing**

Look back at your response to the Writing First activity on page 77. Consulting the Self-Assessment Checklist below, evaluate the paragraph you wrote. Then, prepare a final draft of your paragraph.

☑ SELF-ASSESSMENT CHECKLIST:
Writing a Process Paragraph

☐ Do you have a clearly worded topic sentence that states your paragraph's main idea?

☐ Does your topic sentence identify the process you will discuss?

☐ Does your topic sentence indicate whether you will be explaining a process or giving instructions?

☐ Have you included all the steps in the process?

☐ If your paragraph is set of instructions, have you included all the information readers will need to perform the process?

☐ Do your transitions indicate the order of steps in the process, or do you need to add transitions to make your paragraph more coherent?

☐ Does your paragraph end with a concluding statement that summarizes your main idea?

MOVING FROM PARAGRAPH TO ESSAY

Process

In addition to writing process paragraphs, you may sometimes have to write a **process essay**. For example, in a biology class, you may be required to write an essay in which you discuss the process of cell division. At home, you may decide to write a set of instructions telling family members what to do in case of a fire. *For information on how to write a process essay, see 14D.*

Cause and Effect

PREVIEW

In this chapter, you will learn to write a cause-and-effect paragraph.

■ **WRITING FIRST**

The picture above shows one young woman talking on a cell phone and another typing on a laptop. Look at the picture, and then write a paragraph in which you describe the impact of a particular electronic appliance or gadget on your life or the life of your family—for example, the ATM machine, the cell phone, or the television remote control. Be sure that your topic sentence identifies the item and that the rest of the paragraph discusses how it affects you or your family.

▶ **Word Power**

gadget   a small specialized mechanical or electronic device

impact   (n.) the effect of one thing on another

simplify   to make easier

A What Is Cause and Effect?

Why is the cost of college so high in the United States? How does smoking affect a person's health? What would happen if the city increased its sales tax? How dangerous is the avian flu? All these questions have one thing in common: they try to determine the causes or effects of an action, event, or situation.

A **cause** is something or someone that makes something happen. An **effect** is something brought about by a particular cause. A **cause-and-effect paragraph** helps readers understand why something happened or is happening or shows readers how one thing affects something else.

Cause	*Effect*
Increased airport security ⟶	Long lines at airports
Weight gain ⟶	Health problems
Seatbelt laws passed ⟶	Increased use of seatbelts

When you write a cause-and-effect paragraph, keep the following guidelines in mind:

■ A **cause-and-effect paragraph** should begin with a topic sentence that tells readers whether the paragraph is focusing on causes or on effects (for example, "There are several reasons why the cost of gas is so high" or "Going to the writing center has given me confidence as well as skills").

■ A cause-and-effect paragraph should discuss every important cause or effect, one at a time. The causes or effects should be arranged in some kind of **logical order**—for example, from least important to most important.

■ A cause-and-effect paragraph should end with a concluding statement that sums up the main idea stated in the topic sentence.

A cause-and-effect paragraph generally has the following structure.

Topic Sentence _____

Cause (or effect) #1 _____

_____

Cause (or effect) #2 _____

_____

Cause (or effect) #3 _____

_____

Concluding Statement _____

_____

Causes

The following paragraph focuses on **causes**.

Why Young People Don't Vote

Topic sentence ——————— There are several reasons why young adults do not often vote in national elections. The first reason is that many young people are just not interested in politics. They are busy getting an education or working, and they do not take the time to think about politics or which candidate to vote for. Another reason is that they do not think that their vote is important. They think that because millions of people are voting, their vote will not have an effect on the outcome of an election. A third reason is that many young people do not think that the candidates are speaking to them. They do not think that national issues such as capital gains taxes, Social Security, and Medicare have much to do with them. Finally, many young people are turned off by politics and politicians. As far as they are concerned, politicians just want to get elected and will say anything to get votes. Until these issues are addressed, many

Causes arranged in
logical order

Concluding statement ——————— young people will continue to stay away from the polls.

— Moniquetta Hall (student)

Effects

The following paragraph focuses on **effects**.

Global Warming

Topic sentence ——————— Climate change caused by global warming would have several negative effects. One effect would be an increase in the number of intense storms. Large hurricanes and other types of storms would damage property and kill many people. Another effect would be a rise in sea level. As the earth warms, the polar ice would melt and raise the level of the earth's oceans. Coastal cities and low-lying areas would probably be flooded. Still another effect would be the spread of certain kinds of diseases. Many diseases, now found only in warm areas, would spread to areas that were once cool but then became warm. Malaria and yellow fever, for example, could become as common in the United States as they are in Africa and Southeast Asia. Finally, climate change associated with global warming would affect agriculture. Farming areas, such as the Midwest, where American farmers grow corn and wheat, would become dry. As a result, there would be food shortages, and many people could go

Effects arranged in
logical order

Concluding statement ——————— hungry. No one knows for certain what will happen, but if global warming continues, our lives will certainly be affected.

—Jackie Hue (student)

Transitions in cause-and-effect paragraphs, as illustrated in the two paragraphs above, introduce individual causes or effects. They may also show the connections between a cause and its effects or between an effect

and its causes. In addition, they may indicate which cause or effect is more important than another.

Transitions for Cause and Effect

accordingly	moreover	the first (second, third) reason
another cause	since	
another effect	so	the most important cause
as a result	the first (second, third, final) cause	the most important effect
because		therefore
consequently	the first (second, third, final) effect	
for		
for this reason		

GRAMMAR IN CONTEXT **Cause and Effect**

When you write a cause-and-effect paragraph, you should be careful not to confuse the words *affect* and *effect*. *Affect* is a verb meaning "to influence." *Effect* is a noun meaning "result."

effect

One ~~affect~~ would be an increase in the number of storms. (*effect* is a noun)

No one knows for certain what will happen, but if global

affected

warming continues, our lives will certainly be ~~effected~~. (*affect* is a verb.)

For more information on effect *and* affect, *see Chapter 34.*

◆ PRACTICE 7-1

Read this cause-and-effect paragraph. Then, follow the instructions below.

The Benefits of Day Care

Since our son has been in day care, I have noticed several positive changes. The first change I noticed is that he has learned lots of new words. Because he talks to the other children and to the teachers, his vocabulary is increasing. Every day, he comes home with another word or expression that he has learned.

■ **Culture Clue**

Day care is childcare that is available during the day while parents work.

Another change I have noticed is that he has learned to play with other children. Before he was in day care, my son was around only one other child, his sister. Now, he is with a whole group of children, many older than he is. As a result, he has learned to share his toys and to play with others. The final change I have noticed is that my son has become more independent. He has learned how to tie his shoes as well as how to dress himself in the morning. Before he went to day care, he depended on me to dress him. Now, he does it all by himself. Because of all the benefits that I have seen, I am glad that we put our son in day care.

—Simon Blest (student)

1. Underline the topic sentence of the paragraph.

2. List the words that tell you the writer is moving from one effect to another in the paragraph. The first answer has been listed for you.

   The first change _____

   _____

   _____

3. List the effects the writer describes. The first effect has been listed for you.

   He has learned new words. _____

   _____

   _____

4. Circle the transitional words and phrases the writer uses to identify effects.

5. Underline the paragraph's concluding statement.

◆ **PRACTICE 7-2**

▶ **Word Power**

vandalism the deliberate destruction or damage of property

Following are four possible topic sentences for cause-and-effect paragraphs. After each topic sentence, list the effects that could result from the cause identified in the topic sentence. For example, if you were writing a paragraph about the effects of excessive drinking on campus, you could list low grades, health problems, and vandalism.

1. Having a baby can change your life.

   _____

   _____

   _____

2. Learning a second language has many advantages.

_____

_____

_____

3. MP3 players have been a huge success for a number of reasons.

_____

_____

_____

4. Impulse buying can have negative effects on a person's finances.

_____

_____

_____

■ Culture Clue
Impulse buying is
purchasing something
without planning or
thought.

◆ **PRACTICE 7-3**

List three causes that could support each of the following topic sentences.

1. The causes of teenage obesity are easy to identify.

_____

_____

_____

2. Chronic unemployment can have many causes.

_____

_____

_____

3. The high cost of college tuition is not easy to explain.

_____

_____

_____

4. There are several reasons why professional athletes' salaries are high.

_____

_____

_____

■ **Culture Clue**

Wal-Mart is a discount
store with locations
worldwide. In the United
States, people often
protest the opening
of Wal-Mart stores.

B **Writing a Cause-and-Effect Paragraph**

When Sean Jin was asked to write a cause-and-effect essay for his composition class, he had no trouble thinking of a topic because of a debate that was going on in his hometown about building a Wal-Mart superstore there. He decided to write a paragraph that discussed the effects that such a store would have on the local economy.

His instructor told the class the main problem they could have in planning a cause-and-effect essay is making sure that a **causal relationship** exists—that one event actually causes another. In other words, just because one event follows another closely in time, students should not assume that the second event caused the first.

With this advice in mind, Sean listed the effects a Wal-Mart would have on his small town. Here is Sean's list of effects.

> Provide new jobs
>
> Offer low-cost items
>
> Pay low wages
>
> Push out small businesses

After reviewing his list of effects, Sean wrote the following first draft of his paragraph.

> Wal-Mart can have good and bad effects on a small town. It provides jobs. A large store needs a lot of employees. So, many people from the area will be able to find work. Wal-Mart's prices are low. Families that don't have much money may be able to buy things they can't afford to buy at other stores. Not all of Wal-Mart's effects are positive. Wal-Mart pays employees less than other stores. Wal-Mart provides jobs, but those jobs don't pay very much. When Wal-Mart comes into an area, many small businesses are forced to close. They just can't match Wal-Mart's prices or stock as much merchandise as Wal-Mart can.

When he finished his draft, Sean went to the writing center and met with a tutor. After going over his paragraph with the tutor, Sean decided to make several changes.

■ He decided to sharpen his topic sentence to tie his discussion of Wal-Mart to the small town in which he lived.

■ He decided to add more details about Wal-Mart.

■ He decided to add transitional words and phrases to emphasize the positive and negative effects he identifies.

■ He decided to add a concluding statement that would reinforce his main idea.

After making these changes, he continued revising and editing his paragraph. Here is his final draft.

Wal-Mart Comes to Town

When Wal-Mart comes to a small town like mine, it can have good and bad effects. One beneficial effect is that it provides jobs. A large Wal-Mart superstore needs a lot of employees. So, many people will be able to find work. In my rural town, almost 10 percent of the people are out of work. Wal-Mart could give these people a chance to improve their lives. Another positive effect that Wal-Mart will have is to keep prices low. For this reason, families that don't have much money will be able to buy things they couldn't afford to buy at other stores. My own observations show that some items at my local Wal-Mart are as much as 20 percent cheaper than those at other stores. Not all of Wal-Mart's effects are positive, however. One negative effect Wal-Mart can have is that it can actually lower wages in an area. My aunt, who works at Wal-Mart, says that beginning workers earn between $8 and $10 an hour. This is less than they would get in stores that pay union wages. Another negative effect Wal-Mart can have is to drive other, smaller businesses out. When Wal-Mart comes into an area, many small businesses are forced to close. They just can't match Wal-Mart's prices or selection of merchandise. It is clear that although Wal-Mart can have a number of good effects, it can also have some bad ones.

- Topic sentence sharpened

- Details added

- Transitions added

- Concluding statement added

◆ **PRACTICE 7-4**

Now, you are ready to write a cause-and-effect paragraph. Choose one of the following topics (or choose your own topic) for a paragraph that examines causes or effects. Then, on a separate sheet of paper, use one or more of the strategies described in 1C to help you think of as many causes or effects as you can for the topic you have chosen.

Why a current television show or movie is so popular
Some causes (or effects) of stress
The negative health effects of junk food
Why teenagers (or adults) drink
The reasons you decided to attend college
The effects of a particular government policy
How becoming a vegetarian might change (or has changed) your life

The benefits of home cooking
Why a particular sport is popular
How an important event in your life influenced you
The possible effects of violent song lyrics on teenagers
The problems of text messaging
Why some people find writing difficult
The major reasons that high school or college students drop out
of school
How managers can get the best (or the worst) from their employees

◆ PRACTICE 7-5

Review your notes on the topic you chose in Practice 7-4, and create a cluster diagram. Write the topic you have chosen in the center of the page, and draw arrows branching out to specific causes or effects.

◆ PRACTICE 7-6

Choose a few of the most important causes or effects from the cluster diagram you made in Practice 7-5, and list them here.

_____

_____

_____

_____

_____

_____

◆ PRACTICE 7-7

Reread your list of causes or effects from Practice 7-6. Then, draft a topic sentence that introduces your topic and communicates the point you will make about it.

_____

_____

_____

◆ PRACTICE 7-8

List the causes or effects you will discuss in your paragraph, arranging them in an effective order—for example, from least to most important.

1. _____

2. _____

3. _____

4. _____

◆ PRACTICE 7-9

Draft your cause-and-effect paragraph.

◆ PRACTICE 7-10

Consulting the Self-Assessment Checklist below, revise your cause-and-effect paragraph.

◆ PRACTICE 7-11

Type a final draft of your cause-and-effect paragraph.

■ **WRITING FIRST: Revising and Editing**

Look back at your response to the Writing First activity on page 88. Consulting the Self-Assessment Checklist below, evaluate the paragraph you wrote. Then, prepare a final draft of your paragraph.

☑ SELF-ASSESSMENT CHECKLIST:
Writing a Cause-and-Effect Paragraph

☐ Do you have a clearly worded topic sentence that states your paragraph's main idea?

☐ Does your topic sentence identify the cause or effect on which your paragraph will focus?

☐ Do you need to add other important causes or effects?

☐ Do you need to explain your causes or effects in more detail?

☐ Do all your details and examples support your paragraph's main idea?

☐ Do your transitions show how your points are related?

☐ Do your transitions clearly introduce each cause or effect, or do you need to add transitions to make your paragraph more coherent?

☐ Does your paragraph end with a concluding statement that summarizes your main idea?

MOVING FROM PARAGRAPH TO ESSAY

Cause and Effect

In addition to writing cause-and-effect paragraphs, you may sometimes have to write a **cause-and-effect essay**. For example, in a political science class, you may write an essay in which you discuss the causes of the famine in Darfur. At work, you may write a memo in which you point out how a new procedure is affecting your job performance. *For information on how to write a cause-and-effect essay, see 14E.*

Comparison and Contrast

PREVIEW

In this chapter, you will learn to write a comparison-and-contrast paragraph.

■ WRITING FIRST

The picture above shows the cast of the popular 1990s television sitcom *Fresh Prince of Bel-Air*. Look at the picture, and then write a comparison-and-contrast paragraph in which you explain how your family's life is different from (or similar to) the life of the family pictured here.

▶ **Word Power**

generation a group of individuals born and living at about the same time

materialistic more concerned with material things than with spiritual or cultural values

upwardly mobile able to advance in social or economic standing

99

A   What Is Comparison and Contrast?

When you buy something — for example, an air conditioner, a car, a hair drier, or a computer—you often comparison-shop, looking at various models to determine how they are alike and how they are different. Eventually, you decide which one you want to buy. In other words, you *compare and contrast*. When you **compare**, you look at how two things are similar. When you **contrast**, you look at how they are different.

Comparison-and-contrast paragraphs can examine just similarities, just differences, or both.

When you write a comparison-and-contrast paragraph, keep the following guidelines in mind:

- A **comparison-and-contrast paragraph** should begin with a topic sentence that tells readers whether the paragraph is going to discuss similarities or differences. The topic sentence should also make clear the focus of the comparison (for example, "Toni Morrison and Maya Angelou have similar ideas about race and society" or "My parents and I have different ideas about success").
- A comparison-and-contrast paragraph should discuss the same or similar points for both subjects, one by one. Points should be arranged in **logical order**—for example, from least important to most important.
- A comparison-and-contrast paragraph should end with a concluding statement that reinforces the main point of the comparison.

There are two kinds of comparison-and-contrast paragraphs: *subject-by-subject comparisons* and *point-by-point comparisons*.

Subject-by-Subject Comparisons

In a **subject-by-subject comparison**, you divide your comparison into two parts and discuss one subject at a time. In the first part of the paragraph, you discuss all your points about one subject. Then, in the second part, you discuss all your points about the other subject, comparing it to the first. (In each part of the paragraph, you discuss the points in the same order.)

A subject-by-subject comparison is best for short paragraphs in which you do not discuss too many points. Because readers are not asked to remember a great many points, they will have little difficulty keeping track of the comparison as they read.

A subject-by-subject comparison generally has the following structure.

Topic Sentence _____

_____

Subject A _____

Point 1_____

_____

Point 2 _____

_____

Point 3 _____

_____

Subject B _____

Point 1 _____

_____

Point 2 _____

_____

Point 3 _____

_____

Concluding Statement _____

_____

The writer of the following paragraph uses a subject-by-subject comparison to compare two places to eat on campus.

Eating on Campus

<u>Food trucks are a good alternative to the campus cafeteria.</u> Eating in the ———— Topic sentence
cafeteria takes a lot of time. Students have to go into a building, wait in line,
walk down some stairs, and find a table. In addition, the cafeteria usually has
a limited variety of food, with only two or three different hot meals and some
prepackaged sandwiches. The food is cooked in advance, and after sitting on a   Subject A:
steam tray for a few hours, it is dry and lukewarm. Finally, food in the cafeteria   Eating in the school
costs a lot. Students who are not on a food plan can easily spend seven or   cafeteria
eight dollars for dinner. In contrast, the food trucks are much quicker than
the cafeteria. Most food trucks serve a meal in less than five minutes. If the
weather is nice, students can sit anywhere on campus and eat. In addition,
the food trucks offer a lot of choice. Some of the trucks, such as the ones
that sell Chinese food, even sell platters. In addition, the food from the trucks   Subject B:
is fresh and hot most of the time. Finally, meals from a food truck usually cost   Eating at the food trucks
less than five dollars. This is a big savings, especially if you are a student on
a tight budget. <u>For busy students, the food trucks are often a better choice</u> ———— Concluding statement
<u>than the cafeteria.</u>

— Dan Lindt (student)

8 A

Point-by-Point Comparisons

When you write a **point-by-point comparison**, you discuss a point about one subject and then discuss the same point for the second subject. You use this alternating pattern throughout the paragraph.

A point-by-point comparison is a better strategy for paragraphs in which you discuss many points. It is also a better choice if the points you are discussing are technical or complicated. Because you compare the two subjects one point at a time, readers will able to see each point of comparison before moving on to the next point.

A point-by-point comparison generally has the following structure.

Topic Sentence _____

_____

Point 1 _____

Subject A _____

_____

Subject B _____

_____

Point 2 _____

Subject A _____

_____

Subject B _____

_____

Point 3 _____

Subject A _____

_____

Subject B _____

_____

Concluding Statement _____

_____

In the following paragraph, the writer uses a point-by-point-comparison to compare baseball and football.

Baseball versus Football

After being a fan for years, I understand how different baseball and football are. First, football is violent, and baseball is not. In football, the object is to tackle a person on the other team. The harder the hit, the better the tackle. In baseball, however, violence is not the object of the game. If a player gets hurt, it is usually an accident, such as when two players run into each other. Next, the words used to describe each game are different. The language of football is the language of war: linemen "blitz," quarterbacks throw "bombs," tacklers "crush" receivers, and games end in "sudden death" overtimes. The language of baseball, however, is peaceful: hitters "sacrifice," runners "slide," and pitchers throw "curves" or "sliders." Finally, the pace of each game is different. Football is played against the clock. When the clock runs out, the game is over. Unlike a football game, a baseball game does not end until nine innings are played or a tie is broken. Theoretically, a game could go on forever. Even though football and baseball are so different, I like them both.

— Deniz Bilgutay (student)

Topic sentence

Point 1: Level of violence

Point 2: Language used to describe games

Point 3: Pace of games

Concluding statement

Transitions are important in a comparison-and-contrast paragraph. Transitions tell readers when you are changing from one point (or one subject) to another. Transitions also make your paragraph more coherent by showing readers whether you are focusing on similarities (for example, *likewise* or *similarly*) or differences (for example, *although* or *in contrast*).

> **■ Culture Clue**
>
> In North American *football*, players carry, throw, or kick the ball. In European football, called *soccer*, players simply kick the ball.

Transitions for Comparison and Contrast

although	one difference . . . another difference
but	one similarity . . . another similarity
even though	on the contrary
however	on the one hand . . . on the other hand
in comparison	similarly
in contrast	though
like	unlike
likewise	whereas
nevertheless	

GRAMMAR IN CONTEXT   Comparison and Contrast

When you write a comparison-and-contrast paragraph, you should state the points you are comparing in **parallel** terms to highlight their similarities or differences.

(continued on following page)

NOT PARALLEL	First, football is violent, and violence isn't seen very often in baseball.
PARALLEL	First, football is violent, and baseball is not.

For more information on revising to make ideas parallel, see Chapter 19.

◆ PRACTICE 8-1

Read this comparison-and-contrast paragraph; then, follow the instructions below.

Immigration: Past and Present

Immigration to the United States is quite different today from what it was a century ago. In the late nineteenth and early twentieth centuries, most immigrants to the United States came from southern and eastern Europe. In the last fifty years, however, about 80 percent of the immigrants have come from Latin America, the Caribbean, and Asia. A hundred years ago, most of the immigrants were uneducated, unskilled, and poor. In contrast, although some more recent immigrants are in similar circumstances, many of them are well-educated professionals who are not poor. Most immigrants a hundred years ago made a conscious effort to blend in. They saw the United States as a melting pot in which they could lose their immigrant identities and become like others in American society. More recent immigrants, however, prefer to keep their distinctive identities while still taking part in American society. Regardless of these differences, most immigrants still come to the United States for the same reasons—to improve themselves economically and to find freedom.

—Jorge Hernandez (student)

1. Underline the topic sentence of the paragraph.

2. Does this paragraph deal mainly with similarities or differences?

   _____ How do you know? _____

3. Is this paragraph a subject-by-subject or point-by-point comparison?

   _____ How do you know? _____

   _____

4. List some of the contrasts the writer describes. The first contrast has
been listed for you.

A century ago, most immigrants came from southern and eastern

Europe; more recently, most have come from Latin America, the

Caribbean, and Asia.

_____

_____

_____

_____

_____

_____

_____

5. Circle the transitional words and phrases the writer uses to contrast
his two subjects.

6. Underline the paragraph's concluding statement.

◆ PRACTICE 8-2

Following are four possible topic sentences. List three similarities or differences for the two subjects being considered in the topic sentence. For
example, if you were writing a paragraph comparing health care provided
by a local clinic with health care provided by a private physician, you
could discuss the cost, the length of waiting time, the quality of care, and
the frequency of follow-up visits.

1. My mother (or father) and I are very much alike (or different).

_____

_____

_____

2. My friends and I have similar views on _____.

_____

_____

_____

3. Democrats and Republicans have two very different ways of trying to
solve the country's problems.

_____

_____

_____

_____

4. Two of my college instructors have very different teaching styles.

_____

_____

_____

_____

B Writing a Comparison-and-Contrast Paragraph

When Jermond Love was asked to write a comparison-and-contrast essay for his composition class, he decided to brainstorm to find a topic that he could write about. When he reviewed his brainstorming notes, he came up with the following possible topics.

Football and soccer

Fast food and home cooking

The difference between my brother and me

Life in Saint Croix versus life in the United States

Jermond decided that he would write about the differences between life in New York City and life in Saint Croix, the Caribbean island on which he was raised. He listed the following subjects that he could compare and contrast. Then, he crossed out the ones he didn't want to write about.

Size

Population

~~Economy~~

Friendliness

~~Businesses~~

Lifestyle

After brainstorming some more, Jermond listed the points he could discuss for each of his four subjects. He began with basic information and then moved on to the idea he wanted to emphasize: the different lifestyles.

Size

    Saint Croix

      Small size

      Small population

      Christiansted and Frederiksted

New York
    Large size
    Large population
    Five boroughs

Lifestyle

    Saint Croix
       Laid back
       Friendly
    New York
       People in a hurry
       Not always friendly

Because he would not be discussing many points in this paragraph and because the points were not very complicated, Jermond decided to use a subject-by-subject organization for his paragraph. He did not think his readers would have much difficulty remembering his points as they moved from one section of his paragraph and the other.

Here is the first draft of Jermond's paragraph.

> Life in Saint Croix is very different from life in New York City. Saint Croix is much smaller than New York City. Saint Croix has a total population of about 60,000 people. The two main towns are Christiansted and Frederiksted. New York City is very large. Its residents are crowded into the five boroughs. The lifestyle in Saint Croix is different from the lifestyle of New York City. In Saint Croix, people operate on "island time." Everyone is friendly. People don't see any point in getting anyone upset. In New York City, people are always in a hurry. They don't take the time to slow down and enjoy life. As a result, people can seem unfriendly. They don't take the time to get to know anyone. I hope when I graduate I can stay in New York City but visit my home in Saint Croix whenever I can.

Jermond put his paragraph aside for a day and then reread it. Although he was generally satisfied with what he had written, he thought that it could be better. To help students revise their paragraphs, his instructor paired students and asked them to read and discuss each other's drafts. After working with a classmate on his draft, Jeremond decided that his topic sentence was clear and specific but that other parts of his paragraph needed revision. He decided to make the following changes.

■ He decided to include more details. Would readers know the location of Saint Croix? Would they know the population of Christiansted and Frederiksted? Would they know what he meant by "island time"?

■ He decided to add transitional words and phrases to show when he moved from one point to the next.

■ He decided to change his concluding statement because it didn't really restate the idea in his topic sentence.

After making these changes, Jermond revised and edited his paragraph.

Saint Croix versus the United States

Life in Saint Croix is very different from life in New York City. One difference between Saint Croix and New York is that Saint Croix is much smaller than New York. Saint Croix, the largest of United States Virgin Islands, has a population of about 60,000 people. The two main towns on the island are Christiansted, with a population of about 3,000 people, and Frederiksted, with a population of about 830. Unlike Saint Croix, New York City is large. It has a population of over 8 million people crowded into the five boroughs of Manhattan, Brooklyn, the Bronx, Queens, and Staten Island. My neighborhood in Brooklyn is more than twice the size of Christiansted and Frederiksted together. Another difference between Saint Croix and New York City is their lifestyles. Life in Saint Croix is slower than life in New York. In Saint Croix, people operate on "island time." Things get done, but people don't rush to do them. When a worker says "later," that can mean "this afternoon," "tomorrow," or even "next week." No one seems to mind, as long as the job gets done. People don't see any point in getting anyone upset. In New York, however, people are always in a hurry. They don't take the time to slow down and enjoy life. Everything is fast—fast food, fast cars, and fast Internet access. As a result, people can seem unfriendly. Although Saint Croix and New York City are different, life is very interesting in both places.

■ Details added

■ Transitions added

■ New concluding statement added

◆ PRACTICE 8-3

Now, you are ready to write a comparison-and-contrast paragraph. Choose one of the topics below (or choose your own topic) for a paragraph exploring similarities or differences. Then, on a separate sheet of paper, use one or more of the strategies described in 1C to help you think of as many similarities and differences as you can for the topic you have chosen. (If you use clustering, create a separate cluster diagram for each of the two subjects you are comparing.)

Two popular television personalities or radio talk-show hosts
Dog owners versus cat owners
Two cars you could consider buying
How you act in two different situations (at home and at work, for example) or with two different sets of people (such as your family and your professors)
Living in the city versus living in the country (or in a small town)
Two Web sites
Men's and women's attitudes toward dating, shopping, or conversation
A movie compared to its sequel

Public school education versus home schooling

Two competing consumer items, such as two car models, two computer
systems, or two video game systems

Two cultures' attitudes toward dating and marriage

Two different kinds of vacations

Two generations' attitudes toward a particular issue or subject (for
example, how people in their forties and people in their teens view
religion, technology, or politics)

◆ PRACTICE 8-4

Review your notes on the topic you chose in Practice 8-3, and decide
whether to focus on similarities or differences. On the following lines, list the
similarities or differences that can best help you develop a comparison-and-
contrast paragraph on the topic you have selected.

_____

_____

_____

_____

◆ PRACTICE 8-5

Reread your list of similarities or differences from Practice 8-4. Then, draft
a topic sentence that introduces your two subjects and indicates whether
your paragraph will focus on similarities or on differences.

_____

_____

_____

◆ PRACTICE 8-6

Decide whether you will write a subject-by-subject or a point-by-point
comparison. Then, use the appropriate outline below to help you plan
your paragraph. Before you begin, decide on the order in which you will
present your points—for example, from least important to most important. (For a subject-by-subject comparison, begin by deciding which subject you will discuss first.)

Subject-by-Subject Comparison

Subject A _____

  Point 1 _____

  Point 2 _____

Point 3 _____

Point 4 _____

Subject B _____

    Point 1 _____

    Point 2 _____

    Point 3 _____

    Point 4 _____

Point-by-Point Comparison

Point 1 _____

    Subject A _____

    Subject B _____

Point 2 _____

    Subject A _____

    Subject B _____

Point 3 _____

    Subject A _____

    Subject B _____

Point 4 _____

    Subject A _____

    Subject B _____

◆ **PRACTICE 8-7**

Draft your comparison-and-contrast essay paragraph.

◆ **PRACTICE 8-8**

Consulting the Self-Assessment Checklist on page 111, revise your comparison-and-contrast paragraph.

◆ **PRACTICE 8-9**

Type a final draft of your comparison-and-contrast paragraph.

■ **WRITING FIRST: Revising and Editing**

Look back at your response to the Writing First activity on page 99. Consulting the Self-Assessment Checklist below, evaluate the paragraph you wrote. Then, prepare a final draft of your paragraph.

☑ SELF-ASSESSMENT CHECKLIST:
Writing a Comparison-and-Contrast Paragraph

- Does the topic sentence clearly state your paragraph's main idea?

- Does the topic sentence indicate whether you are focusing on similarities or on differences?

- Do you need to include more examples of similarities or differences?

- If you have used a subject-by-subject comparison, do transitional words and phrases signal the shift from one subject to another?

- If you have used a point-by-point comparison, do transitional words and phrases lead readers from one point to another?

- Do you need to add transitional words and phrases to make your paragraph more coherent?

- Does your paragraph end with a concluding statement that sums up your main idea?

MOVING FROM PARAGRAPH TO ESSAY

Comparison and Contrast

In addition to writing comparison-and-contrast paragraphs, you may sometimes have to write a **comparison-and-contrast essay**. For example, in a criminal justice class, you may have to compare two recent Supreme Court decisions. At work, you may have to write a memo in which you compare the qualifications of two people who are applying for the same job. *For information on how to write a comparison-and-contrast essay, see 14F.*

PREVIEW

In this chapter, you will learn to write a classification paragraph.

▶ **Word Power**

enthusiastic having great excitement or interest in a subject or cause

fanatic someone who has extreme enthusiasm for a cause

■ **WRITING FIRST**

The picture above shows fans at a baseball game. Look at the picture, and then discuss the various types of fans you might see at a particular sporting event—for example, those who concentrate on the game, those who wave signs and banners, and those who wear costumes or team gear.

A What Is Classification?

When you **classify**, you sort items (people, things, ideas) into categories or groups. You classify when you organize bills into those you have to pay now and those you can pay later, or when you sort the clothes in a dresser drawer into piles of socks, T-shirts, and underwear.

In a **classification paragraph**, you tell readers how items can be sorted into categories or groups. Each category must be **distinct**. In other words, none of the items in one category should also fit into another category. For example, you would not classify novels into mysteries, romances, and paperbacks, because both mystery novels and romance novels could also be paperbacks.

When you write a classification paragraph, keep the following guidelines in mind:

■ A **classification paragraph** should begin with a topic sentence that introduces the subject of the paragraph. It may also identify the categories you will discuss (for example, "Before you go camping, you should sort the items you are thinking of packing into three categories: those that are absolutely necessary, those that could be helpful, and those that are not really necessary").

■ A classification paragraph should discuss each of the categories, one at a time. Your discussion of each category should include enough details and examples to show how it is distinct from the other categories.

■ The categories in a classification paragraph should be arranged in **logical order**—for example, from most important to least important or from smallest to largest.

■ A classification paragraph should end with a concluding statement that reinforces the main point stated in the topic sentence.

A classification paragraph generally has the following structure.

Topic Sentence _____

_____

Category #1_____

_____

Category #2_____

_____

Category #3_____

_____

Concluding Statement _____

_____

The writer of the following paragraph classifies his friends into three groups.

Categories of Friends

Topic sentence ———— My friends can be classified into three groups: those who know want they want out of life, those who don't have a clue, and those who are still searching for goals. Friends in the first category, those who know want they want, are

First category of friend — the most mature. They know exactly what they want to do for the rest of their lives. For this reason, they are the most predictable and the most reliable. They are also the most boring. Friends in the second category, those who don't have a clue, are the most immature. If there is a party the night before a test,

Second category of friend — they will go to the party and try to study when they get back. Although these friends can be a bad influence, they are the most fun. Friends in the last category, those who are searching for goals, are somewhere between the other two types when it comes to maturity. They do not know exactly what they want

Third category of friend — to do with their lives, but they are trying to find a goal. These friends can be unpredictable, but their willingness to try new things makes them the most

Concluding statement ———— interesting. Even though my three groups of friends are completely different, I like all of them.

— Daniel Corey (student)

Transitions are important in a classification paragraph. They tell readers when you are moving from one category to another (for example, *the first type, the second type*). They can also indicate which categories you think are more important than others (for example, *the most important, the least important*).

Transitions for Classification

one kind…another kind	the first group…the last group
one way…another way	the first type…the second type
the first (second, third) category	the most (or least) important group
	the next part

GRAMMAR IN CONTEXT   Classification

When you write a classification paragraph, you may list the categories you are going to discuss. If you use a **colon** to introduce your list, make sure that a complete sentence comes before the colon.

INCORRECT   My friends can be divided into: those who know want they want out of life, those who don't have a clue, and those who are still searching for goals

(continued on following page)

(continued from previous page)

CORRECT My friends can be divided into three groups: those who know want they want out of life, those who don't have a clue, and those who are still searching for goals.

For more information on how to use a colon to introduce a list, see 33D.

◆ PRACTICE 9-1

Read this classification paragraph; then, follow the instructions below.

Three Kinds of Shoppers

Shoppers can be put into three categories: practical, recreational, and professional. The first category is made up of practical shoppers, those who shop because they need something. Practical shoppers go right to the item they are looking for in the store and then leave. They do not waste time browsing or walking aimlessly from store to store. The next category is made up of recreational shoppers, those who shop for entertainment. For them, shopping is like going to the movies or out to dinner. They do it because it is fun. They will spend hours walking through stores looking at merchandise. More often than not, they will not buy anything. For recreational shoppers, it is the activity of shopping that counts, not the purchase itself. The third category is made up of professional shoppers, those who shop because they have to. For them, shopping is a serious business. You can see them in the mall, carrying four, five, or even six bags. Whenever you walk through a mall, you will see all three types of shoppers.

— Kimberley Toomer (student)

1. Underline the topic sentence of the paragraph.

2. What is the subject of the paragraph? _____

3. What three categories does the writer describe?

_____

_____

4. Circle the transitional phrases the writer uses to introduce the three categories.

5. Underline the paragraph's concluding statement.

◆ **PRACTICE 9-2**

List items in each of the following groups, then sort the items into three or four categories.

1. All the items on your desk

_____

_____

_____

Categories: _____

2. Buildings on your college campus

_____

_____

_____

Categories: _____

3. Magazines or newspapers you read

_____

_____

_____

Categories: _____

4. The various parts of a piece of equipment you use for a course or on the job

_____

_____

_____

Categories: _____

B | **Writing a Classification Paragraph**

In a college composition course, Corey Levin participated in a service-learning project at a local Ronald McDonald House, a charity that houses families of seriously ill children receiving treatment at nearby hospitals.

He met several professional athletes there and was surprised to learn that many of them regularly donate time and money to charity.

When Corey was asked by his composition instructor to write a paragraph about what he had learned from his experience, he decided to write a paragraph that classified the ways in which professional athletes give back to their communities. To find ideas to write about, he jotted down the following list of categories.

> Starting charitable foundations
>
> Guidance
>
> Responding to emergencies

Corey then listed examples under each of the three categories.

> Foundations
>   Michael Jordan
>   Troy Aikman
>
> Guidance
>   Shaquille O'Neal
>   The Philadelphia 76ers
>
> Responding to emergencies
>   Ike Reese
>   Vince Carter

After completing this informal outline, Corey drafted a topic sentence for his paragraph: "High-profile athletes find many ways to give back to their communities." Then, using his informal outline as a guide, Corey wrote the following draft of his paragraph.

> High-profile athletes find many ways to give back to their communities. Many athletes as well as teams do a lot to help people. I met some of them when I volunteered at the Ronald McDonald House. For example, Michael Jordan and the Chicago Bulls built a Boys' and Girls' Club on Chicago's West Side. Troy Aikman set up a foundation that builds playgrounds for children's hospitals. Shaquille O'Neal's Shaq's Paq provides guidance for inner-city children. The Philadelphia 76ers visit schools and have donated over five thousand books to local libraries. Ike Reese, of the Atlanta Falcons, collects clothing and food for families that need help. Vince Carter of the New Jersey Nets founded the Embassy of Hope Foundation. It distributes food to needy families at Thanksgiving and hosts a Christmas party for disadvantaged families.

Following his instructor's suggestion, Corey emailed his draft to a classmate for feedback. In her response, the classmate made the following suggestions.

■ Add sentences that clearly identify and explain the three categories you are discussing.
■ Add more details about who the athletes are, and eliminate unnecessary words and phrases.

■ Add transitions to introduce each category.
■ Add a concluding statement that sums up the paragraph's main idea.

With these comments in mind, Corey revised and edited his paragraph. Here is his final draft.

Giving Back

High-profile athletes find many ways to give back to their communities. One way to give back is to start charitable foundations to help young fans. For example, Michael Jordan and the Chicago Bulls built a Boys' and Girls' Club on Chicago's West Side. In addition, Troy Aikman set up a foundation that builds playgrounds for children's hospitals. Another way athletes give back to their communities is by mentoring, or giving guidance to young people. Many high-profile athletes work in programs that encourage young people to stay in school. Shaquille O'Neal's Shaq's Paq provides guidance for inner-city children. The Philadelphia 76ers visit schools and have donated over five thousand books to local libraries. One more way athletes can contribute to their communities is to respond to emergencies. Football player Ike Reese, of the Atlanta Falcons, collects clothing and food for families that need help. Basketball player Vince Carter founded the Embassy of Hope Foundation. It distributes food to needy families at Thanksgiving and hosts a Christmas party for disadvantaged families. These are just some of the ways that high-profile athletes give back to their communities.

■ Sentences defining categories added

■ Transitions added to introduce each category

■ Concluding statement added

◆ PRACTICE 9-3

Now you are ready to write a classification paragraph. Choose one of the topics below (or one of your own choice). Then, on a separate sheet of paper, use one or more of the strategies described in 1C to help you classify the members of the group you have chosen into as many categories as necessary.

Your friends	Popular music
Drivers	Fitness routines
Commuters on public transportation	Useful Web sites
Television shows	Part-time jobs
Employees or bosses	Teachers
Parents or children	Movie sound tracks
Types of success	T-shirt slogans
Radio stations	

◆ PRACTICE 9-4

Review the information you came up with for the topic you chose in Practice 9-3. On the following lines, list three or four categories you can develop in your paragraph.

Category 1: _____

Category 2: _____

Category 3: _____

Category 4: _____

◆ PRACTICE 9-5

Reread the list you made in Practice 9-4. Then, draft a topic sentence that introduces your subject and the categories you will discuss.

_____

_____

_____

◆ PRACTICE 9-6

List below the categories you will discuss in your classification paragraph in the order in which you will discuss them.

1. _____

2. _____

3. _____

4. _____

◆ PRACTICE 9-7

Draft your classification paragraph.

◆ PRACTICE 9-8

Consulting the Self-Assessment Checklist on page 120, revise your classification paragraph.

◆ PRACTICE 9-9

Prepare a final draft of your classification paragraph.

■ **WRITING FIRST: Revising and Editing**

Look back at your response to the Writing First activity on
page 112. Consulting the Self-Assessment Checklist below,
revise your classification paragraph. Then, prepare a final
draft of your paragraph.

☑ SELF-ASSESSMENT CHECKLIST:
Writing a Classification Paragraph

- Do you have a clearly worded topic sentence that states your
  main idea?

- Does your topic sentence identify the categories you will discuss?

- Do all your examples and details support your paragraph's
  main idea?

- Do you need to include more examples or specific explanations?

- Do your transitions clearly indicate which categories are more
  important than others?

- Do your transitions tell readers when you are moving from one
  category to another, or do you need to add more transitions to
  make your paragraph more coherent?

- Does your paragraph end with a concluding statement that
  sums up your main idea?

MOVING FROM PARAGRAPH TO ESSAY

Classification

In addition to writing classification paragraphs, you may sometimes have to write a **classification essay**. For example, a question
on a history exam may ask you to classify those who fought in the
American Revolution. To answer this question, you would have to
put these individuals into three groups: colonists, British soldiers,
and British sympathizers (Tories). For a local library's book sale, you
may have to write a brochure in which you classify books according to subject or reading level. *For information on how to write a
classification essay, see 14G.*

Definition

PREVIEW

In this chapter, you will learn to write a definition paragraph.

American Heritage Dictionary – _Cite This Source_ – _Share This_

dis·re·spect Ⓟ 🔊 (dĭs'rĭ-spĕkt') Pronunciation Key
n.   Lack of respect, esteem, or courteous regard.

tr.v.   **dis·re·spect·ed, dis·re·spect·ing, dis·re·spects**
To show a lack of respect for: _disrespected her elders; disrespected the law._

(_Download Now_ or _Buy the Book_)
The American Heritage® Dictionary of the English Language, Fourth Edition
Copyright © 2006 by Houghton Mifflin Company.
Published by Houghton Mifflin Company. All rights reserved.

Online Etymology Dictionary – _Cite This Source_ – _Share This_
disrespect
   1614 (v.), 1631 (n.), from dis- + respect.

Online Etymology Dictionary, © 2001 Douglas Harper

WordNet – _Cite This Source_ – _Share This_
disrespect

noun
1. an expression of lack of respect
2. a disrespectful mental attitude [ant: esteem]
3. a manner that is generally disrespectful and contemptuous [syn: contempt]

verb
1. show a lack of respect for [ant: abide by]
2. have little or no respect for; hold in contempt [ant: esteem]

WordNet® 3.0, © 2006 by Princeton University.

■ **WRITING FIRST**

The image above is from a Web site showing entries from various dictionaries. Read the entries, and then write a one-paragraph definition of a word you learned in one of your college courses. Assume that your readers are not familiar with the term you are defining.

▶ **Word Power**

denote   to indicate; to refer to specifically

signify   to have meaning or importance

A What Is Definition?

During a conversation, you might say that a friend is stubborn, that a stream is polluted, or that a neighborhood is dangerous. In order to make yourself clear, you have to define what you mean by *stubborn*, *polluted*, or *dangerous*. Like conversations, academic assignments also may involve definition. In a history paper, for example, you might have to define *imperialism*; on a biology exam, you might be asked to define *mitosis*.

A **definition** tells what a word means. When you want your readers to know exactly how you are using a specific term, you define it.

When most people think of definitions, they think of the **formal definitions** they see in a dictionary. Formal definitions have a three-part structure.

- The term to be defined
- The general class to which the term belongs
- The things that make the term different from all other items in the general class to which the term belongs

Term	Class	Differentiation
Ice hockey	is a game	played on ice by two teams on skates who use curved sticks to try to hit a puck into the opponent's goal.
Spaghetti	is a pasta	made in the shape of long, thin strands, usually served with a sauce.

A single-sentence formal definition is often not enough to define a specialized term (*point of view* or *premeditation*, for example), an abstract concept (*happiness* or *success*, for example), or a complicated subject (*stem-cell research*, for example). In these cases, you may need to expand the basic formal definition by writing a definition paragraph. In fact, a **definition paragraph** is an expanded formal definition.

When you write a definition paragraph, keep the following guidelines in mind:

- A **definition paragraph** may begin with the formal definition and then state the main point of the paragraph in the topic sentence.
- A definition paragraph does not follow any one pattern of development; in fact, it may define a term by using any of the patterns discussed in this text. For example, a definition paragraph may explain a concept by *comparing* it to something else or by giving *examples*.
- A definition paragraph should end with a concluding statement that summarizes the main point of the paragraph.

Here is one possible structure for a definition paragraph. Notice that this paragraph uses a combination of **narration** and **exemplification**.

Topic Sentence _____

_____

Point #1 _____

Narration _____

_____

Point #2 _____

Example _____

Example _____

Point #3 _____

Example _____

Example _____

Concluding Statement _____

_____

The writer of the following paragraph uses narration and exemplification to define the term *business casual*.

Business Casual

Business casual means dressing comfortably but looking professional. ——— Topic sentence
Until recently, men and women dressed formally for work. For example, men
wore dark suits and plain ties while women wore dark jackets and skirts. In —— Narration
the 1990s, however, the rise of technology companies in Silicon Valley made
popular a new style of work attire, called *business causal*. Today, business
causal is the accepted form of dress in most businesses. For men, this usually —— Examples of men's
means wearing a collared shirt with no tie and khaki pants, sometimes with   business casual
a sports jacket and loafers. For women, it means wearing a skirt or pants —— Examples of women's
with a blouse or collared shirt. Women can wear low heels or flats. High-tech   business casual
companies can be even more informal. They may even allow employees to wear
jeans and T-shirts to work. While business casual may be the new norm,
every company has its own standards for what is acceptable. ——— Concluding statement
                                        —Chase Durbin (student)

Transitions are important for definition paragraphs. In the paragraph above, the transitional words and phrases *until recently, in the 1990s,* and *today* tell readers when they are moving from one narrative event to another. The transitional phrases *for men* and *for women* introduce examples.

The following box lists some of the transitional words and phrases that are frequently used in definition paragraphs. You can also use the transitional words and phrases associated with the specific pattern (or patterns) that you use to develop your paragraph.

Transitions for Definition

also	often
for example	one characteristic . . . another
however	characteristic
in addition	one way . . . another way
in particular	sometimes
in the 1990s (or another time)	specifically
like	the first kind . . . the second kind

GRAMMAR IN CONTEXT **Definition**

A definition paragraph often includes a formal definition of the term or concept you are going to discuss. When you write your formal definition, be careful not to use the phrase *is where* or *is when*.

Business casual is ~~when you dress~~ *dressing* comfortably but ~~look~~ *looking* professional.

◆ **PRACTICE 10-1**

Read this definition paragraph; then, follow the instructions on page 125.

Writer's Block

Writer's block is the inability to start writing. For nonprofessionals, writer's block almost always involves assigned writing, such as a paper for school or a report for work. Sometimes writer's block is caused by poor preparation. For example, the writer has not set aside enough time to think and make notes. However, even prepared writers with many ideas already on paper can experience writer's block. It is like being tongue-tied, only writer's block is more like being brain-tied. All the ideas keep bouncing around but will not settle into any order, and the writer cannot decide what to say first. Often, the only cure for writer's block is to give up for a while, find something else to do, and try again later.

By doing this, you give your mind a chance to clear and your ideas a chance to regroup and, eventually, to begin flowing.

—Thaddeus Eddy (student)

1. Underline the topic sentence of the paragraph.

2. What is the subject of this definition? _____

3. What is the writer's one-sentence definition of the subject?

_____

_____

4. List some of the specific information the writer uses to define his subject. The first piece of information has been listed for you.

For nonprofessionals, it almost always involves assigned writing.

_____

_____

5. What patterns of development does the writer use in his definition? List them here.

_____

_____

_____

6. Underline the paragraph's concluding statement.

◆ PRACTICE 10-2

Following are four possible topic sentences for definition paragraphs. Each topic sentence includes an underlined word. In the space provided, list two possible patterns of development that you could use to develop a definition of the underlined word. For example, you could define the word *discrimination* by giving examples (exemplification) and by telling a story (narration).

1. During the interview, the job candidate made a sexist comment.

   Possible strategy: _____

   Possible strategy: _____

2. Loyalty is one of the chief characteristics of golden retrievers.

   Possible strategy: _____

   Possible strategy: _____

3. More than forty years after President Johnson's Great Society initiative, we have yet to eliminate poverty in the United States.

Possible strategy: _____

Possible strategy: _____

4. The problem with movies today is that they are just too <u>violent</u>.

Possible strategy: _____

Possible strategy: _____

B Writing a Definition Paragraph

On a history exam, Lorraine Scipio was asked to write a one-paragraph definition of the term *imperialism*. Lorraine had studied for the exam, so she knew what imperialism was. Because she wanted to make sure that she did not leave anything out of her definition (and because she had a time limit), she quickly listed her points on the inside front cover of her exam book. Then, she crossed out two items that did not seem relevant.

A policy of control

Military

~~Lenin~~

Establish empires

Cultural superiority

Raw materials and cheap labor

Africa, etc.

~~Cultural imperialism~~

Nineteenth-century term

Next, Lorraine reorganized her points in the order in which she planned to write about them.

Establish empires

Nineteenth-century term

Cultural superiority

Africa, etc.

Raw materials and cheap labor

A policy of control

Military

Referring to the points on her list, Lorraine wrote the following draft of her definition paragraph. Notice that she uses several different patterns to develop her definition.

The goal of imperialism is to establish an empire. The imperialist country thinks that it is superior to the country it takes over. It justifies its actions

by saying that it is helping the other country. But it isn't. Countries such as Germany, Belgium, Spain, and England have been imperialist in the past. The point of imperialism is to take as much out of the occupied countries as possible. Often, imperialist countries sent troops to occupy other countries and to keep order. As a result, imperialism kept the people in occupied countries in poverty and often broke down local governments and local traditions.

After she finished writing her paragraph, Lorraine read it quickly, making sure that it had answered the exam question. Then, she made the following changes.

- She added a formal definition at the beginning of her paragraph because the exam question asked for a definition.
- She added transitional words and phrases to make the connections between her ideas clearer.
- She added more details to develop her definition.
- She added a concluding statement that summed up the effects of imperialism.

Lorraine made her changes directly on the draft she had written. Then, she edited her paragraph for grammar, punctuation, and mechanical errors, paying particular attention to verb tense. Finally, because she had some extra time, she recopied her revised and edited draft. The final draft of Lorraine's exam answer appears below. (Because this is an exam answer, the paragraph does not have a title.)

Imperialism is a nineteenth-century term that refers to the policy by which one country takes over the land or the government of another country. The goal of imperialism was to establish an empire. The imperialist country thought that it was superior to the country it took over. It justified its actions by saying that it was helping the other country. For instance, countries such as Germany, Belgium, Spain, and England claimed large areas of land in Africa. The point of imperialism was to take as much out of the occupied countries as possible. For example, in South America and Mexico, Spain removed tons of gold from the areas it occupied. It made the natives into slaves and forced them to work in mines. In order to protect their interests, imperialist countries often sent troops to occupy other countries and to keep order. As a result, imperialism kept the people in occupied countries in poverty and often broke down local governments and local traditions. At its worst, European imperialism brought slavery, destruction, and death to many people.

- Topic sentence with formal definition added

- Supporting details added

- Transitions added

- Concluding statement added

FOCUS **Writing Paragraph Answers on Exams**

When you write paragraph answers on exams, you do not have much time to work, so you need to be well prepared. Know your subject well, and memorize important definitions. You may have time to write an outline, a rough draft, and a final draft, but you will have to work quickly. Your final draft should include all the elements of a good paragraph: a topic sentence, supporting details, transitions, and a concluding statement.

◆ **PRACTICE 10-3**

Now, you are ready to write a definition paragraph. Choose one of the topics below (or choose your own topic). Then, on a separate sheet of paper, use one or more of the strategies described in 1C to help you define the term you have chosen to discuss. Name the term, and then describe it, give examples of it, tell how it works, explain its purpose, consider its history or future, or compare it with other similar things. In short, do whatever works best for defining your subject.

A negative quality, such as envy, dishonesty, or jealousy
An ideal, such as the ideal friend or neighborhood
A type of person, such as a worrier or a show-off
A social concept, such as equality, opportunity, or discrimination
An important play or strategy in a particular sport or game
A hobby you pursue or an activity associated with that hobby
A technical term or specific piece of equipment that you use in your job
An object (such as an article of clothing) that is important to your culture or religion
A basic term in a course you are taking
A particular style of music or dancing
A controversial subject whose definition not all people agree on, such as affirmative action, right to life, or gun control
A goal in life, such as success or happiness

◆ **PRACTICE 10-4**

Review your notes for the topic you chose in Practice 10-3. On a separate sheet of paper, list the details that can best help you to develop a definition paragraph.

◆ **PRACTICE 10-5**

Reread your notes from Practice 10-4. Then, draft a topic sentence that summarizes the main point you want to make about the term you are going to define.

_____

_____

◆ **PRACTICE 10-6**

List the ideas you will discuss in your paragraph, arranging them in an effective order.

1. _____

2. _____

3. _____

4. _____

5. _____

◆ **PRACTICE 10-7**

Draft your definition paragraph.

◆ **PRACTICE 10-8**

Consulting the Self-Assessment Checklist on page 130, revise your definition paragraph.

◆ **PRACTICE 10-9**

Type a final draft of your definition paragraph.

■ **WRITING FIRST: Revising and Editing**

Look back at your response to the Writing First activity on page 121. Consulting the Self-Assessment Checklist on page 130, revise your definition paragraph. Then, prepare a final draft of your paragraph.

☑ SELF-ASSESSMENT CHECKLIST:
Writing a Definition Paragraph

- Do you have a clearly worded topic sentence that states your paragraph's main idea?

- Does your topic sentence identify the term you are defining?

- Do all your examples and details support your topic sentence?

- Do you need to add more examples or details to help you define your term?

- Are your transitions appropriate for the pattern (or patterns) of development you use, or do you need to add transitions to make your paragraph more coherent?

- Does your paragraph end with a concluding statement that summarizes your main idea?

MOVING FROM PARAGRAPH TO ESSAY

Definition

In addition to writing definition paragraphs, you may also have to write a **definition essay**. For example, for psychology class, you might have to write an essay in which you define the term *autism*. For a study group at your place of worship, you might be asked to write definitions of *morality* and *goodness*. *For information on how to write a definition essay, see 14H.*

Argument

PREVIEW

In this chapter, you will learn to write an argument paragraph.

■ **WRITING FIRST**

The picture above shows a confrontation between a pro-immigration protestor and a member of an anti-immigration group, the Minutemen Project, in New York City in July 2006. Look at the picture, and then write a paragraph in which you argue for or against one of the following policies.

- Granting guest-worker status to undocumented immigrants
- Outlawing smoking in all public places
- Taxing all purchases made on the Internet
- Requiring everyone in the United States to carry a national identification card
- Reinstituting the military draft in the United States
- Enabling people to vote in federal elections on their home computers

Include examples from your experience or from your reading to support your position.

▶ Word Power
controversy a dispute

debate to discuss or argue about

11 **A**

A **What Is Argument?**

■ **Culture Clue**
Arguing for one's point
of view is central to
American culture. In
fact, the United States
Constitution guarantees
all citizens the right to
express their opinions
without fear of
punishment. This is called
freedom of speech.

When most people hear the word *argument*, they think of the heated ex-changes on television interview programs. These discussions, however, are more like shouting matches than arguments. True **argument** involves tak-ing a well-thought-out position on a **debatable topic**—a topic about which reasonable people may disagree (for example, "Should intelligent design be taught in high school classrooms?" or "Should teenagers who commit felonies be tried as adults?").

In an **argument paragraph**, your purpose is to persuade readers that your position has merit. You attempt to convince people of the strength of your ideas not by shouting but by presenting **evidence**—facts and examples. In the process, you address opposing ideas, and if they are strong, you acknowledge their strengths. If your evidence is solid and your logic is sound, you will present a convincing argument.

FOCUS **Evidence**

There are two kinds of **evidence**—*facts* and *examples*.

1. A **fact** is a piece of information that can be verified. If you make a statement, you should be prepared to support it with facts—for example, statistics, observations, or statements that are accepted as true.

2. An **example** is a specific illustration of a general statement. To be convincing, an example should clearly relate to the point you are making.

When you write an argument paragraph, keep the following guidelines in mind:

■ An **argument paragraph** should begin with a topic sentence that states your position. Using words like *should, should not,* or *ought to* in your topic sentence will make your position clear to readers.

The federal government <u>should</u> lower the tax on gasoline.

The city <u>should not</u> build a new sports stadium.

■ An argument paragraph should present points that support the topic sentence. For example, if your purpose is to argue in favor of placing warning labels on unhealthy snack foods, you should give several rea-sons why this policy should be instituted.

■ An argument paragraph should support each point with **evidence** (facts and examples).

■ An argument paragraph should address and **refute** (argue against) op-posing arguments. By showing that an opponent's arguments are weak or inaccurate, you strengthen your own position.

■ An argument paragraph should end with a strong concluding statement that summarizes the main idea of the paragraph.

An argument paragraph generally has the following structure.

Topic Sentence _____

_____

Point #1 _____

_____

Point #2 _____

_____

Point #3 _____

_____

Opposing Argument #1 (plus refutation) _____

_____

Opposing Argument #2 (plus refutation) _____

_____

Concluding Statement _____

_____

The following paragraph argues in favor of an emergency notification system for college students.

Why Our School Should Install an Emergency Notification System

Our school should install an emergency notification system that would ———Topic sentence
deliver an instant message to students' cell phones in a campus crisis. The first
reason why we should install an emergency notification system is that it is
needed. Currently, it takes an hour or two to inform the whole campus of ⎤
something—for example, that school is closing because of bad weather or that ⎬ Point 1 and examples
a school event has been cancelled. Another reason why we should install an ⎦
emergency notification system is that it will make our campus safer by warning ⎤
students if a crime takes place on campus. For example, when a shooting took
place in 2007 on the campus of Virginia Tech, the school was unable to warn
students to evacuate the campus. The result was that more than thirty people ⎬ Point 2 and examples
were killed. An emergency notification system might have saved the lives of
many of these people. One objection to an emergency notification system is ⎦
that email notification is good enough. Unfortunately, many students check ⎤
their email just once or twice a day. However, most students carry cell phones ⎬ Opposing argument 1
and read instant messages whenever they get them. Another objection is that ⎦ (plus refutation)

11 A

Opposing argument 2
(plus refutation)

Concluding statement

some students do not have cell phones. The same system that delivers instant messages to students, however, could also deliver messages to digital message boards around campus. <u>Because communicating with students in a crisis situation can save lives, our school should install an emergency notification system.</u>

—Ashley Phillips (student)

Transitions are important in argument paragraphs. In the paragraph above, the transitional words and phrases *the first reason* and *another reason* tell readers they are moving from one point to another. In addition, the transitional phrases *one objection* and *another objection* indicate that the writer is addressing two opposing arguments.

Transitions for Argument

accordingly	finally	nonetheless
admittedly	first . . . second . . .	of course
after all	for this reason	on the one hand . . .
although	however	on the other hand
because	in addition	since
but	in conclusion	the first reason
certainly	in fact	therefore
consequently	in summary	thus
despite	meanwhile	to be sure
even so	moreover	truly
even though	nevertheless	

GRAMMAR IN CONTEXT   Argument

When you write an argument paragraph, you need to show the relationships between your ideas. You do this by creating both compound sentences and complex sentences.

COMPOUND SENTENCE   An emergency notification system will help

all of us communicate better. ~~It~~ *, and it* will ensure

our school's safety.

COMPLEX SENTENCE   *Because communicating*

~~Communicating~~ with students in a crisis

situation can save lives. ~~Our~~ *, our* school should

install an emergency notification system.

For more information on how to create compound sentences, see Chapter 16. For more information on how to create complex sentences, see Chapter 17.

◆ **PRACTICE 11-1**

Read this argument paragraph; then see the instructions that follow.

Big Brother in the Workplace

Employers should not routinely monitor the computer use of their employees. Every day, employees use their computers for work-related tasks, and in many companies every keystroke is recorded. In addition, some companies read employees' private email files as well as monitoring the Internet sites they visit. This monitoring violates employees' privacy. It creates an unpleasant work environment because employees feel that someone is always watching them. In fact, at some companies, employees have even been fired for sending personal emails or humorous pictures. Of course, companies that believe computers should be used only for work-related tasks have a point. After all, the company pays for both the computers and the employees' time. The problem with this line of thinking, however, is that it ignores the fact that workers need some downtime in order to work effectively. For this reason, it makes sense to allow some use of computers for personal reasons (to send emails to friends, for example). Unless the company has reason to suspect misuse of company computers, it should not routinely monitor all employees' computers.

—Scott Rathmill (student)

1. Underline the topic sentence of the paragraph.

2. What issue is the subject of the paragraph?

_____

   What is the writer's position?

_____

3. What specific points does the writer use to support his topic sentence?

_____

_____

4. List some of the evidence (facts and examples) that the writer uses to support his points. The first piece of evidence has been listed for you.

   Every keystroke an employee makes is recorded.

_____

_____

_____

5. What other evidence could the writer have used?

_____

_____

_____

_____

6. What opposing argument does the writer address?

_____

7. How does the writer address this argument?

_____

8. Circle the transitional words and phrases the writer uses to move readers through his argument.

9. Underline the paragraph's concluding statement.

◆ **PRACTICE 11-2**

Following are four topic sentences for argument paragraphs. On the lines below, list two or three points that could support each topic sentence. For example, if you were arguing in support of laws requiring motorcycle riders to wear safety helmets, you could say they cut down on medical costs and save lives.

1. Marijuana use for certain medical conditions should be legalized.

_____

_____

_____

2. All student athletes should be paid a salary by their college or university.

_____

_____

_____

3. College students caught cheating should be expelled.

_____

_____

4. The U.S. government should provide free health care.

_____

_____

_____

◆ **PRACTICE 11-3**

Choose one of the topic sentences from Practice 11-2. Then, list two types of evidence that could support each point you listed. For example, if you said that wearing safety helmets saves lives, you could list "accident statistics" and "statements by emergency room physicians."

_____

_____

B   Writing an Argument Paragraph

Phillip Zhu was asked to write an argument paragraph on a topic that interested him. Because he was taking a course in computer ethics, he decided to write about an issue that had been discussed in class: the way employers have recently begun searching social networking sites, such as MySpace, to find information about job applicants.

Phillip had already formed an opinion about this issue, and he knew something about the topic. For this reason, he was able to write a topic sentence right away.

> Employers should not use social networking sites to find information about job applicants.

Phillip then listed the following ideas that he could use to support his topic sentence.

Social networking sites should be private

People exaggerate on social networking sites

Stuff meant to be funny

No one warns applicant

Need email address to register

Expect limited audience

Employers can misinterpret what they find

Employers going where they don't belong

Not an accurate picture

Not fair

Not meant to be seen by job recruiters

Phillip then arranged his ideas into an informal outline.

> Social networking sites should be private
> Need email address to register
> Expect limited audience
> Employers going where they don't belong
>
> People exaggerate on social networking sites
> Stuff meant to be funny
> Not meant to be seen by job recruiters
> No one warns applicant
>
> Employers can misinterpret what they find
> Not an accurate picture
> Not fair

Once Phillip finished his informal outline, he tried to think of possible arguments against his position because he knew he would have to consider and refute these opposing arguments in his paragraph. He came up with two possible arguments against his position.

1. Employers should be able to find out as much as they can.
2. Applicants have only themselves to blame.

Phillip then wrote the following draft of his paragraph.

> Employers should not use social networking sites to find information about job applicants. For one thing, social networking sites should be private. By visiting these sites, employers are going where they do not belong. People also exaggerate on social networking sites. They say things that are not true, and they put things on the sites they would not want job recruiters to see. No one ever tells applicants that recruiters search these sites, so they feel safe posting all kinds of material. Employers can misinterpret what they read. Employers and recruiters need to get as much information as they can. They should not use unfair ways to get this information. Applicants have only themselves to blame for their problems. They need to be more careful about what they put up online. This is true, but most applicants don't know that employers will search social networking sites.

After finishing his draft, Phillip scheduled a conference with his instructor. Together, they went over his paragraph and decided that Phillip needed to make the following changes.

■ He needed to make his topic sentence more specific and more forceful.
■ He needed to add more supporting evidence (facts and examples) to his discussion. For example, what social networking sites is he talking about? Which ones are restricted? How do employers gain access to these sites?
■ He needed to delete irrelevant discussion blaming job applicants for the problem.
■ He needed to add transitional words and phrases to clearly identify the points he is making in support of his argument and also to identify the two opposing arguments he discusses and refutes.
■ He needed to add a strong concluding statement to sum up his argument.

After making these changes, Phillip revised and edited his paragraph. Here is his final draft.

Unfair Searching

Employers should not use social networking sites such as MySpace and Facebook to find information about job applicants. First, social networking sites should be private. People who use these sites do not expect employers to access these sites. However, some employers routinely search these sites to find information about job applicants. Doing this is not right, and it is not fair. By visiting these sites, employers are going where they do not belong. Another reason why employers should not use information from social networking sites is that people frequently exaggerate on them. They say things that are not true, and they post statements and pictures on the sites that they would not want job recruiters to see. Because no one ever tells applicants that recruiters search these sites, they feel safe posting embarrassing pictures or making exaggerated claims about drinking or sex. Finally, employers can misinterpret what they read. As a result, they may reject a good applicant because they take seriously what is meant to be a joke. Of course, employers need to get as much information about a candidate as they can. They should not, however, use unfair ways to get this information. In addition, prospective employers should realize that the profile they see on a social networking site does not accurately represent the job applicant. For these reasons, they should not use these sites to do background checks.

- Topic sentence made more specific

- More evidence added

- Transitions added to introduce points

- Transitions added to introduce opposing arguments

- Concluding statement added

◆ PRACTICE 11-4

Now, you are ready to write an argument paragraph. Choose one of the topics below (or choose your own topic). Then, on a separate sheet of paper, use one or more of the strategies described in 1C to help you focus on a specific issue to discuss in an argument paragraph.

An Issue Related to Your School

Grading policies	Financial aid
Required courses	Student activity fees
Attendance policies	Childcare facilities
Campus security	Sexual harassment policies
Dining facilities	The physical condition of classrooms

An Issue Related to Your Community

The need for a traffic signal, a youth center, or something else you
    think would benefit your community

An action you think local officials should take, such as changing school
    hours, cleaning up a public space, or improving services for the elderly

A new law you would like to see enacted

A current law you would like to see changed

A controversy you have been following in the news

◆ **PRACTICE 11-5**

Once you have chosen an issue in Practice 11-4, write a journal entry
about your position on the issue. Consider the following questions: Why
do you feel the way you do? Do you think many people share your views,
or do you think you are in the minority? What specific actions do you
think should be taken? What objections are likely to be raised against your
position? How might you respond to these objections?

◆ **PRACTICE 11-6**

Review your notes for the topic you chose in Practice 11-4, and select the
points that best support your position. List these points below. Then, list the
strongest arguments against your position.

Supporting points: _____

_____

Opposing arguments: _____

_____

◆ **PRACTICE 11-7**

Draft a topic sentence that clearly expresses the position you will take in
your paragraph.

_____

_____

◆ **PRACTICE 11-8**

In the space provided, arrange the points that support your position in an
order that you think will be convincing to your audience.

1. _____

2. _____

3. _____

4. _____

5. _____

◆ PRACTICE 11-9

In the space provided, list the evidence (facts and examples) that you could use to support each of your points.

Evidence for point 1: _____

_____

Evidence for point 2: _____

_____

Evidence for point 3: _____

_____

◆ PRACTICE 11-10

Draft your argument paragraph.

◆ PRACTICE 11-11

Consulting the Self-Assessment Checklist on page 142, revise your argument paragraph.

◆ PRACTICE 11-12

Type a final draft of your argument paragraph.

■ WRITING FIRST: Revising and Editing

Look back at your response to the Writing First activity on page 131. Consulting the Self-Assessment Checklist on page 142, evaluate the paragraph you wrote. Then, prepare a final draft of your paragraph.

☑ SELF-ASSESSMENT CHECKLIST:
Writing an Argument Paragraph

☐ Do you have a clearly worded topic sentence that states your position on this issue?

☐ Does your topic sentence state your position on a debatable topic?

☐ Does all your evidence support your paragraph's main idea?

☐ Have you included enough evidence to support your points, or do you need to add more?

☐ Do you include transitions to let readers know when you move from one point to another?

☐ Do you include transitions to indicate when you are addressing opposing arguments?

☐ Do you need to add transitions to make your argument more coherent?

☐ Does your paragraph end with a concluding statement that reinforces your position on the issue?

MOVING FROM PARAGRAPH TO ESSAY

Argument

In addition to writing argument paragraphs, you may sometimes have to write an **argument essay**. For example, in a literature class, you may be asked to write an essay about a poem, play, or short story in which you support an argumentative thesis. In an email to a local newspaper, you might argue for a law that taxes motorists who drive into the center of the city. *For information on how to write an argument essay, see 14I.*

UNIT THREE

FOCUS ON ESSAYS

Writing an Essay

PREVIEW

In this chapter, you will learn:

- to understand essay structure (12A)
- to decide on a topic (12B)
- to find ideas to write about (12C)
- to state a thesis (12D)
- to choose supporting points (12E)
- to arrange supporting points (12F)
- to draft your essay (12G)
- to revise your essay (12H)
- to edit your essay (12I)
- to check your essay's format (12J)

■ WRITING FIRST

The picture above shows a person dressed up as a mascot outside of a Jack-in-the-Box fast-food restaurant. Look at the picture, and then think about the worst job you have ever had. This is the topic you will be writing about as you move through this chapter. (If you have never had a job, you may write about a specific task that you disliked or about a bad job that a friend or a relative has had.)

145

Much of the writing you do in school will be longer than a single paragraph. Often, you will be asked to write an **essay**—a group of paragraphs on a single subject. When you write an essay, you follow the same process you do when you write a paragraph: you begin with finding something to say and then move on to choosing and arranging ideas, drafting, revising, and editing.

A Thinking about Paragraphs and Essays

In some ways, paragraphs and essays are similar. Both paragraphs and essays have a single **main idea**. In a paragraph, the **topic sentence** presents the main idea, and the rest of the paragraph supports this main idea with details, facts, and examples. The paragraph often ends with a concluding statement.

Paragraph

A **topic sentence** states the main idea of the paragraph.

Supporting sentences develop the main idea with details and examples.

A **concluding statement** ends the paragraph.

An essay contains a number of paragraphs, each one carrying out a particular function. Even so, essay structure is similar to paragraph structure.

- The essay's first paragraph—the **introduction**—begins with **opening remarks** and closes with a **thesis statement**. This thesis statement, like a paragraph's topic sentence, presents the main idea.
- The **body** of the essay contains several paragraphs that **support** the thesis statement. Each body paragraph begins with a **topic sentence** that states the main idea of the paragraph. The other sentences in the paragraph support the topic sentence with **details** and **examples**.
- The last paragraph—the **conclusion**—ends the essay. The conclusion includes a **concluding statement** that sums up the essay's main idea, perhaps restating the thesis. It ends with **concluding remarks**.

Nearly every essay you will write in college will have a **thesis and support** structure.

Essay

Opening remarks introduce the subject to be discussed in the essay.

A **thesis statement** presents the essay's main idea.

Introduction

A **topic sentence** states the essay's first main point.

Details and **examples** support the topic sentence.

A **topic sentence** states the essay's second main point.

Details and **examples** support the topic sentence.

A **topic sentence** states the essay's third main point.

Details and **examples** support the topic sentence.

— *Body paragraphs*

A **concluding statement** summarizes the essay's main idea, perhaps restating the thesis.

Concluding remarks present the writer's final thoughts on the subject.

— *Conclusion*

The following student essay illustrates this thesis-and-support structure.

Becoming Chinese American

Although I was born in Hong Kong, I have spent most of my life in the United States. However, my parents have always made sure that I did not forget my roots. They always tell stories of what it was like to live in Hong Kong. To make sure my brothers and sisters and I know what is happening in China, my parents subscribe to Chinese cable TV. When we were growing up, we would watch the celebration of the Chinese New Year, the news from Asia, and Chinese movies and music videos. As a result, I value Chinese culture even though I am an American.

— **Introduction**

Thesis statement

The Chinese language is an important part of my life as a Chinese American. Unlike some of my Chinese friends, I do not think Chinese is unimportant or embarrassing. First, I feel that it is my duty as a Chinese American to learn Chinese so that I can pass it on to my children. In addition, knowing Chinese enables me to communicate with my relatives. Because my parents and

(Topic sentence states essay's first main point)

— **First body paragraph**

grandparents do not speak English well, Chinese is our main form of communication. Finally, Chinese helps me identify with my culture. When I speak Chinese, I feel connected to a culture that is over five thousand years old. Without the Chinese language, I would not be who I am.

(Topic sentence states essay's second main point)

Second body paragraph

Chinese food is another important part of my life as a Chinese American. One reason for this is that everything we Chinese people eat has a history and a meaning. At a birthday meal, for example, we serve long noodles and buns in the shape of peaches. This is because we believe that long noodles represent long life and that peaches are served in heaven. Another reason is that to Chinese people, food is a way of reinforcing ties between family and friends. For instance, during a traditional Chinese wedding ceremony, the bride and the groom eat nine of everything. This is because the number nine stands for the Chinese words "together forever." By taking part in this ritual, the bride and groom start their marriage by making Chinese customs a part of their life together.

(Topic sentence states essay's third main point)

Third body paragraph

Religion is the most important part of my life as a Chinese American. At various times during the year, Chinese religious festivals bring together the people I care about the most. During Chinese New Year, my whole family goes to the temple. Along with hundreds of other families, we say prayers and welcome each other with traditional New Year's greetings. After leaving the temple, we all go to Chinatown and eat dim sum until the lion dance starts. As the colorful lion dances its way down the street, people beat drums and throw firecrackers to drive off any evil spirits that may be around. Later that night, parents give children gifts of money in red envelopes that symbolize joy and happiness in the coming year.

Concluding statement

Conclusion

Concluding remarks

My family has taught me how important it is to hold on to my Chinese culture. When I was six, my parents sent me to a Chinese-American grade school. My teachers thrilled me with stories of Fa Mulan, the Shang Dynasty, and the Moon God. I will never forget how happy I was when I realized how special it is to be Chinese. This is how I want my own children to feel. I want them to be proud of who they are and to pass their language, history, and culture on to the next generation.

◆ **PRACTICE 12-1**

Following is an essay organized according to the diagram on pages 146–47. Read the essay, and then answer the questions that follow it.

Maybe you have moved to a new city, so you need to find a new doctor for yourself and your family. Maybe your doctor has retired. Or maybe you need a specialist to help you deal with a difficult medical problem. In any case, your goal is clear: to find a doctor. Several strategies can help you find a good doctor.

— Introduction

First, look for a well-qualified doctor. One way to begin is to identify the best hospital in the area and find a doctor on the staff there. Good doctors are attracted to good hospitals, so this is a good place to start your search. Recommendations from friends and neighbors can also be useful. Once you have some names, find out whether the doctors are board certified in their specific fields. Board certification means that doctors have had extensive training in their specialties. You can find out whether a doctor is board certified by going to the American Board of Medical Specialties Web site.

— First body paragraph

Second, decide what things are important to you. For example, how far are you willing to travel to see the doctor? Also, consider when the doctor is available. Many doctors have office hours only on weekdays. Is this acceptable, or will you need evening or Saturday appointments? Will you be able to see the doctor at any time, or will you have to go to a hospital emergency room? Finally, find out how you will pay for the medical care you receive. If you have medical insurance, find out if the doctor accepts your plan. If you do not have medical insurance, find out what payment options the doctor offers. Will you have to pay the entire bill at once, or will you be able to arrange a payment plan?

— Second body paragraph

Next, make an appointment to visit the office and meet the doctor. If the office seems crowded and disorganized, be on your guard. The doctor may be overscheduled, overworked, understaffed, or simply disorganized. Also, see how long it takes to see the doctor. Unless the doctor is called away to an emergency, you should not have to sit in the waiting room for one or two hours. Finally, see if you feel comfortable talking to the doctor. If the doctor seems rushed or uninterested, take this as an indication of the type of medical care you will get. Finally, both the doctor and the office staff should treat you with respect. They should take the time to ask about your general health and to update your medical records.

— Third body paragraph

Finding a good doctor requires careful planning and a lot of work. You may even have to take the time to see several doctors and assess each one. Remember, though, there are no short cuts. If the result of all your hard work is a qualified doctor who really cares about your well-being, then your time will have been well spent.

— Conclusion

1. Underline the essay's thesis. Then, write it on the lines below.

_____

_____

2. Underline the topic sentence of each body paragraph.

3. What point does the first body paragraph make?

_____

_____

4. What point does the second paragraph make?

_____

_____

5. What point does the third body paragraph make?

_____

_____

6. At what point in the conclusion does the writer restate the essay's thesis?

_____

_____

7. How does the writer develop the points made in the body paragraphs?

Body paragraph 1: _____

_____

Body paragraph 2: _____

_____

Body paragraph 3: _____

_____

B Deciding on a Topic

Most of the essays you will write in college begin as an **assignment** given to you by your instructor. The following assignments are typical of those you might be given in your composition class.

- Decide some things you would change about your school.
- What can college students do to improve the environment?
- Discuss an important decision you made during the past three years.

Because these assignments are so general, you need to narrow them before you can start to write. What specific things would you change? Exactly what could you do to improve the environment? Which decision should you write about? Answering these questions will help you narrow these assignments into **topics** that you can write about.

Assignment	Topic
Discuss some things you would change about your school.	Three things I would change to improve the quality of life at Jackson County Community College
What can college students do to improve the environment?	The campus recycling project
Discuss an important decision you made during the past three years.	Deciding to go back to school

◆ PRACTICE 12-2

Decide whether the following topics are narrow enough for an essay of four or five paragraphs. If a topic is suitable, write *OK* in the blank. If it is not, write in the blank a revised version of the same topic that is narrow enough for a brief essay.

Examples: Successful strategies for quitting smoking _____*OK*_____

Horror movies _____*1950s Japanese monster movies*_____

1. Violence in American public schools _____

2. Ways to improve your study skills _____

3. Using pets as therapy for nursing-home patients _____

4. Teachers _____

5. Safe ways to lose weight _____

■ WRITING FIRST: Flashback

Look back at the Writing First activity on page 145. To narrow the topic to one you can write about, you need to decide which job to focus on. On the lines below, list several jobs you could discuss.

Before you start writing about a topic, you need to find out what you have to say about it. Sometimes ideas may come to you easily. More often, you will have to use specific strategies, such as *freewriting* or *brainstorming*, to help you come up with ideas.

Freewriting

When you **freewrite**, you write for a fixed period of time without stopping. When you do **focused freewriting**, you write with a specific topic in mind. Then, you read what you have written and choose the ideas you think you can use.

The following focused freewriting example was written by a student, Jared White, on the topic "Deciding to go back to school."

> Deciding to go back to school. When I graduated high school, I swore I'd never go back to school. Hated it. Couldn't wait to get out. What was I thinking? How was I supposed to support myself? My dad's friend needed help. He taught me how to paint houses. I made good money, but it was boring. I couldn't picture myself doing it forever. Even though I knew I was going to have to go back to school, I kept putting off the decision. Maybe I was lazy. Maybe I was scared — probably both. I had this fear of being turned down. How could someone who had bad grades all through high school go to college? Also, I'd been out of school for six years. And even if I did get in (a miracle!), how would I pay for it? How would I live? While I was painting, I met a guy who told me that I could get into community college. Tuition was a lot lower than I thought. I just had to push myself to go. Well, here I am — the first one in my family to go to college.

◆ PRACTICE 12-3

Reread Jared White's freewriting. If you were advising Jared, which ideas would you tell him to explore further? Why? Write your answers below.

_____

_____

_____

_____

■ WRITING FIRST: Flashback

Choose two of the jobs you listed for the Flashback activity on page 151. Freewrite about each of them on separate sheets of paper.

(*continued on following page*)

(*continued from previous page*)

Now, choose the job that gave you the most interesting material. On the lines below, write the name of the job. Then, write down the ideas that you would like to develop further.

Job: _____

_____

Ideas: _____

_____

_____

_____

Brainstorming

When you **brainstorm** (either individually or with others in a group), you write down (or type) all the ideas you can think of about a particular topic. After you have recorded as much material as you can, you look over your notes and decide which ideas are useful and which ones are not.

Here are Jared White's brainstorming notes about his decision to go back to school.

Deciding to Go Back to School

Money a problem
No confidence
Other students a lot younger
Paying tuition — how?
No one in family went to college
Friends not in college
Couldn't see myself in college
Relationship with Beth
Considered going to trade school
Computer programmer?
Grades bad in high school
Time for me to grow up
Wondered if I would get in
Found out about community college
Went to Web site
Admission requirements not bad
Afraid — too old, failing out, looking silly
Took time to get used to routine
Found other students like me
Liked studying

◆ **PRACTICE 12-4**

Reread Jared White's brainstorming notes. Which ideas would you advise him to explore further? Write these ideas on the lines below.

_____

_____

_____

_____

■ **WRITING FIRST: Flashback**

Review the freewriting you did in the Flashback activity on pages 152–53. On a separate sheet of paper, brainstorm about the job for which you have found the most interesting ideas. What ideas about the job did you get from brainstorming that you did not get from freewriting? Write these ideas on the lines below.

_____

_____

_____

_____

D Stating Your Thesis

After you have gathered information about your topic, you need to decide what point you want to make about it. You will then express this point in a **thesis statement**: a single sentence that clearly expresses the main idea that you will discuss in the rest of your essay.

Topic	Thesis Statement
Three things I would change about Jackson County Community College	If I could change three things to improve Jackson County Community College, I would expand the food choices, decrease class size in first-year courses, and ship some of my classmates to the North Pole.
The campus recycling project	The recycling project recently begun on our campus should be promoted more actively.
The difficulty of going back to school	I decided that if I really wanted to attend college full-time, I could.

Like a topic sentence, a thesis statement tells readers what to expect. An effective thesis statement has two important characteristics.

1. *An effective thesis statement makes a point about a topic. For this reason, it must do more than state a fact or announce what you plan to write about.*

STATEMENT OF FACT	Many older students are returning to school.
ANNOUNCEMENT	In this essay, I would like to discuss the difficulties many older students have going back to school.
EFFECTIVE THESIS STATEMENT	I decided that if I really wanted to attend college full-time, I could.

A statement of fact is not an effective thesis statement because it gives you nothing to develop in your essay. After all, how much can you say about the *fact* that many older students are returning to school? Likewise, an announcement of what you plan to discuss gives readers no indication of the position you will take on your topic. Remember, an effective thesis statement makes a point.

2. *An effective thesis statement is clearly worded and specific.*

VAGUE THESIS STATEMENT	Television commercials are not like real life.
EFFECTIVE THESIS STATEMENT	Television commercials do not accurately portray women or minorities.

The vague thesis statement above gives readers no sense of the ideas the essay will discuss. It does not say, for example, *why* television commercials are not realistic. The effective thesis statement is more focused. It signals that the essay will discuss television commercials that present unrealistic portrayals of women and minorities.

◆ PRACTICE 12-5

In the space provided, indicate whether each of the following items is a statement of fact (*F*), an announcement (*A*), a vague statement (*VS*), or an effective thesis (*ET*).

Examples

My drive to school takes more than an hour. ___F___

I hate my commute between home and school. ___VS___

1. Students who must commute a long distance to school are at a disadvantage compared to students who live close by. _____

2. In this paper, I will discuss cheating. _____

3. Schools should establish specific policies to discourage students from cheating. _____

4. Cheating is a problem. _____

5. Television commercials are designed to sell products. _____

6. I would like to explain why some television commercials are funny. _____

7. Single parents have a rough time. _____

8. Young people are starting to abuse alcohol and drugs at earlier ages than in the past. _____

9. Alcohol and drug abuse are major problems in our society. _____

10. Families can do several things to help children avoid alcohol and drugs. _____

◆ **PRACTICE 12-6**

Label each of the following thesis statements *VS* if it is too vague, *F* if it is factual, *A* if it is an announcement, or *ET* if it is an effective thesis. On a separate sheet of paper, rewrite those that are not effective thesis statements.

1. Different types of amusement parks appeal to different types of people. _____

2. There are three reasons why Election Day should be a national holiday. _____

3. Every four years, voters in the United States elect a new president. _____

4. My paper will prove that DVDs are better than videotapes. _____

5. The largest fish is the whale shark. _____

6. Scientists once thought that the dinosaurs were killed off by climate change. _____

7. NASCAR drivers could do several things to make their sport safer. _____

8. This paper will discuss the increase in the number of women in the military since the 1970s. _____

9. Movies provide great entertainment. _____

10. Computers have enabled teachers to develop new classroom techniques. _____

■ Culture Clue

NASCAR is the National Association for Stock Car Auto Racing.

◆ **PRACTICE 12-7**

Rewrite the following vague thesis statements.

    Example: My relatives are funny.

                Rewrite: *My relatives think they are funny, but sometimes*

                         their humor can be offensive.

1. Text messaging can save time.
2. Airport security is a hassle.
3. Athletes are paid too much.
4. Many people get their identities from their cars.
5. Being single has lots of advantages.

◆ **PRACTICE 12-8**

A list of broad topics for essays follows. Select five of these topics, narrow them, and generate a thesis statement for each.

   1. Terrorism
   2. Reality television
   3. U.S. immigration policies
   4. Music
   5. Dieting

   6. Required courses
   7. Computer games
   8. Disciplining children
   9. Street sense
 10. Footwear

■ **WRITING FIRST: Flashback**

Review your freewriting and brainstorming from the Flashback activities on pages 152–53 and page 154. Then, write a thesis statement for your essay on the lines below.

Thesis statement: _____

_____

_____

E   **Choosing Supporting Points**

Once you have decided on a thesis statement, look over your freewriting and brainstorming again. Identify the points that best support your thesis, and cross out those that do not.

    Jared White made the following list of supporting points about his decision to go back to school. When he reviewed his list, he crossed out several points that he thought would not support his thesis.

Money a problem
~~No confidence~~
Other students a lot younger
Paying tuition — how?
No one in family went to college
Friends not in college
Couldn't see myself in college
~~Relationship with Beth~~
~~Considered going to trade school~~
~~Computer programmer?~~
Grades bad in high school
~~Time for me to grow up~~
Wondered if I would get in
Found out about community college
Went to Web site
~~Web site answered questions~~
Admission requirements not bad
Afraid — too old, failing out, looking dumb
~~Took time to get used to routine~~
Found other students like me
Liked studying

◆ PRACTICE 12-9

Look at Jared's list of supporting points above. Are there any points he crossed out that you think he should keep? Are there any other points he should cross out? Write your answers on the lines below.

Points to keep: _____

_____

Points to cross out: _____

_____

F   Arranging Supporting Points

After you have selected the points you think will best support your thesis, arrange them into groups. For example, after looking at the list of points above, Jared White saw that his points fell into three groups of excuses for not going back to school: not being able to pay tuition, not being a good student in high school, and not being able to picture himself in college.

After you have come up with your groups, arrange them in the order in which you will discuss them (for example, from general to specific, or

from least important to most important). Then, arrange the supporting points for each group in the same way. This orderly list can serve as a rough outline to guide you as you write.

Jared grouped and listed his points in the following order.

Excuse 1: Not being able to pay tuition
    Money a problem
    Found out about community college
    Went to Web site

Excuse 2: Not being a good student in high school
    Grades bad in high school
    Wondered if I would get in
    Admission requirements not bad

Excuse 3: Not being able to picture myself in college
    No one in family went to college
    Friends not in college
    Afraid—too old, failing out, looking dumb
    Found other students like me
    Liked studying

◆ **PRACTICE 12-10**

Look over Jared's list of points above. Do you think his arrangement is effective? Can you suggest any other ways he might have arranged his points? Write your suggestions on the lines below.

_____

_____

FOCUS **Preparing a Formal Outline**

A list of points like the one that appears above is usually all you need to plan a short essay. However, some writers—especially when they are planning a longer, more detailed essay—like to use a more formal outline.

Formal outlines use a combination of numbered and lettered headings to show the relationships among ideas. For example, the most important (and most general) ideas are assigned a roman numeral; the next most important ideas are assigned capital letters. Each level develops the idea above it, and each new level is indented.

Here is a formal outline of the points that Jared planned to discuss in his essay.

(continued on following page)

(continued from previous page)

Thesis statement: I decided that if I really wanted to attend college full-time, I could.

I. Not being able to pay tuition
  A. Money a problem
  B. Community college
    1. Tuition low
    2. Expenses reasonable
II. Not being a good student in school
  A. Grades bad
    1. Didn't care about high school
    2. Didn't do homework
  B. Anxiety about getting in
  C. Admissions requirements
    1. High school diploma
    2. County residence
    3. Placement tests
III. Not being able to picture myself in college
  A. Family no help
  B. Friends not in college
  C. Fear of going
    1. Too old
    2. Couldn't keep up
  D. Fears disappeared
    1. Found other students like me
    2. Liked studying

■ WRITING FIRST: Flashback

On the lines below, recopy the thesis statement you wrote in the Flashback box on page 157.

_____

_____

Now, review the freewriting and brainstorming you did in response to the Flashback activities on pages 152–53 and page 154. List below the points you plan to use to support your thesis statement. Cross out any points that do not support your thesis statement.

_____   _____

_____   _____

_____   _____

_____   _____

(continued on following page)

(continued from previous page)

Finally, group these points, and arrange the points in each group in an order in which you could write about them.

_____   _____   _____

_____   _____   _____

_____   _____   _____

_____   _____   _____

_____   _____   _____

G Drafting Your Essay

After you have decided on a thesis for your essay and have arranged your points in the order in which you will discuss them, you are ready to draft your essay.

At this stage of the writing process, you should not worry about spelling or grammar or about composing a perfect introduction or conclusion. Your main goal is to get your ideas down so you can react to them. Remember that the draft you are writing will be revised, so leave room for your changes: write on every other line, and leave extra space between lines if you are typing. Follow your rough outline, but don't hesitate to depart from it if you think of new points.

As you draft your essay, be sure that it has a **thesis-and-support** structure—that is, it should state a thesis and support it with details and examples.

Jared White used a thesis-and-support structure in the first draft of his essay.

Going Back to School

I have been out of school since I graduated from high school six years ago. The decision to return to school was one I had a lot of difficulty making. I had been around enough to know that without more education, I'd never get anywhere in life, but I always found reasons for not taking the plunge. However, after a lot of thinking, I realized that my reasons for not going to college were just excuses. I decided that if I really wanted to attend college full-time, I could.

My first excuse for not going to college was that I couldn't afford to go to school full-time. I had worked since I finished high school, but I hadn't put much money away. I kept wondering how I would pay for books and tuition. I needed to support myself and pay for rent, food, and car expenses. I was working as a house painter, and a house I was painting belonged to a college instructor. Painting wasn't hard work, but it was boring. I'd start in the morning and work without a break until lunch. We began talking. When I told him about my situation, he told me I should look at our local community college. I went online and looked at the college's Web site. I found out that tuition was forty dollars a credit, much less than I thought it would be.

Now that I had taken care of my first excuse, I had to deal with my second—that I hadn't been a good student in high school. When I was a teenager, I didn't care much about school. School bored me to death. Now that I was considering going back to school, though, I wondered what price I would have to pay for my laziness and immaturity. The answer to this question was not as bad as I thought it would be. According to the community college's Web site, all I needed to be admitted was a high school diploma and county residence. I would have to take some placement tests, but I would be judged on my ability, not my high school grades. The Web site was easy to navigate, and I had no problem finding information.

I had a hard time picturing myself in college. No one in my family had ever gone to college. My friends were just like me; they all went to work right after high school. I had no role model or mentor who could give me advice. I thought I was just too old for college. After all, I was probably at least six years older than most of the students. How would I be able to keep up with the younger students in the class? I hadn't opened a textbook for years, and I'd never really learned how to study. Most of my fears disappeared during my first few weeks of classes. I saw a lot of students who were as old as I was, and some were even older. Studying didn't seem to be a problem either. I actually enjoyed learning. History, which had put me to sleep in high school, suddenly became interesting. So did math and English. It soon became clear to me that I was going to like being in college.

Going to college as a full-time student has changed my life, both personally and financially. I am no longer the same person I was in high school. I allowed laziness and insecurity to hold me back. Now, I have options that I didn't have before. When I graduate from community college, I plan to transfer to the state university and get a four-year degree.

◆ PRACTICE 12-11

Reread Jared White's first draft. What changes would you suggest he make? What should he add? What should he delete? Write your suggestions on the lines below.

Material to add: _____

_____

_____

_____

Material to delete: _____

_____

_____

_____

_____

■ **WRITING FIRST: Flashback**

On a separate sheet of paper, write a draft of an essay about the job you chose in the Flashback exercise on page 152. Be sure to include the thesis statement you developed in the Flashback exercise on page 157 as well as the points you listed in the Flashback exercise on page 160–61.

H Revising Your Essay

When you **revise** your essay, you resee, rethink, reevaluate, and rewrite your work. Some of the changes you make—such as adding, deleting, or rearranging sentences or even whole paragraphs—will be major. Others will be small—for example, adding or deleting words or phrases.

Before you begin revising, put your essay aside for a time. This "cooling-off" period allows you to see your draft more objectively when you return to it. (Keep in mind that revision is usually not a neat process. When you revise, you write directly on your draft: draw arrows, underline, cross out, and write above lines and in the margins.)

Even when you write on a computer, it is a good idea to print out a draft and revise on it. With a printout, you are able to see a full page—or even two pages next to each other—as you revise. When you have finished, you can type your changes into your document. Do not delete sentences or paragraphs until you are certain you do not need them; instead, move unwanted material to the end of your draft.

To get the most out of revision, read your essay carefully, and use the following checklist as your guide.

☑ SELF-ASSESSMENT CHECKLIST:
Revising Your Essay

- Does your essay have an introduction, a body, and a conclusion?

- Does your introduction include a clearly worded thesis statement that states your essay's main idea?

- Does each body paragraph have a topic sentence?

- Does each topic sentence introduce a point that supports the thesis?

- Does each body paragraph include enough details and examples to support the topic sentence?

- Are the body paragraphs unified, well developed, and coherent?

- Does your conclusion include a concluding statement that restates your thesis or sums up your main idea?

When you **edit** your essay, you check grammar and sentence structure. Then, you look at punctuation, mechanics, and spelling.

As you edit, think carefully about the questions in the Self-Assessment Checklist that follows.

☑ SELF-ASSESSMENT CHECKLIST:
Editing Your Essay

Editing for Common Sentence Problems

- Have you avoided run-ons? (See Chapter 21.)
- Have you avoided sentence fragments? (See Chapter 22.)
- Do your subjects and verbs agree? (See Chapter 23.)
- Have you avoided illogical shifts? (See Chapter 24.)
- Have you avoided misplaced and dangling modifiers? (See Chapter 25.)

Editing for Grammar

- Are your verb forms and verb tenses correct? (See Chapters 26 and 27.)
- Have you used nouns and pronouns correctly? (See Chapter 28.)
- Have you used adjectives and adverbs correctly? (See Chapter 29.)

Editing for Punctuation, Mechanics, and Spelling

- Have you used commas correctly? (See Chapter 31.)
- Have you used apostrophes correctly? (See Chapter 32.)
- Have you used capital letters where they are required? (See 33A.)
- Have you used quotation marks correctly where they are needed? (See 33B.)
- Have you spelled every word correctly? (See Chapter 34.)

When Jared printed out the first draft of his essay about deciding to return to college, he added extra space so he could write his revision and editing changes between the lines. Here is his draft, with his handwritten changes.

The other day, my sociology instructor mentioned that half the students enrolled in college programs across the country were twenty-five or older. His remarks caught my attention because I am one of those students.

~~Going Back to School~~ *Starting Over*
                          ^

I have been out of school since I graduated from high school six years ago.

The decision to return to school was one I had a lot of difficulty making. I had

been around enough to know that without more education, I'd never get anywhere in life, but I always found reasons for not taking the plunge. However, after a lot of thinking, I realized that my reasons for not going to college were just excuses. I decided that if I really wanted to attend college full-time, I could.

My first excuse for not going to college was that I couldn't afford to go to school full-time. I had worked since I finished high school, but I hadn't put much money away. I kept wondering how I would pay for books and tuition. I also needed to support myself and pay for rent, food, and car expenses. *The solution to my problem came unexpectedly.* I was working as a house painter, and a house I was painting belonged to a college instructor. ~~Painting wasn't hard work, but it was boring. I'd start in the morning and work without a break until lunch.~~ *During my lunch break, we* We began talking. When I told him about my situation, he told me I should look at our local community college. I went online and looked at the college's Web site. I found out that tuition was forty dollars a credit, much less than I thought it would be.

The money I'd saved, along with what I could make painting houses on the weekends, could get me through.

Now that I had taken care of my first excuse, I had to deal with my second—that I hadn't been a good student in high school. When I was a teenager, I didn't care much about school. *In fact, school* ~~School~~ bored me ~~to death.~~ Now that I was considering going back to school, though, I wondered what price I would have to pay for my laziness and immaturity. The answer to this question was not as bad as I thought it would be. According to the community college's Web site, all I needed to be admitted was a high school diploma and county residence. I would have to take some placement tests, but I would be judged on my ability, not my high school grades. ~~The Web site was easy to navigate, and I had no problem finding information.~~ *My biggest problem still bothered me:* I had a hard time picturing myself in college. No one in my family had ever gone to college. My friends were just like me; they all went to work right after high school. I had no role model or mentor who could give me advice. *Besides,* I thought I was just too old for college. After all, I was probably at least six years older than most of the students. How would I be able to keep up with the younger students in the class? I hadn't opened a textbook for years, and I'd never really learned how to study. *However, most* ~~Most~~ of my fears disappeared during my first few weeks of classes. I saw a lot of students who were as old as I was,

In class, I would stare out the window or watch the second hand of the clock move slowly around. I never bothered with homework. School just didn't interest me.

and some were even older. Studying didn't seem to be a problem either. I actually enjoyed learning. History, which had put me to sleep in high school, suddenly became interesting. So did math and English. It soon became clear to me that I was going to like being in college.

Going to college as a full-time student has changed my life, both personally and financially. I am no longer the same person I was in high school. *In the past,* I allowed laziness and insecurity to hold me back. Now, I have options that I didn't have before. When I graduate from community college, I plan to transfer to the state university and get a four-year degree. *The other day, one of my instructors asked me if I had ever considered becoming a teacher. The truth is, I never had, but now I might. I'd like to be able to give kids like me the tough, realistic advice I wish someone had given me.*

◆ PRACTICE 12-12

What material did Jared White add to his draft? What did he delete? Write your answers on the following lines.

Material added: _____

_____

Material deleted: _____

_____

Think about why Jared made these changes, and be prepared to discuss his decisions.

When his revisions and edits were complete, Jared proofread his essay to make sure he had not missed any errors. The final revised and edited version of his essay appears below. (Marginal annotations have been added to highlight key features of his paper.)

Jared White
Professor Wilkinson
English 120
7 Oct. 2008

Starting Over

Introduction

The other day, my sociology instructor mentioned that half the students enrolled in college programs across the country are twenty-five or older. His remarks caught my attention because I am one of those students. I have been out of school since I graduated from high school six years ago. The decision

to return to school was one I had a lot of difficulty making. I had been around enough to know that without more education, I would never get anywhere in life, but I always found reasons for not taking the plunge. However, after a lot of thinking, I realized that my reasons for not going to college were just excuses. I decided that if I really wanted to attend college full-time, I could.

    My first excuse for not going to college was that I couldn't afford to go to school full-time. I had worked since I finished high school, but I hadn't put much money away. I kept wondering how I would pay for books and tuition. I also needed to support myself and pay for rent, food, and car expenses. The solution to my problem came unexpectedly. I was working as a house painter, and a house I was painting belonged to a college instructor. During my lunch break, we began talking. When I told him about my situation, he told me I should look at our local community college. I went online and looked at the college's Web site. I found out that tuition was forty dollars a credit, much less than I thought it would be. The money I'd saved, along with what I could make painting houses on the weekends, could get me through.

    Now that I had taken care of my first excuse, I had to deal with my second—that I hadn't been a good student in high school. When I was a teenager, I didn't care much about school. In fact, school bored me. In class, I would stare out the window or watch the second hand on the clock move slowly around. I never bothered with homework. School just didn't interest me. Now that I was considering going back to school, though, I wondered what price I would have to pay for my laziness and immaturity. The answer to this question was not as bad as I thought it would be. According to the community college's Web site, all I needed to be admitted was a high school diploma and county residence. I would have to take some placement tests, but I would be judged on my ability, not my high school grades.

    My biggest problem still bothered me: I had a hard time picturing myself in college. No one in my family had ever gone to college. My friends were just like me; they all went to work right after high school. I had no role model or mentor who could give me advice. Besides, I thought I was just too old for college. After all, I was probably at least six years older than most of the students. How would I be able to keep up with the younger students in the class? I hadn't opened a textbook for years, and I'd never really learned how to study. However, most of my fears disappeared during my first few weeks of classes. I saw a lot of students who were as old as I was, and some were even older. Studying didn't seem to be a problem either. I actually enjoyed learning. History, which had put me to sleep in high school, suddenly became interesting. So did math and English. It soon became clear to me that I was going to like being in college.

    Going to college as a full-time student has changed my life, both personally and financially. I am no longer the same person I was in high school. In the past, I allowed laziness and insecurity to hold me back. Now, I have options that I didn't have before. When I graduate from community college, I plan to transfer to the state university and get a four-year degree. The other day, one of my instructors asked me if I had ever considered becoming a teacher. The truth is, I never had, but now I might. I'd like to be able to give kids like me the tough, realistic advice that I wish someone had given me.

Thesis statement

First main point

Second main point

Body paragraphs

Third main point

Concluding statement

Conclusion

◆ **PRACTICE 12-13**

Reread the final draft of Jared White's essay. Do you think this draft is an improvement over his first draft? What other changes could Jared have made? Write your suggestions here.

_____

_____

_____

_____

_____

■ **WRITING FIRST: Flashback**

Using the Self-Assessment Checklist for revising your essay on page 163 as a guide, evaluate the essay you wrote for the Flashback exercise on page 163. What points can you add to support your thesis more fully? What points can you delete? Can any ideas be stated more clearly? (You may want to get feedback by exchanging essays with another student.) On the following lines, list the changes you think you should make to your draft.

_____

_____

_____

_____

_____

■ **WRITING FIRST: Revising and Editing**

Now, revise the draft of your essay, writing in new material between the lines or in the margins. Then, edit this revised draft using the Self-Assessment Checklist for editing your essay on page 164 to help you find errors in grammar, sentence structure, punctuation, mechanics, and spelling. When you have finished, prepare a final draft of your essay.

J **Checking Your Essay's Format**

The **format** of an essay is the way it looks on a page—for example, the size of the margins, the placement of page numbers, the space between lines. Most instructors expect you to follow a certain format when you type an essay. The essay format illustrated on the following page is commonly used in composition classes.

Essay Format: Sample First Page

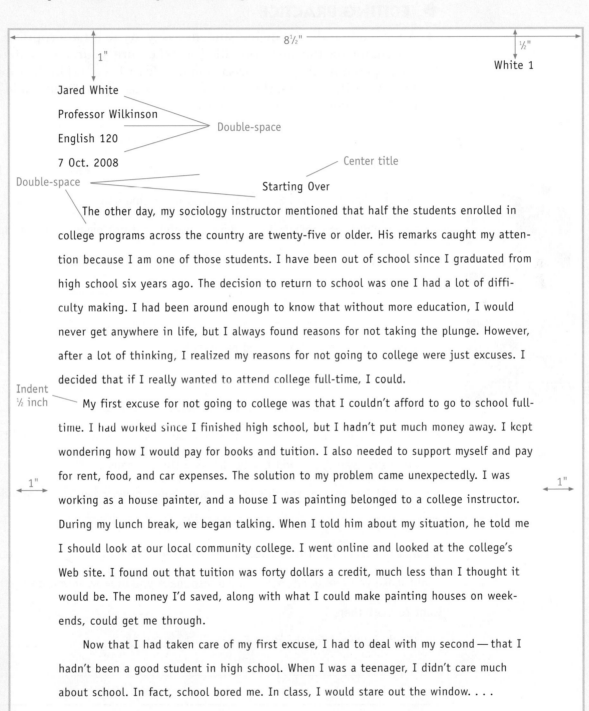

8½"   ½"

1"   White 1

Jared White

Professor Wilkinson

English 120   Double-space

7 Oct. 2008

Double-space   Center title

                                              Starting Over

The other day, my sociology instructor mentioned that half the students enrolled in college programs across the country are twenty-five or older. His remarks caught my attention because I am one of those students. I have been out of school since I graduated from high school six years ago. The decision to return to school was one I had a lot of difficulty making. I had been around enough to know that without more education, I would never get anywhere in life, but I always found reasons for not taking the plunge. However, after a lot of thinking, I realized my reasons for not going to college were just excuses. I decided that if I really wanted to attend college full-time, I could.

Indent ½ inch

My first excuse for not going to college was that I couldn't afford to go to school full-time. I had worked since I finished high school, but I hadn't put much money away. I kept wondering how I would pay for books and tuition. I also needed to support myself and pay for rent, food, and car expenses. The solution to my problem came unexpectedly. I was working as a house painter, and a house I was painting belonged to a college instructor. During my lunch break, we began talking. When I told him about my situation, he told me I should look at our local community college. I went online and looked at the college's Web site. I found out that tuition was forty dollars a credit, much less than I thought it would be. The money I'd saved, along with what I could make painting houses on weekends, could get me through.

1"   1"

Now that I had taken care of my first excuse, I had to deal with my second — that I hadn't been a good student in high school. When I was a teenager, I didn't care much about school. In fact, school bored me. In class, I would stare out the window. . . .

1"

CHAPTER REVIEW

◆ EDITING PRACTICE

1. After reading the following student essay, write an appropriate thesis statement on the lines provided. (Make sure your thesis statement clearly communicates the essay's main idea.) Then, fill in the topic sentences for the second, third, and fourth paragraphs. Finally, add a concluding statement in the conclusion.

Preparing for a Job Interview

I have looked at a lot of books and many Web sites that give advice on how to do well on a job interview. Some recommend practicing your handshake, and others suggest making eye contact. This advice is useful, but not many books tell how to get mentally prepared for an interview. [Thesis statement:] _____

_____

_____

[Topic sentence for the second paragraph:] _____

_____

_____

Woman at job interview

Feeling good about how I look is important, so I usually wear a jacket and tie to an interview. Even if you will not be dressing this formally on the job, try to make a good first impression. For this reason, you should never come to an interview dressed in jeans or shorts. Still, you should be careful not to overdress. For example, wearing a suit or a dressy dress to an interview at a fast-food restaurant might make you feel good, but it could also make you look as if you do not really want to work there.

[Topic sentence for the third paragraph:] _____

_____

_____

Going on an interview is a little like getting ready to take part in a sporting event. You have to go in with the right attitude. If you think you are not going to be successful, chances are that you will not be. So, before I go on any interview,

I spend some time building my confidence. I tell myself that I can do the job and that I will do well in the interview. By the time I get to the interview, I am sure I am the right person for the job.

[Topic sentence for the fourth paragraph:] _____

_____

_____

Most people go to an interview knowing little or nothing about the job. They expect the interviewer to tell them what they will have to do. Once, an interviewer told me that he likes a person who has taken the time to do his or her homework. Since that time, I have always done some research before I go on an interview — even for a part-time job. (Most of the time, my research is nothing more than a quick look at the company Web site.) This kind of research really pays off. At my last interview, for example, I was able to talk in detail about the job I would do. The interviewer must have been impressed because she offered me the job on the spot.

[Concluding statement:] _____

_____

_____

Man coming into a job interview

Of course, following my suggestions will not guarantee that you get a job. You still have to do well at the interview itself. Even so, getting mentally prepared for the interview will give you an advantage over people who do almost nothing before they walk in the door.

2. Write another body paragraph that you could add to the essay above. (This new paragraph will go right before the essay's conclusion.) The topic sentence has been provided for you.

Another way to prepare yourself mentally is to anticipate and answer some typical questions interviewers ask. _____

_____

_____

_____

_____

_____

_____

_____

_____

◆ **COLLABORATIVE ACTIVITIES**

1. On your own, find a paragraph in a magazine or a newspaper about an issue that interests you. Working in a group, select one of the paragraphs. Choose three points about the issue discussed that you could develop in a short essay, and then brainstorm about these points. Finally, write a sentence that could serve as the thesis statement for an essay.

2. Working in a group, come up with thesis statements suitable for essays on three of the following topics.

Living on a budget	Gun safety
YouTube	Fitness
Safe driving	Patriotism
Parenthood	Bad habits
Honesty	How to prepare for a test

3. Exchange your group's three thesis statements with those of another group. Choose the best one of the other group's thesis statements. A member of each group can then read the thesis statement to the class and explain why the group chose the thesis statement it did.

☑ REVIEW CHECKLIST:
Writing an Essay

■ Most essays have a thesis-and-support structure. The thesis statement presents the main idea, and the body paragraphs support the thesis. (See 12A.)

■ Begin by narrowing your assignment to a topic you can write about. (See 12B.)

■ Find ideas to write about. (See 12C.)

■ Identify your main idea, and develop an effective thesis statement. (See 12D.)

■ Choose the points that best support your thesis, and arrange them in the order in which you plan to discuss them. (See 12E and 12F.)

(continued on following page)

(continued from previous page)

- ☐ Write your first draft, making sure your essay has a thesis-and-support structure. (See 12G.)

- ☐ Revise your essay. (See 12H.)

- ☐ Edit your essay. (See 12I.)

- ☐ Make sure your essay's format is correct. (See 12J.)

CHAPTER 13

Introductions and Conclusions

Word Power

monotonous   repetitious; lacking in variety

robotic   mechanical; without original thought

routine   a standard procedure

■   **WRITING FIRST**

The picture above shows Charlie Chaplin caught in a factory machine in the film *Modern Times* (1936). Look at the picture, and then print out a copy of the essay about your worst job that you wrote for Chapter 12. As you go through this chapter, you will be working on the introduction and conclusion of this essay.

When you draft an essay, you usually focus on the **body** because it is the section in which you develop your ideas. A well-constructed essay, however, is more than a series of body paragraphs. It also includes an **introduction** and a **conclusion**, both of which contribute to the overall effectiveness of your essay.

A   Introductions

An **introduction** is the first thing people see when they read your essay. If your introduction is interesting, it will make readers want to read further. If it is not, readers may get bored and stop reading.

   Your introduction should be a full paragraph that moves from general to specific ideas. It should begin with some general **opening remarks** that will draw readers into your essay. The **thesis statement**, a specific sentence that presents the main idea of your essay, usually comes at the end of the introduction. The following diagram illustrates the general shape of your introduction.

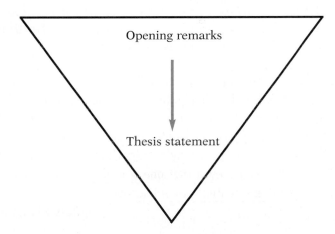

   Here are some options you can experiment with when you write your introductions. (In each of the sample introductory paragraphs that follow, the thesis statement is underlined and labeled.)

Beginning with a Narrative

You can begin an essay with a narrative drawn from your own experience or from a current news event.

> On September 11, 2001, terrorists crashed two airplanes into the twin towers at the World Trade Center. Almost immediately, hundreds of firefighters rushed inside the buildings to try to save as many lives as possible. Their actions saved many people, but half the firefighters — over three hundred — died when the twin towers collapsed. The sad fact is that until a tragedy occurs, most people never think about how difficult a firefighter's job really is.   Thesis statement
>
> — Richard Pogue (student)

Beginning with a Question (or a Series of Questions)

Asking one or more questions at the beginning of your essay is an effective strategy. Because readers expect you to answer the questions, they will want to read further.

> What's wrong with this picture? A teenage girl sits under a Christmas tree, opening her presents. She is excited when she gets a new sweater and the running shoes she has been wanting. On the surface, everything seems fine. However, the girl's parents are uncomfortable because they know that children from developing countries probably worked long hours in sweatshops to make the American teenager's Christmas presents. <u>Instead of feeling guilty, people like this girl's parents should take steps to end child labor and help poor children live better lives.</u>
>
> — Megan Davia (student)

Thesis statement

Beginning with a Definition

A definition at the beginning of your essay can give readers important information. As the following introduction shows, a definition can help explain a complicated idea or a confusing concept.

> The term *good parent* is not easy to define. Some things about being a good parent are obvious — keeping children safe, taking them to the doctor for checkups, helping them with their homework, and staying up with them when they are sick. Other things are not so obvious, however. I found this out last year when I became a volunteer at my daughter's middle school. <u>Until that time, I never would have believed that one morning a week could do so much to improve my daughter's attitude toward school.</u>
>
> — Russ Hightower (student)

Thesis statement

Beginning with a Quotation

An appropriate saying or some interesting dialogue can draw readers into your essay.

> According to the comedian Jerry Seinfeld, "When you're single, you are the dictator of your own life. . . . When you're married, you are part of a vast decision-making body." In other words, before you can do anything when you are married, you have to talk it over with someone else. These words kept going through my mind as I thought about asking my girlfriend to marry me. The more I thought about Seinfeld's words, the more I put off asking. <u>I never thought about the huge price that I would pay for this delay.</u>
>
> — Dan Brody (student)

Thesis statement

Beginning with a Surprising Statement

You can begin your essay with a surprising or unexpected statement. Because your statement takes readers by surprise, it catches their attention.

> Some of the smartest people I know never went to college. In fact, some of them never finished high school. They still know how to save 20 percent on the price of a dinner, fix their own faucets when they leak, get discounted prescriptions, get free rides on a bus to Atlantic City, use public transportation to get anywhere in the city, and live on about twenty-two dollars a day. These are my grandparents' friends. Some people would call them old and poor. <u>I would call them survivors who have learned to make it through life on nothing but a Social Security check.</u>
>
> —Sean Ragas (student)

Thesis statement

FOCUS **What to Avoid in Introductions**

■ Do not begin your essay by announcing what you plan to write about.

> *Phrases to Avoid*
> This essay is about…
> In my essay, I will discuss…

■ Do not apologize for your ideas.

> *Phrases to Avoid*
> Although I don't know much about this subject…
> I might not be an expert, but…

FOCUS **Choosing a Title**

Every essay should have a **title** that suggests the subject of the essay and makes people want to read it.

■ Capitalize all words except for articles (*a, an, the*), prepositions (*at, to, of, around*, and so on), and coordinating conjunctions (*and, but*, and so on), unless they are the first or last word of the title.
■ Do not underline your title or enclose it in quotation marks.
■ Center the title at the top of the first page. Double-space between the title and the first line of your essay.

(continued on following page)

(*continued from previous page*)

As you consider a title for your paper, think about the following options.

■ *A title can highlight a key word or term.*

A "Good" American Citizen
Orange Crush

■ *A title can be a straightforward announcement.*

How to Stop a Car with No Brakes
Don't Hang Up, That's My Mom Calling

■ *A title can establish a personal connection with readers.*

America, Stand Up for Justice and Democracy
Why We Need Animal Experimentation

■ *A title can be a familiar saying or a quotation from your essay itself.*

The Dog Ate My Disk, and Other Tales of Woe

◆ PRACTICE 13-1

Look at the student essays in Chapter 14, locating one introduction you think is particularly effective. On the lines below, explain the strengths of the introduction you chose.

_____

_____

_____

_____

◆ PRACTICE 13-2

Using the different options for creating titles discussed in the Focus box above, write two titles for each of the essays described below.

1. A student writes an essay about three people who disappeared mysteriously: Amelia Earhart, aviator; Ambrose Bierce, writer; and Jimmy Hoffa, union leader. In the body paragraphs, the student describes the circumstances surrounding their disappearances.

_____

_____

2. A student writes an essay arguing against doctors' letting people select the gender of their babies. In the body paragraphs, she presents reasons why she thinks it is unethical.

_____

_____

3. A student writes an essay to explain why America is ready to elect a woman president. In the body paragraphs, the writer gives reasons for his beliefs.

_____

_____

4. A student writes an essay describing the harmful effects of steroids on student athletes. In the body paragraphs, he shows the effects on the heart, brain, and other organs.

_____

_____

5. A student writes an essay explaining why she joined the Navy Reserve. In the body paragraphs, she discusses her need to earn money for college tuition, her wish to learn a trade, and her desire to see the world.

_____

_____

■ **WRITING FIRST: Flashback**

Look back at the introduction of the essay you reprinted for the Writing First activity on page 174. Does it include opening remarks that prepare readers for the essay to follow? Does it include a thesis statement? Will it interest readers? On a separate sheet of paper, draft a different opening paragraph using one of the options illustrated in 13A. Then, on the line below, indicate what kind of introduction you have drafted.

After you have finished drafting a new introduction, think of a new title that will attract your readers' attention. (Use one of the options listed in the "Choosing a Title" Focus box on pages 177–78.) Write your new title on the line below.

Option used for new introduction: _____

B **Conclusions**

Because your conclusion is the last thing readers see, they often judge your entire essay by its effectiveness. For this reason, conclusions should planned, drafted, and revised carefully.

Like an introduction, a **conclusion** should be a full paragraph. It should begin with a specific **concluding statement** that restates the essay's main idea, and it should end with some general **concluding remarks**. The following diagram illustrates the general shape of a conclusion.

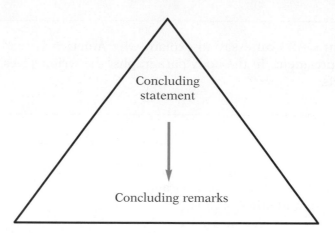

Here are some options you can experiment with when you write your conclusions. (In each of the sample concluding paragraphs that follow, the concluding statement is underlined and labeled.)

Concluding with a Narrative

A narrative conclusion can bring an event discussed in the essay to a logical, satisfying close.

Concluding statement

> Being a firefighter is a challenging and often dangerous job. The firefighters who died on September 11, 2001, show how true this fact is. They rushed into the two burning World Trade towers without thinking about what could happen to them. Even as the buildings were falling down, they continued to help people escape. At the end of the day, they did the job they had been trained to do, and they did it well. These brave people are role models for me and for other volunteer firefighters around the country. They remind all of us of how important the job we do really is.
>
> — Richard Pogue (student)

Concluding with a Prediction

This type of conclusion not only sums up the thesis but also looks to the future.

Concluding statement

> My hesitation cost me more than I ever could have dreamed. When she thought that I didn't want to marry her, Jen broke up with me. For the past three months, I have been trying to get back together with her. We have gone out a few times, and I am trying to convince her to trust me again. I hope that sometime soon we will look back at this situation and laugh. Meanwhile, all I can do is tell Jen that I am sorry and keep hoping.
>
> — Dan Brody (student)

Concluding with a Recommendation

Once you think you have convinced readers that a problem exists, you can make recommendations in your conclusion about how the problem should be solved.

<u>Several steps can be taken to deal with the problem of child labor.</u> First, people should educate themselves about the problem. They can begin by going to Web sites that give information about child labor. Then, they can join an organization such as Human Rights Watch or the Global Fund for Children. These groups sponsor programs that help child laborers in their own countries. Finally, people can stop supporting businesses that benefit either directly or indirectly from child labor. If all of us are committed to change, we can do lot to reduce this problem worldwide.

— Megan Davia (student)

Concluding statement

Concluding with a Quotation

A well-chosen quotation—even a brief one—can be an effective concluding strategy. In the following paragraph, the quotation reinforces the main idea of the essay.

<u>Volunteering at my daughter's middle school has done a lot to help both her and me.</u> She now likes to go to school, and her grades have improved. I now understand how much effort it takes to be a good parent. What I am most proud of is that no one told me what to do. I just figured it out for myself. I guess Dr. Spock was right when he said to parents in his book *Baby and Child Care*, "Trust yourself. You know more than you think you do."

— Russ Hightower (student)

Concluding statement

FOCUS   **What to Avoid in Conclusions**

- Do not introduce any new ideas. Your conclusion should sum up the ideas you discuss in your essay, not open up new lines of thought.
- Do not apologize for your opinions, ideas, or conclusions. Apologies will undercut your readers' confidence in you.

  Phrases to Avoid
  I may not be an expert…
  At least that is my opinion…
  I could be wrong, but…

- Do not use overused phrases to announce your essay is coming to a close.

  Phrases to Avoid
  In summary,…
  In conclusion,…

◆ **PRACTICE 13-3**

Look at the student essays in Chapter 14, locating one conclusion you think is particularly effective. On the lines below, explain the strengths of the conclusion you chose.

_____

_____

_____

_____

■ **WRITING FIRST: Flashback**

Look again at the essay you reprinted for the Writing First activity on page 174. Evaluate your conclusion. Does it include a concluding statement and general concluding remarks? Does it bring your essay to a clear and satisfying close? Will it leave a strong impression on readers? On a separate sheet of paper, try drafting a different concluding paragraph using one of the options illustrated in 13B. Then, on the line below, indicate what kind of conclusion you have drafted.

Option used for new conclusion: _____

■ **WRITING FIRST: Revising and Editing**

Reread your responses to the Flashback activity above and the one on page 179. Are the new paragraphs you wrote more effective than the introduction and conclusion of the essay you wrote in Chapter 12? If so, substitute them for the opening and closing paragraphs of that essay.

CHAPTER REVIEW

◆ EDITING PRACTICE

The following student essay has an undeveloped introduction and conclusion. Decide what introductory and concluding strategy would be best for the essay. Then, on a separate sheet of paper, rewrite both the introduction and the conclusion. Finally, add an interesting title for the essay.

———————

This essay is about three of the most dangerous jobs. They are piloting small planes, logging, and fishing.

Flying a small plane can be dangerous. For example, pilots who fly tiny planes that spray pesticides on farmers' fields do not have to comply with the safety rules for large airplanes. They also have to fly very low in order to spray the right fields. This leaves little room for error. Also, pilots of air-taxis and small commuter planes die in much greater numbers than airline pilots do. In some places, like parts of Alaska, there are long distances and few roads, so many small planes are needed. Their pilots are four times more likely to die than other pilots because of bad weather and poor visibility. In general, flying a small plane can be very risky.

Another dangerous job is logging. Loggers always are at risk of having parts of trees or heavy machinery fall on them. Tree trunks often have odd shapes, so they are hard to control. As a result, they often break loose from equipment that is supposed to move them. In addition, weather conditions, like snow or rain, can cause dangers. Icy or wet conditions increase the risk to loggers, who can fall from trees or slip when they are sawing a tree. Because loggers often work in remote places, it is very hard to get prompt medical aid. As a result, a wound that could be treated in a hospital may be fatal to a logger.

The most dangerous occupation is working in the fishing industry. Like loggers, professional fishermen work in unsafe conditions. They use heavy machinery to pull up nets and to move large amounts of fish. The combination of icy or slippery boat decks and large nets and cages makes the job unsafe. The weather is often very bad, so fishermen are at risk of drowning from falling overboard during a storm.

In fact, drowning is the most common cause of death in this industry. Also, like logging, fishing is done far from hospitals and medical help, so even minor injuries can be very serious.

In conclusion, piloting, logging, and fishing are three of the most dangerous occupations.

◆ COLLABORATIVE ACTIVITIES

1. Bring to class several copies of an essay you wrote for another class. Have each person in your group comment on your essay's introduction and conclusion. Revise the introduction and conclusion in response to your classmates' suggestions.

2. Find a magazine or newspaper article that interests you. Cut off the introduction and conclusion, and bring the body of the article to class. Ask your group to decide on the best strategy for introducing and concluding the article. Then, collaborate on writing new opening and closing paragraphs and an interesting title.

3. Working in a group, think of interesting and appropriate titles for essays on each of the topics listed below. Try to use as many of the different options outlined in the Focus box on pages 177–78 as you can.

The difficulty of living with a roommate
The dangers of gambling
The need for regular exercise
The joys of living in the city (or in the country)
The responsibilities of having a pet
Things that make life easier
The stress of job interviews
The obligation to vote
The advantages of wireless Internet
The problems of being a parent
The need for better public transportation

☑ REVIEW CHECKLIST:
Introductions and Conclusions

    The introduction of your essay should prepare readers for the ideas to follow and should include opening remarks and a thesis statement. It should also create interest. (See 13A.) You can begin an essay with any of the following options.

A narrative	A quotation
A question	A surprising statement
A definition	

(continued on following page)

(continued from previous page)

- Your title should suggest the subject of your essay and make people want to read further. (See 13A.)

- The conclusion of your essay should restate the thesis and make some general concluding remarks. (See 13B.) You can conclude an essay with any of the following options.

  A narrative   A recommendation
  A prediction   A quotation

CHAPTER 14

Patterns of Essay Development

As you learned in Chapters 3 through 11, writers have a variety of options for developing ideas within a paragraph. These options include *exemplification, narration, description, process, cause and effect, comparison and contrast, classification, definition,* and *argument.* When you write an essay, you can use these same patterns of development to help you organize your material.

In your college courses, different assignments and writing situations call for different patterns of essay development.

- If an essay exam question asked you to compare two systems of government, you would use *comparison and contrast*.
- If an English composition assignment asked you to tell about a childhood experience, you would use *narration*.
- If a section of a research paper on environmental pollution called for examples of dangerous waste disposal practices, you would use *exemplification*.

A   Exemplification

Exemplification illustrates a general statement with one or more specific examples. An **exemplification essay** uses specific examples to support a thesis.

Writing an Exemplification Essay
- Make sure your topic calls for exemplification.
- Find ideas to write about.
- Identify your main idea, and write a thesis statement.
- Choose examples and details to support your thesis.
- Arrange your supporting examples in a logical order.
- Draft your essay.
- Revise your essay.
- Edit your essay.

(For detailed information on the process of writing an essay, see Chapter 12.)

FOCUS   Topics for Exemplification

The wording of your assignment may suggest exemplification. For example, you may be asked to *illustrate* or to *give examples*.

Assignment	Thesis Statement
Education Should children be taught only in their native languages or in English as well? Support your answer with examples of specific students' experiences.	The success of students in a bilingual third-grade class suggests the value of teaching elementary school students in English as well as in their native languages.

(continued on following page)

(continued from previous page)

Literature Does William Shakespeare's *Othello* have to end tragically? Illustrate your position with references to specific characters.	Each of the three major characters in *Othello* contributes to the play's tragic ending.
Composition Discuss the worst job you ever had, including plenty of specific examples to support your thesis.	My summer job at a fast-food restaurant was my all-time worst job because of the endless stream of rude customers, the many boring and repetitive tasks I had to perform, and my manager's insensitive treatment of employees.

In an exemplification essay, each body paragraph can develop a single example or discuss several related examples.

FOCUS **Options for Organizing Exemplification Essays**

One Example
per Paragraph

¶1 Introduction
¶2 First example
¶3 Second example
¶4 Third example
¶5 Conclusion

Several Related Examples
per Paragraph

¶1 Introduction
¶2 First group of examples
¶3 Second group of examples
¶4 Third group of examples
¶5 Conclusion

In each body paragraph of your essay, a topic sentence should introduce the example (or group of related examples) that the paragraph will discuss. Each example you select should clearly support your thesis. Transitional words and phrases should introduce your examples and indicate how one example is related to another.

FOCUS **Transitions for Exemplification**

also	furthermore	the most important
besides	in addition	example
finally	moreover	the next example
first	one example . . .	
for example	another example	
for instance	specifically	

Model Exemplification Essay

The following student essay, "Going to Extremes" by Kyle Sims, uses examples to illustrate the characteristics of extreme sports. Two of the body paragraphs group several brief examples together; one paragraph focuses on a single example. Notice how Kyle uses clear topic sentences and helpful transitions to introduce his examples and link them to one another.

Going to Extremes

For years, sports like football, baseball, and basketball have been popular in cities, suburbs, and small rural towns. For some young people, however, these sports no longer seem exciting, especially when compared to "extreme sports," such as snowboarding and BMX racing. Extreme sports are different from more familiar sports because they are dangerous, they are physically challenging, and they require specialized equipment.   1

First, extreme sports are dangerous. For example, snowboarders take chances with snowy hills and unpredictable bumps. They zoom down mountains at high speeds, which is typical of extreme sports. In addition, snowboarders and skateboarders risk painful falls as they do their tricks. Also, many extreme sports, like rock climbing, bungee jumping, and sky diving, are performed at very high altitudes. Moreover, the bungee jumper has to jump from a very high place, and there is always a danger of getting tangled with the bungee cord. People who participate in extreme sports accept—and even enjoy—these dangers.   2

In addition, extreme sports are very difficult. For instance, surfers have to learn to balance surfboards while dealing with wind and waves. Bungee jumpers may have to learn how to do difficult stunts while jumping off a high bridge or a dam. Another example of the physical challenge of extreme sports can be found in BMX racing. BMX racers have to learn to steer a lightweight bike on a dirt track that has jumps and banked corners. These extreme sports require skills that most people do not naturally have. These special skills have to be learned, and participants in extreme sports enjoy this challenge.   3

Finally, almost all extreme sports require specialized equipment. For example, surfers need surfboards that are light but strong. They can choose epoxy boards, which are stronger, or fiberglass boards, which are lighter. They can choose shortboards, which are shorter than seven feet and are easier to maneuver. Or, they can use longboards, which are harder and slower to turn in the water but are easier to learn on. Also, surfers have to get special wax for their boards to keep from slipping as they are paddling out into the water. For surfing in cold water, they need wetsuits that trap their own body heat. Other extreme sports require different kinds of specialized equipment, but those who participate in them are willing to buy whatever they need.   4

Extreme sports have become increasingly popular in recent years, and television has helped to increase their popularity. For example, in 2002 and 2006, snowboarding and other extreme sports were featured in the Winter Olympics. In the future, the Olympics will include skateboarding and BMX   5

racing. Already, the Summer and Winter X Games are televised on ESPN and ABC. Sports like BMX racing, snowboarding, surfing, and snowmobiling get national attention on these programs. With all this publicity, extreme sports are likely to become even more popular.

◆ **PRACTICE 14-1**

1. Underline the thesis statement of "Going to Extremes." On the lines below, restate the thesis in your own words.

_____

_____

2. What examples of extreme sports does Kyle give in paragraph 2?

_____

_____

What examples of dangers does he give in paragraph 3?

_____

In paragraph 4, Kyle discusses surfing, giving examples of the equipment surfers need. List this equipment.

_____

3. How does Kyle introduce his examples? Underline some of the transitional words and phrases that serve this purpose.

4. Is the introduction effective? How else might Kyle have opened his essay?

_____

_____

5. Is the conclusion effective? How else could Kyle have ended his essay?

_____

6. What is this essay's greatest strength? What is its greatest weakness?

Strength: _____

Weakness: _____

GRAMMAR IN CONTEXT | **Exemplification**

When you write an exemplification essay, you may introduce your examples with transitional words and phrases like *First* or *In addition*. If you do, be sure to use a comma after the introductory word or phrase.

First, extreme sports are dangerous.

In addition, extreme sports are very difficult.

Finally, almost all extreme sports require specialized equipment.

For information on using commas with introductory transitional words and phrases, see 31B.

◆ **PRACTICE 14-2**

Following the writing process outlined in Chapter 12, write an exemplification essay on one of the following topics.

Reasons to start (or not to start) college right after high school
The three best products ever invented
What kinds of people or images should appear on U.S. postage stamps? Why?
Advantages (or disadvantages) of being a young parent
Athletes who really are role models
Four items students need to survive in college
What messages do various hip-hop artists send to listeners?
Study strategies that work
Traits of a good employee
Three or four recent national or world news events that gave you hope—
or events that upset or shocked you

◆ **PRACTICE 14-3**

The billboard pictured on the following page shows a public service advertisement promoting addiction awareness. Study the picture carefully, and then write an exemplification essay explaining how this advertisement appeals to its intended audience. For example, does it seem to be trying to inform the public? To frighten people? To get them to do something? Begin by describing the ad. Then, identify the audience you think it hopes to reach, and state your thesis. In the body of your essay, give examples to support your thesis.

> **Word Power**
> **ignorance** the state of being uneducated, unaware, or uninformed
>
> **motivate** to move to action

✔ SELF-ASSESSMENT CHECKLIST:
Writing an Exemplification Essay

- Does your introduction give readers a clear idea of what to expect?

- Does your essay include a thesis that clearly states your essay's main idea?

- Do all your examples support your thesis, or should some be deleted?

- Do you have enough examples to support your thesis, or do you need additional examples?

- Do you have enough transitional words and phrases to introduce your examples?

- Does your conclusion sum up the main idea of your essay?

- What problems did you experience in writing your essay? What would you do differently next time?

B Narration

Narration tells a story, usually presenting a series of events in chronological (time) order, moving from beginning to end. A **narrative essay** can tell a personal story, or it can recount a recent or historical event or a fictional story.

Writing a Narrative Essay

■ Make sure your topic calls for narration.
■ Find ideas to write about.
■ Identify your main idea, and write a thesis statement.
■ Choose events and details to support your thesis.
■ Arrange events in a clear order, usually chronological.
■ Draft your essay.
■ Revise your essay.
■ Edit your essay.

(For detailed information on the process of writing an essay, see Chapter 12.)

FOCUS   Topics for Narration

The wording of your assignment may suggest narration. For example, you may be asked to *tell, trace, summarize events,* or *recount.*

Assignment	*Thesis Statement*
Composition Tell about a time when you had to show courage even though you were afraid.	In extraordinary circumstances, a person can exhibit great courage and overcome fear.
American history Summarize the events that occurred during President Franklin Delano Roosevelt's first one hundred days in office.	Although many thought they were extreme, the measures enacted by Roosevelt during his first one hundred days in office were necessary to fight the economic depression.
Political science Trace the development of the Mississippi Freedom Democratic Party.	As the Mississippi Freedom Democratic Party developed, it found a voice that spoke for equality and justice.

When you write a narrative essay, you can discuss one event or several in each paragraph of your essay.

FOCUS   Options for Organizing Narrative Essays

One Event per Paragraph	*Several Events per Paragraph*
¶1 Introduction	¶1 Introduction
¶2 First event	¶2 First group of events
¶3 Second event	¶3 Second group of events
¶4 Third event	¶4 Third group of events
¶5 Conclusion	¶5 Conclusion

Sometimes, to add interest to your narrative, you may decide not to use exact chronological order. For example, you might begin with the end of your story and then move back to the beginning to trace the events that led to this outcome. However you arrange the events, carefully worded topic sentences and clear transitional words and phrases will help readers follow your narrative.

FOCUS **Transitions for Narration**

after	eventually	next
as	finally	now
as soon as	first . . . second . . .	soon
at first	third	then
at the same time	immediately	two hours (days,
before	later	months, years)
by this time	later on	later
earlier	meanwhile	when

Model Narrative Essay

The following student essay, "Reflections" by Elaina Corrato, is a narrative that relates the events of the day of her thirtieth birthday. Transitional words and phrases link events in chronological order and help keep readers on track.

Reflections

Word Power

milestone an important event; a turning point

Turning thirty did not bother me at all. My list of "Things to Do before I Die" 1 was far from complete, but I knew I had plenty of time to do them. In fact, turning thirty seemed like no big deal to me. If anything, it was a milestone I was happy to be approaching. Unfortunately, other people had different ideas about this milestone, and eventually their ideas made me rethink my own.

As the big day approached, my family kept teasing me about it. My sister 2 kept asking me if I felt any different. She couldn't believe I wasn't upset, but I didn't pay any attention to her. I was looking forward to a new chapter in my life. I liked my job, I was making good progress toward my college degree, and I was healthy and happy. Why should turning thirty be a problem? So, I made no special plans for my birthday, and I decided to treat it as just another day.

My birthday fell on a Saturday that year, and I enjoyed the chance to sleep 3 in. After I got up and had breakfast, I did my laundry and then set out for the supermarket. I rarely put on makeup or fixed my hair on Saturdays. After all, I didn't have to go to work or to school. I was only running errands in the neighborhood. Later on, though, as I waited in line at the deli counter, I caught sight of my reflection in the mirrored meat case. At first, I thought it wasn't really me. The woman staring back at me looked so old! She had bags under her eyes, and she even had a few gray hairs. I was so upset by my reflection that on my way home I stopped and bought a mud mask — guaranteed to make me look younger.

As I walked up the street toward my house, I saw something attached to   4
the front railing. When I got closer, I realized that it was a bunch of balloons,
and they were black balloons. There was also a big sign that said "Over the Hill"
in big black letters. I'd been trying to think about my birthday in positive
terms, but my family seemed to have other ideas. Obviously, it was time for the
mud mask.

After quickly unloading my groceries, I ran upstairs to apply the mask.   5
The box promised a "rejuvenating look," and that was exactly what I wanted.
I spread the sticky brown mixture on my face, and it hardened instantly. As
I sat on my bed, waiting for the mask to work its magic, I heard the doorbell
ring. Then, I heard familiar voices and my husband calling me to come down,
saying that I had company. I couldn't answer him. I couldn't talk (or even
smile) without cracking the mask. At this point, I retreated to the bathroom
to make myself presentable for my friends and family. This task was not easy.

When I managed to scrub off the mud mask, my face was covered with little   6
red pimples. Apparently, my sensitive skin couldn't take the harsh chemicals. At
first, I didn't think the promise of "rejuvenated" skin was what I got. I had to
admit, though, that my skin did look a lot younger. In fact, when I finally went
downstairs to celebrate my birthday, I looked as young as a teenager—a
teenager with acne.

◆ PRACTICE 14-4

1. Underline the thesis statement of "Reflections." Restate it below in
   your own words.

   _____

   _____

   _____

2. Underline the specific transitional words and phrases Elaina uses to
   link events in chronological order.

3. What specific events and situations support Elaina's thesis? List as
   many as you can.

   _____

   _____

   _____

   _____

4. Do you think paragraph 2 is necessary? How would Elaina's essay be
   different without it?

   _____

   _____

   _____

   _____

5. Do you think Elaina's conclusion should restate her thesis and summarize all the events her essay discusses, or is her conclusion effective? Explain your answer.

_____

_____

_____

GRAMMAR IN CONTEXT **Narration**

When you write a narrative essay, you tell a story. When you get caught up in your story, you might sometimes find yourself stringing a list of incidents together without proper punctuation, creating a **run-on**.

INCORRECT As the big day approached, my family kept teasing me about it, my sister kept asking me if I felt any different.

CORRECT As the big day approached, my family kept teasing me about it. My sister kept asking me if I felt any different.

For information on how to identify and correct run-ons, see Chapter 21.

◆ **PRACTICE 14-5**

Following the writing process outlined in Chapter 12, write a narrative essay on one of the following topics.

The story of your education
Your idea of a perfect day
The plot summary of a terrible book or movie
A time when you had to make a split-second decision
Your first confrontation with authority
An important historical event
A day everything went wrong
A story from your family's history
Your employment history, from first to most recent job
A biography of your pet

◆ **PRACTICE 14-6**

The picture on the following page shows a bride and groom at a Las Vegas wedding chapel. Study the picture carefully, and then write a narrative essay that tells the story behind it. (If you prefer, you can write about a wedding you attended.)

▶ **Word Power**
impulsive acting without thought, or without considering the consequences of one's actions

unique one of a kind

■ **Culture Clue**

In Las Vegas, Nevada, couples can marry quickly and cheaply. Many also decide to marry in nontraditional ways. For example, the image shows a couple getting married in their car at a drive-thru wedding service.

☑ SELF-ASSESSMENT CHECKLIST:
Writing a Narrative Essay

- Does your introduction set the scene and introduce important people and places?

- Does your essay include a thesis that clearly states your main idea?

- Are the events you discuss arranged in clear chronological (time) order?

- Do you include enough examples and details to make your narrative interesting?

- Do topic sentences and transitional words and phrases make the sequence of events clear?

- Does your conclusion remind readers why you have told them your story?

- What problems did you experience in writing your essay? What would you do differently next time?

C   Description

Description tells what something looks, sounds, smells, tastes, or feels like. A **descriptive essay** uses details to give readers a clear, vivid picture of a person, place, or object.

Writing a Descriptive Essay

- Make sure your topic calls for description.
- Find ideas to write about.
- Decide what dominant impression you want to convey.
- Choose details that help to convey your dominant impression.
- If possible, write a thesis statement that your details will support.
- Arrange your details in an effective order.
- Draft your essay.
- Revise your essay.
- Edit your essay.

(For detailed information on the process of writing an essay, see Chapter 12.)

FOCUS Topics for Description

The wording of your assignment may suggest description. For example, it may ask you to *describe* or to *tell what an object looks like.*

Assignment	Thesis Statement
Composition Describe a room that was important to you when you were a child.	Pink-and-white striped wallpaper, tall shelves of cuddly stuffed animals, and the smell of Oreos dominated the bedroom I shared with my sister.
Scientific writing Describe a piece of scientific equipment.	The mass spectrometer is a complex instrument, but every part is ideally suited to its function.
Art history Choose one modern painting and describe its visual elements.	The disturbing images crowded together in Pablo Picasso's *Guernica* suggest the brutality of war.

When you plan a descriptive essay, you focus on selecting details that help your readers see what you see, feel what you feel, and experience what you experience. Your goal is to create a single **dominant impression**, a central theme or idea to which all the details relate—for example, the liveliness of a street scene or the quiet of a summer night. This dominant impression unifies the description and gives readers an overall sense of what the person, place, object, or scene looks like (and perhaps what it sounds, smells, tastes, or feels like). Sometimes—but not always—your details will support a thesis, making a point about the subject you are describing.

You can arrange details in a descriptive essay in many different ways. For example, you can move from least to most important details, from top to bottom (or from bottom to top or side to side), or from far to near (or near to far). Each of your essay's body paragraphs may focus on one key characteristic of the subject you are describing or on several related descriptive details.

FOCUS **Options for Organizing Descriptive Essays**

Least to Most Important	Top to Bottom	Far to Near
¶1 Introduction	¶1 Introduction	¶1 Introduction
¶2 Least important details	¶2 Details at top	¶2 Distant details
¶3 More important details	¶3 Details in middle	¶3 Closer details
¶4 Most important details	¶4 Details on bottom	¶4 Closest details
¶5 Conclusion	¶5 Conclusion	¶5 Conclusion

When you describe a person, place, object, or scene, you can use **objective description**, reporting only what your senses of sight, sound, smell, taste, and touch tell you ("The columns were two feet tall and made of white marble"). You can also use **subjective description**, conveying your attitude or your feelings about what you observe ("The columns were tall and powerful looking, and their marble surface seemed as smooth as ice"). Many essays combine these two kinds of description.

Descriptive writing, particularly subjective description, is frequently enriched by **figures of speech**—language that creates special or unusual effects.

■ A **simile** uses *like* or *as* to compare two unlike things.

Her smile was like sunshine.

■ A **metaphor** compares two unlike things without using *like* or *as*.

Her smile was a light that lit up the room.

■ **Personification** suggests a comparison between a nonliving thing and a person by giving the nonliving thing human traits.

The sun smiled down on the crowd.

As you write, use transitional words and expressions to guide readers through your description. (Many of these useful transitions are prepositions or other words and phrases that indicate location or distance.)

14 C

> ### FOCUS Transitions for Description
>
> | | | |
> |---|---|---|
> | above | in front of | outside |
> | behind | inside | over |
> | below | nearby | the least |
> | between | next to | important |
> | beyond | on | the most |
> | in | on one side . . . | important |
> | in back of | on the other side | under |

Model Descriptive Essay

The following student essay, "Boris Kosachev, Russian Pianist" by Danielle McLarin, uses description to create a portrait of a person who was important to her. By combining subjective and objective description and using specific details, Danielle conveys a vivid impression of her childhood piano teacher as strict yet caring.

Boris Kosachev, Russian Pianist

As a daughter of professional musicians, I was encouraged by my parents at 1 an early age to develop my musical talents. After learning the basics with my mother, I began taking lessons with a professional: Boris Kosachev, Russian pianist. While taking lessons with him, I always found Mr. Kosachev unfairly strict and rigid, but now I understand what it was that motivated him.

At first glance, Mr. Kosachev looked like an ordinary little old man: he was 2 nearly eighty years old when I took lessons with him. He was very small even from the perspective of a nine-year-old. He was probably about five foot four, but his miniature features made him appear even smaller. His tiny black eyes were almost hidden by his eyelids, and small spectacles were mounted on his sharp nose. His ears, which stuck out slightly from the sides of his head, were equally small and shaped like rose petals.

His mustache was thick and white, carefully trimmed to the corners of his 3 mouth. In contrast, his eyebrows were unusually thin, with only a few fine white hairs. The hair on his head, however, was as thick as his mustache, and it flowed from his head in thick waves that stood outward from his scalp as if electrically charged. His hair, like his mustache, was white, with a few black strands serving as reminders of his long-ago youth.

By the time I knew Mr. Kosachev, the skin on his cheeks and under his chin 4 drooped from his face in pale, wrinkled layers. The skin on his hands and fingers, however, was tight and thin, making every bone and vein visible as he maneuvered his hands all over the keyboard. Although they were not large, his hands seemed big because of his unusually long, thin fingers.

In the summer, when he wore short sleeves, I noticed how strong and 5 muscular his arms seemed. His torso was thin, but over the years he began to develop a slight belly, possibly because of his strict pianist diet: "You must eat

more Stroganoff. The cream and the meat; they are what good pianists eat. Good physique is good playing." His legs were short and thin, but that did not stop him from leaping quickly to the piano when he heard something he didn't like.

I can still picture him looking over my shoulder as I played each note. 6 As I played, he would usually yell commands in broken English, and he would sometimes resort to Russian curses. Often, however, after I had polished a piece, he would sit behind me in a state of deep meditation with his hands pressed together, his fingers pointing upward to support his chin, his right leg crossed over his left. His eyes remained closed, and they wrinkled slightly only when I would arrive at the *forte* at the end of a *crescendo* a beat too soon or overdramatize the *rubato* of a phrase. Sometimes, he would compliment me on my work — "Ah, you have done much work on this section!" — but most of these compliments were inevitably followed by criticism: "This is falling apart!" "What is these notes?" "You play them wrong."

For most of my time with Mr. Kosachev, I knew little of his life and career. 7 As I learned more about his rigorous training in Russia, I began to understand his harshness and his high expectations for me. Many times, he would say to me, "I only ask you to practice two hours a day. In Russia, I was six years old, and I practice two hours a day. When I was your age, I practice all day after school. Ah, the American life is no good for pianist." Still, it was not until years afterward that I understood Mr. Kosachev's goals for me and for his other students: he wanted us to live up to our potential as artists, and maybe one day to become better pianists than he was and enjoy the prestige that he had dreamed of for himself. For this reason, he held true to the Russian music tradition and work ethic — even in America.

◆ PRACTICE 14-7

1. What dominant impression of her piano teacher does Danielle convey to readers?

_____

2. List the specific details Danielle uses to convey her essay's dominant impression. What other details could she have included?

_____

_____

3. What determines the order in which details are presented in this essay? How else might Danielle have arranged details?

_____

_____

_____

4. This essay contains very few transitions to move readers from one aspect of the subject to the next. Do you think any transitions need to be added? If so, where?

_____

_____

_____

5. Is this essay primarily a subjective or an objective description?

_____

6. What is this essay's greatest strength? What is its greatest weakness?

Strength: _____

Weakness: _____

GRAMMAR IN CONTEXT   Description

When you write a descriptive essay, you may use **modifiers** to describe your subject. If you place modifying words or phrases incorrectly, you create a misplaced modifier that may confuse your readers.

CONFUSING   ┌──────────── MODIFIER ────────────┐
Looking over my shoulder as I played each note,

I can still picture him.

(Is the writer looking over her own shoulder?)

CLEAR   I can still picture **him** looking over my shoulder as
┌──────── MODIFIER ────────┐
I played each note.

For information on how to identify and correct misplaced modifiers, see 25D.

◆ **PRACTICE 14-8**

Following the writing process outlined in Chapter 12, write a descriptive essay on one of the following topics.

An abandoned building
A person or character who
   makes you laugh (or
   frightens you)
Your room (or your closet
   or desk)
A family photograph

A historical site or monument
An advertisement
An object you cherish
Someone whom everyone notices
Someone whom no one notices
The home page of a Web site you
   visit often

◆ **PRACTICE 14-9**

The picture below shows a house surrounded by lush landscaping. Write a real-estate brochure for the house, using your imagination to invent details that describe its setting, exterior, and interior. Your goal in this descriptive essay is to include the kind of positive details that might persuade a prospective buyer to purchase the house.

▶ **Word Power**

mansion a large, stately house

lush characterized by abundant growth

real estate property, including land and buildings

☑ SELF-ASSESSMENT CHECKLIST:
Writing a Descriptive Essay

☐ Does your introduction identify the subject of your description and convey your essay's dominant impression?

☐ Do you describe your subject in enough detail, or do you need to add more details to create a more vivid picture?

☐ Do all the details in your essay support your dominant impression, or should some be deleted?

☐ Are your details arranged in an effective order within your essay and within paragraphs?

☐ Do your topic sentences and transitional words and phrases move readers smoothly from one part of your subject to another?

☐ Does your conclusion reinforce your dominant impression and leave readers with a clear sense of your essay's purpose?

☐ What problems did you experience in writing your essay? What would you do differently next time?

D Process

A **process** is a series of chronological steps that produces a particular re-sult. **Process essays** explain the steps in a procedure, telling how some-thing is (or was) done. A process essay can be organized as either a *process explanation* or a set of *instructions*.

Writing a Process Essay
- Make sure your topic calls for process.
- Decide whether you want to explain a process or write instructions.
- Find ideas to write about.
- Identify your main idea, and write a thesis statement.
- Identify the most important steps in the process.
- List the steps in the process in chronological order.
- Draft your essay.
- Revise your essay.
- Edit your essay.

(For detailed information on the process of writing an essay, see Chapter 12.)

FOCUS Topics for Process

The wording of your assignment may suggest process. For example, you may be asked to *explain a process, give instructions, give direc-tions,* or *give a step-by-step account.*

Assignment	Thesis Statement
American government Explain the process by which a bill becomes a law.	The process by which a bill becomes a law is long and complex, involving numer-ous revisions and a great deal of compromise.
Pharmacy practice Summarize the procedure for conducting a clinical trial of a new drug.	To ensure that drugs are safe and effective, scientists follow strict procedural guidelines for testing and evaluating them.
Technical writing Write a set of instructions for applying for a student internship in a government agency.	If you want to apply for a government internship, you need to follow several important steps.

If your purpose is simply to help readers understand a process, not actu-ally perform it, you will write a process explanation. **Process explanations,**

like the first two examples in the Focus box above, often use present tense verbs ("Once a bill *is* introduced in Congress" or "A scientist first *submits* a funding application") to explain how a procedure is generally carried out. However, when a process explanation describes a specific procedure that was completed in the past, it uses past tense verbs ("The next thing I *did*").

If your purpose is to enable readers to actually perform the steps in a process, you will write instructions. **Instructions**, like the last example in the Focus box on page 204, always use present tense verbs in the form of commands to tell readers what to do ("First, *meet* with your adviser").

Whether your essay is a process explanation or a set of instructions, you can either devote a full paragraph to each step of the process or group a series of minor steps together in a single paragraph.

FOCUS **Options for Organizing Process Essays**

One Step per Paragraph
¶1 Introduction
¶2 First step in process
¶3 Second step in process
¶4 Third step in process
¶5 Conclusion

Several Steps per Paragraph
¶1 Introduction
¶2 First group of steps
¶3 Second group of steps
¶4 Third group of steps
¶5 Conclusion

As you write your process essay, discuss each step in the order in which it is performed, making sure your topic sentences clearly identify the function of each step or group of steps. (If you are writing instructions, you may also include reminders or warnings that readers might need to know when performing the process.)

Transitions are extremely important in process essays because they enable readers to follow the sequence of steps in the process and, in the case of instructions, to perform the process themselves.

FOCUS **Transitions for Process**

after that	immediately	the final step
as	later	the first (second,
as soon as	meanwhile	third) step
at the end	next	then
at the same time	now	the next step
before	once	when
finally	soon	while
first	subsequently	

14 D

■ **Culture Clue**

A *flea market* is a place where many people come together to sell used or inexpensive merchandise.

Model Process Essay

The following student essay, Jen Rossi's "For Fun and Profit," explains the process of selling at a flea market. Because Jen thought most readers would be unlikely to share her interest in her hobby, she did not write her essay in the form of instructions. Instead, she wrote a process explanation, using present tense verbs to explain how she generally proceeds. Notice how clear transitions move readers smoothly through the steps of the process.

For Fun and Profit

My first experience selling items at a flea market was both fun and profitable. In fact, it led to a hobby that is also a continuing source of extra money. That first time took a lot of work, but the routine I established then has made each flea market easier.

The first step in the process is to call to reserve a spot at the flea market. Then, I recruit a helper—usually my brother or one of my roommates—and we get to work.

The next step is sorting through all the items I managed to accumulate since the last flea market. My helper comes in handy here, encouraging me to sell ugly or useless things I may want to hold on to. We make three piles—keep, sell, and trash—and one by one, we place every item in a pile. (Before we decide to sell or throw out an item, I check with all my roommates to make sure I'm not accidentally throwing out one of their prized possessions.)

Next comes pricing the items for sale, which is actually the hardest step for me. It's always difficult to accept the fact that I might have to set a low price for something that has sentimental value for me (a giant stuffed animal, for example). It's just as hard to set a high price on the ugly lamp or old record album that might turn out to be someone's treasure. At my first flea market, I returned with a lot of unsold items, and I later realized I had sold other items too cheaply. I never made these mistakes again.

The next step is my least favorite: packing up items to be sold. I usually borrow my friend's van for the heavy items (boxes of books or dishes, for example). The small items (knickknacks, silk flowers, stray teaspoons) can be transported in my brother's car.

The final steps in my preparation take place on the day before the event. I borrow a couple of card tables from friends of my parents. Then, I go to the bank and get lots of dollar bills and quarters, and I collect piles of newspaper and plastic supermarket bags. Now, my planning is complete.

On the day of the flea market, I get up early, and my helper and I load the two vehicles. When we arrive at the site where the event is to be held, one of us unloads the cars. The other person sets things up, placing small items (such as dishes and DVDs) on the card tables and large items (such as my parents' old lawnmower) on the ground near the tables.

Then, the actual selling begins. Before I can even set up our tables, people start picking through my things, offering me cash for picture frames, pots and pans, and video games. We develop a system as the day goes on: one of us persuades buyers that that old meat grinder or vase is just what they've been looking for, and the other person negotiates the price with prospective buyers. Then, while one of us wraps small items in the newspapers or bags we brought

1

2

3

4

5

6

7

8

(and helps carry large items to people's cars), the other person takes the money and makes change.

Finally, at the end of the day, I count my money and give a share to my helper. We then load all the unsold items into the car and van and bring them back to my apartment. We store them in the back of my closet so it will be easy to pack them up again for the next flea market.

9

—Jen Rossi (student)

◆ PRACTICE 14-10

1. List the major steps in the process of selling at a flea market. Does Jen present them in strict chronological order?

_____

_____

_____

_____

2. What identifies Jen's essay as a process explanation rather than a set of instructions?

_____

_____

3. Underline some of the transitional words and phrases that link the steps in the process. Are any other transitions needed?

_____

_____

_____

_____

4. Underline Jen's thesis statement. Restate it below in your own words.

_____

_____

_____

5. What is the essay's greatest strength? What is its greatest weakness?

Strength: _____

Weakness: _____

GRAMMAR IN CONTEXT Process

When you write a process essay, you may have problems keeping tense, person, and voice consistent throughout. If you shift from one tense, person, or voice to another without good reason, you will confuse your readers.

CONFUSING We make three piles—keep, sell, and trash—and one by one, every item was placed in a pile. (shift from active to passive voice and from present to past tense)

CLEAR We make three piles—keep, sell, and trash—and one by one, we place every item in a pile. (consistent voice and tense)

For information on how to avoid illogical shifts in tense, person, and voice, see Chapter 24.

◆ PRACTICE 14-11

Following the writing process outlined in Chapter 12, write a process essay on one of the following topics. (Note: Before you begin, decide whether a process explanation or a set of instructions will be more appropriate for your purpose.)

An unusual recipe
College registration
Finding an apartment
Applying for a job
Getting dressed for a typical Saturday night
A religious ritual or cultural ceremony
A task you often do at work
A do-it-yourself project that didn't get done
Your own writing process
A self-improvement program (past, present, or future)
How to find something on the Internet

◆ PRACTICE 14-12

▶ **Word Power**

priorities the most important tasks

optimum the most favorable condition for a particular situation

The picture on the following page shows John Belushi as John "Bluto" Blutarsky in the infamous toga party scene from the 1978 film *Animal House*. Study the picture carefully, and then list the steps involved in planning the perfect party. Use this list to help you write a process essay that gives step-by-step instructions in the order in which they need to be done. (Hint: You can devote separate paragraphs to groups of tasks to be done the week before, the day before, the morning of the party, and so on.) Be sure to include any necessary cautions and reminders—for example, "Don't forget to tell your neighbors you're having a party"—to help your readers avoid potential problems.

☑ SELF-ASSESSMENT CHECKLIST:
Writing a Process Essay

☐ Does your introduction identify the process you will discuss and indicate whether you will be explaining the process or writing instructions?

☐ Does your thesis statement present an overview of the process and indicate why you are writing about it?

☐ Do you include every step readers will need to understand (or perform) the process?

☐ Are all the steps you present necessary, or should some be deleted?

☐ Are the steps in the process presented in strict chronological (time) order?

☐ Are related steps grouped in individual paragraphs?

☐ Do topic sentences clearly identify major stages in the process?

☐ Do you include transitional words and phrases that clearly show how the steps in the process are related?

☐ If you are writing instructions, have you included all necessary warnings or reminders?

☐ Does your conclusion effectively sum up your process?

☐ What problems did you experience in writing your essay? What would you do differently next time?

A **cause** makes something happen; an **effect** is a result of a particular cause or event. **Cause-and-effect essays** identify causes or predict effects; sometimes, they do both.

Writing a Cause-and-Effect Essay
- Make sure your topic calls for cause and effect.
- Decide whether your essay will focus on causes, effects, or both.
- Find ideas to write about.
- Identify your main idea, and write a thesis statement.
- Choose causes or effects to support your thesis.
- Arrange causes and effects in an effective order.
- Draft your essay.
- Revise your essay.
- Edit your essay.

(For detailed information on the process of writing an essay, see Chapter 12.)

FOCUS **Topics for Cause and Effect**

The wording of your assignment may suggest cause and effect. For example, the assignment may ask you to *explain why, predict the outcome, list contributing factors, discuss the consequences,* or tell what *caused* something else or how something is *affected* by something else.

Assignment	Thesis Statement
Women's studies What factors contributed to the rise of the women's movement in the 1970s?	The women's movement of the 1970s had its origins in the peace and civil rights movements of the 1960s.
Public health Discuss the possible long-term effects of smoking.	In addition to its well-known negative effects on smokers themselves, smoking also causes significant problems for those exposed to secondhand smoke.
Media and society How has the Internet affected the lives of those who have grown up with it?	The Internet has created a generation of people who learn differently from those in previous generations.

A cause-and-effect essay can focus on causes or on effects. When you write about causes, be sure to examine *all* relevant causes. You should emphasize the cause you consider the most important, but do not forget to consider other causes that may be significant. Similarly,

when you write about effects, consider *all* significant effects of a particular cause, not just the first few that you think of.

If your focus is on finding causes, as it is in the first assignment in the Focus box on the previous page, your introductory paragraph should identify the effect (the women's movement). If your focus is on predicting effects, as it is in the second and third assignments listed there, you should begin by identifying the cause (smoking, the Internet). In the body of your essay, you can devote a full paragraph to each cause (or effect), or you can group several related causes (or effects) together in each paragraph.

FOCUS **Options for Organizing Cause-and-Effect Essays**

Identifying Causes

¶1 Introduction (identifies effect)
¶2 First cause
¶3 Second cause
¶4 Third (and most important) cause
¶5 Conclusion

Predicting Effects

¶1 Introduction (identifies cause)
¶2 First effect
¶3 Second effect
¶4 Third (and most important) effect
¶5 Conclusion

Transitions are important in cause-and-effect essays because they establish causal connections, telling readers that A caused B and not the other way around. They also make it clear that events have a *causal* relationship (A *caused* B) and not just a *sequential* relationship (A *came before* B). Remember, when one event follows another, the second is not necessarily the result of the first. For example, an earthquake may occur the day before you fail an exam, but that doesn't mean the earthquake caused you to fail.

FOCUS **Transitions for Cause and Effect**

accordingly	for this reason	the most impor-
another cause	since	tant cause
another effect	so	the most impor-
as a result	the first (second,	tant effect
because	third) cause	therefore
consequently	the first (second,	
for	third) effect	

Model Cause-and-Effect Essay

The following student essay, "How My Parents' Separation Changed My Life" by Andrea DeMarco, examines the effects of a significant event on

the writer and her family. Andrea begins by identifying the cause—the separation—and then goes on to explain its specific effects on her family and on herself. Notice how transitional words and phrases make the essay's causal connections clear to her readers.

How My Parents' Separation Changed My Life

Until I was eight, I lived the perfect all-American life with my perfect all-American family. I lived in a suburb of Albany, New York, with my parents, my sister and brother, and our dog, Daisy. We had a ping-pong table in the basement, a barbecue in the backyard, and two cars in the garage. My dad and mom were high school teachers, and every summer we took a family vacation. Then, it all changed. My parents' separation made everything different.   1

One day, just before Halloween, when my sister was twelve and my brother was fourteen (Daisy was seven), our parents called us into the kitchen for a family conference. We didn't think anything was wrong at first; they were always calling these annoying meetings. We figured it was time for us to plan a vacation, talk about household chores, or be nagged to clean our rooms. As soon as we sat down, though, we knew this was different. We could tell Mom had been crying, and Dad's voice cracked when he told us the news. They were separating—they called it a "trial separation"—and Dad was moving out of our house.   2

After that day, everything seemed to change. Every Halloween we always had a big jack-o'-lantern on our front porch. Dad used to spend hours at the kitchen table cutting out the eyes, nose, and mouth and hollowing out the insides. That Halloween, because he didn't live with us, things were different. Mom bought a pumpkin, and I guess she was planning to carve it up. But she never did, and we never mentioned it. It sat on the kitchen counter for a couple of weeks, getting soft and wrinkled, and then it just disappeared.   3

Other holidays were also different because Mom and Dad were not living together. Our first Thanksgiving without Dad was pathetic. I don't even want to talk about it. Christmas was different, too. We spent Christmas Eve with Dad and our relatives on his side and Christmas Day with Mom and her family. Of course, we got twice as many presents as usual. I realize now that both our parents were trying to make up for the pain of the separation. The worst part came when I opened my big present from Mom: Barbie's Dream House. This was something I had always wanted. Even at eight, I knew how hard it must have been for Mom to afford it. The trouble was, I had gotten the same thing from Dad the night before.   4

The separation affected each of us in different ways. The worst effect of my parents' separation was not the big events but the disruption in our everyday lives. Dinner used to be a family time, a chance to talk about our day and make plans. But after Dad left, Mom seemed to stop eating. Sometimes she would just have coffee while we ate, and sometimes she wouldn't eat at all. She would microwave some frozen thing for us or heat up soup or cook some hot dogs. We didn't care—after all, now she let us watch TV while we ate—but we did notice.   5

Other parts of our routine changed, too. Because Dad didn't live with us anymore, we had to spend every Saturday and every Wednesday night at his   6

apartment, no matter what else we had planned. Usually, he would take us to dinner at McDonald's on Wednesdays, and then we would go back to his place and do our homework or watch TV. That wasn't too bad. Saturdays were a lot worse. We really wanted to be home, hanging out with our friends in our own rooms in our own house. Instead, we had to do some planned activity with Dad, like go to a movie or a hockey game.

By the end of the school year, my parents had somehow worked things out,   7 and Dad was back home again. That June, at a family conference around the kitchen table, we made our summer vacation plans. We decided on Williamsburg, Virginia, the all-American vacation destination. So, things were back to normal, but I wasn't, and I'm still not. Now, ten years later, my mother and father are all right, but I still worry they'll split up again. And I worry about my own future husband and how I will ever be sure he's the one I'll stay married to. As a result of what happened in my own family, it is hard for me to believe any relationship is forever.

◆ **PRACTICE 14-13**

1. Underline Andrea's thesis statement. Restate it below in your own words.

_____

_____

_____

2. What specific effects of her parents' separation does Andrea identify?

_____

_____

_____

3. Underline the transitional words and phrases that make the causal connections in Andrea's essay clear to her readers.

4. Is Andrea's relatively long concluding paragraph effective? Why or why not? Do you think it should be shortened or divided into two paragraphs?

_____

_____

_____

5. Is Andrea's straightforward title effective, or should she have used a more creative or eye-catching title? Can you suggest an alternative?

_____

_____

_____

6. What is this essay's greatest strength? What is its greatest weakness?

Strength: _____

Weakness: _____

GRAMMAR IN CONTEXT **Cause and Effect**

When you write a cause-and-effect essay, you may have trouble remembering the difference between *affect* and *effect*.

The worst ~~affect~~ *effect* of my parents' separation was not the big events but the disruption in our everyday lives. (*effect* is a noun)

The separation ~~effected~~ *affected* each of us in different ways. (*affect* is a verb)

For information on *affect* and *effect*, see Chapter 34.

◆ **PRACTICE 14-14**

Following the writing process outlined in Chapter 12, write a cause-and-effect essay on one of the following topics.

A teacher's positive (or negative) effect on you
Why you voted a certain way in a recent election (or why you did not vote)
Why the popularity of soap operas has been steadily declining
How your life would be different if you dropped out of school (or quit your job)
How a particular invention (for example, the cell phone) has changed your life
Why text messaging is so popular
A movie or book that changed the way you look at life
How a particular season (or day of the week) affects your mood
How having a child would change (or has changed) your life
How a particular event made you grow up

◆ **PRACTICE 14-15**

The picture on page 215 shows a happy couple, recent lottery winners, with a sign announcing their prize. Imagine you have won a multi-million-dollar

lottery. How would your life change? Write a cause-and-effect essay that discusses specific ways in which your life would be different.

▶ **Word Power**

annuity annual payment of an allowance or income

windfall a sudden, unexpected piece of good luck

▦ **Culture Clue**

A *lottery* is a form of gambling. People buy tickets that are drawn at random on a specified date. Then, prizes are given to the winners.

☑ SELF-ASSESSMENT CHECKLIST:
Writing a Cause-and-Effect Essay

- Does your introduction give readers an overview of the topic you will discuss?

- Does your thesis statement indicate whether your essay will focus on causes or on effects?

- Do you identify all causes or effects relevant to your topic, or do you need to add any?

- Have you arranged causes and effects to indicate which are more important than others?

- Does each body paragraph identify and explain one particular cause or effect (or several closely related causes or effects)?

- Do you include enough transitional words and phrases to make your essay's cause-and-effect connections clear?

- Does your conclusion reinforce the causal relationships you discuss? If necessary, revise to make your emphasis clearer.

- What problems did you experience in writing your essay? What would you do differently next time?

F **Comparison and Contrast**

Comparison identifies similarities; **contrast** identifies differences. **Comparison-and-contrast essays** explain how two things are alike or how they are different; sometimes, they discuss both similarities and differences.

Writing a Comparison-and-Contrast Essay

■ Make sure your topic calls for comparison and contrast.
■ Find ideas to write about.
■ Decide whether you want to discuss similarities, differences, or both.
■ Identify your main idea and write a thesis statement.
■ Identify specific points of comparison or contrast to support your thesis.
■ Decide whether to structure your essay as a point-by-point or subject-by-subject comparison.
■ Draft your essay.
■ Revise your essay.
■ Edit your essay.

(For detailed information on the process of writing an essay, see Chapter 12.)

FOCUS **Topics for Comparison and Contrast**

The wording of your assignment may suggest comparison and contrast—for example, by asking you to *compare, contrast, discuss similarities,* or *identify differences.*

Assignment	Thesis Statement
Philosophy What basic similarities do you find in the beliefs of Henry David Thoreau and Martin Luther King Jr.?	Although King was more politically active, both he and Thoreau strongly supported the idea of civil disobedience.
Nutrition How do the diets of native Japanese and Japanese Americans differ?	As they become more and more assimilated, Japanese Americans consume more fats than native Japanese do.
Literature Contrast the two sisters in Alice Walker's short story "Everyday Use."	Unlike Maggie, Dee—her more successful, better-educated sister—has rejected her family's heritage.

When you organize a comparison-and-contrast essay, you can choose either a *point-by-point* or a *subject-by-subject* arrangement. A **point-by-point** comparison alternates between the two subjects you are comparing or contrasting, moving back and forth from one subject to the other. A **subject-by-subject** comparison treats its two subjects separately, first fully discussing one subject and then moving on to consider the other subject. In both kinds of comparison-and-contrast essays, the same points are discussed in the same order for both subjects.

FOCUS   **Options for Organizing Comparison-and-Contrast Essays**

Point-by-Point Comparison

¶1 Introduction (identifies subjects to be compared or contrasted)

¶2 First point discussed for both subjects

¶3 Second point discussed for both subjects

¶4 Third point discussed for both subjects

¶5 Conclusion

Subject-by-Subject Comparison

¶1 Introduction (identifies subjects to be compared or contrasted)

¶¶2–3 First subject discussed

¶¶4–5 Second subject discussed

¶6 Conclusion

The transitional words and phrases you use in a comparison-and-contrast essay tell readers whether you are focusing on similarities or on differences. Transitions also help move readers through your essay from one subject to the other and from one point of comparison or contrast to the next.

FOCUS   **Transitions for Comparison and Contrast**

although	likewise
but	nevertheless
even though	on the contrary
however	on the one hand . . . on the other hand
in comparison	similarly
in contrast	unlike
instead	whereas
like	

Model Comparison-and-Contrast Essay

The following student essay, "Another Ordinary Day" by Nisha Jani, contrasts teenage boys and girls by going through a typical day in the lives of "Johnny" and "Jane." A point-by-point comparison, Nisha's essay alternates between her two subjects, treating the same points in the same order for each. Her topic sentences identify the part of the day each paragraph will discuss, and transitional words and phrases clearly signal shifts from one subject to the next.

Another Ordinary Day

"Boys are from Jupiter and get stupider / Girls are from Mars and become   1
movie stars / Boys take a bath and smell like trash / Girls take a shower and
smell like a flower." As simple playground songs like this one suggest, the two
sexes are very different. As adults, men and women have similar goals, values,
and occupations, but as children and teenagers, boys and girls often seem to
belong to two different species. In fact, from the first moment of the day
to the last, the typical boy and girl live very different lives.

The sun rises, and the alarm clock signals the beginning of another day for   2
Johnny and Jane, two seventh-grade classmates. Johnny, an average thirteen-
year-old boy, wakes up late and has to hurry. He throws on his favorite jeans,
a baggy T-shirt, and a baseball cap. Then, he has a hearty high-cholesterol
breakfast and runs out of the house to school, usually forgetting some vital
book or homework assignment. Jane, unlike Johnny, wakes up early and takes
her time. She takes a long shower and then blow-dries her hair. For Jane,
getting dressed can be a very difficult process, one that often includes taking
everything out of her closet and calling friends for advice. After she makes her
decision, she helps herself to some food (probably low- or no-fat) and goes off
to school, making sure she has with her everything she needs.

School is a totally different experience for Johnny and Jane. Johnny will   3
probably sit in the back of the classroom with a couple of other guys, throwing
paper airplanes and spitballs. These will be directed at the males they do not
like and the females they think are kind of cute. (However, if their male friends
ever ask the boys about these girls, they will say girls are just losers and deny
that they like any of them.) On the opposite side of the classroom, however,
Jane is focused on a very different kind of activity. At first, it looks as if she is
carefully copying the algebra notes that the teacher is putting on the board,
but her notes have absolutely nothing to do with algebra. Instead, she is
writing about boys, clothes, and other topics that are much more important to
her than the square root of one hundred twenty-one. She proceeds to fold the
note into a box or other creative shape, which can often put origami to shame.
As soon as the teacher turns her back, the note is passed and the process
begins all over again.

Lunch, a vital part of the school day, is also very different for Johnny and   4
Jane. On the one hand, for Johnny and his friends, it is a time to compare
baseball cards, exchange sports facts, and of course tell jokes about every
bodily function imaginable. In front of them on the table, their trays are filled
with pizza, soda, fries, and chips, and this food is their main focus. For Jane,
on the other hand, lunch is not about eating; it is a chance to exchange the

▶ **Word Power**

origami   the Japanese art
of folding paper into shapes
representing birds or
animals

latest gossip about who is going out with whom. The girls look around to see
what people are wearing, what they should do with their hair, and so on. Jane's
meal is quite a bit smaller than Johnny's: it consists of a small low-fat yogurt
and half a bagel (if she feels like splurging, she will spread some cream cheese
on the bagel).

After school, Johnny and Jane head in different directions. Johnny rushes   5
home to get his bike and meets up with his friends to run around and play
typical "guy games," like pick-up basketball or touch football. Johnny and his
friends play with every boy who shows up, whether they know him or not. They
may get into physical fights and arguments, but they always plan to meet up
again the next day. In contrast to the boys, Jane and her friends are very
selective. Their circle is a small one, and they do everything together. Some
days, they go to the mall (they will not necessarily buy anything there, but they
will consider the outing productive anyway because they will have spent time
together). Most days, though, they just talk, with the discussion ranging from
school to guys to lipstick colors. When Jane gets home, she will most likely run
to the phone and talk for hours to the same three or four girls.

At the age of twelve or thirteen, boys and girls do not seem to have   6
very much in common. Given this situation, it is amazing that boys and girls
grow up to become men and women who interact as neighbors, friends, and
coworkers. What is even more amazing is that so many grow up to share lives
and raise families together, treating each other with love and respect.

◆ PRACTICE 14-16

1. Underline Nisha's thesis statement. Restate it below in your own
words.

_____

_____

_____

2. Does Nisha's opening paragraph identify the subjects she will discuss?
Will she focus on similarities or on differences?

_____

_____

_____

3. Nisha's essay is a point-by-point comparison. What four points does
she discuss for each of her two subjects?

_____

_____

_____

4. Underline some transitional words and phrases Nisha uses to move
readers from one subject (Johnny) to the other (Jane).

5. Reread Nisha's topic sentences. What do they contribute to the essay?

_____

_____

_____

_____

6. What is this essay's greatest strength? What is its greatest weakness?

Strength: _____

Weakness: _____

GRAMMAR IN CONTEXT   **Comparison and Contrast**

When you write a comparison-and-contrast essay, you need to present the points you are comparing or contrasting in **parallel** terms to highlight their similarities or differences.

┌─────PARALLEL─────┐
Johnny, an average thirteen-year-old boy, wakes up late and has

to hurry.

┌─────PARALLEL─────┐
Jane, unlike Johnny, wakes up early and takes her time.

For information on revising to make ideas parallel, see Chapter 19.

◆ **PRACTICE 14-17**

Following the writing process outlined in Chapter 12, write a comparison-and-contrast essay on one of the following topics.

Two coworkers
Two movie heroes
How you expect your life to be different from the lives of your parents
Men's and women's ideas about their body images
Two ways of studying for an exam
Risk-takers and people who play it safe
Country and city living (or you can compare suburban living with either)
Two popular magazines (features, ads, target audiences, pictures)
Two actors

◆ **PRACTICE 14-18**

The pictures below show two famous war memorials. Study the two photographs carefully, and then write an essay in which you compare them, considering both what the monuments look like and their emotional impact on you.

Iwo Jima memorial statue at Arlington National Cemetery

Vietnam Veterans Memorial in Washington, D.C.

14 G

☑ SELF-ASSESSMENT CHECKLIST:
Writing a Comparison-and-Contrast Essay

- Does your introduction identify the two subjects you will compare and contrast?

- Does your thesis statement indicate whether your essay will examine similarities or differences?

- Have you discussed all significant points of comparison or contrast that apply to your two subjects?

- Have you treated similar points for both of your two subjects?

- Is your essay's organization consistent with either a point-by-point comparison or a subject-by-subject comparison?

- Does each topic sentence clearly identify the subject and the point of comparison or contrast being discussed?

- Do you include enough transitional words and phrases to move readers from one subject or point to another?

- Does your conclusion remind readers what your two subjects are and whether you have focused on similarities or differences?

- What problems did you experience during the process of writing your essay? What would you do differently next time?

G Classification

Classification is the act of sorting items into appropriate categories. **Classification essays** divide a whole (your subject) into parts and sort various items into categories.

Writing a Classification Essay
- Make sure your topic calls for classification.
- Find ideas to write about.
- Identify your main idea and write a thesis statement.
- Decide what categories you will discuss.
- Sort examples and details into categories.
- Arrange your categories in an effective order.
- Draft your essay.
- Revise your essay.
- Edit your essay.

(For detailed information on the process of writing an essay, see Chapter 12.)

FOCUS Topics for Classification

The wording of your assignment may suggest classification. For example, you may be asked to consider *kinds, types, categories, components, segments,* or *parts of a whole.*

Assignment	Thesis Statement
Business What kinds of courses are most useful for students planning to run their own businesses?	Courses dealing with accounting, management, interpersonal communication, and computer science offer the most useful skills for future business owners.
Biology List the components of blood and explain the function of each.	Red blood cells, white blood cells, platelets, and plasma have distinct functions.
Education Classify elementary school children according to their academic needs.	The elementary school population includes special-needs students, students with reading and math skills at or near grade level, and academically gifted students.

As a rule, each paragraph of a classification essay examines a separate category—a different part of the whole. For example, a paragraph could focus on one kind of course in the college curriculum, one component of the blood, or one type of child. Within each paragraph, you discuss the individual items that you have put into a particular category—for example, accounting courses, red blood cells, or gifted students. If you consider some categories less important than others, you may decide to discuss those minor categories together in a single paragraph, devoting full paragraphs only to the most significant categories.

FOCUS Options for Organizing Classification Essays

One Category in Each Paragraph	Major Categories in Separate Paragraphs; Minor Categories Grouped Together
¶1 Introduction (identifies whole and its major categories)	¶1 Introduction (identifies whole and its major categories)
¶2 First category	¶2 Minor categories
¶3 Second category	¶3 First major category
¶4 Third category	¶4 Second (and more important) major category
¶5 Conclusion	¶5 Conclusion

In a classification essay, topic sentences identify the category or categories discussed in each paragraph. Transitional words and phrases signal movement from one category to the next and may also tell readers which categories you consider more (or less) important.

FOCUS **Transitions for Classification**

one kind . . . another kind the final type	the first (second, third) category the last group	the most important component the next part

---

Model Classification Essay

The following student essay, "Selling a Dream" by Rob O'Neal, classifies American car names into categories on the basis of the kind of message they communicate to consumers. Notice that Rob discusses one category in each of his body paragraphs, using clear topic sentences to identify and define each kind of car name and relate each category to the group as a whole.

Selling a Dream

The earliest automobiles were often named after the men who manufactured them — Ford, Studebaker, Nash, Olds, Chrysler, Dodge, Chevrolet, and so on. More recently, however, American car makers have been competing to see what kinds of names will sell the most cars. Many car names seem to be chosen simply for how they sound: Alero, Corvette, Neon, Probe, Caprice. Many others, however, are designed to sell specific dreams to consumers. Americans always seem to want to be, do, and become something different. They want to be tough and brave, to explore new places, to take risks. With the names that auto manufacturers choose for their cars, they appeal to Americans' deepest desires. 1

Some American cars are named for places people dream of traveling to. Park Avenue, Malibu, Riviera, Seville, Tahoe, Yukon, Aspen, and Durango are some names that suggest escape — to New York City, California, Europe, the West. Other place names — Sebring, Daytona, and Bonneville, for example — are associated with the danger and excitement of car racing. And then there is the El Dorado, a car named for a fictional paradise: a city of gold. 2

Other car names convey rough and tough, even dangerous, images. Animal names fall into this category, with models like Ram, Bronco, and Mustang suggesting powerful, untamed beasts. Other cars in the "rough and tough" category include those that suggest the wildness of the Old West: Wrangler and Rodeo, for example. Because the American auto industry is centered near Detroit, Michigan, where many cities have Indian names, cars named for the cities where they are manufactured inherited these names. Thus, cars called Cadillac, Pontiac, and Cherokee recall the history of Indian nations, and these too might suggest the excitement of the untamed West. 3

The most interesting car names in terms of the dream they sell, however, are those that suggest exploration and discovery. Years ago, some car names honored real explorers, like DeSoto and LaSalle. Now, model names only sell an abstract idea. Still, American car names like Blazer, Explorer, Navigator, Mountaineer, Expedition, Caravan, and Voyager (as well as the names of foreign cars driven by many Americans, such as Nissan's Pathfinder and Quest and Honda's Passport, Pilot, and Odyssey) have the power to make drivers feel they are blazing new trails and discovering new worlds — when in fact they may simply be carpooling their children to a soccer game or commuting to work.

4

Today, the car is an ordinary piece of machinery, a necessity for many people. Clearly, the automobile is no longer seen as the amazing invention it once was. Despite the fact that most people take the existence of cars for granted, however, manufacturers still try to make consumers believe they are buying more than just transportation. But whether we drive a Malibu, Mustang, Cherokee, or Expedition — or even a "royal" LeBaron or Marquis—we eventually realize that we are driving cars, not magic carpets.

5

◆ PRACTICE 14-19

1. What three categories of car names does Rob discuss in his essay?

_____

_____

_____

2. Is Rob's treatment of the three categories similar? Does he give the same kind of information for each kind of car name?

_____

_____

_____

3. How do Rob's topic sentences move readers from one category to the next? How do they link the three categories?

_____

_____

_____

_____

4. Underline Rob's thesis statement. Restate it below in your own words.

_____

_____

_____

5. Should Rob have included additional examples in each category? Should he have included any additional categories?

_____

_____

_____

6. What is this essay's greatest strength? What is its greatest weakness?

Strength: _____

Weakness: _____

GRAMMAR IN CONTEXT Classification

When you write a classification essay, you may want to list the categories you are going to discuss or the examples in each category. If you do, use a **colon** to introduce your list, and make sure that a complete sentence comes before the colon.

> Many car names seem to be chosen simply for how they sound: Alero, Corvette, Neon, Probe, Caprice.

For information on how to use a colon to introduce a list, see 33D.

◆ **PRACTICE 14-20**

Following the writing process outlined in Chapter 12, write a classification essay on one of the following topics.

Types of teachers (or bosses)
Ways to lose (or gain) weight
Things hanging on your walls
Kinds of moods
Kinds of stores in your
    community shopping
    district or mall
Traits of oldest children, middle
    children, and youngest children
Kinds of desserts
Workers you encounter in a
    typical day
Popular music
College students' clothing choices
Kinds of tattoos

▶ **Word Power**
finicky hard to please

glutton a person who eats without moderation

◆ **PRACTICE 14-21**

The picture on the following page shows people eating a meal at a restaurant in New York City's Chinatown. Look at the photo, and think about all the kinds of food you eat in a typical week. Then, write an essay in which

you classify the foods you eat. The categories you create can classify the food according to convenience, country of origin, ease of preparation, healthfulness, or where it is consumed.

☑ SELF-ASSESSMENT CHECKLIST:
Writing a Classification Essay

- Does your introduction identify the subject of your classification?

- Does your thesis statement identify the categories you will discuss?

- Does each topic sentence clearly identify the category or categories the paragraph discusses?

- Do all your categories support your essay's thesis?

- Have you treated each major category similarly and with equal thoroughness?

- Do you include enough transitional words and phrases to lead readers from one category to the next?

- Does your conclusion review the major categories your essay discusses?

- What problems did you experience in writing your essay? What would you do differently next time?

H   Definition

Definition explains the meaning of a term or concept. A **definition essay** presents an *extended definition,* using various patterns of development to move beyond a simple dictionary definition.

Writing a Definition Essay

■ Make sure your topic calls for definition.
■ Find ideas to write about.
■ Identify your main idea and write a thesis statement.
■ Decide what patterns of development to use to support your thesis.
■ Arrange supporting examples and details in an effective order.
■ Draft your essay.
■ Revise your essay.
■ Edit your essay.

(For detailed information on the process of writing an essay, see Chapter 12.)

FOCUS   Topics for Definition

The wording of your assignment may suggest definition. For example, you may be asked to *define* or *explain* or to answer the question *What is x?* or *What does x mean?*

Assignment	Thesis Statement
Art Explain the meaning of the term *performance art.*	Unlike more conventional forms of art, *performance art* extends beyond the canvas.
Biology What did Darwin mean by the term *natural selection?*	*Natural selection,* popularly known as "survival of the fittest," is a good deal more complicated than most people think.
Psychology What is *attention deficit disorder?*	*Attention deficit disorder* (ADD), once narrowly defined as a childhood problem, is now known to affect adults as well as children.

As the thesis statements above suggest, definition essays can be developed in various ways. For example, you can define something by telling how it occurred (narration), by describing its appearance (description), by giving a series of examples (exemplification), by telling how it operates (process), by telling how it is similar to or different from something else

(comparison and contrast), or by discussing its parts (classification). Some definition essays use a single pattern of development; others combine several patterns of development, perhaps using a different one in each paragraph.

FOCUS **Options for Organizing Definition Essays**

Single Pattern of Development	*Combination of Several Different Patterns of Development*
¶1 Introduction (identifies term to be defined)	¶1 Introduction (identifies term to be defined)
¶2 Definition by example	¶2 Definition by description
¶3 Additional examples	¶3 Definition by example
¶4 Additional examples	¶4 Definition by comparison and contrast
¶5 Conclusion	¶5 Conclusion

The kinds of transitions used in a definition essay depend on the specific pattern or patterns of development in the essay.

FOCUS **Transitions for Definition**

also	like
for example	one characteristic . . . another characteristic
in addition	one way . . . another way
in particular	specifically

Model Definition Essay

The following student essay, "Street Smart" by Kristin Whitehead, defines the term *street smart*. In the essay's introduction, Kristin defines her term briefly; in the essay's body paragraphs, she develops her definition further. Notice that the topic sentences of Kristin's three body paragraphs repeat a key phrase to remind readers of her essay's subject.

Street Smart

I grew up in a big city, so I was practically born street smart. I learned the hard way how to act and what to do, and so did my friends. To us, being street smart meant having common sense. We wanted to be cool, but we needed to be safe, too. Now I go to college in a big city, and I realize that not everyone here grew up the way I did. Many students are from suburbs or rural areas, and they are either terrified of the city or totally ignorant of city life.

1

The few suburban or rural students who are willing to venture downtown are not street smart — but they should be. Being street smart is a vital survival skill, one that everyone should learn.

For me, being street smart means knowing how to protect my possessions. Friends of mine who are not used to city life insist on wearing all their jewelry when they go downtown. I think this is asking for trouble, and I know better. I always tuck my chain under my shirt and leave my gold earrings home. Another thing that surprises me is how some of my friends wave their money around. They always seem to be standing on the street, trying to count their change or stuff dollars into their wallets. Street-smart people make sure to put their money safely away in their pockets or purses before they leave a store. A street-smart person will also carry a backpack, a purse strapped across the chest, or no purse at all. A person who is not street smart carries a purse loosely over one shoulder or dangles it by its handle. Again, these people are asking for trouble.

Being street smart also means protecting myself. It means being aware of my surroundings at all times and looking alert. A lot of times, I have been downtown with people who kept stopping on the street to talk about where they should go next or walking up and down the same street over and over again. A street-smart person would never do this. It is important that I look as if I know where I am going at all times, even if I don't. Whenever possible, I decide on a destination in advance, and I make sure I know how to get there. Even if I am not completely sure where I am headed, I make sure my body language conveys my confidence in my ability to reach my destination.

Finally, being street smart means protecting my life. A street-smart person does not walk alone, especially after dark, in an unfamiliar neighborhood. A street-smart person does not ask random strangers for directions; when lost, he or she asks a shopkeeper for help. A street-smart person takes main streets instead of side streets. When faced with danger or the threat of danger, a street-smart person knows when to run, when to scream, and when to give up money or possessions to avoid violence.

So how does someone get to be street smart? Some people think it is a gift, but I think it is something almost anyone can learn. Probably the best way to learn how to be street smart is to hang out with people who know where they are going.

◆ **PRACTICE 14-22**

1. Underline Kristin's thesis statement. Restate it below in your own words.

_____

2. In your own words, define the term *street smart*. Why does this term require more than a one-sentence definition?

_____

_____

_____

3. Where does Kristin use examples to develop her definition? Where does she use comparison and contrast?

_____

_____

_____

4. What phrase does Kristin repeat in the topic sentences to tie her three body paragraphs together?

_____

5. Kristin's conclusion is quite a bit shorter than her other paragraphs. What, if anything, do you think she should add to this paragraph?

_____

_____

6. What is this essay's greatest strength? What is its greatest weakness?

Strength: _____

Weakness: _____

GRAMMAR IN CONTEXT   Definition

When you write a definition essay, you may begin with a one-sentence definition that you expand in the rest of your essay. When you write your definition sentence, do not use the phrases *is when* or *is where*.

means knowing

For me, being street smart ~~is when I know~~ how to protect my

possessions.

means protecting

Being street smart is also ~~where I protect~~ myself.

For information on how to structure a definition sentence, see the Grammar in Context box in 10A.

◆ PRACTICE 14-23

Following the writing process outlined in Chapter 12, write a definition essay on one of the following topics.

Upward mobility	Responsibility	Courage
Peer pressure	Procrastination	Happiness
Competition	Security	Home
Success		

14 I

▶ **Word Power**
nuclear family a family unit
made up of a mother and
father and their children

◆ **PRACTICE 14-24**

The pictures on page 233 show various kinds of families. Look at the pictures, and then write an essay in which you define *family*. In what ways do the family groups shown on the following page fit (or not fit) your definition?

☑ SELF-ASSESSMENT CHECKLIST:
Writing a Definition Essay

   ▢ Does your introduction identify the term your essay will define and provide a brief definition?

   ▢ Does your thesis statement indicate why you are defining the term?

   ▢ Do you use appropriate patterns of development to develop your definition, or should you explore other options?

   ▢ Do topic sentences clearly lead readers from one part of your definition to the next?

   ▢ Are all your details and examples clearly related to the term you are defining, or should some be deleted?

   ▢ Do you include enough transitional words and phrases to clearly link your ideas, or do you need to add transitions?

   ▢ Does your conclusion sum up your essay's main points and remind readers why you are defining the term?

   ▢ What problems did you experience in writing your essay? What would you do differently next time?

I Argument

Argument takes a stand on a debatable issue—that is, an issue that has two sides (and can therefore be debated). An **argument essay** uses different kinds of *evidence*—facts, examples, and expert opinion—to persuade readers to accept a position.

An African-American couple

A mixed-race family

A two-father family

A father helps his children with homework

Writing an Argument Essay
- ■ Make sure your topic calls for argument.
- ■ Find ideas to write about.
- ■ Decide on the position you will support, and write a thesis state-ment that clearly expresses this position.
- ■ List points in support of your thesis.
- ■ Arrange your points in an effective order.
- ■ Support each point with evidence.
- ■ Consider arguments against your position.
- ■ Draft your essay.
- ■ Revise your essay.
- ■ Edit your essay.

(For detailed information on the process of writing an essay, see Chapter 12.)

FOCUS **Topics for Argument**

The wording of your assignment may suggest argument. For example, you may be asked to *debate, argue, consider, give your opin-ion, take a position,* or *take a stand.*

Assignment	Thesis Statement
Composition Explain your position on a current social issue.	People should be able to invest some of their Social Security contribu-tions in the stock market.
American history Do you believe that General Lee was responsible for the South's defeat at the Battle of Gettysburg? Why or why not?	Because Lee refused to listen to the advice given to him by General Longstreet, he is largely responsible for the South's defeat at the Battle of Gettysburg.
Ethics Should physician-assisted suicide be legalized?	Although many people think physician-assisted suicide should remain illegal, it should be legal in certain situations.

An argument essay can be organized *inductively* or *deductively.* An **inductive argument** moves from the specific to the general—that is, from a group of specific observations to a general conclusion based on these observations. An essay on the first topic in the Focus box above, for example, could be an inductive argument. It could begin by presenting facts, examples, and expert opinion about the benefits of investing in the stock market and end with the conclusion that people should be able to invest part of their Social Security contributions in the stock market.

A **deductive argument** moves from the general to the specific. A deductive argument begins with a **major premise** (a general statement that the writer believes his or her audience will accept) and then moves to a **minor premise** (a specific instance of the belief stated in the major premise). It ends with a **conclusion** that follows from the two premises. For example, an essay on the last topic in the Focus box above could be a deductive argument. It could begin with the major premise that all terminally ill patients who are in great pain should be given access to physician-assisted suicide. It could then go on to state and explain the minor premise that a particular patient is both terminally ill and in great pain, offering facts, examples, and the opinions of experts to support this premise. The essay could conclude that this patient should, therefore, be allowed the option of physician-assisted suicide. The deductive argument presented in the essay would have three parts.

MAJOR PREMISE   All terminally ill patients who are in great pain should be allowed to choose physician-assisted suicide.

MINOR PREMISE   John Lacca is a terminally ill patient who is in great pain.

CONCLUSION   Therefore, John Lacca should be allowed to choose physician-assisted suicide.

Before you present your argument, think about whether your readers are likely to be hostile toward, neutral toward, or in agreement with your position. Once you understand your audience, you can decide which points to make in support of your argument.

Begin each paragraph of your argument essay with a topic sentence that clearly states a point in support of your thesis. Throughout your essay, try to include specific examples that will make your arguments persuasive. Keep in mind that arguments that rely just on generalizations are not as convincing as those that include vivid details and specific examples. Finally, strive for a balanced, moderate tone, and avoid name-calling or personal attacks.

FOCUS Options for Organizing Argument Essays

Inductive Argument
¶1 Introduction
¶2 First point (supported by facts, examples, and expert opinion)
¶3 Second point
¶4 Third point
¶5 Identification and refutation of opposing arguments
¶6 Conclusion

Deductive Argument
¶1 Introduction
¶2 Major premise stated and explained
¶3 Minor premise stated and explained
¶4 Evidence supporting minor premise presented
¶5 Opposing arguments identified and refuted
¶6 Conclusion

In addition to presenting your case, your essay should also briefly summarize arguments *against* your position and **refute** them (that is, argue against them or prove them false) by identifying factual errors or errors in logic. If an opposing argument is particularly strong, concede its strength—but try to point out some weaknesses as well. If you deal with opposing arguments in this way, your audience will see you as a fair and reasonable person.

Transitions are extremely important in argument essays because they not only signal the movement from one part of the argument to another but also relate specific points to one another and to the thesis statement.

FOCUS **Transitions for Argument**

accordingly	granted	of course
admittedly	however	on the one
although	in addition	hand . . . on the
because	in conclusion	other hand
but	indeed	since
certainly	in fact	so
consequently	in summary	therefore
despite	meanwhile	thus
even so	moreover	to be sure
even though	nevertheless	truly
finally	nonetheless	
first, second . . .	now	

Model Argument Essay

The following student paper, "Amnesty for Undocumented Immigrants" by Peter Charron, is an argument essay. Peter takes a strong stand, and he supports his thesis with specific facts, examples, and expert opinion.

Amnesty for Undocumented Immigrants

More than twelve million undocumented immigrants now live in the United   1
States. Is it practical to send them all back home? Should they be allowed to stay? Despite their illegal entry, if they have worked and raised their families in the United States for years, these people should be allowed to stay in this country and, eventually, to become American citizens.

Many people object to the idea of amnesty, an official pardon for past   2
illegal acts. Certainly, in this case, amnesty would forgive immigrants for entering the country illegally. However, this amnesty would not come without penalty. First, they would be heavily fined. In addition, they would have to show that they have jobs and can speak English. Moreover, to become American citizens, they would have to wait at least thirteen years. So, even though they would be granted amnesty, they still would be punished for entering the United States illegally.

Undocumented immigrants come to this country to work, and they   3
often take low-wage jobs that businesses would otherwise find difficult or
impossible to fill. For example, undocumented immigrants often work as
migrant laborers — planting, cultivating, and picking crops like lettuce and
tomatoes. In the Southwest, where there are many Mexican immigrants, laborers
often work in the construction industry. The meat packing, landscaping, and
hotel industries also use immigrant workers, not all of whom are in this country
legally. Finally, the health care industry needs more and more people every year
who will work for low pay as caregivers, providing personal care to the elderly
and disabled. It would be very hard to fill all these jobs without illegal
immigrants.

Giving amnesty to undocumented immigrants is not a perfect solution, but   4
it would solve many problems. Now, these immigrants feel they have to hide
from authorities because they are afraid they will be deported. Therefore, they
may delay seeking needed medical care. Instead, they may wind up in a hospital
emergency room when they are seriously ill. This is expensive for everyone. In
addition, children of undocumented immigrants often cannot attend college
because college scholarships require documents — and, even if students can
afford the tuition, they must be legal in order to get even a part-time job.
Consequently, it is very hard for undocumented immigrants to improve their
lives or the lives of their children.

People who oppose immigration amnesty say that it would encourage   5
disrespect for the law. This may be so. Nevertheless, in this case, there is no
good alternative. It would be impossible to track down and deport the more
than twelve million immigrants now in the United States illegally. Moreover,
even if it were possible, a huge labor shortage would result. Another objection
to the idea of amnesty is the claim that undocumented immigrants take jobs
away from American citizens. However, according to the Department of Labor,
this is not true. In fact, undocumented immigrants tend to work at jobs that
citizens are unwilling to take. Finally, some say that the American way of life
is being weakened by illegal immigrants. However, just the opposite is true:
the United States has always been enriched by immigrants, whether legal or
not. In fact, immigration is the lifeblood of the nation.

Granted, undocumented immigrants broke the law when they entered the   6
country. However, even if it were possible to send them all back, the results
would be disastrous for them and for the nation. Therefore, the best solution
is to find a way to allow them to stay. By coming to America, they have shown
that they want to work. They should be allowed to do so. Thus, America can
continue to be a nation of immigrants.

◆ **PRACTICE 14-25**

1. Underline the essay's thesis statement. In your own words, tell what
   position Peter takes in his essay.

   _____

   _____

2. List the facts and examples Peter uses to support his thesis. Where does he include expert opinion?

_____

_____

_____

_____

_____

_____

3. Can you think of any that he doesn't mention?

_____

_____

_____

_____

4. Underline the transitional words and phrases Peter uses to move his argument along.

5. Throughout his essay, Peter acknowledges that some immigrants have broken the law. Do you think this is a good idea? Why or why not?

_____

_____

_____

_____

6. Where does Peter address opposing arguments? What other arguments should he have addressed?

_____

_____

_____

_____

_____

7. What is this essay's greatest strength? What is its greatest weakness?

Strength: _____

Weakness: _____

> **GRAMMAR IN CONTEXT**   **Argument**

When you write an argument essay, you need to show the relationships between your ideas by combining sentences to create **compound sentences** and **complex sentences**.

Undocumented immigrants come to this country to work. ~~They~~ *, and they* often take low-wage jobs that businesses would otherwise find difficult or impossible to fill. (compound sentence)

Now, these immigrants feel they have to hide from authorities. ~~They~~ *because they* are afraid they will be deported. (complex sentence)

For information on how to create compound sentences, see Chapter 16. For information on how to create complex sentences, see Chapter 17.

◆ **PRACTICE 14-26**

Following the writing process outlined in Chapter 12, write an argument essay on one of the following topics.

Teenagers who commit serious crimes should (or should not) be tried as adults.

Citizens without criminal records should (or should not) be permitted to carry concealed weapons.

Human beings should (or should not) be used in medical research experiments.

Parents should (or should not) be permitted to use government vouchers to pay private school tuition.

College financial aid should (or should not) be based solely on merit.

Government funds should (or should not) be used to support the arts.

Public high schools should (or should not) be permitted to distribute condoms to students.

The minimim wage should (or should not) be raised to ten dollars an hour.

College athletes should (or should not) be paid to play.

Convicted felons should (or should not) lose the right to vote.

◆ **PRACTICE 14-27**

The picture on next page shows a driver texting on his cell phone. Many states are considering (or have already adopted) a ban on cell phone use by drivers in moving vehicles. Look at the picture, and then write an argument essay in which you argue either that such a ban is a good idea or that the convenience of cell phones outweighs the possible risk of accidents.

> **Word Power**
> **multitasking** doing several tasks at the same time
>
> **hazardous** dangerous

✓ SELF-ASSESSMENT CHECKLIST:
Writing an Argument Essay

- ☐ Does your introduction present the issue you will discuss and clearly state your position?

- ☐ Is your topic debatable—that is, does the issue you discuss really have two sides?

- ☐ Does your thesis statement clearly express the stand you take on the issue?

- ☐ Have you considered whether readers are likely to be hostile toward, neutral toward, or in agreement with your position— and have you chosen your points accordingly?

- ☐ Is your essay structured as either an inductive argument or a deductive argument?

- ☐ Have you summarized and refuted the major arguments against your position?

- ☐ Do you have enough evidence to support your points?

- ☐ Do all your points clearly support your position?

- ☐ Do you include enough transitional words and phrases to help readers follow the logic of your argument?

- ☐ Does your conclusion follow logically from the points you have made in your essay—and does it summarize and reinforce your main points?

- ☐ What problems did you experience in writing your essay? What would you do differently next time?

✔ REVIEW CHECKLIST:
Patterns of Essay Development

- Exemplification essays use specific examples to support a thesis. (See 14A.)

- Narrative essays tell a story by presenting a series of events in chronological order. (See 14B.)

- Descriptive essays use details to give readers a clear, vivid picture of a person, place, or object. (See 14C.)

- Process essays explain the steps in a procedure, telling how something is (or was) done or how to do something. (See 14D.)

- Cause-and-effect essays identify causes or predict effects. (See 14E.)

- Comparison-and-contrast essays explain how two things are alike or how they are different. (See 14F.)

- Classification essays divide a whole into parts and sort various items into categories. (See 14G.)

- Definition essays use various patterns of development to develop an extended definition. (See 14H.)

- Argument essays take a stand on a debatable issue, using evidence to persuade readers to accept a position. (See 14I.)

UNIT FOUR

WRITING EFFECTIVE SENTENCES

Writing Simple Sentences

PREVIEW

In this chapter, you will learn

- to identify a sentence's subject (15A)
- to identify prepositions and prepositional phrases (15B)
- to distinguish a prepositional phrase from a subject (15B)
- to identify a sentence's verb (15C)

▶ **Word Power**

idol someone who is admired or adored

role model a person who serves as a model for other people to imitate

emulate to strive to equal or excel

■ **WRITING FIRST**

The picture above shows British soccer superstar David Beckham, who now plays for the LA Galaxy. Look at the picture, and then write about a person with whom you would like to trade places. What appeals to you about this person's life?

A **sentence** is a group of words that expresses a complete thought. Every sentence includes both a <u>subject</u> and a <u>verb</u>.

<u>David Beckham</u> <u>is</u> a soccer player.

A Subjects

Every sentence includes a subject. The **subject** of a sentence tells who or what is being talked about in the sentence. Without a subject, a sentence is not complete. In the following three sentences, the subject is underlined.

<u>Derek Walcott</u> won the 1992 Nobel Prize in literature.

<u>He</u> was born in St. Lucia.

<u>St. Lucia</u> is an island in the Caribbean.

The subject of a sentence can be a noun or a pronoun. A **noun** names a person, place, or thing—*Derek Walcott, St. Lucia*. A **pronoun** takes the place of a noun—*I, you, he, she, it, we, they,* and so on.

The subject of a sentence can be *singular* or *plural*. A **singular subject** is one person, place, or thing *(Derek Walcott, St. Lucia, he)*.

A **plural subject** is more than one person, place, or thing *(poems, people, they)*.

Walcott's <u>poems</u> have been collected in books.

A plural subject that joins two subjects with *and* is called a **compound subject**.

<u>St. Lucia and Trinidad</u> are Caribbean islands.

◆ PRACTICE 15-1

In the paragraph below, underline the subject of each sentence.

Example: The poet's <u>parents</u> were both teachers.

ON THE WEB
Visit *Exercise Central* at
bedfordstmartins.com/writingfirst
for more practice.

(1) Derek Walcott was born in 1930. (2) His ancestors came from Africa, the Netherlands, and England. (3) Walcott spent his early years on the Caribbean island of St. Lucia. (4) Writing occupied much of his time. (5) His early poems were published in Trinidad. (6) He later studied in Jamaica and in New York. (7) Walcott eventually became a respected poet. (8) He was a visiting lecturer at Harvard in 1981. (9) In 1990, he published *Omeros*. (10) This long poem about classical Greek heroes is set in the West Indies. (11) In 1992, the poet won a Nobel Prize. (12) Walcott later collaborated with songwriter Paul Simon on *The Capeman*, a Broadway musical.

◆ **PRACTICE 15-2**

Underline the subject in each sentence. Then, write *S* above singular subjects and *P* above plural subjects. Remember, compound subjects are plural.

Example: <u>Agritainment</u> introduces tourists to agriculture and entertainment at the same time.

1. Today, tourists can have fun on working farms.

2. In the past, visitors came to farms just to pick fruits and vegetables.

3. Now, some farms have mazes and petting zoos.

4. One farm has a corn maze every year.

5. Sometimes the maze is in the shape of a train.

6. Visitors can also enjoy giant hay-chute slides, pedal go-carts, and hayrides.

7. Working farms start agritainment businesses to make money.

8. However, insurance companies and lawyers worry about the dangers of agritainment.

9. Tourists have gotten animal bites, fallen from rides and machinery, and gotten food poisoning.

10. Agritainment, like other businesses, has advantages and disadvantages.

■ **WRITING FIRST: Flashback**

Look back at your response to the Writing First activity on page 245. Underline the subject of each of your sentences. Then, list all the subjects on the lines below.

_____   _____

_____   _____

_____   _____

_____   _____

_____   _____

Now, write *S* beside each singular subject and *P* beside each plural subject. (Remember that a compound subject is plural.)

B **Prepositional Phrases**

A **prepositional phrase** consists of a **preposition** (a word such as *on, to, in,* or *with*) and its **object** (the noun or pronoun it introduces).

Preposition	+	Object	=	Prepositional Phrase
on		the stage		on the stage
to		Nia's house		to Nia's house
in		my new car		in my new car
with		them		with them

Because the object of a preposition is a noun or a pronoun, it may seem to be the subject of a sentence. However, the object of a preposition can never be the subject of a sentence. To identify a sentence's true subject, cross out each prepositional phrase. (Remember, every prepositional phrase is introduced by a preposition.)

subject prep phrase
The <u>cost</u> ~~of the repairs~~ was astronomical.

prep phrase ・ *prep phrase* ・ *subject*
~~At the end of the novel~~, ~~after an exciting chase~~, the <u>lovers</u> flee
prep phrase
~~to Mexico~~.

Frequently Used Prepositions

about	before	except	off	toward
above	behind	for	on	under
across	below	from	onto	underneath
after	beneath	in	out	until
against	beside	inside	outside	up
along	between	into	over	upon
among	beyond	like	through	with
around	by	near	throughout	within
as	despite	of	to	without
at	during			

◆ **PRACTICE 15-3**

Each of the following sentences includes at least one prepositional phrase. To identify each sentence's subject, begin by crossing out each prepositional phrase. Then, underline the subject of the sentence.

Example: ~~In presidential elections~~, third-party <u>candidates</u> have attracted many voters.

(1) With more than 27 percent of the vote, Theodore Roosevelt was the strongest third-party presidential candidate in history. (2) In the 1912 election, Roosevelt ran second to Woodrow Wilson. (3) Before Roosevelt,

no third-party candidate had won a significant number of votes. (4) In recent years, however, some candidates of other parties have done quite well. (5) In 1968, George C. Wallace of the American Independent Party won 13 percent of the vote. (6) In 1980, John B. Anderson, an Independent, got almost 7 percent of the vote. (7) With nearly 19 percent of the popular vote, Ross Perot ran a strong race against Democrat Bill Clinton and Republican George Bush in 1992. (8) In 2000, with the support of many environmentalists, Ralph Nader ran for the presidency. (9) In 2004, Nader was also on the ballot in many states. (10) The two-party system of the United States has survived despite many challenges by third-party candidates.

■ WRITING FIRST: Flashback

Look back at your response to the Writing First activity on page 245. Have you used any prepositional phrases? List them on the lines below.

_____ _____ _____ _____

_____ _____ _____ _____

_____ _____ _____ _____

_____ _____ _____ _____

C Verbs

In addition to its subject, every sentence also includes a verb. This **verb** (also called a **predicate**) tells what the subject does or connects the subject to words that describe or rename it. Without a verb, a sentence is not complete.

Action Verbs

An **action verb** tells what the subject does, did, or will do.

Nomar Garciaparra <u>plays</u> baseball.
Renee <u>will drive</u> to Tampa on Friday.
Amelia Earhart <u>flew</u> across the Atlantic.

Action verbs can also show mental and emotional actions.

Travis always <u><u>worries</u></u> about his job.

Sometimes, the subject of a sentence performs more than one action. In this case, the sentence includes two or more action verbs joined to form a **compound predicate**.

He <u><u>hit</u></u> the ball, <u><u>threw</u></u> down his bat, and <u><u>ran</u></u> toward first base.

ON THE WEB

Visit *Exercise Central* at **bedfordstmartins.com/writingfirst** for more practice.

◆ PRACTICE 15-4

In the following sentences, underline each action verb twice. Some sentences contain more than one action verb.

1. Many critics see one romance novel as just like another.

2. The plot usually involves a beautiful young woman, the heroine, in some kind of danger.

3. A handsome stranger offers his help.

4. At first, the heroine distrusts him.

5. Then, another man enters the story and wins the heroine's trust.

6. Readers, however, see this man as an evil villain.

7. Almost too late, the heroine too realizes the truth.

8. Luckily, the handsome hero returns and saves her from a nasty fate.

9. Many readers enjoy the predictable plots of romance novels.

10. However, most literary critics dislike these books.

Linking Verbs

A **linking verb** does not show action. Instead, it connects the subject to a word or words that describe or rename it. The linking verb tells what the subject is (or what it was, will be, or seems to be).

A googolplex <u><u>is</u></u> an extremely large number.

Many linking verbs, like *is*, are forms of the verb *be*. Other linking verbs refer to the senses (*look, feel,* and so on).

The photocopy <u><u>looks</u></u> blurry.
Some students <u><u>feel</u></u> anxious about the future.

Frequently Used Linking Verbs

act	feel	seem
appear	get	smell
be (am, is, are,	grow	sound
was, were)	look	taste
become	remain	turn

◆ PRACTICE 15-5

In the following sentences, underline each linking verb twice.

1. Urban legends are folk tales created to teach a lesson.

2. One familiar urban legend is the story of Hookman.

3. According to this story, a young couple is alone in Lovers' Lane.

4. The lovers are in a car, listening to a radio announcement.

5. An escaped murderer is nearby.

6. The murderer's left hand is a hook.

7. The young woman becomes hysterical.

8. Suddenly, Lovers' Lane seems very dangerous.

9. Later, they are shocked to see a hook hanging from the passenger door handle.

10. The purpose of this legend is to convince young people to avoid dangerous places.

◆ PRACTICE 15-6

Underline every verb in each of the following sentences twice. Remember that a verb can be an action verb or a linking verb.

Example: Infomercials <u>are</u> long television commercials.

(1) The word *infomercial* comes from the words *information* and *commercial*. (2) Like commercials, infomercials sell products. (3) Unlike commercials, infomercials sell products directly to viewers. (4) Infomercial hosts are "experts" or celebrities. (5) Some infomercials use talk show or news report formats. (6) Many infomercial products are available only on television. (7) Famous products include the Food Saver, Mighty Putty, and the Ginsu knife. (8) Many infomercial products are not good bargains. (9) Still, television viewers love to buy them. (10) Infomercials earn $2 billion every year.

Helping Verbs

Many verbs consist of more than one word. For example, the verb in the following sentence consists of two words.

Minh <u>must make</u> a decision about his future.

In this sentence, *make* is the **main verb**, and *must* is a **helping verb**.

FOCUS **Helping Verbs**

Helping verbs (also called **auxiliary verbs**) include forms of *be*, *have*, and *do* as well as the words *must, will, can, could, may, might, should,* and *would*.

- ■ Some helping verbs, such as forms of *be* and *have*, combine with main verbs to give information about when the action occurs.
- ■ Forms of *do* combine with main verbs to form questions and negative statements.
- ■ Some helping verbs indicate willingness (*can*), possibility (*may*), necessity (*should*), obligation (*must*), and so on.

A sentence's **complete verb** is made up of a main verb plus any helping verbs that accompany it. In the following sentences, the complete verb is underlined twice, and the helping verbs are checkmarked.

Minh <u><u>should have gone</u></u> earlier.

<u><u>Did</u></u> Minh <u><u>ask</u></u> the right questions?

Minh <u><u>will work</u></u> hard.

Minh <u><u>can</u></u> really <u><u>succeed</u></u>.

FOCUS **Helping Verbs with Participles**

Participles, such as *going* and *gone*, cannot stand alone as main verbs in a sentence. They need a helping verb to make them complete.

INCORRECT   Minh going to the library.

CORRECT   Minh <u>is going</u> to the library.

INCORRECT   Minh gone to the library.

CORRECT   Minh <u>has gone</u> to the library.

◆ **PRACTICE 15-7**

The verbs in the sentences that follow consist of a main verb and one or more helping verbs. In each sentence, underline the complete verb twice, and put a check mark above the helping verb(s).

Example: The Salk polio vaccine <u>was given</u> to more than a million schoolchildren in 1954.

(1) By the 1950s, parents had become terrified of polio. (2) For years, it had puzzled doctors and researchers. (3) Thousands had become ill each year in the United States alone. (4) Children should have been playing happily. (5) Instead, they would get very sick. (6) Polio was sometimes called infantile paralysis. (7) In fact, it did cause paralysis in children and in adults as well. (8) Some patients could breathe only with the help of machines called iron lungs. (9) Others would remain in wheelchairs for life. (10) By 1960, Jonas Salk's vaccine had reduced the incidence of polio in the United States by more than 90 percent.

■ **WRITING FIRST: Flashback**

Look back at your response to the Writing First activity on page 245. In each sentence, underline the complete verb twice, and put a check mark above each helping verb. Then, copy the helping verbs on the lines below.

_____ _____ _____ _____

_____ _____ _____ _____

■ **WRITING FIRST: Revising and Editing**

Look back at your response to the Writing First activity on page 245. Circle every action verb. Then, try to replace some of them with different action verbs that express more precisely what the subject of each sentence is, was, or will be doing. For example, you might replace *like* with *admire* or *respect*.

CHAPTER REVIEW

◆ **EDITING PRACTICE**

Read the following student essay. Underline the subject of each sentence once, and underline the complete verb of each sentence twice. If you have trouble locating the subject, try crossing out the prepositional phrases. The first sentence has been done for you.

Hip-Hop Pioneer

Hip-hop is extremely popular ~~among young people~~. Russell Simmons is one of the most important people in hip-hop. He started the record label Def Jam. Simmons is responsible for getting hip-hop music accepted by mainstream audiences. Simmons also showed the world a successful black-owned business.

Simmons was born in Queens, New York, in 1957. He began to promote hip-hop in 1978. Simmons started to represent rap artists with his production company, Rush Productions. One of his clients was his own brother, Joseph. Simmons called Joseph's group Run-D.M.C. With producer Rick Rubin, Simmons started the Def Jam record label. Def Jam's artists had a rebellious quality. Many listeners loved them.

Def Jam was soon known as a creative company. It introduced the work of many black artists (as well as some white groups) to a multicultural audience. Def Jam released recordings of Public Enemy, the Beastie Boys, and other hip-hop artists. The movie *Krush Groove* dramatized the founding of the company. It was a big success with fans of hip-hop. In 1991, Simmons began the HBO Series *Def Comedy Jam*. This series featured the uncensored comedy of many black comedians, including Martin Lawrence, Chris Rock, and Jamie Foxx. Simmons also made some movies. One was *The Nutty Professor*. This film marked the comeback of actor Eddie Murphy.

Russell Simmons is a very successful businessman. In addition to Def Jam, Simmons started other businesses. One of them was Phat Farm, a line of clothing for men. Phat Farm was followed by Baby Phat. This was a line of women's clothing. Simmons also started *One World*. This magazine focused on the hip-hop lifestyle. In addition, he founded an advertising agency, Rush Media Company. In

Russell Simmons at the NAACP Image Awards, 2007

The Beastie Boys at the MTV Video Music Awards, 2004

1999, Simmons sold his share of Def Jam for $100 million. By then, he was highly respected as both a music promoter and a businessman.

In the past, hip-hop was criticized as a fad. Now, however, hip-hop has entered the broader American culture. More than anyone, Russell Simmons has been responsible for hip-hop's success.

◆ COLLABORATIVE ACTIVITIES

1. Fold a sheet of paper in half vertically. Working in a group of three or four students, spend two minutes listing as many nouns as you can in the column to the left of the fold. When your time is up, exchange papers with another group of students. Limiting yourselves to five minutes, write an appropriate action verb beside each noun. Each noun will now be the subject of a short sentence.

2. Choose five short sentences from those you wrote for Collaborative Activity 1. Working in the same group, collaborate to create more fully developed sentences. First, expand each subject by adding words or prepositional phrases that give more information about the subject. (For example, you could expand *boat* to *the small, leaky boat with the red sail*.) Then, expand each sentence further, adding ideas after the verb. (For example, the sentence *The boat bounced* could become *The small, leaky boat with the red sail bounced helplessly on the water*.)

3. Work in a group of three or four students to write one original sentence for each of the linking verbs listed on page 251. When you have finished, exchange papers with another group. Now, try to add words and phrases to the other group's sentences to make them more interesting.

☑ REVIEW CHECKLIST:
Writing Simple Sentences

▪ A sentence expresses a complete thought. The subject tells who or what is being talked about in the sentence. (See 15A.)

▪ A prepositional phrase consists of a preposition and its object (the noun or pronoun it introduces). (See 15B.)

▪ The object of a preposition cannot be the subject of a sentence. (See 15B.)

▪ An action verb tells what the subject does, did, or will do. (See 15C.)

▪ A linking verb connects the subject to a word or words that describe or rename it. (See 15C.)

▪ Many verbs are made up of more than one word. The complete verb in a sentence includes the main verb plus any helping verbs. (See 15C.)

CHAPTER 16

Writing Compound Sentences

■ **WRITING FIRST**

The picture above shows a high school graduation with two of the graduating students holding their children. Look at the picture, and then write a letter to the president of your college explaining why your campus needs a day-care center. (If your school already has a day-care center, explain why it deserves continued—or increased—funding.)

The most basic kind of sentence, a **simple sentence**, consists of a single **independent clause**: one <u>subject</u> and one <u>verb</u>.

European <u>immigrants</u> <u>arrived</u> at Ellis Island.

A **compound sentence** is made up of two or more simple sentences (independent clauses).

A Using Coordinating Conjunctions

One way to form a compound sentence is by joining two independent clauses with a **coordinating conjunction** preceded by a comma.

European immigrants arrived at Ellis Island, <u>but</u> Asian immigrants arrived at Angel Island.

> ► **Word Power**
>
> **coordinate** equal in importance, rank, or degree

Coordinating Conjunctions

and	for	or	yet
but	nor	so	

Coordinating conjunctions join two ideas of equal importance. They describe the relationship between two ideas, showing how and why the ideas are related. Different coordinating conjunctions have different meanings.

■ To indicate addition, use *and.*

He acts like a child, <u>and</u> people think he is cute.

■ To indicate contrast or contradiction, use *but* or *yet.*

He acts like a child, <u>but</u> he is an adult.

He acts like a child, <u>yet</u> he longs to be taken seriously.

■ To indicate a cause-and-effect relationship, use *so* or *for.*

He acts like a child, <u>so</u> we treat him like one.

He acts like a child, <u>for</u> he craves attention.

■ To present alternatives, use *or.*

He acts like a child, <u>or</u> he is ignored.

■ To eliminate alternatives, use *nor.*

He does not act like a child, <u>nor</u> does he look like one.

FOCUS **Commas with Coordinating Conjunctions**

When you use a coordinating conjunction to link two independent clauses into a single compound sentence, always put a comma before the coordinating conjunction.

We can stand in line all night, or we can go home now.

Remember, though, not to use a comma before a coordinating conjunction unless it links two *complete independent clauses*.

INCORRECT   We can stand in line all night, or go home now.

CORRECT   We can stand in line all night or go home now.

ON THE WEB
Visit *Exercise Central* at
bedfordstmartins.com/writingfirst
for more practice.

◆ PRACTICE 16-1

Fill in the coordinating conjunction—*and, but, for, nor, or, so,* or *yet*—that most logically links the two parts of each compound sentence. Remember to insert a comma before each coordinating conjunction.

Example: Fairy tales have been told by many people around the

world , _but_ the stories by two German brothers may be the most

famous.

(1) Jakob and Wilhelm Grimm lived in the nineteenth century_____ they wrote many well-known fairy tales. (2) Most people think fondly of fairy tales _____the Brothers Grimm wrote many unpleasant and violent stories. (3) In their best-known works, children are abused _____ endings are not always happy. (4) Either innocent children are brutally punished for no reason ___they are neglected. (5) For example, in "Hansel and Gretel," the stepmother mistreats the children _____their father abandons them in the woods. (6) In this story, the events are horrifying _____the ending is still happy. (7) The children outwit the evil adults _____they escape unharmed. (8) Apparently, they are not injured physically____are they harmed emotionally. (9) Nevertheless, their story can hardly be called pleasant ____it remains a story of child abuse and neglect.

◆ **PRACTICE 16-2**

Join each of the following pairs of independent clauses with a coordinating conjunction. Be sure to place a comma before the coordinating conjunction.

Example: A computer makes drafting essays easier. ~~It~~ also makes
, and it

revision easier.

1. Training a dog to heel is difficult. Dogs naturally resist strict control.

2. A bodhran is an Irish drum. It is played with a wooden stick.

3. Students should spend two hours of study time for each hour of class time. They may not do well in the course.

4. Years ago, students wrote their lessons on slates. The teacher could correct each student's work individually.

5. Each state in the United States has two senators. The number of representatives depends on a state's population.

6. In 1973, only 2.5 percent of those in the U.S. military were women. By 2008, that percentage had increased to 20 percent.

7. A "small craft advisory" warns boaters of bad weather conditions. These conditions can be dangerous to small boats.

8. A DVD looks like a CD. It can hold fifteen times as much information.

9. Hip-hop fashions include sneakers and baggy pants. These styles are very popular among today's young men.

10. Multiple births have become more and more common. Even septuplets have a reasonable chance of survival today.

◆ **PRACTICE 16-3**

Add coordinating conjunctions to combine some of the simple sentences in the following paragraph. Remember to put a comma before each coordinating conjunction you add.

Example: Years ago, few Americans lived to be one hundred. ~~Today,~~
, but today,

there are over 32,000 centenarians.

(1) Diet, exercise, and family history may explain centenarians' long lives. (2) This is not the whole story. (3) A recent study showed surprising similarities among centenarians. (4) They did not all avoid tobacco and

alcohol. (5) They did not have low-fat diets. (6) In fact, they ate relatively large amounts of fat, cholesterol, and sugar. (7) Diet could not explain their long lives. (8) They did, however, share four key traits. (9) First, all the centenarians were optimistic about life. (10) All were positive thinkers. (11) They also had deep religious faith. (12) In addition, they had all continued to lead physically active lives. (13) They remained mobile even as elderly people. (14) Finally, all were able to adapt to loss. (15) They had all lost friends, spouses, or children. (16) They were able to get on with their lives.

◆ **PRACTICE 16-4**

Write another simple sentence to follow each of the sentences below. Then, connect the sentences with a coordinating conjunction and the correct punctuation.

> **Example:** Many patients need organ transplants/, *but there is a serious*
>
> *shortage of organ donors.*

1. Smoking in bed is dangerous. _____

   _____

2. Some cars are equipped with GPS systems. _____

   _____

3. Diamonds are very expensive. _____

   _____

4. Kangaroos carry their young in pouches. _____

   _____

5. Dancing is good exercise. _____

   _____

6. Motorcycle helmet laws have been dropped in some states. _____

   _____

7. Some businesses sponsor bowling leagues for their employees. _____

   _____

8. Pretzels are a healthier snack than potato chips. _____

   _____

9. Many so-called juices actually contain very little real fruit juice. _____

_____

10. People tend to resist change. _____

_____

■ **WRITING FIRST: Flashback**

Look back at your response to the Writing First activity on page 256. If you see any compound sentences, bracket them. If you see any pairs of simple sentences that could be combined into one compound sentence, rewrite them below, joining them with appropriate coordinating conjunctions.

1. _____

_____

2. _____

_____

3. _____

_____

Be sure each of your new compound sentences includes a comma before the coordinating conjunction.

B   Using Semicolons

Another way to create a compound sentence is by joining two simple sentences (independent clauses) with a **semicolon**.

The AIDS quilt contains thousands of panels; each panel is rectangular.

A semicolon generally connects clauses whose ideas are closely linked.

◆ **PRACTICE 16-5**

Each of the following items consists of one simple sentence. Create a compound sentence for each item by changing the period to a semicolon and then adding another simple sentence.

Example: My brother is addicted to fast food/; *he eats it every day.*

■ **Culture Clue**

The *AIDS Memorial Quilt* is a huge quilt whose individual squares celebrate the lives of people who have died from AIDS, Acquired Immune Deficiency Syndrome.

1. Fast-food restaurants are an American institution. _____

_____

2. Families often eat at these restaurants. _____

_____

3. Many teenagers work there. _____

_____

4. McDonald's is known for its hamburgers. _____

_____

5. KFC is famous for its fried chicken. _____

_____

6. Taco Bell serves Mexican-style food. _____

_____

7. Pizza Hut specializes in pizza. _____

_____

8. Many fast-food restaurants offer some low-fat menu items. _____

_____

9. Some offer recyclable packaging. _____

_____

10. Some even have playgrounds. _____

_____

■ **Culture Clue**

Fast food is inexpensive food that can be prepared and served quickly, such as hamburgers, french fries, milkshakes, etc.

■ **WRITING FIRST: Flashback**

Look back at your response to the Writing First activity on page 256. Do you see any pairs of simple sentences that you could connect with semicolons? If so, rewrite them on the lines below, linking each pair with a semicolon.

_____

_____

_____

_____

_____

C   Using Transitional Words and Phrases

Another way to create a compound sentence is by combining two simple sentences (independent clauses) with a **transitional word or phrase**. When you use a transitional word or phrase to join two sentences, a semicolon always comes *before* the transitional word or phrase, and a comma always comes *after* it.

> Some college students receive grants; however, others must take out loans.

> He had a miserable time at the party; in addition, he lost his wallet.

Frequently Used Transitional Words

also	instead	still
besides	later	subsequently
consequently	meanwhile	then
eventually	moreover	therefore
finally	nevertheless	thus
furthermore	now	
however	otherwise	

Frequently Used Transitional Phrases

after all	in comparison
as a result	in contrast
at the same time	in fact
for example	in other words
for instance	of course
in addition	on the contrary

Adding a transitional word or phrase makes the connection between ideas in a sentence clearer and more precise than it would be if the ideas were linked with just a semicolon. Different transitional words and phrases convey different meanings.

- Some signal addition (*also, besides, furthermore, in addition, moreover,* and so on).

  > I have a lot on my mind; also, I have a lot of things to do.

- Some make causal connections (*therefore, as a result, consequently, thus,* and so on).

  > I have a lot on my mind; therefore, it is hard to concentrate.

16 C

■ Some indicate contradiction or contrast (*nevertheless, however, in contrast, still,* and so on).

> I have a lot on my mind; <u>still</u>, I must try to relax.

■ Some present alternatives (*instead, on the contrary, otherwise,* and so on).

> I have a lot on my mind; <u>otherwise</u>, I could relax.

> I will try not to think; <u>instead</u>, I will relax.

■ Some indicate time sequence (*eventually, finally, at the same time, later, meanwhile, now, subsequently, then,* and so on).

> I have a lot on my mind; <u>meanwhile</u>, I still have work to do.

◆ PRACTICE 16-6

Add semicolons and commas where required to set off transitional words and phrases that join two independent clauses.

Example: Ketchup is a popular condiment; therefore, it is available in almost every restaurant.

ON THE WEB
Visit *Exercise Central* at
bedfordstmartins.com/writingfirst
for more practice.

> ► **Word Power**
> **condiment** a prepared
> sauce or pickle used to add
> flavor to food

(1) Andrew F. Smith, a food historian, wrote a book about the tomato later he wrote a book about ketchup. (2) This book, *Pure Ketchup*, was a big project in fact Smith worked on it for five years. (3) The word *ketchup* may have come from a Chinese word however Smith is not certain of the word's origins. (4) Ketchup has existed since ancient times in other words it is a very old product. (5) Ketchup has changed a lot over the years for example special dyes were developed in the nineteenth century to make it red. (6) Smith discusses many other changes for instance preservative-free ketchup was invented in 1907. (7) Ketchup is now used by people in many cultures still salsa is more popular than ketchup in the United States. (8) Today, designer ketchups are being developed meanwhile Heinz has introduced green and purple ketchup in squeeze bottles. (9) Some of today's ketchups are chunky in addition some ketchups are spicy. (10) Ketchup continues to change however Smith is now working on a book about the history of popcorn.

◆ PRACTICE 16-7

Consulting the lists of transitional words and phrases on page 263, choose a word or phrase that logically connects each pair of independent

clauses below into one compound sentence. Be sure to punctuate appropriately.

Example: Every year since 1927, *Time* magazine has chosen a Man
of the Year/ ~~The~~ Man of the Year has not always been a man.

    ; however, the

(1) The Man of the Year must have greatly influenced the previous year's events. The choice is often a prominent politician. (2) In the 1920s and 1930s, world leaders were often chosen. Franklin Delano Roosevelt was chosen twice. (3) During World War II, Hitler, Stalin, Churchill, and Roosevelt were all chosen. Stalin was featured twice. (4) Occasionally, the Man of the Year was not an individual. In 1950, it was The American Fighting Man. (5) Only a few women have been selected. Queen Elizabeth II of England was featured in 1952. (6) Very few people of color have been named Man of the Year. Martin Luther King Jr. was honored in 1963. (7) The Man of the Year is not always a person. The Computer was selected in 1982 and Endangered Earth in 1988. (8) In 2006, *Time* did not choose a specific person. Its person of the year was "You."

◆ PRACTICE 16-8

Add the suggested transitional word or phrase to each of the simple sentences below. Then, create a compound sentence by adding a new independent clause to follow it. Be sure to punctuate correctly.

Example: Commuting students do not really experience campus life. (however)

Commuting students do not really experience campus life; however, there are

some benefits to being a commuter.

1. Campus residents may have a better college experience. (still)

    _____

    _____

2. Living at home means students can have home-cooked meals. (in contrast)

    _____

    _____

3. Commuters have a wide choice of jobs in the community. (on the other hand)

_____

_____

4. Commuters get to live with their families. (however)

_____

_____

5. There are also some disadvantages to being a commuter. (for example)

_____

_____

6. Unlike dorm students, most commuters have family responsibilities. (in fact)

_____

_____

7. Commuters might have to help take care of their parents or grandparents. (in addition)

_____

_____

8. Commuters might need a car to get to school. (consequently)

_____

_____

9. Younger commuters may be under the watchful eyes of their parents. (of course)

_____

_____

10. Commuting to college has pros and cons. (therefore)

_____

_____

◆ **PRACTICE 16-9**

Using the specified topics and transitional words and phrases, create five compound sentences. Be sure to punctuate appropriately.

Example
Topic: fad diets
Transitional phrase: for example

People are always falling for fad diets; for example, some people eat only

pineapple to lose weight.

1. *Topic:* laws to protect people with disabilities
Transitional phrase: in addition

_____

_____

2. *Topic:* single men and women as adoptive parents
Transitional word: however

_____

_____

3. *Topic:* prayer in public schools
Transitional word: therefore

_____

_____

4. *Topic:* high school proms
Transitional word: also

_____

_____

5. *Topic:* course requirements at your school
Transitional word: instead

_____

_____

■ **WRITING FIRST: Flashback**

Look back at your response to the Writing First activity on
page 256. Have you used any transitional words or phrases to
link independent clauses? If so, check to make sure that you
have punctuated them correctly. Then, check to see that you
have used the word or phrase that best shows the relationship
between the ideas in the two independent clauses. Revise your
work if necessary.

■ **WRITING FIRST: Revising and Editing**

Look back at your response to the Writing First activity on page 256. Now, try to add one of the new compound sentences you created in the Flashback activities on pages 261 and 262. Then, check each compound sentence to make sure you have used the coordinating conjunction or transitional word or phrase that best conveys your meaning and that you have punctuated these sentences correctly. When you have finished, look over a piece of writing you have done in response to another assignment, and try combining some pairs of simple sentences into compound sentences.

CHAPTER REVIEW

◆ EDITING PRACTICE

Read the following student essay. Then, create compound sentences by linking pairs of simple sentences where appropriate, joining them with a coordinating conjunction, a semicolon, or a transitional word or phrase. Remember to put commas before coordinating conjunctions and to use semicolons and commas correctly with transitional words and phrases. The first two sentences have been combined for you.

■ **Culture Clue**

Ukraine is a country in Eastern Europe that borders Russia.

Map of Ukraine

My Grandfather's Life

My great-grandparents were born in Ukraine,͟ ̶T̶h̶e̶y̶ raised my grandfather in *, but they* western Pennsylvania. The ninth of their ten children, he had a life I cannot begin to imagine. To me, he was my big, strong, powerful grandfather. He was also a child of poverty.

My great-grandfather worked for the American Car Foundry. The family lived in a company house. They shopped at the company store. In 1934, my great-grandfather was laid off. He went to work digging sewer lines for the government. At that time, the family was on welfare. Every week, they were entitled to get food rations. My grandfather would go to pick up the food. The family desperately needed the prunes, beans, flour, margarine, and other things.

For years, my grandfather wore his brothers' hand-me-down clothes. He wore thrift-shop shoes with cardboard over the holes in the soles. He was often hungry. He would sometimes sit by the side of the railroad tracks, waiting for the engineer to throw him an orange. My grandfather would do any job to earn a quarter. Once, he weeded a mile-long row of tomato plants. For this work, he was paid twenty-five cents and a pack of NECCO wafers.

My grandfather saved his pennies. Eventually, he was able to buy a used bicycle for two dollars. He dropped out of school at fourteen and got a job. The family badly needed his income. He woke up every day at 4 a.m.. He rode his bike to his job at a meatpacking plant. He worked for fifty cents a day.

In 1943, at the age of seventeen, my grandfather joined the U.S. Navy. He discovered a new world. For the first time in his life, he had enough to eat. He was always first in line at the mess hall. He went back for seconds and thirds before anyone else. After the war ended in 1945, he was discharged from the Navy. He went to work in a meat market in New York City. The only trade he knew was the meat business. Three years later, when he had saved enough to open his own store, Pete's Quality Meats, he knew his life of poverty was finally over.

> **Culture Clue**
> *NECCO* (New England Confectionery Company) dates back to 1847 and is the oldest candy manufacturer in the United States.

World War II sailor

◆ COLLABORATIVE ACTIVITIES

1. Working in a small group, pair each of the simple sentences in the left-hand column below with a sentence in the right-hand column to create ten compound sentences. Use as many different coordinating conjunctions as you can to connect the independent clauses. Be sure each coordinating conjunction you choose conveys a logical relationship between ideas, and remember to put a comma before each one. You may use some of the listed sentences more than once. *Note:* Many different combinations—some serious and factually accurate, some humorous—are possible.

Some dogs wear little sweaters.	Many are named Hamlet.
Pit bulls are raised to fight.	They live in groups.
Bonobos are pygmy chimpanzees.	One even sings Christmas carols.
	They can wear bandanas.
Many people fear Dobermans.	They can play Frisbee.
Leopards have spots.	Many live in equatorial Zaire.
Dalmations can live in firehouses.	Some people think they are gentle.
Horses can wear blankets.	They don't get cold in winter.
All mules are sterile.	They are half horse and half donkey.
Great Danes are huge dogs.	
Parrots can often speak.	They can be unpredictable.

2. Work in a group of three or four students to create a cast of five characters for a movie, a television pilot, or a music video. Working individually, write five descriptive simple sentences—one about each character. Then, exchange papers with another student. Add a semicolon and a transitional word or phrase to each sentence on the list to create five new compound sentences.

Example

ORIGINAL   Mark is a handsome heartthrob.
SENTENCE

NEW SENTENCE   Mark is a handsome heartthrob; unfortunately, he has green dreadlocks.

☑ REVIEW CHECKLIST:
Writing Compound Sentences

- ▢ A compound sentence is made up of two simple sentences (independent clauses).

- ▢ A coordinating conjunction—*and, but, for, nor, or, so,* or *yet*—can join two independent clauses into one compound sentence. A comma always comes before the coordinating conjunction. (See 16A.)

- ▢ A semicolon can join two independent clauses into one compound sentence. (See 16B.)

- ▢ A transitional word or phrase can also join two independent clauses into one compound sentence. When it joins two independent clauses, a transitional word or phrase is always preceded by a semicolon and followed by a comma. (See 16C.)

Writing Complex Sentences

PREVIEW

In this chapter, you will learn

- to identify complex sentences (17A)
- to use subordinating conjunctions to form complex sentences (17B)
- to use relative pronouns to form complex sentences (17C)

■ WRITING FIRST

In 1963, the U.S. government began requiring that all cigarette packages include a warning label. The picture above shows some of these labels. Look at the picture, and then write about a law that you think should be passed, and explain why you think this law is necessary.

▶ **Word Power**
legislation a propsed or enacted law

enact to make into law

As you learned in Chapter 16, an **independent clause** can stand alone as a sentence.

INDEPENDENT   The art <u>exhibit</u> <u>was</u> controversial.
CLAUSE

However, a **dependent clause** cannot stand alone as a sentence.

DEPENDENT   Because the art exhibit was controversial
CLAUSE

What happened because the exhibit was controversial? To answer this question, you need to add an independent clause that completes the idea begun in the dependent clause. The result is a **complex sentence**—a sentence that consists of one independent clause and one or more dependent clauses.

┌──────────── DEPENDENT CLAUSE ────────────┐ ┌── INDEPENDENT CLAUSE ──┐
COMPLEX   Because the art exhibit was controversial, many people came
SENTENCE to see the paintings.

◆ PRACTICE 17-1

In the blank following each of the items below, indicate whether the group of words is an independent clause (*IC*) or a dependent clause (*DC*).

Example: The American diner began as a covered horse-drawn lunch

wagon. __*IC*__

1. When lunch wagons added stools and counters in the late 1800s. _____

2. Some expanded lunch wagons had fancy woodwork and glass. _____

3. Because of laws that restricted operating hours. _____

4. Lunch wagon operators started opening diners. _____

5. The name *diner* came from railroad dining cars. _____

6. Because some diners were converted railroad cars. _____

7. Diners added bathrooms, booths, and landscaping in the 1920s to attract female customers. _____

8. Even though many diners moved from cities to suburbs after World War II. _____

9. Diners later competed with fast-food restaurants by adding brick walls and shingled roofs. _____

■ **Culture Clue**

A *diner* is a type of informal restaurant that serves typically American food (e.g., pancakes, hamburgers, sandwiches, and coffee). It usually includes a counter to sit at as well as booths or tables.

10. Who by the 1980s made railroad-style diners popular again in the United States and Europe. _____

◆ PRACTICE 17-2

In the blank following each of the items below, indicate whether the group of words is an independent clause (*IC*) or a dependent clause (*DC*).

Example: When novelist Toni Morrison was born in Ohio in 1931.

_DC_

1. As a young reader, Toni Morrison liked the classic Russian novelists.

   _____

2. After she graduated from Howard University with a bachelor's degree in English. _____

3. Morrison based her novel *The Bluest Eye* on a childhood friend's prayers to God for blue eyes. _____

4. While she raised two sons as a single mother and worked as an editor at Random House. _____

5. As her reputation as a novelist grew with the publication of *Song of Solomon* and *Tar Baby*. _____

6. Her picture appeared on the cover of *Newsweek* in 1981. _____

7. Before her novel *Beloved* won the 1988 Pulitzer Prize for fiction. _____

8. *Beloved* was later made into a film starring Oprah Winfrey. _____

9. In 1993, Morrison became the first African-American woman to win the Nobel Prize in Literature. _____

10. Who published the novel *Paradise* in 1998 to mixed reviews. _____

B   Using Subordinating Conjunctions

One way to form a complex sentence is to use a **subordinating conjunction**—a word like *although* or *because*—to join two simple sentences (independent clauses).

> **Word Power**
> **subordinate** (adj) being lower in rank or position; secondary in importance

TWO SIMPLE SENTENCES	Muhammad Ali was stripped of his heavyweight title for refusing to go into the army. Many people admired his antiwar position.

COMPLEX SENTENCE ┌─────── DEPENDENT CLAUSE ───────┐ **Although Muhammad Ali was stripped of his heavy-** **weight title for refusing to go into the army,** many people admired his antiwar position.

Frequently Used Subordinating Conjunctions

after	even though	since	whenever
although	if	so that	where
as	if only	than	whereas
as if	in order that	that	wherever
as though	now that	though	whether
because	once	unless	while
before	provided that	until	
even if	rather than	when	

Different subordinating conjunctions express different relationships between dependent and independent clauses.

Relationship between Clauses	Subordinating Conjunction	Example
Time	after, before, since, until, when, when-ever, while	When the whale surfaced, Ahab threw his harpoon.
Reason or cause	as, because	Scientists scaled back the project because the government cut funds.
Result or effect	in order that, so that	So that students' math scores will improve, many schools have begun special programs.
Condition	even if, if, unless	The rain forest may disappear unless steps are taken immediately.
Contrast	although, even though, though	Although Thomas Edison had almost no formal education, he was a successful inventor.
Location	where, wherever	Pittsburgh was built where the Allegheny and Monongahela Rivers meet.

FOCUS Punctuating with Subordinating Conjunctions

In a complex sentence, use a comma after the dependent clause. Do not use a comma after the independent clause.

```
┌──────── DEPENDENT CLAUSE ────────┐ ┌── INDEPENDENT CLAUSE ──┐
Although she wore the scarlet letter, Hester carried herself
proudly.
```

```
┌──────── INDEPENDENT CLAUSE ────────┐ ┌──────── DEPENDENT CLAUSE ────────┐
Hester carried herself proudly although she wore the scarlet
letter.
```

◆ PRACTICE 17-3

In the blank in each of the sentences below, write an appropriate subordinating conjunction. Look at the list of subordinating conjunctions on page 274 to help you choose a conjunction that establishes a logical relationship between the two clauses it links. (The required punctuation has already been added.)

Example: _____*When*_____ he was only six years old, Freddy Adu was playing soccer games with grown men.

(1) Freddy Adu's family moved from Ghana to the United States _____ he was still a young boy. (2) Freddy did not play organized soccer _____ he was in the fourth grade. (3) _____ he was still a teenager, Freddy became one of America's most famous soccer players. (4) His talent for soccer excites even professional players and coaches _____ they see him play. (5) _____ he was thirteen, he has been recruited by some of the best teams in the world. (6) One team offered his mother $750,000 _____ Freddy would play for them. (7) _____ she needed the money, his mother turned down every offer. (8) The offers kept coming in _____ Freddy continued to win major competitions for young players. (9) _____ Freddy joined DC United, he became the highest-paid player in American soccer. (10) In 2007, _____ his contract was cancelled, Adu transferred to a team based in Lisbon, Portugal.

ON THE WEB
Visit *Exercise Central* at
bedfordstmartins.com/writingfirst
for more practice.

◆ **PRACTICE 17-4**

Combine each of the following pairs of sentences to create one complex sentence. Use a subordinating conjunction from the list on page 274 to indicate the relationship between the dependent and independent clauses in each sentence. Make sure you include a comma where one is required.

> **Example:** Orville and Wilbur Wright built the first powered plane/
> *although they*
> ~~They~~ had no formal training as engineers.
> ^

1. Professional midwives are used widely in Europe, In the United States, they usually practice only in areas with few doctors.

2. John Deere constructed his first steel plow in 1837, A new era began in farming.

3. Stephen Crane describes battles in *The Red Badge of Courage.* He never saw a war.

4. Elvis Presley died in 1977, Thousands of his fans gathered in front of his mansion.

5. Jonas Salk developed the first polio vaccine in the 1950s, The number of polio cases in the United States declined.

6. The salaries of baseball players rose in the 1980s, Some sportswriters predicted a drop in attendance at games.

7. The Du Ponts arrived from France in 1800. American gunpowder was not as good as French gunpowder.

8. Margaret Sanger opened her first birth-control clinic in America in 1916, She was arrested and put in jail.

9. Thaddeus Stevens thought plantation land should be given to freed slaves, He disagreed with Lincoln's peace terms for the South.

10. Steven Spielberg directed some very popular movies. He did not win an Academy Award until *Schindler's List* in 1993.

■ WRITING FIRST: Flashback

Look back at your response to the Writing First activity on page 271. Identify two pairs of simple sentences that could be combined with subordinating conjunctions. On the lines below, combine each pair into a complex sentence by making one sentence a dependent clause. Check to make sure you have punctuated your new sentences correctly.

_____

_____

_____

_____

C   Using Relative Pronouns

Another way to form a complex sentence is to use **relative pronouns** (*who, that, which,* and so on) to join two simple sentences (independent clauses).

TWO SIMPLE SENTENCES   Pit bulls were originally bred in England. They can be very aggressive.

                                                ┌─────── DEPENDENT CLAUSE ───────┐
COMPLEX SENTENCE   Pit bulls, which were originally bred in England, can be very aggressive.

Note: The relative pronoun always refers to a word in the independent clause.

Relative Pronouns

that	which	whoever	whomever
what	who	whom	whose

Different relative pronouns show different relationships between the ideas in the independent and dependent clauses they link.

TWO SIMPLE SENTENCES   Nadine Gordimer comes from South Africa. She won the Nobel Prize in Literature in 1991.

COMPLEX SENTENCE   Nadine Gordimer, who won the Nobel Prize in Literature in 1991, comes from South Africa.

TWO SIMPLE SENTENCES	Last week I had a job interview. It went very well.
COMPLEX SENTENCE	Last week I had a job interview that went very well.
TWO SIMPLE SENTENCES	Transistors have replaced vacuum tubes in radios and televisions. They were invented in 1948.
COMPLEX SENTENCE	Transistors, which were invented in 1948, have replaced vacuum tubes in radios and televisions.

ON THE WEB

Visit *Exercise Central* at
bedfordstmartins.com/writingfirst
for more practice.

◆ PRACTICE 17-5

In each of the following complex sentences, underline the dependent clause once, and underline the relative pronoun twice. Then, draw an arrow from the relative pronoun to the noun or pronoun to which it refers.

Example: MTV, which was the first TV channel devoted to popular music videos, began in 1981.

1. MTV's very first music video, which was performed by a group called the Buggles, contained the lyric "Video killed the radio star."

2. MTV's early videos were simple productions that recorded the singers in live studio performances.

3. Recording executives, who did not like MTV at first, soon realized the power of music videos.

4. Music videos became big productions that featured many settings, special effects, and dancers.

5. The Cars' song "You Might Think" won the award for best video at the first MTV music awards, which aired in September 1984.

6. The game show *Remote Control,* which made fun of *Jeopardy,* began on MTV in 1987.

7. The fashion program *House of Style* became popular in 1989 because of supermodel Cindy Crawford, who was its first host.

8. *The Real World,* a reality series that featured a group of young people living together in New York City, also became popular then.

9. That same year, governor Bill Clinton, who would soon be elected president, met with young voters on MTV.

10. Today, MTV, which devotes less and less time to music videos, produces many hours of original programming.

◆ PRACTICE 17-6

Combine each of the following pairs of simple sentences into one complex sentence. Use the relative pronoun that follows each pair.

Example: Many young Americans perform community service as part of their education. They are learning valuable skills. (who)

Many young Americans, who perform community service as part of their

education, are learning valuable skills.

1. Their work is called service-learning. It benefits both the participants and the communities. (which)

_____

_____

2. A service-learning project meets a community need. It is sponsored either by a school or by the community. (which)

_____

_____

3. The young people work at projects such as designing neighborhood playgrounds. They are not paid. (who)

_____

_____

4. These are challenging projects. They give young people satisfaction. (that)

_____

5. Designing a playground teaches them to communicate. It requires teamwork. (which)

_____

_____

■ **WRITING FIRST: Flashback**

Look back at your response to the Writing First activity on page 271. Identify two simple sentences that could be combined with a relative pronoun into one complex sentence. (If you cannot find two appropriate sentences, write two new ones.) On the lines below, write the new complex sentence.

_____

_____

_____

_____

■ **WRITING FIRST: Revising and Editing**

Look back at your response to the Writing First activity on page 271. Try adding one of the new complex sentences you created in the Flashback activities on page 277 and above. Then, check to make sure there are no errors in your use of subordinating conjunctions and relative pronouns. Finally, make sure that you have punctuated correctly.

CHAPTER REVIEW

◆ **EDITING PRACTICE**

Read the following student essay. Then, revise it by combining pairs of simple sentences with subordinating conjunctions or relative pronouns. Be sure to choose subordinating conjunctions and relative pronouns that indicate the relationship between the two sentences you combine. Check your punctuation carefully. The first sentence has been revised for you.

Community Artist

When
I was in tenth grade at West Philadelphia High School in Philadelphia, I took

an art class. One day, my teacher started to talk about the free Philadelphia Mural

Arts Program. We could sign up for it. I needed something to do after school and

during the summer. I didn't know much about the program. I signed up and was

accepted. It turned out to be a rewarding experience.

Graffiti on wall

My teacher told us about the beginning of the Mural Arts program. It started in 1984 as a spinoff of the Philadelphia Anti-Graffiti Network. Philadelphia had a serious problem. The problem was graffiti. Graffiti artists had painted on buildings all over the city. A solution to the problem was the Philadelphia Anti-Graffiti Network. This program offered graffiti artists an alternative. They could give up graffiti. They would not be prosecuted. They enjoyed painting. They could paint murals instead of graffiti on public buildings. They could create landscapes, portraits of local heroes, and abstract designs. The former graffiti artists had once been lawbreakers. They could now help build community spirit.

By 1996, the Philadelphia Anti-Graffiti Network was concentrating on eliminating graffiti, and the Mural Arts Program was working to improve the community. It no longer worked with graffiti offenders. It started after-school and summer programs for students. The Mural Arts Program got national recognition in 1997. President Clinton helped paint a mural. So far, the Mural Arts Program has completed more than 2,300 murals. This is more than any other public art program in the country.

Mural created by the Philadelphia Mural Arts Program

I joined the Mural Arts program in 2007. With my fellow students, I visited some of the murals. We came from all over the city. The best part of the program took place in the summer. We learned to use computers to turn our ideas into works of art. We worked with an artist. We actually got to paint parts of her mural on the walls of a building. People walk or drive by the building. They can see our work.

I learned a lot in this program. All the students had to work together. We also worked with artists and members of the community. We helped the community create a mural. At first, I didn't care about art. Now I really appreciate it. I am grateful to my tenth-grade art teacher. He got me interested in the Mural Arts Program.

◆ COLLABORATIVE ACTIVITIES

1. Working in a group of four students, make a list of three or four of your favorite television shows. Divide into pairs, and with your partner, write two simple sentences describing each show. Next, use subordinating conjunctions or relative pronouns to combine each pair of sentences into one complex sentence. With your group, discuss how the ideas in each complex sentence are related, and make sure you have used the subordinating conjunction or relative pronoun that best conveys this relationship.

EXAMPLE: *The Brady Bunch* portrays a 1970s family. It still
appeals to many viewers.

Although *The Brady Bunch* portrays a 1970s family,
it still appeals to many viewers.

2. Imagine that you and the members of your group live in a neighbor-hood where workers are repairing underground power lines. As they work, the workers talk loudly and use foul language. Write a letter of complaint to the power company in which you explain that the work-ers' behavior is offensive to you and to your children. Tell the company that you want the offensive behavior to end. Write the first draft of your letter in simple sentences. After you have written this draft, work as a group to combine as many sentences as you can with subordinat-ing conjunctions and relative pronouns.

3. Assume you are in a competition to determine which collaborative group in your class is best at writing complex sentences. Working in a group, prepare a letter to your instructor in which you present the strengths of your group. Be sure to use a subordinating conjunction or relative pronoun in each of the sentences in your letter. Finally, as a class, evaluate the letters from the groups, and choose the letter that most successfully convinces you that its group is best.

☑ REVIEW CHECKLIST:
Writing Complex Sentences

- A complex sentence consists of one independent clause (simple sentence) combined with one or more dependent clauses. (See 17A.)

- Subordinating conjunctions—such as *although, after, when, while,* and *because*—can join two independent clauses into one complex sentence. (See 17B.)

- Always use a comma after the dependent clause in the sentence. Do not use a comma after the independent clause. (See 17B.)

- Relative pronouns—such as *who, which,* and *that*—can also join two independent clauses into one complex sentence. The relative pronoun shows the relationship between the ideas in the two independent clauses that it links. (See 17C.)

Writing Varied Sentences

PREVIEW

In this chapter, you will learn

- to vary sentence types (18A)
- to vary sentence openings (18B)
- to combine sentences (18C)
- to mix long and short sentences (18D)

■ WRITING FIRST

The picture above shows items on display at the Rock and Roll Hall of Fame and Museum in Cleveland, Ohio. Look at the picture, and then write about a museum exhibit that would include artifacts from your favorite musicians. What items would you include? What would you expect each item to communicate about the music and the time the songs were recorded?

▶ **Word Power**

memorabilia things worthy of remembering

nostalgia a longing for people or things that are no longer present

artifact object of historical interest

Sentence variety is important because a paragraph of varied sentences flows more smoothly, is easier to read and understand, and is more interesting than one in which all the sentences are structured in the same way.

A   Varying Sentence Types

Most English sentences are **statements**. Others are **questions** or **exclamations**. One way to vary your sentences is to use an occasional question or exclamation where it is appropriate.

In the following paragraph, a question and an exclamation add variety.

Over a period of less than twenty years, the image of African Americans in television sitcoms seemed to change dramatically, reflecting the changing status of black men and women in American society. But had

Question anything really changed? In *Beulah,* the 1950 sitcom that was the first to star an African-American woman, the title character was a maid. Her friends were portrayed as irresponsible and not very smart. *Amos 'n' Andy,* which also appeared in the 1950s, continued these negative stereotypes of black characters. In 1968, with the civil rights movement at its height, the NBC comedy hit *Julia* portrayed a black woman in a much more favorable light. A widowed nurse, raising a small boy on her own, Julia was a dedicated professional and a devoted mother. The image of the African American was certainly more positive, but the character was no more balanced or three-dimensional than earlier black characters had been. Julia was not

Exclamation an object of ridicule; instead, she was a saint!

◆ PRACTICE 18-1

Revise the following paragraph by changing one of the statements into a question and one of the statements into an exclamation.

Example: The cell phone may be making the wristwatch obsolete. (statement)

Is the cell phone making the wristwatch obsolete? (question)

(1) As cell phones and other small electronic devices become more common, fewer people are wearing watches. (2) Most cell phones, Black-Berries, Game Boys, and music players tell the time. (3) In addition, cell phone clocks offer very accurate time. (4) This is because they set themselves with satellite signals. (5) They also adjust automatically to time-zone changes. (6) Typical wristwatches cannot compete with these convenient features. (7) After all, unlike the newer gadgets, watches are not computers. (8) However, watches do remain appealing for other rea-sons. (9) Many people use them as fashion accessories or status symbols. (10) For other, more old-fashioned people, the watch is essential.

■ **WRITING FIRST: Flashback**

Look back at your response to the Writing First activity on page 283. What questions does your writing answer? Write one or two questions on the lines below.

Question 1: _____

_____

Question 2: _____

_____

If you can, add one of these questions to your discussion.
    If you think an exclamation would be an appropriate addition to your writing, suggest one below.

Exclamation: _____

_____

Where could you add this exclamation?

B   Varying Sentence Openings

Varying the way you begin your sentences is another way to add life to your writing. When all the sentences in a paragraph begin in the same way, your writing is likely to seem dull and repetitive. In the following para-graph, for example, every sentence begins with the subject.

18 **B**

▶ **Word Power**

amphibians cold-blooded vertebrates, such as frogs, that live both in the water and on land

Scientists have been observing a disturbing phenomenon. The population of frogs, toads, and salamanders has been declining. This decline was first noticed in the mid-1980s. Some reports blamed chemical pollution. Some biologists began to suspect that a fungal disease was killing these amphibians. The most reasonable explanation seems to be that the amphibians' eggs are threatened by solar radiation. This radiation penetrates the thinned ozone layer, which used to shield them from the sun's rays.

Beginning with Adverbs

Instead of opening every sentence in a paragraph with the subject, you can try beginning with one or more **adverbs**.

Scientists have been observing a disturbing phenomenon. <u>Gradually but steadily</u>, the population of frogs, toads, and salamanders has been declining. This decline was first noticed in the mid-1980s. Some reports blamed chemical pollution. Some biologists began to suspect that a fungal disease was killing these amphibians. <u>However</u>, the most reasonable explanation seems to be that the amphibians' eggs are threatened by solar radiation. This radiation penetrates the thinned ozone layer, which used to shield them from the sun's rays.

◆ **PRACTICE 18-2**

ON THE WEB

Visit *Exercise Central* at **bedfordstmartins.com/writingfirst** for more practice.

Underline the adverb in each of the following sentences, and then rewrite the sentence so that the adverb appears at the beginning. Be sure to punctuate correctly.

Example: The artist Tupac Amaru Shakur was <u>occasionally</u> known by the names 2Pac, Makaveli, or Pac.

Occasionally, the artist Tupac Amaru Shakur was known by the names

2Pac, Makaveli, or Pac.

1. Tupac was initially a roadie and backup dancer for the rap group Digital Underground.

_____

_____

2. He then released the album *2Pocalypse Now,* praised and criticized because of its frank lyrics.

_____

_____

3. Tupac next faced conflicts with rival rap artists, leading to his being shot and spending time in prison.

_____

_____

4. Tupac was generally known for his top-selling albums, but he also was a movie actor, a poet, and a social activist.

_____

_____

5. His influence continued, however, after his 1996 murder, and some fans even believe that he is still alive.

_____

_____

◆ **PRACTICE 18-3**

Underline the adverb in each of the following sentences, and then rewrite the sentence so that the adverb appears at the beginning. Be sure to punctuate correctly.

Example: An internship is <u>usually</u> a one-time work or service experience related to a student's career plans.

Usually, an internship is a one-time work or service experience related

to a student's career plans.

1. Internships are sometimes paid or counted for academic credit.

_____

2. A student who wants an internship should first talk to an academic advisor.

_____

3. The student should next write a résumé listing job experience, education, and interests.

_____

_____

4. The student can then send the résumé to organizations that are looking for interns.

_____

_____

5. Going to job fairs and networking are often good ways to find internships.

◆ PRACTICE 18-4

In each of the following sentences, fill in the blank with an appropriate adverb. Be sure to punctuate correctly.

    Example: *Slowly,*   the sun crept over the horizon.

1. _____ the speeding car appeared from out of nowhere.

2. _____ it crashed into the guard rail.

3. _____ the car jackknifed across the highway.

4. _____ drivers behind the car slammed on their brakes.

5. _____ someone called 911.

6. _____ a wailing siren could be heard.

7. _____ the ambulance arrived.

8. _____ emergency medical technicians went to work.

9. _____ a police officer was on hand to direct traffic.

10. _____ no one was badly hurt in the accident.

Beginning with Prepositional Phrases

Another way to create sentence variety is to begin some sentences with prepositional phrases. A **prepositional phrase** (such as *along the river* or *near the diner*) is made up of a preposition and its object.

    <u>In recent years</u>, scientists have been observing a disturbing phenomenon. Gradually but steadily, the population of frogs, toads, and salamanders has been declining. This decline was first noticed in the mid-1980s. <u>At first</u>, some reports blamed chemical pollution. <u>After a while</u>, some biologists began to suspect that a fungal disease was killing these amphibians. However, the most reasonable explanation seems to be that the amphibians' eggs are threatened by solar radiation. This radiation penetrates the thinned ozone layer, which used to shield them from the sun's rays.

◆ PRACTICE 18-5

Underline the prepositional phrase in each of the following sentences, and then rewrite the sentence so that the prepositional phrase appears at the beginning. Be sure to punctuate correctly.

Example: Very few American women worked in factories before the 1940s.

Before the 1940s, very few American women worked in factories.

1. Many male factory workers became soldiers during World War II.

_____

2. The U.S. government encouraged women to take factory jobs in the war's early years.

_____

_____

3. Over six million women took factory jobs between 1942 and 1945.

_____

4. A new female image emerged with this greater responsibility and independence.

_____

_____

5. Many women wore pants for the first time.

_____

6. Most lost their factory jobs after the war and returned to "women's work."

_____

_____

◆ PRACTICE 18-6

In each of the following sentences, fill in the blank with an appropriate prepositional phrase. Be sure to punctuate correctly.

Example: *At the start of the New York marathon,* Justin felt as if he could run forever.

1. _____ he warmed up by stretching and bending.

2. _____ all the runners were crowded together.

3. _____ they crossed a bridge over the Hudson River.

4. _____ the route became steeper and steeper.

5. _____ Justin grabbed some water from a helpful onlooker.

6. _____ he staggered across the finish line.

◆ **PRACTICE 18-7**

Every sentence in the following paragraph begins with the subject, but several sentences contain prepositional phrases or adverbs that could be moved to the beginning. To vary the sentence openings, move prepositional phrases to the beginnings of three sentences, and move adverbs to the beginnings of two other sentences. Be sure to place a comma after these introductory prepositional phrases and adverbs.

In the Cuban-American community, people
Example: ~~People in the Cuban-American community~~ often mention
           ^
José Julian Martí as one of their heroes.

(1) José Martí was born in Havana in 1853, when Cuba was a colony of Spain. (2) He had started a newspaper demanding Cuban freedom by the time he was sixteen years old. (3) The Spanish authorities forced him to leave Cuba and go to Spain in 1870. (4) He published his first pamphlet calling for Cuban independence while in Spain. openly continuing his fight. (5) He later lived for fourteen years in New York City. (6) He started the journal of the Cuban Revolutionary Party during his time in New York. (7) Martí's essays and poems argued for Cuba's freedom. (8) He died in battle against Spanish soldiers in Cuba, passionately following up his words with actions.

■ **WRITING FIRST: Flashback**

Look back at your response to the Writing First activity on page 283. Identify one sentence that you could begin with an adverb and one that you could begin with a prepositional phrase. (Note that the adverb or prepositional phrase may already be somewhere in the sentence.) Write the revised sentences on the lines below.

1. _____,_____
   (Adverb)

   _____

2. _____,_____
   (Prepositional phrase)

   _____

C Combining Sentences

You can also create sentence variety by experimenting with different ways of combining sentences.

Using -ing Modifiers

A **modifier** identifies or describes other words in the sentence. You can use an -*ing* modifier to combine two sentences.

TWO SENTENCES   Duke Ellington composed more than a thousand songs. He worked hard to establish his reputation.

COMBINED WITH   Composing more than a thousand songs, Duke
-*ing* MODIFIER   Ellington worked hard to establish his reputation.

When the two sentences above are combined, the -*ing* modifier (*composing more than a thousand songs*) describes the new sentence's subject (*Duke Ellington*).

◆ PRACTICE 18-8

Use an -*ing* modifier to combine each of the following pairs of sentences into a single sentence. Eliminate any unnecessary words, and use a comma to set off each -*ing* modifier. When you are finished, underline the -*ing* modifier in each sentence.

Example: Green parties date from the 1970s. They work to save the environment.

Dating from the 1970s, Green parties work to save the environment.

1. Green parties operate from the bottom up. They believe in organizing neighborhoods first.

   _____

   _____

2. The German Green Party organized locally against nuclear power. It won seats in a national election.

   _____

   _____

3. Green parties grew quickly. They were established in seventy-two countries by 2001.

   _____

4. The Green movement has spread beyond the Green Party. It has made people care about the environment.

_____

_____

5. The Green movement has enlisted the support of celebrities to stop global warming. It has led to such events as the Live Earth concerts.

_____

_____

6. Many people now work to save the environment. They recycle and buy "green" products.

_____

_____

◆ PRACTICE 18-9

To complete each of the following sentences, fill in the blank with an appropriate *-ing* modifier. Be sure to punctuate correctly.

> **Example:** _Selling candy door to door,_ the team raised money for new uniforms.

1. _____ the judge called for order in the courtroom.

2. _____ the miners found silver instead.

3. _____ migrating birds often travel long distances in the early fall.

4. _____ fans waited patiently to buy tickets for the concert.

5. _____ the child seemed frightened.

◆ PRACTICE 18-10

Complete each of the following sentences by adding an appropriate independent clause after the *-ing* modifier. Be sure to punctuate correctly.

> **Example:** Blasting its siren _, the fire truck raced through the busy streets._

1. Stepping up to home plate _____

_____

2. Traveling at high speeds _____

_____

3. Broiling in the ninety-degree weather _____

_____

4. Looking both ways _____

_____

5. Talking to a group of news reporters _____

_____

Using *-ed* Modifiers

You can also use an *-ed* modifier to combine two sentences.

TWO SENTENCES   Nogales is located on the border between Arizona and Mexico. It is a bilingual city.

COMBINED WITH
-ed MODIFIER   Located on the border between Arizona and Mexico, Nogales is a bilingual city.

When the two sentences above are combined, the *-ed* modifier (*located on the border between Arizona and Mexico*) describes the new sentence's subject (*Nogales*).

◆ PRACTICE 18-11

Use an *-ed* modifier to combine each of the following pairs of sentences into a single sentence. Eliminate any unnecessary words, and use a comma to set off each *-ed* modifier. When you are finished, underline the *-ed* modifer in each sentence.

Example: Miguel Sabado was interested in helping teenagers. He invented Entertainment-Education.

Interested in helping teenagers, Miguel Sabado invented Entertainment-

Education.

1. Sabado was influenced by Albert Bandura. He believed that a person's behavior could change his or her environment.

_____

_____

2. Sabado was trained as a TV producer in Mexico. He created soap operas in which teenagers dealt with social problems.

_____

_____

3. Mexican soap operas are called telenovelas. They are a very popular form of entertainment.

_____

4. Viewers were very involved with Sabado's characters. They identified with the characters' problems.

_____

5. Viewers were encouraged to change their lives. Nearly a million went to literacy classes because of a telenovela character.

_____

_____

6. Some Mexicans were deprived of access to TV. They got Sabado's message through radio soap operas.

_____

_____

7. Some teenagers were introduced to Entertainment-Education through radio talk shows. They worked through problems with hosts their own age.

_____

_____

8. Sabado's programs have been adopted in other countries. They have helped teenagers in Asia and Africa.

_____

_____

9. Many programs have focused on family planning. These programs have reduced the number of births wherever they are broadcast.

_____

_____

10. Miguel Sabado was inspired to help teenagers in Mexico. He has now helped teenagers all over the world.

_____

_____

◆ **PRACTICE 18-12**

To complete each of the following sentences, fill in the blank with an appropriate *-ed* modifier. Be sure to punctuate correctly.

Example: _Buried for many years,_ the treasure was discovered by accident.

1. _____ the child started crying when the storm began.

2. _____ the hikers rested on the rocks at the top of the mountain.

3. _____ the small boat almost sank.

4. _____ the balloons in Macy's Thanksgiving Day parade soared above the crowds.

5. _____ family stories help families keep their traditions alive.

◆ **PRACTICE 18-13**

Complete each of the following sentences by adding an appropriate independent clause after the -*ed* modifier. Be sure to punctuate correctly.

Example: Promoted as children's books _, the Harry Potter stories also_ _appeal to adults_ .

1. Annoyed by her parents _____

_____

2. Abandoned in the woods for three days _____

_____

3. Bored by the same old routine _____

_____

4. Confronted with the evidence _____

_____

5. Asked whether or not they supported the president _____

_____

Using Compound Subjects or Compound Predicates

A **compound subject** consists of two nouns or pronouns, usually joined by *and*. A **compound predicate** consists of two verbs, usually joined by *and*. You can use a compound subject or a compound predicate to combine two sentences.

TWO SENTENCES	Elijah McCoy was an African-American inventor. Garrett Morgan was also an African-American inventor.
COMBINED (COMPOUND SUBJECT)	Elijah McCoy and Garrett Morgan were African-American inventors.
TWO SENTENCES	Arundhati Roy's first novel, *The God of Small Things*, appeared in 1997. It won the Pulitzer Prize.
COMBINED (COMPOUND PREDICATE)	Arundhati Roy's first novel, *The God of Small Things*, appeared in 1997 and won the Pulitzer Prize.

◆ **PRACTICE 18-14**

Create a compound subject by combining each of the following pairs of sentences into one sentence.

Example: For many businesses, following trends is essential. Predicting future fads is also essential.

For many businesses, following trends and predicting future fads are essential.

_____

1. Many clothing companies rely on trend forecasters to help them predict trends. Technology companies often rely on trend forecasters as well.

_____

_____

2. Understanding consumer desires is part of the forecaster's job. Figuring out how to meet those desires is another part of the job.

_____

_____

3. Analysis of past trends helps forecasters collect the information they need. Extensive market research helps them collect information as well.

_____

_____

4. Of course, surprises are always possible in the world of forecasting. Failures are always possible, too.

_____

_____

ON THE WEB

Visit *Exercise Central* at **bedfordstmartins.com/writingfirst** for more practice.

5. Predicting what people will want is impossible. Knowing for certain
what people will buy is also impossible.

_____

_____

◆ PRACTICE 18-15

Create a compound predicate by combining each of the following pairs of
sentences into a single sentence.

Example: The inventor Thomas Edison left school at an early age.
He first made his living selling newspapers.

The inventor Thomas Edison left school at an early age and first made his

living selling newspapers.

1. Despite his lack of formal education, Edison had a quick mind. He also
showed a talent for problem solving.

_____

_____

2. A job as a telegraph operator gave him an interest in electricity. It also
led him to experiment with inventions.

_____

_____

_____

3. Edison patented the earliest phonograph in 1878. He created the first
practical light bulb the following year.

_____

_____

4. His experiments brought electricity into people's homes. They also
made "moving pictures" possible.

_____

_____

_____

5. Edison held many patents. He made a fortune from his inventions.

_____

_____

6. Edison worked in New Jersey. He had laboratories there in West Orange and Menlo Park.

_____

_____

◆ PRACTICE 18-16

Combine each of the following pairs of sentences into one sentence by creating a compound subject or a compound predicate. Remember that a compound subject joined by *and* takes a plural verb.

Example: Several years ago, the NCAA Presidents Commission wanted to reform college athletic programs/ ~~It~~ recommended a number of changes. (compound predicate)

and

(1) College presidents wanted to improve the academic performance of college athletes. Their supporters also wanted to improve the academic performance of college athletes. (2) They wanted to raise the number of required core courses for entering freshmen. They also wanted to increase the required SAT scores. (3) A second proposal required athletes to earn a certain number of credits every year. It set a minimum grade point average for them. (4) At first, many athletic directors saw the changes as unfair. They resisted them. (5) Many coaches believe standardized test scores are biased. They do not want them used to screen student athletes. (6) However, many athletes under the old system had fallen behind academically. They often failed to graduate. (7) The new rules, supporters claimed, would give student athletes a fair chance. They also keep them on the graduation track.

Using Appositives

An **appositive** is a word or word group that identifies, renames, or describes a noun or pronoun. Creating an appositive is often a good way to combine two sentences about the same subject.

TWO SENTENCES C. J. Walker was the first American woman to become a self-made millionaire. She marketed a line of hair-care products for black women.

COMBINED C. J. Walker, the first American woman to become a self-made millionaire, marketed a line of hair-care products for black women.

In the example above, the appositive appears in the middle of a sentence. However, an appositive can also come at the beginning or at the end of a sentence.

The first American woman to become a self-made millionaire, C. J. Walker marketed a line of hair-care products for black women. (appositive at the beginning)

Several books have been written about C. J. Walker, the first American woman to become a self-made millionaire. (appositive at the end)

◆ PRACTICE 18-17

Use appositives to combine each of the following pairs of sentences into one sentence. Note that the appositive may appear at the beginning, in the middle, or at the end of the sentence. Be sure to use commas appropriately.

ON THE WEB

Visit *Exercise Central* at
bedfordstmartins.com/writingfirst
for more practice.

Example: On Friday, I will take my car to Joe's Garage, Joe's is a shop that replaces mufflers.

1. The iPhone is a product released by Apple in 2007. It is not only a phone but a camera, a multimedia player, and a Web browser.

2. The Edmonton Corn Maze in Alberta, Canada, is one of the largest mazes in North America. It covers fifteen acres of ground and usually takes visitors an hour to complete.

3. When British soccer star David Beckham retired from playing in his own country, he came to play for a U.S. team. That team is the LA Galaxy.

4. Musician Angélique Kidjo sings in several different languages, including French, English, Yoruba, and Fon. She is a native of Benin.

5. Stepping outside for a cigarette is an activity that used to be acceptable at most workplaces. It is now being banned by many companies.

◆ PRACTICE 18-18

Use appositives to combine each of the following pairs of sentences into one sentence. Note that the appositive may appear at the beginning, in the middle, or at the end of the sentence. Be sure to use commas appropriately.

Example: Wikipedia is a popular online information source, It is available in more than two hundred languages.

(1) Wikipedia is one of the largest reference sites on the Web. It is different from other encyclopedias in many ways. (2) This site is a constant work-in-progress. It allows anyone to add, change, or correct information in its articles. (3) For this reason, researchers have to be careful when using information from Wikipedia. Wikipedia is a source that may contain factual errors. (4) The older articles are the ones that have been edited and corrected the most. These often contain the most trustworthy information. (5) Despite some drawbacks, Wikipedia has many notable advantages. These advantages include free and easy access, up-to-date information, and protection from author bias.

■ **WRITING FIRST: Flashback**

Look back at your response to the Writing First activity on page 283. Find two or three pairs of sentences that you think could be combined. On the lines below, combine each pair of sentences into a single sentence, using one of the methods discussed in 18C. Use a different method for each pair of sentences.

1. _____

_____

2. _____

_____

3. _____

_____

D **Mixing Long and Short Sentences**

A paragraph of short, choppy sentences—or a paragraph of long, rambling sentences—can be monotonous. By mixing long and short sentences, perhaps combining some simple sentences to create compound and complex sentences, you can create a more interesting paragraph.

In the following paragraph, the sentences are all short, and the result is boring and hard to follow.

The world's first drive-in movie theater opened on June 6, 1933. This drive-in was in Camden, New Jersey. Automobiles became more popular. Drive-ins did too. By the 1950s, there were more than four thousand drive-ins in the United States. Over the years, the high cost of land led to a decline in the number of drive-ins. So did the rising popularity of television. Soon, the drive-in movie theater had almost disappeared. It was replaced by the multiplex. In 1967, there were forty-six drive-ins in New Jersey. Today, only one is still open. That one is the Delsea Drive-in in Vineland, New Jersey.

The revised paragraph that appears below is more interesting and easier to read. (Note that the final short sentence is retained for emphasis.)

The world's first drive-in movie theater opened on June 6, 1933, in Camden, New Jersey. As automobiles became more popular, drive-ins did too, and by the 1950s, there were more than four thousand drive-ins in the United States. Over the years, the high cost of land and the rising popularity of television led to a decline in the number of drive-ins. Soon, the drive-in movie theater had almost disappeared, replaced by the multiplex. In 1967, there were forty-six drive-ins in New Jersey, but today, only one is still open. That one is the Delsea Drive-in in Vineland, New Jersey.

◆ **PRACTICE 18-19**

The following paragraph contains a series of short, choppy sentences that can be combined. Revise the paragraph so that it mixes long and short sentences. Be sure to use commas and other punctuation appropriately.

Example: Kente cloth has special significance for many African Americans; ~~Some~~ *, but some* other people do not understand this significance.

ON THE WEB
Visit *Exercise Central* at
bedfordstmartins.com/writingfirst
for more practice.

■ **Culture Clue**
In *drive-in movie theaters*, cars park in front of large, outdoor movie screens.

(1) Kente cloth is made in western Africa. (2) It is produced primarily by the Ashanti people. (3) It has been worn for hundreds of years by African royalty. (4) They consider it a sign of power and status. (5) Many African Americans wear kente cloth. (6) They see it as a link to their heritage. (7) Each pattern on the cloth has a name. (8) Each color has a special significance. (9) For example, red and yellow suggest a long and healthy life. (10) Green and white suggest a good harvest. (11) African women may wear kente cloth as a dress or head wrap. (12) African-American women, like men, usually wear strips of cloth around their shoulders. (13) Men and women of African descent wear kente cloth as a sign of racial pride. (14) It often decorates college students' gowns at graduation.

■ **WRITING FIRST: Flashback**

Look back at your response to the Writing First activity on page 283. Count the number of words in each sentence.

Then, write a new short sentence to follow your longest sentence.

New sentence: _____

_____

_____

_____

■ **WRITING FIRST: Revising and Editing**

Look back at your response to the Writing First activity on page 283. Using the strategies discussed in this chapter that seem appropriate, revise your writing so that your sentences are varied, interesting, and smoothly connected. (You may want to incorporate sentences you wrote for the Flashback activities on pages 285, 290, 300, and above.) When you are finished, revise some sentences in an assignment you have completed for another course.

CHAPTER REVIEW

◆ **EDITING PRACTICE**

The following student essay lacks sentence variety. All of its sentences are statements beginning with the subject, and it includes a number of short, choppy sentences. Using the strategies discussed in this chapter, revise the essay to achieve greater sentence variety. The first sentence has been edited for you.

Toys by Accident

Many popular toys and games are the result of accidents. People try to invent ^when people^
one thing but discover something else instead. Sometimes they are not trying to

invent anything at all. They are completely surprised to find a new product.

Play-Doh is one example of an accidental discovery. Play-Doh is a popular pre-school toy. Play-Doh first appeared in Cincinnati. A company made a compound to clean wallpaper. They sold it as a cleaning product. The company then realized that this compound could be a toy. Children could mold it like clay. They could use it again and again. The new toy was an immediate hit. Play-Doh was first sold in 1956. Since then, more than two billion cans of Play-Doh have been sold.

Play-Doh

The Slinky was discovered by Richard James. He was an engineer. At the time, he was trying to invent a spring to keep ships' instruments steady at sea. He tested hundreds of springs of varying sizes, metals, and tensions. None of them worked. One spring fell off the desk and "walked" down a pile of books. It went end over end onto the floor. He thought his children might enjoy playing with it. James took the spring home. They loved it. Every child in the neighborhood wanted one. The first Slinky was demonstrated at Gimbel's Department Store in Philadelphia in 1945. All four hundred Slinkys were sold within ninety minutes. The Slinky is simple and inexpensive. The Slinky is still popular with children today.

Slinky

The Frisbee was also discovered by accident. According to one story, a group of Yale University students were eating pies from a local bakery. The bakery was called Frisbies. They finished eating the pies. They started throwing the empty pie tins around. A carpenter in California made a plastic version. He called it the Pluto Platter. The Wham-O company bought the patent on the product. Wham-o renamed it the Frisbee after the bakery. This is how the Frisbee came to be.

Frisbee

Some new toys are not developed by toy companies. Play-Doh, the Frisbee, and the Slinky are examples of very popular toys that were discovered by accident. Play-Doh started as a cleaning product. The Slinky was discovered by an engineer who was trying to invent something else. The Frisbee was invented by students having fun. The toys were discovered unexpectedly. All three toys have become classics.

◆ COLLABORATIVE ACTIVITIES

1. Read the following list of sentences. Working in a small group, change one sentence to a question and one to an exclamation. Then, add adverbs or prepositional phrases at the beginning of several of the sentences in the list.

Many well-known African-American writers left the United States in the years following World War II.
Many went to Paris.
Richard Wright was a novelist.
He wrote *Native Son* and *Black Boy*.
He wrote *Uncle Tom's Children*.
He left the United States for Paris in 1947.
James Baldwin wrote *Another Country, The Fire Next Time,* and *Giovanni's Room.*
He also wrote essays.
He came to Paris in 1948.
Chester Himes was a detective story writer.
He arrived in Paris in 1953.
William Gardner Smith was a novelist and journalist.
He also left the United States for Paris.
These expatriates found Paris more hospitable than America.
They also found it less racist.

2. Continuing to work in your group, use the strategies discussed and illustrated in 18C to help you combine the sentences on the list above into a varied and interesting paragraph. (You may keep the sentences in the order in which they appear.)

3. When your group's revisions are complete, trade paragraphs with another group and further edit the other group's paragraph to improve sentence variety and coherence.

☑ REVIEW CHECKLIST:
Writing Varied Sentences

- Vary sentence types. (See 18A.)

- Vary sentence openings. (See 18B.)

- Combine sentences. (See 18C.)

- Mix long and short sentences. (See 18D.)

Using Parallelism

PREVIEW

In this chapter, you will learn

- to recognize parallel structure (19A)
- to use parallel structure (19B)

■ **WRITING FIRST**

The picture above shows a street scene in the Old Town neighborhood of Chicago. Look at the picture, and then discuss three positive things about your own neighborhood, school, or workplace. Support your statements with specific examples.

▶ **Word Power**

enlighten to give insight to; to educate

enrich to make fuller or more rewarding

inspire to stimulate to action; to motivate

A **Recognizing Parallel Structure**

Parallelism means using matching words, phrases, clauses, and sentence structure to highlight similar items in a sentence. When you use parallelism, you are telling readers that certain ideas are related. By repeating similar grammatical structures to express similar ideas, you create sentences that are clearer and easier to read.

In the following examples, the individual elements in the parallel sentences are balanced; the elements in the other sentences are not.

Parallel	*Not Parallel*
Please leave <u>your name</u>, <u>your number</u>, and <u>your message</u>.	Please leave <u>your name</u>, <u>your number</u>, and <u>you should also leave a message</u>.
I plan to <u>graduate from high school</u> and <u>become a nurse</u>.	I plan to <u>graduate from high school</u>, and then <u>becoming a nurse would be a good idea</u>.
The grass was <u>soft</u>, <u>green</u>, and <u>sweet smelling</u>.	The grass was <u>soft</u>, <u>green</u>, and <u>the smell was sweet</u>.
<u>Making the team</u> was one thing; <u>staying on it</u> was another.	<u>Making the team</u> was one thing; <u>to stay on it</u> was another.
<u>We can register</u> for classes in person, or <u>we can register</u> by email.	<u>We can register</u> for classes in person, or <u>registering by email</u> is another option.

◆ **PRACTICE 19-1**

ON THE WEB
Visit *Exercise Central* at
bedfordstmartins.com/writingfirst
for more practice.

In the following sentences, decide whether the underlined words and phrases are parallel. If so, write *P* in the blank. If not, rewrite the sentences so that the ideas they express are presented in parallel terms.

Examples: Our letter carrier is <u>sloppy</u>, <u>unfriendly</u>, and <u>undependable</u>.

  P
  ___

When choosing a candidate, voters may need to know whether or not the
          trustworthy,
candidates are <u>likable</u>, <del>their trustworthiness</del>, and <del>if they are</del> honest.____
                ^

1. I just bought <u>some lettuce</u> and <u>mushrooms</u>, and <u>three pounds of tomatoes</u>. ____

2. Do you want it done <u>quickly</u>, or do you want it done <u>well</u>? ____

3. The plumber needs to <u>repair a leaky pipe</u>, <u>replace a missing faucet</u>, and <u>a toilet that is running should be fixed</u>. ____

4. When John was a college student, he <u>was on the football team</u> and <u>played baseball</u>, and <u>was on the basketball team</u>. _____

5. Our vacation turned out to be <u>relaxing</u> but <u>expensive</u>. _____

6. On my refrigerator are magnets from <u>my accountant</u>, <u>the doctor I went to see for the first time last week</u>, and <u>my dentist</u>. _____

7. <u>Show me a neat desk</u>, and I will <u>show you an empty mind</u>. _____

8. At my tenth high-school reunion, I was surprised to find that I enjoyed <u>meeting my old classmates</u>, <u>walking around the school</u>, and <u>I even had a good time talking with the principal</u>. _____

9. I just <u>washed the floor</u>. Can you <u>vacuum the rug</u>? _____

10. Our old car <u>has poor gas mileage</u>, <u>its windshield leaks when it rains</u>, and <u>its brakes don't work very well</u>. _____

■ WRITING FIRST: Flashback

Look back at your response to the Writing First activity on page 305, and underline the parallel words, phrases, and clauses. Revise, if necessary, to make sure that comparable ideas are presented in parallel terms.

B Using Parallel Structure

Parallel structure is especially important in *paired items, comparisons,* and *items in a series.*

Paired Items

Use parallel structure when you connect ideas with a **coordinating conjunction**—*and, but, for, nor, or, so,* and *yet.*

George believes in <u>doing a good job</u> and <u>minding his own business</u>.
You can <u>pay me now</u> or <u>pay me later</u>.

Also use parallel structure for paired items joined by *both . . . and, not only . . . but also, either . . . or, neither . . . nor,* and *rather . . . than.*

Jan is both <u>artistically talented</u> and <u>mechanically inclined</u>.

The group's new recording not only has a dance beat but also has thought-provoking lyrics.

I'd rather eat one worm by itself than eat twenty worms with ice cream.

Items in a Series

Use parallel structure for items in a series—words, phrases, or clauses.

Every Wednesday I have English, math, and psychology.

Increased demand, high factory output, and a strong dollar will help the economy.

She is a champion because she stays in excellent physical condition, puts in long hours of practice, and has an intense desire to win.

Items in a List or in an Outline

Use parallel structure for items in a numbered or bulleted list.

There are three reasons to open an Individual Retirement Account (IRA):
1. To save money
2. To reduce taxes
3. To be able to retire

Use parallel structure for the elements in an outline.

A. Basic types of rocks
   1. Igneous
   2. Sedimentary
   3. Metamorphic

◆ **PRACTICE 19-2**

Fill in the blanks in the following sentences with parallel words, phrases, or clauses of your own that make sense in context.

Example: At the lake, we can _____go for a swim_____, _____paddle a canoe_____, and _____play volleyball_____.

ON THE WEB

Visit *Exercise Central* at
bedfordstmartins.com/writingfirst
for more practice.

1. When I get too little sleep, I am _____, _____, and _____.

2. I am good at _____ but not at _____.

3. My ideal mate is _____ and _____.

4. I define success not only as _____ but also as _____.

5. I use my computer for both _____ and _____.

6. I like _____ and _____.

7. You need three qualities to succeed at college: _____,

_____, and _____.

8. I enjoy not only _____ but also _____.

9. I would rather _____ than _____.

10. Football _____, but baseball _____.

◆ PRACTICE 19-3

Rewrite the following sentences so that matching ideas are presented in parallel terms. Add punctuation as needed.

Example: Some experts believe homework is harmful to learning, and also it is harmful to children's health and to family life.

Some experts believe homework is harmful to learning, to children's health,

and to family life.

1. Experts who object to homework include Dorothy Rich and Harris Cooper, and another expert, Alfie Kohn, also objects to homework.

   _____

   _____

2. Harris Cooper of Duke University says that middle school students do not benefit from more than one and a half hours of homework, and more than two hours of homework does not benefit high school students.

   _____

   _____

   _____

   _____

3. In his book *The Homework Myth*, Alfie Kohn says that homework creates family conflict, and stress is also created in children.

   _____

   _____

4. Kohn suggests that children could do other things after school to develop their bodies and minds, and they could also do some things to develop their family relationships.

   _____

   _____

5. Kohn believes that instead of doing homework, children could interview parents about family history and also chemistry could be learned through cooking.

_____

_____

_____

6. Harris Cooper advises that homework should take a short amount of time and should advance learning and also reading skills should be promoted.

_____

_____

_____

7. There seems to be no relationship between the amount of homework assigned and students are getting lower test scores.

_____

_____

_____

8. For example, students in countries that assign less homework, such as Japan and Denmark, score higher on achievement tests than American students, and the Czech Republic does too.

_____

_____

_____

9. Students in countries that assign more homework, such as Greece and Thailand, score lower on achievement tests than American students; in Iran, they also assign more homework.

_____

_____

_____

10. All critics of homework agree that elementary students receive too much homework, middle school students receive too much homework, and too much homework is done by high school students.

_____

_____

_____

■ WRITING FIRST: Flashback

Look back at your response to the Writing First activity on page 305. On the lines below, write two new sentences that you could add, and then revise them as follows: (1) In one sentence, use a coordinating conjunction, such as *and* or *but;* (2) in a second sentence, present items in a series; (3) in the third sentence, present items in a list. When you have finished, check to make sure that you have used parallel structure in each sentence and that you have punctuated correctly.

1. _____

_____

_____

_____

2. _____

_____

_____

_____

3. _____

_____

_____

_____

■ WRITING FIRST: Revising and Editing

Look back at your response to the Writing First activity on page 305, and try to add one or more of the sentences you wrote for the Flashback activity above. Then, revise your work, correcting faulty parallelism and adding parallel constructions where necessary. When you are finished, do the same for another assignment you are currently working on.

CHAPTER REVIEW

◆ **EDITING PRACTICE**

Read the following student essay, which contains examples of faulty parallelism. Identify the sentences you think need to be corrected, and make the changes required to achieve parallelism. Be sure to supply all words necessary for clarity, grammar, and sense. Add punctuation as needed. The first error has been edited for you.

Self-Made Men and Women

wealth.

Many self-made people rise from poverty to ~~being wealthy.~~ They often have little formal education. Or they don't have any formal education at all. However, they want to succeed. They rely on strength, being ambitious and they are determined.

Oprah Winfrey is a good example of a strong woman. She came from a very poor family. The ability to overcome difficult conditions was one of her traits. First, she lived with her grandmother on a Mississippi farm, and then she was brought to live with her mother in Milwaukee, Wisconsin. During this time, she was abused by several relatives. When she was thirteen, she was sent to Nashville, Tennessee, to live with her father. He used strict discipline. She was also taught to value education. Through her own determination and because she was very ambitious, Winfrey got a job at a local broadcasting company. This started her career. Today, she is one of the most powerful people in the world, and she also has more money than almost anyone.

Self-made people are ambitious. Although self-made men and women do not start at the top, eventually the top is reached by them. Most remember their first jobs. For example, Mark Cuban, a sports entrepreneur, who also owns broadcasting companies, recalls that when he was twelve years old, he sold garbage bags door-to-door. Now, he owns the Dallas Mavericks. Other self-made people did laundry, were pizza makers, worked as janitors, and had the job of cleaning out cars and shoveling snow at a used-car lot. They did not let these kinds of jobs keep them from their goals.

Oprah Winfrey

Mark Cuban

The most important characteristic of self-made people is that they are determined. They are not only self-confident, but doing a job better is important to them. They want to make a difference in other people's lives. Sometimes, these characteristics are seen in business, as with Richard Branson, the owner of Virgin Records and Virgin Atlantic Airlines. Sometimes, we see these qualities in the political area, as with Margaret Thatcher, former prime minister of Great Britain, whose father was an ordinary shopkeeper. Also, there is former president Bill Clinton, born in the small town of Hope, Arkansas, who grew up in a family with a violent stepfather who was an alcoholic. All of these self-made men and women wanted to accomplish something important. Success was found by them.

A Virgin Airlines plane

In present-day society, it has become important to get a good education. In fact, education is seen as the key to success. However, the characteristics of self-made people are also important qualities of self-made men and women. They are curious. They also have a lot of ambition and they have the quality of being determined. Without these qualities, they could not succeed.

◆ **COLLABORATIVE ACTIVITIES**

1. Working in a group, list three or four qualities that you associate with each word in the following pairs.

   Brothers/sisters
   Teachers/students
   Parents/children
   City/country
   Fast food/organic food
   Movies/TV shows
   Work/play

2. Write a compound sentence comparing each of the above pairs of words. Use a coordinating conjunction to join the clauses, and make sure each sentence uses clear parallel structure, mentions both words, and includes the qualities you listed for the words in Collaborative Activity 1.

   _____

   _____

3. Choose the three best sentences your group has written for Collaborative Activity 2. Assign one student from each group to write these sentences on the board so the entire class can read them. The class can then decide which sentences use parallelism most effectively.

> ☑ REVIEW CHECKLIST:
> Using Parallelism
>
> ☐ Use matching words, phrases, clauses, and sentence structure to highlight similar items or ideas. (See 19A.)
>
> ☐ Use parallel structure with paired items. (See 19B.)
>
> ☐ Use parallel structure for items in a series. (See 19B.)
>
> ☐ Use parallel structure for items in a list or in an outline. (See 19B.)

Using Words Effectively

PREVIEW

In this chapter, you will learn

- to use specific words (20A)
- to use concise language (20B)
- to avoid slang (20C)
- to avoid clichés (20D)
- to use similes and metaphors (20E)
- to avoid sexist language (20F)

■ WRITING FIRST

The picture above shows a house in the country. Look at the picture, and then describe your dream house. Would it resemble the house in the picture, or would it be different? How? What would be inside the house? Be as specific as possible.

> ▶ **Word Power**
>
> **appealing** attractive or interesting
>
> **ideal** a model of perfection; the best of its kind
>
> **practical** useful

Specific words refer to particular people, places, things, ideas, or qualities. **General words** refer to entire classes or groups. Sentences that contain specific words are more precise and vivid than those that contain only general words.

Sentences with General Words	Sentences with Specific Words
While walking in the woods, I saw an <u>animal</u>.	While walking in the woods, I saw a <u>baby skunk</u>.
<u>Someone</u> decided to run for Congress.	<u>Rebecca</u> decided to run for Congress.
<u>Weapons</u> are responsible for many murders.	<u>Saturday night specials</u> are responsible for many murders.
Denise bought new <u>clothes</u>.	Denise bought a new <u>blue vest</u>.
I really enjoyed my <u>meal</u>.	I really enjoyed my <u>pepperoni pizza</u>.
Darrell had always wanted a <u>classic car</u>.	Darrell had always wanted a <u>black 1957 Chevy convertible</u>.

FOCUS **Using Specific Words**

One way to strengthen your writing is to avoid general words like *good, nice,* or *great.* Instead, take the time to think of more specific words. For example, when you say the ocean looked *pretty,* do you really mean that it *sparkled, glistened, rippled, foamed, surged,* or *billowed?*

◆ **PRACTICE 20-1**

ON THE WEB
Visit *Exercise Central* at
bedfordstmartins.com/writingfirst
for more practice.

In the following passage, the writer describes an old store in the town of Nameless, Tennessee. Underline the specific words in the passage that help you imagine the scene the writer describes. The first sentence has been done for you.

(1) The old store, lighted only by <u>three fifty-watt bulbs</u>, smelled of <u>coal oil</u> and <u>baking bread</u>. (2) In the middle of the rectangular room, where the oak floor sagged a little, stood an iron stove. (3) To the right was a wooden table with an unfinished game of checkers and a stool made from an apple-tree stump. (4) On shelves around the walls sat earthen jugs with corncob stoppers, a few canned goods, and some of

the two thousand old clocks and clockworks Thurmond Watts owned.
(5) Only one was ticking; the others he just looked at.

—WILLIAM LEAST HEAT-MOON, *Blue Highways*

◆ PRACTICE 20-2

In the blank beside each of the five general words below, write a more specific word. Then, use the more specific word in an original sentence.

    Example: child *six-year-old*

    All through dinner, my six-year-old chattered excitedly about his first day of

    school.

1. emotion _____

_____

_____

2. building _____

_____

_____

3. said _____

_____

_____

4. animal _____

_____

_____

5. went _____

_____

_____

◆ PRACTICE 20-3

The following one-paragraph application for a job uses general words. Choose a job that you might want to apply for. Then, rewrite the paragraph on a separate page, substituting specific language for the general language of the original and adding details where necessary. Start by making the first sentence, which identifies the job, more specific: for example, "I would like to apply for the dental technician position you advertised on March 15 in the *Post*." Go on to include specific information about your background and qualifications. Expand the original paragraph into a three-paragraph letter.

I would like to apply for the position you advertised in today's paper. I graduated from high school and am currently attending college. I have taken several courses that have prepared me for the duties the position requires. I also have several personal qualities that I think you would find useful in a person holding this position. In addition, I have had certain experiences that qualify me for such a job. I would appreciate the opportunity to meet with you to discuss your needs as an employer. Thank you.

■ **WRITING FIRST: Flashback**

Look back at your response to the Writing First activity on page 315. Find several general words, and write those words on the lines below. For each word, substitute another word that is more specific.

General Words   *Specific Alternatives*

_____   _____

_____   _____

_____   _____

B   **Using Concise Language**

Concise language says what it has to say in as few words as possible. Too often, writers use words and phrases that add nothing to a sentence's meaning. A good way to test a sentence for these words is to see if crossing them out changes the sentence's meaning. If the sentence's meaning does not change, you can assume that the words you crossed out are unnecessary.

> *The*
> ~~It is clear that the~~ United States was not ready to fight World War II.

> *To*
> ~~In order to~~ follow the plot, you must make an outline.

Sometimes, you can replace several unnecessary words with a single word.

> *Because*
> ~~Due to the fact that~~ I was tired, I missed my first class.

Unnecessary repetition—saying the same thing twice for no reason—can also make your writing wordy. When you revise, delete repeated words and phrases that add nothing to your sentences.

My instructor told me the book was ~~old-fashioned and~~ outdated. (An old-fashioned book is outdated.)

The ~~terrible~~ tragedy of the fire could have been avoided. (A tragedy is *always* terrible.)

FOCUS **Using Concise Language**

The following phrases add nothing to a sentence. You can usually delete or condense them with no loss of meaning.

Wordy	*Concise*
It is clear that	(delete)
It is a fact that	(delete)
The reason is because	Because
The reason is that	Because
It is my opinion that	I think/I believe
Due to the fact that	Because
Despite the fact that	Although
At the present time	Today/Now
At that time	Then
In most cases	Usually
In order to	To
In the final analysis	Finally
Subsequent to	After

◆ **PRACTICE 20-4**

To make the following sentences more concise, eliminate any unnecessary repetition, and delete or condense wordy expressions.

> **Example:** ~~It is a fact that each individual~~ *Each* production of *Sesame Street* around the world is geared toward the local children ~~in that region.~~

(1) In order to meet the needs of international children all over the world, Sesame Workshop helps produce versions of its popular show *Sesame Street* in other countries outside the United States. (2) Due to the fact that each country has different issues and concerns, the content of these shows varies. (3) In most cases, the producers focus on and concentrate on the cultural diversity in their country. (4) In order to develop the most appropriate material for their shows, producers also consult with and listen to local educators and child development experts, people who are experts in the field. (5) At the present time, versions of *Sesame Street* exist in a wide variety of places and countries. They include Mexico, Russia, South Africa, Bangladesh, and Egypt. (6) Created in 1972,

■ **Culture Clue**

Sesame Street is an American educational children's television program that began in 1969 and still runs today. Its popular puppet characters are called Muppets.

Mexico's *Plaza Sésamo* is one of the oldest international versions, having been around longer than versions in other countries. (7) This Spanish-language show includes and brings in familiar and well-known characters like Elmo and Cookie Monster as well as unique and original characters like Abelardo and Pancho. (8) Like all versions of *Sesame Street, Plaza Sésamo*'s main and most important focus is on educating and teaching children about letters, numbers, and the diverse world around them.

■ **WRITING FIRST: Flashback**

Look back at your response to the Writing First activity on page 315. Identify a sentence that contains unnecessary repetition. Rewrite the sentence on the lines below, editing it so it is more concise.

_____

_____

C ▏ Avoiding Slang

Slang is nonstandard language that calls attention to itself. It is usually associated with a particular social group—musicians, computer users, or teenagers, for example. Often, it is used for emphasis or to produce a surprising or original effect. (Because it is very informal, slang has no place in your college writing.)

                                easy
My psychology exam was really ~~sweet~~.

                       relax ^
On the weekends, I like to ~~chill~~ and watch old movies on TV.

If you have any question about whether a term is slang or not, look it up in a dictionary. If the term is identified as *slang* or *informal,* find a more suitable term.

◆ **PRACTICE 20-5**

Edit the following sentences, replacing the slang expressions with clearer, more precise words and phrases.

                        yelled at me
Example: My father ~~lost it~~ when I told him I crashed the car.

1. Whenever I get bummed, I go outside and jog.

2. Tonight I'll have to leave by 11 because I'm wiped out.

3. I'm not into movies or television.

4. Whenever we get into an argument, my boyfriend knows how to push my buttons.

5. I really lucked out when I got this job.

■ **WRITING FIRST: Flashback**

Look back at your response to the Writing First activity on page 315. See if any sentences contain slang. If they do, rewrite the sentences on the lines below, replacing the slang terms with more suitable words or phrases.

_____

_____

_____

D **Avoiding Clichés**

Clichés are expressions—such as "easier said than done" and "last but not least"—that have been used so often that they have lost their meaning. These worn-out expressions get in the way of clear communication.

When you identify a cliché in your writing, replace it with a direct statement—or, if possible, with a fresher expression.

CLICHÉ When school was over, she felt free ~~as a bird~~.

CLICHÉ These days, you have to be ~~sick as a dog~~ *seriously ill* before you are

admitted to a hospital.

FOCUS **Avoiding Clichés**

Here are examples of some clichés you should avoid in your writing.

better late than never   break the ice
beyond a shadow of a doubt   broad daylight

(continued on following page)

> *(continued from previous page)*
>
> face the music   selling like hotcakes
> give 110 percent   the bottom line
> happy as a clam   think outside the box
> hard as a rock   tried and true
> it goes without saying   water under the bridge
> play God   what goes around comes
> pushing the envelope   around
> raining cats and dogs

ON THE WEB
Visit *Exercise Central* at
bedfordstmartins.com/writingfirst
for more practice.

◆ **PRACTICE 20-6**

Cross out any clichés in the following sentences. Then, either substitute a fresher expression or restate the idea more directly.

free of financial worries

Example: Lottery winners often think they will be ~~on easy street~~ for the rest of their lives.

(1) Many people think that a million-dollar lottery jackpot allows the winner to stop working like a dog and start living high on the hog. (2) All things considered, however, the reality for lottery winners is quite different. (3) For one thing, lottery winners who hit the jackpot do not always receive their winnings all at once; instead, yearly payments—for example, $50,000—can be paid out over twenty years. (4) Of that $50,000 a year, close to $20,000 goes to taxes and anything else the lucky stiff already owes the government, such as student loans. (5) Next come relatives and friends with their hands out, leaving winners between a rock and a hard place. (6) They can either cough up gifts and loans or wave bye-bye to many of their loved ones. (7) Adding insult to injury, many lottery winners lose their jobs because employers think that, now that they are "millionaires," they no longer need to draw a salary. (8) Many lottery winners wind up way over their heads in debt within a few years. (9) In their hour of need, many might like to sell their future payments to companies that offer lump-sum payments of forty to forty-five cents on the dollar. (10) This is easier said than done, however, because most state lotteries do not allow winners to sell their winnings.

■ **WRITING FIRST: Flashback**

Look back at your response to the Writing First activity on
page 315. If you have used any clichés, list them below. Then,
either replace each cliché with a more direct statement, or
think of a more original way of expressing the idea.

Cliché   *Revised*

_____   _____

_____   _____

_____   _____

E   Using Similes and Metaphors

A **simile** is a comparison of two unlike things that uses *like* or *as*.

His arm hung at his side <u>like</u> a broken branch.

He was <u>as</u> content <u>as</u> a cat napping on a windowsill.

A **metaphor** is a comparison of two unlike things that does not use *like* or *as*.

Invaders from another world, the dandelions conquered my garden.

He was a beast of burden, hauling cement from the mixer to the
building site.

The force of similes and metaphors comes from the surprise of seeing
two seemingly unlike things being compared. Used in moderation, similes
and metaphors can make your writing more lively and more interesting.

◆ **PRACTICE 20-7**

Use your imagination to complete each of the following items by creating
three original similes.

   Example: A boring class is like *toast without jam.*

                            a four-hour movie.

                            a bedtime story.

1. A good friend is like   _____

                                _____

                                _____

2. A thunderstorm is like   _____

                                _____

                                _____

3. A workout at the gym is like _____

_____

_____

◆ **PRACTICE 20-8**

Think of a person you know well. Using that person as your subject, fill in each of the following blanks to create metaphors. Try to complete each metaphor with more than a single word, as in the example.

Example: If _my baby sister_ were an animal, _she_ would be

a curious little kitten.

1. If _____ were a musical instrument, _____ would be _____

_____

2. If _____ were a food, _____ would be _____

_____

3. If _____ were a means of transportation, _____ would be _____

_____

4. If _____ were a natural phenomenon, ____ would be _____

_____

5. If _____ were a toy, _____ would be _____

_____

■ **WRITING FIRST: Flashback**

Look back at your response to the Writing First activity on page 315. Find two sentences that could be enriched with a simile or a metaphor. Rewrite these two sentences on the lines below, adding a simile to one sentence and a metaphor to the other.

Sentence with simile _____

_____

Sentence with metaphor _____

_____

F | **Avoiding Sexist Language**

Sexist language refers to men and women in insulting terms. Sexist language is not just words like *stud* or *babe,* which many people find objectionable. It can also be words or phrases that unnecessarily call attention to gender or that suggest a job or profession is held only by a man (or only by a woman) when it actually is not.

You can avoid sexist language by being sensitive and using a little common sense. There is always an acceptable nonsexist alternative for a sexist term.

Sexist	*Nonsexist*
man, mankind	humanity, humankind, the human race
businessman	executive, business person
fireman, policeman, mailman	firefighter, police officer, letter carrier
male nurse, woman engineer	nurse, engineer
congressman	member of Congress, representative
stewardess, steward	flight attendant
man and wife	man and woman, husband and wife
manmade	synthetic
chairman	chair, chairperson
anchorwoman, anchorman	anchor
actor, actress	actor

FOCUS **Avoiding Sexist Language**

Do not use *he* when your subject could be either male or female.

Sexist: Everyone should complete his assignment by next week.

You can correct this problem in three ways.

■ *Use* he or she *or* his or her.

Everyone should complete his or her assignment by next week.

■ *Use plural forms.*

Students should complete their assignment by next week.

■ *Eliminate the pronoun.*

Everyone should complete the assignment by next week.

◆ **PRACTICE 20-9**

Edit the following sentences to eliminate sexist language.

                                                       or her (or omit "his")

Example: A doctor should be honest with his patients.

1. Many people today would like to see more policemen patrolling the streets.

2. The attorneys representing the plaintiff are Geraldo Diaz and Mrs. Barbara Wilkerson.

3. Every soldier picked up his weapons.

4. Christine Fox is the female mayor of Port London, Maine.

5. Travel to other planets will be a significant step for man.

■ **WRITING FIRST: Flashback**

Look back at your response to the Writing First activity on page 315. Have you used any words or phrases that unnecessarily call attention to gender? Have you used *he* when your subject could be either male or female? Rewrite on the following lines any sentences in which these problems occur. Then, cross out the sexist language, and substitute acceptable nonsexist alternatives.

_____

_____

_____

_____

■ **WRITING FIRST: Revising and Editing**

Look back at your response to the Writing First activity on page 315. Revise the paragraph, making sure your language is as specific as possible, and avoid using clichés or sexist expressions. Be sure to incorporate the revisions you made in this chapter's Flashback activities. When you have finished, revise another writing assignment you are currently working on.

CHAPTER REVIEW

◆ EDITING PRACTICE

Read the following student essay carefully and then revise it. Make sure that your revision is concise, uses specific words, and includes no slang, sexist language, or clichés. Add an occasional simile or metaphor if you like. The first sentence has been edited for you.

Unexpected Discoveries

When we hear the word "accident," we think of bad things, *, like dented fenders and broken glass.* But accidents can be good, too. Modern science has made advances as a result of accidents. It is a fact that a scientist sometimes works like a dog for years in his laboratory, only to make a weird discovery because of a mistake.

The most famous example of a good, beneficial accident is the discovery of penicillin. A scientist, Alexander Fleming, had seen many soldiers die of infections after they were wounded in World War I. All things considered, many more soldiers died due to the fact that infections occurred than from wounds. Fleming wanted to find a drug that could put an end to these terrible, fatal infections. One day in 1928, Fleming went on vacation, leaving a pile of dishes in the lab sink. As luck would have it, he had been growing bacteria in those dishes. When he came back, he noticed that one of the dishes looked moldy. What was strange was that near the mold, the bacteria were dead as a doornail. It was crystal clear to Fleming that the mold had killed the bacteria. He had discovered penicillin, the first antibiotic.

Alexander Fleming

Everyone has heard the name "Goodyear." It was Charles Goodyear who made a discovery that changed and revolutionized the rubber industry. In the early nineteenth century, rubber products became thin and runny in hot weather and cracked in cold weather. One day in 1839, Goodyear accidentally dropped some rubber mixed with sulfur on a hot stove. It changed color and turned black. After being cooled, it could be stretched, and it would return to its original size and shape. This kind of rubber is now used in tires and in many other products.

Another thing was also discovered because of a lab accident involving rubber. In 1953, Patsy Sherman, a female chemist for the 3M company, was trying to find

Charles Goodyear

Patsy Sherman

a new type of rubber. She created a batch of man-made, synthetic liquid rubber. Some of the liquid accidentally spilled onto a lab assistant's new white canvas sneaker. Her assistant used everything but the kitchen sink to clean the shoe, but nothing worked. Over time, the rest of the shoe became dirty, but the part where the spill had hit was still clean as a whistle. Sherman realized that she had found something that could actually keep fabrics clean by doing a number on dirt. The 3M Corporation named this brand new product Scotchguard.

A scientist can be clumsy and careless, but sometimes his mistakes lead to great and important discoveries. Penicillin, better tires, and Scotchguard are examples of products that were the result of scientific accidents.

◆ COLLABORATIVE ACTIVITIES

1. Photocopy two or three paragraphs of description from a romance novel, a western novel, or a mystery novel. Bring your paragraphs to class. Working in a group, choose one paragraph that seems to need clearer, more specific language.
2. As a group, revise the paragraph you chose for Collaborative Activity 1, making it as specific as possible and eliminating any clichés or sexist language.
3. Exchange your revised paragraph from Collaborative Activity 2 with the paragraph revised by another group and check the other group's work. Make any additional changes you think your paragraph needs.

☑ REVIEW CHECKLIST:
Using Words Effectively

- Use specific words that convey your ideas clearly and precisely. (See 20A.)
- Use concise language that says what it has to say in the fewest possible words. (See 20B.)
- Avoid slang. (See 20C.)
- Avoid clichés. (See 20D.)
- Whenever possible, use similes and metaphors to make your writing more lively and more interesting. (See 20E.)
- Avoid sexist language. (See 20F.)

Read the following student essay. Then, edit it by creating more effective sentences. Combine simple sentences into compound or complex sentences, use parallelism, create varied sentences, and use words that are concise, specific, and original. The first editing change has been made for you.

Eating Street Food

Street food, food cooked and served at a portable stand is extremely popular in the United States. ~~Street~~ ^{Usually, street} food customers ~~usually~~ get their food quickly, ^{and} ~~They~~ do not pay much. Some regional or ethnic foods are sold as street food, Then, they become popular There are concerns about the cleanliness and freshness of street food. These problems can be avoided. It is a fact that street food has many advantages.

Street food is the original fast food. Street food is both fast and cheap. Customers usually do not have much time to wait for it to be cooked. Vendors have to offer food that can be made beforehand or prepared quickly. The original U.S. street food is the hot dog. It can be steamed ahead of time and quickly be put into a bun. Some customers want things like relish, onions, or chili. They can be added. Street food does not cost as much as restaurant food. Vendors usually have to buy a license in order to sell food at a particular location. They do not have to rent a store, pay waiters and waitresses, and supply tablecloths and dishes therefore they can charge much less than a restaurant. Street food customers don't have to make the commitment of time and money required at a sit-down restaurant. They don't have to tip the server either. Customers cannot sit at tables, however. There are no tables. They have to eat while standing or walking. Customers often don't have much time. This situation suits them. Students need fast and cheap food, especially on college campuses. Food carts make them happy as a clam.

Street food is often regional or ethnic. Vendors sell cheese steaks and soft pretzels in Philadelphia. They sell reindeer sausages in Alaska. They sell tacos and tamales in Mexican neighborhoods. In Chicago, customers can buy kielbasa sandwiches and pierogies. Often, food carts offer ethnic foods to customers

Hot dog vendor

Mexican snacks

who are tasting them for the first time. A person can see if he likes Indian curry, Israeli falafel, Italian panini, or a gyro from Greece. Because of the success of street vendors, many ethnic foods have gone mainstream and are now offered in sit-down restaurants.

Falafel cart

There is some concern about the safety of street food. Refrigeration may be limited or nonexistent. Cleanliness sometimes can be a problem. Food from a street-corner cart may be safer than food cooked in a restaurant kitchen. In the restaurant, it may sit for a long time. Also, due to the fact that food carts may lack refrigeration, very fresh ingredients are often used. Still, customers should follow some tips for buying street food. The food should be kept covered until it is cooked. The money and food should not be touched by the same individual. Local customers are a good guide to the best street food. They know where the food is freshest. A long line usually indicates a good and safe source of street food.

In the United States, street food is especially varied. In the United States, there are many immigrants. Food is an important part of culture. The popularity of ethnic street food can be a sign that the immigrants' culture has been accepted.

UNIT FIVE

SOLVING COMMON SENTENCE PROBLEMS

Run-Ons

PREVIEW

In this chapter, you will learn

- to recognize run-ons (21A)
- to correct run-ons in five different ways (21B)

■ **WRITING FIRST**

In the picture above, a child snacks in front of the television. Why do you think so many American children are physically out of shape? What do you think can be done about this problem? Look at the picture, and then try to answer these questions.

▶ **Word Power**

lethargic tired, sluggish

obese extremely overweight

sedentary accustomed to sitting or getting little exercise

333

334

21 **A**

SOLVING
COMMON
SENTENCE
PROBLEMS

A **Recognizing Run-Ons**

A **sentence** consists of at least one independent clause—one subject and one verb.

College costs are rising.

A **run-on** is an error that occurs when two sentences are joined incorrectly. There are two kinds of run-ons: *fused sentences* and *comma splices*.

A **fused sentence** occurs when two sentences are joined without any punctuation.

FUSED SENTENCE   [College costs are rising] [many students are worried.]

A **comma splice** occurs when two sentences are joined with just a comma.

COMMA SPLICE   [College costs are rising], [many students are worried.]

◆ **PRACTICE 21-1**

Some of the sentences in the following paragraph are correct, but others are run-ons. In the answer space after each sentence, write *C* if the sentence is correct, *FS* if it is a fused sentence, and *CS* if it is a comma splice.

Example: Using a screen reader is one way for blind people to access the Web, two popular programs are JAWS for Windows and Window-Eyes. _*CS*_

(1) The Internet should be accessible to everyone, this is not always the case. _*C*_ (2) Many blind computer users have trouble finding information on the Web. _*C*_ (3) Often, this is the result of poor Web design it is the designer's job to make the site accessible. _*C*_ (4) Most blind people use special software called screen readers, this technology translates text into speech or Braille. _*CS*_ (5) However, screen readers do not always work well the information is sometimes hard to access. _*C*_ (6) Web sites need to be understandable to all Internet users. _*C*_ (7) The rights of blind Internet users may be protected by the Americans with Disabilities Act (ADA). _*C*_ (8) We will have to wait for more cases to come to trial then we will know more. _*CS*_ (9) Meanwhile, we have to rely on software companies to make the necessary changes, this will take some time. _*C*_ (10) However, there are incentives for these companies; the 1.5 million blind users are all potential customers. _____

■ WRITING FIRST: Flashback

Look back at your response to the Writing First activity on page 333. Do you see any run-ons? If so, underline them.

B Correcting Run-Ons

FOCUS **Correcting Run-Ons**

You can correct run-ons in five ways.

1. *Use a period to create two separate sentences.*
   College costs are rising. Many students are worried.

2. *Use a coordinating conjunction (*and, but, or, nor, for, so,
   or yet) *to connect ideas.*
   College costs are rising, and many students are worried.

3. *Use a semicolon to connect ideas.*
   College costs are rising; many students are worried.

4. *Use a semicolon followed by a transitional word or
   phrase to connect ideas.*
   College costs are rising; as a result, many students are
   worried.

5. *Use a dependent word (*although, because, when, *and so
   on) to connect ideas.*
   Because college costs are rising, many students are worried.

---

1. **Use a period to create two separate sentences.** Be sure each sentence begins with a capital letter and ends with a period.

INCORRECT (FUSED SENTENCE)	Gas prices are very high some people are buying hybrid cars.
INCORRECT (COMMA SPLICE)	Gas prices are very high, some people are buying hybrid cars.
CORRECT	Gas prices are very high. Some people are buying hybrid cars. (two separate sentences)

336

SOLVING
COMMON
SENTENCE
PROBLEMS

21 B

◆ **PRACTICE 21-2**

Correct each of the following run-ons by using a period to create two separate sentences. Be sure both of your new sentences begin with a capital letter and end with a period.

> **Example:** Stephen Colbert used to appear on *The Daily Show with Jon Stewart,* ~~now,~~ *. Now,* he has his own show called *The Colbert Report.*

1. In June 2007, Gordon Brown became prime minister of the United Kingdom, he replaced Tony Blair.

2. New York–style pizza usually has a thin crust Chicago-style "deep-dish pizza" has a thick crust.

3. Last week, Soraya won a text-messaging contest the prize for being the fastest was five hundred dollars.

4. In some parts of Canada's Northwest Territory, the only way to transport supplies is over frozen lakes being an ice road trucker is one of the most dangerous jobs in the world.

5. In 1961, the first Six Flags theme park opened in Arlington, Texas, the six flags represent the six governments that have ruled the area that is now Texas.

2. **Use a coordinating conjunction to connect ideas.** If you want to indicate a particular relationship between ideas—for example, cause and effect or contrast—you can connect two independent clauses with a coordinating conjunction (*and, but, or, nor, for, so,* or *yet*) that makes this relationship clear. Always place a comma before the coordinating conjunction.

INCORRECT (FUSED SENTENCE)	Some schools require students to wear uniforms other schools do not.
INCORRECT (COMMA SPLICE)	Some schools require students to wear uniforms, other schools do not.
CORRECT	Some schools require students to wear uniforms, but other schools do not. (clauses connected with the coordinating conjunction *but,* preceded by a comma)

◆ **PRACTICE 21-3**

Correct each of the following run-ons by using a coordinating conjunction (*and, but, or, nor, for, so,* or *yet*) to connect ideas. Be sure to put a comma before each coordinating conjunction.

Example: Many college students use Facebook to keep up with old
friends ⌄ they also use it to find new ones. *, and*

anb 8 o

1. A car with soft tires gets poor gas mileage, keeping tires inflated is a

   good way to save money on gas.

2. It used to be difficult for football fans to see the first-down line on tel-

   evision, the computer-generated yellow line makes it much easier. *But now*

3. Indonesia has more volcanoes than any other country in the world, the *But*

   United States has the biggest volcano in the world, Mauna Loa in Hawaii.

4. Chefs can become famous for cooking at popular restaurants they can

   become famous for hosting television shows.

5. Overcrowded schools often have to buy portable classrooms or trailers

   this is only a temporary solution.

3. **Use a semicolon to connect ideas.** If you want to indicate a particularly close connection—or a strong contrast—between two ideas, use a
   semicolon.

INCORRECT (FUSED SENTENCE)	Most professional basketball players go to college most professional baseball players do not.
INCORRECT (COMMA SPLICE)	Most professional basketball players go to college, most professional baseball players do not.
CORRECT	Most professional basketball players go to college; most professional baseball players do not. (clauses connected with a semicolon)

◆ PRACTICE 21-4

Correct each of the following run-ons by using a semicolon to connect
ideas. Do not use a capital letter after the semicolon unless the word that
follows it is a proper noun.

Example: From 1930 until 2006, Pluto was known as a planet ⌄ it is now

known as a "dwarf planet."

1. Of all the states, Alaska has the highest percentage of Native American

   residents 16 percent of Alaskans are of Native descent.

2. Satellites and global positioning systems (GPS) can help farmers to

   better understand the needs of their crops, these new methods are part

   of a trend called "precision agriculture."

338

SOLVING
COMMON
SENTENCE
PROBLEMS

21 B

3. Enforcing traffic laws can be difficult; some cities use cameras to photograph anyone who runs a red light.

4. Old landfills can sometimes be made into parks; Cesar Chavez Park in Berkeley, California, is one example.

5. Freestyle motocross riders compete by doing jumps and stunts; some famous FMX riders are Corey Hart, Nate Adams, and Travis Pastrana.

4. **Use a semicolon followed by a transitional word or phrase to connect ideas.** To indicate a specific relationship between two closely related ideas, add a transitional word or phrase after the semicolon.

INCORRECT (FUSED SENTENCE)	Finding a part-time job can be challenging some-times it is even hard to find an unpaid internship.
INCORRECT (COMMA SPLICE)	Finding a part-time job can be challenging, some-times it is even hard to find an unpaid internship.
CORRECT	Finding a part-time job can be challenging; in fact, sometimes it is even hard to find an unpaid intern-ship. (clauses connected with a semicolon followed by the transitional phrase *in fact*)

Some Frequently Used Transitional Words and Phrases

as a result	in addition	now
finally	in fact	still
for example	moreover	therefore
for instance	nevertheless	thus
however		

For more complete lists of transitional words and phrases, see 16C.

◆ PRACTICE 21-5

Correct each of the following run-ons by using a semicolon, followed by the transitional word or phrase in parentheses, to connect ideas. Be sure to put a comma after the transitional word or phrase.

Example: When babies are first born, they can only see black and
; still,
white most baby clothes and blankets are made in pastel colors. (still)

1. Restaurant goers can expect to come across different condiments in different regions of the country, few tables in the Southwest are with-out a bottle of hot sauce. (for example)

2. Every April, millions of people participate in TV-Turnoff Week by not watching television they read, hang out with family and friends, and generally enjoy their free time. (instead)

3. Today, few people can count on company pension plans, thirty years ago, most people could. (however)

4. Bottled water can be a waste of money tap water is free. (after all)

5. Dog breeders who run "puppy mills" are only concerned with making money they are not particularly concerned with their dogs' well-being. (unfortunately)

FOCUS **Connecting Ideas with Semicolons**

Run-ons often occur when you use a transitional word or phrase to join two independent clauses *without also using a semicolon.*

INCORRECT (FUSED SENTENCE)	It is easy to download information from the Internet however it is not always easy to evaluate the information.
INCORRECT (COMMA SPLICE)	It is easy to download information from the Internet, however it is not always easy to evaluate the information.

To correct this kind of run-on, put a semicolon before the transitional word or phrase, and put a comma after it.

CORRECT	It is easy to download information from the Internet; however, it is not always easy to evaluate the information.

---

5. **Use a dependent word to connect ideas.** When one idea is dependent on another, you can connect the two ideas by adding a dependent word, such as *when, who, although,* or *because.*

INCORRECT (FUSED SENTENCE)	American union membership was high in the mid-twentieth century it has declined in recent years.
INCORRECT (COMMA SPLICE)	American union membership was high in the mid-twentieth century, it has declined in recent years.

340

21 B

SOLVING
COMMON
SENTENCE
PROBLEMS

■ **Culture Clue**

Labor unions are groups of workers who band together to achieve common goals such as fair wages, safety, and security.

ON THE WEB

Visit *Exercise Central* at **bedfordstmartins.com/writingfirst** for more practice.

CORRECT   Although American union membership was high in the mid-twentieth century, it has declined in recent years. (clauses connected with the dependent word *although*)

CORRECT   American union membership, which was high in the mid-twentieth century, has declined in recent years. (clauses connected with the dependent word *which*)

Some Frequently Used Dependent Words

after	eventually	until
although	if	when
as	instead	which
because	since	who
before	that	
even though	unless	

For complete lists of dependent words, including subordinating conjunctions and relative pronouns, see 17B and 17C.

◆ **PRACTICE 21-6**

Correct each of the following run-ons and comma splices by adding a dependent word. Consult the list above to help you choose a logical dependent word. Be sure to use correct punctuation.

Example: *Even though the* ~~The~~ court found him guilty, his fans still believed he was innocent.

1. The Dragon Boat Festival is a traditional Chinese celebration, it occurs every year on the fifth day of the fifth month of the Chinese calendar.

2. Many people now know that tanning damages the skin, most people use sunscreen.

3. Successful auctions often depend on experienced auctioneers, they encourage the audience to keep bidding.

4. The tide goes out in the late afternoon, we can collect shells.

5. Kevin's arm span is greater than his height, he has a positive "ape index."

◆ **PRACTICE 21-7**

Correct each of the following run-ons in one of these four ways: by creating two separate sentences, by using a coordinating conjunction, by using a semicolon, or by using a semicolon followed by a transitional word or phrase. Remember to put a semicolon before, and a comma after, each transitional word or phrase.

> **Example:** Twenty-five percent of Americans under the age of fifty have
>   , and
> one or more tattoos ^ 50 percent of Americans under the age of twenty-
> five have one or more tattoos.

1. Coffee came to Italy in 1600 Pope Clement "baptized" the Muslim beverage for Christians.

2. Skateboarding is a male-dominated sport only 26 percent of skateboarders are women.

3. Some heavy metal musicians have been influenced by classical music, however they have taken their music in a very different direction.

4. *I Know What You Did Last Summer* breaks teen horror movie stereotypes eventually, the main characters save their friends and take responsibility for their actions.

5. Some people believe that the Harry Potter books promote witchcraft, other feel that the books promote positive values, such as as friendship and courage.

6. Shakespeare portrayed Richard III as evil, the Richard III Society claims that Richard was a virtuous king.

7. Iceland is the country with the highest percentage of children born out of wedlock the figure is 62 percent.

8. Philip K. Dick was a science fiction writer his book *Do Androids Dream of Electric Sheep?* was made into the movie *Blade Runner.*

9. David Beckham is a soccer star from England he came to the United States to help promote soccer here.

10. Asperger's syndrome is a form of autism people with Asperger's have high intelligence but poor social skills.

342

SOLVING
COMMON
SENTENCE
PROBLEMS

21 B

◆ **PRACTICE 21-8**

Correct each run-on in the following paragraph in the way that best indicates the relationship between ideas. Be sure to use appropriate punctuation.

Example: After World War II, New York City's Coney Island went

through a period of decline/ many people are now working to revive

the magical seaside resort.

; however, (above "/")

(1) In the late nineteenth century, Coney Island was famous, in fact, it was legendary. (2) It had beaches, hotels, racetracks, and a stadium, every summer, Coney Island was crowded. (3) By the turn of the century, it was best known for three amusement parks these parks were Luna Park, Steeplechase, and Dreamland. (4) Today, all three of these parks are closed, most of the original Coney Island is gone. (5) However, three of the Island's most famous rides remain they are preserved as official historic sites. (6) One of these rides is the Wonder Wheel, it is a 150-foot-high Ferris wheel. (7) The other two rides are the Cyclone roller coaster and the Parachute Jump. (8) Today's visitors come to experience these old favorites they also come to see Coney Island's new attractions. (9) One of these attractions is Keyspan Park, it is home to a minor-league baseball team called the Brooklyn Cyclones. (10) Both new and traditional events also keep visitors coming to Coney Island, The Mermaid Parade, the Coney Island Film Festival, and the annual hot-dog eating contest are particular favorites.

■ **WRITING FIRST: Flashback**

For each run-on or comma you identified in the Flashback activity on page 335, write two possible corrected versions on the lines below.

_____

_____

_____

_____

_____

■ **WRITING FIRST: Revising and Editing**

Look back at your responses to the Writing First activity on page 333 and the Flashback activities on page 335 and above. For each run-on you found, choose the revision that best conveys your meaning, and revise your Writing First activity accordingly. If you do not find any run-ons in your own writing, work with a classmate to correct his or her writing, or edit the work you did for another assignment.

CHAPTER REVIEW

◆ **EDITING PRACTICE: PARAGRAPH**

Read the following student paragraph, and revise it to eliminate run-ons. Correct each run-on in the way that best indicates the relationship between ideas, and be sure to punctuate correctly. The first error has been corrected for you.

The Moken People

The Moken people of Southeast Asia are one of the last groups of "sea gypsies."
                    , where
They live on the water in the Andaman Sea they hunt and gather all of their own
                            ^
food. For nine months of the year, the Moken make their homes on wooden boats,

344

21 B

SOLVING
COMMON
SENTENCE
PROBLEMS

these boats are known as *kabang*. The Moken only settle on land during the three-month monsoon season, it is too dangerous to be on the water then. Their diving skills are excellent they know a great deal about the water and sea life. This knowledge may be what saved the Moken people from the deadly 2004 tsunami. They understood that the receding water meant danger, they were able to escape to higher ground. Amazingly, only one Moken man was reported killed by the tsunami more than 2,000 others survived. Unfortunately, there are many threats to the Moken people's unique way of life, it is unclear how much longer they will be able to preserve their culture.

Moken people on the water

◆ **EDITING PRACTICE: ESSAY**

Read the following student essay, and revise it to eliminate run-ons. Correct each run-on in the way that best indicates the relationships between ideas, and be sure to punctuate correctly. The first error has been corrected for you.

Comic-Book Heroes

Comic-book heroes have a long history, ~~they~~ *They* originated in comic strips and radio shows. In the "Golden Age" of comic books, individual superheroes were the most popular characters, then teams and groups of superheroes were introduced. Today, some of these superheroes can be found in the movies. Over the years, superheroes have remained very popular.

One of the first comic-book heroes was Popeye. Popeye had no supernatural powers, he battled his enemy, Bluto, with strength that he got from eating spinach. Another early comic-book hero was The Shadow he fought crime while wearing a cape and mask. The Shadow first appeared in comic books in 1930 later the character had his own radio show.

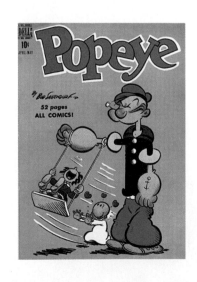

The late 1930s and 1940s are considered the Golden Age of comic books, it was then that many famous comic-book heroes were introduced. The first Superman comic appeared in 1939. Superman came out from behind his identity as meek Clark Kent, he could fly "faster than a speeding bullet." Superman was the first comic-book hero who clearly had superhuman ability to fight evil. Batman was different from Superman he had no real superpowers. Also, Superman was decent and moral, Batman was willing to break the rules. Wonder Woman appeared in 1941, she

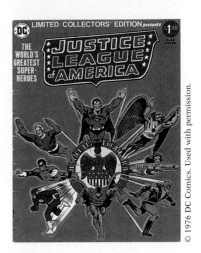

could catch a bullet in one hand. She could re-grow a limb, she could tell when someone was not telling the truth. Wonder Woman truly had superhuman qualities.

Superheroes sometimes had help. Batman had Robin, Wonder Woman had her sister, Wonder Girl. Sometimes there were superhero teams, these were groups of superheroes who helped each other fight evil. The first team was the Justice League of America its members included Superman, Batman, and Wonder Woman. Eventually, the Justice League fought against threats to the existence of the earth these threats even included alien invasions. Another superhero team was the X-Men they were mutants with supernatural abilities.

Now, comic books are not as popular as they used to be, however, superheroes can still be found in popular movies. Superman has been the main character in many movies there have also been several successful Batman, Spiderman, and Fantastic Four movies. Apparently, people still want to see superheroes fight evil and win.

◆ COLLABORATIVE ACTIVITIES

1. Find an interesting paragraph in a newspaper or magazine article or on the Web. Working in a small group, recopy it onto a separate sheet of paper, creating run-ons. Exchange exercises with another group.
2. Work in a small group to correct each run-on and comma splice in an exercise prepared by another group of students. When you have finished, return the exercise to the group that created it.
3. Continuing to work with members of your group, evaluate the other group's work on your exercise, comparing it to the original newspaper or magazine paragraph. Pay particular attention to punctuation. Where the students' version differs from the original, decide whether their version is incorrect or whether it represents an acceptable (or even superior) alternative to the original.

☑ REVIEW CHECKLIST:
Run-Ons

▪ A run-on is an error that occurs when two sentences are joined incorrectly. (See 21A.)

▪ A fused sentence occurs when two sentences are incorrectly joined without any punctuation. (See 21A.)

(continued on following page)

346

SOLVING
COMMON
SENTENCE
PROBLEMS

21 B

(continued from previous page)

- A comma splice occurs when two sentences are joined with just a comma. (See 21A.)

- Correct a run-on in one of the following ways.

  - By creating two separate sentences.

    _____. _____.

  - By using a coordinating conjunction.

    _____, [coordinating conjunction] _____.

  - By using a semicolon.

    _____; _____.

  - By using a semicolon followed by a transitional word or phrase.

    _____; [transitional word or phrase], _____.

  - By using a dependent word.

    [Dependent word] _____, _____.

    _____ [dependent word] _____.

  (See 21B.)

Sentence Fragments

CHAPTER

22

PREVIEW

In this chapter, you will learn

- to recognize sentence fragments (22A)
- to correct missing-subject fragments (22B)
- to correct phrase fragments (22C)
- to correct *-ing* fragments (22D)
- to correct dependent clause fragments (22E)

▶ **Word Power**
transform   to change completely

empower   to give strength or power to

■ WRITING FIRST

The picture above shows an advertisement for the Apple iPod. Look at the picture, and then imagine you are writing a magazine ad for your favorite beverage, footwear, or health or beauty product. Describe the product you chose, including a few possible advertising slogans.

347

348

SOLVING
COMMON
SENTENCE
PROBLEMS

22 **A**

A **sentence fragment** is an incomplete sentence. Every sentence must include at least one subject and one verb, and every sentence must express a
complete thought. If a group of words does not do *all* these things, it is a
fragment and not a sentence—even if it begins with a capital letter and
ends with a period.

The following is a complete sentence.

s   v

SENTENCE   The <u>actors</u> in the play <u>were</u> very talented. (includes both a
subject and a verb and expresses a complete thought)

Because a sentence must have both a subject and a verb and express a
complete thought, the following groups of words are not complete sentences; they are fragments.

FRAGMENT (NO VERB)	The actors in the play. (What point is being made about the actors?)
FRAGMENT (NO SUBJECT)	Were very talented. (Who were very talented?)
FRAGMENT (NO SUBJECT OR VERB)	Very talented. (Who was very talented?)
FRAGMENT (DOES NOT EXPRESS COMPLETE THOUGHT)	Because the actors in the play were very talented. (What happened because they were very talented?)

FOCUS   **Identifying Fragments**

Sentence fragments almost always appear next to complete
sentences.

┌───── COMPLETE SENTENCE ─────┐ ┌────── FRAGMENT ──────┐
Celia took two electives. Physics 320 and Spanish 101.

The fragment above does not have a subject or a verb. The complete
sentence that comes before it, however, has both a subject (*Celia*)
and a verb (*took*).

Often, you can correct a sentence fragment by attaching it to a
nearby sentence that supplies the missing words.

Celia took two electives, Physics 320 and Spanish 101.

◆ **PRACTICE 22-1**

Some of the following items are fragments, and others are complete sentences. On the line following each item, write *F* if it is a fragment and *S* if
it is a complete sentence.

Example: Star formations in the night sky. _____F_____

1. To save as much as possible for retirement. _____

2. The judge gave her a two-year sentence. _____

3. A birthday on Christmas Day. _____

4. Because he lost ten pounds on his new diet. _____

5. Working in the garden and fixing the roof. _____

6. Sonya flew to Mexico. _____

7. Starts in August in many parts of the country. _____

8. And slept in his own bed last night. _____

9. Famous for her movie roles. _____

10. A phone that plays music and takes photos. _____

◆ **PRACTICE 22-2**

In the following passage, some of the numbered groups of words are missing a subject, a verb, or both. Identify each fragment by labeling it *F*. Then, decide how each fragment could be attached to another word group to create a complete new sentence. Finally, rewrite the entire passage, using complete sentences, on the lines provided.

Example: Martha Grimes, Ruth Rendell, and Deborah Crombie

write detective novels. _____ Set in England. _____F_____

Rewrite: *Martha Grimes, Ruth Rendell, and Deborah Crombie write*

detective novels set in England.

(1) Sara Paretsky writes detective novels. _____ (2) Such as *Burn Marks* and *Guardian Angel*. _____ (3) These novels are about V. I. Warshawski. _____ (4) A private detective. _____ (5) V. I. lives and works in Chicago. _____ (6) The Windy City. _____ (7) Every day as a detective. _____ (8) V. I. takes risks. _____ (9) V. I. is tough. _____ (10) She is also a woman. _____

Rewrite:

_____

_____

_____

_____

350

SOLVING
COMMON
SENTENCE
PROBLEMS

22 **A**

◆ **PRACTICE 22-3**

In the following paragraph, some of the numbered groups of words are missing a subject, a verb, or both. First, underline each fragment. Then, decide how each fragment could be attached to a nearby word group to create a complete new sentence. Finally, rewrite the entire paragraph, using complete sentences, on the lines provided.

Example: Gatorade was invented at the University of Florida. <u>To help the Florida Gators fight dehydration.</u>

Rewrite: *Gatorade was invented at the University of Florida to help the Florida Gators fight dehydration.*

(1) Doctors discovered that football players were losing electrolytes and carbohydrates. (2) Through their sweat. (3) They invented a drink. (4) That replaced these important elements. (5) Gatorade tasted terrible. (6) But did its job. (7) The Florida Gators survived a very hot season. (8) And won most of their games. (9) Now, Gatorade is used by many college and professional football teams. (10) As well as in baseball, basketball, tennis, golf, and soccer.

Rewrite:

_____

_____

_____

_____

_____

_____

■ **WRITING FIRST: Flashback**

Look back at your response to the Writing First activity on page 347. Do all your sentences seem complete? If you think any are not complete, copy them on the lines below.

_____

_____

_____

_____

B   **Missing-Subject Fragments**

Every sentence must include both a subject and a verb. If the subject is left out, the sentence is incomplete. In the following example, the first word group is a sentence. It includes both a subject (*He*) and a verb (*packed*). However, the second word group is a fragment. It includes a verb (*took*) but no subject.

┌────────── SENTENCE ──────────┐┌─────── FRAGMENT ───────┐
He packed his books and papers. And also took an umbrella.

One way to correct this kind of fragment is to attach it to the sentence that comes right before it. This sentence often contains the missing subject.

CORRECT   He packed his books and papers and also took an umbrella.

Another way to correct this kind of fragment is to add the missing subject.

CORRECT   He packed his books and papers. He also took an umbrella.

◆ **PRACTICE 22-4**

Each of the following items includes a missing-subject fragment. Using one of the two methods explained above, correct each fragment.

Example: Back-to-school sales are popular with students. And with their parents.

Back-to-school sales are popular with students and with their parents.   or

Back-to-school sales are popular with students. The sales are also popular

with their parents.

1. Quitting smoking is very hard. But can add years to people's lives.

   _____

   _____

2. Some retailers give a lot of money to charity. And even donate part of their profits.

   _____

   _____

3. Geography bees resemble spelling bees. But test the contestants' knowledge of countries around the world.

   _____

   _____

4. School uniforms are often preferred by parents. And preferred by school principals.

   _____

   _____

352

22 B

SOLVING
COMMON
SENTENCE
PROBLEMS

5. During the Cold War, the Soviet Union and the United States were rivals. But never actually fought a war with each other.

_____

_____

6. Scooters have been around for many years. And have recently become popular again.

_____

_____

7. With cosmetic surgery, people can look younger. And feel younger, too.

_____

8. Online shopping sites sometimes offer free shipping. Or have lower prices than local stores.

_____

_____

9. Pro football linemen can weigh more than 300 pounds. But are still able to run fast.

_____

_____

10. Using an electric toothbrush can be good for one's teeth. And promote healthy gums.

_____

_____

■ **WRITING FIRST: Flashback**

Look back at your response to the Writing First activity on page 347. Does every word group that is punctuated as a sentence include a subject? On the lines below, correct any missing-subject fragments you find.

_____

_____

_____

_____

_____

C   Phrase Fragments

Every sentence must include a subject and a verb. A **phrase** is a group of words that is missing a subject or a verb or both. When you punctuate a phrase as if it is a sentence, you create a fragment. You can usually correct a phrase fragment in your writing by attaching it to the sentence that comes directly before it.

An **appositive** identifies, renames, or describes a noun or a pronoun. An appositive phrase cannot stand alone as a sentence. To correct an appositive fragment, attach it to the sentence containing the nouns or pronouns that the appositive identifies.

                                                                ⌐— FRAGMENT —

INCORRECT   He decorated the room in his favorite colors. Brown and black.

CORRECT   He decorated the room in his favorite colors, brown and black.

Sometimes a word or expression like *including, such as, for example,* or *for instance* introduces an appositive. Even if an appositive phrase is introduced by one of these expressions, it is still a fragment.

                                                            ⌐—FRAGMENT—

INCORRECT   A balanced diet should include high-fiber foods. Such as leafy vegetables, fruits, beans, and whole-grain bread.

CORRECT   A balanced diet should include high-fiber foods, such as leafy vegetables, fruits, beans, and whole-grain bread.

A **prepositional phrase** consists of a preposition and its object. A prepositional phrase cannot stand alone as a sentence. To correct a prepositional phrase fragment, attach it to the sentence that comes directly before it.

                                          ⌐——— FRAGMENT ———⌐

INCORRECT   She promised to stand by him. In sickness and in health.

CORRECT   She promised to stand by him in sickness and in health.

An **infinitive** consists of *to* plus the base form of the verb (*to be, to go, to write*). An infinitive phrase (*to be free, to go home, to write a novel*) cannot stand alone as a sentence. You can usually correct an infinitive phrase fragment by attaching it to the sentence that comes directly before it.

                                          ⌐——— FRAGMENT ———

INCORRECT   Eric considered dropping out of school. To start his own business.

CORRECT   Eric considered dropping out of school to start his own business.

ON THE WEB
Visit *Exercise Central* at
bedfordstmartins.com/writingfirst
for more practice.

> ■ **Culture Clue**
>
> The most famous infinitive phrase comes from Shakespeare's play *Hamlet:* "To be or not to be, that is the question."

22 C

You can also add the words necessary to complete the sentence.

CORRECT Eric considered dropping out of school. He wanted to start his own business.

◆ **PRACTICE 22-5**

In the following paragraph, some of the numbered groups of words are phrase fragments. First, identify each fragment by labeling it *F*. Then, decide how each fragment could be attached to an adjacent sentence to create a complete new sentence. Finally, rewrite the entire paragraph, using complete sentences, on the lines provided.

Example: A maze is a type of puzzle in which a person has to find his or her way. _____ Through a complicated route. ___*F*___

Rewrite: *A maze is a type of puzzle in which a person has to find his or her way through a complicated route.*

(1) Mazes have been constructed out of paving stones, cornfields, and rooms. _____ (2) Connected by doors. _____ (3) Printed mazes can be solved with a pen or pencil. _____ (4) During the 1970s, many books and magazines published printed mazes. _____ (5) For children and adults. _____ (6) There are no foolproof ways to escape. _____ (7) From a maze. _____ (8) One strategy is to keep turning to either the right or the left. _____ (9) To keep from getting lost. _____ (10) Mazes can be fun to explore. _____ (11) On foot or on paper. _____

Rewrite:

_____

_____

_____

_____

_____

_____

◆ **PRACTICE 22-6**

In the following paragraph, some of the numbered groups of words are phrase fragments. First, underline each fragment. Then, decide how each fragment could be attached to an adjacent sentence to create a complete new sentence. Finally, rewrite the entire paragraph, using complete sentences, on the lines provided.

Example

Nurses' uniforms have changed a lot. <u>Over the years.</u>

Rewrite: *Nurses' uniforms have changed a lot over the years.*

(1) Originally, nurses' uniforms looked like nuns' habits because nuns used to take care. (2) Of sick people. (3) In the late 1800s, a student of Florence Nightingale created a brown uniform. (4) With a white apron and cap. (5) This uniform was worn by student nurses at her school. (6) The Florence Nightingale School of Nursing and Midwifery. (7) Eventually, nurses began to wear white uniforms, white stockings, white shoes, and starched white caps. (8) To stress the importance of cleanliness. (9) Many older people remember these uniforms. (10) With affection. (11) Today, most nurses wear bright, comfortable scrubs. (12) To help patients (especially children) feel more at ease.

Rewrite:

_____

_____

_____

_____

_____

_____

_____

◆ **PRACTICE 22-7**

Each of the following items is a phrase fragment, not a sentence. Correct each fragment by adding any words needed to turn the fragment into a complete sentence. (You may add words before or after the fragment.)

Example: During World War I. *A flu epidemic killed millions of people during World War I. or During World War I, a flu epidemic killed millions of people.*

1. To be the best player on the team. _____

_____

356

SOLVING
COMMON
SENTENCE
PROBLEMS

22 D

2. From a developing nation in Africa. _____

_____

3. Such as tulips or roses. _____

_____

4. Behind door number 3. _____

_____

5. Including my parents and grandparents. _____

_____

6. With a new car in the driveway. _____

_____

7. To make a difficult career decision. _____

_____

8. For a long time. _____

_____

9. Turkey, stuffing, potatoes, and cranberry sauce. _____

_____

10. In less than a year. _____

_____

■ **WRITING FIRST: Flashback**

Look back at your response to the Writing First activity on
page 347. Are any phrases incorrectly punctuated as sentences?
On the lines below, correct each phrase fragment you find.
(Hint: In most cases, you will be able to attach the fragment
to the sentence that comes right before it.)

_____

_____

_____

D *-ing* **Fragments**

Every sentence must include a subject and a verb. If the verb is incomplete, a word group is a fragment, not a sentence.

An *-ing* verb cannot be a complete verb. It needs a **helping verb** to
complete it. An *-ing* verb, such as *looking*, cannot stand alone in a sentence

without a helping verb (*is looking,* *was looking,* *were looking,* and so on). When you use an *-ing* verb without a helping verb, you create a fragment.

┌─────────── FRAGMENT ───────────┐

INCORRECT   The twins are full of mischief. Always looking for trouble.

One way to correct an *-ing* fragment is to attach it to the sentence that comes right before it.

CORRECT   The twins are full of mischief, always looking for trouble.

Another way to correct an *-ing* fragment is to add a subject and a helping verb.

CORRECT   The twins are full of mischief. They are always looking for trouble.

FOCUS *Being*

The *-ing* verb *being* is often used incorrectly as if it were a complete verb.

INCORRECT   I decided to take a nap. The outcome being that I slept through calculus class.

To correct this kind of fragment, substitute a form of the verb *be* that can serve as the main verb in a sentence—for example, *is, was, are,* or *were.*

CORRECT   I decided to take a nap. The outcome was that I slept through calculus class.

◆ **PRACTICE 22-8**

Each of the following items includes an *-ing* fragment. In each case, correct the fragment by attaching it to the sentence before it.

Example: Certain tips can help grocery shoppers. Saving them a lot of money.

Certain tips can help grocery shoppers, saving them a lot of money.

1. Always try to find a store brand. Costing less than the well-known and widely advertised brands.

_____

_____

358

SOLVING
COMMON
SENTENCE
PROBLEMS

22 D

2. Look for a product's cost per pound. Comparing it to the cost per pound of similar products.

_____

_____

3. Learn which stores are best for different kinds of products. Understanding that some stores are good only for certain items.

_____

_____

4. Examine sale-priced fruits and vegetables. Checking carefully for damage or spoilage.

_____

_____

5. Buy different brands of the same product. Trying each one to see which brand you like best.

_____

_____

◆ **PRACTICE 22-9**

All of the following are fragments. Turn each fragment into a complete sentence by adding a subject and a helping verb. Write your revised sentence on the line below each fragment.

Example: Running down the stairs.

Revised: _Jane and her dog were running down the stairs._

1. Trying to decide where to live.

Revised: _____

_____

2. Sleeping whenever he could.

Revised: _____

_____

3. Learning to be a good neighbor.

Revised: _____

_____

4. Turning off all the lights in the house.

Revised: _____

_____

5. Volunteering to help.

Revised: _____

_____

6. Really feeling optimistic about the future.

Revised: _____

_____

7. Always complaining about the lab manual.

Revised: _____

_____

8. Deciding whether or not to get a new cell phone.

Revised: _____

_____

9. Minding their own business.

Revised: _____

_____

10. Finally handing me the car keys.

Revised: _____

_____

■ WRITING FIRST: Flashback

Look back at your response to the Writing First activity on
page 347. Underline any *-ing* modifiers you find. Are the sentences in which they appear complete? Correct each fragment
you find. Then, write your corrected sentences on the lines below.

_____

_____

_____

_____

360

SOLVING
COMMON
SENTENCE
PROBLEMS

22 **E**

E **Dependent Clause Fragments**

Every sentence must include a subject and a verb. A sentence must also express a complete thought.

A **dependent clause** is a group of words that is introduced by a **dependent word**, such as *although, because, that,* or *after.* A dependent clause includes a subject and a verb, but it does not express a complete thought. Therefore, it cannot stand alone as a sentence. To correct a dependent clause fragment, you must complete the thought.

The following dependent clause is incorrectly punctuated as if it were a sentence.

FRAGMENT   After Simon won the lottery.

This sentence fragment includes both a subject (*Simon*) and a complete verb (*won*), but it does not express a complete thought. What happened after Simon won the lottery? To turn this fragment into a sentence, you need to complete the thought.

SENTENCE   After Simon won the lottery, <u>he quit his night job.</u>

Some dependent clauses are introduced by dependent words called **subordinating conjunctions**.

FRAGMENT   Although Marisol had always dreamed of coming to America.

This sentence fragment includes a subject (*Marisol*) and a complete verb (*had dreamed*), but it is not a sentence; it is a dependent clause introduced by the subordinating conjunction *although.*

To correct this kind of fragment, attach it to an **independent clause** (a simple sentence) to complete the idea. (You can often find the independent clause you need right before or right after the fragment.)

SENTENCE   Although Marisol had always dreamed of coming to America, <u>she did not have enough money for the trip until 1985.</u>

FOCUS **Subordinating Conjunctions**

after	even though	since	whenever
although	if	so that	where
as	if only	than	whereas
as if	in order that	that	wherever
as though	now that	though	whether
because	once	unless	while
before	provided that	until	
even if	rather than	when	

For information on how to use subordinating conjunctions, see 17B.

FOCUS Correcting Dependent Clause Fragments

The simplest way to correct a dependent clause fragment is just to cross out the dependent word (the subordinating conjunction or relative pronoun) that makes the idea incomplete.

~~Although~~ Marisol had always dreamed of coming to America.

However, when you delete the dependent word, readers may have trouble seeing the connection between the new sentence and the one before or after it. A better way to revise is to attach the dependent clause fragment to an independent clause, as illustrated on page 360.

Other dependent clauses are introduced by dependent words called **relative pronouns**.

FRAGMENT   Novelist Richard Wright, <u>who</u> came to Paris in 1947.

FRAGMENT   A quinceañera, <u>which</u> celebrates a Latina's fifteenth birthday.

FRAGMENT   A key World War II battle <u>that</u> was fought on the Pacific island of Guadalcanal.

Each of the above sentence fragments includes a subject (*Richard Wright, quinceañera, battle*) and a complete verb (*came, celebrates, was fought*). However, they are not sentences because they do not express complete thoughts. In each case, a relative pronoun creates a dependent clause.

To correct each of these fragments, add the words needed to complete the thought.

SENTENCE   Novelist Richard Wright, who came to Paris in 1947, <u>spent the rest of his life there</u>.

SENTENCE   A quinceañera, which celebrates a Latina's fifteenth birthday, <u>signifies her entrance into womanhood</u>.

SENTENCE   A key World War II battle that was fought on the Pacific island of Guadalcanal <u>took place in 1943</u>.

ON THE WEB
Visit *Exercise Central* at
bedfordstmartins.com/writingfirst
for more practice.

FOCUS Relative Pronouns

that	who	whomever
what	whoever	whose
which	whom	

For information on how to use relative pronouns, see 17C.

362

SOLVING
COMMON
SENTENCE
PROBLEMS

22 E

◆ **PRACTICE 22-10**

Correct each of these dependent clause fragments in two ways. First, turn the fragment into a complete sentence by adding an independent clause to complete the idea. Second, delete the subordinating conjunction or relative pronoun that makes the idea incomplete.

> **Example:** Before it became a state.
>
> Revised: *Before it became a state, West Virginia was part of Virginia.*
>
> Revised: *It became a state.*

1. Because many homeless people are mentally ill.

Revised: _____

_____

Revised: _____

_____

ON THE WEB
Visit *Exercise Central* at
bedfordstmartins.com/writingfirst
for more practice.

2. The film that frightened me.

Revised: _____

_____

Revised: _____

_____

3. Although raccoons can be found living wild in many parts of the United States.

Revised: _____

_____

Revised: _____

_____

4. People who drink and drive.

Revised: _____

_____

Revised: _____

_____

5. Some parents who are too strict with their children.

Revised: _____

_____

Revised: _____

_____

6. Whenever a new semester begins.

Revised: _____

_____

Revised: _____

_____

7. The Vietnam War, which led to widespread protests in the United States.

Revised: _____

_____

Revised: _____

_____

8. Animals that are used in medical research.

Revised: _____

_____

Revised: _____

_____

9. Unless something is likely to change.

Revised: _____

_____

Revised: _____

_____

10. Although it is a very controversial issue.

Revised: _____

_____

Revised: _____

_____

◆ PRACTICE 22-11

All of the following are fragments. Some are phrases incorrectly punctuated as sentences, others do not have a complete verb, and still others are dependent clauses punctuated as sentences. Turn each fragment into a complete sentence, writing the revised sentence on the line below the fragment. Whenever possible, try creating two different revisions.

Example: Waiting in the dugout.

Revised: *Waiting in the dugout, the players chewed tobacco.*

364

SOLVING
COMMON
SENTENCE
PROBLEMS

22 E

Revised: *The players were waiting in the dugout.*

1. Because three-year-olds are still very attached to their parents.

Revised: _____

_____

Revised: _____

_____

2. Going around in circles.

Revised: _____

_____

Revised: _____

_____

3. To win the prize for the most unusual costume.

Revised: _____

_____

Revised: _____

_____

4. Students who thought they could not afford to go to college.

Revised: _____

_____

Revised: _____

_____

5. On an important secret mission.

Revised: _____

_____

Revised: _____

_____

6. Although many instructors see cheating as a serious problem.

Revised: _____

_____

Revised: _____

_____

7. Hoping to get another helping of chocolate fudge cake.

Revised: _____

_____

Revised: _____

_____

8. The rule that I always felt was the most unfair.

Revised: _____

_____

Revised: _____

_____

9. A really exceptional worker.

Revised: _____

_____

Revised: _____

_____

10. Finished in record time.

Revised: _____

_____

Revised: _____

_____

■ **WRITING FIRST: Flashback**

Look back at your response to the Writing First activity on page 347. Underline every subordinating conjunction you find, and underline *which, that,* and *who* wherever you find them. Do any of these words introduce a dependent clause that is punctuated as if it is a sentence? On the lines below, correct each fragment you find either by deleting the subordinating conjunction or relative pronoun or by attaching the fragment to another word group to create a complete sentence.

_____

_____

_____

(*continued on following page*)

366

SOLVING
COMMON
SENTENCE
PROBLEMS

22 E

(continued from previous page)

_____

_____

_____

■ WRITING FIRST: Revising and Editing

Look back at your response to the Writing First activity on page 347. Incorporating corrections from all the Flashback activities in this chapter, revise your work. Then, check one more time to make sure every sentence is complete.

CHAPTER REVIEW

◆ EDITING PRACTICE: PARAGRAPH

Read the following student paragraph, which includes incomplete sentences. Underline each fragment. Then, correct the fragment by attaching it to an adjacent sentence that completes the idea. Be sure to punctuate correctly. The first fragment has been underlined and corrected for you.

My First Job

When I was in high school, I worked as a salesperson, <del>In</del> *in* a retail clothing store. I always seemed to be running. Constantly straightening the same racks over and over again. When the store was busy, it was very hectic. Not all the customers were patient. Or polite. Some lost their tempers. Because they couldn't find a particular size or color. Then, they took their anger out on me. On slow nights, when the store was almost empty. I was restless and bored. Eventually, I found a more rewarding position. At a preschool for developmentally delayed children.

An Old Navy store in New York City

◆ EDITING PRACTICE: ESSAY

Read the following student essay, which includes incomplete sentences. Underline each fragment. Then, correct the fragment by attaching it to an

adjacent sentence that completes the idea. Be sure to punctuate correctly. The first fragment has been underlined and corrected for you.

Bad Behavior at the Movies

Some people have completely stopped/ ~~Going~~ *going* to the movies. They have not stopped because they dislike the movies but because they dislike the rude moviegoers. Who ruin their experience. One big problem is irritating cell phone use. There are also problems with noise. And with sharing the theater space with strangers. All these issues can make going to the movies seem like more trouble than it is worth.

Cell phones cause all sorts of problems. In movie theaters. People are told to turn off their phones. But do not always do so. Loud cell-phone conversations can be infuriating. To people who want to hear the movie. When a phone rings during the movie. It is especially annoying. Some moviegoers even complain that bright text message screens distract them. From the movie. Of course, theaters could use jammers. To block all cell-phone signals. Unfortunately, this would also block incoming emergency calls.

Noise in the movies also comes from other sources. Such as crying babies. People pay money to watch a movie. Not to listen to a baby screaming. Crinkling candy wrappers are also annoying. In addition, some moviegoers insist on talking to each other. During the movie. In fact, they may make watching a movie an interactive event. Talking to the actors and telling them what they should do next. If they have seen the movie before, they may say lines of dialogue before the actors do. Spoiling the suspense for everyone else. Sometimes people even talk about various subjects. That have nothing to do with the movie. In all these cases, the noise is a problem. For anyone who wants to watch the movie and hear the actors on the screen.

Mother and baby at the movies

Finally, going to the movies requires sharing the theater with other people. Who are neither relatives nor friends. Unfortunately, many people behave in movie theaters the same way they behave at home. When they are watching television. They may put their feet up on the seats in front of them. Making it impossible for others to sit there. Moviegoers become very annoyed if someone sits right in front of them. And

Couple kissing in movie theater

368

SOLVING
COMMON
SENTENCE
PROBLEMS

22 E

blocks their view of the screen. Of course, these issues do not come up at home. Where friends and relatives can easily work out any problems.

Irritating movie behavior has driven many people to abandon movie theaters and turn to pay-per-view or DVDs. To end this rude behavior, moviegoers need to become aware of the needs of others. And make a real effort to change their behavior. Selfishness is the problem; thinking about other people is the solution.

◆ COLLABORATIVE ACTIVITIES

1. Exchange workbooks with another student, and read each other's responses to the Writing First activity on page 347. On a separate sheet of paper, list five fragments that describe the product your partner has written about. When your own workbook is returned to you, revise each fragment written by your partner, creating a complete sentence for each one. Finally, add one of these new sentences to your own Writing First activity.

2. Working in a group of three or four students, add different subordinating conjunctions to sentences *a* through *d* below to create several different fragments. (See 17B for a list of subordinating conjunctions.) Then, turn each of the resulting fragments into a complete sentence by adding a word group that completes the idea.

Example

Sentence	*Fragment*	*New sentence*
I left the party.	As I left the party	As I left the party, I fell.
	After I left the party	After I left the party, the fun stopped.
	Until I left the party	Until I left the party, I had no idea it was so late.

Sentences

a. My mind wanders.
b. She caught the ball.
c. He made a wish.
d. Disaster struck.

3. Working in a group of three or four students, build as many sentences as you can from the fragments listed below. Use your imagination to create as many creative sentences as you can.

Example

Fragment Knowing he has an incredible memory

Sentences Zack, knowing he has an incredible memory, wonders how he managed to forget everything he learned about chemistry.
Knowing he has an incredible memory, Monty the Magnificent is confident that he can amaze his audience.

Fragments

a. wandering in the desert
b. never worrying about anything
c. looking for his ideal mate
d. always using as much ketchup as possible
e. starting a new job

☑ REVIEW CHECKLIST:
Sentence Fragments

▪ A sentence fragment is an incomplete sentence. Every sentence must include a subject and a verb and express a complete thought. (See 22A.)

▪ Every sentence must include a subject. (See 22B.)

▪ Phrases cannot stand alone as sentences. (See 22C.)

▪ Every sentence must include a complete verb. (See 22D.)

▪ Dependent clauses cannot stand alone as sentences. (See 22E.)

Subject-Verb Agreement

■ WRITING FIRST

The picture above, a painting by Ralph Fasanella called *Baseball Panorama*, shows players and fans at a baseball game. Look at the picture, and then describe what is happening on the field and in the stands. (Use present tense verbs.)

▶ **Word Power**

spectacle a large-scale public show or event

reaction a response

anticipation an expectation

A   Understanding Subject-Verb Agreement

A sentence's subject (a noun or a pronoun) and its verb must **agree**: singular subjects take singular verbs, and plural subjects take plural verbs.

The <u>museum</u> <u>opens</u> at ten o'clock. (singular noun subject *museum* takes singular verb *opens*)

The <u>museums</u> <u>open</u> at ten o'clock. (plural noun subject *museums* takes plural verb *open*)

<u>She</u> always <u>watches</u> the eleven o'clock news. (singular pronoun subject *she* takes singular verb *watches*)

<u>They</u> always <u>watch</u> the eleven o'clock news. (plural pronoun subject *they* takes plural verb *watch*)

Subject-Verb Agreement with Regular Verbs

	Singular	**Plural**
First person	I play	Molly and I/we play
Second person	you play	you play
Third person	he/she/it plays	they play
	the man plays	the men play
	Molly plays	Molly and Sam play

◆ **PRACTICE 23-1**

Underline the correct form of the verb in each of the following sentences. Make sure the verb agrees with its subject.

Example: Radio stations (<u>broadcast</u>/broadcasts) many kinds of music.

(1) Most music fans (know/knows) about salsa, a popular style of Latin music. (2) However, they (need/needs) a little education when it comes to ranchera, a blend of several traditional forms of Mexican music. (3) These forms (include/includes) mariachi music as well as ballads and waltz-like tunes. (4) Ranchera (appeal/appeals) to a wide audience of Americans of Mexican descent. (5) Its performers (sell/sells) millions of records a year, and often they (top/tops) *Billboard*'s Latin charts. (6) In fact, Mexican recordings (outsell/outsells) any other form of Latin music in the United States. (7) This popularity (surprise/surprises) many people. (8) Older ranchera lovers (tend/tends) to be first-generation, working-class immigrants, but more and more young listeners (seem/seems) drawn to ranchera. (9) Whenever one

ON THE WEB
Visit *Exercise Central* at
bedfordstmartins.com/writingfirst
for more practice.

372

SOLVING
COMMON
SENTENCE
PROBLEMS

23 A

Los Angeles nightclub (host/hosts) a ranchera night, it (draw/draws) a large number of English-speaking fans in their twenties. (10) Clearly, ranchera musicians (deserve/deserves) more attention from the music industry.

◆ **PRACTICE 23-2**

Fill in the blank with the correct present tense form of the verb.

Example: Americans _____*commute*_____ an average of 25 minutes to work each day. (commute)

(1) "Extreme commuters" _____ at least 90 minutes getting to work. (spend) (2) Their commutes _____ much longer than the average American's trip to work. (take) (3) Sometimes, an extreme commuter even _____ state lines to get to work. (cross) (4) Often, a person _____ an extra-long commute for housing reasons. (choose) (5) Far outside the city, the "exurbs" _____ more affordable houses. (offer) (6) A more rural area usually _____ more peaceful surroundings as well. (provide) (7) Many extreme commuters _____ the time they spend commuting. (hate) (8) Others _____ the time they get to think, talk to other commuters, or listen to music. (enjoy) (9) In any case, extreme commuters usually _____ such a long way to work because they have to. (travel) (10) For better or worse, more and more people _____ extreme commuters every year. (become)

■ **WRITING FIRST: Flashback**

Look back at your response to the Writing First activity on page 370. Choose two sentences that contain present tense verbs, and rewrite the sentences on the lines below. Underline the subject of each sentence once and the verb twice. If the subject and verb of each sentence do not agree, correct them.

_____

_____

_____

_____

B **Compound Subjects**

The subject of a sentence is not always a single word. It can also be a **compound subject**, made up of two or more words. To avoid subject-verb agreement problems with compound subjects, follow these rules.

■ When the parts of a compound subject are connected by *and,* the compound subject takes a plural verb.

> John and Marsha share an office.

■ When the parts of a compound subject are connected by *or,* the verb agrees with the part of the subject that is closer to it.

> The mayor or the council members meet with community
>
> groups.
>
> The council members or the mayor meets with community
>
> groups.

◆ **PRACTICE 23-3**

Underline the correct form of the verb in each of the following sentences. Make sure that the verb agrees with its compound subject.

Example: Gloves or a scarf (make/makes) a good wintertime gift.

1. Cars and trucks (fill/fills) the municipal parking lot each day.

2. Grapes or an apple (provide/provides) a nutritious addition to a lunch.

3. A guard and a video monitoring system (watch/watches) the bank's
   lobby during business hours.

4. A vegetable or french fries (come/comes) with the steak dinner.

5. A pianist or a guitarist (play/plays) at the club every weekend.

6. Nurses or nurse practitioners (offer/offers) round-the-clock patient
   care.

7. According to an old saying, fish and houseguests (smell/smells) bad
   after three days.

8. Flowers or a get-well balloon (cheer/cheers) people up when they are ill.

9. The restaurant owner or her daughter always (greet/greets) customers.

10. A sliding glass door or French windows (allow/allows) light into a
    room.

▶ **Word Power**
municipal   relating to a
town, city, or a local
government

374

23 C

SOLVING
COMMON
SENTENCE
PROBLEMS

■ **WRITING FIRST: Flashback**

Look at the two sentences you wrote for the Flashback activity on page 372. Rewrite them with compound subjects. In each sentence, make sure the compound subjects agree with the verb.

_____

_____

_____

_____

C   *Be, Have, and* **Do**

The verbs *be, have,* and *do* are irregular in the present tense. For this reason, they can present problems with subject-verb agreement. Memorizing their forms is the only sure way to avoid such problems.

Subject-Verb Agreement with Be

	Singular	*Plural*
First person	I am	we are
Second person	you are	you are
Third person	he/she/it is	they are
	Tran is	Tran and Ryan are
	the boy is	the boys are

Subject-Verb Agreement with Have

	Singular	*Plural*
First person	I have	we have
Second person	you have	you have
Third person	he/she/it has	they have
	Shana has	Shana and Robert have
	the student has	the students have

Subject-Verb Agreement with Do

	Singular	*Plural*
First person	I do	we do
Second person	you do	you do
Third person	he/she/it does	they do
	Ken does	Ken and Mia do
	the book does	the books do

◆ **PRACTICE 23-4**

Fill in the blank with the correct present tense form of the verb *be, have,* or *do.*

Example: Sometimes, people __do__ damage without really meaning to. (do)

(1) Biologists __is__ serious worries about the damage that invading species of animals can cause. (have) (2) The English sparrow _____ one example. (be) (3) It __have__ a role in the decline in the number of bluebirds. (have) (4) On the Galapagos Islands, cats __are__ another example. (be) (5) Introduced by early explorers, they currently __do__ much damage to the eggs of the giant tortoises that live on the islands. (do) (6) Scientists today __are__ worried about a new problem. (be) (7) This __is__ a situation caused by wildlife agencies that put exotic fish into lakes and streams. (be) (8) They __do__ this to please those who enjoy fishing. (do) (9) Although popular with people who fish, this policy __have__ major drawbacks. (have) (10) It __has__ one drawback in particular: many species of fish have been pushed close to extinction. (have)

ON THE WEB
Visit *Exercise Central* at
bedfordstmartins.com/writingfirst
for more practice.

■ **WRITING FIRST: Flashback**

Look back at your response to the Writing First activity on page 370. Have you used a form of *be, have,* or *do* in any of your sentences? If so, copy these sentences on the lines below. Have you used the correct forms of *be, have,* and *do?* Correct any agreement errors.

_____

_____

_____

_____

376

SOLVING
COMMON
SENTENCE
PROBLEMS

23 D ✓

D   Words between Subject and Verb

Don't be confused when a group of words (for example, a prepositional phrase) comes between the subject and the verb. These words do not affect subject-verb agreement.

CORRECT   High <u>levels</u> of mercury <u>occur</u> in some fish.

CORRECT   <u>Water</u> in the fuel lines <u>causes</u> an engine to stall.

CORRECT   <u>Food</u> between the teeth <u>leads</u> to decay.

An easy way to identify the subject of the sentence is to cross out the words that come between the subject and the verb.

High levels ~~of mercury~~ occur in some fish.

Water ~~in the fuel lines~~ causes an engine to stall.

Food ~~between the teeth~~ leads to decay.

ON THE WEB
Visit *Exercise Central* at
bedfordstmartins.com/writingfirst
for more practice.

FOCUS   Words between Subject and Verb

Look out for words such as *in addition to, along with, together with, as well as, except,* and *including.* Phrases introduced by these words do not affect subject-verb agreements.

<u>St. Thomas</u>, ~~along with St. Croix and St. John~~, <u>is</u> part of the United States Virgin Islands.

◆ **PRACTICE 23-5** ✓

In each of the following sentences, cross out the words that separate the subject and the verb. Then, underline the subject of the sentence once and the verb that agrees with the subject twice.

Example: The <u>messages</u> ~~on the phone~~ (<u>say</u>/says) that Carol is out of town.

1. Each summer, <u>fires</u> ~~from lightning~~ (cause/<u>causes</u>) a great deal of damage.

2. Global <u>warming</u> ~~from pollution~~ (make/<u>makes</u>) the earth hotter.

3. <u>One</u> ~~out of ten men~~ (<u>gets</u>/get) prostate cancer.

4. The wood <u>stove</u> ~~in the living room~~ (heat/<u>heats</u>) the entire house.

5. Trans fat in a variety of foods (lead/leads) to increased rates of heart disease.

6. A good set of mechanic's tools (costs/cost) a lot of money.

7. New Orleans, along with other Gulf Coast cities, (suffers/suffer) from severe flooding.

8. The United States as well as Germany and Japan (produces/produce) the world's best cars.

9. Fans at a concert (gets/get) angry if the band is late.

10. The book on the table (look/looks) like an interesting story.

■ **WRITING FIRST: Flashback**

Look back at your response to the Writing First activity on page 370. Can you find any sentences in which a prepositional phrase comes between the subject and the verb? If so, write each subject and verb on the lines below.

Subject   Verb

_____   _____

_____   _____

_____   _____

_____   _____

Now, correct any errors in subject-verb agreement.

E **Collective Noun Subjects**

Collective nouns are words (such as *family* and *audience*) that name a group of people or things but are singular. Because they are singular, they always take singular verbs.

          s   v
The team practices five days a week in the gym.

Frequently Used Collective Nouns

army	club	family	jury
association	committee	gang	mob
band	company	government	team
class	corporation	group	union

378

SOLVING
COMMON
SENTENCE
PROBLEMS

23 F

◆ **PRACTICE 23-6**

Fill in the blank with the correct present tense form of the verb.

Example: The club _____is_____ supposed to meet every Tuesday. (be)

1. The jury usually _____ a verdict after much discussion. (reach)

2. Before the exam, the class _____ into study groups. (break)

3. Each year, the family _____goes_____ to the beach for a vacation. (go)

4. Every year, the corporation _____ a new health plan for its

   employees. (establish)

5. A group of lions _____ resting under the trees. (be)

■ **WRITING FIRST: Flashback**

Look back at your response to the Writing First activity on page 370. Can you find any sentences that have collective nouns as subjects? If so, check carefully to make sure the subjects and verbs agree. If they do not, revise each incorrect sentence. Write the correct form of each verb on the lines below.

Collective Noun Subject   *Verb*

_____   _____

_____   _____

F **Indefinite Pronoun Subjects**

Indefinite pronouns—*anybody, everyone,* and so on—do not refer to a particular person, place, or idea.

Most indefinite pronouns are singular and take singular verbs.

    s   v
No one likes getting up early.

     s   v
Everyone likes to sleep late.

     s   v
Somebody likes beets.

Singular Indefinite Pronouns

another	either	neither	one
anybody	everybody	nobody	somebody
anyone	everyone	no one	someone
anything	everything	nothing	something
each	much		

A few indefinite pronouns (*both, many, several, few, others*) are plural and take plural verbs.

  s   v
Many were left homeless by the flood.

FOCUS **Indefinite Pronouns as Subjects**

If a prepositional phrase comes between the indefinite pronoun and the verb, cross out the prepositional phrase to help you identify the sentence's subject.

  s   v
Each ~~of the boys~~ has a bike.

  s   v
Many ~~of the boys~~ have bikes.

◆ **PRACTICE 23-7**

Circle the correct verb in each sentence.

Example: Each of the three streams in our area ((is)/are) polluted.

1. One of the streams no longer (have/has) any fish.

2. Another (contain/contains) a lot of algae.

3. Everybody (want/wants) to improve the situation.

4. However, no one (are/is) willing to do anything.

5. Somebody (need/needs) to take the lead.

6. Everyone (know/knows) that pollution is difficult to control.

7. Neither of the candidates (seem/seems) willing to act.

8. Whenever anyone (ask/asks) them for suggestions, neither (have, has) any.

ON THE WEB
Visit *Exercise Central* at
bedfordstmartins.com/writingfirst
for more practice.

▶ **Word Power**

algae water-dwelling organisms that look like plants but have no roots, stems, or leaves

380

23 G

SOLVING
COMMON
SENTENCE
PROBLEMS

9. According to the candidates, everything possible (is/are) being done.

10. One of my friends (say/says) that she will not vote for either candidate.

■ **WRITING FIRST: Flashback**

Look back at your response to the Writing First activity on page 370. Do any of your sentences contain indefinite pronoun subjects? Write each indefinite pronoun subject and its verb on the lines below. Do all the verbs agree with their indefinite pronoun subjects? Correct any errors below.

Indefinite Pronoun Subject   *Verb*

_____   _____

_____   _____

_____   _____

_____   _____

_____   _____

_____   _____

G Verbs before Subjects

A verb always agrees with its subject—even if the verb comes *before* the subject. In questions, for example, word order is reversed, with the verb coming before the subject or with the subject coming between two parts of the verb.

       V   S
Where is the bank?

   V   S   V
Are you going to the party?

If you have trouble identifying the subject of a question, answer the question with a statement. (In the statement, the subject will come before the verb.)

     V   S   S   V
Where is the bank? The bank is on Walnut Street.

FOCUS **There Is and There Are**

When a sentence begins with *there is* or *there are*, the word *there* is not the subject of the sentence. The subject comes after the form of the verb *be*.

> v   s
> There is one chief justice on the Supreme Court.

> v   s
> There are nine justices on the Supreme Court.

◆ **PRACTICE 23-8**

Underline the subject of each sentence, and circle the correct form of the verb.

> **Example:** Who (is/are) the baseball player who broke Hank Aaron's
>
> home run record?

1. Where (do/does) snakes go in the winter?

2. Why (do/does) people who cannot afford them buy lottery tickets?

3. (Is/Are) there any states that do not follow Daylight Savings Time?

4. How (do/does) an immigrant become a citizen?

5. There (is/are) three branches of government in the United States.

6. There (is/are) one way to improve vocabulary—read often.

7. There (is/are) some money available for financial aid.

8. There (is/are) four steps involved in changing the oil in a car.

9. What (is/are) the country with the highest literacy rate?

10. Where (do/does) the football team practice in the off season?

Culture Clue

In the United States, *Daylight Savings Time* provides more usable daylight hours during the spring, summer, and fall months. This helps people to decrease their energy consumption.

382

23 G

SOLVING
COMMON
SENTENCE
PROBLEMS

■ WRITING FIRST: Flashback

Look back at your response to the Writing First activity on page 370. Do you have any sentences in which the verb comes before the subject? If so, write these sentences on the lines below. Then, check carefully to make sure the subjects and verbs agree. If they do not, revise each incorrect sentence here.

_____

_____

_____

_____

_____

■ WRITING FIRST: Revising and Editing

Look back at your response to the Writing First activity on page 370. Incorporating changes and corrections from this chapter's Flashback activities, revise your work, making sure all your verbs agree with their subjects.

CHAPTER REVIEW

◆ EDITING PRACTICE: PARAGRAPH

Read the following student paragraph, which includes errors in subject-verb agreement. Decide whether or not each of the underlined verbs agrees with its subject. If it does not, cross out the verb, and write in the correct form. If it does, write *C* above the verb. The first sentence has been done for you.

Conflict Diamonds

Today, many people <u>know</u> [C] about conflict diamonds, and most <u>wants</u> [want] this violent trade to end. These illegal diamonds <u>comes</u> from countries where there <u>are</u> civil war. Most often, the origin of these stones <u>is</u> an unstable central or west African nation. Rebel groups in these countries <u>mines</u> the diamonds and <u>sells</u> them to

Couple choosing an engagement ring

raise money for weapons. In the process, local people, who <u>does</u> not benefit from the sale of the diamonds, often <u>gets</u> hurt or killed. How <u>does</u> a person who wants to buy a diamond avoid buying a conflict diamond? Once a diamond <u>reach</u> the store, neither a customer nor a gem expert <u>have</u> the ability to see its history just by looking at it. However, a consumer can ask for proof that the diamond <u>is</u> "conflict-free." Each of the diamonds in a store <u>are</u> supposed to have an official certificate to prove that it <u>is</u> legal.

◆ **EDITING PRACTICE: ESSAY**

Read the following student essay, which includes errors in subject-verb agreement. Decide whether each of the underlined verbs agrees with its subject. If it does not, cross out the verb, and write in the correct form. If it does, write *C* above the verb. The first sentence has been done for you.

■ Culture Clue
Pickup trucks have large open cargo areas behind the cab; *station wagons* are four-door cars with long cargo areas behind the seats; *SUVs* are sport utility vehicles.

Party in the Parking Lot

Fun at football games <u>are</u> (*is*) not limited to cheering for the home team. Many people <u>arrives</u> four or five hours early, <u>sets</u> up grills in the parking lot, and <u>start</u> cooking. Typically, fans <u>drives</u> to the stadium in a pickup truck, a station wagon, or an SUV. They <u>open</u> up the tailgate, <u>puts</u> out the food, and <u>enjoys</u> the atmosphere with their friends. In fact, tailgating <u>is</u> so popular that, for some fans, it is more important than the game itself.

What <u>do</u> it take to tailgate? First, most tailgaters <u>plan</u> their menus in advance. To avoid forgetting anything, they <u>makes</u> lists of what to bring. Paper plates, along with a set of plastic glasses, <u>make</u> it unnecessary to bring home dirty dishes. Jugs of water <u>is</u> essential, and damp towels <u>helps</u> clean up hands and faces. Also, light-weight chairs or another type of seating <u>is</u> important.

At the game, parking near a grassy area or at the end of a parking row <u>are</u> best. This location <u>give</u> tailgaters more space to cook and eat. If the food <u>are</u> ready two hours before the game <u>start</u>, there <u>is</u> plenty of time to eat and to clean up.

Some tailgaters <u>buys</u> expensive equipment. The simple charcoal grill <u>have</u> turned into a combination grill, cooler, and fold-out table with a portable awning. There <u>is</u> grills with their own storage space. Other grills <u>swings</u> out from the

Tailgaters deep-frying a turkey

Tailgating in stadium parking lot

384

SOLVING
COMMON
SENTENCE
PROBLEMS

23 G

*Eagles and Patriots fans at
Superbowl XXXIX (2005)*

tailgate to provide easy access to the vehicle's storage area. Some deluxe grills even <u>has</u> their own beer taps, TVs, and sinks.

Whatever equipment tailgaters <u>brings</u> to the game, the most important factors <u>is</u> food and companionship. There <u>is</u> a tradition of sharing food and swapping recipes with other tailgaters. Most tailgaters <u>loves</u> to meet one another and compare notes on recipes. For many, the tailgating experience <u>is</u> more fun than the game itself.

◆ COLLABORATIVE ACTIVITIES

1. Working in a group of four students, list ten nouns (five singular and five plural)—people, places, or things—on the left-hand side of a sheet of paper. Beside each noun, write the present tense form of a verb that could logically be used with the noun. Exchange papers with another group, and check to see that singular nouns are used with singular verbs and plural nouns are used with plural verbs.

2. Working with your group, expand each noun-and-verb combination you listed in Collaborative Activity 1 into a complete sentence. Next, write a sentence that could logically follow each of these sentences, using a pronoun as the subject of the new sentence. Make sure the pronoun you choose refers to the noun in the previous sentence, as in this example: *Alan watches three movies a week. He is addicted to films.* Check to be certain the subjects in your sentences agree with the verbs.

3. Exchange the final version of your edited Writing First activity with another student in your group. Answer the following questions about each sentence in your partner's work.

   ■ Does the sentence contain a compound subject?
   ■ Does the sentence contain words that come between the subject and the verb?
   ■ Does the sentence contain an indefinite pronoun used as a subject?
   ■ Does the sentence contain a verb that comes before the subject?

   As you answer these questions, check to make sure all the verbs agree with their subjects. When your own work is returned to you, make any necessary corrections.

✔ REVIEW CHECKLIST:
Subject-Verb Agreement

- ☐ Singular subjects (nouns and pronouns) take singular verbs, and plural subjects take plural verbs. (See 23A.)

- ☐ Special rules govern subject-verb agreement with compound subjects. (See 23B.)

- ☐ The irregular verbs *be, have,* and *do* often present problems with subject-verb agreement in the present tense. (See 23C.)

- ☐ Words that come between the subject and the verb do not affect subject-verb agreement. (See 23D.)

- ☐ Collective nouns are singular and take singular verbs. (See 23E.)

- ☐ Most indefinite pronouns, such as *no one* and *everyone,* are singular and take a singular verb when they serve as the subject of a sentence. A few are plural and take plural verbs. (See 23F.)

- ☐ A sentence's subject and verb must always agree, even if the verb comes before the subject. (See 23G.)

PREVIEW

In this chapter, you will learn to avoid

- illogical shifts in tense (24A)
- illogical shifts in person (24B)
- illogical shifts in voice (24C)

■ **Culture Clue**

Take Your Daughter to Work Day was created by the Ms. Foundation for Women in 1993 in order to expose young women to career opportunities. In 2003, the program was expanded to include sons.

▶ **Word Power**

aspire to strive toward a goal

encourage to inspire with hope or confidence

nurture to nourish; to bring up

■ **WRITING FIRST**

The picture above shows a mother and daughter in an office on Take Your Daughter to Work Day. Look at the picture, and then write about what parents can do to help their children succeed in their careers. How can parents motivate their children to set appropriate goals and work to achieve them?

A **shift** occurs whenever a writer changes **tense**, **person**, or **voice**. As you write and revise, be sure that any shifts you make are **logical**—that is, that they occur for a reason.

A Shifts in Tense

Tense is the form a verb takes to show when an action takes place or when a situation occurs. Some shifts in tense are necessary—for example, to indicate a change from past time to present time.

LOGICAL SHIFT   When they first <u>came</u> out, cell phones <u>were</u> large and bulky, but now they <u>are</u> small and compact.

An **illogical shift in tense** occurs when a writer shifts from one tense to another for no apparent reason.

ILLOGICAL SHIFT   The dog walked to the fireplace. Then, he circles twice and IN TENSE   lies down in front of the fire. (shift from past tense to present tense)

REVISED   The dog walked to the fireplace. Then, he circled twice and lay down in front of the fire. (consistent use of past tense)

REVISED   The dog walks to the fireplace. Then, he circles twice and lies down in front of the fire. (consistent use of present tense)

◆ PRACTICE 24-1

Edit the following sentences to correct illogical shifts in tense. If a sentence is correct, write *C* in the blank.

ON THE WEB
Visit *Exercise Central* at
bedfordstmartins.com/writingfirst
for more practice.

Examples

During World War II, the 100th Battalion of the 442nd Combat Infantry

were
Regiment was made up of young Japanese Americans who ~~are~~ eager to
                                                      ^
serve in the U.S. Army. _____

The 100th Battalion of the 442nd Infantry is the only remaining United

States Army Reserve ground combat unit that fought in World War II.

___*C*___

(1) At the start of World War II, 120,000 Japanese Americans are sent

to relocation camps because the government feared that they might be

disloyal to the United States. _____ (2) However, in 1943, the United

388

SOLVING
COMMON
SENTENCE
PROBLEMS

24 B

States needed more soldiers, so it sends recruiters to the camps to ask for volunteers. _____ (3) The Japanese-American volunteers are organized into the 442nd Combat Infantry Regiment. _____ (4) The soldiers of the 442nd Infantry fought in some of the bloodiest battles of the war, including the invasion of Italy at Anzio and a battle in Bruyeres, France, where they capture over two hundred enemy soldiers. _____ (5) When other U.S. troops are cut off by the enemy, the 442nd Infantry soldiers were sent to rescue them. _____ (6) The Japanese-American soldiers suffered the highest casualty rate of any U.S. unit and receive over eighteen thousand individual decorations. _____ (7) Former senator Daniel Inouye of Hawaii, a Japanese American, was awarded the Distinguished Service Cross for his bravery in Italy and has to have his arm amputated. _____ (8) The 442nd Infantry was awarded more decorations than any other combat unit of its size and earns eight Presidential Unit citations. _____ (9) Today, the dedication and sacrifice of the 442nd Infantry was seen as evidence that Japanese Americans were patriotic and committed to freedom and democracy. _____ (10) The bravery of the 442nd Infantry during World War II paved the way for today's desegregated American military. _____

> ■ **WRITING FIRST: Flashback**
>
> Look back at your response to the Writing First activity on page 386. Check each sentence to make sure it includes no illogical shifts from one tense to another. If you find an incorrect sentence, rewrite it on the lines below, correcting the illogical shifts in tense.
>
> _____
>
> _____
>
> _____

B **Shifts in Person**

Person is the form a pronoun takes to show who is speaking, spoken about, or spoken to.

Person		
	Singular	*Plural*
First person	I	we
Second person	you	you
Third person	he, she, it	they

An **illogical shift in person** occurs when a writer shifts from one person to another for no apparent reason.

ILLOGICAL SHIFT   The hikers were told that you had to stay on the trail. (shift from third person to second person)

REVISED   The hikers were told that they had to stay on the trail. (consistent use of third person)

ILLOGICAL SHIFT   Anyone can learn to cook if you practice. (shift from third person to second person)

REVISED   You can learn to cook if you practice. (consistent use of second person)

REVISED   Anyone can learn to cook if he or she practices. (consistent use of third person)

◆ **PRACTICE 24-2**

The following sentences contain illogical shifts in person. Edit each sentence so that it uses pronouns consistently. Be sure to change any verbs that do not agree with the new subjects.

Example: Before a person finds a job in the fashion industry,
he or she has
~~you have~~ to have some experience.
^

(1) Young people who want careers in the fashion industry do not always realize how hard you will have to work. (2) They think that working in the world of fashion will be glamorous and that you will quickly make a fortune. (3) In reality, no matter how talented you are, a recent college graduate entering the industry is paid only about $22,000 a year. (4) The manufacturers who employ new graduates expect you to work at least three years at this salary before you are promoted. (5) A young designer may get a big raise if you are very talented, but this is unusual. (6) New employees have to pay their dues, and you soon

ON THE WEB
Visit *Exercise Central* at
bedfordstmartins.com/writingfirst
for more practice.

■ Culture Clue
Pay their dues is a phrase meaning that people must work hard, learn, and be loyal for years before earning respect.

390

SOLVING
COMMON
SENTENCE
PROBLEMS

24 C

realize that most of your duties are boring. (7) An employee may land a job as an assistant designer but then find that you have to color in designs that have already been drawn. (8) Other beginners discover that you spend most of your time typing up orders. (9) If a person is serious about working in the fashion industry, you have to be realistic. (10) For most newcomers to the industry, the ability to do what you are told to do is more important than your talent.

■ **WRITING FIRST: Flashback**

Look back at your response to the Writing First activity on page 386. Check each sentence to make sure it includes no illogical shifts in person. If you find an incorrect sentence, rewrite it on the lines below, correcting illogical shifts in person.

_____

_____

_____

C **Shifts in Voice**

Voice is the form a verb takes to indicate whether the subject is acting or is acted upon. When the subject of a sentence is acting, the sentence is in the **active voice**. When the subject of a sentence is acted upon, the sentence is in the **passive voice**.

ACTIVE VOICE   Nat Turner organized a slave rebellion in August 1831. (Subject *Nat Turner* is acting.)

PASSIVE VOICE   A slave rebellion was organized by Nat Turner in 1831. (Subject *rebellion* is acted upon.)

An **illogical shift in voice** occurs when a writer shifts from active to passive voice or from passive to active voice for no apparent reason.

ILLOGICAL SHIFT   J. D. Salinger wrote *The Catcher in the Rye,* and *Franny*
IN VOICE   *and Zooey* was also written by him. (active to passive)

REVISED   J. D. Salinger wrote *The Catcher in the Rye,* and he also wrote *Franny and Zooey.* (consistent use of active voice)

ILLOGICAL SHIFT   Radium was discovered by Marie Curie in 1910, and
IN VOICE   she won a Nobel Prize in chemistry in 1911. (passive to
                   active)

REVISED   Marie Curie discovered radium in 1910, and she won
                   a Nobel Prize in chemistry in 1911. (consistent use of
                   active voice)

FOCUS **Correcting Illogical Shifts in Voice**

The active voice is stronger and more direct than the passive voice.
For this reason, you should usually use the active voice in your college writing.

To change a sentence from the passive to the active voice, determine who or what is acting, and make this noun the subject of a
new active voice sentence.

PASSIVE VOICE   The campus escort service is used by my friends.
                 (*My friends* are acting.)

ACTIVE VOICE   My friends use the campus escort service.

◆ **PRACTICE 24-3**

The following sentences contain illogical shifts in voice. Revise each
sentence by changing the underlined passive voice verb to the active voice.

Example

Two teachers believed they could help struggling students in New York

City schools, so "Chess in the Schools" was founded by them in 1986.

Two teachers believed they could help struggling students in New York

City schools, so they founded "Chess in the Schools" in 1986.

1. Chess develops critical thinking skills, and self-discipline and self-
   esteem are developed by players, too.

   _____

   _____

2. Because players face complicated chess problems, good problem-solving
   skills are developed by them.

   _____

   _____

ON THE WEB
Visit *Exercise Central* at
bedfordstmartins.com/writingfirst
for more practice.

392

SOLVING
COMMON
SENTENCE
PROBLEMS

24 C

3. Student chess players improve their concentration, and reading and math skills <u>can be improved</u> through this better concentration.

_____

_____

4. Chess teaches students how to lose as well as win, and that ability <u>will be needed</u> by students throughout their lives.

_____

_____

5. "Chess in the Schools" also helps keep students out of trouble because of the conflict resolution skills <u>developed</u> by them.

_____

_____

■ **WRITING FIRST: Flashback**

Look back at your response to the Writing First activity on page 386. Check each sentence to make sure it includes no illogical shifts in voice. If you find an incorrect sentence, rewrite it on the lines below, correcting illogical shifts in voice.

_____

_____

_____

_____

_____

_____

■ **WRITING FIRST: Revising and Editing**

Look back at your response to the Writing First activity on page 386. Revise any illogical shifts in tense, person, or voice by incorporating the changes and corrections you made in this chapter's Flashback activities. When you have finished, check for illogical shifts in another assignment you are currently working on.

CHAPTER REVIEW

◆ EDITING PRACTICE: PARAGRAPH

Read the following student paragraph, which includes illogical shifts in tense, person, and voice. Edit the passage to eliminate the unnecessary shifts, making sure subjects and verbs agree. The first error has been corrected for you.

The Origin of Baseball Cards

The first baseball cards appeared in the late 1800s. These cardboard pictures ~~are~~ *were* put in packs of cigarettes. Some people collected the cards. The cigarette companies use the cards to encourage people to buy its products. By the early twentieth century, it was found by candy makers that they could use baseball cards to sell its candy to children. As a result, they developed new marketing plans. For example, each Cracker Jack box contains a baseball card. In 1933, gum manufacturers put bubblegum in packs of baseball cards. Children could trade these cards. Sometimes, children would put cards in the spokes of their bike wheels. The cards made noise when the wheels turns. Eventually, the bubblegum was dropped by the card manufacturers, and people collected just the cards. Still, collecting baseball cards was just a hobby for children until the 1970s, when dealers began to sell his rarest cards at high prices. Today, baseball-card collectors were mainly adults who are interested in investment, not baseball.

WAGNER, PITTSBURG

1909 Honus Wagner baseball card, which sold for over two million dollars in 2000.

▪ Culture Clue

Cracker Jack is the brand name of an American snack food that consists of caramel-covered popcorn and nuts. Boxes of Cracker Jacks contain small, inexpensive toy prizes inside.

◆ EDITING PRACTICE: ESSAY

Read the following student essay, which includes illogical shifts in tense, person, and voice. Edit the passage to eliminate the unnecessary shifts, making sure subjects and verbs agree. When possible, change passive voice constructions to active voice constructions. The first sentence has been edited for you.

The Mixing of Cultures

Some immigrants to the United States think that to become American, they have to give up ~~your~~ *their* ethnic identity. Others, however, realize that you can become American without losing their identity. To me, this was the strength of the United States: as a Filipino American, you can be both Filipino and American.

Flag of the Philippines

394

SOLVING
COMMON
SENTENCE
PROBLEMS

24 C

When a family moves to the United States from the Philippines, you try to keep your native language. Although most Filipinos know how to speak English, Tagalog, is also spoken by them, usually at home. However, English is often spoken with an accent. In the United States, parents don't want their children to have a foreign accent, so they made their children speak the English that they learn in school. At the same time, parents wanted their children to learn Tagalog so that they can speak with their relatives when visiting the Philippines. As a result, parents often teach them Tagalog when the children are teens.

Many Filipino Americans decorated their houses to remind themselves of the Philippines. For example, bamboo and rattan chairs and cabinets are often used to give their homes a tropical look. Bamboo placemats, ebony wood carvings, and macramé or seashell plant hangers may also be used. Sometimes their chandeliers and even curtains are made of capiz, which was a thin, laminated shell. Baskets and bowls are often made by Philippine tribes. With these decorative touches, a Filipino-American family can make his or her house like a house in the Philippines.

In the Philippines, food reflected many cultures, including Indian, Spanish, and Chinese. For example, the staple food is rice, which is eaten by most people several times a day. Along with rice, Filipinos eat a stew made with peanuts and pork. The spices included garlic and ginger. Tropical fruit is common, especially coconut and mangoes. You can buy all these foods in the United States.

A Filipino who wants to hold on to your ethnic background can enjoy life in America. Here, cultures mix and enrich one another. Each culture had something to offer: its food, its language, and its traditions. At the same time, America had something to offer each culture: economic opportunity, education, and freedom.

Filipino-American family

◆ COLLABORATIVE ACTIVITIES

1. On a separate sheet of paper, write five sentences that include shifts from present to past tense, some logical and some illogical. Exchange papers with another person in your group, and revise any incorrect sentences.

2. As a group, make up a test with five sentences containing illogical shifts in tense, person, and voice. Exchange tests with another group in the class. After you have taken their test, compare your answers with theirs.

3. As a group, choose five words from the list below, and use each as the subject of a sentence. Make sure each sentence includes a pronoun that refers to the subject.

Example: Teachers must know their students.

anybody	children	a parent	something
anyone	everybody	people	teachers
anything	everyone	raccoons	a woman
a book	no one	someone	workers

Make sure the sentences you have written do not include any illogical shifts in person.

✔ REVIEW CHECKLIST:
Illogical Shifts

    ■ An illogical shift in tense occurs when a writer shifts from one tense to another for no apparent reason. (Sec 24A.)

    ■ An illogical shift in person occurs when a writer shifts from one person to another for no apparent reason. (See 24B.)

    ■ An illogical shift in voice occurs when a writer shifts from active to passive voice or from passive to active voice for no apparent reason. (See 24C.)

Misplaced and Dangling Modifiers

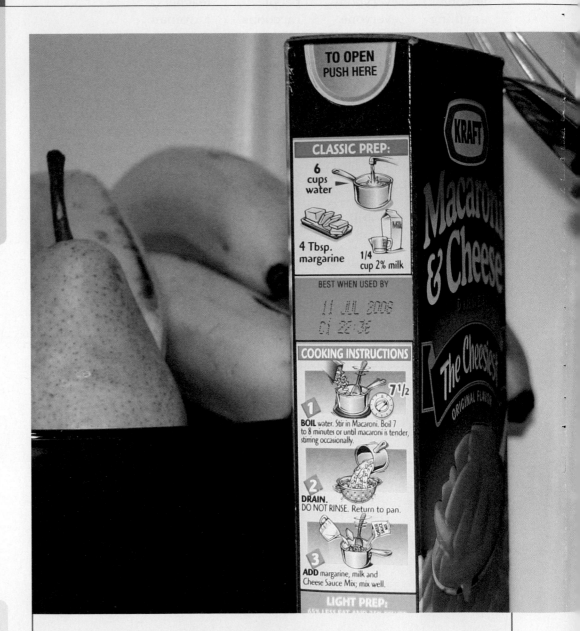

■ WRITING FIRST

The picture above shows instructions for making macaroni and cheese. Read these instructions, and then write a recipe for your favorite dish. Begin by introducing the recipe; then, list the ingredients, and explain how to prepare the dish.

A **modifier** is a word or word group that **modifies** (identifies or describes) another word in a sentence. To avoid confusion, a modifier should be placed as close as possible to the word it modifies.

Many word groups that act as modifiers are introduced by *-ing* (present participle) or *-ed* (past participle) modifiers.

> Using his garage as a workshop, Steve Jobs invented the personal computer.

> Rejected by Hamlet, Ophelia goes mad and drowns herself.

Used correctly, *-ing* and *-ed* modifiers can provide useful information. Used incorrectly, these types of modifiers can be troublesome. For this reason, when you write, you should watch out for misplaced and dangling *-ing* and *-ed* modifiers.

A Correcting Misplaced Modifiers

A **misplaced modifier** appears to modify the wrong word because it is placed incorrectly in the sentence. To correct this problem, move the modifier so it is as close as possible to the word it is supposed to modify (usually directly before it).

> INCORRECT   Sarah fed the dog wearing her pajamas. (Was the dog wearing Sarah's pajamas?)
>
> CORRECT   Wearing her pajamas, Sarah fed the dog.
>
> INCORRECT   Dressed in a raincoat and boots, I thought my son was prepared for the storm. (Who was dressed in a raincoat and boots?)
>
> CORRECT   I thought my son, dressed in a raincoat and boots, was prepared for the storm.

ON THE WEB
Visit *Exercise Central* at
bedfordstmartins.com/writingfirst
for more practice.

◆ PRACTICE 25-1

Underline the modifier in each of the following sentences. Then, draw an arrow to the word it modifies.

Example: Helping people worldwide, Doctors Without Borders is a group of volunteer medical professionals.

1. Suffering from famine and other disasters, some people are unable to help themselves.

2. Feeding and healing them, Doctors Without Borders improves their lives.

398

SOLVING
COMMON
SENTENCE
PROBLEMS

25 A

3. Responding to a recent earthquake, doctors arrived within three days to help with the relief effort.

4. Setting up refugee camps in Thailand, the group quickly helped its first survivors.

5. Some doctors, chartering a ship called *The Island of Light*, once provided medical aid to people escaping Vietnam by boat.

ON THE WEB
Visit *Exercise Central* at
bedfordstmartins.com/writingfirst
for more practice.

◆ PRACTICE 25-2

Rewrite the following sentences, which contain misplaced modifiers, so that each modifier clearly refers to the word it logically modifies.

Example: Mark ate a pizza standing in front of the refrigerator.

Standing in front of the refrigerator, Mark ate a pizza.

1. The cat broke the vase frightened by a noise.

_____

_____

2. Running across my bathroom ceiling, I saw two large, hairy bugs.

_____

_____

3. Lori looked at the man sitting in the chair with red hair.

_____

_____

4. *ET* is a film about an alien directed by Steven Spielberg.

_____

_____

5. Covered with chocolate sauce, Fred loves ice cream sundaes.

_____

_____

6. After reading the poem, the meaning became clear to me.

_____

_____

7. The deer was hit by a car running across the street.

_____

_____

8. Dressed in a beautiful wedding gown, the groom watched the bride walk

down the aisle.

_____

_____

9. The exterminator sprayed the insect wearing a mask.

_____

_____

10. With a mysterious smile, Leonardo da Vinci painted the *Mona Lisa*.

_____

_____

■ **WRITING FIRST: Flashback**

Look back at your response to the Writing First activity on
page 396. Do any sentences contain misplaced modifiers?
On the lines below, rewrite each incorrect sentence by placing
the modifier as close as possible to the word it modifies.

_____

_____

_____

_____

B **Correcting Dangling Modifiers**

A **dangling modifier** "dangles" because the word it modifies does not
appear in the sentence. Often, a dangling modifier comes at the beginning
of a sentence and seems to modify the word that follows it.

Using my computer, the report was finished in two days.

In the sentence above, the modifier *Using my computer* seems to be modifying *the report*. But this makes no sense. (How can the report use a computer?) The word the modifier should logically refer to is not in the
sentence. To correct this sentence, you need to supply the missing word.

400

SOLVING
COMMON
SENTENCE
PROBLEMS

25 B

Using my computer, I finished the report in two days.

To correct a dangling modifier, supply a word to which the modifier can logically refer.

INCORRECT   Moving the microscope's mirror, the light can be directed onto the slide. (Can the light move the mirror?)

CORRECT   Moving the microscope's mirror, you can direct the light onto the slide.

INCORRECT   Paid in advance, the furniture was delivered. (Was the furniture paid in advance?)

CORRECT   Paid in advance, the movers delivered the furniture.

◆ PRACTICE 25-3

ON THE WEB

Visit *Exercise Central* at
bedfordstmartins.com/writingfirst
for more practice.

Each of the following sentences contains a dangling modifier. To correct each sentence, add a word to which the modifier can logically refer.

Example: Waiting inside, my bus passed by.

Waiting inside, I missed my bus.

1. Paid by the school, the books were sorted in the library.

   _____

   _____

2. Pushing on the brakes, my car would not stop for the red light.

   _____

   _____

3. Short of money, the trip was canceled.

   _____

4. Working overtime, his salary almost doubled.

   _____

5. Angered by the noise, the concert was called off.

   _____

   _____

6. Using the correct formula, the problem was easily solved.

   _____

   _____

7. Tired and hungry, the assignment was finished by midnight.

_____

_____

8. Sitting on a park bench, the pigeons were fed.

_____

9. Staying in bed on Sunday, the newspaper was read from beginning to end.

_____

_____

10. Driving for a long time, my leg began to hurt.

_____

_____

◆ **PRACTICE 25-4**

Complete the following sentences, making sure to include a word to which each modifier can logically refer.

Example: Dancing with the man of her dreams, *she decided it was*

time to wake up.

1. Blocked by the clouds, _____

_____

2. Applying for financial aid, _____

_____

3. Settled into his recliner chair, _____

_____

4. Fearing that they might catch a cold, _____

_____

5. Hearing strange noises through the wall, _____

_____

6. Soaked by the rain, _____

_____

7. Playing poker until after midnight, _____

_____

Culture Clue

Poker is a popular card game in which players make bets.

402

SOLVING
COMMON
SENTENCE
PROBLEMS

25 B

8. Lighting the candles, _____

_____

9. Donated by disaster aid groups, _____

_____

10. Wearing their best clothes, _____

_____

■ **WRITING FIRST: Flashback**

Look back at your response to the Writing First activity on page 396. Do any of your sentences contain dangling modifiers? On the lines below, rewrite any sentence that contains a dangling modifier, making sure to include a word to which the modifier can logically refer.

1. _____

_____

_____

2. _____

_____

_____

■ **WRITING FIRST: Revising and Editing**

Look back at your repose to the Writing First activity on page 396. Add two sentences to your recipe, one with an *-ing* modifier and one with an *-ed* modifier. Then, check your work for any misplaced or dangling modifiers.

CHAPTER REVIEW

◆ EDITING PRACTICE: PARAGRAPH

Read the following student paragraph, which includes modification errors. Rewrite sentences where necessary to correct misplaced and dangling modifiers. In some cases, you may have to supply a word to which the modifier can logically refer. The first incorrect sentence has been corrected for you.

Beyond Mickey Mouse

For more than twenty years, Pixar computer animation studios have produced
thousands of pictures were provided by artists
movies. Sketched by hand before Pixar, ~~artists provided thousands of pictures~~ for
                                          ^
traditional animated films. Led by Steve Jobs, animation was revolutionized by

Pixar. Using computers, special software was used by animators to create speech

and movement. Invented by Pixar, animators were able to achieve startling lifelike

effects. The typical Pixar plot shows characters growing as they move into the

world. Encouraging this growth, the characters' friends offer advice and guidance.

The first sucessful Pixar film was *Toy Story*. Completed in 1995, the use of

computer animation made *Toy Story* a success. *Toy Story* was followed by *A Bug's*

Life, Finding Nemo, and *The Incredibles*. Bringing in more than $525 million,

audiences made these movies very successful. In 2006, Disney bought Pixar

for $7.4 billion. Now, the company that pioneered traditional animation eighty

years ago owns Pixar.

Scene from Toy Story

◆ EDITING PRACTICE: ESSAY

Read the following student essay, which includes modification errors. Rewrite sentences to correct dangling and misplaced modifiers. In some cases, you will have to supply a word to which the modifier can logically refer. The first sentence has been corrected for you.

Eating as a Sport

                                   often
After eating a big meal, ~~the food often makes~~ you feel stuffed. Imagine how
                                   ^
someone participating in competitive eating feels. To win, you have to eat more

food faster than anyone else. Training for days, many different kinds of food

are eaten in these contests. For example, contestants eat chicken wings, pizza,

ribs, hot dogs, and even matzo balls. Training for events, competitive eating

404

25 B

SOLVING
COMMON
SENTENCE
PROBLEMS

is considered a sport by participants. By winning, a good living can be made by a competitive eater. Considered dangerous by some, competitive eaters and their fans nevertheless continue to grow.

The way it works is that each competitor eats the same weight or portion of food. Giving the signal, the competitors begin eating. Breaking the food in pieces or just eating the food whole, any technique can be used. The competitors, soaked in water, can make the food softer. They can even eat hot dogs separately from their buns. Good competitors are usually not overweight. In fact, some are quite thin. Keeping the stomach from expanding, competitors are hurt by extra fat. By drinking large amounts of water, their stomachs stretch and increase their chances of winning. This is one technique many competitors use when they train.

The International Federation of Competitive Eating watches over the contests to make sure they are fair and safe. Providing the dates and locations, contests are listed on its Web site. Often, contests are held at state fairs. Also listing participants, prizes, and rankings of winners, new participants are invited. Before entering the contests, their eating specialty and personal profile must be indicated by new participants. Competitors must also be at least eighteen years old.

Joey Chestnut (left) and Takeru Kobayashi at a hot dog–eating contest in Coney Island

Many competitive eaters participate in lots of contests. For example, weighing only 100 pounds, 8.1 pounds of sausage was eaten in only 10 minutes by Sonya Thomas. At another contest, she ate 46 crab cakes in 10 minutes. Held in the United States, some participants come from other countries. For instance, Takeru Kobayashi, who comes from Japan, once ate 18 pounds of cow brains in 15 minutes. Winners usually get cash prizes. The largest prize, $20,000, was awarded in a hot dog–eating contest at Coney Island, which was televised by ESPN. By eating 66 hot dogs and their buns in 12 minutes, the contest was won by Joey Chestnut, a professional speed eater. Almost 50,000 people attended the contest in person, and millions watched on television.

Joey Chestnut wins contest

■ Culture Clue

ESPN—The Entertainment and Sports Programming Network—is dedicated to broadcasting sports 24 hours a day.

There is some concern about competitive eating. By stretching the stomach, a person's health may be affected. There is also concern about obesity and overeating. Worried about choking, events should have doctors present some people argue. Still, many people like to watch these contests, and they seem to be getting more popular each year.

◆ COLLABORATIVE ACTIVITIES

1. Working in a group of five or six students, make a list of five *-ing* modifiers and five *-ed* modifiers. Exchange your list with another group, and complete one another's sentences.

    Examples
    <u>Typing</u> as fast as he could, *John could not wait to finish his screenplay.*
    <u>Frightened</u> by a snake, *the horse ran away.*

2. Working in a team of three students, compete with other teams to compose sentences that contain outrageous and confusing dangling or misplaced modifiers. As a class, correct the sentences. Then, vote on which group wrote the best sentences.

3. In a group of four or five students, find examples of confusing dangling and misplaced modifiers in magazines and newspapers. Rewrite the sentences, making sure each modifier is placed as close as possible to the word it describes.

☑ REVIEW CHECKLIST:
Misplaced and Dangling Modifiers

- Correct a misplaced modifier by placing the modifier as close as possible to the word it modifies. (See 25A.)

- Correct a dangling modifier by supplying a word to which the dangling modifier can logically refer. (See 25B.)

Read the following student essay, which contains run-ons, sentence fragments, errors with subject-verb agreement, illogical shifts, and dangling and misplaced modifiers. Edit the essay to correct the errors. The first error has been corrected for you.

Not In My Back Yard

NIMBY, a term that was coined in 1980, stands for "Not In My Back Yard." "NIMBYs" are people who are against certain changes in their communities, ~~Even~~ *even* though these changes will benefit the general population. For example, NIMBYs may oppose new public housing, "big box" stores, prisons, airports, or highways. Because may harm the community. These people also fear the presence in their neighborhoods of certain groups. Such as people with disabilities. They did not want these people. To live anywhere near them. NIMBYs have raised important issues. About the conflict between the rights of the individual and the rights of the population as a whole.

NIMBYs are suspicious of the government, they worry that the government will ignore their community's needs. For example, the government may say new jobs will be available, however, what if the jobs pay low wages? What if the new employers force locally owned small stores out of business? Low-income housing may be badly needed, but what if one of the results are a reduction in the value of nearby property? What if the strains on schools and traffic is unacceptable? NIMBYs always worry about these questions.

NIMBYs do understand that certain facilities must be built or improved nevertheless, they worry that each change may have their own negative effects. For example, needing new airport runways in order to reduce delays, NIMBYs object to the increased noise it causes. Although new sources of energy is badly needed, NIMBYs oppose the noise pollution. That windmills would bring to their community. New sites may be needed to dispose of hazardous waste, but NIMBYs are afraid of leaking waste containers. That may contaminate homes and neighborhoods.

Demonstrators protest a proposed Wal-Mart Supercenter

Wind turbines in California

Finally, there is always going to be fears. Of the unknown. Group homes for people with physical disabilities and mental illness is often a problem for NIMBYs. They are also opposed to having sex offenders living in their community. Of course, no one wants a dangerous criminal living in their neighborhood. However, if someone has completed the required prison sentence, they have to live somewhere. Some of these negative attitudes is a result of lack of information others are based on a parent's real concerns about the safety of their children. Parents did not quarrel with the right of sex offenders to find a place to live they just do not want them to live anywhere near their children. NIMBYs feel that they have to protect themselves and their families.

Disabled resident and aide at group home for children

The conflicts of NIMBY involve a real moral dilemma. On the one hand, belief in the importance of individuals mean that people should rely on themselves, not on government. On the other hand, belief in social responsibility means that people should think about the well-being of others. The conflict between these two positions may be very difficult to resolve. Because sometimes the needs of the individual is in conflict with the needs of the general community.

UNIT SIX

UNDERSTANDING BASIC GRAMMAR

Verbs: Past Tense

PREVIEW

In this chapter, you will learn

- to understand regular verbs in the past tense (26A)
- to understand irregular verbs in the past tense (26B)
- to deal with problem verbs in the past tense (26C and 26D)

Washoe, Barrier-Breaking Chimp, Dies at 42

Washoe, a West African–born chimpanzee who became the first nonhuman to learn American Sign Language (ASL), died on October 30ᵗʰ, 2007, after a brief illness. She was 42.

Born in 1965, Washoe was sold to the United States Air Force and brought to North America, where she was adopted by two scientists, Drs. Allen and Beatrix Gardner, at the University of Nevada, Reno. Although she was a research animal, Washoe was raised at the scientists' home in Washoe County, Nevada, from which she got her name. There, the couple taught her to sign using ASL.

Until that time, scientists had been unsuccessful in teaching chimps to master spoken human languages. The Gardners' ground-breaking work, known as the Washoe Project, taught Washoe to communicate basic ideas by means of a nonverbal human language. Eventually, Washoe mastered 250 signs. She also picked up signs from observing human interactions, and she successfully taught ASL to her adoptive chimp son, Loulis. In 1980, Washoe moved with scientists Deborah and Roger Fouts to the Chimpanzee and Human Communications Institute at Central Washington University, in Ellensburg, Washington. Here,

she became the matriarch of the four resident chimps at the Institute, and she spent the rest of her life.

Washoe enjoyed looking through books, magazines, and catalogues (particularly shoe catalogues); she had a strong interest in footwear. "She always checked out your shoes, and if you had new ones she'd sign for you to show them to her," said Dr. Jensvold, assistant director of the CHCI. Considered loyal, kind, and fair in her treatment of her caretakers and her chimp friends, Washoe lived beyond the average lifespan for chimpanzees in captivity and made a great impact on the scientific community at large.

■ WRITING FIRST

Look at the obituary above, and then write your own obituary. (Refer to yourself by name or by *he* or *she*.) As you write, assume that you have led a long life and have achieved almost everything you hoped you would. Be sure to include the accomplishments for which you would most like to be remembered. Remember to use transitional words and phrases that clearly show how one event in your life relates to another.

▶ **Word Power**
accomplishment something completed successfully; an achievement

longevity long life

objective a goal

Tense is the form a verb takes to show when an action or situation takes place. The **past tense** indicates that an action occurred in the past.

A Regular Verbs

Regular verbs form the past tense by adding either *-ed* or *-d* to the **base form** of the verb (the present tense form of the verb that is used with *I*).

We register<u>ed</u> for classes yesterday.
Walt Disney produce<u>d</u> short cartoons in 1928.

Regular verbs that end in *-y* form the past tense by changing the *y* to *i* and adding *-ed*.

tr<u>y</u>	tr<u>ied</u>
appl<u>y</u>	appl<u>ied</u>

◆ PRACTICE 26-1

Change the regular verbs in the following sentences to the past tense. Cross out the present tense form of each underlined verb, and write the past tense form above it.

                                        visited

Example: Every year, my mother ~~visits~~ her family in Bombay, India.

(1) She always returns with designs on her hands and feet. (2) In India, women called henna artists create these patterns. (3) Henna originates in a plant found in the Middle East, India, Indonesia, and northern Africa. (4) Many women in these areas use henna to color their hands, nails, and parts of their feet. (5) Men dye their beards as well as the manes and hooves of their horses. (6) They also color animal skins with henna. (7) In India, my mother always celebrates the end of the Ramadan religious fast by going to a "henna party." (8) A professional henna artist attends the party to apply new henna decorations to the women. (9) After a few weeks, the henna designs wash off. (10) In the United States, my mother's henna designs attract the attention of many people.

ON THE WEB
Visit *Exercise Central* at
bedfordstmartins.com/writingfirst
for more practice.

■ **WRITING FIRST: Flashback**

Look back at your response to the Writing First activity on page 411. Underline the past tense verbs that end in -ed and -d. Then, write them on the lines below.

_____	_____	_____
_____	_____	_____
_____	_____	_____

B   Irregular Verbs

Unlike regular verbs, whose past tense forms end in -ed or -d, **irregular verbs** have irregular forms in the past tense. In fact, their past tense forms may look very different from their present tense forms.

The following chart lists the base form and past tense form of many of the most commonly used irregular verbs.

Irregular Verbs in the Past Tense

Base Form	Past	Base Form	Past
awake	awoke	drive	drove
be	was, were	eat	ate
beat	beat	fall	fell
become	became	feed	fed
begin	began	feel	felt
bet	bet	fight	fought
bite	bit	find	found
blow	blew	fly	flew
break	broke	forgive	forgave
bring	brought	freeze	froze
build	built	get	got
buy	bought	give	gave
catch	caught	go (goes)	went
choose	chose	grow	grew
come	came	have	had
cost	cost	hear	heard
cut	cut	hide	hid
dive	dove (dived)	hold	held
do	did	hurt	hurt
draw	drew	keep	kept
drink	drank	know	knew

(continued on following page)

(continued from previous page)

Base Form	Past	Base Form	Past
lay (to place)	laid	sing	sang
lead	led	sit	sat
leave	left	sleep	slept
let	let	speak	spoke
lie (to recline)	lay	spend	spent
light	lit	spring	sprang
lose	lost	stand	stood
make	made	steal	stole
meet	met	stick	stuck
pay	paid	sting	stung
quit	quit	swear	swore
read	read	swim	swam
ride	rode	take	took
ring	rang	teach	taught
rise	rose	tear	tore
run	ran	tell	told
say	said	think	thought
see	saw	throw	threw
sell	sold	understand	understood
send	sent	wake	woke
set	set	wear	wore
shake	shook	win	won
shine	shone (shined)	write	wrote

◆ **PRACTICE 26-2**

ON THE WEB

Visit *Exercise Central* at
bedfordstmartins.com/writingfirst
for more practice.

In the following sentences, fill in the correct past tense form of each irregular verb in parentheses. Use the chart above to help you find the correct irregular verb form. If you cannot find a particular verb on the chart, look it up in a dictionary.

> **Example:** In 1987, Connie and Howard Cleary ___*began*___ (begin) a movement to improve safety on college campuses.

(1) Connie and Howard Cleary's daughter, Jeanne, _____ (be) murdered on the Lehigh University campus. (2) Jeanne _____ (think) she was safe. (3) However, her attacker _____ (get) into her dorm room through three different doors that had been left unlocked. (4) Shockingly, Jeanne's attacker actually _____ (go) to Lehigh. (5) Shattered by the loss of their daughter, her parents _____ (do) not withdraw into their pain. (6) Instead, they _____ (feel) that the best memorial to their daughter would be the prevention of similar crimes, so they founded Security on Campus, Inc. (7) SOC _____ (make) legal information

available to victims of crimes on college campuses. (8) Because of the efforts of SOC, Congress _____ (write) a law that forced colleges to disclose their crime statistics. (9) Colleges also _____ (have) to explain how they tried to protect their students. (10) Because of this law, the number of campus crimes _____ (fall).

■ WRITING FIRST: Flashback

Look back at your response to the Writing First activity on page 411. Circle each irregular past tense verb you find. Then, write each one in the column on the left. In the column on the right, write the verb's base form. (If necessary, consult the list of irregular verbs on pages 413–14 or a dictionary.)

Past Tense	Base Form
_____	_____
_____	_____
_____	_____
_____	_____
_____	_____
_____	_____

C Problem Verbs: *Be*

The irregular verb *be* can cause problems because it has two different past tense forms—*was* for singular subjects and *were* for second person singular subjects as well as for plural subjects. (All other English verbs have just one past tense form.)

Carlo was interested in becoming a city planner. (singular)

They were happy to help out at the school. (plural)

Past Tense Forms of the Verb Be

	Singular	**Plural**
First person	I was tired.	We were tired.
Second person	You were tired.	You were tired.
Third person	He was tired.	
	She was tired.	They were tired.
	It was tired.	
	The man was tired.	Frank and Billy were tired.

26 C

ON THE WEB
Visit *Exercise Central* at
bedfordstmartins.com/writingfirst
for more practice.

Culture Clue
NASA is the National
Aeronautics and Space
Administration.

◆ **PRACTICE 26-3**

Edit the following passage for errors in the use of the verb *be*. Cross out any underlined verbs that are incorrect, and write the correct forms above them. If a verb form is correct, label it *C*.

Example: Before 1990, there ~~was~~ *were* no female Hispanic astronauts in the NASA program.

(1) Although there had never been a Hispanic woman astronaut, it <u>was</u> impossible for NASA to ignore Ellen Ochoa's long career in physics and engineering. (2) When Ochoa <u>was</u> young, her main interests <u>was</u> music, math, and physics. (3) After getting a degree in physics at San Diego State University, she <u>were</u> considering a career in music or business. (4) However, she <u>was</u> convinced by her mother to continue her education. (5) In 1983, Ochoa <u>was</u> studying for a doctorate in electrical engineering at Stanford University when the first female astronaut, Sally Ride, flew on the space shuttle. (6) Ochoa <u>were</u> inspired by Sally Ride to become an astronaut. (7) More than 2,000 people <u>was</u> also inspired to apply for the astronaut program. (8) In 1990, Ochoa <u>was</u> picked to fly into space. (9) On one of her flights, she <u>was</u> a mission specialist and used a remote-controlled robotic arm to catch a satellite. (10) After four space flights, Ochoa <u>were</u> made Director of Flight Crew Operations.

■ **WRITING FIRST: Flashback**

Look back at your response to the Writing First activity on page 411. Find all the sentences in which you use the past tense of *be*. Copy two or three of these sentences on the lines below, and underline each subject of the verb *be*. Make sure you have used the correct form of the verb in each case.

1. _____

_____

2. _____

_____

3. _____

_____

D Problem Verbs: *Can/Could* and *Will/Would*

The helping verbs *can/could* and *will/would* present problems because their past tense forms are sometimes confused with their present tense forms.

Can/Could

Can, a present tense verb, means "is able to" or "are able to."

First-year students <u>can</u> apply for financial aid.

Could, the past tense of *can*, means "was able to" or "were able to."

Escape artist Harry Houdini claimed that he <u>could</u> escape from any prison.

Will/Would

Will, a present tense verb, talks about the future from a point in the present.

A solar eclipse <u>will</u> occur in ten months.

Would, the past tense of *will*, talks about the future from a point in the past.

I told him yesterday that I <u>would</u> think about it.

Would is also used to express a possibility or wish.

If we stuck to our budget, we <u>would</u> be better off.
Laurie <u>would</u> like a new stuffed animal.

FOCUS *Will* and *Would*

Note that *will* is used with *can* and that *would* is used with *could*.

I will feed the cats if I can find their food.

I would feed the cats if I could find their food.

◆ PRACTICE 26-4

Circle the appropriate helping verb from the choices in parentheses.

Example: People who don't want to throw things away (can, could) rent a self-storage unit.

(1) In the past, warehouse storage (will, would) provide a place to

store excess items. (2) However, people (will, would) have to hire moving

ON THE WEB
Visit *Exercise Central* at
bedfordstmartins.com/writingfirst
for more practice.

▶ **Word Power**
warehouse a large building
for storing goods

vans and (can, could) hardly ever have access to their stored items.

(3) They (will, would) have to sign an expensive long-term contract.

(4) Now, however, they (can, could) take advantage of a new industry.

(5) They (can, could) store possessions in a space as small as a closet or as large as a house. (6) With self-storage, people (can, could) easily move their belongings in and out of the storage unit. (7) When they need more space, they (will, would) be able to get it. (8) In fact, the managers of self-storage facilities (can, could) suggest how much space owners (will, would) need. (9) The only person who (can, could) get into the self-storage unit is the person who has rented it. (10) If people need a hand truck to move their belongings, they (can, could) usually borrow one. (11) All in all, using self-storage (can, could) solve a lot of problems for people with too many possessions.

■ WRITING FIRST: Flashback

Look back at your response to the Writing First activity on page 411. On the following lines, write a few sentences in the first person ("I") that describe what you would have accomplished if you had had the chance. Be sure to use *could* and *would* in your sentences.

_____

_____

_____

_____

_____

_____

■ WRITING FIRST: Revising and Editing

Look back at your response to the Writing First activity on page 411. Make sure you have used the correct past tense form for each of your verbs. If you have not, cross out the incorrect form, and write the proper past tense form of the verb above the line.

CHAPTER REVIEW

◆ **EDITING PRACTICE**

Read the following student essay, which includes errors in past tense verb forms. Decide whether each of the underlined past tense verbs is correct. If the verb is correct, write *C* above it. If it is not, cross out the verb, and write in the correct past tense form. The first sentence has been corrected for you. (If necessary, consult the list of irregular verbs on pages 413–14.)

Healing

The window seat ~~were~~ ^{was} our favorite place to sit. I piled pillows on the ledge and <u>spended</u> several minutes rearranging them. Then, my friend and I <u>lied</u> on our backs and propped our feet on the wall. We <u>sat</u> with our arms around our legs and <u>thinked</u> about the mysteries of life.

We stared at the people on the street below and <u>wonder</u> who they <u>was</u> and where they <u>was</u> going. We imagined that they <u>can</u> be millionaires, foreign spies, or drug smugglers. We believed that everyone except us <u>leaded</u> wonderful and exciting lives.

I <u>heard</u> a voice call my name. Reluctantly, I <u>standed</u> up, tearing myself away from my imaginary world. My dearest and oldest friend — my teddy bear — and I came back to the real world. I grabbed Teddy and <u>brung</u> him close to my chest. Together, we <u>go</u> into the cold dining room, where twelve other girls <u>sit</u> around a table eating breakfast. None of them looked happy.

In the unit for eating disorders, meals <u>was</u> always tense. Nobody <u>wants</u> to eat, but the nurses watched us until we <u>eated</u> every crumb. I <u>set</u> Teddy on the chair beside me and stared gloomily at the food on our plate. I closed my eyes and <u>taked</u> the first bite. I <u>feeled</u> the calories adding inches of ugly fat. Each swallow <u>were</u> like a nail being ripped from my finger. At last, it <u>was</u> over. I had survived breakfast.

Days passed slowly. Each passing minute <u>was</u> a victory. After a while, I learned how to eat properly. I learned about other people's problems. I also learned that people loved me. Eventually, even Teddy stopped feeling sorry for me. I <u>begun</u> to

Mary-Kate Olsen, who has suffered from anorexia

■ **Culture Clue**

Anorexia nervosa is an eating disorder in which the patient loses his or her appetite and ability to eat adequately.

Home page for anorexia treatment Web site

smile — and laugh. Sometimes, I even considered myself happy. My doctors

challenged me — and, surprisingly, I <u>rised</u> to the occasion.

◆ COLLABORATIVE ACTIVITIES

1. Working in a group of three or four students, choose a famous living figure — an actor, a sports star, or a musician, for example — and brainstorm together to list details about this person's life. Then, working on your own, use the details to write a profile of the famous person.

2. Working in a group, list several current problems that you think could be solved within ten or fifteen years. Each member of the group should then select a problem from the list and write a paragraph or two describing how the problem could be solved. As a group, arrange the paragraphs so that they form the body of an essay. Develop a thesis statement, write an introduction and a conclusion, and then revise the body paragraphs of the essay.

3. Form a group with three other students. What national or world events do you remember most clearly? Take ten minutes to list news events that you think have defined the last five years. On your own, write a short essay in which you discuss the significance of the three or four events that the members of your group agree were the most important.

☑ REVIEW CHECKLIST:
Verbs: Past Tense

- The past tense is the form a verb takes to show that an action occurred in the past. (See 26A.)

- Regular verbs form the past tense by adding either *-ed* or *-d* to the base form of the verb. (See 26A.)

- Irregular verbs have irregular forms in the past tense. (See 26B.)

- *Be* has two different past tense forms — *was* for singular subjects and *were* for second person singular subjects as well as for plural subjects. (See 26C.)

- *Could* is the past tense of *can*. *Would* is the past tense of *will*. (See 26D.)

Verbs: Past Participles

PREVIEW

In this chapter, you will learn

- to identify regular past participles (27A)
- to identify irregular past participles (27B)
- to use the present perfect tense (27C)
- to use the past perfect tense (27D)
- to use past participles as adjectives (27E)

■ WRITING FIRST

The picture above shows a dance class. Look at the picture, and then write about an activity—a hobby or a sport, for example—that you have been involved in for a relatively long time. Begin by identifying the activity and stating why it has been important to you. Then, describe the activity, paying particular attention to what you have gained from it over the years.

▶ **Word Power**

benefit something that promotes well-being

diversion something that distracts or relaxes the mind

A **Regular Past Participles**

Every verb has a past participle form. The **past participle** form of a regular verb is identical to its past tense form. Both are formed by adding either *-ed* or *-d* to the **base form** of the verb (the present tense form of the verb that is used with the pronoun *I*).

PAST TENSE
He earn<u>ed</u> a fortune.

PAST PARTICIPLE
He has earn<u>ed</u> a fortune.

PAST TENSE
He creat<u>ed</u> a work of art.

PAST PARTICIPLE
He has creat<u>ed</u> a work of art.

◆ **PRACTICE 27-1**

Fill in the correct past participle form of each regular verb in parentheses.

Example: Recently, vacationers have __*discovered*__ (discover) some new opportunities to get away from it all and to do good at the same time.

(1) Volunteer vacationers have _____ (visit) remote areas to build footpaths, cabins, and shelters. (2) Groups such as Habitat for Humanity have _____ (offer) volunteers a chance to build homes in low-income areas. (3) Habitat's Global Village trips have _____ (raise) awareness about the lack of affordable housing in many countries. (4) Participants in Sierra Club programs have _____ (donate) thousands of work hours all over the United States. (5) Sometimes these volunteers have _____ (join) forest service workers to help restore wilderness areas. (6) They have _____ (clean) up trash at campsites. (7) They have also _____ (remove) nonnative plants. (8) Some volunteer vacationers have _____ (travel) to countries such as Costa Rica, Russia, and Thailand to help with local projects. (9) Other vacationers have _____ (serve) as English teachers. (10) Volunteering vacations have _____ (help) to strengthen cross-cultural understanding.

■ **WRITING FIRST: Flashback**

Look back at your response to the Writing First activity on page 421. Identify each helping verb (a form of the verb *have*) that is followed by a regular past participle (ending in *-ed* or *-d*).

(*continued on following page*)

(*continued from previous page*)

Write each helping verb and past participle on the lines below.

Helping Verb	*Regular Past Participle*
_____	_____
_____	_____
_____	_____
_____	_____

B Irregular Past Participles

Irregular verbs nearly always have irregular past participles. Irregular verbs do not form the past participle by adding -*ed* or -*d* to the base form of the verb.

The following chart lists the base form, the past tense form, and the past participle of the most commonly used irregular verbs.

Irregular Past Participles

Base Form	Past Tense	Past Participle
awake	awoke	awoken
be (am, are)	was (were)	been
beat	beat	beaten
become	became	become
begin	began	begun
bet	bet	bet
bite	bit	bitten
blow	blew	blown
break	broke	broken
bring	brought	brought
build	built	built
buy	bought	bought
catch	caught	caught
choose	chose	chosen
come	came	come
cost	cost	cost
cut	cut	cut
dive	dove, dived	dived

(*continued on following page*)

(continued from previous page)

Base Form	Past Tense	Past Participle
do	did	done
draw	drew	drawn
drink	drank	drunk
drive	drove	driven
eat	ate	eaten
fall	fell	fallen
feed	fed	fed
feel	felt	felt
fight	fought	fought
find	found	found
fly	flew	flown
forgive	forgave	forgiven
freeze	froze	frozen
get	got	got, gotten
give	gave	given
go	went	gone
grow	grew	grown
have	had	had
hear	heard	heard
hide	hid	hidden
hold	held	held
hurt	hurt	hurt
keep	kept	kept
know	knew	known
lay (to place)	laid	laid
lead	led	led
leave	left	left
let	let	let
lie (to recline)	lay	lain
light	lit	lit
lose	lost	lost
make	made	made
meet	met	met
pay	paid	paid
quit	quit	quit
read	read	read
ride	rode	ridden
ring	rang	rung
rise	rose	risen
run	ran	run
say	said	said
see	saw	seen
sell	sold	sold
send	sent	sent
set	set	set
shake	shook	shaken

(continued on following page)

(continued from previous page)

Base Form	Past Tense	Past Participle
shine	shone, shined	shone, shined
sing	sang	sung
sit	sat	sat
sleep	slept	slept
speak	spoke	spoken
spend	spent	spent
spring	sprang	sprung
stand	stood	stood
steal	stole	stolen
stick	stuck	stuck
sting	stung	stung
swear	swore	sworn
swim	swam	swum
take	took	taken
teach	taught	taught
tear	tore	torn
tell	told	told
think	thought	thought
throw	threw	thrown
understand	understood	understood
wake	woke, waked	woken, waked
wear	wore	worn
win	won	won
write	wrote	written

◆ PRACTICE 27-2

Fill in the correct past participle of each irregular verb in parentheses. Refer to the chart above as needed. If you cannot find a particular verb on the chart, look it up in a dictionary.

Example: Occasionally, a wildfire has ____*caught*____ (catch) firefighters unprepared.

(1) Wildfires have always _____ (be) a part of nature. (2) In some case cases, fires have _____ (come) and _____ (go) without causing much destruction. (3) In other cases, fires have _____ (cost) people a lot of time, money, and pain. (4) All of us have _____ (have) to accept the fact that healthy forests occasionally burn. (5) However, according to some people, wildfires have _____ (become) more threatening in recent years. (6) One reason is that more

ON THE WEB
Visit *Exercise Central* at
bedfordstmartins.com/writingfirst
for more practice.

people have _____ (build) houses close to wooded areas.
(7) In addition, many areas of the United States have _____
(see) unusually hot and dry weather. (8) Occasionally, fires have
_____ (sweep) through acres of forest before firefighters could set
up firebreaks. (9) However, firefighters have _____ (do) their best
to stop fires that threaten people's property. (10) In all cases, firefighting
agencies have _____ (make) protection of human life their first
priority.

◆ **PRACTICE 27-3**

Edit the following paragraph for errors in irregular past participles. Cross
out any underlined past participles that are incorrect, and write in the
correct form above them. If the verb form is correct, label it *C*.

> **Example:** In recent years, some people have ~~standed~~ up against over-
> seas sweatshops.
>
> *stood*
> ^

(1) Buying products from overseas sweatshops has became

controversial over the last few decades. (2) American manufacturers

have sended their materials to developing countries where employees

work under terrible conditions for very low wages. (3) Violations of basic

U.S. labor laws—such as getting extra pay for overtime and being paid

on time—have lead to protests. (4) Low-wage workers in developing

countries have finded themselves facing dangerous working conditions

as well as verbal and sexual abuse. (5) Even well-known retailers—such

as Sears, Tommy Hilfiger, and Target—have gotten in trouble for selling

items made in sweatshops. (6) Recently, colleges have be criticized for

using overseas sweatshops to make clothing featuring school names.

(7) Students have spoke out against such practices, and schools have

had to respond. (8) While some manufacturers may have losed money by

increasing wages for overseas workers, they have understanded that this

is the right thing to do. (9) They have made a promise to their customers

that they will not employ sweatshop labor. (10) Still, consumers have not always <u>forgave</u> manufacturers who have a history of such practices.

■ **WRITING FIRST: Flashback**

Look back at your response to the Writing First activity on page 421, and identify each helping verb (a form of the verb *have*) that is followed by an irregular past participle. Then, write each helping verb and irregular past participle on the lines below.

Helping Verb   *Irregular Past Participle*

_____   _____

_____   _____

_____   _____

_____   _____

C The Present Perfect Tense

The past participle can be used to form different verb tenses. For example, the past participle can be combined with the present tense forms of *have* to form the **present perfect tense**.

The Present Perfect Tense

(have *or* has + *past participle*)

Singular	**Plural**
I <u>have gained</u>.	We <u>have gained</u>.
You <u>have gained</u>.	You <u>have gained</u>.
He <u>has gained</u>.	They <u>have gained</u>.
She <u>has gained</u>.	
It <u>has gained</u>.	

■ Use the present perfect tense to indicate an action that began in the past and continues into the present.

> PRESENT PERFECT   The <u>nurse</u> <u>has worked</u> at the Welsh Mountain clinic for two years. (The working began in the past and continues into the present.)

■ Use the present perfect tense to indicate that an action has just occurred.

> PRESENT PERFECT   I <u>have</u> just <u>eaten</u>. (The eating has just occurred.)

ON THE WEB
Visit *Exercise Central* at
bedfordstmartins.com/writingfirst
for more practice.

◆ PRACTICE 27-4

Circle the appropriate verb tense (past tense or present perfect) from the choices in parentheses.

Example: When I (visited, have visited) Montreal, I was surprised to discover a truly bilingual city.

(1) When I was in Montreal, I (heard, have heard) both English and French. (2) Montreal (kept, has kept) two languages because of its history. (3) Until 1763, Montreal (belonged, has belonged) to France. (4) Then, when France (lost, has lost) the Seven Years War, the city (became, has become) part of England. (5) When I was there last year, most people (spoke, have spoken) both French and English. (6) Although I (knew, have known) no French, I (found, have found) that I was able to get along quite well. (7) For example, all the museums (made, have made) their guided tours available in English. (8) Most restaurants (offered, have offered) bilingual menus. (9) There (were, have been) even English radio and television stations and English newspapers. (10) In Montreal, I (felt, have felt) at home and at the same time in a foreign country.

◆ PRACTICE 27-5

■ **Culture Clue**
A *poll* is a collection of opinions from individuals or groups of people that is used for analysis. Pollsters are the workers who conduct polls.

Fill in the appropriate verb tense (past tense or present perfect) of the verb in parentheses.

Example: Before the last presidential election, most major newspapers and TV news channels ____conducted____ (conduct) their own polls.

Intensive Pronouns

Intensive pronouns always appear directly after their antecedents, and they are used for emphasis.

I myself have had some experience in sales and marketing.

The victim himself collected the reward.

They themselves were uncertain of the significance of their findings.

ON THE WEB
Visit *Exercise Central* at
bedfordstmartins.com/writingfirst
for more practice.

◆ PRACTICE 28-16

Fill in the correct reflexive or intensive pronoun in each of the following sentences.

> **Example:** The opening act was exciting, but the main attraction
>
> _____*itself*_____ was boring.

1. My aunt welcomed her visitors and told them to make _____

   at home.

2. Mysteriously, migrating birds can direct _____ through

   clouds, storms, and moonless nights.

3. The First Lady _____ gave a speech at the political rally.

4. We all finished the marathon without injuring _____.

5. Even though the government offered help to people who lived in the

   flooded areas, the homeowners _____ did most of the re-

   building.

6. Sometimes he finds _____ daydreaming in class.

7. The guide warned us to watch _____ because the path was

   slippery.

8. The senators were not happy about committing _____ to

   vote for lower taxes.

9. She gave _____ a manicure.

10. Although everyone else in my family can sing or play a musical instru-

    ment, I _____ am tone deaf.

Culture Clue

The *First Lady* is the wife of the president of the United States.

(continued from previous page)

used in a compound or a pronoun used in a comparison? If
so, write the sentences here, making sure you have used the
appropriate pronoun case.

_____

_____

_____

Now, circle any uses of *who* and *whom* in your writing. Have
you used these pronouns correctly?

I   Reflexive and Intensive Pronouns

Two special kinds of pronouns, *reflexive pronouns* and *intensive pronouns*,
end in *-self* (singular) or *-selves* (plural). Although the functions of the two
kinds of pronouns are different, their forms are identical.

Reflexive and Intensive Pronouns

Singular Forms

Antecedent	*Reflexive or Intensive Pronoun*
I	myself
you	yourself
he	himself
she	herself
it	itself

Plural Forms

Antecedent	*Reflexive or Intensive Pronoun*
we	ourselves
you	yourselves
they	themselves

Reflexive Pronouns

Reflexive pronouns indicate that people or things did something to themselves or for themselves.

Rosanna lost herself in the novel.

You need to watch yourself when you mix those solutions.

Mehul and Paul made themselves cold drinks.

To determine whether to use the subjective or objective case for a pronoun in the second part of a compound, follow the same rules that apply for a pronoun that is not part of a compound.

■ If the compound in which the pronoun appears is the sentence's subject, use the subjective case.

> <u>Toby and I</u> [not *me*] like jazz.
>
> <u>He and I</u> [not *me*] went to the movies.

■ If the compound is an object, use the objective case.

> The school sent <u>my father and me</u> [not *I*] the financial aid forms.
>
> This argument is between <u>her and me</u> [not *I*].

FOCUS **Choosing Pronouns in Compounds**

To determine which pronoun case to use in a compound that joins a noun and a pronoun, rewrite the sentence with just the pronoun.

> Toby and [*I* or *me*?] like jazz.
>
> I like jazz. (not *Me like jazz*)
>
> Toby and I like jazz.

◆ **PRACTICE 28-13**

In the following sentences, the underlined pronouns are part of compounds. Check them for correct subjective or objective case. If a correction needs to be made, cross out the pronoun, and write the correct form above it. If the pronoun is correct, write *C* above it.

Example: There are millions of blogs available on the Internet, but

only a few of them are read by my brother and ~~I~~.
                                                    me

(1) My brother Dan and <u>me</u> love to read blogs. (2) Our parents make fun of <u>him</u> and <u>I</u> for how much time <u>him</u> and <u>me</u> spend on the computer every day reading <u>them</u>. (3) <u>Them</u> and their friends do not see what makes blogs so interesting to <u>us</u> and to so many other readers. (4) They do not understand how addictive reading blogs can be for curious people

like <u>he</u> and <u>I</u>. (5) <u>Him</u> and his friends follow several political blogs, and <u>them</u> and <u>him</u> often contribute their opinions. (6) One of their favorite sites is The Onion, where <u>they</u> read about current political events. (7) My friends and <u>me</u> prefer to look at more personal sites, ones that seem more like diaries. (8) In particular, <u>them</u> and <u>I</u> like to follow travel blogs written by ordinary people all over the world. (9) Reading these lets <u>we</u> and anyone else who is interested read about places we have never seen. (10) This opportunity to hear about other people's experiences and opinions is the reason my brother and <u>me</u> got interested in blogs in the first place.

Pronouns in Comparisons

Sometimes, a pronoun appears after the word *than* or *as* in the second part of a **comparison**.

> John is luckier <u>than</u> <u>I</u>.
>
> The inheritance changed Raymond as much <u>as</u> <u>her</u>.

- If the pronoun is a subject, use the subjective case.

  > John is luckier <u>than</u> <u>I</u> [am].

- If the pronoun is an object, use the objective case.

  > The inheritance changed Raymond as much <u>as</u> [it changed] <u>her</u>.

FOCUS **Choosing Pronouns in Comparisons**

Sometimes, the pronoun you use can change your sentence's meaning. For example, if you say, "I like Cheerios more than *he*," you mean that you like Cheerios more than the other person likes them.

> I like Cheerios more than he [does].

If, however, you say, "I like Cheerios more than *him*," you mean that you like Cheerios more than you like the other person.

> I like Cheerios more than [I like] him.

◆ **PRACTICE 28-14**

Each of the following sentences includes a comparison with a pronoun following the word *than* or *as*. Write in each blank the correct form (subjective or objective) of the pronoun in parentheses. In brackets, add the word or words needed to complete the comparison.

Example: Many people are better poker players than ____*I [am]*____ (I/me).

1. The survey showed that most people like the candidate's wife as much as _____ (he/him).

2. No one enjoys shopping more than _____ (she/her).

3. My brother and Aunt Cecile were very close, so her death affected him more than _____ (I/me).

4. No two people could have a closer relationship than _____ (they/them).

5. My neighbor drives better than _____ (I/me).

6. He may be as old as _____ (I/me), but he does not have as much work experience.

7. That jacket fits you better than _____ (I/me).

8. The other company had a lower bid than _____ (we/us), but we were awarded the contract.

The Pronouns *Who* and *Whom, Whoever* and *Whomever*

To determine whether to use *who* or *whom* (or *whoever* or *whomever*), you need to know how the pronoun functions within the clause in which it appears.

■ When the pronoun is the subject of the clause, use *who* or *whoever*.

> I wonder <u>who</u> wrote that song. (*Who* is the subject of the clause *who wrote that song*.)

> I will vote for <u>whoever</u> supports the youth center. (*Whoever* is the subject of the clause *whoever supports the youth center*.)

■ When the pronoun is the object, use *whom* or *whomever*.

> <u>Whom</u> do the police suspect? (*Whom* is the direct object of the verb *suspect*.)

> I wonder <u>whom</u> the song is about. (*Whom* is the object of the preposition *about* in the clause *whom the song is about*.)

> Vote for <u>whomever</u> you prefer. (*Whomever* is the object of the verb *prefer* in the clause *whomever you prefer*.)

FOCUS *Who* and *Whom*

To determine whether to use *who* or *whom*, try substituting another pronoun for *who* or *whom* in the clause. If you can substitute *he* or *she*, use *who*; if you can substitute *him* or *her*, use *whom*.

> [Who/Whom] wrote a love song? <u>He</u> wrote a love song.

> [Who/Whom] was the song about? The song was about <u>her</u>.

The same test will work for *whoever* and *whomever*.

♦ **PRACTICE 28-15**

Circle the correct form of *who* or *whom* (or *whoever* or *whomever*) in parentheses in each sentence.

Example: With (who/whom) did Rob collaborate?

1. The defense team learned (who/whom) was going to testify for the prosecution.

2. (Who/Whom) does she think she can find to be a witness?

3. I think the runner (who/whom) crosses the finish line first will be the winner.

4. They will argue their case to (whoever/whomever) will listen.

5. It will take time to decide (who/whom) the record holder is.

6. Take these forms to the clerk (who/whom) is at the front desk.

7. We will have to penalize (whoever/whomever) misses the first training session.

8. (Who/Whom) did Kobe take to the prom?

9. We saw the man (who/whom) fired the shots.

10. To (who/whom) am I speaking?

ON THE WEB

Visit *Exercise Central* at **bedfordstmartins.com/writingfirst** for more practice.

■ **WRITING FIRST: Flashback**

Look back at your response to the Writing First activity on page 436. Can you find any sentences that contain a pronoun

(continued on following page)

(1) For years, Americans _____ (rely) on opinion polls to predict which candidate is most likely to become president. (2) Over the years, these polls _____ (become) more accurate as pollsters have learned how to avoid errors. (3) In the process, pollsters _____ (change) the methods they use to contact people. (4) Until 1986, interviewers _____ (knock) on doors to ask people questions. (5) More recently, public opinion polls _____ (use) randomly selected telephone numbers. (6) However, because many people have cell phones with unlisted numbers, some observers _____ (question) the accuracy of the telephone sampling method. (7) In other words, despite all the improvements that polls _____ (undergo), they are still far from perfect. (8) Nevertheless, when Americans were asked to evaluate the accuracy of polls, most people _____ (say) that they predict election results fairly accurately.

■ **WRITING FIRST: Flashback**

Look back at your response to the Writing First activity on page 421. Choose three sentences with past tense verbs, and rewrite them below, changing past tense to present perfect tense. How does your revision change the meaning of each sentence?

1. _____

_____

_____

2. _____

_____

_____

3. _____

_____

_____

The past participle can also be used to form the **past perfect tense**, which consists of the past tense of *have* plus the past participle.

The Past Perfect Tense

(had + *past participle*)

Singular	**Plural**
I had returned.	We had returned.
You had returned.	You had returned.
He had returned.	They had returned.
She had returned.	
It had returned.	

Use the past perfect tense to show that an action occurred before another past action.

PAST PERFECT TENSE   PAST TENSE

Chief Sitting Bull <u>had fought</u> many battles before he <u>defeated</u> General Custer. (The fighting was done by Sitting Bull before he defeated Custer.)

◆ **PRACTICE 27-6**

Circle the appropriate verb tense (present perfect or past perfect) from the choices in parentheses.

Example: Although the children (have eaten/had eaten) dinner, they still had room for ice cream.

1. Ren wondered where he (has left/had left) his keys.

2. He now believes he (has lost/had lost) them.

3. The receptionist told the interviewer that the applicant (has arrived/ had arrived).

4. The interviewer says that she (has waited/had waited) for an hour.

5. The jury decided that the defendant (has lied/had lied) on the witness stand.

6. The jury members are still discussing the case although they (have been/had been) in the jury room for three days.

ON THE WEB
Visit *Exercise Central* at
bedfordstmartins.com/writingfirst
for more practice.

7. By the time I reached the restaurant, I (have decided/had decided) to order a pepperoni pizza.

8. By the time my pizza is ready, I usually (have finished/had finished) my pinball game.

9. The DVD (has been/had been) playing for only ten minutes when I ejected it.

10. This movie is excellent; I (have seen/had seen) it at least five times.

■ **WRITING FIRST: Flashback**

Look back at your response to the Flashback activity on page 429. Rewrite your three present perfect tense sentences on the following lines, this time changing them to the past perfect tense. How do your revisions change the meaning of each sentence?

1. _____

_____

_____

2. _____

_____

_____

3. _____

_____

_____

E **Past Participles as Adjectives**

In addition to functioning as verbs, past participles can also function as adjectives modifying nouns that follow them.

I cleaned up the broken glass.

The exhausted runner finally crossed the finish line.

Past participles are also used as adjectives after **linking verbs**, such as *seemed* or *looked*.

Jason seemed surprised.

He looked shocked.

◆ **PRACTICE 27-7**

Edit the following passage for errors in past participle forms used as adjectives. Cross out any underlined participles that are incorrect, and write the correct form above them. If the participle form is correct, label it *C*.

                                                                  C
Example: College students are often <u>worried</u> about money.

(1) College students are <u>surprise</u> when they find <u>preapprove</u> applications for credit cards in their mail. (2) Credit-card companies also recruit <u>targeted</u> students through booths that are <u>locate</u> on campus. (3) The booths are <u>design</u> to attract new customers with offers of gifts. (4) Why have companies gone to all this trouble to attract <u>qualified</u> students? (5) Most older Americans already have at least five credit cards that are <u>stuff</u> in their wallets. (6) Banks and credit-card companies see younger college students as a major <u>untapped</u> market. (7) According to experts, students are a good credit risk because <u>concern</u> parents usually bail them out when they cannot pay a bill. (8) Finally, people tend to feel emotionally <u>tic</u> to their first credit card. (9) Companies want to be the first card that is <u>acquire</u> by a customer. (10) For this reason, credit-card companies target <u>uninform</u> college students.

■ **WRITING FIRST: Flashback**

Look back at your response to the Writing First activity on page 421. Choose three nouns you used in your writing, and list them in the right-hand column below. Then, think of a past participle that can modify each noun, and write the modifier in the left-hand column.

Past Participle   *Noun*

1. _____   _____

2. _____   _____

3. _____   _____

■ **WRITING FIRST: Revising and Editing**

Look back at your response to the Writing First activity on
page 421. Do you need to revise your use of past participles
and perfect tenses? Cross out any incorrect verb forms, and
write your corrections above them. When you have finished,
check the past participles and perfect tenses in another writing
assignment on which you are currently working.

CHAPTER REVIEW

◆ **EDITING PRACTICE**

Read the following student essay, which includes errors in the use of
past participles and in the use of the perfect tenses. Decide whether each
of the underlined items is correct. If it is correct, write *C* above it. If it
is not, write in the correct verb form. The first error has been corrected
for you.

Young Voters and the Power of the Internet

In the past, most young Americans ~~have paid~~ *paid* little attention to national
elections. Over the last few years, however, participation among young voters <u>has
increase</u>. It seems that young people <u>have began</u> to realize their power. Several
factors <u>had been</u> responsible for this shift, including concerns about the war in
Iraq and about climate change. However, the Internet <u>has</u> also <u>played</u> an important
role in boosting young people's interest in politics.

Many businesses <u>have turn</u> to the Internet to reach customers, especially
young ones. Similarly, political campaigns <u>have find</u> that they can attract voters by
using the Internet. For example, both Democrats and Republicans <u>had used</u> email
to convince voters to support candidates. At the same time, Web sites and blogs
<u>have create</u> interest in politics.

For example, in the 2008 primaries, all of the major candidates <u>have worked</u> to
make their Web sites and blogs more attractive to young people. Most candidates

*A viewer asks candidates a
question during CNN YouTube
presidential debate*

■ **Culture Clue**

The word *primaries* refers
to primary elections. In
the United States, voters
nominate one candidate
from each party (usually
Democratic or Republican)
during the primaries.

Home page for Senator Barack Obama's presidential Web site.

Home page for Senator John McCain's presidential Web site.

had links to Facebook, MySpace, and YouTube. On his Web site, Democrat Barack Obama has offered to text-message campaign updates to his supporters. Republican John McCain has created McCainSpace, a place where visitors could set up their own Web sites. These additions has made it easier for young people to get involve in those candidates' campaigns.

Perhaps more important, the Internet has provide many ways for young people to communicate with one another. Using a variety of social networking sites, young people had been able to voice their political opinions and organize meetings and rallies. Some youth-oriented sites have start to offer video forums as well. For example, Generation Engage has use Apple's iChat to link eighteen- to twenty-four-year-olds with political leaders. Before the Internet, this kind of communication have not been possible.

While a few years ago many young people have felt disconnected from politics, recent polls have showed that young voters now feel optimistic about their ability to influence an election's outcome. The Internet has been responsible for this sense of involvement. Undoubtedly, the Internet will continue to encourage young people's participation in politics for years to come.

◆ **COLLABORATIVE ACTIVITIES**

1. Exchange Writing First activities with another student. Read each other's work, making sure that past participles are used correctly.
2. Assume that you are a restaurant employee who has been nominated for the Employee of the Year Award. To win this award (along with a thousand-dollar prize), you have to explain in writing what you have done during the past year to deserve this honor. Write a letter to your supervisor and the awards committee. When you have finished, trade papers with another student and edit his or her letter. Read all the letters to the class, and have the class decide which is the most convincing.

✔ REVIEW CHECKLIST:
Verbs: Past Participles

- ☐ The past participle of regular verbs is formed by adding *-ed* or *-d* to the base form. (See 27A.)

- ☐ Irregular verbs usually have irregular past participles. (See 27B.)

- ☐ The past participle is combined with the present tense forms of *have* to form the present perfect tense. (See 27C.)

- ☐ The past participle is used to form the past perfect tense, which consists of the past tense of *have* plus the past participle. (See 27D.)

- ☐ The past participle can function as an adjective. (See 27E.)

Nouns and Pronouns

▶ **Word Power**

compelling extremely forceful

escapist providing distraction from reality

mesmerizing hypnotic

■ **WRITING FIRST**

The picture above shows the characters from the TV show *The Simpsons*. Look at the picture, and then write about why you like a particular TV show, musician or group, or movie. Assume your readers are not familiar with the subject you are writing about.

A Identifying Nouns

A **noun** is a word that names a person (*singer, Jay Z*), an animal (*dolphin, Flipper*), a place (*downtown, Houston*), an object (*game, Scrabble*), or an idea (*happiness, Darwinism*).

A **singular noun** names one thing. A **plural noun** names more than one thing.

FOCUS   **Common and Proper Nouns**

Most nouns, called **common nouns**, begin with lowercase letters.

    character   holiday

Some nouns, called **proper nouns**, name particular people, animals, places, objects, or events. A proper noun always begins with a capital letter.

    Homer Simpson   Labor Day

B Forming Plural Nouns

Most nouns that end in consonants add -*s* to form plurals. Other nouns add -*es* to form plurals. For example, most nouns that end in -*o* add -*es* to form plurals. Other nouns, whose singular forms end in -*s*, -*ss*, -*sh*, -*ch*, -*x*, or -*z*, also add -*es* to form plurals. (Some nouns that end in -*s* or -*z* double the *s* or *z* before adding -*es*.)

Singular	Plural
street	streets
radio	radios
gas	gases
class	classes
bush	bushes
church	churches
fox	foxes
quiz	quizzes

Irregular Noun Plurals

Some nouns form plurals in unusual ways.

■ Nouns whose plural forms are the same as their singular forms

Singular	Plural
a deer	a few deer
this species	these species
a television series	two television series

■ Nouns ending in *-f* or *-fe*

Singular	Plural
each half	both halves
my life	our lives
a lone thief	a gang of thieves
one loaf	two loaves
the third shelf	several shelves

Exceptions: *roof* (plural *roofs*), *proof* (plural *proofs*), *belief* (plural *beliefs*)

■ Nouns ending in *-y*

Singular	Plural
another baby	more babies
every worry	many worries

Note that when a vowel (*a, e, i, o, u*) comes before the *y*, the noun has a regular plural form: *monkey* (plural *monkeys*), *day* (plural *days*).

■ Hyphenated compound nouns

Singular	Plural
Lucia's sister-in-law	Lucia's two favorite sisters-in-law
a mother-to-be	twin mothers-to-be
the first runner-up	all the runners-up

Note that the plural ending is attached to the compound's first word: *sister, mother, runner*.

■ Miscellaneous irregular plurals

Singular	Plural
that child	all children
a good man	a few good men
the woman	lots of women
my left foot	both feet
a wisdom tooth	my two front teeth
this bacterium	some bacteria

◆ **PRACTICE 28-1**

Next to each of the following singular nouns, write the plural form of the noun. Then, circle the irregular noun plurals.

Examples: bottle ___*bottles*___   child ___(*children*)___

1. headache _____
2. life _____
3. foot _____
4. chain _____
5. deer _____
6. honey _____
7. bride-to-be _____
8. woman _____
9. loaf _____
10. kiss _____

11. beach _____
12. duty _____
13. son-in-law _____
14. species _____
15. wife _____
16. city _____
17. elf _____
18. tooth _____
19. catalog _____
20. patty _____

◆ **PRACTICE 28-2**

Proofread the underlined nouns in the following paragraph, checking to make sure singular and plural forms are correct. If a correction needs to be made, cross out the noun, and write the correct form above it. If the noun is correct, write *C* above it.

Example: Getting through security lines at ~~airportes~~ *airports* has become difficult.

(1) Since September 11, 2001, <u>traveler-to-bes</u> have had to think carefully about what they pack in their carry-on luggage. (2) All airlines now have to protect the <u>lifes</u> of the <u>men</u> and <u>woman</u> who fly on their planes. (3) Currently, airlines allow two <u>piece</u> of carry-on luggage, including <u>pursess</u>, laptop computers, and <u>briefcase</u>. (4) Prescription medications can be carried through security <u>checkpointes</u>. (5) However, because of concerns about <u>explosivess</u>, travelers can bring only three-ounce <u>containeres</u> of gels, <u>liquides</u>, and <u>aerosols</u>. (6) Each <u>travelers</u> has to put these <u>item</u> in a single clear zip-lock plastic bag, which will be inspected by security <u>personnels</u>. (7) Also, <u>people</u> are usually asked to take off their <u>shoeses</u> at the checkpoint and place them in <u>bins</u> for X-ray inspection. (8) Most sharp items, such as box <u>cutterz</u> and ice <u>pickes</u>, cannot be

brought through security but can be packed in checked <u>suitcases</u>. (9) At some airports, there are long <u>delayes</u> in the security lines as screeners carry out their <u>dutys</u>. (10) Nevertheless, these security <u>procedur</u> help protect travelers and airplane <u>crewes</u>.

■ **WRITING FIRST: Flashback**

Look back at your response to the Writing First activity on page 436. Circle each noun. Write any plural nouns on the lines below, and circle any irregular plurals.

_____ _____ _____ _____

_____ _____ _____ _____

C | **Identifying Pronouns**

A **pronoun** is a word that refers to and takes the place of a noun or another pronoun.

> Michelle was really excited because <u>she</u> had finally found a job that made <u>her</u> happy. (*She* refers to *Michelle*; *her* refers to *she*.)

In the sentence above, the pronouns *she* and *her* take the place of the noun *Michelle*.

> Pronouns, like nouns, can be singular or plural.

■ Singular pronouns (*I, he, she, it, him, her,* and so on) always take the place of singular nouns or pronouns.

> Geoff left his jacket at work, so <u>he</u> went back to get <u>it</u> before <u>it</u> could be stolen. (*He* refers to *Geoff*; *it* refers to *jacket*.)

■ Plural pronouns (*we, they, our, their,* and so on) always take the place of plural nouns or pronouns.

> Jessie and Dan got up early, but <u>they</u> still missed <u>their</u> train. (*They* refers to *Jessie and Dan*; *their* refers to *they*.)

■ The pronoun *you* can be either singular or plural.

> When the volunteers met the mayor, they said, "We really admire <u>you</u>." The mayor replied, "I admire <u>you</u>, too." (In the

first sentence, *you* refers to *the mayor*; in the second sentence, *you* refers to *the volunteers*.)

FOCUS **Demonstrative Pronouns**

Demonstrative pronouns—*this, that, these*, and *those*—point to one or more items.

- *This* and *that* point to one item: <u>This</u> is a work of fiction, and <u>that</u> is a nonfiction book.
- *These* and *those* point to more than one item: <u>These</u> are fruits, but <u>those</u> are vegetables.

◆ **PRACTICE 28-3**

In the following sentences, fill in each blank with an appropriate pronoun.

Example: Ever since __*I*__ had my first scuba-diving experience, __*I*__ have wanted to search for sunken treasure.

(1) Three friends and _____ decided to explore an area off the Florida coast where a shipwreck had occurred almost three hundred years ago. (2) The first step was to get a boat; _____ all decided to buy a used rubber boat with a fifteen-horsepower engine. (3) _____ had hardly been used and was in very good condition. (4) _____ needed some equipment, including an anchor, but _____ didn't have to buy a metal detector because my friends already had two of _____. (5) If there was treasure on the bottom of the ocean, _____ would find it. (6) _____ stayed in the boat while my friends made the first dive. (7) At first, _____ found only fish and sea worms, but _____ didn't give up. (8) Finally, one of the metal detectors started beeping because _____ had located a cannon and two cannonballs. (9) Then, it started beeping again; this time, _____ had found some pieces of pottery and an old pistol. (10) Although our group didn't find any coins, _____ were all very happy with the results.

■ **WRITING FIRST: Flashback**

Look back at your response to the Writing First activity on page 436. In the column on the left, list all the pronouns you used. In the column on the right, list the noun or pronoun each pronoun refers to and takes the place of.

Pronoun

Noun

D **Pronoun-Antecedent Agreement**

The word that a pronoun refers to is called the pronoun's **antecedent**. In the following sentence, the noun *leaf* is the antecedent of the pronoun *it*.

The leaf turned yellow, but it did not fall.

A pronoun must always agree with its antecedent. If an antecedent is singular, as it is in the sentence above, the pronoun must be singular. If the antecedent is plural, as it is in the sentence below, the pronoun must also be plural.

The leaves turned yellow, but they did not fall.

If an antecedent is feminine, the pronoun that refers to it must also be feminine.

Melissa passed her driver's exam with flying colors.

If an antecedent is masculine, the pronoun that refers to it must also be masculine.

Matt wondered what courses he should take.

If an antecedent is **neuter** (neither masculine nor feminine), the pronoun that refers to it must also be neuter.

Lee's car broke down, but she refused to fix it again.

◆ **PRACTICE 28-4**

In the following sentences, circle the antecedent of each underlined pronoun. Then, draw an arrow from the pronoun to the antecedent it refers to.

Example: College students today often fear they will be the victims of crime on campus.

ON THE WEB
Visit *Exercise Central* at
bedfordstmartins.com/writingfirst
for more practice.

(1) Few campuses are as safe as they should be, experts say. (2) However, crime on most campuses is probably no worse than it is in any other community. (3) Still, students have a right to know how safe their campuses are. (4) My friend Joyce never walks on campus without her can of Mace. (5) Joyce believes she must be prepared for the worst. (6) Her boyfriend took a self-defense course that he said was very helpful. (7) My friends do not let fear of crime keep them from enjoying the college experience. (8) We know that our school is doing all it can to make the campus safe.

◆ **PRACTICE 28-5**

Fill in each blank in the following passage with an appropriate pronoun.

Example: Kenny Howard was a pioneer in the customizing of cars and trucks; since the 1950s, ___*he*___ has created award-winning designs.

(1) Kenny Howard, also known as "Von Dutch," was born in 1929 in Los Angeles, where _____ learned a lot from his father, a sign painter. (2) By the time Howard was ten years old, _____ was doing professional pin striping and painting unique decorations on motorcycles. (3) Howard branched out, and eventually _____ began decorating cars as well. (4) Customers wanted Howard's designs, so _____ offered him a lot of money. (5) Even after he doubled his rates, the customers still came, and _____ demanded his services. (6) Howard was an inventor, too; for

example, _____ invented motorized roller skates. (7) Howard's logo was the "flying eyeball," which _____ put on motorcycles, cars, and knives. (8) In the 1950s, _____ did more than anyone else to create the hot rod culture.

■ WRITING FIRST: Flashback

Look back at your response to the Writing First activity on page 436. Underline each pronoun in your paragraph, circle its antecedent, and draw an arrow from each pronoun to its antecedent. Do all your pronouns agree with their antecedents? If not, correct your pronouns.

E Special Problems with Agreement

Certain kinds of antecedents can cause problems for writers because they cannot easily be identified as singular or plural.

Compound Antecedents

A **compound antecedent** consists of two or more words connected by *and* or *or*.

■ Compound antecedents connected by *and* are plural, and they are used with plural pronouns.

> During World War II, Belgium and France tried to protect their borders.

■ Compound antecedents connected by *or* may take a singular or a plural pronoun. The pronoun always agrees with the word that is closer to it.

> Is it possible that European nations or Russia may send its [not *their*] troops?

> Is it possible that Russia or European nations may send their [not *its*] troops?

◆ PRACTICE 28-6

In each of the following sentences, underline the compound antecedent, and circle the connecting word (*and* or *or*). Then, circle the appropriate pronoun in parentheses.

Example: Marge and Homer Simpson love (his or her/their) children very much in spite of the problems they cause.

1. Either *24* or *Lost* had the highest ratings for any television show in (its/their) final episode of the season.

2. In *South Park*, Geek 1 and Geek 2 help create a time machine out of (his/their) friend Timmy's wheelchair.

3. Both Netflix and Blockbuster offer (its/their) movie rentals online.

4. Either cable stations or the networks hire attractive anchors to host (its/their) prime-time shows.

5. Recent movies and documentaries about penguins have delighted (its/their) audiences.

6. In baseball, pitchers and catchers communicate (his or her/their) plays with hand signals.

7. Either Playstation2 or Xbox gives (its/their) players many hours of gaming fun.

8. In summer, many parents and children enjoy spending (his or her/their) time at water parks.

9. Hurricanes or tornadoes can be frightening to (its/their) victims.

Indefinite Pronoun Antecedents

Most pronouns refer to a specific person or thing. However, **indefinite pronouns** do not refer to any particular person or thing.

Most indefinite pronouns are singular.

Singular Indefinite Pronouns

another	everybody	no one
anybody	everyone	nothing
anyone	everything	one
anything	much	somebody
each	neither	someone
either	nobody	something

When an indefinite pronoun antecedent is singular, use a singular pronoun to refer to it.

Everything was in its place. (*Everything* is singular, so it is used with the singular pronoun *its*.)

FOCUS Indefinite Pronouns with *Of*

The singular indefinite pronouns *each, either, neither,* and *one* are often used in phrases with *of—each of, either of, neither of,* or *one of*—followed by a plural noun. Even in such phrases, these indefinite pronoun antecedents are always singular and take singular pronouns.

Each of the routes has its [not *their*] own special challenges.

A few indefinite pronouns are plural.

Plural Indefinite Pronouns

both
few
many
others
several

When an indefinite pronoun antecedent is plural, use a plural pronoun to refer to it.

They all wanted to graduate early, but few received their diplomas in

January. (*Few* is plural, so it is used with the plural pronoun *their.*)

FOCUS Using *His* or *Her* with Indefinite Pronouns

Even though the indefinite pronouns *anybody, anyone, everybody, everyone, somebody, someone,* and so on are singular, many people use plural pronouns to refer to them.

Everyone must hand in their completed work before 2 P.M.

This usage is widely accepted in spoken English. Nevertheless, indefinite pronouns like *everyone* are singular, and written English requires a singular pronoun.

However, using the singular pronoun *his* to refer to *everyone* suggests that *everyone* refers to a male. Using *his or her* is more accurate because the indefinite pronoun can refer to either a male or a female.

Everyone must hand in his or her completed work before 2 P.M.

(*continued on following page*)

(continued from previous page)

When used over and over again, *he or she, him or her*, and *his or her* can create wordy or awkward sentences. Whenever possible, use plural forms.

All students must hand in their completed work before 2 P.M.

◆ **PRACTICE 28-7**

In the following sentences, first circle the indefinite pronoun. Then, circle the pronoun in parentheses that refers to the indefinite pronoun antecedent.

Example: (Each) of the lacrosse players will have ((his or her)/their) own locker at training camp.

1. Everyone likes to choose (his or her/their) own class schedule.

2. Somebody left (his or her/their) iPod on the bus.

3. Many of the contestants gave (his or her/their) best performance for the *American Idol* judges.

4. Someone in the audience left (his or her/their) cell phone on during the performance.

5. Neither of the dogs wanted to have (its/their) coat brushed.

6. The soccer coach personally gave each of the players (his or her/their) trophy.

7. Both of the soldiers donated (his or her/their) cars to Purple Heart, an organization that helps veterans.

8. No one should ever give (his or her/their) Social Security number to telephone solicitors.

9. Anyone who works hard in college can usually receive (his or her/their) degree.

10. Everyone loves receiving greeting cards on (his or her/their) birthday.

◆ **PRACTICE 28-8**

Edit the following sentences for errors in pronoun-antecedent agreement.
When you edit, you have two options: either substitute *its* or *his or her* for
their to refer to the singular antecedent, or replace the singular antecedent
with a plural word.

> **Examples:** Everyone is responsible for ~~their~~ *his or her* own passport and money.
>
> *All*
> ~~Each~~ of the children took their books out of their backpacks.

1. Either of the hybrid cars comes with their own tax rebate.

2. Anyone who loses their locker key must pay $5.00 for a new one.

3. Everyone loves seeing their home team win.

4. Somebody left their scarf and gloves on the subway.

5. Almost everyone waits until the last minute to file their tax returns.

6. Each student returned their library books on time.

7. Everything needed to build the model airplane comes in their kit.

8. Anyone who wants to succeed needs to develop their public speaking
   skills.

9. One of the hockey teams just won their first Olympic medal.

10. No one leaving the show early will get their money back.

Collective Noun Antecedents

Collective nouns are words (like *band* and *team*) that name a group of
people or things but are singular. Because they are singular, collective
noun antecedents are used with singular pronouns.

> The band played on, but it never played our song.

Frequently Used Collective Nouns

army	club	gang	mob
association	committee	government	posse
band	company	group	team
class	family	jury	union

◆ **PRACTICE 28-9**

Circle the collective noun antecedent in the following sentences. Then, circle the correct pronoun in parentheses.

> **Example:** The (jury) returned with ((its)/their) verdict.

1. The company offers good benefits to (its/their) employees.

2. All five study groups must hand in (its/their) projects by Tuesday.

3. Any government should care about the welfare of (its/their) citizens.

4. The Asian Students Union is sponsoring a party to celebrate (its/their) twentieth anniversary.

5. Every family has (its/their) share of problems.

6. To join the electricians' union, applicants had to pass (its/their) test.

7. Even the best teams have (its/their) bad days.

8. The orchestra has just signed a contract to make (its/their) first recording.

9. The math class did very well with (its/their) new teacher.

10. The club voted to expand (its/their) membership.

◆ **PRACTICE 28-10**

Edit the following passage for correct pronoun-antecedent agreement. First, circle the antecedent of each underlined pronoun. Then, cross out any pronoun that does not agree with its antecedent, and write the correct form above it. If the pronoun is correct, write *C* above it.

> *C*
> **Example:** Many Americans believe that the (country) is ready for its
>
> first female president.

(1) Before 1920, most American women could not have their say in government because they were not allowed to vote. (2) However, in the mid-1800s, women began to demand her right to vote—or "woman suffrage." (3) Supporters of woman suffrage believed everyone, regardless of their gender, should be able to vote. (4) Susan B. Anthony and Elizabeth Cady Stanton, who were leaders of the suffrage movement, put her energies into fighting for an amendment to the U.S. Constitution. (5) Finally, in

1919, the House of Representatives and the states gave <u>its</u> approval to the Nineteenth Amendment, which gave American women the right to vote. (6) Now, almost one hundred years later, nothing in government seems out of reach if a woman is willing to work hard for <u>it</u>. (7) For example, in 2007, Nancy Pelosi became the first female Speaker of the House of Representatives, making <u>them</u> one of the most powerful people in the U.S. government. (8) In 2008, Senator Hillary Clinton came close to winning <u>her</u> party's nomination for president. (9) In the future, more and more women will likely earn <u>his or her</u> way into America's top positions.

■ **WRITING FIRST: Flashback**

Look back at your response to the Writing First activity on page 436. Does your paragraph contain any antecedents that are compounds, indefinite pronouns, or collective nouns? If so, list them below.

Compounds	*Indefinite Pronouns*	*Collective Nouns*
_____	_____	_____
_____	_____	_____
_____	_____	_____
_____	_____	_____
_____	_____	_____

Have you used the correct pronoun to refer to each of these antecedents? If not, correct your pronouns.

F   **Vague and Unnecessary Pronouns**

Vague and unnecessary pronouns clutter up your writing and make it hard to understand. Eliminating them will make your writing clearer and easier for readers to follow.

Vague Pronouns

A pronoun should always refer to a specific antecedent. When a pronoun—such as *they* or *it*—has no antecedent, readers will be confused.

VAGUE PRONOUN On the news, <u>they</u> said baseball players would strike. (Who said baseball players would strike?)

VAGUE PRONOUN <u>It</u> says in today's paper that our schools are over-crowded. (Who says schools are overcrowded?)

When you use *they* or *it* as the subject of a sentence, be sure the pronoun refers to a specific word in the sentence. If it does not, either delete it, or replace it with a noun.

REVISED <u>The news report</u> said baseball players would strike.

REVISED <u>An editorial</u> in today's paper says that our schools are overcrowded.

Unnecessary Pronouns

When a pronoun comes directly after its antecedent, it is unnecessary.

UNNECESSARY PRONOUN The librarian, <u>he</u> told me I should check the database.

In the sentence above, the pronoun *he* serves no purpose. Readers do not need to be directed back to the pronoun's antecedent (the noun *librarian*) because it appears right before the pronoun. The pronoun should therefore be deleted.

REVISED The librarian told me I should check the database.

◆ PRACTICE 28-11

The following sentences contain vague or unnecessary pronouns. Revise each sentence on the line below it.

Example: On the Web site, they advertised a special offer.

The Web site advertised a special offer.

1. In Jamaica, they have green mountains and spectacular scenery.

_____

2. My hamster, he loves his exercise wheel.

_____

3. In the biography it told a story of triumph over poverty.

_____

4. The baby's toys, they were made in China.

_____

5. Her best friend, she lives across the street.

_____

6. On *Jeopardy!*, they have to give the answers in the form of questions.

_____

7. These peaches, they don't look ripe to me.

_____

8. On televisions all over the world, they watched the moon landing.

_____

9. The antique plate, it almost fell off the table.

_____

10. In her class, they do not use a textbook.

_____

■ **WRITING FIRST: Flashback**

Look back at your response to the Writing First activity on page 436. Do any of your sentences contain vague or unnecessary pronouns? If so, revise the sentences on the lines below, and correct them.

_____

_____

_____

_____

G **Pronoun Case**

A **personal pronoun** refers to a particular person or thing. Personal pronouns change form according to their function in a sentence. Personal pronouns can be *subjective*, *objective*, or *possessive*.

Personal Pronouns

Subjective	Objective	Possessive
I	me	my, mine
he	him	his
she	her	her, hers
it	it	its

(continued on following page)

(continued from previous page)

Subjective	Objective	Possessive
we	us	our, ours
you	you	your, yours
they	them	their, theirs
who	whom	whose
whoever	whomever	

Subjective Case

When a pronoun is a subject, it is in the **subjective case**.

Finally, <u>she</u> realized that dreams could come true.

Objective Case

When a pronoun is an object, it is in the **objective case**.

If Joanna hurries, she can stop <u>him</u>. (The pronoun *him* is the direct object of the verb *can stop*.)

Professor Miller sent <u>us</u> information about his research. (The pronoun *us* is the indirect object of the verb *sent*.)

Marc threw the ball to <u>them</u>. (The pronoun *them* is the object of the preposition *to*.)

Possessive Case

When a pronoun shows ownership, it is in the **possessive case**.

Hieu took <u>his</u> lunch to the meeting. (The pronoun *his* indicates that the lunch belongs to Hieu.)

Debbie and Kim decided to take <u>their</u> lunches, too. (The pronoun *their* indicates that the lunches belong to Debbie and Kim.)

◆ PRACTICE 28-12

In the following passage, fill in the blank after each pronoun to indicate whether the pronoun is subjective (*S*), objective (*O*), or possessive (*P*).

Example: Famous criminals Bonnie Parker and Clyde Barrow committed their __*P*__ crimes during the 1930s.

(1) With their _____ gang, Bonnie and Clyde robbed a dozen banks

as well as many stores and gas stations. (2) In small towns, they _____

terrorized the police. (3) Capturing them _____ seemed impossible.

(4) To many Americans, however, their _____ crimes seemed exciting.

(5) Because Bonnie was a woman, she _____ was especially fascinating to

them _____. (6) During their _____ crimes, Bonnie and Clyde would often

carry a camera, take photographs of themselves, and send them _____ to

the newspapers, which were happy to publish them _____. (7) By the

time they _____ were killed in an ambush by Texas and Louisiana law

officers, Bonnie and Clyde were famous all over the United States.

(8) They _____ were the first celebrity criminals.

■ **WRITING FIRST: Flashback**

Look back at your response to the Writing First activity on
page 436. On the following lines, list all the personal pronouns
you have used, classifying them as subjective, objective, or
possessive.

Subjective	*Objective*	*Possessive*
_____	_____	_____
_____	_____	_____
_____	_____	_____

Have you used correct pronoun case in every sentence? Make
any necessary corrections.

H   **Special Problems with Pronoun Case**

When you are trying to determine which pronoun case to use, three kinds
of pronouns can cause problems: pronouns in compounds, pronouns in
comparisons, and the pronouns *who* and *whom* (or *whoever* and
whomever).

Pronouns in Compounds

Sometimes a pronoun is linked to a noun or to another pronoun with *and*
or *or* to form a **compound**.

The teacher and I met for an hour.

He or she can pick up Jenny at school.

■ **WRITING FIRST: Flashback**

Look back at your response to the Writing First activity on
page 436. Have you used any reflexive or intensive pronouns?
If so, list them here.

Reflexive pronouns: _____

Intensive pronouns: _____

If not, write two new sentences, one using a reflexive pronoun
and one using an intensive pronoun.

_____

_____

■ **WRITING FIRST: Revising and Editing**

Look back at your response to the Writing First activity on
page 436. Change every singular noun to a plural noun and
every plural noun to a singular noun, editing your pronouns so
singular pronouns refer to singular nouns and plural pronouns
refer to plural nouns. (Be sure to edit verbs as well, making
sure singular subjects take singular verbs and plural subjects
take plural verbs.)

CHAPTER REVIEW

◆ **EDITING PRACTICE**

Read the following student essay, which includes noun and pronoun
errors. Check for errors in plural noun forms, pronoun case, and pronoun-
antecedent agreement. Then, make any editing changes you think are
necessary. The first sentence has been edited for you.

Cell Phone Misbehavior

manners
Good ~~manneres~~ used to mean using the right fork and holding the door
open for others. Today, however, people may find that good manners are more
complicated than it used to be. New inventions have led to new challenges.
Cell phones, in particular, have created some problems.

Apple iPhone

Man using cell phone on bus

One problem is the "cell yell," which is the tendency of a person to shout while they are using their cell phones. Why do we do this? Maybe we do not realize how loud we are talking. Maybe we yell out of frustration. Anyone can become angry when they lose a call. Dead batterys can be infuriating. Unfortunately, the yeller annoys everyone around them.

Even if cell-phone users theirselves speak normally, other people can hear them. My friends and me are always calling each other, and we do not always pay attention to whom can hear us. The result is that other people are victims of "secondhand conversations." These conversations are not as bad for people's health as secondhand smoke, but it is just as annoying. Whom really wants to hear about the private lifes of strangers? Restrooms used to be private; now, whomever is in the next stall can overhear someone's private cell phone conversation and learn their secrets.

Also, some cell-phone user seem to think that getting his calls is more important than anything else that might be going on. Phones ring, chirp, or play silly tunes at concertes, in classrooms, at weddings, in churchs, and even at funerals. Can you picture a grieving family at a cemetery having their service interrupted by a ringing phone? People should not have to be told to turn off his or her cell phones at times like these.

In the United States, there are more than 150 million cell phones. Many people hate their cell phones, but they do not think they can live without it. The problem is that cell phones became popular before there were any rules for its use. However, even if the government passed laws about cell-phone behavior, they would have a tough time enforcing it. It seems obvious that us cell phone users should not need laws to make us behave ourself and use ordinary courtesy.

◆ **COLLABORATIVE ACTIVITIES**

1. Working in a group, fill in the following chart, writing one noun on each line. If the noun is a proper noun, be sure to capitalize it.

Cars	Trees	Foods	Famous Couples	Cities
_____	_____	_____	_____	_____
_____	_____	_____	_____	_____

_____ _____ _____ _____ _____

_____ _____ _____ _____ _____

_____ _____ _____ _____ _____

_____ _____ _____ _____ _____

_____ _____ _____ _____

Now, using as many of the nouns listed above as you can, write a one-paragraph news article that describes an imaginary event. Exchange your work with another group, and check the other group's article to be sure the correct pronoun refers to each noun. Return the articles to their original groups for editing.

2. Working in a group, write a silly story that uses each of these nouns at least once: _Martians, eggplant, MTV, toupee, kangaroo, Iceland, bat, herd,_ and _kayak_. Then, exchange stories with another group. After you have read the other group's story, edit it so that it includes all of the following pronouns: _it, its, itself, they, their, them, themselves._ Return the edited story to its authors. Finally, reread your group's story, and check to make sure pronoun-antecedent agreement is clear and correct.

☑ REVIEW CHECKLIST:
Nouns and Pronouns

- [ ] A noun is a word that names something. A singular noun names one thing; a plural noun names more than one thing. (See 28A.)

- [ ] Most nouns add _-s_ or _-es_ to form plurals. Some nouns have irregular plural forms. (See 28B.)

- [ ] A pronoun is a word that refers to and takes the place of a noun or another pronoun. (See 28C.)

- [ ] The word a pronoun refers to is called the pronoun's antecedent. A pronoun and its antecedent must always agree. (See 28D.)

- [ ] Compound antecedents connected by _and_ are plural and are used with plural pronouns. Compound antecedents connected by _or_ may take singular or plural pronouns. (See 28E.)

- [ ] Most indefinite pronoun antecedents are singular and are used with singular pronouns; some are plural and are used with plural pronouns. (See 28E.)

(continued on following page)

(continued from previous page)

- Collective noun antecedents are singular and are used with singular pronouns. (See 28E.)

- A pronoun should always refer to a specific antecedent. (See 28F.)

- Personal pronouns can be in the subjective, objective, or possessive case. (See 28G.)

- Pronouns present special problems when they are used in compounds and comparisons. The pronouns *who* and *whom* and *whoever* and *whomever* can also cause problems. (See 28H.)

- Reflexive and intensive pronouns must agree with their antecedents. (See 28I.)

Adjectives and Adverbs

PREVIEW

In this chapter, you will learn

- to understand the difference between adjectives and adverbs (29A)
- to identify demonstrative adjectives (29A)
- to form comparatives and superlatives of adjectives and adverbs (29B)

▶ **Word Power**

tutor a private instructor

extracurricular outside the regular course of study

socialize to engage in activities with others

cohort a group united by common experiences

■ **WRITING FIRST**

The picture above shows children being home schooled by their mother. Look at the picture, and then write about the advantages and disadvantages of being educated at home by parents instead of at school by professional teachers.

A   Identifying Adjectives and Adverbs

Adjectives and adverbs are words that modify (identify or describe) other words. They help make sentences more specific and more interesting.

An **adjective** answers the question *What kind? Which one?* or *How many?* Adjectives modify nouns or pronouns.

> The Turkish city of Istanbul spans two continents. (*Turkish* modifies the noun *city*, and *two* modifies the noun *continents*.)

> It is *fascinating* because of its location and history. (*Fascinating* modifies the pronoun *it*.)

FOCUS   **Demonstrative Adjectives**

Demonstrative adjectives—*this, that, these,* and *those*—do not describe other words. They simply identify particular nouns.

This and *that* identify singular nouns and pronouns.

> This Web site is much more up-to-date than that one.

These and *those* identify plural nouns.

> These words and phrases are French, but those expressions are Creole.

An **adverb** answers the question *How? Why? When? Where?* or *To what extent?* Adverbs modify verbs, adjectives, or other adverbs.

> Traffic moved steadily. (*Steadily* modifies the verb *moved*.)

> Still, we were quite impatient. (*Quite* modifies the adjective *impatient*.)

> Very slowly, we moved into the center lane. (*Very* modifies the adverb *slowly*.)

> **FOCUS** Distinguishing Adjectives from Adverbs
>
> Many adverbs are formed when *-ly* is added to an adjective form.
>
> | *Adjective* | *Adverb* |
> |---|---|
> | slow | slowly |
> | nice | nicely |
> | quick | quickly |
> | real | really |
>
> ADJECTIVE Let me give you one <u>quick</u> reminder. (*Quick* modifies the noun *reminder*.)
>
> ADVERB He <u>quickly</u> changed the subject. (*Quickly* modifies the verb *changed*.)

◆ PRACTICE 29-1

In the following sentences, circle the correct form (adjective or adverb) from the choices in parentheses.

Example: Women who are (serious/seriously) walkers or runners need to wear athletic shoes that fit.

ON THE WEB
Visit *Exercise Central* at
bedfordstmartins.com/writingfirst
for more practice.

(1) Doctors have found that many athletic shoes are (poor/poorly) designed for women. (2) Women's athletic shoes are (actual/actually) just smaller versions of men's shoes. (3) As a result, they do not provide a (true/truly) comfortable fit. (4) Studies have shown that to get a shoe that fits (comfortable/comfortably) in the heel, most women must buy one that fits too (tight/tightly) at the front of the foot. (5) This can have a (real/really) negative impact on their athletic performance. (6) Some manufacturers now market athletic shoes that are designed (specific/specifically) for women. (7) Experts say that women must become informed consumers and choose (careful/carefully) when they shop for athletic shoes. (8) They should shop for shoes (immediate/immediately) after exercising or at the end of a work day, when the foot is at its largest. (9) Experts advise that athletic shoes should feel (comfortable/comfortably) from the moment they are tried on.

> **FOCUS** *Good* and *Well*
>
> Be careful not to confuse *good* and *well*. Unlike regular adjectives, whose adverb forms add *-ly*, the adjective *good* is irregular. Its adverb form is *well*.
>
> ADJECTIVE   Fred Astaire was a good dancer. (*Good* modifies the noun *dancer*.)
>
> ADVERB   He danced especially well with Ginger Rogers. (*Well* modifies the verb *danced*.)
>
> Always use *well* when you are describing a person's health.
>
> He really didn't feel well [not *good*] after eating the entire pizza.

◆   **PRACTICE 29-2**

Circle the correct form (*good* or *well*) in the sentences below.

Example: It can be hard for some people to find a (good/well) job that they really like.

(1) Some people may not do (good/well) sitting in an office. (2) Instead, they may prefer to find jobs that take advantage of their (good/well) physical condition. (3) Such people might consider becoming smoke jumpers—firefighters who are (good/well) at parachuting from small planes into remote areas to battle forest fires. (4) Smoke jumpers must be able to work (good/well) even without much sleep. (5) They must also handle danger (good/well). (6) They look forward to the (good/well) feeling of saving a forest or someone's home. (7) As they battle fires, surrounded by smoke and fumes, smoke jumpers may not feel very (good/well). (8) Sometimes, things go wrong; for example, when their parachutes fail to work (good/well), jumpers may be injured or even killed. (9) Smoke jumpers do not get paid particularly (good/well). (10) However, they are proud of their strength and endurance and feel (good/well) about the value of their work.

■ **WRITING FIRST: Flashback**

Look back at your response to the Writing First activity on page 465. Underline each adjective and adverb, and draw an arrow from each to the word it identifies or describes. Do all adjectives modify nouns or pronouns? Do all adverbs modify verbs, adjectives, or other adverbs? Have you used *good* and *well* correctly? On the lines below, revise any sentences that use adjectives or adverbs incorrectly.

_____

_____

_____

_____

B   Comparatives and Superlatives

The **comparative** form of an adjective or adverb compares two people or things. Adjectives and adverbs form the comparative with *-er* or *more*. The **superlative** form of an adjective or adverb compares more than two things. Adjectives and adverbs form the superlative with *-est* or *most*.

ADJECTIVES   This film is <u>dull</u> and <u>predictable</u>.

COMPARATIVE   The film I saw last week was even <u>duller</u> and <u>more predictable</u> than this one.

SUPERLATIVE   The film I saw last night was the <u>dullest</u> and <u>most predictable</u> one I've ever seen.

ADVERB   For a beginner, Jane did needlepoint <u>skillfully</u>.

COMPARATIVE   After she had watched the demonstration, Jane did needlepoint <u>more skillfully</u> than Rosie.

SUPERLATIVE   Of the twelve beginners, Jane did needlepoint the <u>most skillfully</u>.

Forming Comparatives and Superlatives

Adjectives

■ One-syllable adjectives generally form the comparative with *-er* and the superlative with *-est*.

great   greater   greatest

■ Adjectives with two or more syllables form the comparative with *more* and the superlative with *most*.

> wonderful   more wonderful   most wonderful

Exception: Two-syllable adjectives ending in *-y* add *-er* or *-est* after changing the *y* to an *i*.

> funny   funnier   funniest

Adverbs

■ All adverbs ending in *-ly* form the comparative with *more* and the superlative with *most*.

> efficiently   more efficiently   most efficiently

■ Some other adverbs form the comparative with *-er* and the superlative with *-est*.

> soon   sooner   soonest

Solving Special Problems with Comparatives and Superlatives

The following rules will help you avoid errors with comparatives and superlatives.

■ Never use both *-er* and *more* to form the comparative or both *-est* and *most* to form the superlative.

> Nothing could have been <u>more awful</u>. (not *more awfuller*)

> Space Mountain is the <u>most frightening</u> (not *most frighten-ingest*) ride at Disney World.

■ Never use the superlative when you are comparing only two things.

> This is the <u>more serious</u> (not *most serious*) of the two problems.

■ Never use the comparative when you are comparing more than two things.

> This is the <u>worst</u> (not *worse*) day of my life.

◆ PRACTICE 29-3

Fill in the correct comparative form of the word supplied in parentheses.

> **Example:** Children tend to be _____*noisier*_____ (noisy) than adults.

1. Traffic always moves _____ (slow) during rush hour than late at night.

2. The weather report says temperatures will be _____ (cold) tomorrow.

3. Some elderly people are _____ (healthy) than younger people.

4. It has been proven that pigs are _____ (intelligent) than dogs.

5. When someone asks you to repeat yourself, you usually answer _____ (loud).

6. The _____ (tall) of the two buildings was damaged by the earthquake.

7. They want to teach their son to be _____ (respectful) of women than many young men are.

8. Las Vegas is _____ (famous) for its casinos than for its natural resources.

9. The WaterDrop is _____ (wild) than any other ride in the amusement park.

10. You must move _____ (quick) if you expect to catch the ball.

◆ **PRACTICE 29-4**

Fill in the correct superlative form of the word supplied in parentheses.

Example: When people buy tickets to a concert or sporting event, _____*most frequently*_____ (frequently) they have to purchase them from Ticketmaster.

(1) Ticketmaster remains the _____ (large) seller of sports and entertainment tickets in the country. (2) It has maintained that position by being the _____ (successful) at making deals to keep rival agencies from selling tickets for large arenas and stadiums. (3) However, the _____ (new) ticketing companies are starting to challenge Ticketmaster's long-standing monopoly. (4) _____ (recently), Major League Baseball (MLB) bought rival company Tickets.com, ending Ticketmaster's control of MLB ticket sales. (5) Stubhub, the _____ (popular) ticket resale site, has also given Ticketmaster serious competition. (6) The success of

▶ **Word Power**
monopoly a group or company which has exclusive control over a product or a service

these competitors is _____ (directly) related to customers'
dissatisfaction with Ticketmaster. (7) One of the _____
(frequent) complaints against Ticketmaster is that its service fees are the
_____ (high) in the business. (8) Wisely, each of its competitors has tried to have the _____ (small) possible markup
on its ticket sales.

FOCUS *Good/Well* and *Bad/Badly*

Most adjectives and adverbs form the comparative with *-er* or *more*
and the superlative with *-est* or *most*. The adjectives *good* and *bad*
and their adverb forms *well* and *badly* are exceptions.

Adjective	Comparative Form	Superlative Form
good	better	best
bad	worse	worst

Adverb	Comparative Form	Superlative Form
well	better	best
badly	worse	worst

◆ PRACTICE 29-5

Fill in the correct comparative or superlative form of *good, well, bad,* or
badly.

Example: She is at her ___*best*___ (good) when she is under pressure.

1. Today in track practice, Luisa performed _____ (well) than she
   has in weeks.

2. In fact, she ran her _____ (good) time ever in the fifty meter.

3. When things are bad, we wonder whether they will get _____
   (good) or _____ (bad).

4. I've had some bad meals before, but this is the _____ (bad).

5. The world always looks _____ (good) when you're in love than
   when you're not.

6. Athletes generally play the _____ (badly) when their concentration is poorest.

7. The Sport Shop's prices may be good, but Athletic Attic's are the _____ (good) in town.

8. There are _____ (good) ways to solve conflicts than by fighting.

9. People seem to hear _____ (well) when they agree with what you're saying than when they don't agree with you.

10. Of all the children, Manda took the _____ (good) care of her toys.

■ **WRITING FIRST: Flashback**

Look back at your response to the Writing First activity on page 465. Copy the adjectives and adverbs from your writing in the column on the left. Then, write the comparative and superlative forms for each adjective or adverb in the other columns. (Remember that some adjectives and adverbs do not have comparative or superlative forms.)

Adjective or Adverb	*Comparative Form*	*Superlative Form*
_____	_____	_____
_____	_____	_____
_____	_____	_____
_____	_____	_____
_____	_____	_____
_____	_____	_____

■ **WRITING FIRST: Revising and Editing**

Look back at your response to the Writing First activity on page 465. Have you used enough adjectives and adverbs to convey your ideas clearly to readers? Add or substitute words as needed to make your writing more specific and more interesting. Then, delete any unnecessary adjectives and adverbs.

CHAPTER REVIEW

◆ EDITING PRACTICE

Read the following student essay, which includes errors in the use of adjectives and adverbs. Make any changes necessary to correct adjectives incorrectly used for adverbs and adverbs incorrectly used for adjectives. Also correct any errors in the use of comparatives and superlatives and in the use of demonstrative adjectives. Finally, try to add some adjectives and adverbs that you feel would make the writer's ideas clearer or more specific. The first sentence has been edited for you.

Starting Over

A wedding can be the *most joyful* ~~joyfullest~~ occasion in two people's lives, the beginning of a couple's most happiest years. For some unlucky women, however, a wedding can be the worse thing that ever happens; it is the beginning not of their happiness but of their battered lives. As I went through the joyful day of my wedding, I wanted bad to find happiness for the rest of my life, but what I hoped and wished for did not come true.

I was married in the savannah belt of the Sudan in the eastern part of Africa, where I grew up. I was barely twenty-two years old. The first two years of my marriage progressed peaceful, but problems started as soon as our first child was born.

Many American women say, "If my husband hit me just once, that would be it. I'd leave." But those attitude does not work in cultures where tradition has overshadowed women's rights and divorce is not accepted. All women can do is accept their sadly fate. Battered women give many reasons for staying in their marriages, but fear is the commonest. Fear immobilizes these women, ruling their decisions, their actions, and their very lives. This is how it was for me.

Of course, I was real afraid whenever my husband hit me. I would run to my mother's house and cry, but she would always talk me into going back and being more patiently with my husband. Our tradition discourages divorce, and wife-beating is taken for granted. The situation is really quite ironic: the religion I practice sets harsh punishments for abusive husbands, but tradition has so overpowered religion that the laws do not really work very good.

Map of Sudan

Sudanese wedding ceremony

One night, I asked myself whether life had treated me fair. True, I had a high school diploma and two of the beautifullest children in the world, but all this was not enough. I realized that to stand up to the husband who treated me so bad, I would have to achieve a more better education than he had. That night, I decided to get a college education in the United States. My husband opposed my decision, but with the support of my father and mother, I was able to begin to change my life. My years as a student and single parent in the United States have been real difficult for me, but I know I made the right choice.

◆ **COLLABORATIVE ACTIVITIES**

1. Working in a small group, write a plot summary for an imaginary film. Begin with one of the following three sentences.

   ■ Dirk and Clive were sworn enemies, but that night on Boulder Ridge they vowed to work together just this once, for the good of their country.

   ■ Genevieve entered the room in a cloud of perfume, and when she spoke, her voice was like velvet.

   ■ The desert sun beat down on her head, but Susanna was determined to protect what was hers, no matter what the cost.

2. Trade summaries with another group. Add as many adjectives and adverbs as you can to the other group's summary. Make sure each modifier is appropriate.

3. Reread your own group's plot summary and edit it carefully, paying special attention to the way adjectives and adverbs are used.

☑ REVIEW CHECKLIST:
Adjectives and Adverbs

- Adjectives modify nouns or pronouns. (See 29A.)

- Demonstrative adjectives—*this, that, these,* and *those*—identify particular nouns. (See 29A.)

- Adverbs modify verbs, adjectives, or other adverbs. (See 29A.)

- To compare two people or things, use the comparative form of an adjective or adverb. To compare more than two people or things, use the superlative form of an adjective or adverb. (See 29B.)

- The adjectives *good* and *bad* and their adverb forms *well* and *badly* have irregular comparative and superlative forms. (See 29B.)

CHAPTER 30

Grammar and Usage for ESL Writers

■ WRITING FIRST

The image above, a painting by Childe Hassam, shows American flags displayed on the Fourth of July, Independence Day. Look at the picture, and then explain how you and your family celebrate a holiday that is important to you. Use present tense.

Learning English as a second language involves more than just learning grammar. In fact, if you have been studying English as a second language, you may know more about English grammar than many native speakers do. However, you will still need to learn the conventions and rules that most native speakers already know.

▶ **Word Power**

commemorate to show respect for; to celebrate

culture behavior and customs of a particular group

A   Subjects in Sentences

English requires that every sentence state its subject. In addition, every dependent clause must also have a subject.

> INCORRECT   Elvis Presley was only forty-two years old when died. (When who died?)
>
> CORRECT   Elvis Presley was only forty-two years old when he died.

When the real subject follows the verb and the normal subject position before the verb is empty, it must be filled by a "dummy" subject, such as *it* or *there*.

> INCORRECT   Is hot in this room.
>
> CORRECT   It is hot in this room.

> INCORRECT   Are many rivers in my country.
>
> CORRECT   There are many rivers in my country.

Standard English also does not permit a two-part subject in which the second part of the subject is a pronoun referring to the same person or thing as the first part.

> INCORRECT   The Caspian Sea it is the largest lake in the world.
>
> CORRECT   The Caspian Sea is the largest lake in the world.

◆ PRACTICE 30-1

Each of the following sentences is missing the subject of a dependent or an independent clause. On the lines after each sentence, rewrite it, adding an appropriate subject. Then, underline the subject you have added.

Example: Because college students often have very little money, are always looking for inexpensive meals.

Because college students often have very little money, they are always looking

for inexpensive meals.

ON THE WEB
Visit *Exercise Central* at **bedfordstmartins.com/writingfirst** for more practice.

1. Ramen noodles are a popular choice for students because are cheap, tasty, and easy to prepare.

_____

_____

2. In minutes, a student can enjoy hot noodles flavored with chicken, shrimp, or beef, and sell vegetarian versions, too.

_____

_____

3. Although high in carbohydrates (a good source of energy), also contain saturated and trans fats and few vitamins or minerals.

_____

_____

4. Cookbooks provide special recipes for preparing ramen noodles; include "Ramen Shrimp Soup" and "Ramen Beef and Broccoli."

_____

_____

5. Not just popular with American college students, are also popular in many other countries around the world.

_____

_____

6. The noodles have even found their way to the International Space Station, where enjoy them in space.

_____

_____

7. The noodles originated in China many years ago, where were deep fried so that they could be stored for a long time without spoiling.

_____

_____

8. For today's college students, however, spoilage is not a problem because are usually eaten long before their expiration date.

_____

_____

◆ **PRACTICE 30-2**

The following sentences contain unnecessary two-part subjects. Rewrite each sentence correctly on the lines provided.

Example: Travelers to China they often visit the Great Wall.

Travelers to China often visit the Great Wall.

ON THE WEB
Visit *Exercise Central* at
bedfordstmartins.com/writingfirst
for more practice.

1. The first parts of the Great Wall they were built around 200 A.D.

2. The Great Wall it was built to keep out invading armies.

3. The sides of the Great Wall they are made of stone, brick, and earth.

4. The top of the Great Wall it is paved with bricks, forming a roadway for horses.

5. The Great Wall it is the only man-made object that can be seen by astronauts in space.

■ **WRITING FIRST: Flashback**

Look back at your response to the Writing First activity on page 476. Does every sentence state its subject? Underline the subject of each sentence. If a sentence does not have a subject, add one. If any sentence has a two-part subject, cross out the unnecessary pronoun.

B   Plural Nouns

In English, most nouns add -s to form plurals. Every time you use a noun, ask yourself whether you are talking about one item or more than one, and choose a singular or plural form accordingly. Consider this sentence.

ON THE WEB

Visit *Exercise Central* at
bedfordstmartins.com/writingfirst
for more practice.

CORRECT The <u>books</u> in both <u>branches</u> of the <u>library</u> are deteriorating.

The three nouns in this sentence are underlined: one is singular (*library*), and the other two are plural (*books, branches*). The word *both* is not enough to indicate that *branch* is plural even though it might be obvious that there are many books in any branch of a library. Even if a sentence includes information that tells you that a noun is plural, you must always use a form of the noun that shows explicitly that it is plural.

◆ PRACTICE 30-3

Underline the plural nouns in the following sentences. (Not all of the sentences contain plural nouns.)

Example: Mass immigration and lack of employment created unexpected social <u>problems</u> in the United States in the nineteenth century.

1. In 1850, New York City estimated that about thirty thousand homeless children lived on its streets.

2. The children were considered "orphans" because their parents had died, lost jobs, or were ill.

3. A social service agency in New York City suggested a solution to this problem.

4. The solution was to send these children to America's heartland—to states like Iowa, Kansas, and Arkansas.

5. There, the children could be accepted into families and help with farming and other chores.

6. In 1854, the first trainload of orphans was shipped to western cities and towns.

7. The children were lined up in a local hall, looked over, and selected by interested families.

8. Then, the remaining children got back on the train and went on to the next town to go through the process again.

9. Most of the children found happy homes and loving parents, but others were treated like servants by their new families.

10. By 1930, social service agencies had begun to reconsider the plan and stopped the orphan trains.

WRITING FIRST: Flashback

Look back at your response to the Writing First activity on page 476. On the lines below, list all the plural nouns you used.

_____ _____ _____ _____

_____ _____ _____ _____

Does each plural noun have a form that shows the noun is plural? Correct any errors you find.

C Count and Noncount Nouns

A **count noun** names one particular thing or a group of particular things that can be counted: *a teacher, a panther, a bed, an ocean, a cloud, an ice cube; two teachers, many panthers, three beds, two oceans, several clouds, some ice cubes.* A **noncount noun** names things that cannot be counted: *gold, cream, sand, blood, smoke, water.*

Count nouns usually have a singular form and a plural form: *cube, cubes.* Noncount nouns usually have only a singular form: *water.* Note how the nouns *cube* and *water* differ in the way they are used in sentences.

CORRECT   The glass is full of ice cubes.

CORRECT   The glass is full of water.

INCORRECT   The glass is full of waters.

CORRECT   The glass contains five ice cubes.

CORRECT   The glass contains some water.

INCORRECT   The glass contains five waters.

Often, the same idea can be expressed with either a count noun or a noncount noun.

Count	Noncount
people (plural of *person*)	humanity [*not* humanities]
tables, chairs, beds	furniture [*not* furnitures]
letters	mail [*not* mails]
supplies	equipment [*not* equipments]
facts	information [*not* informations]

Some words can be either count or noncount, depending on the meaning intended.

COUNT   He had many interesting underline{experiences} at his first job.

NONCOUNT   It is often difficult to get a job if you do not have underline{experience}.

FOCUS Count and Noncount Nouns

Here are some guidelines for using count and noncount nouns.

■ Use a count noun to refer to a living animal, but use a noncount noun to refer to the food that comes from that animal.

COUNT   There are three live lobsters in the tank.

NONCOUNT   This restaurant specializes in lobster.

■ If you use a noncount noun for a substance or class of things that can come in different varieties, you can often make that noun plural if you want to talk about those varieties.

NONCOUNT   Cheese is a rich source of calcium.

COUNT   Many different cheeses come from Italy.

■ If you want to shift attention from a concept in general to specific examples of it, you can often use a noncount noun as a count noun.

NONCOUNT   You have a great deal of talent.

COUNT   My talents do not include singing.

◆ **PRACTICE 30-4**

ON THE WEB
Visit *Exercise Central* at
bedfordstmartins.com/writingfirst
for more practice.

In each of the following sentences, identify the underlined word as a count or noncount noun. If it is a noncount noun, circle the *N* following the sentence, but do not write in the blank. If it is a count noun, circle the *C*, and then write the plural form of the noun in the blank.

Examples: Psychologists, sociologists, and anthropologists work in

the field of behavioral <u>science</u>. (N) C _____

They all have the same <u>goal</u>: to understand human behavior. N (C)

_____goals_____

1. Each type of scientist has a different <u>approach</u> to solving a problem.

   N   C   _____

2. An <u>example</u> is the problem of homeless people on our cities' streets.

   N   C   _____

3. Sociologists concentrate on the social causes of <u>homelessness</u>.   N   C

   _____

4. They might study how <u>unemployment</u> contributes to a rise in the number of homeless people.   N   C _____

5. A <u>shortage</u> of inexpensive housing can also cause someone to lose his or her home. N   C _____

6. A sociologist could next question how a <u>society</u> deals with homeless people. N   C _____

7. Psychologists, on the other hand, are interested in the <u>individual</u>.
   N   C _____

8. Their focus would be on how a homeless <u>person</u> feels and thinks.
   N   C _____

9. Anthropologists are interested in studying culture, a society's <u>system</u> of beliefs and its ways of doing things. N   C _____

10. An anthropologist might focus on how the <u>homeless</u> find food and shelter and on how they raise their children.   N   C _____

■ **WRITING FIRST: Flashback**

Look back at your response to the Writing First activity on page 476. On the lines below, list all the noncount nouns you used.

Noncount nouns: _____

_____

_____

_____

_____

Have you used noncount nouns correctly? Check to make sure you have not used a plural ending on any of your noncount nouns, and correct any errors you find.

D   **Determiners with Count and Noncount Nouns**

Determiners are adjectives that *identify* rather than describe the nouns they modify. Determiners may also *quantify* nouns (that is, indicate an amount or a number).

Determiners include the following words.

- Articles: *a, an, the*
- Demonstrative pronouns: *this, these, that, those*
- Possessive pronouns: *my, our, your, his, her, its, their*
- Possessive nouns: *Sheila's, my friend's,* and so on
- *Whose, which, what*
- *All, both, each, every, some, any, either, no, neither, many, most, much, a few, a little, few, little, several, enough*
- All numerals: *one, two,* and so on

When a determiner is accompanied by one or more other adjectives, the determiner always comes first. For example, in the phrase *my expensive new digital watch, my* is a determiner; you cannot put *expensive, new, digital,* or any other adjective before *my.*

A singular count noun must always be accompanied by a determiner—for example, *my watch* or *the new digital watch,* not just *watch* or *new digital watch.* However, noncount nouns and plural count nouns sometimes have determiners but sometimes do not. *This honey is sweet* and *Honey is sweet* are both acceptable, as are *These berries are juicy* and *Berries are juicy.* (In each case, the meaning is different.) You cannot say, *Berry is juicy,* however; say instead, *This berry is juicy, Every berry is juicy,* or *A berry is juicy.*

FOCUS **Determiners**

Some determiners can be used only with certain types of nouns.

- *This* and *that* can be used only with singular nouns (count or noncount): *this berry, that honey.*
- *These, those, a few, few, many, both,* and *several* can be used only with plural count nouns: *these berries, those apples, a few ideas, few people, many students, both sides, several directions.*
- *Much, little,* and *a little* can be used only with noncount nouns: *much affection, little time, a little honey.*
- *Some, enough, all,* and *most* can be used only with noncount or plural count nouns: *some honey, some berries; enough trouble, enough problems; all traffic, all roads; most money, most coins.*
- *A, an, every, each, either,* and *neither* can be used only with singular count nouns: *a berry, an elephant, every possibility, each citizen, either option, neither candidate.*

◆ **PRACTICE 30-5**

In each of the following sentences, circle the more appropriate choice from each pair of words or phrases in parentheses.

ON THE WEB
Visit *Exercise Central* at
bedfordstmartins.com/writingfirst
for more practice.

Examples

Volcanoes are among the most destructive of (all/every) natural forces on earth.

People have always been fascinated and terrified by (this/these) force of nature.

1. Not (all/every) volcano is considered a danger.

2. In (major some/some major) volcanic eruptions, huge clouds rise over the mountain.

3. (A few violent/Violent a few) eruptions are so dramatic that they blow the mountain apart.

4. (Most/Much) volcanic eruptions cannot be predicted.

5. Since the 1400s, (many/much) people—almost 200,000—have lost their lives in volcanic eruptions.

6. When a volcano erupts, (little/a little) can be done to prevent property damage.

7. (Many/Much) lives can be saved, however, if people in the area are evacuated in time.

8. Unfortunately, by the time people realize an eruption is about to take place, there is rarely (many/enough) time to escape.

9. Volcanoes can be dangerous, but they also produce (a little/some) benefits.

10. For example, (a few/a little) countries use energy from underground steam in volcanic areas to produce electric power.

■ **WRITING FIRST: Flashback**

Look back at your response to the Writing First activity on page 476. On the lines that follow, list all the determiners you used in your writing.

(continued on following page)

(continued from previous page)

Determiners: _____

_____

_____

_____

_____

Have you used count and noncount nouns correctly after these determiners? Correct any errors you find.

E Articles

The **definite article** *the* and the **indefinite articles** *a* and *an* are determiners that tell readers whether the noun that follows is one they can identify (*the book*) or one they cannot yet identify (*a book*).

The Definite Article

When the definite article *the* is used with a noun, the writer is saying to readers, "You can identify which particular thing or things I have in mind. The information you need to make that identification is available to you. Either you have it already, or I am about to give it to you."

Readers can find the necessary information in the following ways.

■ By looking at other information in the sentence

> Meet me at the corner of Main Street and Lafayette Road.

In this example, *the* is used with the noun *corner* because other words in the sentence tell readers which particular corner the writer has in mind: the one located at Main and Lafayette.

■ By looking at information in other sentences

> Aisha ordered a slice of pie and a cup of coffee. The pie was delicious. She asked for a second slice.

Here, *the* is used before the word *pie* in the second sentence to indicate that it is the same pie identified in the first sentence. Notice, however, that the noun *slice* in the third sentence is preceded by an indefinite article (*a*) because it is not the same slice referred to in the first sentence.

■ By drawing on general knowledge

> The earth revolves around the sun.

Here, *the* is used with the nouns *earth* and *sun* because readers are expected to know which particular things the writer is referring to.

FOCUS Definite Articles

Always use *the* (rather than *a* or *an*) in the following situations.

■ Before the word *same: the same day*
■ Before the superlative form of an adjective: *the youngest son*
■ Before a number indicating order or sequence: *the third time*

Indefinite Articles

When an indefinite article is used with a noun, the writer is saying to readers, "I don't expect you to have enough information right now to identify a particular thing that I have in mind. I do, however, expect you to recognize that I'm referring to only one item."

Consider the following sentences.

We need <u>a</u> table for our computer.

I have <u>a</u> folding table; maybe you can use that.

In the first sentence, the writer is referring to a hypothetical table, not an actual one. Because the table is indefinite to the writer, it is clearly indefinite to the reader, so *a* is used, not *the*. The second sentence refers to an actual table, but because the writer does not expect the reader to be able to identify the table specifically, it is also used with *a* rather than *the*.

> ▶ **Word Power**
> **hypothetical** assumed or supposed; not supported by evidence

FOCUS Indefinite Articles

Unlike the definite article (*the*), the indefinite articles *a* and *an* occur only with singular count nouns. *A* is used when the next sound is a consonant, and *an* is used when the next sound is a vowel. In choosing *a* or *an*, pay attention to sound rather than to spelling: *a house, a year, a union,* but *an hour, an uncle.*

No Article

Only noncount and plural count nouns can stand without articles: *butter, chocolate, cookies, strawberries* (but <u>a</u> *cookie* or <u>the</u> *strawberry*).

Nouns without articles can be used to make generalizations.

<u>Infants</u> need <u>affection</u> as well as <u>food</u>.

Here, the absence of articles before the nouns *infants, affection,* and *food* indicates that the statement is not about particular infants, affection, or food but about infants, affection, and food in general. Remember not to

use *the* in such sentences; in English, a sentence like *The infants need affection as well as food* can only refer to particular, identifiable infants, not to infants in general.

Articles with Proper Nouns

Proper nouns can be divided into two classes: names that take *the* and names that take no article.

- Names of people usually take no article unless they are used in the plural to refer to members of a family, in which case they take *the*: *Napoleon, Mahatma Gandhi* (but *the Parkers*).
- Names of places that are plural in form usually take *the*: *the Andes, the United States*.
- The names of most places on land (cities, states, provinces, and countries) take no article: *Salt Lake City, Mississippi, Alberta, Japan*. The names of most bodies of water (rivers, seas, and oceans, although not lakes or bays) take *the*: *the Mississippi, the Mediterranean, the Pacific* (but *Lake Erie, San Francisco Bay*).
- Names of streets take no article: *Main Street*. Names of unnumbered highways take *the*: *the Belt Parkway*.

ON THE WEB
Visit *Exercise Central* at
bedfordstmartins.com/writingfirst
for more practice.

◆ PRACTICE 30-6

In the following passage, decide whether each blank needs a definite article (*the*), an indefinite article (*a* or *an*), or no article. If a definite or indefinite article is needed, write it in the space provided. If no article is needed, leave the space blank.

Example: Vicente Fox was born on _____ July 2, 1942, in _*the*_ Mexican capital of Mexico City.

(1) Vicente was _____ second of nine children born to José Luis Fox, _____ wealthy farmer, and Mercedes Quesada. (2) When Vicente was only four days old, _____ Fox family went to live in San Francisco del Rincón, in _____ state of Guanajuato. (3) Vicente Fox studied _____ business administration at the Universidad Iberoamericana in Mexico City. (4) He then moved to _____ United States, where he received _____ degree in management at _____ Harvard University. (5) When he returned to Mexico, he went to work for Coca-Cola, and over _____ next fifteen years, he climbed _____ corporate ladder and became _____ company's youngest manager and eventually Coca-Cola's president for Mexico and _____ Latin America. (6) Fox entered _____ politics by joining _____ National

Action Party during _____ 1980s. (7) In 1988, he was elected to _____

Congress. (8) _____ few years later, in 1991, he ran for _____ post of

governor of Guanajuato but lost. (9) Four years later, however, he won by

_____ landslide. (10) In 1999, Fox took _____ leave of absence as governor

to run in _____ presidential elections. (11) In one interview during his

campaign, he said he wanted to rebuild Mexico into _____ country

"where _____ security and _____ justice prevail, where no one is above

_____ law." (12) After promoting himself as _____ "down-to-earth man of

_____ people," on July 2, 2000, Vicente Fox became _____ first opposition

candidate to reach _____ presidency of _____ Republic of Mexico, and

he served until 2006.

■ **WRITING FIRST: Flashback**

Look back at your response to the Writing First activity on page
476. Circle each definite article (*the*) and indefinite article (*a* or
an) you have used. Have you used articles correctly? Correct
any errors you find.

F   **Negative Statements and Questions**

Negative Statements

To form a negative statement, add the word *not* directly after the first helping verb of the complete verb.

> Global warming has been getting worse.
>
> Global warming has <u>not</u> been getting worse.

When there is no helping verb, a form of the verb *do* must be inserted
before *not*.

> Automobile traffic contributes to pollution.
>
> Automobile traffic <u>does not</u> contribute to pollution.

However, if the main verb is *am, is, are, was*, or *were*, do not insert a form
of *do* before *not*: *Harry was late. Harry was <u>not</u> late.*

Remember that when *do* is used as a helping verb, the form of *do* used
must match the tense and number of the original main verb. Note that in
the negative statement above, the main verb loses its tense and appears in
the base form (*contribute*, not *contributes*).

Questions

To form a question, move the helping verb that follows the subject to the position directly before the subject.

> The governor <u>is</u> trying to compromise.
> <u>Is</u> the governor trying to compromise?

> The governor <u>is</u> working on the budget.
> <u>Is</u> the governor working on the budget?

The same rule applies even when the verb is in the past or future tense.

> The governor <u>was</u> trying to lower state taxes.
> <u>Was</u> the governor trying to lower state taxes?

> The governor <u>will</u> try to get reelected.
> <u>Will</u> the governor try to get reelected?

As with negatives, when the verb does not include a helping verb, you must supply a form of *do*. To form a question, put the correct form of *do* directly before the subject.

> The governor <u>works</u> hard.
> <u>Does</u> the governor <u>work</u> hard?

> The governor <u>improved</u> life in his state.
> <u>Did</u> the governor <u>improve</u> life in his state?

However, if the main verb is *am, is, are, was,* or *were,* do not insert a form of *do* before the verb. Instead, move the main verb to before the subject: *Harry was late.* <u>Was Harry late?</u>

Note: The helping verb never comes before the subject if the subject is a question word, such as *who* or *which*.

> <u>Who</u> is talking to the governor?
> <u>Which</u> bills have been vetoed by the governor?

◆ PRACTICE 30-7

Rewrite each of the following sentences in two ways: first, turn the sentence into a question; then, rewrite the original sentence as a negative statement.

Example: Her newest album is selling as well as her first one.

Question: <u>Is her newest album selling as well as her first one?</u>

Negative statement: <u>Her newest album is not selling as well as her first one.</u>

1. Converting metric measurements to the U.S. system is difficult.

Question: _____

Negative statement: _____

_____

ON THE WEB
Visit *Exercise Central* at
bedfordstmartins.com/writingfirst
for more practice.

2. The early frost damaged some crops.

Question: _____

_____

Negative statement: _____

_____

3. That family was very influential in the early 1900s.

Question: _____

_____

Negative statement: _____

_____

4. Most stores in malls are open on Sundays.

Question: _____

_____

Negative statement: _____

_____

5. Choosing the right gift is a difficult task.

Question: _____

_____

Negative statement: _____

_____

6. Most great artists are successful during their lifetimes.

Question: _____

Negative statement: _____

_____

7. The lawyer can verify the witness's story.

Question: _____

_____

Negative statement: _____

_____

8. American cities are as dangerous as they were thirty years ago.

Question: _____

_____

Negative statement: _____

_____

9. The British royal family is loved by most of the British people.

   Question: _____

   _____

   Negative statement: _____

   _____

10. Segregation in the American South ended with the Civil War.

    Question: _____

    Negative statement: _____

    _____

■ **WRITING FIRST: Flashback**

Look back at your response to the Writing First activity on page 476. Do you see any negative statements? If so, check to make sure you have formed them correctly. Then, on the lines below, write a question that you could add to your writing.

Question: _____

_____

Check carefully to make sure you have formed the question correctly.

G Verb Tense

In English, a verb's form must indicate when an action took place (for instance, in the past or in the present). Always use the appropriate tense of the verb even if the time is obvious or if the sentence includes other indications of time (such as *two years ago* or *at present*).

INCORRECT Albert Einstein emigrate from Germany in 1933.

CORRECT Albert Einstein emigrated from Germany in 1933.

> ■ **WRITING FIRST: Flashback**
>
> Look back at your response to the Writing First activity on
> page 476. Are all your verbs in the present tense? Correct
> any errors you find.

H   Stative Verbs

Stative verbs usually tell that someone or something is in a state that will
not change, at least for a while.

Hiro <u>knows</u> American history very well.

Most English verbs show action, and these action verbs can be used
in the progressive tenses. The **present progressive** tense consists of the
present tense of *be* plus the present participle (*I am going*). The **past progressive** tense consists of the past tense of *be* plus the present participle
(*I was going*). Unlike verbs, however, stative verbs are rarely used in the
progressive tenses.

INCORRECT   Hiro <u>is knowing</u> American history very well.

CORRECT   Hiro <u>knows</u> American history very well.

> **FOCUS** Stative Verbs
>
> Verbs that are stative—such as *know, understand, think, believe,
> want, like, love,* and *hate*—often refer to mental states. Other stative
> verbs include *be, have, need, own, belong, weigh, cost,* and *mean.*
> Certain verbs of sense perception, like *see* and *hear,* are also stative
> even though they can refer to momentary events as well as to un-
> changing states.

Many verbs have more than one meaning, and some of these verbs are
active with one meaning but stative with another. An example is the verb
weigh.

ACTIVE   The butcher <u>weighs</u> the meat.

STATIVE   The meat <u>weighs</u> three pounds.

In the first sentences above, the verb *weigh* means "to put on a scale"; it is
active, not stative. In the second sentence, however, the same verb means
"to have weight," so it is stative, not active. It would be unacceptable to say,

ON THE WEB

Visit *Exercise Central* at
bedfordstmartins.com/writingfirst
for more practice.

"The meat is weighing three pounds," but "The butcher is weighing the meat" would be correct.

◆ **PRACTICE 30-8**

In each of the following sentences, circle the verb or verbs. Then, correct any problems with stative verbs by crossing out the incorrect verb tense and writing the correct verb tense above the line. If the verb is correct, write *C* above it.

                        know

Example: Police officers ~~are knowing~~ that fingerprint identification

C

(is) one of the best ways to catch criminals.

1. As early as 1750 B.C., ancient Babylonians were signing their identities with fingerprints on clay tablets.

2. By 220 A.D., the Chinese were becoming aware that ink fingerprints could identify people.

3. However, it was not until the late 1800s that anyone was believing that criminal identification was possible with fingerprints.

4. Nowadays, we know that each person is having unique patterns on the tips of his or her fingers.

5. When police study a crime scene, they want to see whether the criminals have left any fingerprint evidence.

6. There is always a layer of oil on the skin, and police are liking to use it to get fingerprints.

7. Crime scene experts are often seeing cases where the criminals are touching their hair and pick up enough oil to leave a good fingerprint.

8. The police are needing to judge whether the fingerprint evidence has been damaged by sunlight, rain, or heat.

9. In the courtroom, juries often weigh fingerprint evidence before they are deciding on their verdict.

10. The FBI is collecting millions of fingerprints, which police departments can compare with the fingerprints they find at crime scenes.

■ **WRITING FIRST: Flashback**

Look back at your response to the Writing First activity on page 476. Can you identify any stative verbs? If so, list them here.

Stative verbs: _____ _____ _____

_____ _____ _____

Check carefully to be sure you have not used any of these verbs in a progressive tense. Correct any errors you find.

I Modal Auxiliaries

A **modal auxiliary** (such as *can, may, might,* or *must*) is a helping verb that is used with another verb to express ability, possibility, necessity, intent, obligation, and so on.

I <u>can</u> imagine myself in Hawaii.

Modal auxiliaries usually intensify the dominant verb's meaning:

I <u>must</u> run as fast as I can.

You <u>ought to</u> lose some weight.

Modal Auxiliaries

can	ought to
could	shall
may	should
might	will
must	would

FOCUS Modal Auxiliaries

Modal auxiliaries can be used

■ To express physical ability

I can walk faster than my brother.

■ To express the possibility of something occurring

He might get the job if his interview goes well.

(continued on following page)

(continued from previous page)

■ To express or request permission

> **May** I use the restroom in the hallway?

■ To express necessity

> I **must** get to the train station on time.

■ To express a suggestion or advice

> To be healthy, you **should** [or **ought to**] exercise and eat balanced meals.

■ To express intent

> I **will** try to study harder next time.

■ To express a desire

> **Would** you please answer the telephone?

◆ **PRACTICE 30-9**

In the exercise below, circle the correct modal auxiliary.

Example: (May/(Would)) you help me complete the assignment?

1. It doesn't rain very often in Arizona, but today it looks like it (can/might).

2. I know I (will/ought to) call my aunt on her birthday, but I always find an excuse.

3. Sarah (should/must) study for her English exam, but she prefers to spend time with her friends.

4. John (can/would) be the best person to represent our class.

5. Many people believe they (could/should) vote in every election.

6. All students (will/must) bring two pencils, a notebook, and a dictionary to class every day.

7. (Would/May) you show me the way to the post office?

8. I (could/should) not ask for more than my health, my family, and my job.

9. Do you think they (could/can) come back tomorrow to finish the painting job?

10. A dog (should/might) be a helpful companion for your disabled father.

J   Gerunds

A **gerund** is a verb form ending in *-ing* that always acts as a noun.

> <u>Reading</u> the newspaper is one of my favorite things to do on Sundays.

Just like a noun, a gerund can be used as a subject, a direct object, a subject complement, or the object of a preposition.

FOCUS Gerunds

■ A gerund can be a subject.

   Playing tennis is one of my hobbies.

■ A gerund can be a direct object.

   My brother influenced my racing.

■ A gerund can be a subject complement.

   The most important thing is winning.

■ A gerund can be the object of a preposition.

   The teacher rewarded him for passing.

◆ **PRACTICE 30-10**

To complete the sentences below, fill in the blanks with the gerund form of
the verb provided in parentheses.

Example: _____*Typing*_____ (type) is a skill that every girl used to

learn in high school.

1. _____ (eat) five or six smaller meals throughout the day is

healthier than eating two or three big meals.

2. In the winter, there is nothing better than _____ (skate) outdoors on a frozen pond.

3. The household task I dread the most is _____ (clean).

4. The fish avoided the net by _____ (swim) faster.

5. _____ (quit) is easier than accomplishing a goal.

6. Her parents praised her for _____ (remember) their anniversary.

7. Her favorite job is _____ (organize) the files.

8. I did not like his _____ (sing).

9. For me, _____ (cook) is relaxing.

10. The best way to prepare for the concert is by _____ (practice).

■ **WRITING FIRST: Flashback**

Look back at your response to the Writing First activity on page 476. Have you used any gerunds in your writing? On the lines below, list any *-ing* verb forms that you have used as nouns.

Gerunds: _____

_____

_____

Have you used each gerund correctly as a subject, a direct object, a subject complement, or the object of a preposition? Make any necessary corrections.

K Placing Modifiers in Order

Adjectives and other modifiers that come before a noun usually follow a set order.

Required Order

■ Determiners always come first in a series of modifiers: *these* fragile *glasses*. The determiners *all* or *both* always precede any other determiners: *all these glasses*.

■ If one of the modifiers is a noun, it must come directly before the noun it modifies: *these wine glasses*.

■ Descriptive adjectives are placed between the determiners and the noun modifiers: *these fragile wine glasses*. If there are two or more descriptive adjectives, the following order is preferred.

Preferred Order

■ Adjectives that show the writer's attitude generally precede adjectives that merely describe: *these lovely fragile wine glasses*.
■ Adjectives that indicate size generally come early: *these lovely large fragile wine glasses*.

◆ **PRACTICE 30-11**

Arrange each group of modifiers in the correct order, and rewrite the complete phrase in the blank.

ON THE WEB
Visit *Exercise Central* at
bedfordstmartins.com/writingfirst
for more practice.

> **Example:** (annual, impressive, the, publisher's) report
>
> *the publisher's impressive annual report*

1. (brand-new, a, apartment, high-rise) building

   _____

2. (gifted, twenty-five-year-old, Venezuelan, this) author

   _____

3. (successful, short-story, numerous) collections

   _____

4. (her, all, intriguing, suspense) novels

   _____

5. (publisher's, best-selling, the, three) works

   _____

6. (main, story's, two, this) characters

   _____

7. (young, a, strong-willed) woman

   _____

8. (middle-aged, attractive, the, British) poet

   _____

9. (exquisite, wedding, an, white) gown

   _____

10. (extravagant, wedding, an) reception

    _____

■ **WRITING FIRST: Flashback**

Look back at your response to the Writing First activity on page 476. Have you used several modifiers before a single noun? If so, list below all the modifiers and the noun that follows them.

Modifiers: _____ _____ _____ Noun:_____

Modifiers: _____ _____ _____ Noun:_____

Have you arranged the modifiers in the correct order? Make any necessary corrections.

L **Choosing Prepositions**

A **preposition** introduces a noun or pronoun and links it to other words in the sentence. The word the preposition introduces is called the object of the preposition.

A preposition and its object combine to form a **prepositional phrase**: *on the table, near the table, under the table*.

> I thought I had left the book <u>on</u> the table or somewhere <u>near</u> the table, but I found it <u>under</u> the table.

The prepositions *at, in,* and *on* sometimes cause problems for non-native speakers of English. For example, to identify the location of a place or an event, you can use *at, in,* or *on.*

- The preposition *at* specifies an exact point in space or time.

  > The museum is <u>at</u> 1000 Fifth Avenue. Let's meet there <u>at</u> 10:00 tomorrow morning.

- Expanses of space or time are treated as containers and therefore require *in.*

  > Women used to wear long skirts <u>in</u> the early 1900s.

- *On* must be used in two cases: with names of streets (but not with exact addresses) and with days of the week or month.

  > We will move into our new office <u>on</u> 18th Street either <u>on</u> Monday or <u>on</u> March 12.

■ **WRITING FIRST: Flashback**

Look back at your response to the Writing First activity on page 476. Put a check mark above every use of *at, in,* and *on,*

(continued on following page)

(continued from previous page)

and then write the prepositional phrase each word introduces on the lines below.

Prepositional phrases: _____

_____

_____

Have you used each of these prepositions correctly? Correct any errors you find.

M Prepositions in Familiar Expressions

Many familiar expressions end with prepositions. Learning to write clearly and **idiomatically**—following the conventions of written English—means learning which preposition is used in such expressions. Even native speakers of English sometimes have trouble choosing the correct preposition.

The sentences that follow illustrate idiomatic use of prepositions in various expressions. Note that sometimes different prepositions are used with the same word. For example, both *on* and *for* can be used with *wait* to form two different expressions with two different meanings (*He waited on their table*; *She waited for the bus*). Which preposition you choose depends on your meaning. (In the list that follows, pairs of similar expressions that end with different prepositions are bracketed.)

Expression with Preposition	*Sample Sentence*
acquainted with	During orientation, the university offers workshops to make sure that students are <u>acquainted with</u> its rules and regulations.
addicted to	I think Abby is becoming <u>addicted to</u> pretzels.
agree on (a plan or objective)	It is vital that all members of the school board <u>agree on</u> goals for the coming year.
agree to (a proposal)	Striking workers finally <u>agreed to</u> the terms of management's offer.
angry about or at (a situation)	Taxpayers are understandably <u>angry about</u> (or <u>at</u>) the deterioration of city recreation facilities.
angry with (a person)	When the mayor refused to hire more police officers, his constituents became <u>angry with</u> him.
approve of	Amy's adviser <u>approved of</u> her decision to study in Guatemala.
bored with	Salah got <u>bored with</u> economics, so he changed his major to psychology.
capable of	Hannah is a good talker, but she is not <u>capable of</u> acting as her own lawyer.

consist of	The deluxe fruit basket <u>consisted of</u> five pathetic pears, two tiny apples, a few limp bunches of grapes, and one lonely kiwi.
contrast with	Coach Headley's relaxed style <u>contrasts</u> sharply <u>with</u> Coach Pauley's more formal approach.
convenient for	The proposed location of the new day-care center is <u>convenient for</u> many families.
deal with	Many parents and educators believe it is possible to <u>deal with</u> the special needs of autistic children in a regular classroom.
depend on	Children <u>depend on</u> their parents for emotional as well as financial support.
differ from (something else)	A capitalist system <u>differs from</u> a socialist system in its view of private ownership.
differ with (someone else)	When Miles realized that he <u>differed with</u> his boss on most important issues, he handed in his resignation.
emigrate from	My grandfather and his brother <u>emigrated from</u> the part of Russia that is now Ukraine.
grateful for (a favor)	If you can arrange an interview next week, I will be very <u>grateful for</u> your time and trouble.
grateful to (someone)	Jerry Garcia was always <u>grateful to</u> his loyal fans.
immigrate to	Many Cubans want to leave their country and <u>immigrate to</u> the United States.
impatient with	Keshia often gets <u>impatient with</u> her four younger brothers.
interested in	Tomiko had always been <u>interested in</u> computers, so no one was surprised when she became a Web designer.
interfere with	College athletes often find that their dedication to sports <u>interferes with</u> their schoolwork.
meet with	I hope I can <u>meet with</u> you soon to discuss my research project.
object to	The defense attorney <u>objected to</u> the prosecutor's treatment of the witness.
pleased with	Most of the residents are <u>pleased with</u> the mayor's crackdown on crime.
protect against	Nobel Prize winner Linus Pauling believed that large doses of vitamin C could <u>protect</u> people <u>against</u> the common cold.
reason with	When two-year-olds have tantrums, it is nearly impossible to <u>reason with</u> them.
reply to	If no one <u>replies to</u> our ad within two weeks, we will advertise again.
responsible for	Should teachers be held <u>responsible for</u> their students' low test scores?

similar to	The blood sample found at the crime scene was remarkably <u>similar to</u> one found in the suspect's residence.
specialize in	Dr. Casullo is a dentist who <u>specializes in</u> periodontal surgery.
succeed in	Lisa hoped her MBA would help her <u>succeed in</u> a business career.
take advantage of	Some consumer laws are designed to prevent door-to-door salespeople from <u>taking advantage of</u> buyers.
wait for (something to happen)	Many parents of teenagers experience tremendous anxiety while <u>waiting for</u> their children to come home at night.
wait on (in a restaurant)	We sat at the table for twenty minutes before someone <u>waited on</u> us.
worry about	Why <u>worry about</u> things you cannot change?

FOCUS **Using Prepositions in Familiar Expressions: Synonyms**

Below is a list of familiar expressions that have similar meanings. They can often be used in the same contexts.

acquainted with, familiar with
addicted to, hooked on
angry with (a person), upset
   with
bored with, tired of
capable of, able to
consists of, has, contains,
   includes
deal with, address (a problem)
depend on, rely on
differ from (something else),
   be different from
differ with (someone else),
   disagree
emigrate from, move from
   (another country)
grateful for (a favor),
   thankful for
immigrate to, move to
   (another country)

interested in, fascinated by
interfere with, disrupt
meet with, get together with
object to, oppose
pleased with, happy with
protect against, guard
   against
reply to, answer
responsible for, accountable for
similar to, almost the
   same as
succeed in, attain success in
take advantage of, use an
   opportunity to
wait for (something to
   happen), expect
wait on (in a restaurant),
   serve

ON THE WEB

Visit *Exercise Central* at
bedfordstmartins.com/writingfirst
for more practice.

◆ **PRACTICE 30-12**

In the following passage, fill in each blank with the correct preposition.

Example: Like other struggling artists, writers often make a living

working ____*in*____ restaurants and waiting ____*on*____ customers.

(1) Most writers, even those who succeed _____ the literary

world, need day jobs to help pay _____ food and rent. (2) Many

_____ them work _____ related fields—for example, _____

bookstores, _____ publishing houses, or _____ newspapers.

(3) Some take advantage _____ their talents and devote themselves

_____ teaching others _____ language and literature. (4) For

example, _____ the 1990s, *Harry Potter* author J. K. Rowling worked

as a teacher _____ Portugal and _____ Britain. (5) _____

the 1960s and 70s, students _____ Howard University _____

Washington, DC, could enroll _____ classes taught _____ Nobel

Prize–winner Toni Morrison. (6) Other writers work _____ fields un-

related _____ writing. (7) For instance, poet William Carlos Williams

was a medical doctor who wrote poetry only _____ the evenings.

(8) Science fiction writer Isaac Asimov worked _____ Boston Univer-

sity _____ the department _____ biochemistry. (9) Occasionally,

an aspiring writer has friends and family who approve _____ his or

her goals, and he or she can depend _____ them _____ help.

(10) However, many family members, wanting to protect young writers

_____ poverty, object _____ or interfere _____ their

ambitions.

■ **WRITING FIRST: Flashback**

Look back at your response to the Writing First activity on
page 476. Have you used any of the expressions listed on
pages 501–3? If so, bracket each expression. Have you used the
correct prepositions? Make any necessary corrections.

N Prepositions in Phrasal Verbs

A **phrasal verb** consists of two words, a verb and a preposition, that are joined to form an idiomatic expression. Many phrasal verbs are **separable**. This means that a direct object can come between the verb and the preposition. However, some phrasal verbs are **inseparable**; that is, the preposition must always come immediately after the verb.

Separable Phrasal Verbs

In many cases, phrasal verbs may be split, with the direct object coming between the two parts of the verb. When the direct object is a noun, the second word of the phrasal verb can come either before or after the object.

In the sentence below, *fill out* is a phrasal verb. Because the object of the verb *fill out* is a noun (*form*), the second word of the verb can come either before or after the verb's object.

CORRECT   Please fill out the form.

CORRECT   Please fill the form out.

When the object is a pronoun, however, these phrasal verbs must be split, and the pronoun must come between the two parts of the verb.

INCORRECT   Please fill out it.

CORRECT   Please fill it out.

Some Common Separable Phrasal Verbs

ask out	give away	put back	throw away
bring up	hang up	put on	try out
call up	leave out	set aside	turn down
carry out	let out	shut off	turn off
drop off	make up	take down	wake up
fill out	put away	think over	

Remember, when the object of the verb is a pronoun, these phrasal verbs must be split, and the pronoun must come between the two parts (for example, *take it down, put it on, let it out,* and *make it up*).

Inseparable Phrasal Verbs

Some phrasal verbs, however, cannot be separated; that is, the preposition cannot be separated from the verb. This means that a direct object cannot come between the verb and the preposition.

INCORRECT   Please go the manual over carefully.

CORRECT   Please go over the manual carefully.

Notice that in the correct sentence on the previous page, the direct object (*manual*) comes right after the preposition (*over*).

Some Common Inseparable Phrasal Verbs

come across	run across	show up
get along	run into	stand by
go over	see to	

ON THE WEB
Visit *Exercise Central* at
bedfordstmartins.com/writingfirst
for more practice.

◆ **PRACTICE 30-13**

In each of the following sentences, look closely at the phrasal verb, and decide whether the preposition is placed correctly in the sentence. If it is, write *C* in the blank after the sentence. If the preposition needs to be moved, edit the sentence.

> ■ **Culture Clue**
> A *suburb* is a residential area directly outside a city.

Example: People who live in American suburbs are often surprised to come across wild animals in their neighborhoods. __*C*__

1. In one case, a New Jersey woman found that a hungry bear woke up her from a nap one afternoon. _____

2. She called the police, hung up the phone, and ran for her life. _____

3. Actually, although it is a good idea to stay from bears away, most wild bears are timid. _____

4. When there is a drought, people are more likely to run into bears and other wild animals. _____

5. The amount of blueberries and other wild fruit that bears eat usually drops in dry weather off. _____

6. Bears need to put on weight before the winter, so they may have to find food in suburban garbage cans. _____

7. It is a good idea for families to go their plans over to safeguard their property against bears. _____

8. People should not leave pet food out overnight, or else their dog may find that a hungry bear has eaten its dinner. _____

9. If people have a bird feeder in the yard, they should put away it during the autumn. _____

10. As the human population grows, more and more houses are built in formerly wild areas, so bears and people have to learn to get along with each other. _____

■ **WRITING FIRST: Flashback**

Look back at your response to the Writing First activity on page 476. Have you used any phrasal verbs? If so, list them here.

_____   _____

_____   _____

_____   _____

Have you placed the preposition correctly in each case? Make any necessary corrections.

■ **WRITING FIRST: Revising and Editing**

Look back at your response to the Writing First activity on page 476. Then, review all your Flashback activities, and be sure you have made all necessary corrections in grammar and usage. When you have finished, add any additional transitional words and phrases you need to make the holiday celebration you have described clear to your readers.

CHAPTER REVIEW

◆ **EDITING PRACTICE**

Read the following student essay, which includes errors in the use of subjects, articles and determiners, and stative verbs, as well as errors with prepositions in idiomatic expressions. Check each underlined word or phrase. Add any missing words, and cross out any words used incorrectly, writing the correct words above the line. If the underlined word or phrase is correct, write *C* above it. The title of the essay has been edited for you.

How to Succeed <s>on</s> ⁱⁿ Multinational Business

Success in multinational business often <u>depends in</u> the ability to understand other countries' cultures. Understanding how cultures <u>differ to</u> our own, however, is only one key to <u>these</u> success. In addition, is crucial that businesses learn to adapt to different cultures. <u>The ethnocentrism</u> is the belief that one's own culture has <u>a</u>

best way of doing things. In international business, is necessary to set aside this belief. A company cannot uses the same methods overseas as it uses at home. If a company tries to sell exactly the same product in a different country, could be problems.

To avoid problems, a company it should do a few market research. For example, when McDonald's opened restaurants on India, realized that beef burgers would not work in a country where many people believe that cows are sacred. Instead, burgers were created out of ground chickens. For India's many vegetarians, McDonald's created several different vegetable patty. McDonald's understood that both the religious and cultural characteristic of the country had to be considered if its new restaurants were going to succeed.

Similarly, American company should always find out what the name of a product means in the new language. For example, the General Motors tried to sell a car called the Chevy Nova in Spanish-speaking countries. Unfortunately, although *nova* means "bright star" in English, *no va* means "doesn't go" in Spanish, so it was not good name to use in Spanish-speaking countries. If General Motors' businesspeople had been capable to speaking and understanding the language, they must have chosen a different name. Communicating directly with customers make everyone more comfortable and efficient.

It is many aspects of a country that must be understood before successful international business can be carried out. To protect from legal errors, a company needs to understand the country's legal system, which may be very different from its home country's legal system. May be necessary to get licenses to export products onto other countries. The role of women is also likely to be different; without knowing this, businesspeople might unintentionally be rude. Also, much personal interactions in other countries may give the wrong impression to someone who is inexperienced. For example, in Latin American countries, people are often standing close together and touch each other when they are talking. Americans may feel uncomfortable in such a situation unless understand it.

McDonald's in Egypt

Auto executives from China, Japan, and the United States

Business meeting in Kuwait

Over time, the marketplace <u>is becoming</u> more global. In <u>those</u> setting, individuals from numerous cultures come together. To perform effectively, an international company must hire people with the right <u>experiences</u>. To <u>deal with</u> other cultures, multinational companies <u>inside</u> today's global market must have good <u>informations</u> and show other cultures the highest <u>respects</u>.

◆ COLLABORATIVE ACTIVITIES

1. Working in a small group, make a list of ten prepositional phrases that include the prepositions *above, around, at, between, from, in, on, over, under,* and *with.* Use appropriate nouns as objects of these prepositions, and use as many modifying words as you wish. (Try, for example, to write something like *above their hideous wedding portrait,* not just *above the picture.*)
2. Exchange lists with another group. Still working collaboratively, compose a list of ten sentences, each including one of the other group's ten prepositional phrases. Give your list of ten sentences to another group.
3. Working with this new list of ten sentences, substitute a different prepositional phrase for each one that appears in a sentence. Make sure each sentence still makes sense.

☑ REVIEW CHECKLIST:
Grammar and Usage for ESL Writers

- In almost all cases, English sentences must state their subjects. (See 30A.)

- In English, most nouns add *-s* to form plurals. Always use a form that indicates that a noun is plural. (See 30B.)

- English nouns may be count nouns or noncount nouns. A count noun names one particular thing or a group of particular things (*a teacher, oceans*). A noncount noun names something that cannot be counted (*gold, sand*). (See 30C.)

- Determiners are adjectives that identify rather than describe the nouns they modify. Determiners may also indicate amount or number. (See 30D.)

- The definite article *the* and the indefinite articles *a* and *an* are determiners that indicate whether the noun that follows is one readers can identify (*the book*) or one they cannot yet identify (*a book*). (See 30E.)

(continued on following page)

(continued from previous page)

- To form a negative statement, add the word *not* directly after the first helping verb of the complete verb. To form a question, move the helping verb that follows the subject to the position directly before the subject. (See 30F.)

- A verb's form must indicate when an action took place. (See 30G.)

- Stative verbs indicate that someone or something is in a state that will not change, at least for a while. Stative verbs are rarely used in the progressive tenses. (See 30H.)

- A modal auxiliary is a helping verb that expresses ability, possibility, necessity, intent, obligation, and so on. (See 30I.)

- A gerund is a verb form ending in *-ing* that is always used as a noun. (See 30J.)

- Adjectives and other modifiers that come before a noun usually follow a set order. (See 30K.)

- The prepositions *at, in,* and *on* sometimes cause problems for nonnative speakers of English. (See 30L.)

- Many familiar expressions end with prepositions. (See 30M.)

- A phrasal verb consists of two words, a verb and a preposition, that are joined to form an idiomatic expression. (See 30N.)

Read the following student essay, which includes errors in the use of verbs, nouns, pronouns, adjectives, and adverbs, as well as ESL errors. Make any changes necessary to correct the basic grammar of the sentences. The first sentence has been edited for you.

The Mystery of the Bermuda Triangle

The Bermuda Triangle is an area in the Atlantic Ocean also ~~know~~ *known* as the Devil's Triangle. Its size, between 500,000 and 1.5 million square miles, depends on who you are believing. Strange events happen there.

During the past century, more than fifty ships and twenty airplanes have disappeared to these area. According to some people, a mysterious force causes ships and planes to vanish in the Bermuda Triangle. Everyone who hears about the mystery has to decide for themselves what to believe. However, according to the U.S. Coast Guard, the explanations are not mysterious.

The stories about odd these occurrences they may have started as early as 1492. When Columbus sailed through the area, him and his crew seen unusual lights in the sky. In addition, his compass reacted strangely. Now, is believed that the lights came from a meteor that crashed into the ocean. The peculiar compass readings were probably cause from the fact that in this area magnetic compasses point toward true north rather than magnetic north. This variation can cause navigators to sail off course.

The modern Bermuda Triangle legend started in 1945, when Flight 19, compose of five U.S. Navy Avenger torpedo bombers, disappeared while on a routine training mission. Rescue plane that has been sent to search for them also disappeared. Six aircraft and twenty-seven man vanished. Not only were their lifes lost, but no bodies were ever found. Were a mysterious force responsible? Although the events themselves seem strange, there are several good explanation. First, all the crew members except his leader were trainees. It is quite possibly that they flied through a magnetic storm or that the leader's compass was not working. If so, they would have become confused of their location. Radio transmissions were unreliable because of a bad weather and a broken receiver in one of the

Map of Bermuda Triangle

One of the torpedo bombers that vanished in the Bermuda Triangle in 1945

511

planes. The crew leader was not functioning very good. The leader told his pilots to head east; he thought that they were over the Gulf of Mexico. However, they were flying up the Atlantic coastline, so his instructions sent him further out to sea. If the planes crashed into the ocean at night, it is not likely there would have been any survivors. No wreckage was ever recover.

After Flight 19 disappeared, storys start to appear about the events that have occurred. The odd compass readings, the problems with radio transmissions, and the missing wreckage lead to strange tales. Some people believe that the missing ships and planes were taken by UFOs (unidentified flying objects) to a different dimension. Others think that those whom disappeared were kidnapped from aliens from other planets. However, there are most convincing explanations. The fact that magnetic compasses point toward true north in this area is now well known. It is also well known that the weather patterns in the southern Atlantic and Caribbean areas is unpredictable. In addition, human error may have been involved. For these reason, the tales of the Bermuda Triangle are clearly science fiction, not fact.

Missing Ship Recalls 1918 Disappearance
Newspaper headline

Coast Guard Hunting Tanker With 43 Men
Newspaper headline

UNIT SEVEN

UNDERSTANDING PUNCTUATION, MECHANICS, AND SPELLING

Using Commas

PREVIEW

In this chapter, you will learn

- to use commas in a series (31A)
- to use commas to set off introductory phrases and transitional words and phrases (31B)
- to use commas with appositives (31C)
- to use commas to set off nonrestrictive clauses (31D)
- to use commas in dates and addresses (31E)
- to avoid unnecessary commas (31F)

▶ **Word Power**

subsidized assisted or supported financially

low-density sparsely settled; not crowded

■ WRITING FIRST

The pictures above show houses in disrepair and the public housing units that replaced them. Look at the pictures, and then write about an ideal public housing complex for low-income families. Where should it be located? What kinds of buildings should be constructed? What facilities and services should be offered to residents?

■ Culture Clue

Public housing is government-sponsored housing offered at lower rents to people who need financial assistance.

515

A **comma** is a punctuation mark that separates words or groups of words within sentences. In this way, commas keep ideas distinct from one another.

In earlier chapters, you learned to use a comma between two simple sentences (independent clauses) linked by a coordinating conjunction to form a compound sentence.

> Some people are concerned about global warming, but others are not.

You also learned to use a comma after a dependent clause that comes before an independent clause in a complex sentence.

> Although bears in the wild can be dangerous, hikers can take steps to protect themselves.

In addition, commas are used to set off directly quoted speech or writing from the rest of the sentence.

> John F. Kennedy said, "Ask not what your country can do for you; ask what you can do for your country."

As you will learn in this chapter, commas have several other uses as well.

■ **Culture Clue**

John F. Kennedy was the thirty-fifth president of the United States. He served from 1961 until his assassination in 1963.

A Commas in a Series

Use commas to separate all elements in a **series** of three or more words or word groups (phrases or clauses).

> Leyla, Zack, and Kathleen campaigned for Representative Lewis.
>
> Leyla, Zack, or Kathleen will be elected president of Students for Lewis.
>
> Leyla made phone calls, licked envelopes, and ran errands for the campaign.
>
> Leyla is president, Zack is vice president, and Kathleen is treasurer.

FOCUS Using Commas in a Series

Newspapers and magazines usually omit the comma before the coordinating conjunction in a series. However, in college writing you should always use a comma before the coordinating conjunction.

> Leyla, Zack, and Kathleen worked on the campaign.

(continued on following page)

(*continued from previous page*)

> Exception: Do not use *any* commas if all the items in a series are separated by coordinating conjunctions.
>
> > Leyla or Zack or Kathleen will be elected president of Students for Lewis.

◆ **PRACTICE 31-1**

Edit the following sentences for the use of commas in a series. If the sentence is correct, write *C* in the blank.

ON THE WEB
Visit *Exercise Central* at
bedfordstmartins.com/writingfirst
for more practice.

Examples

Costa Rica produces bananas, cocoa, and sugar cane. ____*C*____

The pool rules state that there is no running/ or jumping/ or diving.

_____

1. The musician plays guitar bass and drums. _____

2. The organization's goals are feeding the hungry, housing the homeless, and helping the unemployed find work. ____*C*____

3. *The Price Is Right*, *Let's Make a Deal*, and *Jeopardy!* are three of the longest-running game shows in television history. ____*C*____

4. In native Hawaiian culture, yellow was worn by the royalty red was worn by priests and a mixture of the two colors was worn by others of high rank. ____*C*____

5. The diary Anne Frank kept while her family hid from the Nazis is insightful, touching and sometimes humorous. _____

6. A standard bookcase is sixty inches tall forty-eight inches wide and twelve inches deep. _____

7. Most coffins manufactured in the United States are lined with bronze, or copper, or lead. ____*C*____

8. Young handsome and sensitive, Leonardo DiCaprio was the 1990s answer to the 1950s actor James Dean. _____

9. California's capital is Sacramento, its largest city is Los Angeles, and its oldest settlement is San Diego. _____

10. Watching television, playing video games, and riding a bicycle are some of the average ten-year-old boy's favorite pastimes. _____

■ **WRITING FIRST: Flashback**

Look back at your response to the Writing First activity on page 515. If you have included a series of three or more words or word groups in any of your sentences, copy it here. Did you use commas correctly to separate elements in the series? If not, correct your punctuation. If no sentence includes a series, write a new sentence that does on the lines below.

_____

_____

B Commas with Introductory Phrases and Transitional Words and Phrases

Use a comma to set off an **introductory phrase** from the rest of the sentence.

In the event of a fire, proceed to the nearest exit.

Walking home, Nelida decided to change her major.

To keep fit, people should try to exercise regularly.

Also use commas to set off **transitional words or phrases** whether they appear at the beginning, in the middle, or at the end of a sentence.

In fact, Thoreau spent only one night in jail.

He was, of course, bailed out by a friend.

He did spend more than two years at Walden Pond, however.

FOCUS Using Commas in Direct Address

Always use commas to set off the name of someone whom you are **addressing** (speaking to) directly, whether the name appears at the beginning, in the middle, or at the end of a sentence.

(continued on following page)

(continued from previous page)

Molly, come here and look at this.

Come here, Molly, and look at this.

Come here and look at this, Molly.

◆ PRACTICE 31-2

Edit the following sentences for the use of commas with introductory phrases. If the sentence is correct, write *C* in the blank.

ON THE WEB
Visit *Exercise Central* at
bedfordstmartins.com/writingfirst
for more practice.

Examples

In recent years, illegal anabolic steroids have become popular among some athletes despite their dangerous side effects. _____

In the Olympics, these steroids are banned. __C__

(1) In doping scandals, athletes have also tested positive for human growth hormones. __✓__ (2) Among track and field athletes, doping has been especially common. _____ (3) Disappointing thousands of fans, two Greek sprinting stars, refused to participate in a drug test at the Athens Olympics. __✓__ (4) Because of their refusal to take the test, they were not allowed to run. _____ (5) In a recent case of steroid abuse, professional wrestler Chris Benoit killed his family and himself. _____ (6) In professional baseball, the home-run record of Barry Bonds has been questioned because of his suspected steroid use. _____ (7) As a result of athletes' fame many children, and young adults see them as role models. _____ (8) Because of their steroid use, young people may think that they can use these drugs, too. _____ (9) In spite of the dangers of steroids young athletes, may think only of becoming stronger and faster. _____ (10) Even with the short-term benefits, young people should avoid using steroids. __C__

Culture Clue

Doping is slang for taking drugs such as steroids in order to improve one's performance in sports.

◆ PRACTICE 31-3

Edit the following sentences for the use of commas with transitional words and phrases. If the sentence is correct, write *C* in the blank.

Example: Eventually' most people build a personal credit history.

(1) Often, establishing credit can be difficult. _____ (2) College students, for example, often have no credit history of their own, especially if their parents pay their bills. _____ (3) Similarly, some married women have no personal credit history. _____ (4) In fact, their credit cards may be in their husbands' names. _____. (5) As a result, they may be unable to get their own loans. __*C*__ (6) Of course, one way to establish credit is to apply for a credit card at a local department store. _____ (7) Also, it is relatively easy to get a gas credit card. _____ (8) It is important, to pay these credit card bills promptly, however. _____ (9) In addition, having checking, and savings accounts can help to establish financial reliability. _____ (10) Finally, people who want to establish a credit history can sign an apartment lease and pay the rent regularly to show that they are good credit risks. __*C*__

■ **WRITING FIRST: Flashback**

Look back at your response to the Writing First activity on page 515. Underline any introductory phrases and transitional words and phrases. Have you set off each of these with commas where appropriate? Revise any incorrect sentences on the lines below, adding commas where needed.

_____

_____

_____

_____

C **Commas with Appositives**

Use commas to set off an **appositive**—a word or word group that identifies, renames, or describes a noun or a pronoun.

I have visited only one country, Canada, outside the United States. (*Canada* is an appositive that identifies the noun *country*.)

Carlos Santana, leader of the group Santana, played at Woodstock in 1969. (*Leader of the group Santana* is an appositive that identifies *Carlos Santana*.)

A really gifted artist, he is also a wonderful father. (*A really gifted artist* is an appositive that describes the pronoun *he*.)

■ **Culture Clue**
The Woodstock Music and Art Fair took place in Bethel, New York. The historic festival featured thirty-two of the best musical acts playing to a large counterculture audience.

FOCUS **Using Commas with Appositives**

Most appositives are set off by commas whether they fall at the beginning, in the middle, or at the end of a sentence.

A dreamer, he spent his life thinking about what he could not have.

He always wanted to build a house, a big white one, overlooking the ocean.

He finally built his dream house, a log cabin.

◆ **PRACTICE 31-4**

Underline the appositive in each of the following sentences. Then, check each sentence for the correct use of commas to set off appositives, and add any missing commas. If the sentence is correct, write *C* in the blank.

ON THE WEB
Visit *Exercise Central* at **bedfordstmartins.com/writingfirst** for more practice.

Example: Wendy Kopp, a student at Princeton University, proposed the Teach For America program to help minority students get a better education. _____

1. Guglielmo Marconi, a young Italian inventor, sent the first wireless message across the Atlantic Ocean in 1901. _____

2. A member of the boy band, 'N Sync, Justin Timberlake, established a career as a solo musician and actor. _____

3. HTML hypertext markup language, consists of the codes used to create Web documents. _____

4. William Filene, founder of Filene's Department Store, invented the "bargain basement." _____

5. Known as NPR National Public Radio, presents a wide variety of programs. _____

6. On the southwest coast of Nigeria lies Lagos a major port. _____

7. Home of the 2008 Olympics, Beijing continues to have serious problems with its air quality. _____

8. Lightning a strong electrical charge can be both beautiful and dangerous. _____

9. A plant that grows on mountains and in deserts, the fern is surprisingly adaptable. __*C*__

10. Golf a game developed in Scotland, is very popular in the United States. __*C*__

■ **WRITING FIRST: Flashback**

Look back at your response to the Writing First activity on page 515. Have you used any appositives? Underline each one. Have you set off appositives with commas? Revise any incorrectly punctuated sentences on the lines that follow.

_____

_____

_____

_____

D **Commas with Nonrestrictive Clauses**

Clauses are often used to add information within a sentence. In some cases, you need to add commas to set off these clauses; in other cases, commas are not required.

Use commas to set off **nonrestrictive clauses**, clauses that are not essential to a sentence's meaning. Do not use commas to set off **restrictive clauses**.

▶ **Word Power**

restrict to keep within limits

restrictive limiting

■ A **nonrestrictive clause** does *not* contain essential information. Nonrestrictive clauses are set off from the rest of the sentence by commas.

Telephone calling-card fraud, which cost consumers and phone companies four billion dollars last year, is increasing.

Here, the clause between the commas (underlined) provides extra information to help readers understand the sentence, but the sentence would still communicate the same idea without this information.

Telephone calling-card fraud is increasing.

■ A **restrictive clause** contains information that is essential to a sentence's meaning. Restrictive clauses are *not* set off from the rest of the sentence by commas.

Many rock stars who recorded hits in the 1950s made little money from their songs.

In the sentence above, the clause *who recorded hits in the 1950s* supplies specific information that is essential to the idea the sentence is communicating: it tells readers which group of rock stars made little money. Without the clause, the sentence does not communicate the same idea because it does not tell which rock stars made little money.

Many rock stars made little money from their songs.

FOCUS *Which, That, and Who*

■ *Which* always introduces a nonrestrictive clause.

> The job, which had excellent benefits, did not pay well. (clause set off by commas)

■ *That* always introduces a restrictive clause.

> He accepted the job that had the best benefits. (no commas)

■ *Who* can introduce either a restrictive or a nonrestrictive clause.

> RESTRICTIVE   Many parents who work feel a lot of stress. (no commas)

> NONRESTRICTIVE   Both of my parents, who have always wanted the best for their children, have worked two jobs for years. (clause set off by commas)

◆ **PRACTICE 31-5**

Edit the following sentences so that commas set off all nonrestrictive clauses. (Remember, commas are *not* used to set off restrictive clauses.) If a sentence is correct, write *C* in the blank.

Example: A museum exhibition that celebrates the Alaska highway

tells the story of its construction. _____*C*_____

(1) During the 1940s, a group of African-American soldiers who

defied the forces of nature and human prejudice were shipped to Alaska.

ON THE WEB
Visit *Exercise Central* at
bedfordstmartins.com/writingfirst
for more practice.

_____ (2) They built the Alaska highway which stretches twelve hundred miles across Alaska. _____ (3) The troops who worked on the highway have received little attention in most historical accounts. _____ (4) The highway which cut through some of the roughest terrain in the world was begun in 1942. _____ (5) The Japanese had just landed in the Aleutian Islands which lie west of the tip of the Alaska Peninsula. _____ (6) Military officials, who oversaw the project, doubted the ability of the African-American troops. _____ (7) As a result, they made them work under conditions, that made construction difficult. _____ (8) The troops who worked on the road proved their commanders wrong by finishing the highway months ahead of schedule. _____ (9) In one case, white engineers, who surveyed a river, said it would take two weeks to bridge. _____ (10) To the engineers' surprise, the soldiers who worked on the project beat the estimate. _____ (11) A military report that was issued in 1945 praised them. _____ (12) It said the goals that the African-American soldiers achieved would be remembered through the ages. _____

■ **WRITING FIRST: Flashback**

Look back at your response to the Writing First activity on page 515. Make sure you have included commas to set off nonrestrictive clauses and have *not* set off restrictive clauses with commas.

E   **Commas in Dates and Addresses**

Dates

Use commas in dates to separate the day of the week from the month and the day of the month from the year.

The first Cinco de Mayo we celebrated in the United States was Tuesday, May 5, 1998.

When a date that includes commas does not fall at the end of a sentence, place a comma after the year.

> Tuesday, May 5, 1998, was the first Cinco de Mayo we celebrated in the United States.

Addresses

Use commas in addresses to separate the street address from the city and the city from the state or country.

> The office of the famous fictional detective Sherlock Holmes was located at 221b Baker Street, London, England.

When an address that includes commas falls in the middle of a sentence, place a commas after the state or country.

> The office at 221b Baker Street, London, England, belonged to the famous fictional detective Sherlock Holmes.

◆ **PRACTICE 31-6**   *skip real.*

Edit the following sentences for the correct use of commas in dates and addresses. Add any missing commas, and cross out any unnecessary commas. If the sentence is correct, write *C* in the blank.

ON THE WEB
Visit *Exercise Central* at
bedfordstmartins.com/writingfirst
for more practice.

Examples

June 3, 1988, is the day my parents were married. _____

Their wedding took place in Santiago, Chile. _____

1. The American Declaration of Independence was approved on July 4, 1776. _____

2. The Pelican Man's Bird Sanctuary is located at 1705 Ken Thompson, Parkway, Sarasota, Florida. _____

3. At 175 Carlton Avenue, Brooklyn, New York, is the house where Richard Wright began writing *Native Son*. _____

4. I found this information in the February 12, 1994, issue of the *New York, Times*. _____

5. The Mexican hero Father Miguel Hidalgo y Costilla was shot by a firing squad on June 30, 1811. _C_____

6. In the Palacio de Gobierno at Plaza de Armas, Guadalajara, Mexico is a mural of the famous revolutionary. _v____

7. The Pueblo Grande Museum is located at 1469 East Washington Street Phoenix Arizona. _____

8. Brigham Young led the first settlers into the valley that is now Salt Lake City, Utah, in 1847. _____

9. St. Louis Missouri was the birthplace of writer Maya Angelou, but she spent most of her childhood in Stamps Arkansas. _____

10. Some records list the writer's birthday as May 19 1928 while others indicate she was born on April 4 1928. _____

F Unnecessary Commas

In addition to knowing where commas are required, it is also important to know when *not* to use commas.

■ Do not use a comma before the first item in a series.

INCORRECT *Duck Soup* starred, Groucho, Chico, and Harpo Marx.

CORRECT *Duck Soup* starred Groucho, Chico, and Harpo Marx.

■ Do not use a comma after the last item in a series.

INCORRECT Groucho, Chico, and Harpo Marx, starred in *Duck Soup*.

CORRECT Groucho, Chico, and Harpo Marx starred in *Duck Soup*.

■ Do not use a comma between a subject and a verb.

INCORRECT Students and their teachers, should try to respect one another.

CORRECT Students and their teachers should try to respect one another.

■ Do not use a comma before the coordinating conjunction that separates the two parts of a compound predicate.

INCORRECT The transit workers voted to strike, and walked off the job.

CORRECT The transit workers voted to strike and walked off the job.

■ Do not use a comma before the coordinating conjunction that separates the two parts of a compound subject.

INCORRECT The transit workers, and the sanitation workers voted to strike.

CORRECT The transit workers and the sanitation workers voted to strike.

■ Do not use a comma to set off a restrictive clause.

INCORRECT People, who live in glass houses, should not throw stones.

CORRECT People who live in glass houses should not throw stones.

■ Finally, do not use a comma before a dependent clause that follows an independent clause.

INCORRECT He was exhausted, because he had driven all night.

CORRECT He was exhausted because he had driven all night.

◆ **PRACTICE 31-7**

Some of the following sentences contain unnecessary commas. Edit to eliminate unnecessary commas. If the sentence is correct, write *C* in the blank following it.

Example: Both the Dominican Republic, and the republic of Haiti occupy the West Indian island of Hispaniola. _____

1. The capital of the Dominican Republic, is Santo Domingo. _____

2. The country's tropical climate, generous rainfall, and fertile soil, make the Dominican Republic suitable for many kinds of crops. _____

3. Some of the most important crops are, sugarcane, coffee, cocoa, and rice. _____

4. Mining is also important to the country's economy, because the land is rich in many ores. _____

5. Spanish is the official language of the Dominican Republic, and Roman Catholicism is the state religion. _____

6. In recent years, resort areas have opened, and brought many tourists to the country. _____

7. Tourists who visit the Dominican Republic, remark on its tropical beauty. _____

8. Military attacks, and political unrest have marked much of the Dominican Republic's history. _____

9. Because the republic's economy has not always been strong, many Dominicans have immigrated to the United States. _____

10. However, many Dominican immigrants maintain close ties to their
home country, and return often to visit. _____

■ **WRITING FIRST: Flashback**

Look back at your response to the Writing First activity on
page 515. Check your work carefully to make sure you have
not used commas in any of the situations listed in 31F. Make
any necessary corrections.

■ **WRITING FIRST: Revising and Editing**

Look back at your response to the Writing First activity on
page 515. Then, make the following additions.

1. Add a sentence that includes a series of three or more words
or word groups.

2. Add introductory phrases to two of your sentences.

3. Add an appositive to one of your sentences.

4. Add a transitional word or phrase to one of your sentences
(at the beginning, in the middle, or at the end).

5. Add a nonrestrictive clause to one of your sentences.

When you have made all the additions, reread your work to
check your use of commas in the new material.

CHAPTER REVIEW

◆ **EDITING PRACTICE**

Read the following student essay, which includes errors in comma use.
Add commas where necessary between items in a series and with introductory phrases, transitional words and phrases, appositives, and nonrestrictive clauses. Cross out any unnecessary commas. The first sentence
has been edited for you.

Brave Orchid

One of the most important characters in The Woman Warrior, Maxine Hong Kingston's autobiographical work, is Brave Orchid, Kingston's mother. Brave Orchid, a complex character is an imaginative storyteller, who tells vivid tales of China. A quiet woman she nevertheless impresses her classmates with her intelligence. She is also a traditional woman. However, she will stop at nothing to make her family exactly what she wants it to be. Brave Orchid strongly believes in herself; even so, she sees herself as a failure.

Maxine Hong Kingston

In her native China Brave Orchid trains to be a midwife. The other women in her class envy her independence brilliance and courage. One day Brave Orchid bravely confronts the Fox Spirit, and tells him he will not win. First, she tells him she can endure any pain that he inflicts on her. Next, she gathers together the women in her dormitory to burn the ghost away. After this event, the other women admire her even more.

Working hard Brave Orchid becomes a midwife in China. After coming to America, however, she cannot work as a midwife. Instead, she works in a Chinese laundry, and picks tomatoes. None of her classmates in China would have imagined this outcome. During her later years in America Brave Orchid becomes a woman, who is overbearing and domineering. She bosses her children around, she tries to ruin her sister's life and she criticizes everyone and everything around her. Her daughter, a straight-A student is the object of her worst criticism.

Brave Orchid's intentions are good. Nevertheless she devotes her energy to the wrong things. She wants the people around her to be as strong as she is. Because she bullies them however she eventually loses them. In addition she is too busy criticizing her daughter's faults to see all her accomplishments. Brave Orchid an independent woman and a brilliant student never achieves her goals. She is hard on the people around her, because she is disappointed in herself.

Map of China

◆ COLLABORATIVE ACTIVITIES

1. Bring a homemaking, sports, or fashion magazine to class. Working in a small group, look at the people pictured in the ads. In what roles are men most often depicted? In what roles are women most often

presented? Identify the three or four most common roles for each sex, and give each kind of character a descriptive name—*jock* or *mother*, for example.

2. Working on your own, choose one type of character from the list your group made in Collaborative Activity 1. Then, write a paragraph in which you describe this character's typical appearance and habits. Refer to the appropriate magazine pictures to support your characterization.

3. Collaborating with other members of your group, write two paragraphs, one discussing how men are portrayed in ads and one discussing how women are portrayed.

4. Circle every comma in the paragraph you wrote for Collaborative Activity 2. Then, work with your group to explain why each comma is used. If no one in your group can explain why a particular comma is used, cross it out.

✔ REVIEW CHECKLIST:
Using Commas

- ☐ Use commas to separate all elements in a series of three or more words or word groups. (See 31A.)

- ☐ Use commas to set off introductory phrases and transitional words and phrases from the rest of the sentence. (See 31B.)

- ☐ Use commas to set off appositives from the rest of the sentence. (See 31C.)

- ☐ Use commas to set off nonrestrictive clauses. (See 31D.)

- ☐ Use commas to separate parts of dates and addresses. (See 31E.)

- ☐ Avoid unneccessary commas. (See 31F.)

Using Apostrophes

PREVIEW

In this chapter, you
will learn

- to use apostrophes to
  form contractions (32A)
- to use apostrophes to
  form possessives (32B)
- to revise incorrect use
  of apostrophes (32C)

■ **WRITING FIRST**

The picture above shows a mechanic working on a car.
Certain jobs have traditionally been considered "men's
work," and others have been viewed as "women's work."
Although the workplace has changed considerably in
recent years, some things have remained the same.

    Look at the picture above, and then discuss the tasks
that are considered "men's work" and "women's work" at
your job or in your current household. Be sure to give
examples of the responsibilities of different people you
discuss. (*Note:* Contractions, such as *isn't* or *don't*, are
acceptable in this informal response.)

▶ **Word Power**
gender sexual identity
(masculine or feminine)

stereotype (n) a conven-
tional, usually oversimplified,
opinion or belief; (v) to
develop a fixed opinion of
an individual or group

An **apostrophe** is a punctuation mark that is used in two situations: to form a contraction and to form the possessive of a noun or an indefinite pronoun.

<table>
<tr><td>**A**</td><td>**Apostrophes in Contractions**</td></tr>
</table>

A **contraction** is a word that uses an apostrophe to combine two words. The apostrophe takes the place of omitted letters.

> I <u>didn't</u> (*did not*) realize how late it was.
>
> <u>It's</u> (*it is*) not right for cheaters to go unpunished.

Frequently Used Contractions

I + am = I'm	are + not = aren't
we + are = we're	can + not = can't
you + are = you're	do + not = don't
it + is = it's	will + not = won't
I + have = I've	should + not = shouldn't
I + will = I'll	let + us = let's
there + is = there's	that + is = that's
is + not = isn't	who + is = who's

ON THE WEB

Visit *Exercise Central* at
bedfordstmartins.com/writingfirst
for more practice.

◆ PRACTICE 32-1

In the following sentences, add apostrophes to contractions if needed. If the sentence is correct, write *C* in the blank.

Example: ~~Whats~~ *What's* the deadliest creature on earth? _____

(1) Bacteria and viruses, which we cant see without a microscope, kill many people every year. _____ (2) When we speak about the deadliest creatures, however, usually were talking about creatures that cause illness or death from their poison, which is called venom. _____ (3) After your bitten, stung, or stuck, how long does it take to die? _____ (4) The fastest killer is a creature called the sea wasp, but it isn't a wasp at all. _____ (5) The sea wasp is actually a fifteen-foot-long jellyfish, and although its not aggressive, it can be deadly. _____ (6) People who've gone swimming off the coast of Australia have encountered this creature. _____ (7) While jellyfish found off the Atlantic coast of the United States

can sting, they arent as dangerous as the sea wasp, whose venom is

deadly enough to kill sixty adults. _____ (8) A person whos been stung by

a sea wasp has anywhere from thirty seconds to four minutes to get help

or die. _____ (9) Oddly, it's been found that something as thin as

pantyhose worn over the skin will prevent these stings. _____ (10) Also,

theres an antidote to the poison in the stings that can save the lives of

victims. _____

■ **WRITING FIRST: Flashback**

Look back at your response to the Writing First activity on
page 531, and underline any contractions. Have you used
apostrophes correctly to replace the missing letters? Recopy
all the contractions correctly on the lines below. Then, rewrite
the contractions as two separate words.

Contractions   *Separate Words*

_____ = _____ + _____

_____ = _____ + _____

_____ = _____ + _____

B   **Apostrophes in Possessives**

Possessive forms of nouns and pronouns show ownership. Nouns and
indefinite pronouns do not have special possessive forms. Instead, they
use apostrophes to indicate ownership.

Singular Nouns and Indefinite Pronouns

To form the possessive of singular nouns (including names) and indefinite
pronouns, add an apostrophe plus an *s*.

> Cesar Chavez's goal (*the goal of Cesar Chavez*) was justice for Amer-
> ican farm workers.
>
> The strike's outcome (*the outcome of the strike*) was uncertain.
>
> Whether it would succeed was anyone's guess (*the guess of anyone*).

> **FOCUS**   **Singular Nouns Ending in -s**
>
> Even if a singular noun already ends in -s, add an apostrophe plus
> an s to form the possessive.
>
> The class's next assignment was a research paper.
>
> Dr. Ramos's patients are participating in a clinical trial.

Plural Nouns

Most plural nouns end in -s. To form the possessive of plural nouns ending in -s (including names), add just an apostrophe (not an apostrophe
plus an s).

The two drugs' side effects (*the side effects of the two drugs*) were
quite different.

The Johnsons' front door (*the front door of the Johnsons*) is red.

Some irregular noun plurals do not end in -s. If a plural noun does not
end in -s, add an apostrophe plus an s to form the possessive.

The men's room is right next to the women's room.

◆ PRACTICE 32-2

ON THE WEB

Visit *Exercise Central* at
bedfordstmartins.com/writingfirst
for more practice.

Rewrite the following phrases, changing the noun or indefinite pronoun
that follows *of* to the possessive form. Be sure to distinguish between singular and plural nouns.

Examples

the mayor of the city _____*the city's mayor*_____

the uniforms of the players _____*the players' uniforms*_____

1. the video of the singer _____

2. the scores of the students _____

3. the favorite band of everybody _____

4. the office of the boss _____

5. the union of the players _____

6. the specialty of the restaurant _____

7. the bedroom of the children _____

8. the high cost of the tickets _____

9. the dreams of everyone _____

10. the owner of the dogs _____

■ **WRITING FIRST: Flashback**

Look back at your response to the Writing First activity on page 531. Circle any possessive forms of nouns or indefinite pronouns. Have you used apostrophes correctly to form these possessives? If not, rewrite them correctly in the appropriate columns below.

Singular Nouns	*Indefinite Pronouns*	*Plural Nouns*
_____	_____	_____
_____	_____	_____

C   **Incorrect Use of Apostrophes**

Be careful not to confuse a plural noun (*boys*) with the singular possessive form of the noun (*boy's*). Never use an apostrophe with a plural noun unless the noun is possessive.

> Termites can be dangerous <u>pests</u> [not *pest's*].

> The <u>Velezes</u> [not *Velez's*] live on Maple Drive, right next door to the *Browns* [not *Brown's*].

Also be careful not to use apostrophes with possessive pronouns that end in *-s: theirs* (not *their's*), *hers* (not *her's*), *its* (not *it's*), *ours* (not *our's*), and *yours* (not *your's*).

FOCUS   **Possessive Pronouns**

Be especially careful not to confuse possessive pronouns with sound-alike contractions. Possessive pronouns never include apostrophes.

Possessive Pronoun	*Contraction*
The dog bit its master.	It's (*it is*) time for breakfast.
The choice is theirs.	There's (*there is*) no place like home.
Whose house is this?	Who's (*who is*) on first?
Is this your house?	You're (*you are*) late again.

ON THE WEB
Visit *Exercise Central* at
bedfordstmartins.com/writingfirst
for more practice.

◆ **PRACTICE 32-3**

Check the underlined words in the following sentences for correct use of apostrophes. If a correction needs to be made, cross out the word, and write the correct version above it. If the noun or pronoun is correct, write *C* above it.

      C
Example: The president's views were presented after several other
speakers   *theirs.*
speaker's first presented their's.

1. Parent's should realize that when it comes to disciplining children, the responsibility is there's.

2. It's also important that parents offer praise for a child's good behavior.

3. In it's first few week's of life, a dog is already developing a personality.

4. His and her's towels used to be popular with couple's, but it's not so common to see them today.

5. All the Ryan's spent four year's in college and then got good jobs.

6. From the radio came the lyrics "You're the one who's love I've been waiting for."

7. If you expect to miss any class's, you will have to make arrangements with someone who's willing to tell you you're assignment.

8. No other school's cheerleading squad ever tried as many tricky stunts as our's did.

9. Surprise test's are common in my economics teacher's class.

10. Jazz's influence on many mainstream musician's is one of the book's main subject's.

■ **WRITING FIRST: Flashback**

Look back at your response to the Writing First activity on page 531. Circle each plural noun. Then, circle each possessive pronoun that ends in -*s*. Have you incorrectly used an apostrophe with any of the circled words? If so, revise your work.

■ WRITING FIRST: Revising and Editing

Look back at your response to the Writing First activity on page 531. Because this is an informal exercise, contractions are acceptable; in fact, they may be preferable because they give your writing a conversational tone. Edit your writing so that you have used contractions in all possible situations.

Now, add two sentences—one that includes a singular possessive noun and one that includes a plural possessive noun. Make sure these two new sentences fit smoothly into your writing and that they use apostrophes correctly in possessives and contractions.

CHAPTER REVIEW

◆ EDITING PRACTICE

Read the following student essay, which includes errors in the use of apostrophes. Edit it to eliminate errors by crossing out incorrect words and writing corrections above them. (Note that this is an informal response paper, so contractions are acceptable.) The first sentence has been edited for you.

The Women of Messina

In William ~~Shakespeares'~~ *Shakespeare's* play <u>Much Ado about Nothing</u>, the women of Messina, whether they are seen as love objects or as ~~shrew's,~~ *shrews,* have very few options. A womans role is to please a man. She can try to resist, but she will probably wind up giving in. The plays two women, Hero and Beatrice, are very different. Hero is the obedient one. Heroes cousin, Beatrice, tries to challenge the rules of the mans world in which she lives. However, in a place like Messina, even women like Beatrice find it hard to get the respect that should be their's.

Right from the start, we are drawn to Beatrice. Shes funny, she has a clever comment for most situation's, and she always speaks her mind about other peoples behavior. Unlike Hero, she tries to stand up to the men in her life, as we see in her and Benedicks conversations. But even though Beatrice's intelligence is obvious, she often mocks herself. Its clear that she doesn't have much self-esteem. In fact, Beatrice is'nt the strong woman she seems to be.

▶ **Word Power**
shrew a scolding woman

William Shakespeare

Shakespeare's Globe Theater

Ultimately, Beatrice does get her man, and she will be happy—but at what cost? Benedicks' last word's to her are "Peace! I will stop your mouth." Then, he kisses her. The kiss is a symbolic end to their bickering. It is also the mark of Beatrices defeat. She has lost. Benedick has shut her up. Now, she will be Benedick's wife and do what he wants her to do. Granted, she will have more say in her marriage than Hero will have in her's, but she is still defeated. Even Beatrice, the most rebellious of Messinas women, finds it impossible to achieve anything of importance in this male-dominated society.

◆ COLLABORATIVE ACTIVITIES

1. Working in a group of four and building on your individual responses to the Writing First exercise at the beginning of the chapter, consider which specific occupational and professional roles are still associated largely with men and which are associated primarily with women. Make two lists, heading one "women's jobs" and one "men's jobs."

2. Now, work in pairs, with one pair of students in each group concentrating on men and the other pair on women. Write a paragraph that attempts to justify why the particular jobs you listed should or should not be restricted to one gender. In your discussion, list the various qualities men or women possess that qualify (or disqualify) them for particular jobs. Use possessive forms whenever possible—for example, *women's energy* (not *women have energy*).

3. Bring to class a book, magazine, or newspaper whose style is informal—for example, a romance novel, *TV Guide*, your school newspaper, or even a comic book. Working in a group, circle every contraction you can find on one page of each publication, and substitute for each contraction the words it combines. Are your substitutions an improvement? (You may want to read a few paragraphs aloud before you reach a conclusion.)

✔ REVIEW CHECKLIST:
Using Apostrophes

- Use apostrophes to form contractions. (See 32A.)

- Use an apostrophe plus an *s* to form the possessive of singular nouns and indefinite pronouns, even when a noun ends in *-s*. (See 32B.)

- Use an apostrophe alone to form the possessive of plural nouns ending in *-s*, including names. If a plural noun does not end in *-s*, add an apostrophe plus an *s*. (See 32B.)

- Do not use apostrophes with plural nouns unless they are possessive. Do not use apostrophes with possessive pronouns. (See 32C.)

Understanding Mechanics

PREVIEW

In this chapter, you will learn

- to capitalize proper nouns (33A)
- to punctuate direct quotations (33B)
- to set off titles (33C)
- to use minor punctuation marks correctly (33D)

■ WRITING FIRST

The picture above shows a familiar scene from the classic 1939 film *The Wizard of Oz*. Look at the picture, and then write about a memorable scene from your favorite movie. Begin by giving the film's title and listing the names of the major stars and the characters they play. Then, tell what happens in the scene, quoting a few words of dialogue if possible.

> ▶ **Word Power**
> **empathize** to identify with
>
> **plot** a series of events in a narrative or drama

539

A | Capitalizing Proper Nouns

A **proper noun** names a particular person, animal, place, object, or idea. Proper nouns are always capitalized. The list that follows explains and illustrates specific rules for capitalizing proper nouns.

> **Culture Clue**
>
> A *census* is an official population count; it often includes details of residents' race, gender, and occupation.

1. Always capitalize names of **races, ethnic groups, tribes, nationalities, languages, and religions**.

   The census data revealed a diverse community of Caucasians, African Americans, and Asian Americans, with a few Latino and Navajo residents. Native languages included English, Korean, and Spanish. Most people identified themselves as Catholic, Protestant, or Muslim.

2. Capitalize names of **specific people and the titles that accompany them**. In general, do not capitalize titles used without a name.

   In 1994, President Nelson Mandela was elected to lead South Africa.

   The newly elected fraternity president addressed the crowd.

3. Capitalize names of **specific family members and their titles**. Do not capitalize words that identify family relationships, including those introduced by possessive pronouns.

   The twins, Aunt Edna and Aunt Evelyn, are Dad's sisters.

   My aunts, my father's sisters, are twins.

4. Capitalize names of **specific countries, cities, towns, bodies of water, streets, and so on**. Do not capitalize words that do not name specific places.

   The Seine runs through Paris, France.

   The river runs through the city.

5. Capitalize names of **specific geographical regions**. Do not capitalize such words when they specify direction.

   William Faulkner's novels are set in the South.

   Turn right at the golf course, and go south for about a mile.

6. Capitalize names of **specific buildings and monuments**. Do not capitalize general references to buildings and monuments.

   He drove past the Liberty Bell and looked for a parking space near City Hall.

   He drove past the monument and looked for a parking space near the building.

> **Culture Clue**
>
> The *Liberty Bell* is a national symbol of freedom in the United States. It was rung on July 8, 1776, to announce the adoption of the Declaration of Independence.

7. Capitalize names of **specific groups, clubs, teams, and associations**. Do not capitalize general references to such groups.

   The Teamsters Union represents workers who were at the stadium for the Republican Party convention, the Rolling Stones concert, and the Phillies-Astros game.

The union represents workers who were at the stadium for the political party's convention, the rock group's concert, and the baseball teams' game.

8. Capitalize names of **specific historical periods, events, and documents**. Do not capitalize nonspecific references to periods, events, or documents.

> The Emancipation Proclamation was signed during the Civil War, not during Reconstruction.

> The document was signed during the war, not during the postwar period.

■ **Culture Clue**
President Lincoln issued the *Emancipation Proclamation* to free slaves in the southern territories on January 1, 1863.

9. Capitalize **names of businesses, government agencies, schools, and other institutions**. Do not capitalize nonspecific references to such institutions.

> The Department of Education and Apple Computer have launched a partnership project with Central High School.

> A government agency and a computer company have launched a partnership project with a high school.

10. Capitalize **brand names**. Do not capitalize general references to kinds of products.

> While Jeff waited for his turn at the Xerox machine, he drank a can of Coke.

> While Jeff waited for his turn at the copier, he drank a can of soda.

11. Capitalize **titles of specific academic courses**. Do not capitalize names of general academic subject areas, except for proper nouns— for example, a language or a country.

> Are Introduction to American Government and Biology 200 closed yet?

> Are the introductory American government course and the biology course closed yet?

12. Capitalize **days of the week, months of the year, and holidays**. Do not capitalize the names of seasons.

> The Jewish holiday of Passover usually falls in April.

> The Jewish holiday of Passover falls in the spring.

◆ **PRACTICE 33-1**

Edit the following sentences, capitalizing letters or changing capitals to lowercase where necessary.

> **Example:** I know ̶C̶hicago well because my ̶m̶other grew up there
>
> and my ̶A̶unt ̶J̶ean and ̶U̶ncle ̶A̶mos still live there.

ON THE WEB
Visit *Exercise Central* at
bedfordstmartins.com/writingfirst
for more practice.

1. Located in the midwest on lake Michigan, chicago is an important port city and the site of o'hare international airport, one of the Nation's busiest.

2. The financial center of the city is Lasalle street, and the lakefront is home to Grant park, where there are many Museums and monuments.

3. To the North of the city, soldier field is home to the chicago bears, the city's football team, and wrigley field is home to the chicago cubs, a national league Baseball Team.

4. In the mid-1600s, the site of what is now Chicago was visited by father jacques marquette, a catholic missionary to the ottawa and huron tribes, who lived in the area.

5. By the 1700s, the city was a trading post run by john kenzie.

6. The city grew rapidly in the 1800s, and immigrants included germans, irish, italians, poles, greeks, and chinese, along with african americans who migrated from the south.

7. Today, Chicago's skyline is marked by many Skyscrapers, built by businesses like the john hancock company, sears, and amoco.

8. To find out more about their city, some Chicago Residents take History classes; northwestern university's School of continuing studies offers one called chicago history in the 20th century.

■ **WRITING FIRST: Flashback**

Look back at your response to the Writing First activity on page 539. Underline every proper noun. Does each proper noun begin with a capital letter? On the lines below, correct any that do not.

_____   _____   _____

_____   _____   _____

A **direct quotation** shows the *exact* words of a speaker or writer. Direct quotations are always placed in quotation marks.

A direct quotation is usually accompanied by an **identifying tag**, a phrase (such as "she said") that names the person being quoted. In the following sentences, the identifying tag is underlined.

<u>Lauren said</u>, "My brother and Tina have gotten engaged."

A <u>famous advertiser wrote</u>, "Don't sell the steak; sell the sizzle."

When a quotation is a complete sentence, it begins with a capital letter and ends with a period, a question mark, or an exclamation point. When a quotation falls at the end of a sentence (as in the two examples above) the period is placed *inside* the quotation marks.

If the quotation is a question or an exclamation, the question mark or an exclamation point is also placed *inside* the quotation marks.

The instructor asked, "Has anyone read *Sula*?"

Officer Warren shouted, "Hold it right there!"

If the quotation itself is not a question or an exclamation, the question mark or exclamation point goes *outside* the quotation marks.

Did Joe really say, "I quit"?

I can't believe he really said, "I quit"!

FOCUS **Indirect Quotations**

A direct quotation shows someone's *exact* words, but an **indirect quotation** simply summarizes what was said or written.
Do not use quotation marks with indirect quotations.

DIRECT QUOTATION   Martin Luther King Jr. said, "I have a dream."

INDIRECT QUOTATION   Martin Luther King Jr. said that he had a dream.

The rules for punctuating direct quotations with identifying tags are summarized below.

■ When the identifying tag comes **before the quotation**, it is followed by a comma.

<u>Alexandre Dumas wrote</u>, "Nothing succeeds like success."

33 B

■ When the identifying tag comes **at the end of a sentence**, it is followed by a period. A comma inside the closing quotation marks separates the quotation from the identifying tag.

"Life is like a box of chocolates," stated Forrest Gump.

■ When the quotation is a question or an exclamation, a question mark or exclamation point separates the quotation from the identifying tag.

"Is that so?" his friends wondered.

"That's amazing!" he cried.

■ When the identifying tag comes **in the middle of the quoted sentence**, it is followed by a comma. The first part of the quotation is also followed by a comma, placed inside the quotation marks. Because the part of the quotation that follows the identifying tag is not a new sentence, it does not begin with a capital letter.

"This is my life," Bette insisted, "and I'll live it as I please."

■ When the identifying tag comes **between two quoted sentences**, it is preceded by a comma and followed by a period. (The second quoted sentence begins with a capital letter.)

"Producer Berry Gordy is an important figure in the history of music," Tony explained. "He was the creative force behind Motown records."

◆ **PRACTICE 33-2**

ON THE WEB
Visit *Exercise Central* at
bedfordstmartins.com/writingfirst
for more practice.

The following sentences contain direct quotations. First, underline the identifying tag. Then, punctuate the quotation correctly, adding capital letters as necessary.

Example: "Why, Darryl asked, "are teachers so strict about deadlines?"

1. We who are about to die salute you said the gladiators to the emperor.

2. When we turned on the television, the newscaster was saying ladies and gentlemen, we have a new president-elect.

3. The bigger they are said boxer John L. Sullivan the harder they fall.

4. Do you take Michael to be your lawfully wedded husband asked the minister.

5. Lisa Marie replied I do.

6. If you believe the *National Enquirer* my friend always says then you'll believe anything.

7. When asked for the jury's verdict, the foreperson replied we find the defendant not guilty.

8. I had felt for a long time that if I was ever told to get up so a white person could sit Rosa Parks recalled I would refuse to do so.

9. Yabba dabba doo Fred exclaimed this brontoburger looks great.

10. Where's my money Addie Pray asked you give me my money!

■ **WRITING FIRST: Flashback**

Look back at your response to the Writing First activity on page 539. Make sure that you have enclosed any direct quotations in quotation marks, placed other punctuation correctly, and capitalized where necessary. Revise any incorrectly punctuated quotations on the lines below.

_____

_____

_____

C **Setting Off Titles**

Some titles are typed in *italics* (or <u>underlined</u> to indicate italics). Others are enclosed in quotation marks. The following box shows how to set off different kinds of titles.

Italicized Titles	*Titles in Quotation Marks*
Books: *How the García Girls Lost Their Accents*	Book chapters: "Understanding Mechanics"
Newspapers: *Miami Herald*	Short stories: "The Tell-Tale Heart"
Magazines: *People*	
Long poems: *John Brown's Body*	Essays and articles: "The Suspected Shopper"
Plays: *Death of a Salesman*	Short poems: "Richard Cory"

(continued on following page)

(continued from previous page)

Italicized Titles	*Titles in Quotation Marks*
Films: *The Rocky Horror Picture Show*	Songs and speeches: "America the Beautiful"; "The Gettysburg Address"
Television or radio series: *Battlestar Galactica*	Individual episodes of television or radio series: "The Montgomery Bus Boycott" (an episode of the PBS series *Eyes on the Prize*)

FOCUS **Capital Letters in Titles**

Capitalize the first letters of all important words in a title. Do not capitalize an **article** (*a, an, the*), a **preposition** (*to, of, around,* and so on), or a **coordinating conjunction** (*and, but,* and so on)—unless it is the first or last word of the title or subtitle (*On the Road;* "To an Athlete Dying Young"; *No Way Out; And Quiet Flows the Don*).

◆ **PRACTICE 33-3**

ON THE WEB
Visit *Exercise Central* at
bedfordstmartins.com/writingfirst
for more practice.

Edit the following sentences, capitalizing letters as necessary in titles.

     Example: Eudora Welty's "a worn path" is a very moving short story.

1. The 1959 movie *plan nine from outer space* has been called the worst picture of all time.

2. Gary Larson's cartoon collections include the books *a prehistory of the far side* and *wiener dog art*.

3. Everyone should read Martin Luther King Jr.'s "i have a dream" speech and his essay "letter from birmingham jail."

4. Bruce Springsteen's album *the rising* includes the songs "lonesome day," "into the fire," and "my city of ruins."

5. CBS has had hits with *CSI, CSI: miami,* and *CSI: new york.*

◆ **PRACTICE 33-4**

In the following sentences, underline titles or place them in quotation marks. (Remember that titles of books and other long works are underlined, and titles of stories, essays, and other shorter works are enclosed in quotation marks.)

Examples: An article in the <u>New York Times</u> called "Whoopi Goldberg Joins <u>The View</u>" talks about a television talk show hosted by women.

1. In addition to her television show, Oprah Winfrey publishes a magazine called O.

2. At the beginning of most major American sporting events, the crowd stands for The Star Spangled Banner.

3. People who want to purchase new computers often compare the different brands in Consumer Reports magazine.

4. The theme song from the TV show 30 Rock has been nominated for an Emmy award.

5. Edgar Allan Poe has written several mysterious short stories, two of which are called The Tell-Tale Heart and The Black Cat.

6. The popular Broadway show The Producers was based on a 1968 movie.

7. Lance Armstrong, who won the Tour de France bicycle race, wrote a book about his fight with cancer called It's Not About the Bike.

8. In a college textbook called Sociology: A Brief Introduction, the first chapter is titled The Essence of Sociology.

■ WRITING FIRST: Flashback

Look back at your response to the Writing First activity on page 539. Have you underlined the film's title? Have you used capital letters where necessary in the title? Make any corrections on the lines below.

_____

_____

D Using Minor Punctuation Marks

The Colon

■ Use a **colon** to introduce a direct quotation.

Our family motto is a simple one: "Accept no substitutes."

■ Use a colon to introduce an explanation, a clarification, or an example.

> Only one thing kept him from climbing Mt. Everest: fear of heights.

■ Use a colon to introduce a list.

> I left my job for four reasons: boring work, poor working conditions, low pay, and a terrible supervisor.

The Dash

Use **dashes** to set off important information.

> She parked her car—a red Firebird—in a towaway zone.

Parentheses

Use **parentheses** to enclose material that is relatively unimportant.

> The weather in Portland (a city in Oregon) was overcast.

◆ PRACTICE 33-5

ON THE WEB
Visit *Exercise Central* at
bedfordstmartins.com/writingfirst
for more practice.

Add colons, dashes, and parentheses to the following sentences where necessary.

Example: Megachurches (those with more than two thousand worshippers at a typical service) have grown in popularity since the 1950s.

1. Megachurches though Protestant are not always affiliated with the main Protestant denominations.

2. Services in megachurches are unique preaching is accompanied by contemporary music and video presentations.

3. Although many of these churches are evangelical actively recruiting new members, people often join because of friends and neighbors.

4. Megachurches tend to keep their members because they encourage all kinds of activities for example, hospitality committees, bible study groups, and orientations.

5. Worshippers say that their services are upbeat full of joy and spirituality.

6. Megachurches in nearly all cases use technology to organize and communicate with their members.

7. The largest of these churches with ten thousand members would be unable to function without telecommunications.

8. Some even offer services in a format familiar to their younger members the podcast.

9. Critics of megachurches and there are some believe they take up too much tax-exempt land.

10. Other critics fear that smaller churches already struggling to keep members will lose worshippers to these huge congregations and eventually have to close.

■ **WRITING FIRST: Flashback**

Look back at your response to the Writing First activity on page 539. Do you see anywhere to add a quotation, an example, or a list that could be introduced by a colon? Write your possible additions here.

Quotation: _____

Example: _____

List: _____

■ **WRITING FIRST: Revising and Editing**

Look back at your response to the Writing First activity on page 539. If you have quoted any dialogue from the film, try varying the placement of the identifying tags you have used. If you did not include any lines of dialogue, try adding one or two. Then, add the quotation, example, or list from the above Flashback activity to your writing. Be sure to introduce this new material with a colon, and make sure that a complete sentence comes before the colon. Finally, edit your work for proper use of capital letters, quotation marks, and underlining.

*Man dying of the plague,
fourteenth or fifteenth century.*

INFLUENZA
FREQUENTLY COMPLICATED WITH
PNEUMONIA
IS PREVALENT AT THIS TIME THROUGHOUT AMERICA.
THIS THEATRE IS CO-OPERATING WITH THE DEPARTMENT OF HEALTH.
YOU MUST DO THE SAME
IF YOU HAVE A COLD AND ARE COUGHING AND
SNEEZING- DO NOT ENTER THIS THEATRE
GO HOME AND GO TO BED UNTIL YOU ARE WELL
Coughing, Sneezing or Spitting Will Not Be
Permitted In The Theatre. In case you
must cough or Sneeze, do so in your own hand-
kerchief, and if the Coughing or Sneezing
Persists Leave The Theatre At Once.
This Theatre has agreed to co-operate with
the Department Of Health in disseminating
the truth about Influenza, and thus serve
a great educational purpose.
**HELP US TO KEEP CHICAGO THE
HEALTHIEST CITY IN THE WORLD**
JOHN DILL ROBERTSON
COMMISSIONER OF HEALTH

*Public health quarantine poster
for 1918 flu epidemic*

■ **Culture Clue**
NPR stands for National
Public Radio.

CHAPTER REVIEW

◆ **EDITING PRACTICE**

Read the following student essay, which includes errors in capitalization
and punctuation and in the use of direct quotations and titles. Correct any
errors you find. The first sentence has been edited for you.

A Threat to Health

Pandemics are like Ẹpidemics, only more widespread, perhaps even including
the whole Ẉorld. In a pandemic, a serious Disease spreads very easily. In the past,
there have been many pandemics, and some exist today. In the future, in spite of
advances in Medicine, there will still be pandemics. In fact, scientists agree that
not every pandemic can be prevented.

Probably the best-known pandemic is the bubonic plague. It killed about
one-third of the Population of europe during the middle ages. Some areas suffered
more than others. According to Philip ziegler in his book the black Death, at least
half the people in florence, Italy, died in one year. Many years later, in 1918, a flu
pandemic killed more than 50 million people worldwide, including hundreds of
thousands in the United states.

Unfortunately, pandemics have not disappeared. AIDS, for example, is a current
pandemic. Philadelphia the 1993 movie starring denzel washington and tom hanks
is still one of the most moving depictions of the heartbreak of AIDS. The rate of
AIDS infection is over 30 percent in parts of africa, and the disease is increasing
on other Continents as well. So far, efforts to find an AIDS vaccine have failed.
Dr. anthony s. Fauci discussed recent AIDS research on NPR's series All things
considered in a program called Search for an HIV vaccine expands.

Although some pandemic diseases, such as Smallpox, have been wiped out by
Vaccination, new pandemics remain a threat. Many viruses and Bacteria change
in response to treatment, so they may become resistant to Vaccination and
Antibiotics. Also, with modern transportation, a disease can move quickly from
Country to Country. For example, the disease known as severe acute respiratory
syndrome (SARS) began in china but was spread to other countries by travelers.

Hundreds died as a result of the SARS pandemic between November 2002 and july 2003. Birds also remain a threat because they can transmit disease. It is obviously impossible to prevent birds from flying from one country to another. Markos kyprianou, health commissioner of the European union, has said that I am concerned that birds in Turkey have been found with the bird flu Virus. He said, There is a direct relationship with viruses found in Russia, Mongolia and china. If this Virus changes so that it can move easily from birds to Humans, bird flu could become the next pandemic.

Public Health Officials are always on the lookout for diseases with three characteristics they are new, they are dangerous, and they are very contagious. Doctors try to prevent them from becoming Pandemics. However, they continue to warn that some Pandemics cannot be prevented.

Mother wearing mask to protect herself against SARS

◆ COLLABORATIVE ACTIVITIES

1. Work in a small group to list as many items in each of the following five categories as you can: planets, islands, bands, automobile models, sports teams. Be sure all your items are proper nouns, and use capital letters where necessary.

   On the lines below, write five original sentences, using one proper noun from each category in each sentence.

   ■ _____

   _____

   ■ _____

   _____

   ■ _____

   _____

   ■ _____

   _____

   ■ _____

   _____

   When you are finished, exchange papers with another group, and check for correct use of capital letters.

2. Imagine that you and the other members of your group are the nominations committee for this year's Emmy, Oscar, or Grammy Awards.

■ **Culture Clue**

Some entertainment awards in the United States are the *Emmy* (Television Arts and Sciences), the *Oscar* (Motion Picture Arts and Sciences), and the *Grammy* (Recording Arts and Sciences).

Work together to compile a list of categories and several nominees for each category, deciding as a group when to use capital letters.

Trade lists with another group. From each category, select the individual artist or work you believe deserves to win the award. Write a sentence about each winner, explaining why each is the best in its category.

When you have finished, exchange papers with another group. Check one another's papers for correct use of capitals, quotation marks, and underlining.

3. Working in pairs, write a conversation between two characters, real or fictional, who have very different positions on a particular issue. Place all direct quotations within quotation marks, and include identifying tags that clearly indicate which character is speaking. (Begin a new paragraph each time a new person speaks.)

Exchange your conversations with another pair of students, and check their work to see that all directly quoted speech is set within quotation marks and that capital letters and other punctuation are used correctly.

☑ REVIEW CHECKLIST:
Understanding Mechanics

- Capitalize proper nouns. (See 33A.)

- Always place direct quotations within quotation marks. (See 33B.)

- In titles, capitalize all important words. Use italics or quotation marks to set off titles. (See 33C.)

- Use colons, dashes, and parentheses to set off material from the rest of the sentence. (See 33D.)

Understanding Spelling

PREVIEW

In this chapter, you will learn

- to become a better speller (34A)

- to know when to use *ie* and *ei* (34B)

- to understand prefixes (34C)

- to understand suffixes (34D)

- to identify commonly confused words (34E)

■ **WRITING FIRST**

In an effort to improve discipline and boost self-esteem, a number of elementary schools across the country have begun requiring students to wear uniforms. The picture above shows a group of students at one such school. Look at the picture, and then write about whether or not you think elementary school students should be required to wear uniforms such as the ones in the picture.

▶ **Word Power**

conducive to leading to; contributing to

economical thrifty

individuality the quality of being distinct from others

A **Becoming a Better Speller**

Improving your spelling may take time, but the following steps can make this task a lot easier.

1. **Use a spell checker.** When you write on a computer, always use your spell checker. It will correct most misspelled words and also identify many typos, such as transposed or omitted letters. Keep in mind, however, that spell checkers do not identify typos that create other words (*then/than*, *form/from*, or *big/beg*, for example) or words that you have used incorrectly (*their/there* or *its/it's*, for example).

2. **Proofread carefully.** Even if you have used a spell checker, always proofread your papers for spelling before you hand them in.

3. **Use a dictionary.** As you proofread your papers, circle words whose spellings you are unsure of. After you have finished your draft, look up these words in a print or online dictionary.

4. **Keep a personal spelling list.** Write down all the words you misspell. Whenever your instructor returns one of your papers, look for misspelled words—usually circled and marked *sp*. Add these to your personal spelling list.

5. **Look for patterns in your misspelling.** Do you consistently misspell words with *ei* combinations? Do you have trouble forming plurals? Once you figure out which errors you make most frequently, you can take steps to eliminate them.

6. **Learn the basic spelling rules.** Memorize the spelling rules in this chapter, especially those that apply to areas in which you are weak. Remember that each rule can help you spell many words correctly.

7. **Review the list of commonly confused words in 34E.** If you have problems with any of these word pairs, add them to your personal spelling list.

8. **Use memory cues.** Memory cues help you remember how to spell certain words. For example, remembering that *definite* contains the word *finite* will help you remember that *definite* is spelled with an *i*, not an *a*.

9. **Learn to spell some of the most frequently misspelled words.** Identify any words on the list below that give you trouble, and add them to your personal spelling list.

Frequently Misspelled Words

across	calendar	describe	finally
all right	cannot	develop	forty
a lot	careful	disappoint	fulfill
already	careless	early	generally
argument	cemetery	embarrass	government
beautiful	certain	entrance	grammar
becoming	conscience	environment	harass
beginning	definite	everything	height
believe	definitely	exercise	holiday
benefit	dependent	experience	integration

(*continued on following page*)

(continued from previous page)

intelligence	occurrences	receive	tomatoes
interest	occurring	recognize	truly
interfere	occurs	reference	until
judgment	personnel	restaurant	usually
loneliness	possible	roommate	Wednesday
medicine	potato	secretary	weird
minute	potatoes	sentence	window
necessary	prejudice	separate	withhold
noticeable	prescription	speech	woman
occasion	privilege	studying	women
occur	probably	surprise	writing
occurred	professor	tomato	written

FOCUS **Vowels and Consonants**

Because English pronunciation is not always a reliable guide for spelling, most people find it useful to memorize some spelling rules. Knowing which letters are vowels and which are consonants will help you understand the spelling rules presented in this chapter.

Vowels: a, e, i, o, u

Consonants: b, c, d, f, g, h, j, k, l, m, n, p, q, r, s, t, v, w, x, z

The letter *y* may be considered either a vowel or a consonant, depending on how it is pronounced. In *young, y* acts as a consonant because it has the sound of *y;* in *truly,* it acts as a vowel because it has the sound of *ee.*

B *ie* and *ei*

Memorize this rule: *i* comes before *e* except after *c*, or when the *ei* sound is pronounced *ay.*

i *before* e	*except after* c	*or when* ei *is pronounced* ay
achieve	ceiling	eight
believe	conceive	freight
friend	deceive	neighbor
		weigh

> **FOCUS** **Exceptions to the "*i* before *e*" Rule**
>
> There are some exceptions to the "*i* before *e*" rule. The exceptions
> follow no pattern, so you must memorize them.
>
> | | | | |
> |---|---|---|---|
> | ancient | either | leisure | seize |
> | caffeine | foreign | neither | species |
> | conscience | height | science | weird |

◆ **PRACTICE 34-1**

Proofread the underlined words in the following sentences for correct
spelling. If a correction needs to be made, cross out the incorrect word,
and write the correct spelling above it. If the word is spelled correctly,
write *C* above it.

                                            C   *receive*

    Example: It was a relief to ~~recieve~~ the good news.

1. Be sure to <u>wiegh</u> the pros and cons before making important decisions,

   particularly those involving <u>friends</u>.

2. When your <u>beliefs</u> are tested, you may be able to <u>acheive</u> a better

   understanding of yourself.

3. In our <u>society</u>, many people <u>decieve</u> themselves into <u>beleiving</u> that they

   are better than everyone else.

4. <u>Cheifly</u> because they have been lucky, they have reached a certain

   <u>height</u> in the world.

5. They think that the blood running through <u>their</u> <u>viens</u> makes them

   belong to a higher <u>species</u> than the average person.

> ■ **WRITING FIRST: Flashback**
>
> Look back at your response to the Writing First activity on
> page 553. Underline any words that have *ie* or *ei* combina-
> tions, and check a dictionary to make sure they are spelled
> correctly. Correct any spelling errors on the lines below.
>
> _____   _____
>
> _____   _____

C   Prefixes

A **prefix** is a group of letters added at the beginning of a word that changes the word's meaning. Adding a prefix to a word never affects the spelling of the original word.

dis + service = disservice   pre + heat = preheat
un + able = unable   un + natural = unnatural
co + operate = cooperate   over + rate = overrate

◆ **PRACTICE 34-2**

Write in the blank the new word that results when the specified prefix is added to each of the following words.

Example: dis + respect = _disrespect_

1. un + happy = _____

2. tele + vision = _____

3. pre + existing = _____

4. dis + satisfied = _____

5. un + necessary = _____

6. non + negotiable = _____

7. im + patient = _____

8. out + think = _____

9. over + react = _____

10. dis + solve = _____

ON THE WEB
Visit *Exercise Central* at
bedfordstmartins.com/writingfirst
for more practice.

■ **WRITING FIRST: Flashback**

Look back at your response to the Writing First activity on page 553. Underline any words that have prefixes, and check a dictionary to make sure each word is spelled correctly. Correct any spelling errors on the lines below.

_____   _____

_____   _____

D   Suffixes

A **suffix** is a group of letters added to the end of a word that changes the word's meaning or its part of speech. Adding a suffix to a word can change the spelling of the original word.

Words Ending in Silent *e*

If a word ends with a silent (unpronounced) *e*, drop the *e* if the suffix begins with a vowel.

DROP THE *E*

hope + ing = hoping   dance + er = dancer

continue + ous = continuous   insure + able = insurable

EXCEPTIONS

change + able = changeable   courage + ous = courageous

notice + able = noticeable   replace + able = replaceable

Keep the *e* if the suffix begins with a consonant.

KEEP THE *E*

hope + ful = hopeful   bore + dom = boredom

excite + ment = excitement   same + ness = sameness

EXCEPTIONS

argue + ment = argument   true + ly = truly

judge + ment = judgment   nine + th = ninth

◆ PRACTICE 34-3

Write in the blank the new word that results from adding the specified suffix to each of the following words.

Examples

insure + ance = _____*insurance*_____

love + ly = _____*lovely*_____

ON THE WEB

Visit *Exercise Central* at
bedfordstmartins.com/writingfirst
for more practice.

1. lone + ly = _____   6. microscope + ic = _____

2. use + ful = _____   7. nine + th = _____

3. revise + ing = _____   8. indicate + ion = _____

4. desire + able = _____   9. effective + ness = _____

5. true + ly = _____   10. arrange + ment = _____

Words Ending in *-y*

When you add a suffix to a word that ends in *-y*, change the *y* to an *i* if the letter before the *y* is a consonant.

CHANGE *Y* TO *I*

beauty + ful = beautiful   busy + ly = busily

try + ed = tried   friendly + er = friendlier

EXCEPTIONS

■   If the suffix starts with an *i*, keep the *y*.

    cry + ing = crying   baby + ish = babyish

■ When you add a suffix to certain one-syllable words, keep the *y*.

shy + er = shyer   dry + ness = dryness

Keep the *y* if the letter before the *y* is a vowel.

KEEP THE Y

annoy + ance = annoyance   enjoy + ment = enjoyment
play + ful = playful   display + ed = displayed

EXCEPTIONS

day + ly = daily   say + ed = said
gay + ly = gaily   pay + ed = paid

◆ PRACTICE 34-4

Write in the blank the new word that results from adding the specified suffix to each of the following words.

Examples

study + ed = _____*studied*_____

employ + ment = _____*employment*_____

1. happy + ness = _____   6. annoy + ing = _____

2. convey + or = _____   7. destroy + er = _____

3. deny + ing = _____   8. twenty + eth = _____

4. carry + ed = _____   9. cry + ed = _____

5. ready + ness = _____   10. lonely + ness = _____

Doubling the Final Consonant

When you add a suffix that begins with a vowel—for example, *-ed*, *-er*, or *-ing*—sometimes you need to double the final consonant in the original word. Do this (1) if the last three letters of the word have a consonant-vowel-consonant (cvc) pattern *and* (2) if the word has one syllable (or if the last syllable is stressed).

FINAL CONSONANT DOUBLED

drum	+ ing	=	drumming	(cvc—one syllable)
bat	+ er	=	batter	(cvc—one syllable)
pet	+ ed	=	petted	(cvc—one syllable)
commit	+ ed	=	committed	(cvc—stress is on last syllable)
occur	+ ing	=	occurring	(cvc—stress is on last syllable)

FINAL CONSONANT NOT DOUBLED

answer	+ ed	=	answered	(cvc—stress is not on last syllable)
happen	+ ing	=	happening	(cvc—stress is not on last syllable)
act	+ ing	=	acting	(no cvc)

◆ **PRACTICE 34-5**

Write in the blank the new word that results from adding the specified suffix to each of the following words.

Examples

rot + ing = _____rotting_____

narrow + er = ___narrower___

1. hope + ed = _____
2. shop + er = _____
3. rest + ing = _____
4. combat + ed = _____
5. reveal + ing = _____

6. open + er = _____
7. unzip + ed = _____
8. trap + ed = _____
9. refer + ing = _____
10. omit + ed = _____

■ **WRITING FIRST: Flashback**

Look back at your response to the Writing First activity on page 553. Underline any words that have suffixes, and check a dictionary to make sure each word is spelled correctly. Correct any spelling errors on the lines below.

_____   _____

_____   _____

E **Commonly Confused Words**

Accept/Except *Accept* means "to receive something." *Except* means "with the exception of" or "to leave out or exclude."

"I <u>accept</u> your challenge," said Alexander Hamilton to Aaron Burr.

Everyone <u>except</u> Darryl visited the museum.

Affect/Effect *Affect* is a verb meaning "to influence." *Effect* is a noun meaning "result."

Carmen's job could <u>affect</u> her grades.

Overexposure to sun can have a long-term <u>effect</u> on skin.

All ready/Already *All ready* means "completely prepared." *Already* means "previously, before."

Serge was <u>all ready</u> to take the history test.

Gina had <u>already</u> been to Italy.

Brake/Break   *Brake* is a noun that means "a device to slow or stop a vehicle." *Break* is a verb meaning "to smash" or "to detach" and sometimes a noun meaning either "a gap" or "interruption" or "a stroke of luck."

> Peter got into an accident because his foot slipped off the <u>brake</u>.
>
> Babe Ruth thought no one would ever <u>break</u> his home run record.
>
> The baseball game was postponed until there was a <u>break</u> in the bad weather.

Buy/By   *Buy* means "to purchase." *By* is a preposition meaning "close to," "next to" or "by means of."

> The Stamp Act forced colonists to <u>buy</u> stamps for many public documents.
>
> He drove <u>by</u> but did not stop.
>
> He stayed <u>by</u> her side all the way to the hospital.
>
> Malcolm X wanted "freedom <u>by</u> any means necessary."

◆ PRACTICE 34-6

Proofread the underlined words in the following sentences for correct spelling. If a correction needs to be made, cross out the incorrect word, and write the correct spelling above it. If the word is spelled correctly, write *C* above it.

ON THE WEB
Visit *Exercise Central* at
bedfordstmartins.com/writingfirst
for more practice.

>   *accept*   *C*
> **Example:**   We must ~~except~~ the fact that the human heart can <u>break</u>.

1. The <u>affects</u> of several new AIDS drugs have <u>all ready</u> been reported.

2. *Consumer Reports* gave high ratings to the <u>breaks</u> on all the new cars tested <u>accept</u> one.

3. Advertisements urge us to <u>by</u> a new product even if we <u>already</u> own a similar item.

4. If you <u>except</u> the charges for a collect telephone call, you will probably have to <u>brake</u> your piggy bank to pay their bill.

5. Cigarette smoking <u>affects</u> the lungs <u>by</u> creating deposits of tar that make breathing difficult.

Conscience/Conscious   *Conscience* is a noun that refers to the part of the mind that urges a person to choose right over wrong. *Conscious* is an adjective that means "aware" or "deliberate."

> After he cheated at cards, his <u>conscience</u> started to bother him.
>
> As she walked through the woods, she became <u>conscious</u> of the hum of insects.
>
> Elliott made a <u>conscious</u> decision to stop smoking.

Everyday/Every day   *Everyday* is a single word that means "ordinary" or "common." *Every day* is two words that mean "occurring daily."

> *I Love Lucy* was a successful comedy show because it appealed to everyday people.

> Every day, Lucy and Ethel would find a new way to get into trouble.

Fine/Find   *Fine* means "superior quality" or "a sum of money paid as a penalty." *Find* means "to locate."

> He sang a fine solo at church last Sunday.

> Demi had to pay a fine for speeding.

> Some people still use a willow rod to find water.

Hear/Here   *Hear* means "to perceive sound by ear." *Here* means "at or in this place."

> I moved to the front so I could hear the speaker.

> My great-grandfather came here in 1883.

Its/It's   *Its* is the possessive form of *it*. *It's* is the contraction of *it is* or *it has*.

> The airline canceled its flights because of the snow.

> It's twelve o'clock, and we are late.

> Ever since it's been in the accident, the car has rattled.

◆ **PRACTICE 34-7**

Proofread the underlined words in the following sentences for correct spelling. If a correction needs to be made, cross out the incorrect word, and write the correct spelling above it. If the word is spelled correctly, write *C* above it.

> **Example:**   It's often difficult for celebrities to adjust to ~~every day~~ life.

1. Hear at Simonson's Fashions, we try to make our customers feel that everyday is a sale day.

2. My uncle was a find person, and its a shame that he died so young.

3. That inner voice you hear is your conscious telling you how you should behave.

4. In the every day world of work and school, it can be hard to fine the time to relax and enjoy life.

5. By the time I became conscience of the cracked pipe, it's leak had done a lot of damage.

Know/No/Knew/New   *Know* means "to have an understanding of" or "to have fixed in the mind." *No* means "not any," "not at all," or "not one." *Knew* is the past tense form of the verb *know*. *New* means "recent or never used."

> I <u>know</u> there will be a lunar eclipse tonight.
>
> You have <u>no</u> right to say that.
>
> He <u>knew</u> how to install a <u>new</u> light switch.

Lie/Lay   *Lie* means "to rest or recline." The past tense of *lie* is *lay*. *Lay* means "to put or place something down." The past tense of *lay* is *laid*.

> Every Sunday, I <u>lie</u> in bed until noon.
>
> They <u>lay</u> on the grass until it began to rain, and then they went home.
>
> Tammy told Carl to <u>lay</u> his cards on the table.
>
> Brooke and Cassia finally <u>laid</u> down their hockey sticks.

Loose/Lose   *Loose* means "not fixed or rigid" or "not attached securely." *Lose* means "to mislay" or "to misplace."

> In the 1940s, many women wore <u>loose</u>-fitting pants.
>
> I never gamble because I hate to <u>lose</u>.

Passed/Past   *Passed* is the past tense of the verb *pass*. It means "moved by" or "succeeded in." *Past* is a noun or an adjective meaning "earlier than the present time."

> The car that <u>passed</u> me was doing more than eighty miles an hour.
>
> David finally <u>passed</u> his driving test.
>
> The novel was set in the <u>past</u>.
>
> The statement said that the bill was <u>past</u> due.

Peace/Piece   *Peace* means "the absence of war" or "calm." *Piece* means "a part of something."

> The British prime minister tried to achieve <u>peace</u> with honor.
>
> My <u>peace</u> of mind was destroyed when the flying saucer landed.
>
> "Have a <u>piece</u> of cake," said Marie.

◆ **PRACTICE 34-8**

Proofread the underlined words in the following sentences for correct spelling. If a correction needs to be made, cross out the incorrect word, and write the correct spelling above it. If the word is spelled correctly, write *C* above it.

Example: Although the soldiers stopped fighting, a *peace*/~~piece~~ treaty was never signed.

1. Because he was late for the job interview, he was afraid he would <u>loose</u> his chance to work for the company.

2. While she <u>laid</u> down for a nap, her children cooked dinner and cleaned the house.

3. There will be <u>know</u> wool sweaters on sale before the holidays.

4. The <u>past</u> chair of the committee left a lot of unfinished business.

5. The broken knife found in the trash turned out to be a <u>peace</u> of the murder weapon.

Principal/Principle *Principal* means "first" or "highest" or "the head of a school." *Principle* means "a law or basic assumption."

She had the <u>principal</u> role in the movie.

I'll never forget the day the <u>principal</u> called me into his office.

It was against his <u>principles</u> to lie.

Quiet/Quit/Quite *Quiet* means "free of noise" or "still." *Quit* means "to leave a job" or "to give up." *Quite* means "actually" or "very."

Jane looked forward to the <u>quiet</u> evenings at the lake.

Sammy <u>quit</u> his job and followed the girls into the parking lot.

"You haven't <u>quite</u> got the hang of it yet," she said.

After practicing all summer, Tamika got <u>quite</u> good at tennis.

Raise/Rise *Raise* means "to elevate" or "to increase in size, quantity, or worth." The past tense of *raise* is *raised*. *Rise* means "to stand up" or "to move from a lower position to a higher position." The past tense of *rise* is *rose*.

Carlos <u>raises</u> his hand whenever the teacher asks for volunteers.

They finally <u>raised</u> the money for the down payment.

The crowd <u>rises</u> every time their team scores a touchdown.

Kim <u>rose</u> before dawn so she could see the eclipse.

Sit/Set *Sit* means "to assume a sitting position." The past tense of *sit* is *sat*. *Set* means "to put down or place" or "to adjust something to a desired position." The past tense of *set* is *set*.

I usually <u>sit</u> in the front row at the movies.

They <u>sat</u> at the clinic waiting for their names to be called.

Elizabeth <u>set</u> the mail on the kitchen table and left for work.

Every semester I <u>set</u> goals for myself.

Suppose/Supposed *Suppose* means "to consider" or "to assume." *Supposed* is both the past tense and the past participle of *suppose*. *Supposed* also means "expected" or "required." (Note that when *supposed* has this meaning, it is always followed by *to*.)

<u>Suppose</u> researchers were to find a cure for cancer.

We <u>supposed</u> the movie would be over by ten o'clock.

You were <u>supposed</u> to finish a draft of the report by today.

◆ **PRACTICE 34-9**

Proofread the underlined words in the following sentences for correct spelling. If a correction needs to be made, cross out the incorrect word, and write the correct spelling above it. If the word is spelled correctly, write *C* above it.

    Example: Boarding the plane took <u>quite</u>ᶜ a long time because of the security process.

1. Jackie was <u>suppose</u> to mow the lawn and trim the bushes last weekend.

2. It is important to <u>sit</u> the computer in a place where the on-off switch can be reached.

3. If you <u>raise</u> the window, a pleasant breeze will blow into the bedroom.

4. The <u>principle</u> reason for her <u>raise</u> to the position of <u>principal</u> of the school was hard work.

5. We were all told to <u>sit</u> and wait for the crowd to become <u>quite</u>.

Their/There/They're *Their* is the possessive form of the pronoun *they*. *There* means "at or in that place." *There* is also used in the phrases *there is* and *there are*. *They're* is the contraction of "they are."

    They wanted poor people to improve <u>their</u> living conditions.

    I put the book over <u>there</u>.

    <u>There</u> are three reasons I will not eat meat.

    <u>They're</u> the best volunteer firefighters I've ever seen.

Then/Than *Then* means "at that time" or "next in time." *Than* is used in comparisons.

    He was young and naive <u>then</u>.

    I went to the job interview and <u>then</u> stopped off for coffee.

    My dog is smarter <u>than</u> your dog.

Threw/Through *Threw* is the past tense of *throw*. *Through* means "in one side and out the opposite side" or "finished."

    Satchel Paige <u>threw</u> a baseball more than ninety-five miles an hour.

    It takes almost thirty minutes to go <u>through</u> the tunnel.

    "I'm <u>through</u>," said Clark Kent, storming out of Perry White's office.

To/Too/Two *To* means "in the direction of." *Too* means "also" or "more than enough." *Two* denotes the numeral 2.

    During spring break, I am going <u>to</u> Disney World.

    My roommates are coming <u>too</u>.

    The microwave popcorn is <u>too</u> hot to eat.

"If we get rid of the Tin Man and the Cowardly Lion, the <u>two</u> of us can go to Oz," said the Scarecrow to Dorothy.

Use/Used   *Use* means "to put into service" or "to consume." *Used* is both the past tense and past participle of *use*. *Used* also means "accustomed." (Note that when *used* has this meaning, it is followed by *to*.)

I <u>use</u> a soft cloth to clean my glasses.

"Hey! Who <u>used</u> all the hot water?" he yelled from the shower.

Marisol had <u>used</u> all the firewood during the storm.

After two years in Alaska, they got <u>used</u> to the short winter days.

◆ **PRACTICE 34-10**

Proofread the underlined words in the following sentences for correct spelling. If a correction needs to be made, cross out the incorrect word, and write the correct spelling above it. If the word is spelled correctly, write *C* above it.

Example: Because of good nutrition, people are taller <u>~~then~~</u> ^{than} they <u>~~use~~</u> ^{used}

to be in the past.

1. The power went out in the dorms, and many students <u>then</u> went <u>too</u> the library to study.

2. Whenever he <u>through</u> out the trash, he walked <u>threw</u> the back yard on his way <u>two</u> the alley.

3. Get your tickets before <u>their</u> all gone.

4. I <u>use</u> to think that my ancestors all came from northern Europe, but I recently learned that some <u>used</u> to live in South Africa.

5. The countries that signed the peace treaty have not lived up to <u>they're</u> responsibilities.

Weather/Whether   *Weather* refers to temperature, humidity, precipitation, and so on. *Whether* is used to introduce alternative possibilities.

The *Farmer's Almanac* says that the <u>weather</u> this winter will be severe.

<u>Whether</u> or not this prediction will be correct is anyone's guess.

Where/Were/We're   *Where* means "at or in what place." *Were* is the past tense of *are*. *We're* is the contraction of "we are."

Where are you going, and <u>where</u> have you been?

Charlie Chaplin and Mary Pickford <u>were</u> popular stars of silent movies.

<u>We're</u> doing our back-to-school shopping early this year.

Whose/Who's *Whose* is the possessive form of *who*. *Who's* is the contraction of either "who is" or "who has."

My roommate asked, "<u>Whose</u> book is this?"

"<u>Who's</u> there?" squealed the second little pig as he leaned against the door.

<u>Who's</u> been blocking the driveway?

Your/You're *Your* is the possessive form of *you*. *You're* is the contraction of "you are."

"You should have worn <u>your</u> running shoes," said the hare as he passed the tortoise.

"<u>You're</u> too kind," said the tortoise sarcastically.

◆ PRACTICE 34-11

Proofread the underlined words in the following sentences for correct spelling. If a correction needs to be made, cross out the incorrect word, and write the correct spelling above it. If the word is spelled correctly, write *C* above it.

Example: As citizens, ~~were~~ *we're* all concerned with <u>where</u> *C* our country is going.

1. The police are attempting to discover <u>who's</u> fingerprints <u>were</u> left at the scene of the crime.

2. Cancer does not care <u>weather</u> <u>your</u> rich or poor, young or old.

3. Santa Fe, <u>were</u> I lived for many years, has better <u>weather</u> than New Jersey has.

4. Whenever we listen to politicians debate, <u>were</u> likely to be wondering <u>whose</u> telling the truth.

5. You should take <u>your</u> time before deciding <u>weather</u> to focus <u>your</u> energy on school or on work.

■ WRITING FIRST: Flashback

Look back at your response to the Writing First activity on page 553. Identify any words that appear on the lists of commonly confused words (on the preceding pages), and check to make sure you have spelled them correctly. Correct any misspelled words, and then write them here.

_____   _____

_____   _____

■ WRITING FIRST: Revising and Editing

Type your response to the Writing First activity on page 553 (if you have not already done so). Proofread carefully for spelling errors, then run a spell check. Did the computer pick up all the errors? Which did it identify? Which did it miss? Correct the spelling errors the computer identified as well as the ones that you found while proofreading. (You can also check spelling in this way in a longer writing assignment you are currently working on.)

CHAPTER REVIEW

◆ EDITING PRACTICE

Read the following student essay, which includes spelling errors. Identify the words you think are misspelled; then, look them up in a dictionary. Finally, cross out each incorrectly spelled word, and write the correct spelling above the line. The first error has been corrected for you.

Coming Home

When my Uncle Joe, a soldier in the United States Marine Corps, ~~returnned~~ *returned*

from Iraq, I was glad he was home. He had fullfilled his responsibility and was

safe. My family welcomed him at the airport with flags and flowers. He hugged us

all and looked thriled to be home. However, returning to civilian life turned out

to be more difficult for him then any of us had expected.

U.S. soldiers in combat in Iraq

Being in the military is very different from any other expereince. Soldeirs are trained to kill. To do this, they have to forget what they have been taught in the passed about not harming others. They have to get use to ignoring what their conscious tells them to do and become less sensitive to others' feelings. Also, to survive, they have to be suspitious of everything around them. They must be alert at all times. Most important, thier emotions must be controled. In combat, they have to function like machines: when given an order, they must follow it. They're own lives and those of there fellow soldiers depend on obedeince.

War changed Uncle Joe, and I learned that this was true of many veterans. Although insensitivity and suspicion are necesary for a soldier, niether one is of much use in civilian life. For example, when my uncle overeacted about a dirty dish left on the kitchen counter, his wife became confused and upset. Similarly, when his family asked him about the war, he became annoied and refussed to talk about it. His family did not understand. As a result, he felt isolated from his freinds and family. When he slept, he had nightmares about being back in combat. He also missed his fellow Marines.

Welcome home crowd for returning U.S. soldiers

Before he returned home, Uncle Joe had looked forward to returning to his job in an insurence company. However, his feelings about his career changed, to. He had become used to the strick dicsipline of the military. As a Marine, my uncle always knew what apropriate behavior was. At work, however, there was no officer to give him orders; although he had a boss, there seemed to be alot of choice about what was considered acceptible. He had much more freedom, but he did not quite know what to do with it. Also, Uncle Joe missed the job security of the military. At home, everthing seemed to be uncertin; people lost their jobs everyday without much warning, and entire companies went bankrupt.

Yellow ribbon decal in support of U.S. troops

What my uncle went threw was similiar to what many of his buddys experienced. Even with counseling, it took him a long time to be able to trust the people around him. Eventually, he was able to become more sensitive to the feelings of others, and he tryed to rely on his civilian friends and family the way he had relied on his fellow Marines. Ocasionaly, he still has nightmares about the war, but they ocurr less often. For Uncle Joe, the war did not end when he came home. Returning home was just the begining of his own personal struggle.

◆ **COLLABORATIVE ACTIVITIES**

1. Working in pairs, compare responses to the Writing First activity on page 553. How many misspelled words did each of you find? How many errors did you and your partner have in common?

2. Are there any patterns of misspelling in your Writing First activities? What types of spelling errors seem most common?

3. Collaborate with your partner to make a spelling list for the two of you, and then work with other groups to create a spelling list for the whole class. When you have finished, determine which types of errors are most common.

☑ REVIEW CHECKLIST:
Understanding Spelling

  ☐ Follow the steps to becoming a better speller. (See 34A.)

  ☐ *I* comes before *e*, except after *c* or in any *ay* sound. (See 34B.)

  ☐ Adding a prefix to a word never affects the word's spelling. (See 34C.)

  ☐ Adding a suffix to a word may change the word's spelling. (See 34D.)

  ☐ When a word ends with silent *e*, drop the *e* if the suffix begins with a vowel. Keep the *e* if the suffix begins with a consonant. (See 34D.)

  ☐ When you add a suffix to a word that ends with a *y*, change the *y* to an *i* if the letter before the *y* is a consonant. Keep the *y* if the letter before the *y* is a vowel. (See 34D.)

  ☐ When you add a suffix that begins with a vowel — for example, *-ed*, *-er*, or *-ing* — sometimes you need to double the final consonant in the original word. Do this (1) if the last three letters of the word have a consonant-vowel-consonant (cvc) pattern *and* (2) if the word has one syllable (or if the last syllable is stressed). (See 34D.)

  ☐ Learn to spell the most commonly confused words. (See 34E.)

UNIT REVIEW

Read the following student essay, which includes various errors. Then, edit the essay by correcting errors in punctuation, mechanics, and spelling. The first sentence has been corrected for you. (Because this is an informal essay, contractions are acceptable.)

Education Internship: First Year

On ~~september 15 2004~~ *September 15, 2004,* I ~~recieved~~ *received* a copy of my college schedule in the ~~male.~~ *mail.* I learned that from nine to ten on monday's and wednesday's, I would be an intern at the accellerated learning laboratory school (the ALL school). This would be my first chance to be in a classroom when I wasnt a student. On the first day of class I got to the school extra early. After I signed in I put on my yellow visitors badge, and met the teacher irene Dennis. I was nervus but ready.

Ms. dennis told me that most of the children were in third, or fourth grade, accept for too girls. One of them was sue a sixth grader. She coudnt read at all. At the beggining of the day, the children were suppose to be reading, writting or studing math. When I looked at them, though I saw that most of them were daydreamming. It was hard to get them to pay attenntion to there work.

At nine oclock it was time for they're group work. Ms dennis students all went to diferrent classrooms, and interracted with other children. The students were studying africa, with three teacher's responsible for about thirty children. Each group had been given one country to focuss on. They had to learn about the food people ate, and the close they wore. Because it was the end of the month the students were wraping up they're study of the Continent and completeing worksheets.

Intern and students in a classroom

My first job was to help Luke a fifth grader. Lukes problem was that he tended to waist time and get distracted. However I gave him alot of firm advise and eventualy got him to work independantly. Next, I moved on too help Randy a boy who thought he new all the answers. Randy had a hard time expresing himself. "Its an easy question" he'd say, but than he'd give the wrong answer. By the time I had both Luke and Randy working on they're own it was time for us to return to our orriginal classroom.

Now Ms. dennis asked me to work with a girl named Tien. Originaly from vietnam she was twelve years old and didnt speak english very well. On a peace of paper she had written, "Happy birthen to you." When I told her that she had spelled a word wrong, she saw her error right away. Then, she wrote the whole sentance again, this time with the corect spelling. I wanted to spend more time with her, but it was almost time for me to leeve.

Classroom bulletin boards

The principle was making an announcment over the loudspeaker as I put my coat on. I waved goodbye when I left, and I heard all these little voices saying, "goodbye rebecca." They seemed dissapointed that I was leaving.

"Dont worry" I told them, I'll be back." I didn't come everyday but every Monday and Wednesday for the rest of the year I was there. I loved working with the children and helpping them to improve. I realy felt I was making a diferrence in there lifes.

Classroom bulletin boards

In may, 2007 right before the end of the Spring semester I was walking across Campus when I past a little kid. All of a sudden I heard him yell out, "hey she goes to our school." He was pointing at me. I rembered this boy who was from the ALL School. His words had an incredable affect on me. I always used to wonder weather I'd be a teacher oneday. Now I new I would. I use to think that teachers affect on they're students was exaggerated. Now I new better.

UNIT EIGHT

READING ESSAYS

Reading for College

Reading is essential to all your college courses. To get the most out of your reading, you should approach the books and articles you read in a practical way, always asking yourself what information they can offer you. You should also approach assigned readings critically, just as you approach your own writing when you revise.

Reading critically does not mean challenging or arguing with every idea, but it does mean wondering, commenting, questioning, and judging. Most of all, it means being an active rather than a passive reader. Being an **active reader** means participating in the reading process: approaching

a reading assignment with a clear understanding of your purpose, previewing a selection, highlighting and annotating it, and perhaps outlining it—all *before* you begin to respond in writing to what you have read.

To gain an understanding of your **purpose**—your reason for reading—you should start by answering some questions.

Questions about Your Purpose

- Why are you reading?
- Will you be expected to discuss what you are reading? If so, will you discuss it in class or in a conference with your instructor?
- Will you have to write about what you are reading? If so, will you be expected to write an informal response (for example, a journal entry) or a more formal one (for example, an essay)?
- Will you be tested on the material?

Once you understand your purpose, you are ready to begin reading.

A Previewing

When you **preview**, you skim a passage to get a sense of the writer's main idea and key supporting points as well as the general emphasis of the passage. You can begin by focusing on the title, the first paragraph (which often contains a thesis statement or overview), and the last paragraph (which often contains a summary of the writer's points). You should also look for clues to the writer's message in the passage's other **visual signals** (headings, boxes, and so on) as well as in its **verbal signals** (the words and phrases the writer uses to convey order and emphasis).

Using Visual Signals

- Look at the title.
- Look at the **headnote**, a paragraph that introduces the author and gives background about the reading.
- Look at the opening and closing paragraphs.
- Look at each paragraph's first sentence.
- Look at headings.
- Look at *italicized* and **boldfaced** words.
- Look at numbered lists.
- Look at bulleted lists (like this one).

(continued on following page)

(continued from previous page)

■ Look at graphs, charts, tables, photographs, and so on.
■ Look at any information that is boxed.
■ Look at any information that is in color.

Using Verbal Signals

■ Look for phrases that signal emphasis ("The *primary* reason"; "The *most important* idea").
■ Look for repeated words and phrases.
■ Look for words that signal addition (*also, in addition, furthermore*).
■ Look for words that signal time sequence (*first, after, then, next, finally*).
■ Look for words that identify causes and effects (*because, as a result, for this reason*).
■ Look for words that introduce examples (*for example, for instance*).
■ Look for words that signal comparison (*likewise, similarly*).
■ Look for words that signal contrast (*unlike, although, in contrast*).
■ Look for words that signal contradiction (*however, on the contrary*).
■ Look for words that signal a narrowing of the writer's focus (*in fact, specifically, in other words*).
■ Look for words that signal summaries or conclusions (*to sum up, in conclusion*).

When you have finished previewing, you should have a general sense of what the writer wants to communicate.

◆ PRACTICE 35-1

"No Comprendo" ("I Don't Understand") is a newspaper article by Barbara Mujica, a professor of Spanish at Georgetown University in Washington, D.C. In this article, which was published in the *New York Times*, Mujica argues against bilingual education (teaching students in their native language as well as in English).

In preparation for class discussion and for other activities that will be assigned later in this chapter, preview the article. As you read, try to identify the writer's main idea and key supporting points, and then write them on the lines that follow the article on pages 578–79.

NO COMPRENDO

Last spring, my niece phoned me in tears. She was graduating from high school and had to make a decision. An outstanding soccer player, she was offered athletic scholarships by several colleges. So why was she crying? 1

My niece came to the United States from South America as a child. Although she had received good grades in her schools in Miami, she spoke English with a heavy accent, and her comprehension and writing skills were deficient. She was afraid that once she left the Miami environment, she would feel uncomfortable and, worse still, have difficulty keeping up with class work. 2

Programs that keep foreign-born children in Spanish-language classrooms for years are only part of the problem. During a visit to my niece's former school, I observed that all business, not just teaching, was conducted in Spanish. In the office, secretaries spoke to the administrators and the children in Spanish. Announcements over the public-address system were made in an English so fractured that it was almost incomprehensible. 3

I asked my niece's mother why, after years in public schools, her daughter had poor English skills. "It's the whole environment," she replied. "All kinds of services are available in Spanish or Spanglish.[1] Sports and after-school activities are conducted in Spanglish. That's what the kids hear on the radio and in the street." 4

Until recently, immigrants made learning English a priority. But even when they didn't learn English themselves, their children grew up speaking it. Thousands of first-generation Americans still strive to learn English, but others face reduced educational and career opportunities because they have not mastered this basic skill they need to get ahead. 5

According to the 1990 census, 40 percent of the Hispanics born in the United States do not graduate from high school, and the Department of Education says that a lack of proficiency in English is an important factor in the drop-out rate. 6

People and agencies that favor providing services only in foreign languages want to help people who do not speak English, but they may be doing these people a disservice by condemning them to a linguistic ghetto from which they cannot easily escape. 7

And my niece? She turned down all of her scholarship opportunities, deciding instead to attend a small college in Miami, where she will never have to put her English to the test. 8

Writer's main idea

_____

_____

Key supporting points

1. _____

2. _____

1. A mixture of Spanish and English.

3. _____

4. _____

B Highlighting

After you have previewed a passage, read through it carefully, highlighting as you read. **Highlighting** means using underlining and symbols to identify key ideas. This active reading strategy will help you understand the writer's ideas and to make connections among these ideas when you reread. Be selective; don't highlight too much. Remember, you will eventually be rereading every highlighted word, phrase, and sentence—so highlight only the most important, most useful information.

Using Highlighting Symbols

- Underline key ideas—for example, topic sentences.
- Box or circle words or phrases you want to remember.
- Place a check mark (✓) or star (✳) next to an important idea.
- Place a double check mark (✓✓) or double star (✳✳) next to an especially significant idea.
- Draw lines or arrows to connect related ideas.
- Put a question mark (?) beside a word or idea that you need to look up.
- Number the writer's key supporting points or examples.

FOCUS Knowing What to Highlight

You want to highlight what's important—but how do you *know* what's important? As a general rule, you should look for the same **visual signals** you looked for when you did your previewing. Many of the ideas you will need to highlight will probably be found in material that is visually set off from the rest of the text—opening and closing paragraphs, lists, and so on.

Also, continue to look for **verbal signals**—words and phrases like *however, therefore, another reason, the most important point*, and so on—that often introduce key points. Together, these visual and verbal signals will give you clues to the writer's meaning and emphasis.

Here is how a student highlighted an excerpt from a newspaper column, "Barbie at Thirty-Five" by Anna Quindlen.

> But consider the recent study at the University of Arizona investigating the <u>attitudes of white and black teenage girls toward body image</u>. The ✳ attitudes of the white girls were a nightmare. Ninety percent expressed ✓ <u>dissatisfaction with their own bodies</u>, and many said they saw dieting as a kind of all-purpose (panacea.) "I think the reason I would diet would be to gain self-confidence," said one. "I'd feel like it was a way of getting control," said another. And they were curiously united in their description of the (perfect girl.) She's 5 feet 7 inches, weighs just over 100 pounds, has long legs and flowing hair. The researchers concluded, "The ideal girl was a living manifestation of the (Barbie doll.)"
>
> While white girls described an (impossible ideal,) black teenagers talked about appearance in terms of style, attitude, pride, and personality. White respondents talked "thin," black ones "shapely." Seventy percent of the black teenagers said they were <u>satisfied with their weight</u>, and there was ✓ little emphasis on dieting. "We're all brought up and taught to be realistic about life," said one, "and we don't look at things the way you want them to be. You look at them the way they are."

The student who highlighted this passage was preparing to write an essay about eating disorders. Because the excerpt included no visual signals apart from the paragraph divisions, she looked carefully for verbal signals.

The student began her highlighting by underlining and starring the writer's main idea. She then boxed the names of the two key groups the passage compares—*white girls* and *black teenagers*—and underlined two phrases that illustrate how the attitudes of the two groups differ (*dissatisfaction with their own bodies* and *satisfied with their weight*). Check marks in the margin remind the student of the importance of these two phrases, and arrows connect each phrase to the appropriate group of girls.

The student also circled three related terms that characterize white girls' attitudes—*perfect girl, Barbie doll*, and *impossible ideal*—drawing lines to connect them. Finally, she circled the unfamiliar word *panacea* and put a question mark above it to remind herself to look the word up in a dictionary.

◆ **PRACTICE 35-2**

Review the highlighted passage on page 580. How would your own highlighting of this passage be similar to or different from the sample student
highlighting?

◆ **PRACTICE 35-3**

Reread "No Comprendo" (p. 578). As you reread, highlight the article by
underlining and starring main ideas, boxing and circling key words,
checkmarking important points, and drawing lines and arrows to connect
related ideas. Be sure to circle each unfamiliar word and to put a question
mark above it.

C Annotating

As you highlight, you should also *annotate* what you are reading. **Annotating** a passage means making notes—of questions, reactions, reminders,
and ideas for writing or discussion—in the margins or between the lines.
Keeping an informal record of ideas as they occur to you will prepare you
for class discussion and provide a useful source of material for writing.

As you read, asking the following questions will help you make useful
annotations.

Questions for Annotating

■ What is the writer saying? What do you think the writer is suggesting or implying? What makes you think so?

■ What is the writer's purpose (his or her reason for writing)?

■ What kind of audience is the writer addressing?

■ Is the writer responding to another writer's ideas?

■ What is the writer's main idea?

■ How does the writer support his or her points? Does the writer
use facts? Opinions? Both?

■ What kind of supporting details and examples does the writer
use?

■ Does the writer include enough supporting details and examples?

■ What pattern of development does the writer use to arrange his
or her ideas? Is this pattern the best choice?

■ Does the writer seem well informed? Reasonable? Fair?

■ Do you understand the writer's vocabulary?

■ Do you understand the writer's ideas?

■ Do you agree with the points the writer is making?

■ How are the ideas presented in this reading selection like
(or unlike) those presented in other selections you have read?

The following passage, which reproduces the student's highlighting from page 580, also illustrates her annotations.

But consider the recent study at the University of Arizona investigating the attitudes of white and black teenage girls toward body image. The ✗ attitudes of the white girls were a nightmare. Ninety percent expressed

✓ dissatisfaction with their own bodies, and many said they saw dieting as a

= cure-all

kind of all-purpose panacea.? "I think the reason I would diet would be to gain self-confidence," said one. "I'd feel like it was a way of getting control," said another. And they were curiously united in their description of

Need for control, perfection. Why? Media? Parents?

the perfect girl. She's 5 feet 7 inches, weighs just over 100 pounds, has long legs and flowing hair. The researchers concluded, "The ideal girl was a liv-

Barbie doll = plastic, unreal

ing manifestation of the Barbie doll."

While white girls described an impossible ideal, black teenagers talked about appearance in terms of style, attitude, pride, and personality. White respondents talked "thin," black ones "shapely." Seventy percent of the

"Thin" vs. "shapely"

black teenagers said they were satisfied with their weight, and there was ✓

Only 30% dissatisfied — but 90% of white girls

little emphasis on dieting. "We're all brought up and taught to be realistic about life," said one, "and we don't look at things the way you want them to be. You look at them the way they are."   vs. Barbie doll (= unrealistic)

overgeneralization?

With her annotations, this student wrote down the meaning of the word *panacea*, put the study's conclusions and the contrasting statistics into her own words, and recorded questions she intended to explore further.

◆ PRACTICE 35-4

Reread "No Comprendo" (p. 578). As you reread, refer to the Questions for Annotating (p. 581), and use them to guide you as you write down your own thoughts and questions in the margins of the article. Note where you agree or disagree with the writer, and briefly explain why. Quickly summarize any points you think are particularly important. Take time to look up any unfamiliar words you have circled and to write brief definitions. Think of these annotations as your preparation for discussing the article in class and eventually writing about it.

◆ **PRACTICE 35-5**

Trade workbooks with another student, and read over his or her high-lighting and annotating of "No Comprendo." How are your written responses similar to the other student's? How are they different? Do your classmate's responses help you see anything new about the article?

D Outlining

Outlining is another technique you can use to help you understand a reading assignment. Unlike a **formal outline**, which follows strict conventions, an **informal outline** enables you to record a passage's ideas in the order in which they are presented. After you have finished an informal outline of a passage, you should be able to see the writer's emphasis (which ideas are more important than others) as well as how the ideas are related.

FOCUS Making an Informal Outline

1. Write or type the passage's main idea at the top of a sheet of paper. (This will remind you of the writer's focus and help keep your outline on track.)

2. At the left margin, write down the most important idea of the first body paragraph or first part of the passage.

3. Indent the next line a few spaces, and list the examples or details that support this idea. (You can use your computer's Tab key to help you set up your outline.)

4. As ideas become more specific, indent further. (Ideas that have the same degree of importance are indented the same distance from the left margin.)

5. Repeat the process with each body paragraph or part of the passage.

The student who highlighted and annotated the excerpt from Anna Quindlen's "Barbie at Thirty-Five" (pp. 580 and 582) made the following informal outline to help her understand the writer's ideas.

Main idea: Black and white teenage girls have very different attitudes about their body images.

White girls dissatisfied
    90% dissatisfied with appearance
    Dieting = cure-all
       –self-confidence
       –control

Ideal = unrealistic
   –tall and thin
   –Barbie doll
<u>Black girls satisfied</u>
  70% satisfied with weight
  Dieting not important
  Ideal = realistic
    –shapely
    –not thin

◆ PRACTICE 35-6

Working on your own or in a small group, make an informal outline of "No Comprendo" (p. 578). Refer to your highlighting and annotations as you construct your outline. When you have finished, check to make certain your outline accurately represents the writer's emphasis and the relationships among her ideas.

E   Summarizing

Once you have highlighted, annotated, and outlined a passage, you may want to summarize it to help you understand it better. A **summary** retells, *in your own words*, what a passage is about. A summary condenses a passage, so it leaves out all but the main idea and perhaps the key supporting points. A summary omits examples and details, and it does *not* include your own ideas or opinions.

FOCUS   Summarizing a Reading Assignment

1. Review your outline.

2. Consulting your outline, restate the passage's main idea *in your own words*.

3. Consulting your outline, restate the passage's key supporting points. Add transitional words and phrases between sentences where necessary.

4. Reread the original passage to make sure you have not left out anything significant.

Note: To avoid accidentally using the exact language of the original, do not look at the passage while you are writing your summary. If you want to use a distinctive word or phrase from the original passage, put it in quotation marks.

The student who highlighted, annotated, and outlined the excerpt from "Barbie at Thirty-Five" (p. 580) wrote the following summary.

> As Anna Quindlen reports in "Barbie at Thirty-Five," a University of Arizona study found that black and white teenage girls have very different attitudes about their body images. Almost all white girls said they were dissatisfied with their appearance. To them, the "perfect girl" would look like a Barbie doll (tall and very thin). Quindlen sees this attitude as unrealistic. Black girls in the study, however, were generally happy with their weight. They did not say they wanted to be thin; they said they wanted to be "shapely."

◆ PRACTICE 35-7

Write a brief summary of "No Comprendo" (p. 578). Use your outline to guide you, and keep your summary short and to the point. Your summary should be about one-quarter to one-third the length of the original article.

F Writing a Response Paragraph

Once you have highlighted and annotated a reading selection, you are ready to write about it—perhaps in a **response paragraph** in which you record your informal reactions to the writer's ideas.

Because a response paragraph is informal, no special guidelines or rules govern its format or structure. As in any paragraph, however, you should include a topic sentence, support the topic sentence with examples and details, write in complete sentences, and link sentences with appropriate transitions. In a response paragraph, informal style and personal opinions are acceptable.

The student who highlighted, annotated, outlined, and summarized the Quindlen passage wrote this response paragraph.

> Why are white and black girls' body images so different? Why do black girls think it's okay to be "shapely" while white girls want to be thin? Maybe it's because music videos and movies and fashion magazines show so many more white models, all half-starved, with perfect hair and legs. Or maybe white girls get different messages from their parents or from the people they date. Do white and black girls' attitudes about their bodies stay the same when they get older? And what about <u>male</u> teenagers' self-images? Do white and black <u>guys</u> have different body images too?

The process of writing this paragraph was very helpful to the student. The questions she asked suggested some interesting ideas that she could explore in class discussion or in a more fully developed piece of writing.

◆ PRACTICE 35-8

On a separate sheet of paper, write an informal response paragraph expressing your reactions to "No Comprendo" (p. 578) and to the issue of bilingual education.

35 G

Reading in the Classroom, in the Community, and in the Workplace

In college, in your life as a citizen of a community, and in the workplace, you will read material in a variety of different formats—for example, textbooks, newspapers, Web sites, and job-related memos, letters, emails, and reports.

Although the active reading process you have just reviewed can be applied to all kinds of material, various kinds of reading require slightly different strategies during the previewing stage. One reason for this is that different kinds of reading may have different purposes: to present information, to persuade, and so on. Another reason is that the various texts you read are aimed at different audiences, and different audiences require different signals about content and emphasis. For these reasons, you need to look for different kinds of verbal and visual signals when you preview different kinds of reading material.

Reading Textbooks

Much of the reading you do in college is in textbooks (like this one). The purpose of a textbook is to present information, and when you read a textbook, your goal is to understand that information. To do this, you need to figure out which ideas are most important as well as which points support those key ideas and which examples illustrate them.

☑ CHECKLIST:
Reading Textbooks

Look for the following features as you preview.

- **Boldfaced** and *italicized* words, which can indicate terms to be defined.

- Boxed checklists or summaries, which may appear at the ends of sections or chapters

- Bulleted or numbered lists, which may list key reasons or examples or summarize important material

- Diagrams, charts, tables, graphs, photographs, and other visuals that illustrate the writer's points

---

Reading Newspapers

As a student, as an employee, and as a citizen, you read school, community, local, and national newspapers. Like textbooks, newspapers communicate

information. In addition to containing relatively objective news articles, however, newspapers also contain editorials (which aim to persuade) as well as feature articles (which may be designed to entertain as well as to inform).

☑ CHECKLIST:
Reading Newspapers

Look for the following features as you preview.

- The name of the section in which the article appears (News, Business, Lifestyle, Sports, and so on)

- Headlines

- Boldfaced headings within articles

- Labels like *editorial*, *commentary*, or *opinion*, which indicate that an article communicates the writer's own views

- Brief biographical information at the end of an opinion piece

- Phrases or sentences in boldface (to emphasize key points)

- The article's first sentence, which often answers the questions *who, what, why, where, when,* and *how*

- The **dateline**, which tells you the city the writer is reporting from

- Related articles that appear on the same page—for example, boxed information and **sidebars**, short articles that provide additional background on people and places mentioned in the article

- Photographs

■ **Culture Clue**
An *editorial* expresses the opinion of the editor or group of editors of a particular publication.

Reading Web Sites

In schools, businesses, and community settings, people turn to the Web for information. However, because many Web sites have busy, crowded pages, reading one can require you to work hard to distinguish important information from not-so-important material. Some Web sites—particularly those whose **URLs** (electronic addresses) end in .com—may have a persuasive rather than an informative purpose (for example, their purpose may be to sell a product or to promote a political position). Those designated .edu (educational institution) or .org (nonprofit organization) are more likely—although not guaranteed—to present unbiased information. (For more on evaluating Web sites, see Appendix B.)

> ☑ CHECKLIST:
> Reading Web Sites
>
> Look for the following features as you preview.
>
> - URL designation (.com, .org, and so on)
> - Links to other sites (underlined in blue)
> - Graphics
> - Color
> - Headings
> - Boxed material
> - Page layout (placement of images and text on the page)
> - Type size
> - Photographs

Reading on the Job

In your workplace, you will be called on to read memos, letters, emails, and reports. These documents, which may be designed to convey information or to persuade, are often addressed to a group rather than to a single person. (Note that the most important information is often presented *first*—in a subject line or in the first paragraph.)

> ☑ CHECKLIST:
> Reading on the Job
>
> Look for the following features as you preview.
>
> - Numbered or bulleted lists of tasks or problems (numbers indicate the order of the items' importance)
> - In an email, links to the Web
> - In a memo or an email, the person or persons addressed
> - In a memo or an email, the subject line
> - In a memo or a report, headings that highlight key topics or points
> - The first and last paragraphs and the first sentence of each body paragraph, which often contain key information
> - Boldfaced, underlined, or italicized words

✔ REVIEW CHECKLIST:
Reading for College

☐ Preview the material. (See 35A.)

☐ Highlight the material. (See 35B.)

☐ Annotate the material. (See 35C.)

☐ Outline the material. (See 35D.)

☐ Summarize the material. (See 35E.)

☐ Write a response paragraph. (See 35F.)

☐ Use active reading strategies in the classroom, in the community, and in the workplace. (See 35G.)

PREVIEW

In this chapter, you will learn to react critically to essays by professional writers.

The following nineteen essays by professional writers offer interesting material to read, react to, think critically about, discuss, and write about. In addition, these essays illustrate some of the ways you can organize ideas in your own writing.

The essays in this chapter use the nine patterns of development you learned about in Units 1 through 3 of this book: exemplification, narration, description, process, cause and effect, comparison and contrast, classification, definition, and argument. Of course, these patterns are not your only options for arranging ideas in essays; in fact, many essays combine several patterns of development. Still, understanding how each of these nine patterns works will help you choose the most effective organization strategy when you are writing for a particular purpose and audience.

In this chapter, two essays by professional writers illustrate each pattern of development. (For argument, three model essays are included.) Each essay is preceded by a short **headnote**, an introduction that tells you something about the writer and suggests what to look for as you read. Following each selection are five sets of questions. (Questions that you can work on in collaboration with other students are marked with an **asterisk** [*].)

- ■ **Reacting to the Reading** questions suggest guidelines for previewing, highlighting, and annotating the essay.
- ■ **Reacting to Words** questions focus on the writer's word choice.
- ■ **Reacting to Ideas** questions encourage you to respond critically to the writer's ideas and perhaps to consider his or her audience or purpose.
- ■ **Reacting to the Pattern** questions ask you to consider how ideas are arranged within the essay and how they are connected to one another.
- ■ **Writing Practice** suggestions give you opportunities to explore in writing ideas related to the section's readings.

As you read each of the following essays, **preview**, **highlight**, and **annotate** it to help you understand what you are reading. Then, read it more carefully in preparation for class discussion and writing.

A   Exemplification

An **exemplification** essay uses one or more specific examples to support a thesis statement. The two selections that follow, "Don't Call Me a Hot Tamale" by Judith Ortiz Cofer and "The Suspected Shopper" by Ellen Goodman, are exemplification essays. Both writers use a series of short examples to support a thesis.

DON'T CALL ME A HOT TAMALE

Judith Ortiz Cofer

Award-winning poet, novelist, and essayist Judith Ortiz Cofer often writes about her experiences as a Latina—a Hispanic woman—living in a non-Hispanic culture. In "Don't Call Me a Hot Tamale," she discusses how being Puerto Rican has affected her in the world beyond Puerto Rico. Note that her examples illustrate the stereotypes she encounters in reaction to both her heritage and her gender.

On a bus to London from Oxford University, where I was earning some [1] graduate credits one summer, a young man, obviously fresh from a pub, approached my seat. With both hands over his heart, he went down on his knees in the aisle and broke into an Irish tenor's rendition of "Maria" from *West Side Story.* I was not amused. "Maria" had followed me to London, reminding me of a prime fact of my life: You can leave the island of Puerto Rico, master the English language, and travel as far as you can, but if you're a Latina, especially one who so clearly belongs to Rita Moreno's[1] gene pool, the island travels with you.

Growing up in New Jersey and wanting most of all to belong, I lived in [2] two completely different worlds. My parents designed our life as a microcosm of their *casas* on the island—we spoke in Spanish, ate Puerto Rican food bought at the *bodega*, and practiced strict Catholicism complete with Sunday mass in Spanish.

I was kept under tight surveillance by my parents, since my virtue and [3] modesty were, by their cultural equation, the same as their honor. As teenagers, my friends and I were lectured constantly on how to behave as proper *señoritas.* But it was a conflicting message we received, since our Puerto Rican mothers also encouraged us to look and act like women by dressing us in clothes our Anglo schoolmates and their mothers found too "mature" and flashy. I often felt humiliated when I appeared at an American friend's birthday party wearing a dress more suitable for a semiformal. At Puerto Rican festivities, neither the music nor the colors we wore could be too loud.

I remember Career Day in high school, when our teachers told us to [4] come dressed as if for a job interview. That morning, I agonized in front of my closet, trying to figure out what a "career girl" would wear, because the only model I had was Marlo Thomas[2] on TV. To me and my Puerto Rican girlfriends, dressing up meant wearing our mother's ornate jewelry and clothing.

At school that day, the teachers assailed us for wearing "everything at [5] once"—meaning too much jewelry and too many accessories. And it was painfully obvious that the other students in their tailored skirts and silk blouses thought we were hopeless and vulgar. The way they looked at us was a taste of the cultural clash that awaited us in the real world, where prospective employers and men on the street would often misinterpret our tight skirts and bright colors as a come-on.

It is custom, not chromosomes, that leads us to choose scarlet over [6] pale pink. Our mothers had grown up on a tropical island where the natural environment was a riot of primary colors, where showing your skin was one way to keep cool as well as to look sexy. On the island, women felt freer to dress and move provocatively since they were protected by the traditions and laws of a Spanish/Catholic system of morality and machismo, the main rule of which was: *You may look at my sister, but if you touch her I will kill you.* The extended family and church structure provided them with a circle of safety on the island; if a man "wronged" a girl, everyone would close in to save her family honor.

---

1. A Puerto Rican actress, dancer, and singer. She is well known for her role in the movie musical *West Side Story,* a version of Shakespeare's *Romeo and Juliet* featuring Anglos and Puerto Ricans in New York City.
2. Star of a 1966–71 television comedy about a young woman living on her own in New York City.

Off-island, signals often get mixed. When a Puerto Rican girl who is 7
dressed in her idea of what is attractive meets a man from the mainstream
culture who has been trained to react to certain types of clothing as a sexual signal, a clash is likely to take place. She is seen as a Hot Tamale, a sexual firebrand. I learned this lesson at my first formal dance when my date
leaned over and painfully planted a sloppy, overeager kiss on my mouth.
When I didn't respond with sufficient passion, he said in a resentful tone:
"I thought you Latin girls were supposed to mature early." It was only the
first time I would feel like a fruit or vegetable—I was supposed to *ripen*,
not just grow into womanhood like other girls.

These stereotypes, though rarer, still surface in my life. I recently 8
stayed at a classy metropolitan hotel. After having dinner with a friend, I
was returning to my room when a middle-aged man in a tuxedo stepped
directly into my path. With his champagne glass extended toward me, he
exclaimed, "Evita!"[3]

Blocking my way, he bellowed the song "Don't Cry for Me, Argentina." 9
Playing to the gathering crowd, he began to sing loudly a ditty to the tune
of "La Bamba"[4]—except the lyrics were about a girl named Maria whose
exploits all rhymed with her name and gonorrhea.

I knew that this same man—probably a corporate executive, even 10
worldly by most standards—would never have regaled a white woman
with a dirty song in public. But to him, I was just a character in his uni-
verse of "others," all cartoons.

Still, I am one of the lucky ones. There are thousands of Latinas with- 11
out the privilege of the education that my parents gave me. For them every
day is a struggle against the misconceptions perpetuated by the myth of
the Latina as whore, domestic worker or criminal.

Rather than fight these pervasive stereotypes, I try to replace them 12
with a more interesting set of realities. I travel around the U.S. reading
from my books of poetry and my novel. With the stories I tell, the dreams
and fears I examine in my work, I try to get my audience past the particu-
lars of my skin color, my accent or my clothes.

I once wrote a poem in which I called Latinas "God's brown daughters." 13
It is really a prayer, of sorts, for communication and respect. In it, Latin
women pray "in Spanish to an Anglo God / with a Jewish heritage," and they
are "fervently hoping / that if not omnipotent, / at least He be bilingual."

Reacting to the Reading

1. Underline the essay's thesis statement.
2. In the margins of the essay, number the examples Cofer uses to support this thesis.

Reacting to Words

*1. Define these words: *tamale* (title), *rendition* (paragraph 1), *microcosm*
   (2), *ornate* (4), *assailed* (5), *riot* (6), *machismo* (6), *firebrand* (7), *regaled*
   (10), *perpetuated* (11), *pervasive* (12), *omnipotent* (13). Can you suggest
   a synonym for each word that will work in the essay?

3. Eva Perón, wife of Juan Perón, president of Argentina in the 1940s and 1950s. She is the subject of the musical *Evita*.
4. A song with Spanish lyrics popular in the late 1950s.

2. What does the phrase *hot tamale* suggest to you? What do you think Cofer intends it to suggest? Can you think of another word or phrase that might be more effective?

Reacting to Ideas

*1. Cofer states her thesis in paragraph 1: "You can leave the island of Puerto Rico, master the English language, and travel as far as you can, but if you're a Latina, . . . the island travels with you." Restate this thesis in your own words. Do you think this statement applies only to Latinas or to members of other ethnic groups as well? Explain.

2. How, according to Cofer, are the signals sent by dress and appearance interpreted differently in Puerto Rico and "off-island" (paragraph 7)? How does this difference create problems for Cofer? Do you think there is anything she can do to avoid these problems?

Reacting to the Pattern

1. What examples does Cofer use to support her thesis? Do you think she supplies enough examples to convince readers that her thesis is reasonable?

2. Cofer begins her essay with an example. Do you think this is an effective opening strategy? Why or why not? How else might she have begun her essay?

3. All of Cofer's examples are personal experiences. Are they as convincing as statistics or examples from current news articles would be? Are they *more* convincing? Explain.

Writing Practice

1. What positive examples can you think of to counteract the stereotype of the Latina as "whore, domestic worker or criminal" (paragraph 11)? Write a letter to a television network in which you propose the addition of several different Latina characters to actual programs in which they might appear.

2. What do you think Cofer can do to avoid being stereotyped? Write an essay that gives examples of specific things she might do to change the way others see her. In your thesis, state why she should (or should not) make these changes.

3. Do you think others stereotype you because of your heritage—or because of your age, your gender, your dress, or where you live? Write an essay in which you discuss some specific instances of such stereotyping.

THE SUSPECTED SHOPPER

Ellen Goodman

Journalist Ellen Goodman wrote "The Suspected Shopper" for her syndicated newspaper column. Note that although Goodman begins with a single extended example of a "suspected shopper"—herself— she supports her thesis with a series of specific examples of incidents

in which she was suspected. As you read, consider whether the essay (written in 1981) is still relevant to readers today—or whether it is perhaps even more relevant.

It is Saturday, Shopping Saturday, as it's called by the merchants who spread their wares like plush welcome mats across the pages of my newspaper.

But the real market I discover is a different, less eager place than the one I read about. On this Shopping Saturday I don't find welcomes, I find warnings and wariness.

At the first store, a bold sign of the times confronts me: SHOPLIFTERS WILL BE PROSECUTED TO THE FULL EXTENT OF THE LAW.

At the second store, instead of a greeter, I find a doorkeeper. It is his job, his duty, to bar my entrance. To pass, I must give up the shopping bag on my arm. I check it in and check it out.

At the third store, I venture as far as the dressing room. Here I meet another worker paid to protect the merchandise rather than to sell it. The guard of this dressing room counts the number of items I carry in and will count the number of items I carry out.

In the mirror, a long, white, plastic security tag juts out from the blouse tucked into the skirt. I try futilely to pat it down along my left hip, try futilely to zip the skirt.

Finally, during these strange gyrations, a thought seeps through years of dulled consciousness, layers of denial. Something has happened to the relationship between shops and shoppers. I no longer feel like a woman in search of a shirt. I feel like an enemy at Checkpoint Charlie.[1]

I finally, belatedly, realize that I am treated less like a customer these days and more like a criminal. And I hate it. This change happened gradually, and understandably. Security rose in tandem with theft. The defenses of the shopkeepers went up, step by step, with the offenses of the thieves.

But now as the weapons escalate, it's the average consumer, the innocent bystander, who is hit by friendly fire.

I don't remember the first time an errant security tag buzzed at the doorway, the first time I saw a camera eye in a dress department. I accepted it as part of the price of living in a tight honesty market.

In the supermarket, they began to insist on a mug shot before they would cash my check. I tried not to take it personally. At the drugstore, the cashier began to staple my bags closed. And I tried not to take it personally.

Now, these experiences have accumulated until I feel routinely treated like a suspect. At the jewelry store, the door is unlocked only for those who pass judgment. In the junior department, the suede pants are permanently attached to the hangers. In the gift shop, the cases are only opened with a key.

I am not surprised anymore, but I am finally aware of just how unpleasant it is to be dealt with as guilty until we prove our innocence. Anyplace we are not known, we are not trusted. The old slogan, "Let the Consumer Beware," has been replaced with a new slogan: "Beware of the Consumer."

1. A military security checkpoint.

It is no fun to be Belgium[2] in the war between sales and security. 14 Thievery has changed the atmosphere of the marketplace. Merchant distrust has spread through the ventilation system of a whole business, a whole city, and it infects all of us.

At the cashier counter today, with my shirt in hand, I the Accused 15 stand quietly while the saleswoman takes my credit card. I watch her round up the usual suspicions. In front of my face, without a hint of embarrassment, she checks my charge number against the list of stolen credit vehicles. While I stand there, she calls the clearinghouse of bad debtors.

Having passed both tests, I am instructed to add my name, address, 16 serial number to the bottom of the charge. She checks one signature against another, the picture against the person. Only then does she release the shirt into my custody.

And so this Shopping Saturday I take home six ounces of silk and a 17 load of resentment.

Reacting to the Reading

1. Goodman gives a number of examples of incidents in which she was suspected of shoplifting. Highlight these examples.
2. In the margins of the essay, add one or two examples from your personal experience (or from the experiences of your friends) that support Goodman's thesis.

Reacting to Words

*1. Define these words: *futilely* (paragraph 6), *gyrations* (7), *belatedly* (8), *tandem* (8), *errant* (10). Can you suggest a synonym for each word that will work in the essay?
2. What is Goodman's purpose in choosing words like *enemy* (paragraph 7) and *mug shot* (11)? How do they help to support her thesis? Can you find additional words or expressions that serve the same purpose?

Reacting to Ideas

*1. Goodman, an upper-middle-class white woman, uses *we* in the sentence "Anyplace we are not known, we are not trusted" (paragraph 13). Who is this *we*? Do you think Goodman is really part of the group with which she identifies?
2. In paragraph 8, Goodman says the change in attitude she observes is understandable. Do you think she is right?
3. Do you think shoplifting is more or less of a problem today than it was in 1981 when Goodman wrote her essay? What makes you think so?

Reacting to the Pattern

1. In paragraph 8, Goodman states her thesis: "I finally, belatedly, realize that I am treated less like a customer these days and more like a criminal." However, she introduces a number of her examples even before she states this thesis. Why do you think she does this?

2. Country located between France and Germany, which were enemies in several wars.

2. List the specific examples of times when Goodman was "treated less like a customer . . . and more like a criminal" (paragraph 8).

3. How does Goodman arrange the specific examples that support her thesis? Is each discussed in an individual paragraph, or are examples grouped together?

Writing Practice

1. Why do you think people shoplift? Write an exemplification essay in which you discuss a different reason in each body paragraph.

2. Have you ever found yourself torn between giving in to peer pressure and maintaining your own sense of right and wrong? Write an essay in which you use several examples from your own life (or from the lives of your friends) to support the idea that peer pressure can be powerful (or even dangerous).

3. What do you think merchants can do to reduce shoplifting without making shoppers feel like criminals? Using exemplification to organize your ideas, write a letter to a store where you are a regular customer.

B   Narration

A **narrative** essay tells a story by presenting a series of events in chronological order. In the first of the two essays that follow, "The Sanctuary of School," Lynda Barry tells a story about home and family. In the second, "Thirty-Eight Who Saw Murder Didn't Call the Police," Martin Gansberg reports the story of a tragic murder.

THE SANCTUARY OF SCHOOL

Lynda Barry

In her cartoon strip "Ernie Pook's Comeek," which appears in a number of newspapers and magazines, Lynda Barry looks at the world through the eyes of children. Her characters remind adult readers of the complicated world of young people and of the clarity with which they see social situations. In "The Sanctuary of School," Barry tells a story from her own childhood. As you read this essay, note how Barry relates her personal experience to a broader issue.

I was 7 years old the first time I snuck out of the house in the dark. It was winter and my parents had been fighting all night. They were short on money and long on relatives who kept "temporarily" moving into our house because they had nowhere else to go.

My brother and I were used to giving up our bedroom. We slept on the couch, something we actually liked because it put us that much closer to the light of our lives, our television.

At night when everyone was asleep, we lay on our pillows watching it with the sound off. We watched Steve Allen's mouth moving. We watched

Johnny Carson's mouth moving.[1] We watched movies filled with gangsters shooting machine guns into packed rooms, dying soldiers hurling a last grenade and beautiful women crying at windows. Then the sign-off finally came and we tried to sleep.

4 The morning I snuck out, I woke up filled with a panic about needing to get to school. The sun wasn't quite up yet but my anxiety was so fierce that I just got dressed, walked quietly across the kitchen and let myself out the back door.

5 It was quiet outside. Stars were still out. Nothing moved and no one was in the street. It was as if someone had turned the sound off on the world.

6 I walked the alley, breaking thin ice over the puddles with my shoes. I didn't know why I was walking to school in the dark. I didn't think about it. All I knew was a feeling of panic, like the panic that strikes kids when they realize they are lost.

7 That feeling eased the moment I turned the corner and saw the dark outline of my school at the top of the hill. My school was made up of about 15 nondescript portable classrooms set down on a fenced concrete lot in a rundown Seattle neighborhood, but it had the most beautiful view of the Cascade Mountains. You could see them from anywhere on the playfield and you could see them from the windows of my classroom—Room 2.

8 I walked over to the monkey bars and hooked my arms around the cold metal. I stood for a long time just looking across Rainier Valley. The sky was beginning to whiten and I could hear a few birds.

9 In a perfect world my absence at home would not have gone unnoticed. I would have had two parents in a panic to locate me, instead of two parents in a panic to locate an answer to the hard question of survival during a deep financial and emotional crisis.

10 But in an overcrowded and unhappy home, it's incredibly easy for any child to slip away. The high levels of frustration, depression and anger in my house made my brother and me invisible. We were children with the sound turned off. And for us, as for the steadily increasing number of neglected children in this country, the only place where we could count on being noticed was at school.

11 "Hey there, young lady. Did you forget to go home last night?" It was Mr. Gunderson, our janitor, whom we all loved. He was nice and he was funny and he was old with white hair, thick glasses and an unbelievable number of keys. I could hear them jingling as he walked across the playfield. I felt incredibly happy to see him.

12 He let me push his wheeled garbage can between the different portables as he unlocked each room. He let me turn on the lights and raise the window shades and I saw my school slowly come to life. I saw Mrs. Holman, our school secretary, walk into the office without her orange lipstick on yet. She waved.

13 I saw the fifth-grade teacher Mr. Cunningham, walking under the breezeway eating a hard roll. He waved.

14 And I saw my teacher, Mrs. Claire LeSane, walking toward us in a red coat and calling my name in a very happy and surprised way, and suddenly my throat got tight and my eyes stung and I ran toward her crying. It was something that surprised us both.

15 It's only thinking about it now, 28 years later, that I realize I was crying from relief. I was with my teacher, and in a while I was going to sit at

---

1. Steve Allen and Johnny Carson were late-night television hosts.

my desk, with my crayons and pencils and books and classmates all around me, and for the next six hours I was going to enjoy a thoroughly secure, warm and stable world. It was a world I absolutely relied on. Without it, I don't know where I would have gone that morning.

Mrs. LeSane asked me what was wrong and when I said "Nothing," she 16 seemingly left it at that. But she asked me if I would carry her purse for her, an honor above all honors, and she asked if I wanted to come into Room 2 early and paint.

She believed in the natural healing power of painting and drawing for 17 troubled children. In the back of her room there was always a drawing table and an easel with plenty of supplies, and sometimes during the day she would come up to you for what seemed like no good reason and quietly ask if you wanted to go to the back table and "make some pictures for Mrs. LeSane." We all had a chance at it—to sit apart from the class for a while to paint, draw and silently work out impossible problems on 11×17 sheets of newsprint.

Drawing came to mean everything to me. At the back table in Room 2, 18 I learned to build myself a life preserver that I could carry into my home.

We all know that a good education system saves lives, but the people of 19 this country are still told that cutting the budget for public schools is necessary, that poor salaries for teachers are all we can manage and that art, music and all creative activities must be the first to go when times are lean.

Before- and after-school programs are cut and we are told that public 20 schools are not made for baby-sitting children. If parents are neglectful temporarily or permanently, for whatever reason, it's certainly sad, but their unlucky children must fend for themselves. Or slip through the cracks. Or wander in a dark night alone.

We are told in a thousand ways that not only are public schools not 21 important, but that the children who attend them, the children who need them most, are not important either. We leave them to learn from the blind eye of a television, or to the mercy of "a thousand points of light"[2] that can be as far away as stars.

I was lucky. I had Mrs. LeSane. I had Mr. Gunderson. I had an abun- 22 dance of art supplies. And I had a particular brand of neglect in my home that allowed me to slip away and get to them. But what about the rest of the kids who weren't as lucky? What happened to them?

By the time the bell rang that morning I had finished my drawing and 23 Mrs. LeSane pinned it up on the special bulletin board she reserved for drawings from the back table. It was the same picture I always drew—a sun in the corner of a blue sky over a nice house with flowers all around it.

Mrs. LeSane asked us to please stand, face the flag, place our right 24 hands over our hearts and say the Pledge of Allegiance. Children across the country do it faithfully. I wonder now when the country will face its children and say a pledge right back.

Reacting to the Reading

1. Underline passages that describe Barry's home life in negative terms and her school life in positive terms.
2. In the margins of the essay, note the specific features of the two places (home and school) that are contrasted.

---

2. Phrase used by former president George Herbert Walker Bush to promote volunteerism.

Reacting to Words

*1. Define these words: *nondescript* (paragraph 7), *fend* (20). Can you suggest a synonym for each word that will work in the essay?
 2. Look up the word *sanctuary* in a dictionary. Which of the listed definitions do you think comes closest to Barry's meaning?

Reacting to Ideas

 1. In paragraph 10, Barry characterizes herself and her brother as "children with the sound turned off." What do you think she means?
 2. List the ways in which Barry's home and school worlds are different.
*3. What is the main point of Barry's essay—the idea that she wants to convince readers to accept? Is this idea actually stated in her essay? If so, where? If not, do you think it should be?

Reacting to the Pattern

 1. Paragraphs 9–10 and 19–22 interrupt Barry's story. What purpose do these paragraphs serve? Do you think the essay would be more effective if paragraphs 9 and 10 came earlier? If paragraphs 19–22 came after paragraph 24? Explain.
 2. What transitional words and phrases does Barry use to move readers from one event to the next? Do you think her essay needs more transitions? If so, where should they be added?

Writing Practice

 1. Did you see elementary school as a "sanctuary" or as something quite different? Write a narrative essay that conveys to readers what school meant to you when you were a child.
 2. In addition to school, television was a sanctuary for Barry and her brother. Did television watching (or some other activity) serve this function for you when you were younger? Is there some activity that fills this role now? In a narrative essay, write about your own "sanctuary."
 3. What role does college play in your life? Write an article for your school newspaper in which you use narration to tell what school means to you now that you are an adult.

THIRTY-EIGHT WHO SAW MURDER DIDN'T CALL THE POLICE

Martin Gansberg

This newspaper article uses objective language to tell about an incident that occurred in New York City in 1964. As Gansberg reconstructs the crime two weeks after it happened, he gives readers a detailed picture of the sequence of events that led up to a young woman's murder—in full view of thirty-eight of her "respectable, law-abiding" neighbors. As you read, consider how you might have acted if you had been a witness to this tragedy.

For more than half an hour 38 respectable, law-abiding citizens in Queens   1
watched a killer stalk and stab a woman in three separate attacks in Kew
Gardens.

Twice their chatter and the sudden glow of their bedroom lights inter-   2
rupted him and frightened him off. Each time he returned, sought her out,
and stabbed her again. Not one person telephoned the police during the
assault; one witness called after the woman was dead.

That was two weeks ago today.   3

Still shocked is Assistant Chief Inspector Frederick M. Lussen, in   4
charge of the borough's detectives and a veteran of 25 years of homicide
investigations. He can give a matter-of-fact recitation on many murders.
But the Kew Gardens slaying baffles him—not because it is a murder, but
because the "good people" failed to call the police.

"As we have reconstructed the crime," he said, "the assailant had three   5
chances to kill this woman during a 35-minute period. He returned twice
to complete the job. If we had been called when he first attacked, the
woman might not be dead now."

This is what the police say happened beginning at 3:20 a.m. in the   6
staid, middle-class, tree-lined Austin Street area:

Twenty-eight-year-old Catherine Genovese, who was called Kitty by   7
almost everyone in the neighborhood, was returning home from her job as
manager of a bar in Hollis. She parked her red Fiat in a lot adjacent to the
Kew Gardens Long Island Rail Road Station, facing Mowbray Place. Like
many residents of the neighborhood, she had parked there day after day
since her arrival from Connecticut a year ago, although the railroad
frowns on the practice.

She turned off the lights of her car, locked the door, and started to walk   8
the 100 feet to the entrance of her apartment at 82-70 Austin Street, which
is in a Tudor building, with stores on the first floor and apartments on the
second.

The entrance to the apartment is in the rear of the building because the   9
front is rented to retail stores. At night the quiet neighborhood is shrouded
in the slumbering darkness that marks most residential areas.

Miss Genovese noticed a man at the far end of the lot, near a seven-   10
story apartment house at 82-40 Austin Street. She halted. Then, nervously,
she headed up Austin Street toward Lefferts Boulevard, where there is a
call box to the 102nd Police Precinct in nearby Richmond Hill.

She got as far as a street light in front of a bookstore before the man   11
grabbed her. She screamed. Lights went on in the 10-story apartment
house at 82-67 Austin Street, which faces the bookstore. Windows slid
open and voices punctuated the early-morning stillness.

Miss Genovese screamed: "Oh, my God, he stabbed me! Please help   12
me! Please help me!"

From one of the upper windows in the apartment house, a man called   13
down: "Let that girl alone!"

The assailant looked up at him, shrugged, and walked down Austin   14
Street toward a white sedan parked a short distance away. Miss Genovese
struggled to her feet.

Lights went out. The killer returned to Miss Genovese, now trying to   15
make her way around the side of the building by the parking lot to get to
her apartment. The assailant stabbed her again.

"I'm dying!" she shrieked. "I'm dying!"   16

Windows were opened again, and lights went on in many apartments. 17
The assailant got into his car and drove away. Miss Genovese staggered to
her feet. A city bus, O-10, the Lefferts Boulevard line to Kennedy International Airport, passed. It was 3:35 a.m.

The assailant returned. By then, Miss Genovese had crawled to the 18
back of the building, where the freshly painted brown doors to the apartment house held out hope for safety. The killer tried the first door;
she wasn't there. At the second door, 82-62 Austin Street, he saw her
slumped on the floor at the foot of the stairs. He stabbed her a third
time—fatally.

It was 3:50 by the time the police received their first call, from a man 19
who was a neighbor of Miss Genovese. In two minutes they were at the
scene. The neighbor, a 70-year-old woman, and another woman were the
only persons on the street. Nobody else came forward.

The man explained that he had called the police after much delibera- 20
tion. He had phoned a friend in Nassau County for advice and then he had
crossed the roof of the building to the apartment of the elderly woman to
get her to make the call.

"I didn't want to get involved," he sheepishly told police. 21

Six days later, the police arrested Winston Moseley, a 29-year-old 22
business machine operator, and charged him with homicide. Moseley
had no previous record. He is married, has two children and owns a
home at 133-19 Sutter Avenue, South Ozone Park, Queens. On Wednesday,
a court committed him to Kings County Hospital for psychiatric
observation.

When questioned by the police, Moseley also said that he had slain 23
Mrs. Annie May Johnson, 24, of 146-12 133d Avenue, Jamaica, on Feb. 29
and Barbara Kralik, 15, of 174-17 140th Avenue, Springfield Gardens, last
July. In the Kralik case, the police are holding Alvin L. Mitchell, who is said
to have confessed to that slaying.

The police stressed how simple it would have been to have gotten 24
in touch with them. "A phone call," said one of the detectives, "would
have done it." The police may be reached by dialing "O" for operator or
SPring 7-3100.

Today witnesses from the neighborhood, which is made up of one- 25
family homes in the $35,000 to $60,000 range with the exception of the
two apartment houses near the railroad station, find it difficult to explain
why they didn't call the police.

A housewife, knowingly if quite casually, said, "We thought it was a 26
lovers' quarrel." A husband and wife both said, "Frankly, we were afraid."
They seemed aware of the fact that events might have been different. A
distraught woman, wiping her hands in her apron, said, "I didn't want my
husband to get involved."

One couple, now willing to talk about that night, said they heard the 27
first screams. The husband looked thoughtfully at the bookstore where the
killer first grabbed Miss Genovese.

"We went to the window to see what was happening," he said, "but 28
the light from our bedroom made it difficult to see the street." The
wife, still apprehensive, added: "I put out the light and we were able to see
better."

Asked why they hadn't called the police, she shrugged and replied: 29
"I don't know."

A man peeked out from a slight opening in the doorway to his apart-   30
ment and rattled off an account of the killer's second attack. Why hadn't
he called the police at the time? "I was tired," he said without emotion.
"I went back to bed."

It was 4:25 a.m. when the ambulance arrived to take the body of Miss   31
Genovese. It drove off. "Then," a solemn police detective said, "the people
came out."

Reacting to the Reading

1. Place a check mark beside each passage of dialogue Gansberg uses.
2. Add brief marginal annotations next to three of these passages of
   dialogue.

Reacting to Words

*1. Define these words: *staid* (paragraph 6), *shrouded* (9). Can you suggest
   a synonym for each word that will work in the essay?
2. What is Gansberg's purpose in using terms like *respectable* (paragraph 1), *law-abiding* (1), and *good people* (4)? What is your reaction to
   these words?

Reacting to Ideas

1. What reasons do the witnesses give for not coming to Kitty Genovese's
   aid? Why do *you* think no one helped her?
*2. Suppose Genovese's attack were to occur today. How do you think her
   neighbors would react? What might be different about the situation?

Reacting to the Pattern

1. What other patterns could Gansberg have used to develop his essay?
   For instance, could he have used comparison and contrast? Exemplification? Given the alternatives, do you think narration is the best
   choice? Why or why not?
*2. Gansberg uses many transitional words and phrases, including refer-
   ences to specific times, to move readers from one event to the next. List
   as many of these transitions as you can. Do you think more transitions
   should be added?

Writing Practice

1. Write a narrative essay about a time when you were a witness who
   chose not to become involved in events you were observing.
2. Find a brief newspaper article that tells a story about a similar incident in which bystanders witnessed a crime. Expand the article
   into a longer essay, inventing characters, dialogue, and additional
   details.
3. Retell Kitty Genovese's story—but this time, have a witness come to
   her rescue.

36 C

A **descriptive** essay tells what something looks, sounds, smells, tastes, or feels like. It uses details to give readers a clear, vivid picture of a person, place, or object. In "Fish Cheeks," Amy Tan describes a family meal. In "Guavas," Esmeralda Santiago describes a fruit.

FISH CHEEKS

Amy Tan

Born in California shortly after her parents immigrated there from China, Amy Tan started writing at an early age. Author of the best-selling novel *The Joy Luck Club* (1989) and the more recent *Saving Fish from Drowning* (2006), Tan is known for exploring Chinese-American mother-daughter relationships. In the following essay, Tan describes her family's Christmas dinner and the lessons she learns about sharing and appreciating her Chinese heritage. Consider how her descriptions reflect her mixed feelings about the dinner.

1 I fell in love with the minister's son the winter I turned fourteen. He was not Chinese, but as white as Mary in the manger. For Christmas I prayed for this blond-haired boy, Robert, and a slim new American nose.

2 When I found out that my parents had invited the minister's family over for Christmas Eve dinner, I cried. What would Robert think of our shabby *Chinese* Christmas? What would he think of our noisy *Chinese* relatives who lacked proper American manners? What terrible disappointment would he feel upon seeing not a roasted turkey and sweet potatoes but *Chinese* food?

3 On Christmas Eve I saw that my mother had outdone herself in creating a strange menu. She was pulling black veins out of the backs of fleshy prawns. The kitchen was littered with appalling mounds of raw food: a slimy rock cod with bulging fish eyes that pleaded not to be thrown into a pan of hot oil. Tofu, which looked like stacked wedges of rubbery white sponges. A bowl soaking dried fungus back to life. A plate of squid, their backs crisscrossed with knife markings so they resembled bicycle tires.

4 And then they arrived—the minister's family and all my relatives in a clamor of doorbells and rumpled Christmas packages. Robert grunted hello, and I pretended he was not worthy of existence.

5 Dinner threw me deeper into despair. My relatives licked the ends of their chopsticks and reached across the table, dipping them into the dozen or so plates of food. Robert and his family waited patiently for platters to be passed to them. My relatives murmured with pleasure when my mother brought out the whole steamed fish. Robert grimaced. Then my father poked his chopsticks just below the fish eye and plucked out the soft meat. "Amy, your favorite," he said, offering me the tender fish cheek. I wanted to disappear.

6 At the end of the meal my father leaned back and belched loudly, thanking my mother for her fine cooking. "It's a polite Chinese custom to show you are satisfied," explained my father to our astonished guests. The

minister managed to muster up a quiet burp. I was stunned into silence the rest of the night.

After everyone had gone, my mother said to me, "You want to be the same as American girls on the outside." She handed me an early gift. It was a miniskirt in beige tweed. "But inside you must always be Chinese. You must be proud you are different. Your only shame is to have shame." 7

And even though I didn't agree with her then, I knew that she understood how much I had suffered during the evening's dinner. It wasn't until many years later—long after I had gotten over my crush on Robert—that I was able to fully appreciate her lesson and the true purpose behind our particular menu. For Christmas Eve that year, she had chosen all my favorite meals. 8

Reacting to the Reading

*1. Circle all the adjectives in this essay that convey a negative impression—for example, *shabby* and *terrible* in paragraph 2.
2. In the margins, write brief annotations explaining what these negative words add to the essay.

Reacting to Words

*1. Define these words: *appalling* (3), *clamor* (4), *grimaced* (5). Can you suggest a synonym for each word that will work in the essay?
2. Underline each use of the word *Chinese* in this essay. What does the word suggest in each case? Does it suggest something positive, negative, or neutral?

Reacting to Ideas

1. Tan is very nervous about the encounter between her family and Robert's. What do you think she is really afraid of?
*2. What do you think Tan's mother means by "'Your only shame is to have shame'" (paragraph 7)?
3. Why does Tan's mother give her the tweed miniskirt?

Reacting to the Pattern

*1. In paragraph 2, Tan asks, "What would Robert think of our shabby *Chinese* Christmas?" How does this question help to establish the dominant impression Tan wants to convey?
2. In paragraph 3, Tan describes the food that was served; in paragraphs 5 and 6, she describes the people. How do the descriptive details she chooses support the essay's dominant impression?
3. Is this essay primarily subjective or objective description? Explain.

Writing Practice

1. Describe a family meal of your own—either a typical breakfast, lunch, or dinner or a "company" or holiday meal.
2. Describe the Tan family's meal from Robert's point of view. What does he see? How does the scene (and the food) look to him?

GUAVAS

Esmeralda Santiago

Esmeralda Santiago grew up in Puerto Rico as the oldest of eleven children raised by a single mother. The family moved to New York when she was thirteen years old. She has written a childhood memoir, *When I Was Puerto Rican* (1993), and its sequel, *Almost a Woman* (1998), describing the family's move to Brooklyn. After graduating from the High School of the Performing Arts in Manhattan, Santiago spent eight years studying part-time at community colleges before being accepted on full scholarship to Harvard University. In recent years, Santiago has also founded a film and production company, helped found a shelter for battered women, and most recently worked as an editor. As you read this selection, take note of which of the five senses Santiago uses to describe the experience of eating a guava.

Barco que no anda, no llega a puerto.

A ship that doesn't sail, never reaches port.

There are guavas at the Shop & Save. I pick one the size of a tennis ball 1
and finger the prickly stem end. It feels familiarly bumpy and firm. The guava is not quite ripe; the skin is still a dark green. I smell it and imagine a pale pink center, the seeds tightly embedded in the flesh.

A ripe guava is yellow, although some varieties have a pink tinge. The 2
skin is thick, firm, and sweet. Its heart is bright pink and almost solid with seeds. The most delicious part of the guava surrounds the tiny seeds. If you don't know how to eat a guava, the seeds end up in the crevices between your teeth.

When you bite into a ripe guava, your teeth must grip the bumpy sur- 3
face and sink into the thick edible skin without hitting the center. It takes experience to do this, as it's quite tricky to determine how far beyond the skin the seeds begin.

Some years, when the rains have been plentiful and the nights cool, 4
you can bite into a guava and not find many seeds. The guava bushes grow close to the ground, their branches laden with green then yellow fruit that seem to ripen overnight. These guavas are large and juicy, almost seedless, their roundness enticing you to have one more, just one more, because next year the rains may not come.

As children, we didn't always wait for the fruit to ripen. We raided the 5
bushes as soon as the guavas were large enough to bend the branch.

A green guava is sour and hard. You bite into it at its widest point, be- 6
cause it's easier to grasp with your teeth. You hear the skin, meat, and seeds crunching inside your head, while the inside of your mouth explodes in little spurts of sour.

You grimace, your eyes water, and your cheeks disappear as your lips 7
purse into a tight O. But you have another and then another, enjoying the crunchy sounds, the acid taste, the gritty texture of the unripe center. At night, your mother makes you drink castor oil, which she says tastes better than a green guava. That's when you know for sure that you're a child and she has stopped being one.

I had my last guava the day we left Puerto Rico. It was large and juicy, 8
almost red in the center, and so fragrant that I didn't want to eat it because
I would lose the smell. All the way to the airport I scratched at it with my
teeth, making little dents in the skin, chewing small pieces with my front
teeth, so that I could feel the texture against my tongue, the tiny pink pellets of sweet.

Today, I stand before a stack of dark green guavas, each perfectly 9
round and hard, each $1.59. The one in my hand is tempting. It smells
faintly of late summer afternoons and hopscotch under the mango tree.
But this is autumn in New York, and I'm no longer a child.

The guava joins its sisters under the harsh fluorescent lights of the 10
exotic fruit display. I push my cart away, toward the apples and pears of
my adulthood, their nearly seedless ripeness predictable and bittersweet.

Reacting to the Reading

1. The essay begins with a quotation in Spanish, followed by its English
   translation. In a marginal note, explain why you think Santiago opens
   with this quotation.
2. Circle all the words in the essay that convey information about guavas'
   physical appearance (how they look).

Reacting to Words

*1. Define these words: *edible* (paragraph 3), *laden* (4), *enticing* (4), *spurts*
   (6), *grimace* (7), *pellets* (8). Can you suggest a synonym for each word
   that will work in the essay?
*2. Write an alternate one-word title for this selection.

Reacting to Ideas

1. How is the fruit in the Shop & Save different from the fruit of Santiago's childhood?
*2. Is this essay just about guavas, or is it really about something else?
   Explain.

Reacting to the Pattern

1. Santiago begins and ends her essay at the Shop & Save, but her imagination takes her somewhere else. Where? What sends her thoughts
   away from the supermarket?
2. Santiago describes several kinds of guavas. How are they different?
*3. In addition to describing how guavas look, Santiago also describes
   their smell, taste, and feel. Where does she use language that conveys
   how guavas taste? How they smell? How they feel?
4. If Santiago had written a purely objective description, what would she
   have left out? What might she have added?

Writing Practice

1. Write a subjective description of a food you loved when you were a
   child. Try to describe the smell, taste, and feel of the food as well as its
   appearance.

2. Write an essay about a friend or family member with whom you associate a particular food or meal. Include descriptions of that person engaged in eating or in preparing the food.

3. How have your tastes in food changed since you were a child? Trace the development of your food preferences, beginning as far back as you can remember. Be sure to describe the foods that defined each stage of your life.

D   Process

A **process** essay explains the steps in a procedure, telling how something is (or was) done. In "Slice of Life," Russell Baker gives a set of instructions for carving a turkey. In "My First Conk," Malcolm X explains the process he went through to straighten his hair.

SLICE OF LIFE

Russell Baker

Pulitzer Prize–winning columnist and author Russell Baker was known for his keen political insight and sharp social commentary. He was also known for being funny. The source of much of Baker's humor is his deadpan approach, in which he pretends to be completely serious. In the following essay, note how he uses this approach to turn what seems to be a straightforward set of instructions into a humorous discussion of a holiday ritual.

How to carve a turkey: 1

Assemble the following tools—carving knife, stone for sharpening   2
carving knife, hot water, soap, wash cloth, two bath towels, barbells, meat cleaver. If the house lacks a meat cleaver, an ax may be substituted. If it is, add bandages, sutures, and iodine to above list.

Begin by moving the turkey from the roasting pan to a suitable carv-   3
ing area. This is done by inserting the carving knife into the posterior stuffed area of the turkey and the knife-sharpening stone into the stuffed area under the neck.

Thus skewered, the turkey may be lifted out of the hot grease with rel-   4
ative safety. Should the turkey drop to the floor, however, remove the knife and stone, roll the turkey gingerly into the two bath towels, wrap them several times around it and lift the encased fowl to the carving place.

You are now ready to begin carving. Sharpen the knife on the stone   5
and insert it where the thigh joins the torso. If you do this correctly, which is improbable, the knife will almost immediately encounter a barrier of bone and gristle. This may very well be the joint. It could, however, be your thumb. If not, execute a vigorous sawing motion until satisfied that the knife has been defeated. Withdraw the knife and ask someone nearby, in as testy a manner as possible, why the knives at your house are not kept in better carving condition.

Exercise the biceps and forearms by lifting barbells until they are   6
strong enough for you to tackle the leg joint with bare hands. Wrapping

one hand firmly around the thigh, seize the turkey's torso in the other hand and scream. Run cold water over hands to relieve pain of burns.

Now, take a bath towel in each hand and repeat the above maneuver. 7 The entire leg should snap away from the chassis with a distinct crack, and the rest of the turkey, obedient to Newton's law[1] about equal and opposite reactions, should roll in the opposite direction, which means that if you are carving at the table the turkey will probably come to rest in someone's lap.

Get the turkey out of the lap with as little fuss as possible, and con- 8 centrate on the leg. Use the meat cleaver to sever the sinewy leather which binds the thigh to the drumstick.

If using the alternate, ax method, this operation should be performed 9 on a cement walk outside the house in order to preserve the table.

Repeat the above operation on the turkey's uncarved side. You now 10 have two thighs and two drumsticks. Using the wash cloth, soap and hot water, bathe thoroughly and, if possible, go to a movie. Otherwise, look each person in the eye and say, "I don't suppose anyone wants white meat."

If compelled to carve the breast anyhow, sharpen the knife on the stone 11 again with sufficient awkwardness to tip over the gravy bowl on the person who started the stampede for white meat.

While everyone is rushing about to mop the gravy off her slacks, 12 hack at the turkey breast until it starts crumbling off the carcass in ugly chunks.

The alternative method for carving white meat is to visit around the 13 neighborhood until you find someone who has a good carving knife and borrow it, if you find one, which is unlikely.

This method enables you to watch the football game on neighbors' tel- 14 evision sets and also creates the possibility that somebody back at your table will grow tired of waiting and do the carving herself.

In this case, upon returning home, cast a pained stare upon the mound 15 of chopped white meat that has been hacked out by the family carving knife and refuse to do any more carving that day. No one who cares about the artistry of carving can be expected to work upon the mutilations of amateurs, and it would be a betrayal of the carver's art to do so.

Reacting to the Reading

1. Number the steps in the process.
2. Underline or star the cautions and warnings Baker provides for readers.

Reacting to Words

*1. Define these words: *sutures* (paragraph 2), *gingerly* (4), *encased* (4), *torso* (5), *execute* (5), *testy* (5), *chassis* (7). Can you suggest a synonym for each word that will work in the essay?
2. In paragraph 14, Baker uses *herself* to refer to *somebody*. What is your reaction to this pronoun use? What other options did Baker have? Why do you think he chose to use *herself*?

---

1. Sir Isaac Newton, seventeenth-century physicist and mathematician known for formulating the laws of gravity and light and for inventing calculus.

Reacting to Ideas

1. This process is not intended to be taken seriously or followed exactly. How can you tell?
*2. Referring to your response to the first Reacting to the Reading question, list the steps in Baker's process of carving a turkey. Then, cross out all nonessential or humorous material. Are the instructions that remain logically ordered? Clear? Accurate?

Reacting to the Pattern

1. How do you know that this essay is a set of instructions and not an explanation of a process?
*2. Do you think the phrase "How to carve a turkey" is an adequate introduction for this essay? What other kind of introduction might Baker have written?
3. Review the various cautions and warnings that you identified in the second Reacting to the Reading question. Are they all necessary? Explain.

Writing Practice

1. Write a new introductory paragraph for this essay. Then, turn Baker's instructions into a straightforward process explanation, deleting any material you consider irrelevant to your purpose. Be sure to include all necessary articles (*a, an, the*) and transitions.
2. List the steps in a recipe for preparing one of your favorite dishes. Then, expand your recipe into an essay, adding transitions and cautions and reminders. Finally, add opening and closing paragraphs that describe the finished product and tell readers why the dish is worth preparing.
3. Write an essay that explains to your fellow students how you juggle the demands of family, work, and school in a typical day. Organize your essay either as a process explanation or as a set of instructions.

MY FIRST CONK

Malcolm X

Malcolm X (1925–1965) was an influential leader in the 1960s civil rights movement in the United States. Jailed as a young man, he continued his education in prison and later became a charismatic member of the religious organization Nation of Islam. In this essay, Malcolm X explains how he had his hair styled to look like a white man's because he, like many African Americans at the time, was ashamed of his natural hair. Consider the importance of the burning sensation that is part of the "conking" process and how it illustrates his emotional pain.

Shorty soon decided that my hair was finally long enough to be conked. 1
He had promised to school me in how to beat the barber shops' three- and
four-dollar price by making up congolene, and then conking ourselves.

I took the little list of ingredients he had printed out for me, and went to a grocery store, where I got a can of Red Devil lye, two eggs, and two medium-sized white potatoes. Then at a drugstore near the poolroom, I asked for a large jar of vaseline, a large bar of soap, a large-toothed comb and a fine-toothed comb, one of those rubber hoses with a metal spray-head, a rubber apron, and a pair of gloves.

"Going to lay on that first conk?" the drugstore man asked me. I proudly told him, grinning, "Right!"

Shorty paid six dollars a week for a room in his cousin's shabby apartment. His cousin wasn't at home. "It's like the pad's mine, he spends so much time with his woman," Shorty said. "Now, you watch me—"

He peeled the potatoes and thin-sliced them into a quart-sized Mason fruit jar, then started stirring them with a wooden spoon as he gradually poured in a little over half the can of lye. "Never use a metal spoon; the lye will turn it black," he told me.

A jelly-like, starchy-looking glop resulted from the lye and potatoes, and Shorty broke in the two eggs, stirring real fast—his own conk and dark face bent down close. The congolene turned pale-yellowish. "Feel the jar," Shorty said. I cupped my hand against the outside, and snatched it away. "Damn right, it's hot, that's the lye," he said. "So you know it's going to burn when I comb it in—it burns bad. But the longer you can stand it, the straighter the hair."

He made me sit down, and he tied the string of the new rubber apron tightly around my neck, and combed up my bush of hair. Then, from the big vaseline jar, he took a handful and massaged it hard all through my hair and into the scalp. He also thickly vaselined my neck, ears and forehead. "When I get to washing out your head, be sure to tell me anywhere you feel any little stinging," Shorty warned me, washing his hands, then pulling on the rubber gloves, and tying on his own rubber apron. "You always got to remember that any congolene left in burns a sore into your head."

The congolene just felt warm when Shorty started combing it in. But then my head caught fire.

I gritted my teeth and tried to pull the sides of the kitchen table together. The comb felt as if it was raking my skin off.

My eyes watered, my nose was running. I couldn't stand it any longer; I bolted to the washbasin. I was cursing Shorty with every name I could think of when he got the spray going and started soap lathering my head.

He lathered and spray-rinsed, lathered and spray-rinsed, maybe ten or twelve times, each time gradually closing the hot-water faucet, until the rinse was cold, and that helped some.

"You feel any stinging spots?"

"No," I managed to say. My knees were trembling.

"Sit back down, then. I think we got it all out okay."

The flame came back as Shorty, with a thick towel, started drying my head, rubbing hard. *"Easy, man, easy!"* I kept shouting.

"The first time's always worst. You get used to it better before long. You took it real good, homeboy. You got a good conk."

When Shorty let me stand up and see in the mirror, my hair hung down in limp, damp strings. My scalp still flamed, but not as badly; I could bear it. He draped the towel around my shoulders, over my rubber apron, and began again vaselining my hair.

I could feel him combing, straight back, first the big comb, then the fine-tooth one.

Then, he was using a razor, very delicately, on the back of my neck. 19
Then, finally, shaping the sideburns.

My first view in the mirror blotted out the hurting. I'd seen some pretty 20
conks, but when it's the first time, on your *own* head, the transformation,
after the lifetime of kinks, is staggering.

The mirror reflected Shorty behind me. We both were grinning and 21
sweating. And on top of my head was this thick, smooth sheen of shining
red hair—real red—as straight as any white man's.

How ridiculous I was! Stupid enough to stand there simply lost in ad- 22
miration of my hair now looking "white," reflected in the mirror in
Shorty's room. I vowed that I'd never again be without a conk, and I never
was for many years.

This was my first really big step toward self-degradation: when I en- 23
dured all of that pain, literally burning my flesh to have it look like a white
man's hair. I had joined that multitude of Negro men and women in
America who are brainwashed into believing that the black people are
"inferior"—and white people "superior"—that they will even violate and
mutilate their God-created bodies to try to look "pretty" by white standards.

Look around today, in every small town and big city, from two-bit cat- 24
fish and soda-pop joints into the "integrated" lobby of the Waldorf-Astoria,
and you'll see conks on black men. And you'll see black women wearing
these green and pink and purple and red and platinum-blonde wigs.
They're all more ridiculous than a slapstick comedy. It makes you wonder
if the Negro has completely lost his sense of identity, lost touch with
himself.

You'll see the conk worn by many, many so-called "upper class" Ne- 25
groes, and, as much as I hate to say it about them, on all too many Negro
entertainers. One of the reasons that I've especially admired some of them,
like Lionel Hampton and Sidney Poitier, among others, is that they have
kept their natural hair and fought to the top. I admire any Negro man who
has never had himself conked, or who has had the sense to get rid of it—
as I finally did.

I don't know which kind of self-defacing conk is the greater shame— 26
the one you'll see on the heads of the black so-called "middle class" and
"upper class," who ought to know better, or the one you'll see on the heads
of the poorest, most downtrodden, ignorant black men. I mean the legal-
minimum-wage ghetto-dwelling kind of Negro, as I was when I got my
first one. It's generally among these poor fools that you'll see a black kerchief over the man's head, like Aunt Jemima; he's trying to make his conk
last longer, between trips to the barbershop. Only for special occasions is
this kerchief-protected conk exposed—to show off how "sharp" and "hip"
its owner is. The ironic thing is that I have never heard any woman, white
or black, express any admiration for a conk. Of course, any white woman
with a black man isn't thinking about his hair. But I don't see how on earth
a black woman with any race pride could walk down the street with any
black man wearing a conk—the emblem of his shame that he is black.

To my own shame, when I say all of this, I'm talking first of all about 27
myself—because you can't show me any Negro who ever conked more
faithfully than I did. I'm speaking from personal experience when I say of
any black man who conks today, or any white-wigged black woman, that
if they gave the brains in their heads just half as much attention as they do
their hair, they would be a thousand times better off.

Reacting to the Reading

1. In the margins of the essay, number the steps in the process Malcolm X describes.
2. What purpose do paragraphs 22–27 serve? In the margin beside these paragraphs, summarize them in one or two sentences.

Reacting to Words

*1. Define these words: *staggering* (paragraph 20), *vowed* (22), *self-degradation* (23), *multitude* (23), *mutilate* (23), *slapstick* (24), *self-defacing* (26), *downtrodden* (26), *emblem* (26). Can you suggest a synonym for each word that will work in the essay?
2. Exactly what is a conk? Write an objective one-sentence definition that explains what the word means.

Reacting to Ideas

*1. What process is Malcolm X explaining here? What is his motive for explaining this process?
2. Where does Malcolm X mention the pain and discomfort of the process? Why do you think he includes these negative details?
*3. What is Malcolm X's first impression of his finished conk? What does he now think of this reaction?
4. What does Malcolm X mean when he says that a black man with a conk is wearing "the emblem of his shame that he is black" (26)?

Reacting to the Pattern

1. What is the first step in the process? Where in the essay does the process actually end?
2. How can you tell this is a process explanation and not a set of instructions?
3. What materials and equipment are needed for this process? If Malcolm X doesn't expect his readers to perform the process themselves, why does he tell them what items are needed?
4. What cautions does Shorty give Malcolm X? What other cautions do you think should be given to people who are about to conk their hair?

Writing Practice

1. Write an essay explaining a distasteful process that you have experienced. In your essay, try to convince readers that this process should be changed (or eliminated).
2. Write a process essay explaining the daily routine you follow in a job you hold (or held). Include a thesis statement that tells readers how you feel about the job.
3. Write a process essay in which you explain how to perform a particular task at a job — for example, how to keep a potential customer on the phone during a sales call, how to service a piece of equipment, or how to stock shelves in a convenience store.

A **cause-and-effect** essay identifies causes or predicts effects; sometimes, it does both. In "The Poncho Bearer," John Schwartz examines his son's motivation for wearing a poncho every Friday throughout high school. In "The 'Black Table' Is Still There," Lawrence Otis Graham focuses on a troubling social situation at his junior high school.

THE PONCHO BEARER

John Schwartz

A former science writer for the *Washington Post*, John Schwartz now writes about technology for the *New York Times*. In this article, Schwartz reflects on his son's decision to wear a poncho to school every Friday and considers the effects of his son's behavior on his school, his family, and himself. Note how the causes and effects of the poncho-wearing shift as they become accepted by the school and as Schwartz learns more about his son's motives.

1   Sam wears a Mexican poncho to school every Friday.

2   Like a number of things about our middle child, the "why" of it is a mystery. When he started wearing it about two years ago, I guessed that he was perhaps reinterpreting the idea of casual Friday for high school. Or he might have just thought, "I will wear the poncho to school on Friday. See what happens."

3   "Thought" may be too strong a word. The poncho appeared in our home when a boy gave it to our oldest child, Elizabeth. She had no interest in it, but Sammy did. It is brightly colored, or more accurately, blinding. By all rights, he should look stupid. In a weird way, he looks good.

4   As we all know, high school for most teenagers is a time of intense pressure to conform. But at 16, Sam has become something of a quiet joker, a subversive with a smile.

5   Sam has often found ways to stand out in situations where others try to fit in. When we first moved to our little town in New Jersey six years ago, he was entering fifth grade. After watching his new school for a while, he came home one day and told us that there were three kinds of kids: the straight-A kids, the kids who were always in trouble and the class clowns. "I think I have a shot," he said, "at class clown."

6   And so he's always made his own path. He dyed his dark blond hair Corvette red one year, got a buzz cut the next. Always changing, always distinctive, and always with that knowing smile. Then he donned the poncho. And then again. And again. Before long, he was known more as Poncho than Sam in the halls of his school.

7   A couple of his coaches didn't like it; one warned Sam that people would not take him seriously if he continued to wear it. As a compromise during football season, he threw his serape over his jersey, which players are required to wear on game days. Even he seemed to think the combination looked stupid, and ultimately he left the poncho home a couple of days in favor of the team colors.

Sam let us know about the coaches' displeasure—not because he 8
wanted us to intervene, just F.Y.I.

Now, I am not a parent who's going to get upset if my son dresses 9
funny. My parents taught me that lesson in the early 1970s in Galveston,
Tex., when the principal of Ball High School suspended my brother Dick
for having long hair.

My brother thought there was a First Amendment issue at stake, and 10
my dad decided to back him up—literally, to make a federal case of it.
Dick and Dad took the school district to court. It was a risky move; my
father was a state senator, and it was not a popular stand. People called
our home—the number was always listed—and shouted obscenities and
hung up.

We lost the case. And I ended up thinking my father was the kind of 11
guy who would stand up for his children no matter what.

So I never gave Sam any trouble about the poncho. For his part, 12
Sam showed his coaches that he was every bit as serious about sports as
he was silly in his choice of Friday attire. They've seen his determination
when he pushes through the offensive line to take down an opposing quar-
terback. He shows the same drive on the wrestling mat and the lacrosse
field.

With achievement came acceptance. The wrestling team gave out knit 13
caps at the end of the season with the player's name embroidered on the
back. Sam's said "Poncho." At the end of lacrosse season, one of the
coaches gave a speech about all the funny things he had learned that year.
The collection of inside jokes had the players rolling, but the best line was
the last: "I have learned it's O.K. to wear a poncho."

Sammy decided to write an essay for an English class about the 14
poncho. Many mysteries were revealed. He wrote that he started wearing
it because, when he tried it on at home, it made him laugh. He also
acknowledged that it has become something of an obligation.

"Despite the amount of fun I've had with this whole experiment, I do 15
tire of it from time to time. I didn't know what I was getting myself into at
the start, and now it's escalated to the point where if I stop more than half
the school will forget that the weekend is about to come up. I feel obli-
gated. I must fulfill my duty in this strange society of learners to remind
them of the good times ahead, even if they only last a few precious days."

He also included a haiku: 16

A blur of color
I stride as poncho billows
In the strong wind gusts.

The essay concluded with his plan to pass his poncho along "to a pre- 17
determined underclassman who upholds all of the standards necessary to
become the next Poncho Bearer" and who will "Remember that the Poncho Bearer does not own the Poncho, but is merely holding onto it and taking care of it for future generations."

O.K., he seems to have cribbed that from the Patek Philippe ads, But 18
it still brought a lump to my throat. The process of finding yourself only
starts in high school; it goes on through the college years.

Defining yourself is the central question of adolescence. We ask, 19
Am I a jock or a geek? A joker or a hippie? Am I smart? Good looking?
Am I enough like everyone else? Am I distinctive? We are pulled in every
direction. Sam has asked the question and, I think, begun to answer
it well.

And so I have felt pretty good about my own light touch as a parent. 20
That good feeling lasted about a week, until I got an instant message from
my daughter at college:
I got a tattoo today. 21

Reacting to the Reading

1. Underline some of Sam's own words, which his father quotes from
   conversation and from Sam's essay (paragraphs 15–17). What do these
   words tell you about Sam?
2. In paragraphs 9–11, Schwartz discusses his brother Dick. In a marginal note, explain the connection between these paragraphs and the
   rest of the essay. What effect did Dick's experience have on Schwartz?

Reacting to Words

*1. Define these words: *poncho* (title), *reinterpreting* (2), *subversive* (4),
   serape (7), *intervene* (8), *escalated* (15), *predetermined* (17). Can you
   suggest a synonym for each word that will work in the essay?
2. A **haiku** is a three-line poem with seventeen syllables. Because it is so
   short and focuses on a single image, each word must be very carefully
   chosen. Read Sam's haiku in paragraph 16, and try to suggest alternatives for some of his words.

Reacting to Ideas

*1. In paragraph 2, Schwartz says he wants to know why his son Sam
   started wearing a poncho to school; he says, "the 'why' of it is a mystery." Do you understand "the 'why' of it"?
2. What details about Sam's background and family life might help to
   explain his decision to wear the poncho?
3. In paragraph 19, Schwartz says that Sam has "asked the question" and
   "begun to answer it well." What does he mean? Do you think he is right
   about Sam?

Reacting to the Pattern

1. List the reasons Sam gives for wearing the poncho. Then, list the reasons Schwartz suggests. Which reason do you think is most likely?
*2. What effects does Sam's decision to wear the poncho have on his par-
   ents? On his classmates and teammates? On Sam himself?
3. Is this essay's emphasis on causes, on effects, or on both causes and
   effects? Explain.

Writing Practice

1. Assume you are Schwartz's son Sam, now a college student. Write a
   cause-and-effect essay for your composition class in which you explain
   your motives for wearing the poncho in high school.
2. Assume you are the "Poncho Bearer" to whom Sam has entrusted his
   poncho. Write a speech for your fellow high school students in which
   you accept this honor and explain how it will affect you.

3. As this essay acknowledges, the high school years can be a difficult time, and fitting in is not always easy. Write an essay in which you explain what can cause young teenagers to feel out of place and what the possible effects—both positive and negative—of this situation can be. Conclude your essay with some recommendations for helping high school students feel that they belong.

THE "BLACK TABLE" IS STILL THERE

Lawrence Otis Graham

A corporate lawyer and best-selling author, Lawrence Otis Graham is best known for "Invisible Man," an article he wrote about the racism he encountered while working as a busboy at an exclusive country club during a leave from his job as a lawyer. In the following essay, Graham reflects on the "black table," a situation that has continued in the school cafeteria since his junior high days. As you read, note how his conclusions about what motivates people to sit where they sit have changed over the years.

1   During a recent visit to my old junior high school in Westchester County, I came upon something that I never expected to see again, something that was a source of fear and dread for three hours each school morning of my early adolescence: the all-black lunch table in the cafeteria of my predominantly white suburban junior high school.

2   As I look back on 27 years of often being the first and only black person integrating such activities and institutions as the college newspaper, the high school tennis team, summer music camps, our all-white suburban neighborhood, my eating club at Princeton or my private social club at Harvard Law School, the one scenario that puzzled me the most then and now is the all-black lunch table.

3   Why was it there? Why did the black kids separate themselves? What did the table say about the integration that was supposedly going on in home rooms and gym classes? What did it say about the black kids? The white kids? What did it say about me when I refused to sit there, day after day, for three years?

4   Each afternoon, at 12:03 p.m., after the fourth period ended, I found myself among 600 12-, 13- and 14-year-olds who marched into the brightly lit cafeteria and dashed for a seat at one of the 27 blue formica lunch tables.

5   No matter who I walked in with—usually a white friend—no matter what mood I was in, there was one thing that was certain: I would not sit at the black table.

6   I would never consider sitting at the black table.

7   What was wrong with me? What was I afraid of?

8   I would like to think that my decision was a heroic one, made in order to express my solidarity with the theories of integration that my community was espousing. But I was just 12 at the time, and there was nothing heroic in my actions.

9   I avoided the black table for a very simple reason: I was afraid that by sitting at the black table I'd lose all my white friends. I thought that by sitting there I'd be making a racist, anti-white statement.

Is that what the all-black table means? Is it a rejection of white people? I no longer think so. 10

At the time, I was angry that there was a black lunch table. I believed 11 that the black kids were the reason why other kids didn't mix more. I was ready to believe that their self-segregation was the cause of white bigotry.

Ironically, I even believed this after my best friend (who was white) 12 told me I probably shouldn't come to his bar mitzvah because I'd be the only black and people would feel uncomfortable. I even believed this after my Saturday afternoon visit, at age 10, to a private country club pool prompted incensed white parents to pull their kids from the pool in terror.

In the face of this blatantly racist (anti-black) behavior, I still somehow 13 managed to blame only the black kids for being the barrier to integration in my school and my little world. What was I thinking?

I realize now how wrong I was. During that same time, there were at 14 least two tables of athletes, an Italian table, a Jewish girls' table, a Jewish boys' table (where I usually sat), a table of kids who were into heavy metal music and smoking pot, a table of middle class Irish kids. Weren't these tables just as segregationist as the black table? At the time, no one thought so. At the time, no one even acknowledged the segregated nature of these other tables.

Maybe it's the color difference that makes all-black tables or all-black 15 groups attract the scrutiny and wrath of so many people. It scares and angers people; it exasperates. It did those things to me, and I'm black.

As an integrating black person, I know that my decision *not* to join the 16 black lunch table attracted its own kind of scrutiny and wrath from my classmates. At the same time that I heard angry words like "Oreo" and "white boy" being hurled at me from the black table, I was also dodging impatient questions from white classmates: "Why do all those black kids sit together?" or "Why don't you ever sit with the other blacks?"

The black lunch table, like those other segregated tables, is a com- 17 ment on the superficial inroads that integration has made in society. Perhaps I should be happy that even this is a long way from where we started. Yet, I can't get over the fact that the 27th table in my junior high school cafeteria is still known as the "black table"—14 years after my adolescence.

Reacting to the Reading

1. Underline what you consider the three or four most important points Graham makes.
2. Graham asks a number of questions in this essay—for example, in paragraph 3 and in paragraph 7. In marginal annotations, answer two or three of these questions.

Reacting to Words

*1. Define these words: *scenario* (paragraph 2), *espousing* (8), *bar mitzvah* (12), *incensed* (12), *blatantly* (13), *scrutiny* (15), *wrath* (15), *inroads* (17). Can you suggest a synonym for each word that will work in the essay?

2. What images does the phrase *black table* bring to mind? Does it have positive or negative connotations to you? Can you think of another term Graham might use to identify the "black table"?

Reacting to Ideas

*1. Why didn't Graham sit at the black table? Do you understand the forces that motivated him? Do you think he should have sat with the other African-American students?

2. When he was in junior high school, who did Graham think was at fault for the existence of the black table? Who does he now think was at fault? Do you agree with him?

*3. In paragraph 14, Graham considers other lunch tables and asks, "Weren't these tables just as segregationist as the black table?" Answer his question.

Reacting to the Pattern

1. Is Graham's essay primarily about causes or about effects? Explain your answer.

*2. Graham focuses largely on his own experiences and actions. Where, if anywhere, does he consider other forces that could have created segregated lunch tables? Do you think he should have considered other causes? For example, should he have discussed the school administration's role? Housing patterns in his community? Explain your position.

Writing Practice

1. Try to recall the lunch tables in the cafeteria of your own junior high school or middle school. Were they segregated as they were in Graham's school? What factors do you believe led students to sit where they did? Write a cause-and-effect essay that discusses the possible causes of the seating patterns you remember.

2. What do you see as the *effects* of segregated lunch tables? Do you think they are necessarily a bad thing, or do they have advantages? Write a cause-and-effect essay that explores the possible results of such seating patterns.

3. What forms of self-segregation (by race, gender, class, and so on) do you observe in your school, workplace, or community? In an essay, discuss both causes and effects.

F   Comparison and Contrast

A **comparison-and-contrast** essay explains how two things are alike or how they are different; sometimes, it discusses both similarities and differences. In "Resisting My Family History," Indira Ganesan compares her life in India to her life in the United States. In "Men Are from Mars, Women Are from Venus," John Gray compares men and women.

RESISTING MY FAMILY HISTORY

Indira Ganesan

At the age of five, Indira Ganesan emigrated with her family from India to the United States. Now a professor at Long Island University, Ganesan has written two novels about the challenges of being both Indian and American—*The Journey* (1990) and *Inheritance* (1998). The following essay, "Resisting My Family History," describes her visit to India after graduating from high school and compares her life in America with the experiences she has with her relatives in India.

In June 1978, in suburban Nanuet, New York, home to a famous mall, I 1
wore a sari to my high school graduation. The next day it was raining, and my family and I set off for India. Watch out for the cows, wrote my favorite English teacher, tongue-in-cheek, in my yearbook. I'd keep a wary eye out, I thought, packing a dozen cassettes on which I'd recorded my favorite music. My friends stood in the rain with a banner proclaiming "Goodbye, Indira!" I was a heroine, a star for the moment. I was leaving the country.

Though I'd been born there, I didn't want to go to India. What I wanted 2
was to knock on a Broadway producer's door and say, "I'm brown, I'm talented, let me write you a play." My parents, however, believed I needed to embrace my Indian past. I wanted only to escape it, as I wanted to escape anything that spoke to me of tradition or old-fashioned ideas. I was too cool for India, too smart.

I remember the heat in Bombay's airport, so thick it was sliceable; the 3
crush of people who wanted to help or state an opinion after our car developed engine trouble on our way home; the glare of the outdoors; the cool dark of the interiors. My uncle's family welcomed my mother and me into their home in Madras, a city on the southeastern part of the subcontinent, famed for its music festivals and its beach. In Madras I enrolled in a Catholic women's college. Nuns were the teachers, the English language was the norm.

In high school I had edited an underground newspaper, bought my 4
first copy of the *Village Voice*, read the *New York Times* regularly. I believed I was a feminist. In India I was unsure of my role. Above all, I was deeply worried that I'd be married off, that I'd be forced to become a housewife, horror of horrors, and would lose my freedom.

What I discovered in India: people who looked like me. Girls who be- 5
friended me instantly. Girls who told me the truth at once. I was an American, and how everyone knew that—for they all did—escaped me. Wasn't I as brown as they? Or was I giving off an American aura, wearing Wrangler jeans and a T-shirt, speaking hesitant Tamil?

I attended a wedding. I watched some of the funeral preparations fol- 6
lowing the death of my great-uncle. I climbed 500 steps to reach a Jain temple where a priest gave me a blessing that translated roughly as "You will have seven years of good luck followed by seven years more of the same." During a ten-day tour of famous temples, I saw a snake charmer in a parking lot and visited an entire city of priests and ascetics. They let us into a temple's sanctum sanctorum, where we saw the God image in all its splendor. On the day that I returned to my uncle's, I announced to my

grandmother that I was going to become a *sannyasi,* a holy woman. I was 17; my grandmother just laughed.

In India I had the unswerving consideration of my relatives, 25 of whom I met in my first six months. I remember our meals together, and the preparations: the pile of freshly shredded coconut—white, flaky, fragrant with milk; the way sweet dough for *jellabies* would be dropped in hot oil and bob up to perfection. In America I picked at pizza and baked ziti on the school lunch menu; in India I feasted. There were scores of delicious meals, piles of snacks in tins, water always available in an earthen vessel in the kitchen.

And still I felt I was missing out on a superlative year in America, and I was determined to dislike India. I dragged my aunt to see a Woody Allen movie and felt it superior to Indian films, even though they managed to reduce me to tears.

In all of this, I, the *yanqui,* was a source of amusement to the family. They bent over backward to please me that year, and I finally admitted to enjoying myself. I can still recall the din of the streets as I rushed to college in the mornings—bicycles, rickshaws, buses, pedestrians, bikes and yes, even a bull here and there.

Upon arrival at school, we lined up for assembly and the college president led the prayers as hundreds of girls listened, long, sleek braids shining with oil. As a fine arts major, I learned from Sister Mary Ann about Buddhist art and how to apply lapis lazuli. We practiced calligraphy with Sister Bernard, a nun in her nineties who wrote "God Is Great" with a beautiful, firm hand. I remember the broad, wooden desks, the way the crows would gather on the windowsills. Goats ambled through the nearby flower gardens.

Now a teacher myself in San Diego, I have just come back from giving a class on "the travel essay." One of my students suggested that the writer we were studying had formed her opinion of the country she was visiting before traveling there. In a sense, I thought, that is what I did with my year in India. I knew before going that I would like the temples and the food and the embrace of my relatives; I just didn't think it was a place for me, a newly graduated high school senior who dreamed of travel. How wrong I was. It was my year abroad, a high-seas adventure from which I would draw for years to come. In India I took my dreams of becoming a someone and began to be a someone. A someone connected to a history, to a family, to a distinct geography. A someone who had traveled after all.

Reacting to the Reading

1. Identify three points of contrast between India and the United States that Ganesan points out. Draw arrows to link these contrasts, connecting each point about life in India to a matching point about life in the United States.
2. In the margins of the essay, label the content of each paragraph "Life in India," "Life in the U.S.," or "India vs. U.S."

Reacting to Words

*1. Define these words: *sari* (paragraph 1), *aura* (5), *ascetics* (6), *sanctum sanctorum* (6), *unswerving* (7), *din* (9), *rickshaws* (9), *lapis lazuli* (10), *calligraphy* (10). Can you suggest a synonym for each word that will work in the essay?

2. Ganesan uses a few words in Tamil (the language spoken in Madras, India) in her essay. Why does she use these words? Does she define them? Do you think she should have used more?

Reacting to Ideas

1. According to Ganesan, what are the major differences between her life in the United States and her life in India?
*2. Which country do you think Ganesan considers her home? Why?
3. In paragraph 2, Ganesan says, "I was too cool for India, too smart." What does she mean? Does she change her mind after her year in India? How does India change her?

Reacting to the Pattern

1. Is this a point-by-point or a subject-by-subject comparison? Explain.
*2. This essay contrasts Indian and American life, but the writer includes much more information about India than about the United States. Why do you think she does this?
*3. What specific points does Ganesan make about India that she does not make about the United States? Can you supply the missing information?
4. Ganesan begins her essay with a discussion of her high school graduation. Why do you think she mentions that she wore a sari to her graduation?

Writing Practice

1. Write an essay in which you contrast two "worlds" of your own—for example, your home life and your school life, your life in your native country and your life in the United States, or your childhood and your adulthood.
2. Write an essay in which you contrast the food, the dress, or another aspect of two different cultures or geographical regions.
3. Write an article for the travel section of a newspaper about a trip you took. Structure your article as a comparison-and-contrast essay, comparing the place you visited with the place in which you and your readers live.

MEN ARE FROM MARS, WOMEN ARE FROM VENUS

John Gray

Marriage counselor, seminar leader, and author John Gray has written a number of books that examine relationships between men and women. His best-known book, *Men Are from Mars, Women Are from Venus* (1992), suggests that men and women are at times so different that they might as well come from different planets. In the following excerpt from this book, Gray contrasts the different communication styles that he believes are characteristic of men and women. As you read, consider whether Gray's comparison oversimplifies the gender differences he discusses.

The most frequently expressed complaint women have about men is that 1
men don't listen. Either a man completely ignores [a woman] when she
speaks to him, or he listens for a few beats, assesses what is bothering her,
and then proudly puts on his Mr. Fix-It cap and offers her a solution to
make her feel better. He is confused when she doesn't appreciate this ges-
ture of love. No matter how many times she tells him that he's not listening, he doesn't get it and keeps doing the same thing. She wants empathy,
but he thinks she wants solutions.

The most frequently expressed complaint men have about women is 2
that women are always trying to change them. When a woman loves a man
she feels responsible to assist him in growing and tries to help him improve the way he does things. She forms a home-improvement committee,
and he becomes her primary focus. No matter how much he resists her
help, she persists—waiting for any opportunity to help him or tell him
what to do. She thinks she's nurturing him, while he feels he's being con-
trolled. Instead, he wants her acceptance.

These two problems can finally be solved by first understanding why 3
men offer solutions and why women seek to improve. Let's pretend to go
back in time, where by observing life on Mars and Venus—before the
planets discovered one another or came to Earth—we can gain some insights into men and women.

Martians value power, competency, efficiency, and achievement. They 4
are always doing things to prove themselves and develop their power
and skills. Their sense of self is defined through their ability to achieve results. They experience fulfillment primarily through success and accomplishment.

Everything on Mars is a reflection of these values. Even their dress is 5
designed to reflect their skills and competence. Police officers, soldiers,
businessmen, scientists, cab drivers, technicians, and chefs all wear uniforms or at least hats to reflect their competence and power.

They don't read magazines like *Psychology Today*, *Self*, or *People*. They 6
are more concerned with outdoor activities, like hunting, fishing, and racing cars. They are interested in the news, weather, and sports and couldn't
care less about romance novels and self-help books.

They are more interested in "objects" and "things" rather than people 7
and feelings. Even today on Earth, while women fantasize about romance,
men fantasize about powerful cars, faster computers, gadgets, gizmos, and
new more powerful technology. Men are preoccupied with the "things" that
can help them express power by creating results and achieving their goals.

Achieving goals is very important to a Martian because it is a way for 8
him to prove his competence and thus feel good about himself. And for
him to feel good about himself he must achieve these goals by himself.
Someone else can't achieve them for him. Martians pride themselves in
doing things all by themselves. Autonomy is a symbol of efficiency, power,
and competence.

Understanding this Martian characteristic can help women under- 9
stand why men resist so much being corrected or being told what to do. To
offer a man unsolicited advice is to presume that he doesn't know what to
do or that he can't do it on his own. Men are very touchy about this, because the issue of competence is so very important to them.

Because he is handling his problems on his own, a Martian rarely talks 10
about his problems unless he needs expert advice. He reasons: "Why involve someone else when I can do it by myself?" He keeps his problems to

himself unless he requires help from another to find a solution. Asking for help when you can do it yourself is perceived as a sign of weakness.

However, if he truly does need help, then it is a sign of wisdom to get 11 it. In this case, he will find someone he respects and then talk about his problem. Talking about a problem on Mars is an invitation for advice. Another Martian feels honored by the opportunity. Automatically he puts on his Mr. Fix-It hat, listens for a while, and then offers some jewels of advice.

This Martian custom is one of the reasons men instinctively offer 12 solutions when women talk about problems. When a woman innocently shares upset feelings or explores out loud the problems of her day, a man mistakenly assumes she is looking for some expert advice. He puts on his Mr. Fix-It hat and begins giving advice; this is his way of showing love and of trying to help.

He wants to help her feel better by solving her problems. He wants to 13 be useful to her. He feels he can be valued and thus worthy of her love when his abilities are used to solve her problems.

Once he has offered a solution, however, and she continues to be upset 14 it becomes increasingly difficult for him to listen because his solution is being rejected and he feels increasingly useless.

He has no idea that by just listening with empathy and interest he can 15 be supportive. He does not know that on Venus talking about problems is not an invitation to offer a solution.

Venusians have different values. They value love, communication, 16 beauty, and relationships. They spend a lot of time supporting, helping, and nurturing one another. Their sense of self is defined through their feelings and the quality of their relationships. They experience fulfillment through sharing and relating.

Everything on Venus reflects these values. Rather than building highways and tall buildings, the Venusians are more concerned with living together in harmony, community, and loving cooperation. Relationships are more important than work and technology. In most ways their world is the opposite of Mars.

They do not wear uniforms like the Martians (to reveal their competence). On the contrary, they enjoy wearing a different outfit every day, according to how they are feeling. Personal expression, especially of their feelings, is very important. They may even change outfits several times a day as their mood changes.

Communication is of primary importance. To share their personal feelings is much more important than achieving goals and success. Talking and relating to one another is a source of tremendous fulfillment.

This is hard for a man to comprehend. He can come close to understanding a woman's experience of sharing and relating by comparing it to the satisfaction he feels when he wins a race, achieves a goal, or solves a problem.

Instead of being goal oriented, women are relationship oriented; they 21 are more concerned with expressing their goodness, love, and caring. Two Martians go to lunch to discuss a project or business goal; they have a problem to solve. In addition, Martians view going to a restaurant as an efficient way to approach food: no shopping, no cooking, and no washing dishes. For Venusians, going to lunch is an opportunity to nurture a relationship, for both giving support to and receiving support from a friend. Women's restaurant talk can be very open and intimate, almost like the dialogue that occurs between therapist and patient.

On Venus, everyone studies psychology and has at least a master's degree in counseling. They are very involved in personal growth, spirituality, and everything that can nurture life, healing, and growth. Venus is covered with parks, organic gardens, shopping centers, and restaurants. 22

Venusians are very intuitive. They have developed this ability through centuries of anticipating the needs of others. They pride themselves in being considerate of the needs and feelings of others. A sign of great love is to offer help and assistance to another Venusian without being asked. 23

Because proving one's competence is not as important to a Venusian, offering help is not offensive, and needing help is not a sign of weakness. A man, however, may feel offended because when a woman offers advice he doesn't feel she trusts his ability to do it himself. 24

A woman has no conception of this male sensitivity because for her it is another feather in her hat if someone offers to help her. It makes her feel loved and cherished. But offering help to a man can make him feel incompetent, weak, and even unloved. 25

On Venus it is a sign of caring to give advice and suggestions. Venusians firmly believe that when something is working it can always work better. Their nature is to want to improve things. When they care about someone, they freely point out what can be improved and suggest how to do it. Offering advice and constructive criticism is an act of love. 26

Mars is very different. Martians are more solution oriented. If something is working, their motto is don't change it. Their instinct is to leave it alone if it is working. "Don't fix it unless it is broken" is a common expression. 27

When a woman tries to improve a man, he feels she is trying to fix him. He receives the message that he is broken. She doesn't realize her caring attempts to help him may humiliate him. She mistakenly thinks she is just helping him to grow. 28

Reacting to the Reading

1. In marginal annotations, number the specific characteristics of men and women that Gray identifies.
2. Using these characteristics as a guide, make an informal outline for a point-by-point comparison.

Reacting to Words

*1. Define these words: *empathy* (paragraph 1), *nurturing* (2), *autonomy* (8), *unsolicited* (9). Can you suggest a synonym for each word that will work in the essay?
2. Do you think referring to men as Martians and women as Venusians is an effective strategy? What other contrasting labels might work?

Reacting to Ideas

1. Do you think Gray is serious? Why or why not?
*2. Do you think Gray's specific observations about men and women are accurate? Is he stereotyping men and women? Explain.
*3. Do you agree with Gray's general point that men and women seem to be from two different planets? Why or why not?

Reacting to the Pattern

1. This essay is a subject-by-subject comparison. How does Gray signal the movement from the first subject to the second subject? Why do you suppose he chose to write a subject-by-subject rather than a point-by-point comparison?

*2. If you were going to add a more fully developed conclusion to sum up this selection's points, what closing strategy would you use? Do you think the selection needs such a conclusion?

Writing Practice

1. Are young (or adolescent) boys and girls also from two different planets? Take a position on this issue, and support it in a subject-by-subject comparison. In your thesis statement, try to account for the differences you identify between boys and girls.

2. Identify one general area in which you believe men's and women's attitudes, behavior, or expectations are very different—for example, dating, careers, eating habits, sports, housekeeping, or driving. Write a comparison-and-contrast essay (serious or humorous) that explores the differences you identify.

3. Are men and women portrayed differently in television dramas or sitcoms? Choose a program that has several well-developed male and female characters, and contrast the men and the women in terms of their actions and their conversations.

G Classification

A **classification** essay divides a whole into parts and sorts various items into categories. Jo-Ellan Dimitrius and Mark Mazzarella's "Liars" considers four different kinds of liars. Scott Russell Sanders's "The Men We Carry in Our Minds" classifies the working men he has known.

LIARS

Jo-Ellan Dimitrius and Mark Mazzarella

Los Angeles lawyer Jo-Ellan Dimitrius is a jury consultant who worked on some of the best-known criminal trials of the 1980s and 1990s, including the Rodney King and O. J. Simpson cases. Dimitrius has worked in civil and criminal trials to assist lawyers in selecting juries and evaluating witnesses by predicting human behavior. Mark Mazzarella is a practicing trial lawyer in San Diego, California, who writes about the formation and management of impressions in juries. He and Dimitrius have cowritten *Reading People* (1998) and *Put Your Best Foot Forward* (2000). In this essay, Dimitrius and Mazzarella classify liars; as you read, think about how their classification of liars could be useful beyond the courtroom.

If people were all honest with one another, reading them would be a lot easier. The problem is that people lie. I'm not talking about those who are wrong but sincerely believe they are correct, or about the delusional few who genuinely can't tell fact from fantasy. Rather, I'm referring to the one characteristic that is probably the most important in any relationship: truthfulness. And if we assume it's there when it's not—watch out!

Much of the information we gather about someone comes directly from the horse's mouth. If he is lying, the information is wrong, and we're likely to misjudge him. That's why it's so crucial to identify liars as soon as possible, and, if you have reason to doubt a person's honesty, to continue to test it until you're entirely at ease with your conclusion.

I have found that most liars fall into one of four basic categories: the occasional liar, the frequent liar, the habitual liar, and the professional liar.

The Occasional Liar

The occasional liar, like most of us, will lie now and then to avoid an unpleasant situation or because he doesn't want to admit doing something wrong or embarrassing. Also like most of us, he does not like to lie and feels very uncomfortable when he does. Because he's uncomfortable, he'll usually reveal his lie through his appearance, body language, and voice. The stress lying causes him will leak out through such things as poor eye contact, fidgeting, or a change in the tone, volume, or patterns of his speech.

The occasional liar often gives his lie some thought, so it may be logical and consistent with the rest of his story. Because it's well thought out, you probably won't be able to spot the lie by its content or context, or by information from third-party sources. In fact, the occasional liar will seldom lie about something that could be easily verified. Consequently, when dealing with an occasional liar, you need to focus on the various visual and oral clues he exhibits.

The Frequent Liar

The frequent liar recognizes what she's doing but doesn't mind it as much as the occasional liar does, so she lies more regularly. Practice makes perfect: the frequent liar is much less likely to reveal her lie through her appearance, body language, and voice. Also, since it doesn't bother her as much to lie, the typical stress-related symptoms won't be as obvious. Any clues in her appearance, voice, and body language might be rather subtle. Often a better way to detect a frequent liar is to focus on the internal consistency and logic of her statements. Since the frequent liar lies more often, and tends to think her lies through less carefully than the occasional liar, she can get sloppy.

The Habitual Liar

The habitual liar lies so frequently that he has lost sight of what he is doing much of the time. In most cases, if he actually thought about it, he would realize he was lying. But he doesn't much care whether what he's saying is true or false. He simply says whatever comes to mind. Because he doesn't care that he's lying, the habitual liar will give very few, if any, physical or vocal clues that he's being dishonest. But because he gives so little thought to his lies and they come so thick and fast, the habitual liar doesn't bother to keep track of them. As a result they are often inconsistent and obvious.

So while it's hard to detect the physical and vocal clues in a habitual liar, it's easier to spot his inconsistencies. Listen carefully and ask yourself whether the liar is contradicting himself and whether what he's saying makes sense. Asking a third party about the liar's stories will also help you confirm your suspicions.

The habitual liar is fairly uncommon, so most of us are temporarily 8 taken in when we encounter one. An acquaintance of mine told me she worked with a woman for several months before her suspicions that the co-worker was a habitual liar were confirmed by an obvious and quite ridiculous lie. The liar, a brown-eyed brunette, came to work one day sporting blue contact lenses of an almost alien hue. When my friend commented on her lenses, the liar said, "These aren't contacts. They're my real eye color. It's just that I've always worn brown contact lenses before."

More than once, a client has told me that his adversary lies all the time 9 and will undoubtedly lie on the witness stand. I counsel my client not to worry: the habitual liar is the easiest target in a lawsuit. In real life, she can run from one person to another, from one situation to the next, lying as she goes, and no one compares notes. There are no court reporters or transcripts of testimony; no one reveals what every witness has said to every other witness, and nobody pores over everything the liar has written on the subject to see whether it's all consistent. But in litigation, that is exactly what happens—and suddenly the habitual liar is exposed. It's very rewarding to see.

The Professional Liar

The professional liar is the hardest to identify. He doesn't lie indiscrimi- 10 nately, like the habitual liar. He lies for a purpose. For example, a mechanic who routinely cons motorists about their "faulty" transmissions will have his diagnosis carefully prepared. A real estate salesman who doesn't want to acknowledge a leaky roof will respond quickly to an inquiry about the stains on the ceiling with a rehearsed, very spontaneous sounding statement: "That was old damage from a water leak in the attic. All it needs is a little touch-up paint."

The professional liar has thought the lie through and knows exactly 11 what he's going to say, how it will fly, and whether the customer can easily verify it. Such a well-practiced lie will not be revealed by the liar's voice, body language, or appearance. The lie will be consistent, both internally and logically. The only sure way to detect it is to check the liar's statements against entirely independent sources. Have the roof inspected. Get a second opinion from another mechanic. Take nothing for granted.

Before you make a definitive call about someone who is truly impor- 12 tant to you, always ask yourself whether the information you have about him is reliable. Is he being truthful? If your goal is to accurately evaluate someone, you can't afford to skip this step.

Reacting to the Reading

1. Circle the names of the four categories of liar the essay identifies.
2. In the margins of the essay, write a one-sentence definition of each of the four categories. Be sure to use your own words for the definitions.

Reacting to Words

*1. Define these words: *delusional* (paragraph 1), *crucial* (2), *context* (5), *verified* (5), *adversary* (9), *pores* (9), *litigation* (9). Can you suggest a synonym for each word that will work in the essay?

2. When referring to the different types of liars, the writers alternate the pronouns *he* and *she*. Why do you think they do this? Do you find this usage confusing? What other alternatives do they have?

Reacting to Ideas

1. According to the authors, why is it important to identify liars?

*2. Which kind of liar do you see as most dangerous? Why?

*3. Do you think a lie is ever acceptable? Explain.

Reacting to the Pattern

1. What determines the order in which the four kinds of liars are presented? Does this arrangement make sense to you?

2. The writers devote considerably more space to the "habitual liar" and the "professional liar" than to the other two kinds. What material do they include for these two categories and not for the other two? Why do you think they do this?

Writing Practice

1. Write an essay about the different kinds of lies told by "occasional liars." Be sure to include at least three different categories.

2. Using "Liars" as a model, write a classification essay that discusses three or four categories of cheaters. Give each category a name.

3. Write a classification essay about different kinds of heroes. In setting up your categories, consider what motivates people to perform heroic acts.

THE MEN WE CARRY IN OUR MINDS

Scott Russell Sanders

Scott Russell Sanders is a professor of English and an essayist. His essays are personal reflections that include social commentary and philosophical reflection and are often set in the Midwest, where he was born and raised. In "The Men We Carry in Our Minds," Sanders reflects on the working lives of the men he knew when he was a boy and classifies them according to the kind of work they do. His essay discusses not only his boyhood impressions of the work these men did but also the direction his own professional life has taken. As you read, notice how Sanders moves from classifying men's work to comparing men's lives to women's lives.

The first men, besides my father, I remember seeing were black convicts   1
and white guards, in the cottonfield across the road from our farm on the outskirts of Memphis. I must have been three or four. The prisoners wore dingy gray-and-black zebra suits, heavy as canvas, sodden with sweat.

Hatless, stooped, they chopped weeds in the fierce heat, row after row, breathing the acrid dust of boll-weevil poison. The overseers wore dazzling white shirts and broad shadowy hats. The oiled barrels of their shotguns flashed in the sunlight. Their faces in memory are utterly blank. Of course those men, white and black, have become for me an emblem of racial hatred. But they have also come to stand for the twin poles of my early vision of manhood—the brute toiling animal and the boss.

When I was a boy, the men I knew labored with their bodies. They were marginal farmers, just scraping by, or welders, steelworkers, carpenters; they swept floors, dug ditches, mined coal, or drove trucks, their forearms ropy with muscle; they trained horses, stoked furnaces, built tires, stood on assembly lines wrestling parts onto cars and refrigerators. They got up before light, worked all day long whatever the weather, and when they came home at night they looked as though somebody had been whipping them. In the evenings and on weekends they worked on their own places, tilling gardens that were lumpy with clay, fixing broken-down cars, hammering on houses that were always too drafty, too leaky, too small.

The bodies of the men I knew were twisted and maimed in ways visible and invisible. The nails of their hands were black and split, the hands tattooed with scars. Some had lost fingers. Heavy lifting had given many of them finicky backs and guts weak from hernias. Racing against conveyor belts had given them ulcers. Their ankles and knees ached from years of standing on concrete. Anyone who had worked for long around machines was hard of hearing. They squinted, and the skin of their faces was creased like the leather of old work gloves. There were times, studying them, when I dreaded growing up. Most of them coughed, from dust or cigarettes, and most of them drank cheap wine or whiskey, so their eyes looked bloodshot and bruised. The fathers of my friends always seemed older than the mothers. Men wore out sooner. Only women lived into old age.

As a boy I also knew another sort of men, who did not sweat and break down like mules. They were soldiers, and so far as I could tell they scarcely worked at all. During my early school years we lived on a military base, an arsenal in Ohio, and every day I saw GIs in the guardshacks, on the stoops of barracks, at the wheels of olive drab Chevrolets. The chief fact of their lives was boredom. Long after I left the Arsenal I came to recognize the sour smell the soldiers gave off as that of souls in limbo. They were all waiting—for wars, for transfers, for leaves, for promotions, for the end of their hitch—like so many braves waiting for the hunt to begin. Unlike the warriors of older tribes, however, they would have no say about when the battle would start or how it would be waged. Their waiting was broken only when they practiced for war. They fired guns at targets, drove tanks across the churned-up fields of the military reservation, set off bombs in the wrecks of old fighter planes. I knew this was all play. But I also felt certain that when the hour for killing arrived, they would kill. When the real shooting started, many of them would die. This was what soldiers were *for*, just as a hammer was for driving nails.

Warriors and toilers: those seemed, in my boyhood vision, to be the chief destinies for men. They weren't the only destinies, as I learned from having a few male teachers, from reading books, and from watching television. But the men on television—the politicians, the astronauts, the generals, the savvy lawyers, the philosophical doctors, the bosses who gave orders to both soldiers and laborers—seemed as removed and unreal to me as the figures in tapestries. I could no more imagine growing up to become one of these cool, potent creatures than I could imagine becoming a prince.

A nearer and more hopeful example was that of my father, who had [6] escaped from a red-dirt farm to a tire factory, and from the assembly line to the front office. Eventually he dressed in a white shirt and tie. He carried himself as if he had been born to work with his mind. But his body, remembering the earlier years of slogging work, began to give out on him in his fifties, and it quit on him entirely before he turned sixty-five. Even such a partial escape from man's fate as he had accomplished did not seem possible for most of the boys I knew. They joined the Army, stood in line for jobs in the smoky plants, helped build highways. They were bound to work as their fathers had worked, killing themselves or preparing to kill others.

A scholarship enabled me not only to attend college, a rare enough feat [7] in my circle, but even to study in a university meant for the children of the rich. Here I met for the first time young men who had assumed from birth that they would lead lives of comfort and power. And for the first time I met women who told me that men were guilty of having kept all the joys and privileges of the earth for themselves. I was baffled. What privileges? What joys? I thought about the maimed, dismal lives of most of the men back home. What had they stolen from their wives and daughters? The right to go five days a week, twelve months a year, for thirty or forty years to a steel mill or a coal mine? The right to drop bombs and die in war? The right to feel every leak in the roof, every gap in the fence, every cough in the engine, as a wound they must mend? The right to feel, when the layoff comes or the plant shuts down, not only afraid but ashamed?

I was slow to understand the deep grievances of women. This was [8] because, as a boy, I had envied them. Before college, the only people I had ever known who were interested in art or music or literature, the only ones who read books, the only ones who ever seemed to enjoy a sense of ease and grace were the mothers and daughters. Like the menfolk, they fretted about money, they scrimped and made-do. But, when the pay stopped coming in, they were not the ones who had failed. Nor did they have to go to war, and that seemed to me a blessed fact. By comparison with the narrow, ironclad days of fathers, there was an expansiveness, I thought, in the days of mothers. They went to see neighbors, to shop in town, to run errands at school, at the library, at church. No doubt, had I looked harder at their lives, I would have envied them less. It was not my fate to become a woman, so it was easier for me to see the graces. Few of them held jobs outside the home, and those who did filled thankless roles as clerks and waitresses. I didn't see, then, what a prison a house could be, since houses seemed to me brighter, handsomer places than any factory. I did not realize—because such things were never spoken of—how often women suffered from men's bullying. I did learn about the wretchedness of abandoned wives, single mothers, widows; but I also learned about the wretchedness of lone men. Even then I could see how exhausting it was for a mother to cater all day to the needs of young children. But if I had been asked, as a boy, to choose between tending a baby and tending a machine, I think I would have chosen the baby. (Having now tended both, I know I would choose the baby.)

So I was baffled when the women at college accused me and my sex [9] of having cornered the world's pleasures. I think something like my bafflement has been felt by other boys (and by girls as well) who grew up in dirt-poor farm country, in mining country, in black ghettos, in Hispanic barrios, in the shadows of factories, in Third World nations—any place where the fate of men is as grim and bleak as the fate of women. Toilers and warriors. I realize now how ancient these identities are, how deep the tug they exert on men, the undertow of a thousand generations. The

miseries I saw, as a boy, in the lives of nearly all men I continue to see in the lives of many—the body-breaking toil, the tedium, the call to be tough, the humiliating powerlessness, the battle for a living and for territory.

When the women I met at college thought about the joys and privileges 10 of men, they did not carry in their minds the sort of men I had known in my childhood. They thought of their fathers, who were bankers, physicians, architects, stockbrokers, the big wheels of the big cities. These fathers rode the train to work or drove cars that cost more than any of my childhood houses. They were attended from morning to night by female helpers, wives and nurses and secretaries. They were never laid off, never short of cash at month's end, never lined up for welfare. These fathers made decisions that mattered. They ran the world.

The daughters of such men wanted to share in this power, this glory. 11 So did I. They yearned for a say over their future, for jobs worthy of their abilities, for the right to live at peace, unmolested, whole. Yes, I thought, yes yes. The difference between me and these daughters was that they saw me, because of my sex, as destined from birth to become like their fathers, and therefore as an enemy to their desires. But I knew better. I wasn't an enemy, in fact or in feeling. I was an ally. If I had known, then, how to tell them so, would they have believed me? Would they now?

Reacting to the Reading

1. In the margins of the essay, name and number the categories Sanders identifies. If he does not name a particular category, supply a suitable name.
2. Highlight the key ideas in paragraph 8. Then, write a one-sentence summary of this paragraph's ideas in the margin. Be sure to use your own words.

Reacting to Words

*1. Define these words: *sodden* (paragraph 1), *acrid* (1), *overseers* (1), *tilling* (2), *finicky* (3), *toilers* (5), *savvy* (5), *expansiveness* (8), *undertow* (9), *yearned* (11). Can you suggest a synonym for each word that will work in the essay?
2. Suggest two or three alternative names for the categories *warriors* and *toilers* (paragraph 5). Do you think any of your suggestions are better than Sanders's choices?

Reacting to Ideas

1. When Sanders was young, what did he see as his destiny? How did he escape his fate? How else do you think he might have escaped?
2. What were the grievances of the women Sanders met at college? Why did Sanders have trouble understanding these grievances?
*3. Who do you believe has an easier life—men or women? Explain.

Reacting to the Pattern

1. What two types of men did Sanders know when he was young? How are they different? What do they have in common?

2. What kinds of men discussed in the essay do not fit into the two categories Sanders identifies in paragraphs 2 through 4? Why don't they fit?

*3. Sanders does not categorize the women he discusses. Can you think of a few categories into which these women could fit?

Writing Practice

1. Write a classification essay in which you identify and discuss three or four categories of workers (females as well as males) you observed in your community when you were growing up. In your thesis statement, draw a conclusion about the relative status and rewards of these workers' jobs.

2. Consider your own work history as well as your future career. Write a classification essay in which you discuss your experience in several different categories of employment in the past, present, and future. Give each category a descriptive title, and include a thesis statement that sums up your progress.

3. Categorize the workers in your current place of employment or on your college campus.

H   Definition

A **definition** essay presents an extended definition, using other patterns of development to move beyond a simple dictionary definition. In "The Wife-Beater," Gayle Rosenwald Smith defines an item of clothing. In "Why I Want a Wife," Judy Brady defines a family role.

THE WIFE-BEATER

Gayle Rosenwald Smith

Philadelphia lawyer Gayle Rosenwald Smith, who specializes in family law, coauthored *What Every Woman Should Know about Divorce and Custody* (1998). Her articles have been published in newspapers such as the *Chicago Tribune* and the *Philadelphia Inquirer* (where this essay appeared). As you read, think about the connotations of violence and masculinity in Smith's definition of a "wife-beater."

Everybody wears them. The Gap sells them. Fashion designers Dolce and Gabbana have lavished them with jewels. Their previous greatest resurgence occurred in the 1950s, when Marlon Brando's Stanley Kowalski wore one in Tennessee Williams' *A Streetcar Named Desire*. They are all the rage.   1

What are they called?   2

The name is the issue. For they are known as "wife-beaters."   3

A Web search shows that kids nationwide are wearing the skinny-ribbed white T-shirts that can be worn alone or under another shirt. Women have adopted them with the same gusto as men. A search of boutiques shows that these wearers include professionals who wear them,   4

adorned with designer accessories, under their pricey suits. They are available in all colors, sizes and price ranges.

Wearers under 25 do not seem to be disturbed by the name. But I sure am. 5

It's an odd name for an undershirt. And even though the ugly stereotypes behind the name are both obvious and toxic, it appears to be cool to say the name without fear of (or without caring about) hurting anyone. 6

That the name is fueled by stereotype is now an academically established fact, although various sources disagree on exactly when shirt and name came together. The *Oxford Dictionary* defines the term *wife-beater* as: 7
"1. A man who physically abuses his wife and
   2. Tank-style underwear shirts. Origin: based on the stereotype that physically abusive husbands wear that particular type of shirt."

The *World Book Dictionary* locates the origin of the term *wife-beater* in the 1970s, from the stereotype of the Midwestern male wearing an undershirt while beating his wife. The shirts are said to have been popular in the 1980s at all types of sporting events, especially ones at which one sits in the sun and develops "wife-beater marks." The undershirts also attained popularity at wet T-shirt contests, in which the wet, ribbed tees accentuated contestants' breasts. 8

In an article in the style section of the New York Times, Jesse Sheidlower, principal editor of the *Oxford English Dictionary*'s American office, says the association of the undershirt and the term *wife-beater* arose in 1997 from varied sources, including gay and gang subcultures and rap music. 9

In the article, some sources argued that the reference in the term was not to spousal abuse per se but to popular-culture figures such as Ralph Cramden and Tony Soprano. And what about Archie Bunker?[1] 10

It's not just the name that worries me. Fashion headlines reveal that we want to overthrow '90s grunge and return to shoulder pads and hardware-studded suits. Am I reading too much into a fashion statement that the return is also to male dominance where physical abuse is acceptable as a means of control? 11

There has to be a better term. After all, it's a pretty rare piece of clothing that can make both men and women look sexier. You'd expect a term connoting flattery—not violence. 12

Wearers under 25 may not want to hear this, but here it is. More than 4 million women are victims of severe assaults by boyfriends and husbands each year. By conservative estimate, family violence occurs in 2 million families each year in the United States. Average age of the batterer: 31. 13

Possibly the last statistic is telling. Maybe youth today would rather ignore the overtones of the term *wife-beater*. It is also true, however, that the children of abusers often learn the behavior from their elders. 14

Therein lies perhaps the worst difficulty: that this name for this shirt teaches the wrong thing about men. Some articles quote women who felt the shirts looked great, especially on guys with great bodies. One woman stated that it even made guys look "manly." 15

So *manly* equals *violent*? Not by me, and I hope not by anyone on any side of age 25. 16

---

1. Characters in the 1950s sitcom *The Honeymooners*, the HBO series *The Sopranos*, and the 1970s sitcom *All in the Family*.

Reacting to the Reading

1. Smith's essay opens with the sentence, "Everybody wears them." Underline this sentence (if you have not already done so).
2. Place a check mark beside each sentence in the essay that supports this opening statement.

Reacting to Words

*1. Define these words: *lavished* (paragraph 1), *resurgence* (1), *gusto* (4), *toxic* (6), *connoting* (12). Can you suggest a synonym for each word that will work in the essay?
2. Smith uses informal words and expressions—for example, *kids* (4), *pricey* (4), and *Not by me* (16)—as well as contractions. Do you think this informal style weakens her serious message? Explain.

Reacting to Ideas

*1. Beyond defining the term *wife-beater*, what is Smith's purpose for writing this essay? How can you tell?
2. What does Smith actually propose or recommend to her readers? For example, does she think people should stop wearing "wife-beater" T-shirts?
*3. In paragraph 11, Smith asks, "Am I reading too much into a fashion statement . . . ?" Answer her question.

Reacting to the Pattern

*1. Where in her essay does Smith develop her definition with examples? Where does she use description? Can you identify any other patterns of development?
2. Where does Smith present a formal (dictionary) definition of *wife-beater*? Where does she give information about the term's origin? Why does she include this material?

Writing Practice

1. Define another article of clothing that, like the "wife-beater" T-shirt, has taken on some special significance. (For example, you could write about baggy jeans or baseball caps.) Focus on the garment and its wearers (not on its name), discussing the impression the article of clothing makes and the associations it has for its wearers and for others. You can use description and either exemplification or classification to develop your essay.
2. Write an essay in which you define a particular type of student on your campus. Develop your definition with description of the person's typical dress and accessories and examples of his or her habits. If you like, you may also include a brief narrative that illustrates this student's typical behavior. Be sure to provide a one-sentence definition that identifies the person you are discussing.

WHY I WANT A WIFE

Judy Brady

Judy Brady helped found the Toxic Links Coalition, an organization dedicated to exposing the dangers of environmental toxins and their impact on public health. She was also an activist in the women's movement, and her classic essay "Why I Want a Wife" was published in the first issue of *Ms.* magazine (1971). As you read, note how Brady uses examples to support her definition of a wife.

I belong to that classification of people known as wives. I am A Wife. And, not altogether incidentally, I am a mother. 1

Not too long ago a male friend of mine appeared on the scene fresh from a recent divorce. He had one child, who is, of course, with his ex-wife. He is looking for another wife. As I thought about him while I was ironing one evening, it suddenly occurred to me that I, too, would like to have a wife. Why do I want a wife? 2

I would like to go back to school so that I can become economically independent, support myself, and, if need be, support those dependent upon me. I want a wife who will work and send me to school. And while I am going to school I want a wife to take care of my children. I want a wife to keep track of the children's doctor and dentist appointments. And to keep track of mine, too. I want a wife to make sure my children eat properly and are kept clean. I want a wife who will wash the children's clothes and keep them mended. I want a wife who is a good nurturant attendant to my children, who arranges for their schooling, makes sure that they have an adequate social life with their peers, takes them to the park, the zoo, etc. I want a wife who takes care of the children when they are sick, a wife who arranges to be around when the children need special care, because, of course, I cannot miss classes at school. My wife must arrange to lose time at work and not lose the job. It may mean a small cut in my wife's income from time to time, but I guess I can tolerate that. Needless to say, my wife will arrange and pay for the care of the children while my wife is working. 3

I want a wife who will take care of *my* physical needs. I want a wife who will keep my house clean. A wife who will pick up after my children, a wife who will pick up after me. I want a wife who will keep my clothes clean, ironed, mended, replaced when need be, and who will see to it that my personal things are kept in their proper place so that I can find what I need the minute I need it. I want a wife who cooks the meals, a wife who is a *good* cook. I want a wife who will plan the menus, do the necessary grocery shopping, prepare the meals, serve them pleasantly, and then do the cleaning up while I do my studying. I want a wife who will care for me when I am sick and sympathize with my pain and loss of time from school. I want a wife to go along when our family takes a vacation so that someone can continue to care for me and my children when I need a rest and change of scene. 4

I want a wife who will not bother me with rambling complaints about a wife's duties. But I want a wife who will listen to me when I feel the need to explain a rather difficult point I have come across in my course of studies. And I want a wife who will type my papers for me when I have written them. 5

I want a wife who will take care of the details of my social life. When my wife and I are invited out by my friends, I want a wife who will take care of the babysitting arrangements. When I meet people at school that I like and want to entertain, I want a wife who will have the house clean, will prepare a special meal, serve it to me and my friends, and not interrupt when I talk about things that interest me and my friends. I want a wife who will have arranged that the children are fed and ready for bed before my guests arrive so that the children do not bother us. I want a wife who takes care of the needs of my guests so that they feel comfortable, who makes sure that they have an ashtray, that they are passed the hors d'oeuvres, that they are offered a second helping of the food, that their wine glasses are replenished when necessary, that their coffee is served to them as they like it. And I want a wife who knows that sometimes I need a night out by myself.   6

I want a wife who is sensitive to my sexual needs, a wife who makes love passionately and eagerly when I feel like it, a wife who makes sure that I am satisfied. And, of course, I want a wife who will not demand sexual attention when I am not in the mood for it. I want a wife who assumes the complete responsibility for birth control, because I do not want more children. I want a wife who will remain sexually faithful to me so that I do not have to clutter up my intellectual life with jealousies. And I want a wife who understands that *my* sexual needs may entail more than strict adherence to monogamy. I must, after all, be able to relate to people as fully as possible.   7

If, by chance, I find another person more suitable as a wife than the wife I already have, I want the liberty to replace my present wife with another one. Naturally, I will expect a fresh new life; my wife will take the children and be solely responsible for them so that I am left free.   8

When I am through with school and have a job, I want my wife to quit working and remain at home so that my wife can more fully and completely take care of a wife's duties.   9

My God, who *wouldn't* want a wife?   10

Reacting to the Reading

1. Review all the characteristics of a wife that Brady mentions. Then, in the margin, write a one-sentence definition of *wife* that summarizes these characteristics.
2. In the margin beside paragraph 10, answer Brady's concluding question.

Reacting to Words

*1. Define these words: *nurturant* (paragraph 3), *peers* (3), *hors d'oeuvres* (6), *replenished* (6), *adherence* (7), *monogamy* (7). Can you suggest a synonym for each word that will work in the essay?
*2. Brady repeats the word *wife* over and over in her essay. Can you think of other words she could have used instead? How might using these words change her essay?

Reacting to Ideas

1. How do you define *wife*? Is your idea of a wife different from Brady's? If so, exactly what is the difference?

2. What central point or idea do you think Brady wants to communicate to her readers? Does she ever actually state this idea? If not, do you think she should?

*3. Brady's essay was written in 1971. Does her idea of a wife seem dated, or does it still seem accurate to you?

Reacting to the Pattern

1. Does Brady include a formal definition of *wife* anywhere in her essay? If so, where? If not, do you think she should?

*2. Brady develops her definition with examples. What are some of her most important examples?

3. Besides exemplification, what other patterns of development does Brady use to develop her definition?

Writing Practice

1. Assume you are Brady's husband and feel unjustly attacked by her essay. Write her a letter in which you define *husband*, using as many examples as you can to show how overworked and underappreciated you are.

2. Write an essay in which you define your ideal teacher, parent, spouse, or boss.

I Argument

An **argument** essay takes a stand on one side of a debatable issue, using facts, examples, and expert opinion to persuade readers to accept a position. The writers of the three essays that follow—Edwidge Danticat in "Impounded Fathers," Ji-Yeon Yuh in "Let's Tell the Story of All America's Cultures," and Dave Eggers in "Serve or Fail"—attempt to convince readers to accept their positions or at least to acknowledge that they are reasonable.

IMPOUNDED FATHERS

Edwidge Danticat

Encouraged by her parents to become a nurse, Danticat pursued her love of writing instead, earning her undergraduate degree in French literature from Barnard College and a master's degree in fine arts from Brown University. Her books, which explore Haitian culture and identity, include *Breath, Eyes, Memory* (1994), *Krik? Krak?* (1995), and *Brother, I'm Dying* (2007). Consider how the vivid examples of deported fathers and abandoned children in this essay—first published in the *New York Times* on Father's Day 2007—make a strong argument for fairer immigration policies.

My father died in May 2005, after an agonizing battle with lung disease. This is the third Father's Day that I will spend without him since we   1

started celebrating together in 1981. That was when I moved to the United States from Haiti, after his own migration here had kept us apart for 8 long years.

My father's absence, then and now, makes all the more poignant for me the predicament of the following fathers who also deserve to be remembered today.

There is the father from Honduras who was imprisoned, then deported, after a routine traffic stop in Miami. He was forced to leave behind his wife, who was also detained by immigration officials, and his 5- and 7-year-old sons, who were placed in foster care. Not understanding what had happened, the boys, when they were taken to visit their mother in jail, asked why their father had abandoned them. Realizing that the only way to reunite his family was to allow his children to be expatriated to Honduras, the father resigned himself to this, only to get caught up in a custody fight with American immigration officials who have threatened to keep the boys permanently in foster care on the premise that their parents abandoned them.

There is also the father from Panama, a cleaning contractor in his 50s, who had lived and worked in the United States for more than 19 years. One morning, he woke to the sound of loud banging on his door. He went to answer it and was greeted by armed immigration agents. His 10-year asylum case had been denied without notice. He was handcuffed and brought to jail.

There is the father from Argentina who moves his wife and children from house to house hoping to remain one step ahead of the immigration raids. And the Guatemalan, Mexican and Chinese fathers who have quietly sought sanctuary from deportation at churches across the United States.

There's the Haitian father who left for work one morning, was picked up outside his apartment and was deported before he got a chance to say goodbye to his infant daughter and his wife. There's the other Haitian father, a naturalized American citizen, whose wife was deported three weeks before her residency hearing, forcing him to place his 4-year-old son in the care of neighbors while he works every waking hour to support two households.

These families are all casualties of a Department of Homeland Security immigration crackdown cheekily titled Operation Return to Sender. The goals of the operation, begun last spring, were to increase the enforcement of immigration laws in the workplace and to catch and deport criminals. Many women and men who have no criminal records have found themselves in its cross hairs. More than 18,000 people have been deported since the operation began last year.

So while politicians debate the finer points of immigration reform, the Department of Homeland Security is already carrying out its own. Unfortunately, these actions can not only plunge families into financial decline, but sever them forever. One such case involves a father who was killed soon after he was deported to El Salvador last year.

"Something else could be done," his 13-year-old son Junior pleaded to the New York–based advocacy group Families for Freedom, "because kids need their fathers."

Right now the physical, emotional, financial and legal status of American-born minors like Junior can neither delay nor prevent their parents' detention or deportation. Last year, Representative José E. Serrano, a Democrat from New York, introduced a bill that would allow immigration judges to

take into consideration the fates of American-born children while review-ing their parents' cases. The bill has gone nowhere, while more and more American-citizen children continue to either lose their parents or their country.

Where are our much-touted family values when it comes to these chil- 11 dren? Today, as on any other day, they deserve to feel that they have not been abandoned—by either their parents or their country.

Reacting to the Reading

1. Highlight the passage in which Danticat expresses her thesis.
2. Next to that passage, write a marginal note that explains why you believe Danticat places her thesis there. Is it more powerful or less powerful placed in this location? Why?

Reacting to Words

*1. Define these words: *poignant* (paragraph 2), *predicament* (2), *expatriated* (3), *custody* (3), *asylum* (4), *sanctuary* (5), *cheekily* (7), *cross hairs* (7), *sever* (8), *advocacy* (9), *touted* (11). Can you suggest a synonym for each word that will work in the essay?
*2. What does Danticat mean when she says that many innocent immi-grants are caught in the "cross hairs" of Operation Return to Sender? Why does she use this expression?

Reacting to Ideas

1. Why is the predicament of other fathers—men she doesn't know—"poignant" for Danticat?
*2. Reread paragraphs 3–6, and explain their purpose in the essay. Do you think they are effective? Why or why not?
*3. Whom does Danticat seem to blame for the harsh enforcement of immigration laws in the United States? Why?

Reacting to the Pattern

1. How does Danticat's argument convince readers to sympathize with the fate of noncriminal immigrants?
2. Is this an inductive or a deductive argument? Explain.
3. Where, if anywhere, does Danticat introduce arguments against her position? What opposing arguments can you think of? How would you refute them?

Writing Practice

1. Write an argument that takes a position on illegal immigration in your community. Support your thesis with information from your own ex-perience and observations or from recent events as reported by your local news. Be sure to state your position clearly and list specific examples to support your argument.
2. Choose an issue you feel strongly about. Write an email to the editor of your local newspaper in which you take a stand on this issue.

LET'S TELL THE STORY
OF ALL AMERICA'S CULTURES

Ji-Yeon Yuh

In 1970, at the age of five, Ji-Yeon Yuh immigrated to Chicago from Seoul, Korea. After working at *Newsday* and the *Ohama World-Reporter*, she completed a doctorate at the University of Pennsylvania and now teaches history at Northwestern University. She is the author of *Beyond the Shadow of Camptown: Korean Military Brides in America* (2002). The following essay, "Let's Tell the Story of All America's Cultures," was originally published in the *Philadelphia Inquirer*. As you read the essay, consider how Yuh includes opposing viewpoints while still successfully arguing her case.

I grew up hearing, seeing, and almost believing that America was white—albeit with a little black tinged here and there—and that white was best.

The white people were everywhere in my 1970s Chicago childhood: Founding Fathers, Lewis and Clark, Lincoln, Daniel Boone, Carnegie, presidents, explorers, and industrialists galore. The only black people were slaves. The only Indians were scalpers.

I never heard one word about how Benjamin Franklin was so impressed by the Iroquois federation of nations that he adapted that model into our system of state and federal government. Or that the Indian tribes were systematically betrayed and massacred by a greedy young nation that stole their land and called it the United States.

I never heard one word about how Asian immigrants were among the first to turn California's desert into fields of plenty. Or about Chinese immigrant Ah Bing, who bred the cherry now on sale in groceries across the nation. Or that plantation owners in Hawaii imported labor from China, Japan, Korea, and the Philippines to work the sugar cane fields. I never learned that Asian immigrants were the only immigrants denied U.S. citizenship, even though they served honorably in World War 1. All the immigrants in my textbook were white.

I never learned about Frederick Douglass, the runaway slave who became a leading abolitionist and statesman, or about black scholar W.E.B. Du Bois. I never learned that black people rose up in arms against slavery. Nat Turner wasn't one of the heroes in my childhood history class.

I never learned that the American Southwest and California were already settled by Mexicans when they were annexed after the Mexican-American War. I never learned that Mexico once had a problem keeping land-hungry white men on the U.S. side of the border.

So when other children called me a slant-eyed chink and told me to go back where I came from, I was ready to believe that I wasn't really an American because I wasn't white.

America's bittersweet legacy of struggling and failing and getting another step closer to democratic ideals of liberty and equality and justice for all wasn't for the likes of me, an immigrant child from Korea. The history books said so.

Well, the history books were wrong.

Educators around the country are finally realizing what I realized as a teenager in the library, looking up the history I wasn't getting in school.

America is a multicultural nation, composed of many people with varying histories and varying traditions who have little in common except their humanity, a belief in democracy, and a desire for freedom.

America changed them, but they changed America too. 11

A committee of scholars and teachers gathered by the New York State 12 Department of Education recognizes this in their recent report, "One Nation, Many Peoples: A Declaration of Cultural Interdependence."

They recommend that public schools provide a "multicultural educa- 13 tion, anchored to the shared principles of a liberal democracy."

What that means, according to the report, is recognizing that America 14 was shaped and continues to be shaped by people of diverse backgrounds. It calls for students to be taught that history is an ongoing process of discovery and interpretation of the past, and that there is more than one way of viewing the world.

Thus, the westward migration of white Americans is not just a heroic 15 settling of an untamed wild, but also the conquest of indigenous peoples. Immigrants were not just white, but Asian as well. Blacks were not merely passive slaves freed by northern whites, but active fighters for their own liberation.

In particular, according to the report, the curriculum should help chil- 16 dren "to assess critically the reasons for the inconsistencies between the ideals of the U.S. and social realities. It should provide information and intellectual tools that can permit them to contribute to bringing reality closer to the ideals."

In other words, show children the good with the bad, and give them 17 the skills to help improve their country. What could be more patriotic?

Several dissenting members of the New York committee publicly 18 worry that America will splinter into ethnic fragments if this multicultural curriculum is adopted. They argue that the committee's report puts the focus on ethnicity at the expense of national unity.

But downplaying ethnicity will not bolster national unity. The history 19 of America is the story of how and why people from all over the world came to the United States, and how in struggling to make a better life for themselves, they changed each other, they changed the country, and they all came to call themselves Americans.

E pluribus unum. Out of many, one. 20

This is why I, with my Korean background, and my childhood tor- 21 mentors, with their lost-in-the-mist-of-time European backgrounds, are all Americans.

It is the unique beauty of this country. It is high time we let all our chil- 22 dren gaze upon it.

Reacting to the Reading

1. Underline Yuh's thesis statement.
2. In the margin beside the thesis statement, rewrite it in your own words.

Reacting to Words

*1. Define these words: *albeit* (paragraph 1), *galore* (2), *abolitionist* (5), *annexed* (6), *multicultural* (10), *indigenous* (15), *ethnicity* (19). Can you suggest a synonym for each word that will work in the essay?

*2. List the words Yuh uses to refer to various ethnic and racial groups. Do you think any other words would be more appropriate?

Reacting to Ideas

*1. In Yuh's "1970s Chicago childhood" (2), she learned little about the achievements of nonwhites. Is this true for you as well?

2. In paragraphs 2 through 6, Yuh lists the things she didn't learn in school. Give some examples of things you didn't learn in school.

*3. Do you agree with Yuh that the public school curriculum should "tell the story of all America's cultures"? Do you see any problems in such an approach?

Reacting to the Pattern

1. Does Yuh arrange her essay as an inductive argument or as a deductive argument (see 14I)? Explain.

2. Where in her essay does Yuh present an argument against her position? Paraphrase this argument.

3. How does Yuh refute (argue against) the opposing argument she presents? Is her refutation convincing? Why or why not?

Writing Practice

1. Write a letter to your high school principal arguing in favor of (or against) a more multicultural curriculum for your school. Like Yuh, use examples from your own educational experiences to support your thesis.

2. Review a high school or college history textbook—either a recent text or one a parent or older sibling used. Do you think there is too little coverage of minority groups' contributions? Too much? Write an email to the publisher arguing for changes.

3. Do you think public schools should "tell the story of all America's cultures"? Write an essay in which you consider what would be gained (or lost) if such an approach were adopted in all American public schools.

SERVE OR FAIL

Dave Eggers

Author, editor, and publisher Dave Eggers is best known for his memoir *A Heartbreaking Work of Staggering Genius* (2000). The book describes how he raised his brother, Christopher, after his parents' death. Eggers also founded McSweeney's, an independent publishing house, as well as writing centers for children in San Francisco and Brooklyn. In "Serve or Fail," he argues that public service should be required for college students. As you read this essay, consider facts and examples that Eggers uses to persuade his audience.

About now, most recent college graduates, a mere week or two beyond their last final, are giving themselves a nice respite. Maybe they're on a   1

beach, maybe they're on a road trip, maybe they're in their rooms, painting their toenails black with a Q-tip and shoe polish. Does it matter? What's important is that they have some time off.

Do they deserve the time off? Well, yes and no. Yes, because finals week is stressful and sleep-deprived and possibly involves trucker-style stimulants. No, because a good deal of the four years of college is spent playing foosball.

I went to a large state school—the University of Illinois—and during my time there, I became one of the best two or three foosball players in the Land of Lincoln. I learned to pass deftly between my rigid players, to play the corners, to strike the ball like a cobra would strike something a cobra would want to strike. I also mastered the dart game called Cricket, and the billiards contest called Nine-ball. I became expert at whiffle ball, at backyard archery, and at a sport we invented that involved one person tossing roasted chickens from a balcony to a group of us waiting below. We got to eat the parts that didn't land on the patio.

The point is that college is too long—it should be three years—and that even with a full course load and part-time jobs (I had my share) there are many hours in the days and weeks that need killing. And because most of us, as students, saw our hours as in need of killing—as opposed to thinking about giving a few of these hours to our communities in one way or another—colleges should consider instituting a service requirement for graduation.

I volunteered a few times in Urbana-Champaign—at a Y.M.C.A. and at a home for senior citizens—and in both cases it was much too easy to quit. I thought the senior home smelled odd, so I left, and though the Y.M.C.A. was a perfect fit, I could have used nudging to continue—nudging the university might have provided. Just as parents and schools need to foster in young people a "reading habit"—a love of reading that becomes a need, almost an addiction—colleges are best-poised to create in their students a lifelong commitment to volunteering even a few hours a month.

Some colleges, and many high schools, have such a thing in place, and last year Michael R. Veon, a Democratic member of Pennsylvania's House of Representatives, introduced a bill that would require the more than 90,000 students at 14 state-run universities to perform 25 hours of community service annually. That comes out to more than 2 million volunteer hours a year.

College students are, for the most part, uniquely suited to have time for and to benefit from getting involved and addressing the needs of those around them. Unlike high school students, they're less programmed, less boxed-in by family and after-school obligations. They're also more mature, and better able to handle a wide range of tasks. Finally, they're at a stage where exposure to service—and to the people whose lives nonprofit service organizations touch—would have a profound effect on them. Meeting a World War II veteran who needs meals brought to him would be educational for the deliverer of that meal, I would think. A college history major might learn something by tutoring a local middle school class that's studying the Underground Railroad. A connection would be forged; a potential career might be discovered.

A service requirement won't work everywhere. It probably wouldn't be feasible, for example, for community college students, who tend to be transient and who generally have considerable family and work demands. But

exempt community colleges and you would still have almost 10 million college students enrolled in four-year colleges in the United States. If you exempted a third of them for various reasons, that would leave more than 6 million able-bodied young people at the ready. Even with a modest 10-hour-a-year requirement (the equivalent of two mornings a year) America would gain 60 million volunteer hours to invigorate the nation's nonprofit organizations, churches, job corps, conservation groups and college outreach programs.

And with some flexibility, it wouldn't have to be too onerous. Colleges   9
could give credit for service. That is, at the beginning of each year, a student could opt for service, and in return he or she might get credits equal to one class period. Perhaps every 25 hours of service could be traded for one class credit, with a maximum of three credits a year. What a student would learn from working in a shelter for the victims of domestic abuse would surely equal or surpass his or her time spent in racquetball class—at my college worth one full unit.

Alternatively, colleges could limit the service requirement to a student's   10
junior year—a time when the students are settled and have more hours and stability in their schedules. Turning the junior year into a year when volunteering figures prominently could also help colleges bridge the chasm that usually stands between the academic world and the one that lies beyond it.

When Gov. Gray Davis of California proposed a service requirement in   11
1999, an editorial in *The Daily Californian,* the student newspaper at the University of California at Berkeley, opposed the plan: "Forced philanthropy will be as much an oxymoron in action as it is in terms. Who would want to receive community service from someone who is forced to serve? Is forced community service in California not generally reserved for criminals and delinquents?"

First of all, that's putting forth a pretty dim view of the soul of the av-   12
erage student. What, is the unwilling college volunteer going to *throw food* at visitors to the soup kitchen? Volunteering is by nature transformative—reluctant participants become quick converts every day, once they meet those who need their help.

Second, college is largely about fulfilling requirements, isn't it? Stu-   13
dents have to complete this much work in the sciences, that much work in the arts. Incoming freshmen accept a tacit contract, submitting to the wisdom of the college's founders and shapers, who decide which experiences are necessary to create a well-rounded scholar, one ready to make a contribution to the world. But while colleges give their students the intellectual tools for life beyond campus, they largely ignore the part about how they might contribute to the world. That is, until the commencement speech, at which time all the "go forth's" and "be helpful's" happen.

But what if such a sentiment happened on the student's first day?   14
What if graduating seniors already knew full well how to balance jobs, studies, family, and volunteer work in the surrounding community? What if campuses were full of underserved high school students meeting with their college tutors? What if the tired and clogged veins of thousands of towns and cities had the energy of millions of college students coursing through them? What if the student who might have become a foosball power—and I say this knowing how much those skills have enhanced my life and those who had the good fortune to have watched me—became instead a lifelong volunteer? That might be pretty good for everybody.

Reacting to the Reading

1. Where does Eggers state his thesis? Place an asterisk in the margin beside it.
2. Underline any statements in the essay with which you disagree. In the margins, briefly explain why.

Reacting to Words

*1. Define these words: *respite* (paragraph 1), *deftly* (3), *forged* (7), *onerous* (9), *surpass* (9), *chasm* (10), *philanthropy* (11), *oxymoron* (11), *transformative* (12). Can you suggest a synonym for each word that will work in the essay?
2. What does the phrase *service requirement* suggest to you? Does it suggest something positive or negative? What other terms could Eggers have used?

Reacting to Ideas

1. In paragraphs 1 through 3, Eggers discusses the ways college students waste time. Does his assessment seem accurate to you? If it does not seem accurate, do these paragraphs weaken his argument in favor of required community service for college students?
2. Do you agree with Eggers that it is colleges that are "best-poised to create in their students a lifelong commitment to volunteering" (5), or do you think this responsibility lies elsewhere? Explain.
*3. Do you think Eggers is too optimistic about the value of community service to the college student? To the community?

Reacting to the Pattern

1. Is this argument inductive, deductive, or a combination of the two?
2. Do you think Eggers spends enough time considering (and refuting) possible objections to his proposal? Can you think of any objections that he doesn't discuss?
3. Identify some of the many questions Eggers asks in his essay. How do they help to move his argument along?

Writing Practice

1. What is your position on required community service for college students? Write a proposal to your school's president arguing for a community-service requirement—or write an editorial for your school newspaper arguing against such a requirement.
2. Write an essay in which you argue that it is not college students but high school students (or recent college graduates) who are "uniquely suited to have time for and to benefit from getting involved and addressing the needs of those around them" (7).

Strategies for College Success

1 Orientation Strategies

Some strategies come in handy even before school begins, as you orient yourself to life as a college student. In fact, you may already have discovered some of them.

1. *Make sure you have everything you need:* a college catalog, a photo ID, a student handbook, a parking permit, and any other items that entering students at your school are expected to have.
2. *Read your school's orientation materials* (distributed as handouts or posted on the school Web site) carefully. These materials will help you to familiarize yourself with campus buildings and offices, course offerings, faculty members, extracurricular activities, and so on.
3. *Be sure you know your academic adviser's name* (and how to spell it), email address, office location, and office hours. Copy this information into your personal address book.
4. *Get a copy of the library's orientation materials.* These will tell you about the library's hours and services and explain procedures such as how to use the online catalog.
5. *Be sure you know where things are*—not just how to find the library and the parking lot but also where you can do photocopying or buy a newspaper.

2 First-Week Strategies

College can seem like a confusing place at first, but from your first day as a college student, there are steps you can take to help you get your bearings.

1. *Make yourself at home.* Find places on campus where you can get something to eat or drink, and find a good place to study or relax before or between classes. As you explore the campus, try to locate all the things you need to feel comfortable—for example, ATMs, rest rooms, and vending machines.
2. *Know where you are going and when you need to be there.* Check the building and room number for each of your classes and the days and hours the class meets. Copy this information onto the front cover of the appropriate notebook. Pay particular attention to classes with

▶ **Word Power**

networking interacting with others to share information

irregular schedules (for example, a class that meets from 9 a.m. to 10 a.m. on Tuesdays but from 11 a.m. to noon on Thursdays).

3. *Get to know your fellow students*. Networking with other students is an important part of the college experience. Get the name, phone number, and email address of at least one student in each of your classes. If you miss class, you will need to get in touch with someone to find out what material you missed.

4. *Familiarize yourself with each course's syllabus*. At the first meeting of every course, your instructor will hand out a **syllabus**, an outline or summary of course requirements, policies, and procedures. (The syllabus may also be posted on the course's Web page.) A syllabus gives you three kinds of useful information.

   ■ Practical information, such as the instructor's office number and email address and what books and supplies to buy

   ■ Information that can help you plan a study schedule—for example, when assignments are due and when exams are scheduled

   ■ Information about the instructor's policies on absences, grading, class participation, and so on

   Read each syllabus carefully, ask questions about anything you do not understand, refer to all your course syllabi regularly—and do not lose them.

5. *Buy books and supplies*. When you buy your books and supplies, be sure to keep the receipts, and do not write your name in your books until you are certain that you are not going to drop a course. (If you write in a book, you will not be able to return it for a full refund.) If your schedule of courses is not definite, wait a few days to buy your texts. You should, however, buy some items right away: a separate notebook and folder for each course you are taking, a college dictionary, and a pocket **organizer** (see A4). In addition to the books and other items required for a particular course (for example, a lab notebook, a programmable calculator, art supplies), you should buy pens and pencils in different colors, paper clips or a stapler, self-stick notes, highlighter pens, and so on. Finally, you will need to buy a backpack or bookbag in which to keep all these items.

6. *Set up your notebooks*. Establish a separate notebook (or a separate section of a divided notebook) for each of your classes. Write your instructor's name, email address, phone number, and office hours and location on the inside front cover of the notebook; write your own name, address, and phone number on the outside, along with the class location and meeting times. (Notebooks with pocket folders can help you keep graded papers, handouts, and the class syllabus all in one place, near your notes.)

FOCUS Using a Dictionary

Even though your computer has a spell checker, you still need to buy a dictionary. A college dictionary tells you not only how to spell words but also what words mean and how to use them.

3 Day-to-Day Strategies

As you get busier and busier, you find that it is hard to keep everything under control. Here are some strategies to help you as you move through the semester.

1. **Find a place to study.** As a college student, you will need your own private place to work and study. This space should include everything you will need to make your work easier—quiet, good lighting, a comfortable chair, a clean work surface, storage for supplies, and so on.
2. **Set up a bookshelf.** Keep your textbooks, dictionary, calculator, supplies, and everything else you use regularly for your coursework in one place—ideally, in your own workspace. That way, when you need something, you will know exactly where it is.
3. **Set up a study schedule.** Identify thirty- to forty-five-minute blocks of free time before, between, and after classes. Set this time aside for review. Remember, studying should be part of your regular routine, not something you do only the night before an exam.

FOCUS **Skills Check**

Don't wait until you have an assignment due to discover that your computer skills need improvement. Be sure your basic word-processing skills are at the level you need for your work. If you need help, get it right away. Your school's computer lab should be the first place you turn for help with word processing, but writing center and library staff members may also be able to help you.

---

4. **Establish priorities.** It is very important to understand what your priorities are. Before you can establish priorities, however, you have to know which assignments are due first, which ones can be done in steps, and which tasks or steps will be most time consuming. Then, you must decide which tasks are most pressing. For example, studying for a test to be given the next day is more pressing than reviewing notes for a test scheduled for the following week. Finally, you have to decide which tasks are more important than others. For example, studying for a midterm is more important than studying for a quiz, and the midterm for a course you are in danger of failing is more important than the midterm for a course in which you are doing well. Remember, you cannot do everything at once; you need to know what must be done immediately and what can wait.
5. **Check your mail.** Check your campus mailbox and email account regularly—if possible, several times a day. If you miss a message, you miss important information about changes in assignments, canceled classes, or rescheduled quizzes.
6. **Schedule conferences.** Try to meet with each of your instructors during the semester even if you are not required to do so. You might schedule one conference during the second or third week of the semester and

> **Word Power**
> **priorities**   things considered more important than others

another a week or two before a major exam or paper is due. Your instructors will appreciate and respect your initiative.

7. ***Become familiar with the student services available on your campus.*** There is nothing wrong with getting help from your school's writing center or tutoring center or from the center for disabled students (which serves students with learning disabilities as well as physical challenges), the office of international students, or the counseling center, as well as from your adviser or course instructors. Think of yourself as a consumer. You are paying for your education, and you are entitled to—and should take advantage of—all the available services you need.

FOCUS **Asking for Help**

Despite all your careful planning, you may still run into trouble. For example, you may miss an exam and have to make it up; you may miss several days of classes in a row and fall behind in your work; you may have trouble understanding the material in one of your courses; or a family member may get sick. Do not wait until you are overwhelmed to ask for help. If you have an ongoing personal problem or a family emergency, let your instructors and the dean of students know immediately.

---

4 **Time-Management Strategies**

Learning to manage your time is very important for success in college. Here are some strategies you can adopt to make this task easier.

1. ***Use an organizer.*** Whether you prefer a print organizer or an electronic one, you should certainly use one—and use it consistently. If you are most comfortable with paper and pencil, purchase a "week-on-two-pages" academic year organizer (one that begins in September, not January); the "week-on-two-pages" format (see p. 651) gives you more writing room for Monday through Friday than for the weekend, and it also lets you view an entire week at once.

   Carry your organizer with you at all times. At the beginning of the semester, copy down key pieces of information from each course syllabus—for example, the date of every quiz and exam and the due date of every paper. As the semester progresses, continue to write in assignments and deadlines. In addition, enter information such as days when a class will be canceled or will meet in the computer lab or in the library, reminders to bring a particular book or piece of equipment to class, and appointments with instructors or other college personnel. If you like, you can also jot down reminders and schedule appointments that are not related to school—for example, changes in your work hours, a dental appointment, or lunch with a friend.

(In addition to writing notes on the pages for each date, some students like to keep a separate month-by-month "to do" list. Crossing out completed items can give you a feeling of accomplishment—and make the road ahead look shorter.)

The sample organizer pages below show how you can use an organizer to keep track of deadlines, appointments, and reminders. The organizer pages shown on page 652 include not only this information but also a study schedule, with notes about particular tasks to be done each day.

2. *Use a calendar*. Buy a large calendar, and post it where you will see it every morning—on your desk, on the refrigerator, or wherever you keep your keys and your ID. At the beginning of the semester, fill in important dates such as school holidays, work commitments, exam dates, and due dates for papers and projects. When you return from school each day, update the calendar with any new information you have entered into your organizer.

3. *Plan ahead*. If you think you will need help from a writing center tutor to revise a paper that is due in two weeks, don't wait until day thirteen to make an appointment; all the time slots may be filled by then. To be safe, make an appointment for help about a week in advance.

4. *Learn to enjoy downtime*. One final—and important—point to remember is that you are entitled to "waste" a little time. When you have a free minute, take time for yourself—and don't feel guilty about it.

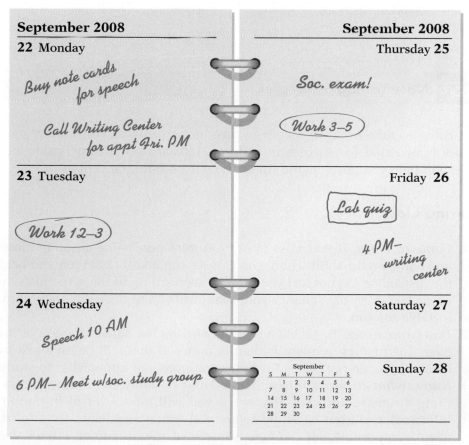

Sample Organizer Page: Deadlines, Appointments, and Reminders Only

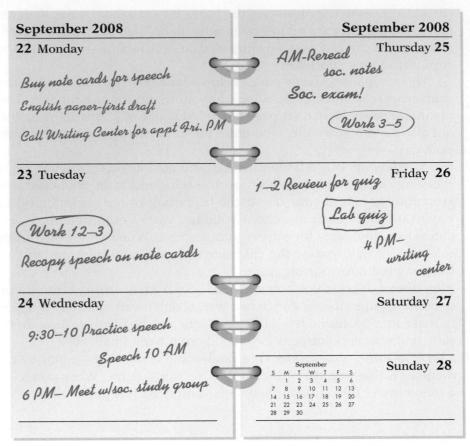

Sample Organizer Page: Deadlines, Appointments, Reminders, and Study Schedule

5   Note-Taking Strategies

Learning to take notes in a college class takes practice, but taking good notes is essential for success in college. Here are some basic guidelines that will help you develop and improve your note-taking skills.

During Class

1. ***Come to class.*** If you miss class, you miss notes—so come to class, and come on time. Sit where you can see the board or screen and hear the instructor. Do not feel you have to keep sitting in the same place in each class every day; change your seat until you find a spot that is comfortable for you.

2. ***Date your notes.*** Begin each class by writing the date at the top of the page. Instructors frequently identify material that will be on a test by dates. If you do not date your notes, you may not know what to study.

3. ***Know what to write down.*** You cannot possibly write down everything an instructor says. If you try, you will miss a lot of important information. Listen carefully *before* you write, and listen for cues to what is important. For example, sometimes the instructor will tell you that something is important or that a particular piece of information

will be on a test. If the instructor emphasizes an idea or underlines it on the board, you should do the same in your notes.

4. *Include examples*. Try to write down an example for each important concept introduced in class—something that will help you remember what the instructor was talking about. (If you do not have time to include examples as you take notes during class, add them when you review your notes.) For instance, if your world history instructor is explaining *nationalism*, you should write down not only a definition but also an example, such as "Germany in 1848."

5. *Write legibly, and use helpful signals*. Use dark (blue or black) ink for your note-taking, but keep a red or green pen handy to highlight important information, jot down announcements (such as a change in a test date), note gaps in your notes, or question confusing points. Do not take notes in pencil, which is hard to read and not as permanent as ink.

6. *Ask questions*. If you do not hear (or do not understand) something your instructor said, or if you need an example to help you understand something, *ask!* Do not, however, immediately turn to another student for clarification. Instead, wait to see if the instructor explains further or if he or she pauses to ask if anyone has a question. If you are not comfortable asking a question during class, make a note of the question and ask the instructor—or send an email—after class.

After Class

1. *Review your notes*. After every class, try to spend ten or fifteen minutes rereading your notes, filling in gaps and examples while the material is still fresh in your mind.

2. *Recopy information*. When you have a break between classes, or when you get home, recopy important pieces of information from your notes. (Some students find it helpful to recopy their notes after every class to reinforce what they have learned, but this can be very time-consuming.)

- Copy announcements (such as quiz dates) onto your calendar.

- Copy reminders (for example, a note to schedule a conference before your next paper is due) into your organizer.

- Copy questions you want to ask the instructor onto the top of the next blank page in your class notebook.

Before the Next Class

1. *Reread your notes*. Leave time to skim the previous class's notes just before each class. This strategy will get you oriented for the next class and will remind you of anything that needs clarification or further explanation. (You might want to give each day's notes a title so you can remember the topic of each class. This can help you find information when you study.)

2. *Ask for help*. Call or email a classmate if you need to fill in missing information; if you still need help, see the instructor during his or her office hours, or come to class early to ask your question before class begins.

6 Homework Strategies

Doing homework is an important part of your education. Homework gives you a chance to practice your skills and measure your progress. If you are having trouble with the homework, chances are you are having trouble with the course. Ask the instructor or teaching assistant for help *now*; do not wait until the day before the exam. Here are some tips for getting the most out of your homework.

1. ***Write down the assignment***. Do not expect to remember an assignment; copy it down. If you are not sure exactly what you are supposed to do, check with your instructor or with another student.
2. ***Do your homework, and do it on time***. Teachers assign homework to reinforce classwork, and they expect homework to be done on a regular basis. It is easy to fall behind in college, but trying to do three—or five—nights' worth of homework in one night is not a good idea. If you do several assignments at once, you not only overload yourself, you also miss important day-to-day connections with classwork.
3. ***Be an active reader***. Get into the habit of highlighting your textbooks and other material as you read.
4. ***Join study groups***. A study group of three or four students can be a valuable support system for homework as well as for exams. If your schedule permits, do some homework assignments—or at least review your homework—with other students on a regular basis. In addition to learning information, you will learn different strategies for doing assignments.

7 Exam-Taking Strategies

Preparation for an exam should begin well before the exam is announced. In a sense, you begin this preparation on the first day of class.

Before the Exam

1. ***Attend every class***. Regular attendance in class—where you can listen, ask questions, and take notes—is the best possible preparation for exams. If you do have to miss a class, arrange to copy (and read) another student's notes *before the next class* so you will be able to follow the discussion.
2. ***Keep up with the reading***. Read every assignment, and read it before the class in which it will be discussed. If you do not, you may have trouble understanding what is going on in class.
3. ***Take careful notes***. Take careful, thorough notes, but be selective. If you can, compare your notes on a regular basis with those of other students in the class; working together, you can fill in gaps or correct errors. Establishing a buddy system will also force you to review your notes regularly instead of just on the night before the exam.

4. *Study on your own*. When an exam is announced, adjust your study schedule—and your priorities—so you have time to review everything. (This is especially important if you have more than one exam in a short period of time.) Over a period of several days, review all your material (class notes, readings, and so on), and then review it again. Make a note of anything you do not understand, and keep track of topics you need to review. Try to predict the most likely questions, and—if you have time—practice answering them.

5. *Study with a group*. If you can, set up a study group. Studying with others can help you understand the material better. However, do not come to group sessions unprepared and expect to get everything from the other students. You must first study on your own.

6. *Make an appointment with your instructor*. Make a conference appointment with the instructor or with the course's teaching assistant a few days before the exam. Bring to this meeting any specific questions you have about course content and about the format of the upcoming exam. (Be sure to review all your study material before the conference.)

7. *Review the material one last time*. The night before the exam is not the time to begin your studying; it is the time to review. When you have finished your review, get a good night's sleep.

During the Exam

By the time you walk into the exam room, you will already have done all you could to get ready for the test. Your goal now is to keep the momentum going and not do anything to undermine all your hard work.

FOCUS **Writing Essay Exams**

If you are asked to write an essay on an exam, remember that what you are really being asked to do is write a **thesis-and-support essay**. Chapter 12 tells you how to do this.

---

1. *Read through the entire exam*. Be sure you understand how much time you have, how many points each question is worth, and exactly what each question is asking you to do. Many exam questions call for just a short answer—*yes* or *no*, *true* or *false*. Others ask you to fill in a blank with a few words, and still others require you to select the best answer from among several choices. If you are not absolutely certain what kind of answer a particular question calls for, ask the instructor or the proctor *before* you begin to write.

2. *Budget your time*. Once you understand how much each section of the exam and each question are worth, plan your time and set your priorities, devoting the most time to the most important questions. If you know you tend to rush through exams, or if you find you often run out of time before you get to the end of a test, you might try checking your

progress when about one-third of the allotted time has passed (for a one-hour exam, check after twenty minutes) to make sure you are pacing yourself appropriately.

3. *Reread each question*. Carefully reread each question *before* you start to answer it. Underline the **key words**—the words that give specific information about how to approach the question and how to phrase your answer.

Remember, even if everything you write is correct, your response is not acceptable if you do not answer the question. If a question asks you to *compare* two novels, writing a *summary* of one of them will not be acceptable.

FOCUS **Key Words**

Here are some helpful key words to look for on exams.

analyze	explain	suggest results,
argue	give examples	effects, outcomes
compare	identify	summarize
contrast	illustrate	support
define	recount	take a stand
demonstrate	suggest causes,	trace
describe	origins, contribut-	
evaluate	ing factors	

---

4. *Brainstorm to help yourself recall the material*. If you are writing a paragraph or an essay, look frequently at the question as you brainstorm. (You can write your brainstorming notes on the inside cover of the exam book.) Quickly write down all the relevant points you can think of—what the textbook had to say, your instructor's comments, and so on. The more information you can think of now, the more you will have to choose from when you write your answer.

5. *Write down the main idea*. Looking closely at the way the question is worded and at your brainstorming notes, write a sentence that states the main idea of your answer. If you are writing a paragraph, this sentence will be your **topic sentence**; if you are writing an essay, it will be your **thesis statement**.

6. *List your main points*. You do not want to waste your limited (and valuable) time making a detailed outline, but an informal outline that lists just your key points is worth the little time it takes. An informal outline will help you plan a clear direction for your paragraph or essay.

7. *Draft your answer*. You will spend most of your time actually writing the answers to the questions on the exam. Follow your outline, keep track of time, and consult your brainstorming notes when you need to—but stay focused on your writing.

8. *Reread, revise, and edit*. When you have finished drafting your answer, reread it carefully to make sure it says everything you want it to say—and that it answers the question.

FOCUS Academic Honesty

Academic honesty—the standard for truth and fairness in work and behavior—is very important in college. Understanding academic honesty goes beyond simply knowing that it is dishonest to cheat on a test. To be sure you are conforming to the rules of academic honesty, you need to pay attention to the following situations.

- Don't reuse papers you wrote in high school. The written work you are assigned in college is designed to help you learn, and your instructors expect you to do the work for the course when it is assigned.
- Don't copy information from a book or article or paste material from a Web site directly into your papers. Using someone else's words or ideas without proper acknowledgment constitutes **plagiarism**, a very serious offense.
- Don't ask another student (or your parents) to help you write or revise a paper. If you need help, ask your instructor or a writing center tutor.
- Don't allow another student to copy your work on a test.
- Don't allow another student to turn in a paper you wrote (or one you helped him or her write).
- Don't work with other students on a take-home exam unless your instructor gives you permission to do so.
- Never buy a paper. Even if you edit it, it is still not your own work.

FOCUS Safety on Campus

Colleges are very concerned about student safety. You should be, too.

- If you drive to school, be sure to lock your car, and always park in a well-lit space.
- If you live on campus, never give your room key or dorm access card to anyone else.
- Be aware of your surroundings at all times, and report strangers loitering on school property to campus police. Also report any suspicious or dangerous behavior—even by fellow students.
- If you live in a building that has buzzer access, don't buzz people in unless you know them. Get in the habit of keeping doors and windows locked.
- Don't wear valuable jewelry or bring large sums of money to class. Keep money, credit cards, and other valuables in a safe place, and don't flash them around.

(*continued on following page*)

(continued from previous page)

- Don't walk alone at night. If you need to be out at night—to go to the library, to your dorm room, or to a public transportation stop, for example—be sure to call your school's van or escort service (even if it means you need to wait). And don't leave a party alone; if you can't get someone you know to walk with you, call for an escort.

- Get in the habit of checking your school newspaper or Web site for crime statistics. If you know what kinds of crimes are most common on your campus and where they generally occur, you will be able to protect yourself.

- Be sure you know where the emergency call stations are located on your campus—and don't hesitate to call campus police for help if you feel threatened.

- If you are stopped by strangers and feel that you are in danger, try to run away. If you can't get away, make as much noise as possible.

- If you are in a situation—for example, at a party—where trouble arises, leave. Don't get involved or try to calm things down.

- Finally, be sure you know how college officials will contact students (for example, by email or by text message) in case of a campuswide weather or crime emergency.

Using Research in Your Writing

In many essays, you use your own ideas to support your points. In other essays—such as argument essays—you may need to supplement your own ideas with **research**: information from outside sources, such as books, magazines, and Internet sites. An expert's opinion, a memorable quotation, or a helpful fact or statistic from an outside source can make your writing more interesting, more authoritative, and more convincing.

When you write an essay that calls for research, you use material from books, periodicals (journals, magazines, and newspapers), and the Internet to support your ideas. You will have an easier time writing your essay if you follow these steps.

1. Choose a topic.
2. Do research.
3. Take notes.
4. Watch out for plagiarism.
5. State your thesis.
6. Make an outline.
7. Write your paper.
8. Document your sources.

1 Choosing a Topic

The first step in writing an essay that calls for research is finding a topic to write about. Before you choose a topic, ask the following questions.

- What is your page limit?
- When is your paper due?
- How many sources are you expected to use?
- What kind of sources are you expected to use?

The answers to these questions will help you tell if your topic is too broad or too narrow.

When May Compton, a student in a composition course, was asked to write a three- to four-page essay that was due in five weeks, she decided that she wanted to write about the counterfeit designer goods that seemed to be for sale everywhere. She knew, however, that the general topic "counterfeit designer goods" would be too broad for her essay.

May was used to seeing sidewalk vendors selling brand-name sunglasses and jewelry. Recently, she and her friends had been invited to a "purse party," where they were able to buy expensive handbags at extremely low prices. Even though these handbags were not identified as fakes, she was sure that they were. Because May was a marketing major, she wondered how these copies were marketed and sold. She also wondered if these counterfeits had any negative effects on consumers. May decided to explore the problem of counterfeit designer merchandise in her paper because she could discuss it in the required number of pages and would be able to finish her paper within the five-week time limit.

2 Doing Research

Finding Information in the Library

The best place to start your research is with the resources of your college library: print and electronic resources that you cannot find anywhere else—including on the Internet. For the best results, you should do your library research systematically. Begin by searching the library's online catalog and electronic databases; then, look for any additional facts or statistics that you need to support your ideas.

FOCUS The Resources of the Library

The Online Catalog

Once you get a general sense of your topic, you can consult the library's catalog. Libraries have **online catalogs** that enable you to use your computer to search all the resources held by the library. By typing in words or phrases related to your topic, you can find books, periodicals, and other materials that you can use in your paper.

Electronic Databases

After consulting the online catalog, you should look at the **electronic databases** that your library subscribes to. These databases enable you to access information from newspapers, magazines, and journals. Some list just citations, while others enable you to retrieve the full text of articles. (You can usually search your library's databases from home or from your dorm room.)

Sources for Facts and Statistics

As you write your paper, you may find that you need certain facts or statistics to support particular points. Works like *Facts on File*, the *Information Please Almanac,* and the *Statistical Abstract of the United States* can help you get such information. These and similar publications are available online; your reference librarian can recommend appropriate sources.

Remember, once you find information in the library, you still have to **evaluate** it—that is, to determine its usefulness and reliability. For example, an article in a respected periodical such as the *New York Times* or the *Wall Street Journal* is more trustworthy and believable than one in a tabloid such as the *National Enquirer* or the *Sun*. You should also look at the date of publication to decide if the book or article is up to date. Finally, consider the author. Is he or she an expert? Does the author have a particular point of view to advance? Your instructor or college librarian can help you select sources that are both appropriate and reliable.

▶ **Word Power**

tabloid a newspaper that emphasizes stories with sensational content

Finding Information on the Internet

The Internet can give you access to a great deal of information that can help you support your points and develop your essay. Most colleges and universities provide Internet access free of charge to students. Once you are online, you need to connect to a **search engine**, a program that helps you find information by sorting through the millions of documents that are available on the Internet. Among the most popular search engines are Google and Yahoo!.

There are three ways to use a search engine to find information.

1. *You can enter a Web site's URL.* All search engines have a box in which you can enter a Web site's electronic address, or **uniform resource locator (URL)**. When you click on the URL or hit your computer's Enter or Return key, the search engine connects you to the Web site. For example, to find information about family members who entered the United States through Ellis Island, you would enter the URL www.ellisislandrecords.com.

2. *You can do a keyword search.* All search engines let you do a **keyword search**. You type a term into a box, and the search engine looks for documents that contain the term, listing all the **hits** (documents containing one or both of these words) that it found. If you type in a broad term like *civil war*, you might get millions of hits—more than you could possibly consider. If this occurs, narrow your search by using a more specific term—*Battle of Gettysburg*, for example. You can focus your search even further by putting quotation marks around the term ("*Battle of Gettysburg*"). When you do this, the search engine will search only for documents that contain this specific phrase.

3. *You can do a subject search.* Some search engines, such as Yahoo!, let you do a **subject search**. First, you choose a broad subject from a list of subjects: *The Humanities, The Arts, Entertainment, Business,* and so on. Each of these general subjects leads you to more specific subjects, until eventually you get to the subtopic that you want. For example, you could start your search on Yahoo with the general topic *Entertainment*. Clicking on this topic would lead you to *Movies* and then to *Movie Reviews*. Finally, you would get to a list of movie reviews that might link to a review of the specific movie you are interested in.

> **FOCUS** Accessing Web Sites: Troubleshooting
>
> Sometimes, your computer will tell you that a site you want to visit is unavailable or does not exist. When this occurs, consider the following possibilities before moving on to another site.
>
> - *Check to make sure the URL is correct.* To reach a site, you have to type its URL accurately. Do not add spaces between items in the address or put a period at the end. Any error will send you to the wrong site—or to no site at all.
> - *Try using just part of the URL.* If the URL is very long, use just the part that ends in *.com* or *.gov*. If this part of the URL doesn't take you where you want to go, you have an incorrect address.
> - *Try revisiting the site later.* Sometimes, Web sites experience technical problems that prevent them from being accessed. Your computer will tell you if a site is temporarily unreachable.

Not every site you access is a valuable source of information. Just as you would with a print source, you should determine whether information you find on the Internet is believable and useful.

May began her research by doing a subject search of her library's online catalog to see what books it listed on her topic. Under the general subject of *counterfeits*, she found the headings *counterfeit coins* and *counterfeit money*. She did not, however, find any books on counterfeit designer goods. She thought that her topic might be too recent for any books to have been published on the subject, so she turned to her library's databases.

A quick look at the Infotrac database showed May that many recent articles had been written about counterfeit designer merchandise. Although some articles just reported police raids on local counterfeiting operations, a few discussed the reasons for counterfeiting and the negative effects of counterfeit goods.

Because May's topic was so current, she found that the Internet was her best source of information. Using the keywords *counterfeit designer goods* and *designer handbags knockoffs*, she located several recent newspaper and magazine articles about her topic. For example, using Google to search for the term *counterfeit designer goods*, she found a site maintained by the Resource for Security Executives that gave recent statistics of counterfeit seizures by the Department of Homeland Security. Using the same search terms on Yahoo!, May found an article in the *Arizona Republic* that discussed the purse parties that are often used to sell counterfeit designer handbags.

3   Taking Notes

Once you have gathered the material you will need, read it carefully, recording any information you think you can use in your essay. As you take notes, you will *paraphrase*, *summarize*, and *quote* your sources. As you do

so, keep your topic in mind; this will help you decide what material is useful. Record your notes on index cards, or in a computer file you have created for this purpose.

Paraphrasing

When you **paraphrase**, you use your own words to present the main ideas of a source, but you keep the order and emphasis of the original. You paraphrase when you want detailed information from the source but not the author's exact words. Paraphrase is useful when you want to make a difficult discussion easier to understand while still giving a clear sense of the original.

FOCUS **Writing a Paraphrase**

1. Read the passage until you understand it.

2. Jot down the main idea of the passage, and list all key supporting points.

3. As you write, follow the order and emphasis of the original.

4. When you revise, make sure you have used your own words and phrasing, and not the words or sentence structure of the original.

5. Document your source.

Here is a passage from the article "Hot Fakes," by Joanie Cox, followed by May's paraphrase.

ORIGINAL

Always pay close attention to the stitching. On a Kate Spade bag, the logo is stitched perfectly straight; it's not a sticker. Most designers stitch a simple label to the inside of their purses. On Chanel bags, however, the interior label is usually stamped and tends to match the color of the exterior. Study the material the bag is made from. A real Chanel Ligne Cambon multipocket bag, for example, is constructed from buttery lambskin leather, not vinyl.

PARAPHRASE

It is often possible to tell a fake designer handbag from a genuine one by looking at the details. For example, items such as logos should not be crooked. You should also look for the distinctive features of a particular brand of handbag. Counterfeiters will not take the time to match colors, and they may use vinyl instead of expensive leather (Cox).

Summarizing

Unlike a paraphrase, which restates the ideas of a source in detail, a **summary** is a general restatement, in your own words, of the main ideas of a passage. For this reason, a summary is always much shorter than the original. Unlike a paraphrase, a summary does not necessarily follow the order or emphasis of the original.

FOCUS **Writing a Summary**

1. Read the passage until you understand it.

2. Jot down the main idea of the passage.

3. As you write, make sure you use your own words, not those of your source.

4. When you revise, make sure your summary contains only the ideas of the source.

5. Document your source.

Here is May's summary of the original passage on page 663.

SUMMARY

Buyers who want to identify fake handbags should check details such as the way the label is sewn and the material the item is made from (Cox).

Quoting

When you quote, you use the author's exact words as they appear in the source, including all punctuation and capitalization. Enclose all words from your source in quotation marks—*followed by appropriate documentation*. Because quotations distract readers, use them only when you think that the author's exact words will add something to your discussion.

FOCUS **When to Quote**

1. Quote when the words of a source are so memorable that to put them into your own words would lessen their impact.

2. Quote when the words of a source are so unique or concise that a paraphrase or summary would change the meaning of the original.

3. Quote when the words of a source add authority to your discussion. The words of a recognized expert can help you make your point convincingly.

QUOTATION

Someone who wants to buy an authentic designer handbag should "pay close attention to the stitching" (Cox).

Integrating Sources

To show readers why you are using a source and to help you integrate source material smoothly into your essay, introduce paraphrases, summaries, and quotations with a phrase that identifies the source or its author. You can position this identifying phrase at various places in a sentence.

As one marketing expert points out, "A real Chanel Ligne Cambon multipocket bag, for example, is constructed from buttery lambskin leather, not vinyl" (Cox).

"A real Chanel Ligne Cambon multipocket bag, for example," says one marketing expert, "is constructed from buttery lambskin leather, not vinyl" (Cox).

"A real Chanel Ligne Cambon multipocket bag, for example, is constructed from buttery lambskin leather, not vinyl," observes one marketing expert (Cox).

FOCUS Integrating Sources

Instead of repeating the word *says,* use some of the words below when you introduce quotations.

admits	concludes	points out
believes	explains	remarks
claims	notes	states
comments	observes	suggests

---

4 Watching Out for Plagiarism

As a rule, you must **document** (give source information for) all words, ideas, or statistics from an outside source. (It is not necessary, however, to document **common knowledge**, factual information widely available in several different reference works.) When you present information from another source as if it is your own (whether you do it intentionally or unintentionally), you commit **plagiarism**—and plagiarism is theft. You can avoid plagiarism by understanding what you must document and what you do not have to document.

FOCUS Avoiding Plagiarism

You should document

- All word-for-word quotations from a source
- All summaries and paraphrases of material from a print or electronic source
- All ideas—opinions, judgments, and insights—of others
- All tables, graphs, charts, and statistics that you get from a source

You do not need to document

- Your own ideas
- Common knowledge
- Familiar quotations

Read the following paragraph from "The Facts on Fakes!" (an unsigned article on the National Association of Resale & Thrift Shops Web site) and the four rules that follow. This material will help you understand the most common causes of plagiarism and show you how to avoid it.

ORIGINAL

Is imitation really the sincerest form of flattery? Counterfeiting deceives the consumer and tarnishes the reputation of the genuine manufacturer. Brand value can be destroyed when a trademark is imposed on counterfeit products of inferior quality—hardly a form of flattery! Therefore, prestigious companies who are the targets of counterfeiters have begun to battle an industry that copies and sells their merchandise. They have filed lawsuits and in some cases have employed private investigators across the nation to combat the counterfeit trade. A quick search of the Internet brings up dozens of press releases from newspapers throughout the country, all reporting instances of law enforcement cracking down on sellers of counterfeit goods by confiscating bogus merchandise and imposing fines.

Rule 1. Document Ideas from Your Sources

PLAGIARISM

When counterfeits are sold, the original manufacturer does not take it as a compliment.

Even though the student writer does not quote her source directly, she must still identify the article as the source of this material because it expresses the article's ideas, not her own.

CORRECT

When counterfeits are sold, the original manufacturer does not take it as a compliment ("Facts").

Rule 2. Place Borrowed Words in Quotation Marks

PLAGIARISM

It is possible to ruin the worth of a brand by selling counterfeit products of inferior quality—hardly a form of flattery ("Facts").

Although the student writer cites the source, the passage incorrectly uses the source's exact words without quoting them. She must quote the borrowed words.

CORRECT (BORROWED WORDS IN QUOTATION MARKS)

It is possible to ruin the worth of a brand by selling "counterfeit products of inferior quality—hardly a form of flattery" ("Facts").

Rule 3. Use Your Own Phrasing

PLAGIARISM

Is copying a design a compliment? Not at all. The fake design not only tries to fool the buyer but also harms the original company. It can ruin the worth of a brand. Because counterfeits are usually of poor quality, they pay the original no compliment. As a result, companies whose products are often copied have started to fight back. They have sued the counterfeiters and have even used private detectives to identify phony goods. Throughout the United States, police have fined people who sell counterfeits and have seized their products ("Facts").

Even though the student writer acknowledges "The Facts on Fakes!" as her source, and even though she does not use the source's exact words, her passage closely follows the order, emphasis, sentence structure, and phrasing of the original. In the following passage, the writer uses her own wording, quoting (and documenting) one distinctive phrase from the source.

CORRECT

According to "The Facts on Fakes!" it is not a compliment when an original design is copied by a counterfeiter. The poor quality of most fakes is "hardly a form of flattery" ("Facts"). The harm to the image of the original manufacturers has caused them to fight back against the counterfeiters, sometimes using their own detectives. As a result, lawsuits and criminal charges have led to fines and confiscated merchandise ("Facts").

Note: Even though the paragraph ends with parenthetical documentation, the quotation requires its own citation.

Rule 4. Distinguish Your Ideas from the Source's Ideas

PLAGIARISM

Counterfeit goods are not harmless. Counterfeiting not only fools the consumer, but it also destroys confidence in the quality of the real thing. Manufacturers know this and have begun to fight back. A number have begun to sue "and in some cases have employed private investigators across the nation to combat the counterfeit trade" ("Facts").

In the passage above, only the quotation in the last sentence seems to be borrowed from the article "The Facts on Fakes!" In fact, however, the ideas in the second sentence also come from this article. The writer should use an identifying phrase to acknowledge the borrowed material in this sentence.

CORRECT

Counterfeit goods are not harmless. According to the article "The Facts on Fakes!" counterfeiting not only fools the consumer, but it also destroys confidence in the quality of the real thing. Manufacturers know this and have begun to fight back. A number have begun to sue "and in some cases have employed private investigators across the nation to combat the counterfeit trade" ("Facts").

FOCUS Avoiding Plagiarism

When you transfer information from Web sites into your notes, you may accidentally "copy and paste" text without noting where the text came from. If you then copy this text into a draft of your paper, you are committing **plagiarism,** the theft of ideas. Every college has rules that students must follow when using words, ideas, and visuals from books, articles, and Internet sources. Consult your school's Web site or student handbook for information on the appropriate use of such information.

---

5 Stating Your Thesis

After you have taken notes, review the information you have gathered, and develop a thesis statement. Your **thesis statement** is a single sentence that states the main idea of your paper and tells readers what to expect. After reviewing her notes, May Compton came up with the following thesis statement for her paper on counterfeit designer goods.

THESIS STATEMENT

People should not buy counterfeit designer merchandise, no matter how tempted they are to do so.

---

6 Making an Outline

Once you have a thesis statement, you are ready to make an outline. Your outline, which covers just the body paragraphs of your paper, can be either a **topic outline** (in which each idea is expressed in a word or a short

phrase) or a **sentence outline** (in which each idea is expressed in a complete sentence). After reviewing her notes, May Compton wrote the following sentence outline for her paper.

    I. Real designer goods are too expensive.
        A. Genuine designer merchandise costs ten times more than it costs to make it.
        B. Even people who can afford it buy fakes.
    II. Buying designer knockoffs is a form of stealing.
        A. The buyer is stealing the work of the original designer.
        B. Counterfeiting operations take jobs away from legitimate workers.
        C. The buyer is stealing the sales taxes that would be paid by the original designer.
   III. Buying designer knockoffs supports organized crime.
        A. The production of designer knockoffs requires money and organization.
        B. Buying knockoffs supports illegal activities.
           1. The profits of selling knockoffs support murder, prostitution, and drugs.
           2. Knockoffs are made in shops that violate the law.
   IV. There is evidence that designer knockoffs support terrorism.
        A. The 1993 World Trade Center bombing has been connected to a counterfeit operation.
        B. The 2001 World Trade Center bombing has been connected to counterfeiting.
        C. The 2004 Madrid train bombing has been connected to counterfeiting.

7 Writing Your Paper

Once you have decided on a thesis and written an outline, you are ready to write a draft of your essay.

- Begin with an **introduction** that includes your thesis statement. Usually, your introduction will be a single paragraph, but sometimes it will be longer.
- In the **body** of your essay, support your thesis statement, with each body paragraph developing a single point. These paragraphs should have clear topic sentences so that your readers will know exactly what points you are making. Use transitional words and phrases to help readers follow your ideas.
- Finally, write a **conclusion** that gives readers a sense of completion. Like your introduction, your conclusion will usually be a single paragraph, but it could be longer. It should reinforce your thesis statement and should end with a memorable sentence.

Remember, you will probably write several drafts of your essay before you hand it in. You can use the Self-Assessment Checklists on pages 163 and 164 to help you revise and edit your paper.

May Compton's completed essay on counterfeit designer goods begins on page 676.

When you **document** your sources, you tell readers where you found the ideas you used in your essay. The Modern Language Association (MLA) recommends the following documentation style for essays that use sources. This format consists of *parenthetical references* in the body of the paper that refer to a *works-cited list* at the end the paper.

Parenthetical References in the Text

A parenthetical reference should include enough information to lead readers to a specific entry in your works-cited list. A typical parenthetical reference consists of the author's last name and the page number (Brown 2). If you use more than one work by the same author, include a shortened form of the title in the parenthetical reference (Brown, "Demand for Fake Designer Goods"). Notice that there is no comma and no *p* or *p.* before the page number.

Whenever possible, introduce information from a source with a phrase that includes the author's name. (If you do this, include only the page number in parentheses.) Place documentation so that it does not interrupt the flow of your ideas, preferably at the end of a sentence.

> As Jonathan Brown observes in "Demand for Fake Designer Goods Is Soaring," as many as 70 percent of buyers of luxury goods are willing to wear designer brands alongside of fakes (2).

In the four special situations listed below, the format for parenthetical references departs from these guidelines.

1. When You Are Citing a Work by Two Authors

> Instead of buying nonbranded items of similar quality, many customers are willing to pay extra for the counterfeit designer label (Grossman and Shapiro 79).

2. When You Are Citing a Work without a Listed Author

> More counterfeit goods come from China than from any other country ("Counterfeit Goods").

3. When You Are Citing a Statement by One Author That Is Quoted in a Work by Another Author

> When speaking of consumers' buying habits, designer Miuccia Prada says, "There is a kind of an obsession with bags" (qtd. in Thomas 23).

4. When You Are Citing an Electronic Source

> A seller of counterfeited goods in California "now faces 10 years in prison and $20,000 in fines" (Cox).

Note: Material downloaded from the Internet or from a library's electronic databases frequently lacks publication information—for example, page numbers. For this reason, the parenthetical references that cite it may contain just the author's name (as in example 4 above) or just a shortened title (as in example 2 above) if the article appears without an author.

FOCUS **Formatting Quotations**

■ **Short quotations** Quotations of no more than four typed lines are run in with the text of your paper. End punctuation comes after the parenthetical reference (which follows the quotation marks).

According to Dana Thomas, customers often "pick up knockoffs for one-tenth the legitimate bag's retail cost, then pass them off as real" ("Terror's Purse Strings").

■ **Long quotations** Quotations of more than four lines are set off from the text of your paper. Begin a long quotation one inch from the left-hand margin, and do not enclose it in quotation marks. Do not indent the first line of a single paragraph. If a quoted passage has more than one paragraph, indent the first line of each paragraph (including the first) one-quarter inch. Introduce a long quotation with a complete sentence followed by a colon, and place the parenthetical reference one space *after* the end punctuation.

In his article, Dana Thomas describes a surprise visit to a factory that makes counterfeit purses:

> On a warm winter afternoon in Guangzhao, I accompanied Chinese police officers on a raid in a decrepit tenement. We found two dozen children, ages 8 to 13, gluing and sewing together fake luxury-brand handbags. The police confiscated everything, arrested the owner and sent the children out. Some punched their timecards, hoping to still get paid. ("Terror's Purse Strings")

The Works-Cited List

The works-cited list includes all the works you **cite** (refer to) in your essay. Use the guidelines in the box on pages 674–75 to help you prepare your list.

The following sample works-cited entries cover the situations you will encounter most often. Follow the formats exactly as they appear here.

B 8

Books

Books by One Author

List the author with last name first. Underline the title. Include the city of publication and a shortened form of the publisher's name—for example, *Bedford* for *Bedford/St. Martin's*. Use the abbreviation *UP* for *University Press*, as in *Princeton UP* and *U of Chicago P*. End with the date of publication.

Russo, Richard. <u>Bridge of Sighs</u>. New York: Knopf, 2007.

Note: MLA recommends that you underline book titles, not put them in italics.

Books by Two or Three Authors

List second and subsequent authors with first name first, in the order in which they are listed on the book's title page.

Buchanan, Andrea J., and Miriam Peskowitz. <u>The Daring Book for Girls</u>.
   New York: Collins, 2007.

Book by More than Three Authors

List only the first author, followed by the abbreviation *et al.* ("and others").

Nelson, Bill, et al. <u>Guide to Computer Forensics and Investigations</u>. 3rd ed.
   Boston: Thomson, 2007.

Two or More Books by the Same Author

List two or more books by the same author in alphabetical order according to title. In each entry after the first, use three unspaced hyphens (followed by a period) instead of the author's name.

Alda, Alan. <u>Never Have Your Dog Stuffed</u>. New York: Arrow, 2007.

---. <u>Things I Overheard While Talking to Myself</u>. New York: Random, 2007.

Edited Book

Thompson, Hunter S. <u>Gonzo</u>. Ed. Steve Crist. Los Angeles: Ammo, 2007.

Translation

Garcia Marquez, Gabriel. <u>Living to Tell the Tale</u>. Trans. Edith Grossman.
   New York: Knopf, 2004.

Revised Edition

Bjelajac, David. <u>American Art: A Cultural History</u>. Rev. ed. New York: Prentice,
   2007.

Anthology

Weiss, M. Jerry, and Helen Weiss, eds. <u>Signet Book of American Essays</u>.
   New York: Signet, 2006.

Essay in an Anthology

    Welty, Eudora. "Writing and Analyzing a Story." <u>Signet Book of American Essays</u>.
        Ed. M. Terry Weiss and Helen Weiss. New York: Signet, 2006. 21-30.

Section or Chapter of a Book

    Gordimer, Nadine. "Loot." <u>"Loot" and Other Stories</u>. New York: Penguin, 2004. 1-6.

Periodicals

Journals

A **journal** is a periodical aimed at readers who know a lot about a particular subject—literature or history, for example. The articles they contain can sometimes be challenging.

Article in a Journal with Continuous Pagination throughout Annual Volume

Some scholarly journals have continuous pagination; that is, one issue might end on page 234, and the next issue would then begin with page 235. In this case, the volume number is followed by the date of publication in parentheses.

    Sauter, Michael J. "Clockwatchers and Stargazers: Time Discipline in Early
        Modern Berlin." <u>American Historical Review</u> 112 (2007): 685-709.

Article in a Journal with Separate Pagination in Each Issue

For a journal in which each issue begins with page 1, the volume number is followed by a period and the issue number and then by the date. Leave no space after the period.

    Sánchez, Maria Carla. "What the Archive Could Not Tell Me." <u>English Language</u>
        <u>Notes</u> 45.1 (2007): 57-66.

Magazines

A **magazine** is a periodical aimed at general readers. For this reason, it contains articles that are easier to understand than those in scholarly journals. Frequently, an article in a magazine does not appear on consecutive pages. For example, it may begin on page 40, skip to page 47, and continue on page 49. If this is the case, your citation should include only the first page, followed by a plus sign.

Article in a Monthly or Bimonthly Magazine

    Edwards, Owen. "Kilroy Was Here." <u>Smithsonian</u> Oct. 2004: 40+.
    Frakes, Dan. "Mac Gems." <u>MacWorld</u> Jan. 2006: 52-55.

Article in a Weekly or Biweekly Magazine (Signed/Unsigned)

    Schley, Jim. "Laid Off and Working Harder than Ever." <u>Newsweek</u> 20 Sept.
        2004: 16.
    "Real Reform Post-Enron." <u>The Nation</u> 4 Mar. 2002: 3.

Newspapers

Article in a Newspaper

    Sullivan, Kevin. "Hustling to Find Classrooms for All in a Diverse Ireland."
        <u>Washington Post</u> 24 Oct. 2007: A12.

Editorial
"Plowing Old Ground." Editorial. <u>Washington Post</u> 23 Oct. 2007: A18.

Internet Sources

Full source information is not always available for Internet sources. When citing Internet sources, include whatever information you can find—ideally, the title of the Internet site (underlined), the date of electronic publication (if available), and the date you accessed the source. Always include the electronic address (URL) enclosed in angle brackets.

Document within a Web Site
"Airman Writes about Life." <u>U.S. Department Of Defense Web Site</u>. 28 Sept. 2007. 1 Oct. 2007 <http://www.defenselink.mil/>.

Personal Site
Bricklin, Dan. Home page. 29 Sept. 2007 <http://www.bricklin.com>.

Article in an Online Reference Book or Encyclopedia
"Sudan." <u>Infoplease World Atlas & Map Library</u>. 2007. 29 Apr. 2008 <http://www.infoplease.com/atlas/>.

Article in a Newspaper
Belson, Ken, and Jill P. Capuzzo. "Towns Rethink Laws against Illegal Immigrants." <u>New York Times on the Web</u> 26 Sept. 2007. 29 Sept. 2008 <http://www.nytimes.com/>.

Editorial
"The Fires This Time." Editorial. <u>New York Times on the Web</u> 24 Oct. 2007. 7 Dec. 2007 <http://www.nytimes.com>.

Article in a Magazine
Patterson, Troy. "The Experience of Actually Watching Live TV." <u>Slate</u> 28 Sept. 2007. 29 Nov. 2007 <http://www.slate.com>.

FOCUS **Preparing the Works-Cited List**

■ Begin the works-cited list on a new page after the last page of your essay.
■ Number the works-cited page as the next page of your essay.
■ Center the heading *Works Cited* one inch from the top of the page; do not underline the heading or place it in quotation marks.
■ Double-space the list.

(continued on following page)

(continued from previous page)

- List entries alphabetically according to the author's last name.
- Alphabetize unsigned articles according to the first major word of the title.
- Begin typing each entry at the left-hand margin.
- Indent second and subsequent lines five spaces (or one-half inch).
- Separate major divisions of each entry—author, title, and publication information—by a period and one space.

Sample Essay Using MLA Style

On the pages that follow is May Compton's completed essay on the topic of counterfeit designer goods. The essay uses MLA documentation style and includes a works-cited page.

B 8

May Compton

Professor DiSalvo

English 100

29 April 2008

The True Price of Counterfeit Goods

At purse parties in city apartments and suburban homes, customers can buy "designer" handbags at impossibly low prices. On street corners, sidewalk vendors sell name-brand perfumes and sunglasses for much less than the list price. On the Internet, buyers can buy fine watches for a fraction of the prices charged by manufacturers. Is this too good to be true? Of course it is. All of these bargains are really knock-offs — copies of the real thing. What the people who buy these items do not know (or prefer not to think about) is that the money they are spending supports organized crime and, sometimes, terrorism. People should not buy counterfeit designer merchandise, no matter how tempted they are to do so.

People who buy counterfeit designer merchandise defend their actions by saying that designer merchandise costs too much. This is certainly true. According to Dana Thomas, the manufacturers of genuine designer merchandise charge more than ten times what it costs to make it. A visitor from Britain, who bought an imitation Gucci purse in New York City for fifty dollars, said, "The real thing is so overpriced. To buy a genuine Gucci purse, I would have to pay over a thousand dollars" (qtd. in "Counterfeit Goods"). Even people who can easily afford to pay the full amount buy fakes. For example, movie stars like Jennifer Lopez openly wear counterfeit goods, and many customers think that if it is all right for celebrities like Lopez to buy fakes, it must also be all right for them too (Malone). As Kim Wallace points out, however, legitimate companies invest a lot of money in designs, fabrics, and salaries. The high prices that these companies charge reflect their costs.

What most people ignore is that buying counterfeit items is really stealing. The FBI estimates that in the United States alone, companies lose about $250 billion as a result of counterfeits (Wallace). In addition, buyers of counterfeit items avoid the state and local sales taxes that legitimate companies pay. Thus, New York City alone loses about a billion dollars every year as a result of the sale of counterfeit merchandise ("Counterfeit Goods"). When this happens, everyone loses. After all, a billion dollars would pay for a lot of police officers and teachers, would fill a lot of potholes, and would pave a lot of streets. Buyers of counterfeit designer goods do not think of themselves as thieves, but that is exactly what they really are.

Introduction

Thesis statement

Paragraph combines paraphrase, quotation, and May's own ideas.

Paragraph contains May's own ideas combined with paraphrases of material from two articles

Compton 2

Buyers of counterfeit merchandise also do not realize that the sale of knock-offs supports organized crime. Most of the profits go to the criminal organization that either makes or imports the counterfeit goods — not to the person who sells the items. In fact, the biggest manufacturer and distributor of counterfeit items is organized crime. Michael Kessler, who heads a company that investigates corporate crime, makes this connection clear when he describes the complicated organization that is needed to make counterfeit perfume:

> They need a place that makes bottles, a factory with pumps to fill the bottles, a printer to make the labels, and a box manufacturer to fake the packaging. Then, they need a sophisticated distribution network, as well as all the cash to set everything up. (qtd. in Malone)

Kessler concludes that only an organized crime syndicate — not any individual — has the money to support this illegal activity. For this reason, anyone who buys counterfeits may also be supporting activities such as prostitution, drug distribution, smuggling of illegal immigrants, gang warfare, extortion, and murder. In addition, the workers who make counterfeits often work in sweatshops where labor and environmental laws are ignored. The illegal factories are often located in countries where children usually work long hours for very low pay (Malone). In fact, as Dana Thomas points out, a worker in China who makes counterfeits earns only a fraction of the salary of a worker who makes the real thing.

Finally, and perhaps most shocking, there is evidence that some of the money earned from the sale of counterfeit designer goods goes to support international terrorism. For example, Kim Wallace reports that during Al-Qaeda training, terrorists are advised to sell fakes to get money for their operations. According to Interpol, an international police organization, the bombing of the World Trade Center in 1993 was paid for in part by the sale of fake T-shirts. Also, evidence suggests that associates of the 2001 bombers of the World Trade Center may have been involved with the production of imitation designer goods (Malone). Finally, the 2004 bombing of commuter trains in Madrid was financed in part by the sale of counterfeits. In fact, an intelligence source states, "It would be more shocking if Al Qaeda *wasn't* involved in counterfeiting. The sums involved are staggering — it would be inconceivable if money were not being raised for their terrorist activities" (qtd. in Malone). Most people would never contribute directly to terrorism, but customers who buy counterfeit purses or fake perfume may be doing just that.

Customers should realize that when they buy counterfeits, they are actually breaking the law. By doing so, they are making it possible for organized crime and

Long quotation is set off from the text

Paragraph contains May's own ideas as well as a paraphrase and a quotation

Conclusion contains May's original ideas, so no documentation is necessary

terrorists to earn money for their illegal activities. Although buyers of counterfeit merchandise justify their actions by saying that the low prices are impossible to resist, they might reconsider if they knew the uses to which their money was going. The truth of the matter is that counterfeit products, such as designer handbags, sunglasses, jewelry, and T-shirts, are "luxuries" that people could do without. By resisting the temptation to buy knock-offs, consumers could help to eliminate the companies that hurt legitimate manufacturers, exploit workers, and perhaps even finance international terrorism.

Compton 4

Works Cited

"Counterfeit Goods Are Linked to Terror Groups." <u>International Herald Tribune</u>
    12 Feb. 2007. 24 Mar. 2008 <http://www.iht.com>.

Malone, Andrew. "Revealed: The True Cost of Buying Cheap Fake Goods." <u>Daily
    Mail</u> 29 July 2007. 25 Mar. 2008 <http://www.dailymail.co.uk>.

Thomas, Dana. "Terror's Purse Strings." Editorial. <u>New York Times</u> 30 Aug. 2007:
    A23.

Wallace, Kim. "A Counter-Productive Trade." <u>Times Daily</u> 29 July 2007. 31 Mar.
    2008 <http://TimesDaily.com>.

Internet source
has no listed
author

Taking Standardized Assessment Tests

During your time as a student, you have probably taken a standardized test. In fact, you've probably taken several. (For example, a student in New York City takes an average of twenty-one standardized tests before graduating from high school.)

The most common standardized tests are exit exams and placement tests. **Exit exams** (like the Georgia Regents' Testing Program) determine whether you are ready to graduate from college. They can also assess whether you are ready to move higher up in a program. **Placement tests** (like the COMPASS and ASSET tests) are designed to place you in classes that are right for your skill level.

Whether you're taking an exit exam or a placement test, there are several things you can do to prepare for them. Adequate preparation will help decrease your anxiety and increase your score.

1 Dealing with Anxiety

Not knowing what to expect from a standardized test can make you anxious. Some amount of test anxiety is natural and can actually help you to work harder and faster. However, if you are too worried, your judgment may be impaired, or you may freeze at the first question, wasting valuable time. The best way to beat test anxiety is to know your test before you take it and then practice as much as you can.

2 Preparing for Standardized Tests

1. *Read.* Learn about your test in advance so you know what it looks like and what kinds of questions it usually asks. In other words, look at examples of previous tests.
2. *Practice.* If you are taking a common exam, go to the test's Web site to look for practice tests and other materials that can help you prepare. If your test is specific to your school, ask your instructor or librarian if a practice test is available. To review specific writing, grammar, and mechanics skills, refer to material covered in *Writing First*. For extra practice questions, go to *Exercise Central* at bedfordstmartins.com/ writingfirst.
3. *Plan your time.* While you take the practice tests, figure out how much time you will need to complete each section, and develop a **time-plan** that tells you how much time to spend on each part of the test

and how much time to spend planning and reviewing. Give yourself extra time for challenging sections, but don't spend all your time there. Then, on test day, write your time-plan in the test's margins, and refer back to it as you work (be sure to ask the exam proctor if you are allowed to write on the exam). Remember to reserve time to review your work at the end.

4. *Be rested and ready.* On the night before the exam, relax. Don't stay up too late, and avoid cramming. Instead, prepare a few days in advance so that you are not stressed out. In the morning, eat a good breakfast and review your time-plan. If you've done your research and taken a few practice tests, you should be ready.

FOCUS **Common Exit Exams and Placement Tests**

The following is a list of common exit exams and placement tests. Use the resources listed below to help you prepare for your test.

Accuplacer

To read more about how to prepare for the test, visit **collegeboard .com/student/testing/accuplacer/index.html** for tips, general information, and sample questions.

COMPASS/ASSET

To get more information about the COMPASS and ASSET tests and to view student guides and samples, visit these Web sites: **act.org/ compass** and **act.org/asset**.

CUNY/ACT

For sample student essays and practice tests for the CUNY/ACT test, visit the Skills Assessment Program's Web site at **rwc.hunter .cuny.edu/act/index.html**.

THEA

For more information on the THEA and for access to a practice test, visit the THEA Web site at **thea.nesinc.com**.

CLAST

For general information on the CLAST, visit the CLAST Web site at **www.firn.edu/doe/sas/clsthome.htm**.

Georgia Regents' Tests

For more information on this test, including a sample reading skills test and a list of approved essay topics, go to **www2.gsu.edu/ ~wwwrtp**.

Multiple-choice questions measure both your ability to remember facts and your critical-thinking skills. These questions often have several answers that seem right. You are expected to find the *best* answer.

1. ***Use your time-plan.*** Before the test, find out what kind of time-keeping device (for example, a watch or a cellphone) you are allowed to bring into the exam. During the test, use the time-plan you developed to help you pace your work.

2. ***Read the directions carefully.*** The directions will tell you how to answer the questions, how much time you have for each question, and how questions will be graded. Keep these directions in mind as you work.

3. ***Answer what is asked.*** Be sure you know exactly what the question is asking. Read the question carefully, and be sure to highlight the question's key words. Think about how to answer the question before you answer it.

4. ***Answer questions in order.*** If you are taking a paper test, stay organized. Answer the questions in order, do not linger too long on any one question, and keep track of answers you have doubts about. After you have answered all the questions, recheck the ones you were uncertain of.

5. ***Try to anticipate the answer.*** Try to answer the question before you read through the answer choices (A, B, C, and D). Then, compare each of the possible choices to the answer you thought of. Be sure to read every word of each possible answer; often, the choices are similar.

6. ***Divide and conquer.*** If you cannot anticipate the answer, check each answer choice against the question. Eliminate any answers you know are incorrect. Of the remaining statements, pick the one that most precisely answers the question. If you are having trouble determining which one is most correct, try focusing on the differences between the remaining answers.

7. ***Consider "All of the above."*** If there is an "All of the above" answer choice and you have determined that at least two answer choices are correct, select "All of the above."

8. ***Identify negatives and absolutes.*** Underline **negative words** like *not*, *but*, *never*, and *except*. Negative words can change a question in important ways. For example, "Choose the answer that is correct" is very different from "Choose the answer that is *not* correct." Be especially alert for double (and even triple) negatives within a sentence. Work out each question's true meaning before you attempt to answer it. (For example, "He was *not* unfriendly" means that he was friendly.) Also underline **absolutes** such as *always*, *never*, and *only*. Answers containing absolutes are often incorrect because exceptions can be found to almost every absolute statement.

9. ***Make an educated guess.*** If you're still not sure which answer to select, make an educated guess. Before guessing, eliminate as many answers as possible. Then, select an answer that uses a qualifying term, like *usually*, *often*, or *most*. If all else fails, choose the answer that you first thought seemed right. Your first instinct is often correct.

10. ***Understand how computer-adaptive tests work.*** If you are taking a computer-adaptive test, keep in mind that the questions get harder as

you answer them correctly. Do not get discouraged if the final questions of each section are very difficult (the final questions affect your score much less than earlier questions do). Also, remember that computer-adaptive tests prevent you from returning to difficult questions. Even so, you should not spend too much time on one question; if you aren't sure, make an educated guess. Finally, be sure to use scratch paper. You will not be able to use the computer to work out answers.

4 Tips for Essay Questions

The essays you write on standardized tests are similar to the essays that you write in class. However, test essays are often scored differently. In addition, some tests might require more than one essay—for example, one essay will assess grammar and mechanics while another will assess critical-thinking skills. Pay close attention to the instructions on your test. Review the points that follow to help you prepare.

1. *Know how to score points.* Before the test, find out how your essay will be scored. Ask your teacher or librarian, look at a practice test, or visit the test's Web site to find out what the test emphasizes. If this information is not available, assume that large issues (like ideas, logic, and organization) will be more important than small ones (like spelling and grammar)—although all of these elements count.

2. *Know what's being asked.* When you take the test, read through each essay question and all of the directions. Make sure you understand them before continuing. Some standardized tests require you to write multiple essays in a limited amount of time; find out in advance if that is the case with your test.

3. *Tackle easy questions first.* Read all the questions, and begin with the one that seems the easiest. Starting strong will help ease your anxiety and give you momentum. In addition, you will score higher if you finish your best work before time runs out.

4. *Make a plan.* Quickly jot down your initial essay ideas. Then, develop a thesis, and make a rough outline of your essay. The few minutes you spend planning will improve your essay's organization and keep you on track as you work.

5. *Get down to business.* On standardized essay tests, keep your writing lean and efficient. Avoid long, complicated introductions. Instead, begin your first paragraph with a sentence that directly answers the essay question and states your thesis. After you've stated your thesis, keep it in mind for the rest of your essay. Look back at the question as you write, and make sure your essay is answering it.

6. *Manage your time.* If you run out of time before you finish writing, quickly jot down an outline of your remaining ideas. If you have time, check your essay, looking for a clear thesis, effective support, appropriate transitions, and a strong concluding statement. Finally, quickly proofread your work and correct any grammatical or mechanical errors.

Looking for a job requires that you understand your goals, look for job leads in the right places, learn about companies and organizations that might employ you, and—most important—learn how to sell yourself.

1 Defining Your Goals

Before you look for a job, you should determine how much time you can devote to work and what you hope to gain from the experience.

1. ***Determine how much time you have.*** How many hours do you think you need to work? How many hours a week *can* you work while still in school? Are those hours distributed throughout the week, or are they all grouped in one or two days? Can you work during regular business hours, or will you need to work evenings?
2. ***Consider unpaid work.*** If you can afford to take an unpaid internship, you can gain the experience you need to get a paying position later on. In addition to exploring existing internships, you can create your own internship by offering to work at an organization without pay so that you can gain experience.

2 Learning about Job Openings

Once you define your goals, you should look for a job in an organized way. The strategies below will help you get the most out of your search.

1. ***Check your college placement office.*** Placement offices generally list both part-time and full-time jobs as well as short-term and temporary positions.
2. ***Scan newspaper and Web listings.*** Many people find jobs through classified advertisements in newspapers or on Web sites. Web sites called **job boards** also post listings and invite job seekers to post their résumés (see D4 for a sample résumé). Here are two of the most popular job boards.

   ■ Monster Board: www.monster.com
   ■ The Job Resource: www.thejobresource.com

3. *Network*. **Networking** means telling instructors, friends, and relatives about your goals and qualifications and finding out who may have helpful information for you.
4. *Keep your eyes open.* Many jobs are never advertised. Some small businesses, for example, rely on word of mouth, signs put in store windows, or flyers posted on campus or community bulletin boards.

3   Marketing Yourself

Once you have found a job you want to apply for, you have to get ready to market yourself to a prospective employer.

1. *Prepare your résumé.* The résumé that you spend hours perfecting usually gets no more than a one-minute review. To increase your résumé's chance of generating interest, you should include most of the following items:

    ■ **Objective** or **Goal** to indicate which position you are suited for

    ■ **Education** and **Experience** to demonstrate your qualifications

    ■ **Special Skills** to illustrate how you are different from others who are applying for the job

    ■ **Activities, Achievements, Honors, Leadership,** and **Interests** to highlight your accomplishments

    ■ **References** to support what you have written about yourself

    Note: Be prepared to update your résumé on a regular basis as your experiences and preferences change. (See D4 for a sample résumé.)
2. *Prepare a cover letter.* Don't simply repeat in the cover letter what your résumé already says. Instead, use the cover letter to make yourself stand out. Show what you know about the organization's needs, and tell how you can benefit the organization. Be sure to address your letter to a specific individual rather than to a general audience such as "To Whom It May Concern." (See D4 for a sample cover letter.)
3. *Prepare for an interview.* Interviews may take place in person or by phone; they may be held on campus or in an employer's office. The interviewer wants to see if you are suited for the job and if you can answer his or her questions.

FOCUS   Interviews: Frequently Asked Questions

Go into an interview prepared to answer the following frequently asked questions.

■ Can you tell me about yourself?
■ Where do you see yourself in five years?
■ How do you respond to criticism?

(continued on following page)

(*continued from previous page*)

- What accomplishment are you most proud of?
- What is your greatest strength? What is your greatest weakness?
- Why did you choose your school? What did you like about it? What did you not like?
- What do you know about our organization?
- Are you willing to relocate or travel?

At the interview, dress appropriately, make eye contact, demonstrate professional behavior (arrive on time, do not smoke, and so on), and sell yourself.

Speak slowly, answer the interviewer's questions fully, and illustrate your points with specific examples from your previous job experiences. If the interviewer asks you a difficult question, take time to think of an answer; don't just say the first thing that comes to your mind, At the end of the interview, thank the interviewer.

4. *Write a follow-up letter*. A strong follow-up letter will make a favorable impression on a potential employer (see D4 for a sample follow-up letter). If you want to expand on an answer that you gave in the interview, this is your chance.

4   Sample Job-Application Materials

An important part of applying for a job is putting together an effective résumé and writing letters of application and follow-up letters. The following examples were written by a student who was applying for a full-time position in the field of hotel management.

Rolando J. Matta

School
321 Topland Avenue
Johnson City, NY 13790
607-737-1111
rjmatta@fhcc.edu

Home
6543 Lincoln Street, 6D
Chicago, IL 60666
312-787-5555
rjmatta@hotmail.com

— Include relevant contact information

OBJECTIVE   Associate innkeeper position in the Chicago area

EDUCATION   Fox Hollow Community College,
                Johnson City, NY 13790
                Major: Hospitality Management
                Expected date of graduation: June 2009
                GPA of 3.4 on a 4.0 scale   ◄——————— Omit GPA if under 3.0
                   Major courses (partial list)
                   Hotel and Restaurant Accounting
                   Hotel-Restaurant Organization and Management
                   Food Purchasing
                   Principles of Food Preparation
                   Executive Housekeeping
                   Hotel Front-Office Operations
                   Hospitality Law

EXPERIENCE   **Hospitality Internship,**
                Grande Hotel, New York, NY
                May 2008 to August 2008
                • Rotated through Front Desk, Housekeeping, and Room
                  Service departments in hands-on and supervisory
                  positions
                • Participated in weekly question-and-answer sessions with
                  key managers
                • Reported on satisfaction of American Bar Association
                  conventioneers
                • Researched cost savings on alternative gifts for returning
                  guests

                Assistant to Meetings Supervisor,
                VIP Executive Suites, Binghamton, NY
                August 2007 to May 2008
                • Coordinated and reviewed setup and breakdown of
                  furniture and refreshments for all meeting rooms
                • Communicated with Audiovisual Department
                • Reviewed all billing against contracts
                • Scheduled appointments for prospective clients with
                  supervisor

OTHER SKILLS   Bilingual (English/Spanish)
ACTIVITIES   Travel in Europe and Latin America; summer cooking
                classes in New York
REFERENCES   Available on request

— Use boldface and bullets to highlight important information

Sample Résumé

321 Topland Avenue
Johnson City, NY 13790
607-737-1111
rjmatta@fhcc.edu

Include your address and the date ——

April 1, 2009

Ms. Jennifer T. White
Manager
Rotunda Hotel and Sports Club
88990 Airport Highway
Chicago, IL 60677

Include the name and address of the person you are writing to ——

Write to a specific person ——►

Dear Ms. White:

Mr. Luigi Cuenca of the Grande Hotel in New York, where I worked last summer, told me that you are looking for a management assistant. I believe my experience at the Grande Hotel and elsewhere has prepared me for this position.

Tell what you know about the organization and what you can bring to it ——►

Since the Rotunda is at O'Hare Airport, I know that many of your guests stay there because of last-minute flight cancellations. For this reason, my experience in responding to frustrated travelers will be of use to you. In addition, I have been reading about the services that hotels in Europe offer to business travelers. I would like to have the opportunity to implement some of these services in the United States.

Politely indicate your availability for an interview ——►

I have enclosed my résumé, and I look forward to talking with you. I will be available for an interview anytime after my final exams on May 30.

Sincerely,

Sign above your typed name ——►

Rolando J. Matta

Rolando J. Matta

Sample Cover Letter

321 Topland Avenue
Johnson City, NY 13790
607-737-1111
rjmatta@fhcc.edu

June 10, 2009

Ms. Jennifer T. White
Manager
Rotunda Hotel and Sports Club
88990 Airport Highway
Chicago, IL 60677

Dear Ms. White:

Thank you for meeting with me earlier today. I appreciated the opportunity ⟵ Thank the interviewer
to speak with you. I especially enjoyed hearing how the Rotunda is similar
to the Grande Hotel in New York City.

The Web site for the hotel in Sydney that we discussed is at ⟵ Provide supplementary information
www.medusa.com.au. On this Web site, you will find photos of
the wall units in each room. These units not only make an attractive
appearance, but they also save space in the closet and in the mini-kitchen.

I am extremely interested in joining your staff and feel certain that I could ⟵ State your enthusiasm directly
contribute much to your organization.   and briefly

Sincerely,

Rolando J. Matta

Rolando J. Matta

Sample Follow-up Letter after an Interview

Answers to Odd-Numbered Exercise Items

Chapter 15

◆ PRACTICE 15-1, page 246
Answers: **1.** subject: Derek Walcott **3.** subject: Walcott **5.** subject: poems **7.** subject: Walcott **9.** subject: he **11.** subject: poet

◆ PRACTICE 15-2, page 247
Answers: **1.** plural subject: tourists **3.** plural subject: farms **5.** singular subject: maze **7.** plural subject: farms **9.** plural subject: Tourists

◆ PRACTICE 15-3, page 248
Answers: **1.** prepositional phrases: With more than 27 percent of the vote; in history; subject: Theodore Roosevelt **3.** prepositional phrases: Before Roosevelt; of votes; subject: candidate **5.** prepositional phrases: In 1968; of the American Independent Party; of the vote; subject: George C. Wallace **7.** prepositional phrases: With nearly 19 percent; of the popular vote; against Democrat Bill Clinton and Republican George Bush; in 1992; subject: Ross Perot **9.** prepositional phrases: In 2004; on the ballot; in many states; subject: Nader

◆ PRACTICE 15-4, page 250
Answers: **1.** see **3.** offers **5.** enters, wins **7.** realizes **9.** enjoy

◆ PRACTICE 15-5, page 251
Answers: **1.** are **3.** is **5.** is **7.** becomes **9.** are

◆ PRACTICE 15-6, page 251
Answers: **1.** comes **3.** sell **5.** use **7.** include **9.** love

◆ PRACTICE 15-7, page 253
Answers: **1.** complete verb: had become; helping verb: had **3.** complete verb: had become; helping verb: had

5. complete verb: would get; helping verb: would **7.** complete verb: did cause; helping verb: did **9.** complete verb: would remain; helping verb: would

Chapter 16

◆ PRACTICE 16-1, page 258
Answers: **1.** and **3.** and **5.** and **7.** so/and **9.** for

◆ PRACTICE 16-2, page 259
Answers: **1.** Training a dog to heel is difficult, for dogs naturally resist strict control. **3.** Students should spend two hours of study time for each hour of class time, or they may not do well in the course. **5.** Each state in the United States has two senators, but the number of representatives depends on a state's population. **7.** A "small craft advisory" warns boaters of bad weather conditions, for these conditions can be dangerous to small boats. **9.** Hip-hop fashions include sneakers and baggy pants, but these styles are very popular among today's young men.

◆ PRACTICE 16-3, page 259
Answers will vary.

◆ PRACTICE 16-4, page 260
Answers will vary.

◆ PRACTICE 16-5, page 261
Answers will vary.

◆ PRACTICE 16-6, page 264
Answers: **1.** Andrew F. Smith, a food historian, wrote a book about the tomato; later, he wrote a book about ketchup. **3.** The word *ketchup* may have come from a Chinese word; however, Smith is not certain of the word's origins. **5.** Ketchup has changed a lot over the years; for example, special dyes were developed in the nineteenth

century to make it red.   **7.** Ketchup is now used by people in many cultures; still, salsa is more popular than ketchup in the United States.   **9.** Some of today's ketchups are chunky; in addition, some ketchups are spicy.

◆ **PRACTICE 16-7, page 264**
Possible edits: **1.** The Man of the Year must have greatly influenced the previous year's events; consequently, the choice is often a prominent politician.   **3.** During World War II, Hitler, Stalin, Churchill, and Roosevelt were all chosen; in fact, Stalin was featured twice.   **5.** Only a few women have been selected; for example, Queen Elizabeth II of England was featured in 1952.   **7.** The Man of the Year is not always a person; in fact, the Computer was selected in 1982 and Endangered Earth in 1988.

◆ **PRACTICE 16-8, page 265**
Possible answers: **1.** Campus residents may have a better college experience; still, being a commuter has its advantages.   **3.** Commuters have a wide choice of jobs in the community; on the other hand, students living on campus may have to take on-campus jobs.   **5.** There are also some disadvantages to being a commuter; for example, commuters may have trouble joining study groups.   **7.** Commuters might have to help take care of their parents or grandparents; in addition, they might have to babysit for younger siblings.   **9.** Younger commuters may be under the watchful eyes of their parents; of course, parents are likely to be stricter than dorm counselors.

◆ **PRACTICE 16-9, page 266**
Answers will vary.

Chapter 17

◆ **PRACTICE 17-1, page 272**
Answers: **1.** Dependent clause   **3.** Dependent clause   **5.** Dependent clause   **7.** Independent clause   **9.** Independent clause

◆ **PRACTICE 17-2, page 273**
Answers: **1.** Independent clause   **3.** Independent clause   **5.** Dependent clause   **7.** Dependent clause   **9.** Independent clause

◆ **PRACTICE 17-3, page 275**
Possible answers: **1.** When   **3.** When   **5.** Since   **7.** Although   **9.** When

◆ **PRACTICE 17-4, page 276**
Possible answers: **1.** Although professional midwives are used widely in Europe, in the United States, they usually practice only in areas with few doctors.   **3.** Stephen Crane describes battles in *The Red Badge of Courage* even though he never saw a war.   **5.** After Jonas Salk developed the first polio vaccine in the 1950s, the number of polio cases in the

United States declined.   **7.** Before the DuPonts arrived from France in 1800, American gunpowder was as good as French gunpowder.   **9.** Because Thaddeus Stevens thought plantation land should be given to freed slaves, he disagreed with Lincoln's peace terms for the South.

◆ **PRACTICE 17-5, page 278**
Answers: **1.** Dependent clause: which was performed by a group called the Buggles; relative pronoun: which; noun: video   **3.** Dependent clause: who did not like MTV at first; relative pronoun: who; noun: executives   **5.** Dependent clause: which aired in September 1984; relative pronoun: which; noun: awards   **7.** Dependent clause: who was its first host; relative pronoun: who; noun: Cindy Crawford   **9.** Dependent clause: who would soon be elected president; relative pronoun: who; noun: Bill Clinton

◆ **PRACTICE 17-6, page 279**
Possible edits: **1.** Their work, which benefits both the participants and the communities, is called service learning.   **3.** The young people, who are not paid, work at projects such as designing neighborhood playgrounds.   **5.** Designing a playground, which requires teamwork, teaches them to communicate.

Chapter 18

◆ **PRACTICE 18-1, page 284**
Answers will vary.

◆ **PRACTICE 18-2, page 286**
Answers: **1.** Adverb: initially; edited sentence: Initially, Tupac was a roadie and backup dancer for the rap group Digital Underground.   **3.** Adverb: next; edited sentence: Next, Tupac faced conflicts with rival rap artists, leading to his being shot and spending time in prison.   **5.** Adverb: however; edited sentence: However, his influence continued after his 1996 murder and some fans even believe that he is still alive.

◆ **PRACTICE 18-3, page 287**
Answers: **1.** Adverb: sometimes; edited sentence: Sometimes, internships are paid or counted for academic credit.   **3.** Adverb: next; edited sentence: Next, the student should write a résumé listing job experience, education, and interests.   **5.** Adverb: often; edited sentence: Often, going to job fairs and networking are good ways to find internships.

◆ **PRACTICE 18-4, page 288**
Answers will vary.

◆ **PRACTICE 18-5, page 288**
Answers: **1.** Prepositional phrase: during World War II; edited sentence: During World War II, many male factory workers became soldiers.   **3.** Prepositional phrase: between 1942 and 1945; edited sentence: Between 1942 and 1945, over six million women took factory jobs.   **5.** Prepositional phrase: for the first time; edited sentence: For the first time, many women wore pants.

◆ **PRACTICE 18-6, page 289**
Answers will vary.

◆ **PRACTICE 18-7, page 290**
Answers will vary.

◆ **PRACTICE 18-8, page 291**
Answers: **1.** Operating from the bottom up, Green parties believe in organizing neighborhoods first. **3.** Growing quickly, Green parties were established in 72 countries by 2001. **5.** Enlisting the support of celebrities to stop global warming, the Green movement has led to such events as the Live Earth concerts.

◆ **PRACTICE 18-9, page 292**
Answers will vary.

◆ **PRACTICE 18-10, page 292**
Answers will vary.

◆ **PRACTICE 18-11, page 293**
Answers: **1.** Influenced by Albert Bandura, Sabado believed that a person's behavior could change his or her environment. **3.** Called telenovelas, Mexican soap operas are a very popular form of entertainment. **5.** Encouraged to change their lives, nearly a million viewers went to literacy classes because of a telenovela character. **7.** Introduced to Entertainment-Education through radio talk shows, some teenagers worked through problems with hosts their own age. **9.** Focused on family planning, these programs have reduced the number of births wherever they are broadcast.

◆ **PRACTICE 18-12, page 294**
Answers will vary.

◆ **PRACTICE 18-13, page 295**
Answers will vary.

◆ **PRACTICE 18-14, page 296**
Answers: **1.** Many clothing companies and technology companies rely on trend forecasters to help them predict trends. **3.** Analysis of past trends and extensive market research help forecasters collect the information they need. **5.** Predicting for certain what people will want and knowing for certain what people will buy are impossible.

◆ **PRACTICE 18-15, page 297**
Answers: **1.** Despite his lack of formal education, Edison had a quick mind and showed a talent for problem solving. **3.** Edison patented the earliest phonograph in 1878 and created the first practical light bulb the following year. **5.** Edison held many patents and made a fortune from his inventions.

◆ **PRACTICE 18-16, page 298**
Answers: **1.** College presidents and their supporters wanted to improve the academic performance of college athletes. **3.** A second proposal required athletes to earn a certain number of credits every year and set a minimum grade point average for them. **5.** Many coaches believe standardized test scores are biased and do not want them used to screen student athletes. **7.** The new rules, supporters claimed, would give student athletes a fair chance and also keep them on the graduation track.

◆ **PRACTICE 18-17, page 299**
Possible edits: **1.** The iPhone, a product released by Apple in 2007, is not only a phone but a camera, a multimedia player, and a Web browser. **3.** When British soccer star David Beckham retired from playing in his own country, he came to play for a U.S. team, the LA Galaxy. **5.** Stepping outside for a cigarette, an activity that used to be acceptable at most workplaces, is now being banned by many companies.

◆ **PRACTICE 18-18, page 299**
Possible edits: **1.** Wikipedia, one of the largest reference sites on the Web, is different from other encyclopedias in many ways. **3.** For this reason, researchers have to be careful when using information from Wikipedia, a source that may contain factual errors. **5.** Despite some drawbacks, Wikipedia has many notable advantages, including free and easy access, up-to-date information, and protection from author bias.

◆ **PRACTICE 18-19, page 301**
Possible edits: Kente cloth is made in western Africa and produced primarily by the Ashanti people. It has been worn for hundreds of years by African royalty who consider it a sign of power and status. Many African Americans wear kente cloth because they see it as a link to their heritage. Each pattern on the cloth has a name, and each color has a special significance. For example, red and yellow suggest a long and healthy life, while green and white suggest a good harvest. Although African women may wear kente cloth as a dress or head wrap, African American women, like men, usually wear strips of cloth around their shoulders. Men and women of African descent wear kente cloth as a sign of racial pride; in fact, it often decorates college students' gowns at graduation.

Chapter 19

◆ **PRACTICE 19-1, page 306**
Answers: **1.** I just bought a head of lettuce, a pint of mushrooms, and three pounds of tomatoes. **3.** The plumber needs to repair a leaky pipe, replace a missing faucet, and fix a running toilet. **5.** Parallel. **7.** Parallel. **9.** Parallel.

◆ **PRACTICE 19-2, page 308**
Answers will vary.

◆ **PRACTICE 19-3, page 309**
Answers: **1.** Experts who object to homework include Dorothy Rich, Harris Cooper, and Alfie Kohn. **3.** In his

book *The Homework Myth*, Alfie Kohn says that homework creates family conflict and creates stress in children. **5.** Kohn believes that instead of doing homework, children could interview parents about family history and learn about chemistry through cooking. **7.** There seems to be no relationship between the amount of homework assigned and students' lower test scores. **9.** Students in countries that assign more homework, such as Greece, Thailand, and Iran, score lower on achievement tests than American students.

Chapter 20

◆ PRACTICE 20-1, page 316
Answers: **1.** three fifty-watt bulbs; coal oil; baking bread **3.** wooden table; unfinished game of checkers; apple-tree stump **5.** none

◆ PRACTICE 20-2, page 317
Answers will vary.

◆ PRACTICE 20-3, page 317
Answers will vary.

◆ PRACTICE 20-4, page 319
Possible edits: **1.** To meet the needs of international children, Sesame Workshop helps produce versions of its popular show *Sesame Street* in other countries. **3.** Usually, the producers focus on the cultural diversity in their country. **5.** Today, versions of *Sesame Street* exist in a variety of countries. They include Mexico, Russia, South Africa, Bangladesh, and Egypt. **7.** This Spanish-language show includes well-known characters like Elmo and Cookie Monster as well as original characters like Abelardo and Pancho.

◆ PRACTICE 20-5, page 320
Possible edits: **1.** Whenever I get upset, I go outside and jog. **3.** I don't like movies or television. **5.** I was really lucky when I got this job.

◆ PRACTICE 20-6, page 322
Answers will vary.

◆ PRACTICE 20-7, page 323
Answers will vary.

◆ PRACTICE 20-8, page 324
Answers will vary.

◆ PRACTICE 20-9, page 326
Possible edits: **1.** Many people today would like to see more police officers patrolling the streets. **3.** All the soldiers picked up their weapons. **5.** Travel to other planets will be a significant step for humanity.

Chapter 21

◆ PRACTICE 21-1, page 334
Answers: **1.** Comma splice **3.** Fused **5.** Fused **7.** Correct **9.** Comma splice

◆ PRACTICE 21-2, page 336
Answers: **1.** In June 2007, Gordon Brown became prime minister of the United Kingdom. He replaced Tony Blair. **3.** Last week, Soraya won a text-messaging contest. The prize for being the fastest was five hundred dollars. **5.** In 1961, the first Six Flags theme park opened in Arlington, Texas. The six flags represent the six governments that have ruled the area that is now Texas.

◆ PRACTICE 21-3, page 336
Possible edits: **1.** A car with soft tires gets poor gas mileage, so keeping tires inflated is a good way to save money on gas. **3.** Indonesia has more volcanoes than any other country in the world, but the United States has the biggest volcano in the world, Mauna Loa in Hawaii. **5.** Overcrowded schools often have to buy portable classrooms or trailers, yet this is only a temporary solution.

◆ PRACTICE 21-4, page 337
Answers: **1.** Of all the states, Alaska has the highest percentage of Native American residents; 16 percent of Alaskans are of Native descent. **3.** Enforcing traffic laws can be difficult; some cities use cameras to photograph anyone who runs a read light. **5.** Freestyle motocross riders compete by doing jumps and stunts; some famous FMX riders are Corey Hart, Nate Adams, and Travis Pastrana.

◆ PRACTICE 21-5, page 338
Possible edits: **1.** Restaurant goers can expect to come across different condiments in different regions of the country; for example, few tables in the Southwest are without a bottle of hot sauce. **3.** Today, few people can count on company pension plans; however, thirty years ago, most people could. **5.** Dog breeders who run "puppy mills" are only concerned with making money; unfortunately, they are not particularly concerned with their dogs' well-being.

◆ PRACTICE 21-6, page 340
Possible edits: **1.** The Dragon Boat Festival is a traditional Chinese celebration that occurs every year on the fifth day of the fifth month of the Chinese calendar. **3.** Successful auctions often depend on experienced auctioneers who encourage the audience to keep bidding. **5.** Since Kevin's arm span is greater than his height, he has a positive "ape index."

◆ PRACTICE 21-7, page 341
Possible edits: **1.** When coffee came to Italy in 1600, Pope Clement "baptized" the Muslim beverage for Christians. **3.** Some heavy metal musicians have been influenced by classical music; however, they have taken their music in a very different direction. **5.** Some people

believe that the Harry Potter books promote witchcraft. Others feel that the books promote positive values, such as friendship and courage. **7.** Iceland is the country with the highest percentage of children born out of wedlock; the figure is 62 percent. **9.** David Beckham is a soccer star from England who came to the United States to help promote soccer here.

◆ **PRACTICE 21-8, page 342**
Possible edits: **1.** In the late nineteenth century, Coney Island was famous; in fact, it was legendary. **3.** By the turn of the century, it was best known for three amusement parks; these parks were Luna Park, Steeplechase, and Dreamland. **5.** However, three of the Island's most famous rides remain. They are preserved as official historic sites. **7.** The other two rides are the Cyclone roller coaster and the Parachute Jump. **9.** One of these attractions is Keyspan Park, which is home to a minor-league baseball team called the Brooklyn Cyclones.

Chapter 22

◆ **PRACTICE 22-1, page 348**
Answers: **1.** Fragment **3.** Fragment **5.** Fragment **7.** Fragment **9.** Fragment

◆ **PRACTICE 22-2, page 349**
Answers: Item 7 is a fragment. *Rewrite:* Sara Paretsky writes detective novels, such as *Burn Marks* and *Guardian Angel.* These novels are about V.I. Warshawski, a private detective. V.I. lives and works in Chicago, the Windy City. Every day as a detective, V.I. takes risks. V.I. is tough. She is also a woman.

◆ **PRACTICE 22-3, page 350**
Rewrite: Doctors discovered that football players were losing electrolytes and carbohydrates through their sweat. They invented a drink that replaced these important elements. Gatorade tasted terrible but did its job. The Florida Gators survived a very hot season and won most of their games. Now, Gatorade is used by many college and professional football teams as well as in baseball, basketball, tennis, golf, and soccer.

◆ **PRACTICE 22-4, page 351**
Possible edits: **1.** Quitting smoking is very hard but can add years to people's lives. **3.** Geography bees resemble spelling bees but test the contestants' knowledge of countries around the world. **5.** During the Cold War, the Soviet Union and the United States were rivals but never actually fought a war with each other. **7.** With cosmetic surgery, people can look younger, and feel younger, too. **9.** Pro football linemen can weigh more than 300 pounds but are still able to run fast.

◆ **PRACTICE 22-5, page 354**
Answers: Items 5, 7, 9, and 11 are fragments. *Possible edits:* Mazes have been constructed out of paving stones, cornfields, and rooms connected by doors. Printed mazes

can be solved with a pen and pencil. During the 1970s, many books and magazines published printed mazes for children and adults. There is no foolproof way to escape from a maze. One strategy is to keep turning to either the right or the left to keep from getting lost. Mazes can be fun to explore on foot or on paper.

◆ **PRACTICE 22-6, page 354**
Answers: Possible edits: Originally, nurses' uniforms looked like nuns' habits because nuns used to take care of sick people. In the late 1800s, a student of Florence Nightingale created a brown uniform with a white apron and cap. This uniform was worn by student nurses at her school, the Florence Nightingale School of Nursing and Midwifery. Eventually, nurses began to wear white uniforms, white stockings, white shoes, and starched white caps to stress the importance of cleanliness. Many older people remember these uniforms with affection. Today, most nurses wear bright, comfortable scrubs to help patients (especially children) feel more at ease.

◆ **PRACTICE 22-7, page 355**
Answers will vary.

◆ **PRACTICE 22-8, page 357**
Answers: **1.** Always try to find a store brand costing less than the well-known and widely advertised brands. **3.** Learn which stores are best for different kinds of products, understanding that some stores are good only for certain items. **5.** Buy different brands of the same product, trying each one to see which brand you like best.

◆ **PRACTICE 22-9, page 358**
Answers will vary.

◆ **PRACTICE 22-10, page 362**
Possible edits: **1.** Many homeless people are mentally ill. **3.** Raccoons can be found living wild in many parts of the United States. **5.** Some parents are too strict with their children. **7.** The Vietnam War led to widespread protests in the United States. **9.** Something is likely to change.

◆ **PRACTICE 22-11, page 363**
Answers will vary.

Chapter 23

◆ **PRACTICE 23-1, page 371**
Answers: **1.** know **3.** include **5.** sell, top **7.** surprises **9.** hosts, draws

◆ **PRACTICE 23-2, page 372**
Answers: **1.** spend **3.** crosses **5.** offer **7.** hate **9.** travel

◆ **PRACTICE 23-3, page 373**
Answers: **1.** fill **3.** watch **5.** plays **7.** smell **9.** greets

◆ **PRACTICE 23-4, page 375**
Answers: **1.** have **3.** has **5.** do **7.** is **9.** has

◆ **PRACTICE 23-5, page 376**
Answers: **1.** Prepositional phrase: from lightning; subject: fires; verb: cause **3.** Prepositional phrase: out of ten men; subject: One; verb: gets **5.** Prepositional phrase: in a variety of foods; subject: Trans fat; verb: leads **7.** Prepositional phrase: along with other Gulf Coast cities; subject: New Orleans; verb: suffers **9.** Prepositional phrase: at a concert; subject: Fans; verb: get

◆ **PRACTICE 23-6, page 378**
Answers: **1.** reaches **3.** goes **5.** is

◆ **PRACTICE 23-7, page 379**
Answers: **1.** has **3.** wants **5.** needs **7.** seems **9.** is

◆ **PRACTICE 23-8, page 381**
Answers: **1.** Subject: snakes; verb: do **3.** Subject: states; verb: Are **5.** Subject: branches; verb: are **7.** Subject: money; verb: is **9.** Subject: country; verb: is

Chapter 24

◆ **PRACTICE 24-1, page 387**
Answers: **1.** were **3.** were **5.** were **7.** had **9.** is

◆ **PRACTICE 24-2, page 389**
Answers: **1.** they **3.** he or she is **5.** he or she is **7.** he or she has **9.** he or she has

◆ **PRACTICE 24-3, page 391**
Answers: **1.** Chess develops critical thinking skills, and players develop self-discipline and self-esteem, too. **3.** Student chess players improve their concentration, and this better concentration can improve reading and math skills. **5.** "Chess in the Schools" also helps keep students in school because of the conflict resolution skills they develop.

Chapter 25

◆ **PRACTICE 25-1, page 397**
Answers: **1.** Modifier: Suffering from famine and other disasters; modifies: people **3.** Modifier: Responding to a recent earthquake; modifies: doctors **5.** Modifier: chartering a ship called *The Island of Light*; modifies: doctors

◆ **PRACTICE 25-2, page 398**
Answers: **1.** Frightened by a noise, the cat broke the vase. **3.** Lori looked at the man with red hair sitting in the chair. **5.** Fred loves ice cream sundaes covered with chocolate sauce. **7.** The deer running across the street was hit by a car. **9.** Wearing a mask, the exterminator sprayed the insect.

◆ **PRACTICE 25-3, page 400**
Answers will vary.

◆ **PRACTICE 25-4, page 401**
Answers will vary.

Chapter 26

◆ **PRACTICE 26-1, page 412**
Answers: **1.** returned **3.** originated **5.** dyed **7.** celebrated **9.** washed

◆ **PRACTICE 26-2, page 414**
Answers: **1.** was **3.** got **5.** did **7.** made **9.** had

◆ **PRACTICE 26-3, page 416**
Answers: **1.** correct **3.** was **5.** correct **7.** were **9.** correct

◆ **PRACTICE 26-4, page 417**
Answers: **1.** would **3.** would **5.** can **7.** will **9.** can **11.** can

Chapter 27

◆ **PRACTICE 27-1, page 422**
Answers: **1.** visited **3.** raised **5.** joined **7.** removed **9.** served

◆ **PRACTICE 27-2, page 425**
Answers: **1.** been **3.** cost **5.** become **7.** seen **9.** done

◆ **PRACTICE 27-3, page 426**
Answers: **1.** become **3.** led **5.** correct **7.** spoken **9.** correct

◆ **PRACTICE 27-4, page 428**
Answers: **1.** heard **3.** belonged **5.** spoke **7.** made **9.** were

◆ **PRACTICE 27-5, page 428**
Answers: **1.** have relied **3.** have changed **5.** have used **7.** have undergone

◆ **PRACTICE 27-6, page 430**
Answers: **1.** had left **3.** had arrived **5.** had lied **7.** had decided **9.** had been

◆ **PRACTICE 27-7, page 432**
Answers: **1.** surprised, preapproved **3.** designed
5. stuffed **7.** concerned **9.** acquired

Chapter 28

◆ **PRACTICE 28-1, page 439**
Answers: **1.** headaches (regular) **3.** feet (irregular)
5. deer (irregular) **7.** brides-to-be (irregular) **9.** loaves
(irregular) **11.** beaches (regular) **13.** sons-in-law
(irregular) **15.** wives (irregular) **17.** elves (irregular)
19. catalogs (regular)

◆ **PRACTICE 28-2, page 439**
Answers: **1.** travelers-to-be **3.** pieces; purses; briefcases
5. explosives; containers; liquids; correct **7.** correct;
shoes; correct **9.** delays; duties

◆ **PRACTICE 28-3, page 441**
Answers: **1.** I **3.** It **5.** we **7.** they; they **9.** it

◆ **PRACTICE 28-4, page 443**
Answers: **1.** Antecedent: campuses; pronoun: they
3. Antecedent: students; pronoun: their **5.** Antecedent:
Joyce; pronoun: she **7.** Antecedent: friends; pronoun:
them

◆ **PRACTICE 28-5, page 443**
Answers: **1.** he **3.** he **5.** they **7.** he

◆ **PRACTICE 28-6, page 444**
Answers: **1.** Compound antecedent: *24* or *Lost*; connecting word: or; pronoun: its **3.** Compound antecedent: Netflix and Blockbuster; connecting word: and;
pronoun: their **5.** Compound antecedent: movies and
documentaries; connecting word: and; pronoun: their
7. Compound antecedent: Playstation2 or Xbox; connecting word: or; pronoun: its **9.** Compound antecedent: Hurricanes or tornadoes; connecting word: or;
pronoun: their

◆ **PRACTICE 28-7, page 447**
Answers: **1.** Indefinite pronoun: Everyone; pronoun: his
or her **3.** Indefinite pronoun: Many; pronoun: their
5. Indefinite pronoun: Neither; pronoun: its **7.** Indefinite
pronoun: Both; pronoun: their **9.** Indefinite pronoun:
Anyone; pronoun: his or her

◆ **PRACTICE 28-8, page 448**
Possible edits: **1.** Either of the hybrid cars comes with its
own tax rebate. **3.** Everyone loves seeing his or her
home team win. **5.** Most people wait until the last
minute to file their tax returns. **7.** Everything needed to
build the model airplane comes in its kit. **9.** One of the
hockey teams just won its first Olympic medal.

◆ **PRACTICE 28-9, page 449**
Answers: **1.** Collective noun: company; pronoun: its
3. Collective noun: government; pronoun: its **5.** Collective noun: family; pronoun: its **7.** Collective noun: teams;
pronoun: their **9.** Collective noun: class; pronoun: its

◆ **PRACTICE 28-10, page 449**
Answers: **1.** Antecedent: women; pronouns: correct
3. Antecedent: everyone; pronoun: his or her **5.** Antecedent: House of Representatives and the states; pronoun: their **7.** Antecedent: Nancy Pelosi; pronoun: her
9. Antecedent: women; pronoun: their

◆ **PRACTICE 28-11, page 451**
Possible edits: **1.** Jamaica has green mountains and
spectacular scenery. **3.** The biography told a story of triumph over poverty. **5.** Her best friend lives across the
street. **7.** These peaches don't look ripe to me. **9.** The
antique plate almost fell off the table.

◆ **PRACTICE 28-12, page 453**
Answers: **1.** Possessive **3.** Objective **5.** Subjective,
objective **7.** Subjective

◆ **PRACTICE 28-13, page 455**
Answers: **1.** I **3.** They; correct **5.** He; they; he **7.** I
9. us

◆ **PRACTICE 28-14, page 457**
Answers: **1.** [they like] him **3.** [it affected] me **5.** I
[do] **7.** [it fits] me

◆ **PRACTICE 28-15, page 458**
Answers: **1** who **3.** who **5.** who **7.** whoever
9. who

◆ **PRACTICE 28-16, page 460**
Answers: **1.** themselves **3.** herself **5.** themselves
7. ourselves **9.** herself

Chapter 29

◆ **PRACTICE 29-1, page 467**
Answers: **1.** poorly **3.** truly **5.** really **7.** carefully
9. comfortable

◆ **PRACTICE 29-2, page 468**
Answers: **1.** well **3.** good **5.** well **7.** well **9.** well

◆ **PRACTICE 29-3, page 470**
Answers: **1.** more slowly **3.** healthier **5.** more loudly
7. more respectful **9.** wilder

◆ **PRACTICE 29-4, page 471**
Answers: **1.** largest **3.** newest **5.** most popular **7.** most
frequent, highest

◆ **PRACTICE 29-5, page 472**
Answers: **1.** better **3.** better, worse **5.** better **7.** best
9. better

Chapter 30

◆ **PRACTICE 30-1, page 477**
Possible edits: **1.** Ramen noodles are a popular choice for students because they are cheap, tasty, and easy to prepare. Subject: they **3.** Although high in carbohydrates (a good source of energy), ramen noodles also contain saturated and trans fats and few vitamins or minerals. Subject: ramen noodles **5.** Not just popular with American college students, ramen noodles are also popular in many other countries around the world. Subject: ramen noodles **7.** The noodles originated in China many years ago, where they were deep fried so that they could be stored for a long time without spoiling. Subject: they

◆ **PRACTICE 30-2, page 479**
Answers: **1.** The first parts of the Great Wall were built around 200 A.D. **3.** The sides of the Great Wall are made of stone, brick, and earth. **5.** The Great Wall is the only man-made object that can be seen by astronauts in space.

◆ **PRACTICE 30-3, page 480**
Answers: **1.** children; streets **3.** No plural nouns **5.** children; families; chores **7.** children; families **9.** children; homes; parents; others; servants; families

◆ **PRACTICE 30-4, page 482**
Answers: **1.** Count: approaches **3.** Noncount **5.** Count: shortages **7.** Count: individuals **9.** Count: systems

◆ **PRACTICE 30-5, page 485**
Answers: **1.** every **3.** A few violent **5.** many **7.** Many **9.** some

◆ **PRACTICE 30-6, page 488**
Answers: **1.** the; a **3.** no article needed **5.** the; the; the; no article needed **7.** no article needed **9.** a **11.** a; no article needed; no article needed; the

◆ **PRACTICE 30-7, page 490**
Answers: **1.** Question: Is converting metric measurements to the U.S. system difficult? Negative statement: Converting metric measurements to the U.S. system is not difficult. **3.** Question: Was that family very influential in the early 1900s? Negative statement: That family was not very influential in the early 1900s. **5.** Question: Is choosing the right gift a difficult task? Negative statement: Choosing the right gift is not a difficult task. **7.** Question: Can the lawyer verify the witness's story? Negative statement: The lawyer cannot verify the witness's story.

9. Question: Is the British royal family loved by most of the British people? Negative statement: The British royal family is not loved by most of the British people.

◆ **PRACTICE 30-8, page 494**
Answers: **1.** Correct **3.** Correct; believed **5.** Correct; correct; correct **7.** often see; touch; correct **9.** Correct; decide

◆ **PRACTICE 30-9, page 496**
Answers: **1.** might **3.** should **5.** should **7.** Would **9.** can

◆ **PRACTICE 30-10, page 497**
Answers: **1.** Eating **3.** cleaning **5.** Quitting **7.** organizing **9.** cooking

◆ **PRACTICE 30-11, page 499**
Answers: **1.** a brand-new high-rise apartment building **3.** numerous successful short-story collections **5.** the publisher's three best-selling works **7.** a strong-willed young woman **9.** an exquisite white wedding gown

◆ **PRACTICE 30-12, page 504**
Answers: **1.** in; for **3.** of; to; about **5.** In; at; in; in; by **7.** in **9.** of; on; for

◆ **PRACTICE 30-13, page 506**
Answers: **1.** In one case, a New Jersey woman found that a hungry bear woke her up from a nap one afternoon. **3.** Actually, although it is a good idea to stay away from bears, most wild bears are timid. **5.** The amount of blueberries and other wild fruit that bears eat usually drops off in dry weather. **7.** It is a good idea for families to go over their plans to safeguard their property against bears. **9.** If people have a bird feeder in the yard, they should put it away during the autumn.

Chapter 31

◆ **PRACTICE 31-1, page 517**
Answers: **1.** The musician plays guitar, bass, and drums. **3.** Correct **5.** The diary Anne Frank kept while her family hid from the Nazis is insightful, touching, and sometimes humorous. **7.** Most coffins manufactured in the United States are lined with bronze, copper, or lead. **9.** California's capital is Sacramento, its largest city is Los Angeles, and its oldest settlement is San Diego.

◆ **PRACTICE 31-2, page 519**
Answers: **1.** Correct **3.** Correct **5.** Correct **7.** As a result of athletes' fame, many children and young adults see them as role models. **9.** In spite of the dangers of steroids, young athletes may think only of becoming stronger and faster.

◆ **PRACTICE 31-3, page 519**
Answers: **1.** Often, establishing credit can be difficult. **3.** Similarly, some married women have no personal

credit history.   **5.** Correct   **7.** Correct   **9.** In addition, having checking and savings accounts can help to establish financial reliability.

◆ **PRACTICE 31-4, page 521**

Answers: **1.** Guglielmo Marconi, a young Italian inventor, sent the first wireless message across the Atlantic Ocean in 1901.   **3.** HTML, hypertext markup language, consists of the codes used to create Web documents.   **5.** Known as NPR, National Public Radio presents a wide variety of programs.   **7.** Correct; appositive: Home of the 2008 Olympics   **9.** Correct; appositive: A plant that grows on mountains and in deserts

◆ **PRACTICE 31-5, page 523**

Answers: **1.** Correct   **3.** Correct   **5.** The Japanese had just landed in the Aleutian Islands, which lie west of the tip of the Alaska Peninsula.   **7.** As a result, they made them work under conditions that made construction difficult.   **9.** In one case, white engineers who surveyed a river said it would take two weeks to bridge.   **11.** Correct

◆ **PRACTICE 31-6, page 525**

Answers: **1.** The American Declaration of Independence was approved on July 4, 1776.   **3.** At 175 Carlton Avenue, Brooklyn, New York, is the house where Richard Wright began writing *Native Son*.   **5.** Correct   **7.** The Pueblo Grande Museum is located at 1469 East Washington Street, Phoenix, Arizona.   **9.** St. Louis, Missouri, was the birthplace of writer Maya Angelou, but she spent most of her childhood in Stamps, Arkansas.

◆ **PRACTICE 31-7, page 527**

Answers: **1.** The capital of the Dominican Republic is Santo Domingo.   **3.** Some of the most important crops are sugarcane, coffee, cocoa, and rice.   **5.** Correct   **7.** Tourists who visit the Dominican Republic remark on its tropical beauty.   **9.** Correct

Chapter 32

◆ **PRACTICE 32-1, page 532**

Answers: **1.** Bacteria and viruses, which we can't see without a microscope, kill many people every year.   **3.** After you're bitten, stung, or stuck, how long does it take to die?   **5.** The sea wasp is actually a fifteen-foot-long jellyfish, and although it's not aggressive, it can be deadly.   **7.** While jellyfish found off the Atlantic coast of the United States can sting, they aren't as dangerous as the sea wasp, whose venom is deadly enough to kill sixty adults.   **9.** Correct

◆ **PRACTICE 32-2, page 534**

Answers: **1.** the singer's video   **3.** everybody's favorite band   **5.** the players' union   **7.** the children's bedroom   **9.** everyone's dreams

◆ **PRACTICE 32-3, page 536**

Answers: **1.** Parents; theirs   **3.** its; weeks   **5.** Ryans; years   **7.** classes; correct; your   **9.** tests; correct

Chapter 33

◆ **PRACTICE 33-1, page 541**

Answers: **1.** Midwest; Lake; Chicago; O'Hare International Airport; nation's   **3.** north; Soldier Field; Chicago Bears; Wrigley Field; Chicago Cubs; National League baseball team   **5.** John Kenzie   **7.** skyscrapers; John Hancock Company; Sears; Amoco

◆ **PRACTICE 33-2, page 544**

Answers: **1.** "We who are about to die salute you," said the gladiators to the emperor.   **3.** "The bigger they are," said boxer John L. Sullivan, "the harder they fall."   **5.** Lisa Marie replied, "I do."   **7.** When asked for the jury's verdict, the foreperson replied, "We find the defendant not guilty."   **9.** "Yabba dabba doo," Fred exclaimed. "This brontoburger looks great."

◆ **PRACTICE 33-3, page 546**

Answers: **1.** The 1959 movie *Plan Nine from Outer Space* has been called the worst picture of all time.   **3.** Everyone should read Martin Luther King, Jr.'s "I Have a Dream" speech and his essay "Letter from Birmingham Jail."   **5.** CBS has had hits with *CSI*, *CSI: Miami*, and *CSI: New York*.

◆ **PRACTICE 33-4, page 546**

Answers: **1.** In addition to her television show, Oprah Winfrey publishes a magazine called *O*.   **3.** People who want to purchase new computers often compare the different brands in *Consumer Reports* magazine.   **5.** Edgar Allan Poe has written several mysterious short stories, two of which are called "The Tell-Tale Heart" and "The Black Cat."   **7.** Lance Armstrong, who won the Tour de France bicycle race, wrote a book about his fight with cancer called *It's Not about the Bike*.

◆ **PRACTICE 33-5, page 548**

Possible edits: **1.** Megachurches—though Protestant—are not always affiliated with the main Protestant denominations.   **3.** Although many of these churches are evangelical (actively recruiting new members), people often join because of friends and neighbors.   **5.** Worshippers say that their services are upbeat: full of joy and spirituality.   **7.** The largest of these churches—with ten thousand members—would be unable to function without telecommunications.   **9.** Critics of megachurches (and there are some) believe they take up too much tax-exempt land.

Chapter 34

◆ **PRACTICE 34-1, page 556**

Answers: **1.** weigh; correct   **3.** Correct; deceive; believing   **5.** Correct; veins; correct

700

◆ **PRACTICE 34-2, page 557**
Answers: **1.** unhappy **3.** preexisting **5.** unnecessary **7.** impatient **9.** overreact

◆ **PRACTICE 34-3, page 558**
Answers: **1.** lonely **3.** revising **5.** truly **7.** ninth **9.** effectiveness

◆ **PRACTICE 34-4, page 559**
Answers: **1.** happiness **3.** denying **5.** readiness **7.** destroyer **9.** cried

◆ **PRACTICE 34-5, page 560**
Answers: **1.** hoped **3.** resting **5.** revealing **7.** unzipped **9.** referring

◆ **PRACTICE 34-6, page 561**
Answers: **1.** effects; already **3.** buy; correct **5.** correct; correct

◆ **PRACTICE 34-7, page 562**
Answers: **1.** Here; every day **3.** Correct; conscience **5.** conscious; its

◆ **PRACTICE 34-8, page 563**
Answers: **1.** lose **3.** no **5.** piece

◆ **PRACTICE 34-9, page 565**
Answers: **1.** supposed **3.** Correct **5.** Correct; quiet

◆ **PRACTICE 34-10, page 566**
Answers: **1.** Correct; to **3.** they're **5.** their

◆ **PRACTICE 34-11, page 567**
Answers: **1.** whose; correct **3.** where; correct **5.** Correct; whether; correct

Acknowledgments

Picture Acknowledgments

3T Bill Aron/PhotoEdit; **3B** James Marshall/The Image Works; **44T** AP Images/Chris Gardner; **44B** Stacy Walsh Rosenstock/NewsCom; **45** Hulton Archive/Getty Images; **49** Miami Dade College Web site homepage: www.mdc.edu/main. Courtesy of Miami Dade College; **59** (c) Lynda Barry. Taken from *One Hundred Demons*. Used courtesy of Darhansoff, Verrill Feldman, Literary Agents; **68** Vic Bider/PhotoEdit; **77** TWISTER® & © 2007 Hasbro, Inc. Used with permission; **88** Scott Tysick/Masterfile Corporation; **99** NBC/Photofest; **112** Chuck Savage, CORBIS; **121** "Disrespect" from Dictionary.com, dictionary.reference.com/browse/disrespect. Courtesy of Online Etymology Dictionary, Houghton Mifflin Harcourt Publishing, and Princeton University; **131** Mike Segar/Reuters/Landov; **145** Spencer Grant/PhotoEdit; **170** Ken Reid/The Image Bank/Getty Images; **171** David Young-Wolff/PhotoEdit; **174** United Artists/Photofest; **183T** Jospeh Sohm/Visions of America/CORBIS; **183B** Mark Kelley/Stone/Getty Images; **186** David Young-Wolff/PhotoEdit; **192** Fred Prouser/Reuters/CORBIS; **197** Digital Vision/Getty Images; **203** Frank Siteman; **209** Universal Pictures/Photofest; **215** Darren McCollester/Getty Images; **221T** Dennis MacDonald/Index Stock; **221B** Richard Pasley/Stock Boston; **227** Michael Schwarz/The Image Works; **233TL** JUPITERIMAGES/Comstock Premium/Alamy; **233TR** Jose Luis Pelaez, Inc./Blend Images/Getty Images; **233 BL** Rachel Epstein/The Image Works; **233BR** Michael Newman/PhotoEdit; **240** Don Mason/Blend Images/Getty Images; **245** Stephen Dunn/Getty Images; **254T** Mark Savage/CORBIS; **254B** Bill Davila/Reuters/Landov; **256** Stephen Ferry/Liaison/Getty Images; **268** Courtesy of the University of Texas Libraries, the University of Texas at Austin; **269** SuperStock, Inc./SuperStock; **271** Eric Fowke/PhotoEdit; **280** Greg Martin/SuperStock; **281** AP Images/Chris Gardner; **283** Ron Kuntz/Reuters/CORBIS; **303T** Daniel Acker/Bloomberg News/Landov; **303C** Dennis Hallinan/Alamy; **303B** Image courtesy of The Advertising Archives; **305** chicagoview/Alamy; **312T** AP Images/Harpo Productions, George Burns; **312B** AP Images/Adrian Wyld/CP; **313** Robert W. Ginn/Alamy; **315** Amanda Clement/Photodisc/Getty Images; **327T** Chris Ware/Keystone Features/Getty Images; **327B** Library of Congress, Digital ID: cph 3a09814; **328** Courtesy 3m Corporation; **329T** John Madre/CORBIS; **329B** Don Smetzer/PhotoEdit; **330** Ryan McGinnis/Alamy; **333** David Young-Wolff/PhotoEdit; **344T** Pierre Perrin/CORBIS SYGMA; **344B** King Features Syndicate; **345** "Limited Collector's Edition" #C-46 © 1976 DC Comics. All Rights Reserved. Used with Permission; **347** AP Images/Jeff Chiu; **366** Frances Roberts/Alamy; **367T** AP Images/Luis Alvarez; **367B** Michael Cogliantry/The Image Bank/Getty Images; **370** Ralph Fasanella/Courtesy of ACA Galleries, New York; **382** Masterfile Corporation; **383T** AP Images/Donna McWillian; **383B** AP Images/Robert E. Klein; **384** Shaun Best/Reuters/CORBIS; **386** Michael Newman/PhotoEdit; **393T** AP Images/Kathy Willens, File; **393B** Picture Quest; **394** Michael Newman/Photo Edit; **396** Gene Anderson; **403** Walt Disney Pictures/Photofest; **404T** AP Images/Seth Wenig; **404B** Bobby Bank/WireImage/Getty Images; **406T** Park Street/PhotoEdit; **406B** Kim Steel/Photographer's Choice/Getty Images; **407** Pamela Chen/Syracuse Newspapers/The Image Works; **411** Central Washington University; **419T** AP Images/Jennifer Graylock; **419B** Courtesy of CRC Health, Cupertino, CA; **421** Bob Stern/The Image Works; **433** STAN HONDA/AFP/Getty Images; **434T** Obama 08. www.barackobama.com/index.php. Courtesy of Barack Obama 2008; **434B** John McCain 2008. www.john mccain.com. Courtesy of John McCain 2008; **436** Fox/Photofest; **462T** AP Images/Paul Sakuma; **462B** Toby Burrows/Digital Vision/Getty Images; **465** Amy Etra/PhotoEdit; **474T** Courtesy of the University of Texas Libraries, The University of Texas at Austin; **474B** Abbas/Magnum Photos; **476** Frederick Childe Hassam/Christie's Images/Superstock; **508T** Stuart Franklin/Magnum Photos; **508C** AP Images/ Eugene Hoshiko; **508B** Jane Smalley/Index Stock; **511T** GraphicMaps.com; **511B** AP Images; **515** Hyungwaon Kang/ Bloomberg News/Landov; **529T** AP Images/Eric Risberg; **529B** Courtesy of the University of Texas Libraries, the University of Texas at Austin; **531** Tony Freeman/PhotoEdit; **537** Library of Congress, Digital ID: cph 3c04495; **538** Art Resource, NY; **539** MGM/Photofest; **550T** The British Library/HIP/The Image Works; **550B** Fair Street Pictures; **551** Kim Cheung/Reuters/Landov; **553** Image Source/Getty Images; **568** Eliana Aponte/Reuters/Landov; **569T** Kayte M. Deioma/PhotoEdit; **569B** Ron

Russek/UPI Photo/Landov; **571** Michael Newman/PhotoEdit; **572T** Spencer Grant/PhotoEdit; **572B** Lon C. Diehl/ PhotoEdit; **575** Gene Anderson.

Text Acknowledgments

Russell Baker. "Slice of Life." From the *New York Times*, November 24, 1974. Copyright © 1974 by The New York Times. All rights reserved. Used by permission and protected by the Copyright Laws of the United States. The printing, copying, redistribution,or retransmission of the Material without express written permission is prohibited.

Lynda Barry. "The Sanctuary of School." From the *New York Times*, Editorial Service, January 5, 1992, page 58. Copyright © 1992 by The New York Times. All rights reserved. Used by permission and protected by the Copyright Laws of the United States. The printing, copying, redistribution, or retransmission of the Material without express written permission is prohibited.

Judy Brady. "Why I Want a Wife." Originally published in the first issue of *Ms* Magazine, 1971. Copyright © 1971 by Judy Brady. Used by permission of the author.

Judith Ortiz Cofer. "Don't Call Me a Hot Tamale." Originally titled "The Myth of the Latin Woman: I Just Met a Girl Named Maria." From *Latin Deli: Prose and Poetry* by Judith Ortiz Cofer. Copyright © 1993 by Judith Ortiz Cofer. Reprinted by permission of University of Georgia Press.

Edwidge Danticat. "Impounded Fathers." From the *New York Times*, Editorial Section, June 17, 2007, page 12. Copyright © 2007 by The New York Times. All rights reserved. Used by permission and protected by the Copyright Laws of the United States. The printing, copying, redistribution, or retransmission of the Material without express written permission is prohibited.

Jo-Ellan Dimitrius and Mark Mazzarella. "Liars." From *Reading People* by Jo-Ellan Dimitrius, Ph.D. and Mark Mazzarella. Copyright © 1998, 1999 by Jo-Ellan Dimitrius, Ph.D. and Mark Mazzarella. Used by permission of Random House, Inc.

Dave Eggers. "Serve or Fail." From the *New York Times*, June 13, 2004, page 13. Copyright © 2004 by The New York Times. All rights reserved. Used by permission and protected by the Copyright Laws of the United States. The printing, copying, redistribution, or retransmission of the Material without express written permission is prohibited.

Indira Ganesan. "Resisting My Family History." First appeared in *Glamour* magazine, September 1994. Copyright © 1994 by Indira Ganesan. Reprinted by permission of the author and the Sandra Dijkstra Literary Agency.

Martin Gansberg. "Thirty-Eight Who Saw Murder Didn't Call the Police." From the *New York Times*, March 27, 1964 issue. Copyright © 1964 by The New York Times. All rights reserved. Used by permission and protected by the Copyright Laws of the United States. The printing, copying, redistribution, or retransmission of the Material without express written permission is prohibited.

Ellen Goodman. "The Suspected Shopper." From *Keeping in Touch* by Ellen Goodman. Copyright © 1985 by The Washington Post Company. Reprinted with the permission of Simon & Schuster Adult Publishing Group. All rights reserved.

Lawrence Otis Graham. "The 'Black Table' Is Still There." From the *New York Times*, February 3, 1991. Op-Ed page. Copyright © 1991 by The New York Times Company. Used by permission.

John Gray. Excerpt from *Men Are from Mars, Women Are from Venus* by John Gray. Copyright © 1992 by John Gray. Reprinted by permission of HarperCollins Publishers.

Malcolm X. "My First Conk." From *The Autobiography of Malcolm X* by Malcolm X and Alex Haley. Copyright © 1964 by Alex Haley and Malcolm X. Copyright © 1965 by Alex Haley and Betty Shabazz. Used by permission of Random House, Inc.

Scott Russell Sanders. "The Men We Carry in Our Minds." First appeared in *Milkweed Chronicle*; from *The Paradise of Bombs*. Copyright © 1984 by Scott Russell Sanders. Reprinted by permission of the author and the author's agents, the Virginia Kidd Agency, Inc.

Esmeralda Santiago. "Guavas." From *When I Was a Puerto Rican* by Esmeralda Santiago. Copyright © 1993 by Esmeralda Santiago. Used by permission of Perseus Books LLC.

John Schwartz. "The Poncho Bearer." From the *New York Times*, Education Life Supplement Section, January 7, 2007 issue. Copyright © 2007 by The New York Times. All rights reserved. Used by permission and protected by the Copyright Laws of the Laws of the United States. The printing, copying, redistribution, or retransmission of the Material without express written permission is prohibited.

Gayle Rosenwald Smith. "The Wife-Beater." From the *Philadelphia Inquirer*, July 2, 2001. Copyright © 2001 by the Philadelphia Inquirer. Used by permission of the publisher.

Amy Tan. "Fish Cheeks." First appeared in *Seventeen Magazine*. Copyright © 1987 by Amy Tan. Reprinted by permission of the author and the Sandra Dijkstra Literary Agency.

Ji-Yeon-Mary Yuhfill. "Let's Tell the Story of All America's Cultures." From the *Philadephia Inquirer*. Copyright © 1991 by the Philadelphia Inquirer. Used by permission of the publisher.

Screenshots

Anorexia Treatment Homepage. Screenshot used by permission of CRC Health, Cupertino, CA. www.anorexia -nervosa-treatment.com.

Frederick Community College Homepage. Screenshot used by permission of Frederick Community College, Frederick MD. www.frederick.edu.

Guilford Technical College Homepage. Screenshot used by permission of Guilford Technical Community College, Jamestown, N.C. – Celebrating 50 Fabulous Years 1958– 2008. www.technet.gtcc.cc.nc.us.

"disrespect." Posted by dictionary.com. Online Etymology Dictionary, © 2001 Douglas Harper. *The American Heritage ® Dictionary of the English Language, Fourth Edition.* Copyright © 2006 by Houghton Mifflin Company. WordNet 3.0. Copyright 2006 by Princeton University. Kernerman English Multilingual Dictionary (Beta Version), © 2000–2006 K Dictionaries Ltd. Used by permission of Online Etymology Dictionary, Houghton Mifflin Harcourt Publishing and Princeton University. All rights reserved.

John McCain homepage. Screenshot used by permission of John McCain 2008. www.johnmccain.com.

Obama08ForAmerica homepage. Screenshot used courtesy of Obama for America. www.barackobama.com.

Index

Note: Page numbers in **bold** type indicate pages where terms are defined.

Correction Symbols

This chart lists symbols that many instructors use to point out writing problems in student papers. Next to each problem is the chapter or section of *Writing First* where you can find help with that problem. If your instructor uses different symbols from those shown here, write them in the space provided.

YOUR INSTRUCTOR'S SYMBOL	STANDARD SYMBOL	PROBLEM
_____	adj	problem with use of adjective 29
_____	adv	problem with use of adverb 29
_____	agr	agreement problem (subject-verb) 23
_____		agreement problem (pronoun-antecedent) 28D, 28E
_____	apos	apostrophe missing or used incorrectly 32
_____	awk	awkward sentence structure 24, 25
_____	cap	capital letter needed 33A
_____	case	problem with pronoun case 28G
_____	cliché	cliché 20D
_____	coh	lack of paragraph coherence 2C
_____	combine	combine sentences 18C
_____	cs	comma splice 21
_____	d	diction (poor word choice) 20
_____	dev	lack of paragraph development 2B
_____	frag	sentence fragment 22
_____	fs	fused sentence 21
_____	ital	italics or underlining needed 33C
_____	lc	lower case; capital letter not needed 33A
_____	para or ¶	indent new paragraph 2
_____	pass	overuse of passive voice
_____	prep	nonstandard use of preposition 30M–N
_____	ref	pronoun reference not specific 28E
_____	ro	run-on sentence 21
_____	shift	illogical shift 24
_____	sp	incorrect spelling 34
_____	tense	problem with verb tense 26, 27
_____	thesis	thesis unclear or not stated 12D–G
_____	trans	transition needed 2C
_____	unity	paragraph not unified 2A
_____	w	wordy, not concise 20B
_____	//	problem with parallelism 19
_____	⊙	problem with comma use 31
_____	⊙	problem with semicolon use 16B, 16C
_____	" "	problem with quotation marks 33B–C
_____	⌒	close up space
_____	^	insert
_____	ℓ	delete
_____	∼	reversed letters or words
_____	X	obvious error
_____	✓	good point, well put